BLACK WOMEN IN WHITE AMERICA

A DOCUMENTARY HISTORY

BLACK WOMEN

IN

WHITE AMERICA

A DOCUMENTARY HISTORY

EDITED BY

GERDA LERNER

VINTAGE BOOKS

A DIVISION OF RANDOM HOUSE, NEW YORK

VINTAGE BOOKS EDITION, FEBRUARY 1973

All rights reserved under International and Pan-American Copyright Conventions. Published in the United States by Random House, Inc., New York, and simultaneously in Canada by Random House of Canada Limited, Toronto. Originally published by Pantheon Books, a division of Random House, Inc., in April 1972.

Library of Congress Cataloging in Publication Data

Lerner, Gerda, 1920–   comp.
    Black women in white America.
    Reprint of the 1972 ed.
    Includes bibliographies.
    1. Women, Negro—Collections. I. Title.
[EL85.86.L4 1973]   301.41′2   72–8643
ISBN 0–394–71880–1

Manufactured in the United States of America

Grateful acknowledgment is extended to the following for permission to reprint copyrighted material, most of which appears in excerpted form unless otherwise indicated:
The Antioch Review: From "Daddy Was a Number Runner" by Louise Meriwether. *The Antioch Review*, Vol. 27, no. 3.
The Christian Science Monitor: Abridgment of "Atlanta self-help," by Robert P. Hey. Copyright © 1968 The Christian Science Publishing Society. All rights reserved. The Dial Press: From *Coming of Age in Mississippi* by Anne Moody. Copyright © 1968 by Anne Moody.
The Dryden Press, Inc.: From *The Journal of Charlotte Forten,* edited by Ray Allen Billington. Copyright by The Dryden Press, Inc.
E. P. Dutton & Co., Inc.: From *Echo in My Soul* by Septima Clark with LeGette Blythe. Copyright © 1962 by Septima Poinsetta Clark.
Friendship Press, New York: From *Twelve Negro Americans* by Mary Jenness. Copyright 1936, Friendship Press, New York.
Hawthorn Books, Inc.: From *Movin' On Up* by Mahalia Jackson with Evan McLeod Wylie. Copyright © 1966 by Mahalia Jackson with Evan McLeod Wylie.
Holt, Rinehart and Winston, Inc.: From *The Trumpet Sounds:* A Memoir of Negro Leadership by Anna Arnold Hedgeman. Copyright © 1964 by Holt, Rinehart and Winston, Inc.
Houghton Mifflin Company: From *Unbought and Unbossed* by Shirley Chisholm. Copyright © 1970 by Shirley Chisholm.
Little, Brown and Company: From *Children of Crisis* by Robert Coles. Copyright © 1964, 1965, 1966, 1967 by Robert Coles.
David McKay Company, Inc.: From *The Third Door:* The Autobiography of an American Negro Woman by Ellen Tarry. Copyright © 1955 by Ellen Tarry. From *The Long Shadow of Little Rock* by Daisy Bates. Copyright © 1962 by Daisy Bates.
Pauli Murray: From "The Negro Woman in the Quest for Equality" by Pauli Murray. Copyright © 1964 by Pauli Murray.

to Daniel

to Stephanie

to the young in spirit

who embrace change and cherish

the infinite variety of

human possibilities

CONTENTS

TEACHING THE FREEDMEN

SCHOOL FOUNDERS

3. A WOMAN'S LOT
BLACK WOMEN ARE SEX OBJECTS FOR WHITE MEN

THE MYTH OF THE "BAD" BLACK WOMAN

THE RAPE OF BLACK WOMEN AS A WEAPON OF TERROR

BLACK WOMEN ATTACK THE LYNCHING SYSTEM

4. MAKING A LIVING
DOING DOMESTIC WORK

FROM SERVICE JOBS TO THE FACTORY

5. SURVIVAL IS A FORM OF RESISTANCE

6. IN GOVERNMENT SERVICE AND POLITICAL LIFE

7. THE MONSTER PREJUDICE
IN THE GRIP OF THE MONSTER

FREEDOM—NOW!

8. "LIFTING AS WE CLIMB"

FROM BENEVOLENT SOCIETIES TO NATIONAL CLUB MOVEMENT

INTERRACIAL WORK

INSIDE A WHITE ORGANIZATION— THE YOUNG WOMEN'S CHRISTIAN ASSOCIATION

GRASS-ROOTS WORK

9. RACE PRIDE

10. BLACK WOMEN SPEAK OF WOMANHOOD

PREFACE

❦ Until the very recent past, black people in America have been denied their history. The discovery of Black history, and its legitimization and acceptance into the body of American history, is progressing at this very time and has already immensely enriched our knowledge of our national past. Black history is beginning to serve whites as an antidote to centuries of racist indoctrination by providing essential knowledge without which a more truly democratic, nonracist society cannot be built. Black history is serving Blacks in a somewhat different sense by arousing pride in a legitimate past, enhancing self-respect and providing heroes and leaders with whom black people can identify.

American women have also been denied their history, but this denial has not yet been as widely recognized. History, in the past largely written by white male historians, has simply failed to ask those questions which would elicit information about the female contribution, the female point of view. Women as a group have been denied knowledge of their legitimate past and have been profoundly affected individually by having to see the world through male eyes. Seeing women cast only in subordinate and inferior positions throughout history and seldom, if ever, learning about female heroines or women of achievement, American girls are conditioned to limit their own life goals and self-esteem. Black women have been doubly victimized by scholarly neglect and racist assumptions. Belonging as they do to two groups which have traditionally been treated as inferiors by American society—Blacks and women—they have been doubly invisible. Their records lie buried, unread, infrequently noticed and even more seldom interpreted. Their names and their achievements are known to only a few specialists. The papers of outstanding figures such as Mary McLeod Bethune, Charlotte Hawkins Brown and Nannie Burroughs are scattered in various libraries, have never been edited nor even partially published. There have been few biographies of black women of the past, fewer monographs, no scholarly interpretive works. The organizational records of black women's organizations are equally scattered, unclassified and unused. This book is an effort to call attention to these unused sources of Black history and to bring another forgotten aspect of the black past to life.

Black people at this moment in history need above all to define themselves autonomously and to interpret their past, their present and their future. This applies to men and women and is a precondition for liberation as well as for any future solutions to the racial problem in the United States. Black people cannot and will not become integrated into American society on any terms but those of self-determination and autonomy. If that is assumed, self-definition and the interpretation of the past is an enormously important and challenging task for black historians.

Having said this, something must be said about the role of the white historian. White scholars, by their culturally conditioned racist assumptions, bear a heavy responsibility for having neglected and distorted the black past. One can expect the present generation of white historians, who are challenged on all sides, to rectify these omissions and distortions in their work, and to do so with a more modest approach to the limitations of their own findings and interpretations than they have done in the past. I am persuaded that black people and white people in America represent two separate cultures, with separate traditions and oftentimes diametrically opposed past experiences. The same probably holds true for men and women, whose roles, history and contributions are on closer examination so greatly separate as to constitute separate cultures. Of course, all groups, men and women, Blacks and whites, members of different nations and races, share in the common universal history. I do not believe that recognizing the existence of large cultural subdivisions means succumbing to separatism, cultural nationalism and a narrow particularistic vision. There is a place for universalistic interpretations of that which is common to all humanity, and there is a place for that which is particular to one group, to one special entity. We accept that there is a world history and a history of France or of India which are not the same, but which fit into similar categories. Our historical perceptions can only be enriched by accepting the fact that so long as sex and race are used to ascribe to people a different rank, role and status, so long will they have a different historical experience from that of the dominant group.

No white historian can ever again approach his work without recognizing that there were black people in the American past whose contributions and whose viewpoint must be considered. Similarly, I believe it is necessary to recognize that there is a female aspect to all history, that women were there and that their special contributions to the building and shaping of society were different from those of men. This difference in quality has up to now meant invisibility and insignificance; it cannot mean this any longer.

Certainly, historians who are members of the culture, or subculture, about which they write will bring a special quality to their material. Their understanding and interpretation is apt to be different from that of an outsider. On the other hand, scholars from outside a culture have frequently had a more challenging vision than those closely involved in and bound by their own culture. Both angles of vision are complementary in arriving at the truth about the past and in finding out "what actually happened." The interpretation of the black past as made by Blacks must be different from that of whites. This does not mean that it can or should only be made by Blacks. It should be made by both groups, and in the clash of opinions, in debate, in the juxtaposition of different interpretations, a richer and fuller and more solidly based history will emerge. In the present volume I have endeavored to let black women speak for themselves. I hope and trust that the rich material here uncovered will stimulate new interpretations and, above all, further research into the black past.

Of necessity a collection such as this cannot be definitive. The source material available is so rich that a representative selection of only the most interesting documents would fill several volumes. This volume, while it contains many documents which are pertinent to a social history of black women, is not in itself such a history. It is, in my opinion, too early to attempt the writing of a social history of black women. The research and monographic work which form the essential groundwork for such a study have yet to be done. In the present work I have endeavored to define the major themes in the history of black women as suggested by source material now available; to bring to light important unknown or little-known documents; and to focus on those women leaders whose influence was recognized and significant in their own time.

Much source material of great interest could not be included, and an arbitrary decision had to be made not to include cultural figures, on the ground that their contributions were somewhat better known to the general public than those of the women whose activities are here documented. The same reasoning led to the decision not to include major documents pertaining to the civil rights struggles of the fifties and sixties, these being relatively well known and easily accessible. Another underlying assumption governing the selection of material for this volume has been that it should not only include historically "important," i.e. known, leaders, but that it should also provide insight into the typical experience of the past by including documents relating to ordinary, anonymous women.

The historiography of this subject imposes limitations of a different kind. In the writing of history or the compiling of documents, the modern historian is dependent on the availability of sources. The kinds of sources collected depend to a large extent on the predilections, interests, prejudices and values of the collectors, archivists and historians of an earlier day. "We have the record of kings and gentlemen ad nauseam and in stupid detail," Dr. W. E. B. DuBois wrote twenty years ago,

> but of the common run of human beings . . . the world has saved all too little of authentic record and tried to forget or ignore even the little saved. With regard to Negroes in America . . . came also the attempt, conscious or unconscious, to excuse the shame of slavery by stressing natural inferiority which would render it impossible for Negroes to make, much less leave, any record of revolt or struggle, any human reaction to utter degradation.*

Similarly, Arthur Schlesinger, Sr., referring to women, complained in 1922: "From reading history textbooks one would think half of our population made only a negligible contribution to history."† The historical sources available reflect the indifferent attention given to women in history. Collected sources predominantly concern middle-class educated women and their activities. The historian relying on such sources can easily fall into an unintended distortion. While this holds true for all women, when one seeks out information concerning black women the distortion becomes compounded. Further, manuscript sources available for the writing of family history have little to offer when it comes to black women. Black history collections, which abound in source material concerning "anonymous people,"

* W. E. B. DuBois, Preface to Herbert Aptheker, ed., *A Documentary History of The Negro People in the United States* (New York: Citadel Press, 1951), p. v.

† Arthur Schlesinger, Sr., *New Viewpoints in American History* (New York: Macmillan Company, 1922), Chap. 6, p. 126.

have failed to pay attention to black women, except for a handful of "leaders."

It was possible to find primary documents pertaining to women in slavery because abolitionists as well as defenders of the slave system collected evidence, including primary sources, pertaining to life under slavery. No comparable interest was manifested by contemporaries or historians in the living conditions of tenant farmers and rural Blacks. What descriptions exist are secondary and frequently biased in that they see Blacks only as passive victims of poverty, discrimination, exploitation and abuse. The great migration to the cities, the transition from rural to urban life, the experience of industrialization as it applied to Blacks, were not generally preserved through primary documents. Economic and descriptive sociological source material is available, though not plentiful, but women are rarely mentioned in it. It is thus due to the limitations of the available documentary record that there are omissions and a certain middle-class bias in this book.

Future interpreters of the history of black women may benefit from approaching this subject not only as a part of Black history in general, but, as is done in this anthology, as part of the history of women in general. A great many facile generalizations about black matriarchy, the black family, black women, black morality are currently circulated without much scholarly evidence and without much basis in careful research. The historian must recognize the complexity, multiplicity and differentiation of this subject. This anthology may serve to highlight some of the directions which research can take to provide a sound foundation for new interpretations.

Black women have always been more conscious of and more handicapped by race oppression than by sex oppression. They have been subject to all the restrictions against Blacks and to those against women. In no area of life have they ever been permitted to attain higher levels of status than white women. Additionally, ever since slavery, they have been sexually exploited by white men through rape or enforced sexual services. These sexual mores, which are characteristic of the relationship of colonizers to the women of the conquered group, function not only symbolically but actually to fasten the badge of inferiority onto the enslaved group. The black man was degraded by being deprived of the power and right to protect his women from white men. The black woman was directly degraded by the sexual attack and, more profoundly, by being deprived of a strong black man on whom she could rely for protection. This slavery pattern was carried into the postslavery period and has only in this century begun to yield to the greater strength and militancy of the black community.

Black women have had an ambiguous role in relation to white society. Because they were women, white society has considered them more docile, less of a threat than black men. It has "rewarded" them by allowing—or forcing—black women into service in the white family. Black women, ever since slavery, have nursed and raised white children, attended white people in sickness and kept white homes running smoothly. Their intimate contact with white people has made them interpreters and intermediaries of the white culture in the black home. At the same time, they have struggled in partnership with their men to keep the black family together and to allow the black community to survive. This dual and often conflicting role has imposed great tensions on black women and has given them unusual strength.

The question of black "matriarchy" is commonly misunderstood. The very term is deceptive, for "matriarchy" implies the exercise of power by women, and black women have been the most powerless group in our entire society. They have consistently had the lowest status in society—the economic and social-political status ranking order consisting of white men, white women, black men, black women. Black women's wages, even today, are lowest of all groups; black women, like white women, were deprived of the ballot until 1920, even though at various times in the North black men of property could vote. After 1920, black women ranked lower than black men in political representation and in access to economic power positions in society, although both rank low compared to all whites.

But the status of black women can be viewed from two different viewpoints: one, as members of the larger society; two, within their own group. When they are considered as Blacks among Blacks, they have higher status within their own group than do white women in white society. This paradox is the direct result of the special relationship of white society to black women: because the lowest-status, lowest-paid jobs in white society are reserved for black women, they often can find work even when black men cannot. In fact, one can say quite definitely that white society has economically pitted black women against black men. For black women, this has meant that they are trained from childhood to become workers, and expect to be financially self-supporting for most of their lives. They know they will have to work, whether they are married or single; work to them, unlike to white women, is not a liberating goal, but rather an imposed lifelong necessity. Until the past decade, the access to the semiskilled and middle range of professional jobs was closed to black women by discrimination; therefore families understood that black girls must either be trained to be teachers or look forward to a lifetime of domestic or low-skilled service work. Black girls thus were given more incentive to complete their advanced education than were black boys, who found that, even with a college degree, job opportunities for them were severely restricted by race discrimination. The financially independent and often better-educated black woman has higher status within her family than some men, although there are many black families with husbands holding steady jobs which follow the usual middle-class family pattern. The greater equality in relations between black men and black women, which are perceived and expressed by many black authors in their writings, may well be due more to the embattled situation of the black family and the constant stress and danger with which it is faced in a hostile world than to any other factor. Certainly it has made a decisive difference in the way the black woman perceives herself and sees her role in society. This alone can adequately explain the resistance most black women feel toward the rhetoric and concepts of the Women's Liberation movement.

As can be seen from the documents in this collection, the black woman's aim throughout her history in America has been for the survival of her family and of her race. While she has for many long periods been forced to socialize her children to a pretended acceptance of discriminatory patterns, she also has managed to imbue them with race pride and a desire for full equality. This dual role has resulted in the unusual resiliency and flexibility of black women and in their oft-repeated stance of dignified passive resistance to oppression. Black women, speaking with many voices and expressing many individual opinions, have been nearly unanimous in their insistence that their own emancipation cannot be separated from the emancipation of their men. Their liberation depends on the liberation of the race and the improvement of the life of the black community. They have shown the pride and strength of people who have endured and survived great oppression. This has given them a sense of their own function in the life of their race and their families and a strong confidence in their own worth. If there is one theme that can emerge from the documentary record here presented, it is the strength, racial pride and sense of community of black women.

ACKNOWLEDGMENTS

❦ I am greatly obliged to the following institutions and their librarians for giving me access to their archives and permission to use their manuscript collections: American Antiquarian Society, Worcester, Massachusetts; Amistad Research Center, Dillard University, New Orleans, Louisianna; Atlanta University, Atlanta, Georgia; Boston Public Library; Columbia University, New York City; Cornell University, Ithaca, New York; William L. Clements Library, University of Michigan, Ann Arbor; Fisk University, Nashville, Tennessee; Library of Congress, Washington, D.C.; The Moorland-Spingarn Collection, Howard University, Washington, D.C.; National Archives, Washington, D.C.; Pennsylvania Historical Society, Philadelphia, Pennsylvania; Schlesinger Library, Radcliffe College, Cambridge, Massachusetts; Schomburg Collection, New York City Public Library; The Sophia Smith Collection, Smith College, Northampton, Massachusetts; and the archives of the Tuskegee Institute, Tuskegee, Alabama.

Special thanks for assistance, advice and courtesy beyond the call of duty are due to: Mrs. Jeanette B. Cheek, Director, The Arthur and Elizabeth Schlesinger Library, Radcliffe College; Miss Elizabeth Duval, Bibliographer (now retired), Sophia Smith Collection, Smith College; Mr. Paul M. Gaston, Director of Research, Southern Regional Council; Mr. Clifton H. Johnson, Director, Amistad Research Center, Dillard University; Mrs. Ann Allen Shockley, Special Collections Librarian, Fisk University; and Mr. Daniel T. Williams, Archivist, Tuskegee Institute. Mrs. Arthur Cort Holden, in generously opening to me her superb private library of rare books, has greatly aided my work.

Many sincere thanks to: Mr. and Mrs. Edward T. James, for sharing with me their research and knowledge; Eleanor Flexner for aiding me with her advice and criticism; Professors Herbert Gutman of the University of Rochester, Nathan I. Huggins of Columbia University, Audre Lord of the City University of New York and Willie Lee Rose of the University of Virginia for their perceptive readings and their helpful critiques, and to Professor Judith Stein of the City College of New York for directing me to an important source. Thanks also to the many others whose suggestions, advice and contacts enabled me to carry through this project.

I am grateful to André Schiffrin of Pantheon Books for his confidence in this work; to Milly Hawk and Verne Moberg for their perceptive and patient editing.

For help in securing the documents in this volume I am indebted to my students and research assistants: Ann Bobroff, Elise Brunelle, Joan Facher, Sally Moore, Eben Smith and John Welch. The technical aspects of my task were greatly lightened by the able assistance of Joy Wolfe.

I am deeply grateful to the Social Science Research Council for a generous grant which provided me with the means necessary to travel to distant archives and the leisure to research and write. I equally appreciate the leave of absence for the year 1970–71 granted me by Sarah Lawrence College, which enabled me to complete this work.

My husband, Carl Lerner, has steadily strengthened and encouraged me by his faith in the validity of this project, his keen critical ability and his understanding of the meaning, theory and practice of women's emancipation.

NOTES ON SOURCES

❦ The historical sources pertaining to black women are rich and varied, almost wholly unexplored and widely scattered. Only very few libraries have arranged their materials in such a way as to make material on black women easily accessible to the researcher. In most cases, such material lies buried within the mass of general historical sources and must be diligently searched out. The card catalogues of most manuscript collections do not keep a listing for "Negro women," although they sometimes may list a few of the Negro women's clubs.

Only a few black women rate separate collections. The Mary Church Terrell Papers at the Library of Congress are an invaluable source not only for the activities of Mrs. Terrell, but for the Negro women's club movement. In the same library are the Booker T. Washington Papers, which include some sources on Margaret Murray Washington. More material on her and her work at Tuskegee can be found in the Tuskegee Institute Library. The papers of Mary McLeod Bethune are widely scattered: some at the Amistad Research Center, Dillard University; some among the Rosenwald Fund Papers at Fisk University. Her newspaper columns are available in the Monroe Work collection of newspaper clippings at Tuskegee Institute. Her work with the National Youth Administration can be traced through the voluminous files of that agency in the National Archives. The bulk of her papers are in private hands and some are at Bethune-Cookman College.

There are Charlotte Hawkins Brown Papers at the Schlesinger Library, Radcliffe College. There are many more of her papers among the incredibly rich and quite unexplored collection at Atlanta University: The Neighborhood Union Papers and those of the Commission on Interracial Cooperation. These two collections are an excellent source for Southern community organizational work by black and white women. Contained in them are papers of a good number of local and state leaders, such as Mrs. Lugenia Hope, whose work and life deserve attention.

For the present work, major Black history and antislavery collections were studied. These include: the manuscript collections of Charles S. Johnson and W. E. B. Dubois at Fisk University; Carter G. Woodson at the Library of Congress; the Monroe Work Papers at Tuskegee Institute; the manuscripts and printed sources of the Schomburg Collection, New York Public Library and of Howard University. Among the antislavery sources used were the following: American Antiquarian Society, Worcester, Massachusetts; Theodore Dwight Weld Collection, William L. Clements Library, University of Michigan; manuscripts division, Boston Public Library; the antislavery collection at Cornell University, Ithaca, New York; the Pennsylvania Historical Society, Philadelphia, Pennsylvania; New York Public Library, New-York Historical Society; and Columbia University. The papers of the American Missionary Association at the Amistad Research Center, Dillard University, are an excellent source for information on teachers and schools during Reconstruction. A thorough reading of the major black newspapers, magazines and publications of the past, as well as of abolitionist and women's rights newspaper sources, yielded much material. The archives of the United States government and records of congressional committee hearings proved to be another valuable source.

Another approach taken was to search the records of white women and their organizations for possible contact with and source material about black women. The major sources of women's history used, in addition to those listed above were: Schlesinger Library, Radcliffe College; Sophia Smith Collection, Smith College; Blackwell Family Papers, Elizabeth Cady Stanton Papers, Library of Congress; Lucy

Chase Manuscript at American Antiquarian Society; and the Lillian Wald Papers at Columbia University.

The organizational records of the major black women's organizations and of those white organizations which had extensive contacts with the black community offer much information about black women and their activities. Among these I have found the YWCA Papers, Smith College; the American Missionary Association files, Amistad Research Center; the NAACP Papers in the Library of Congress; the Committee on Interracial Cooperation and the Neighborhood Union Papers, Atlanta University, of particular interest. The letters to the editor in the black press and in the antislavery press are an interesting source of primary material. Autobiographical writing and oral history furnish much useful information, but these sources must be used with due regard for their limitations. Local records, business directories, the census, health records and community organizational records yielded much useful data.

The section on slavery posed special research problems. Our knowledge of slavery is based on a variety of sources, many of them contradictory. The records of plantation owners and overseers describe plantation life from the owner's point of view. Documents such as birth and death statistics, property records, especially wills, and the business records of slave dealers and owners provide us with the outlines of the property relations and the most common economic practices of the system. Newspapers and legal records are useful sources for the more dramatic or unusual incidents. The records of missionary and reform societies provide some insights into the educational and religious practices related to slaves. In evaluating these records, it is useful to compare the reports of travelers with abolitionist leanings to those with contrary views. A similar approach helps in evaluating the many biographical sources: the diaries, biographies and letters of persons observing the slave system as eyewitnesses.

The vast abolitionist literature is most useful when it represents firsthand eyewitness testimony or documentary material from slaveholders' sources, such as advertisements in Southern papers, letters and statements by slaveholders and court records. The accounts in abolitionist newspapers concerning then current events, such as slave escapes and slave trials, can be validly employed, provided they are compared with and balanced against accounts in the major press.

Slave narratives are a most useful source, since they are presumably written from the slaves' point of view. But a critical evaluation of each narrative is essential, as is a comparative approach. Most of the slave narratives were dictated to or ghost-written by white abolitionists who, consciously or unconsciously, imposed their own biases on the narrative. It must also be kept in mind that almost all slave narratives are the products of escaped or liberated slaves, who are, by definition, men and women of unusual character, intelligence and attainment.

The oral and written testimonies of ex-slaves, compiled after the Civil War and in the 20th century, are another good source, provided one takes into consideration the inaccuracies of old people's memories and the inevitable distortions that occur after a lapse of time. Folklore material—songs, spirituals, tales and jokes—is another valuable source for the culture of the slave.

A general history and regional histories of black women need to be written. The many outstanding women whose selections are included in this book deserve to have biographers, and some, at least, merit collections of their speeches, letters and writings. A study of the Negro women's club movement would yield much undiscovered information about black community life, in which women played a crucial part. The economic contribution of black women deserves a full and scholarly study. The themes are many; the sources are available. It is to be hoped that historians, researchers and writers will turn their talents to this relatively unexplored field.

The term of reference by which Blacks have referred to themselves has changed in the course of history. At any given time, there has usually been a range of differences among Blacks in how they prefer to be designated. In recognition of the emotional and symbolic significance of the choice of a name, which is part of self-definition for individuals as well as for groups, the editor has been guided by the documents in their usage. The terms used in the documents and generally accepted in a given period by the group under discussion were the terms used in the editor's introductions. In a very few instances, "Negro," "Black" or "Afro-American" were used side by side within a sentence in order to avoid a stylistically awkward repetition.

A similar wide range of usage with sensitive connotations concerns the terms "ladies" and "women." As several of the selections show, black women, used to seeing the term "lady" reserved for white women, wished to be called "ladies" and treated as such. Yet members and leaders of Negro women's clubs shared with their white counterparts a dislike for being called "club ladies," a term which had somewhat negative connotations. Feminists of both races always preferred the term "women." Again, editorial usage attempted to follow the spirit and intent of the documents.

In the interest of preserving the authenticity of the documents, grammar, spelling and punctuation have been retained in their original form throughout, even when such usage may seem quaint, erroneous or offensive to the modern reader. Thus, the lower case spelling of the word "Negro," as it occurs in some documents, has been retained. The only word changes made have been slight alterations in spelling and punctuation where these seemed necessary for greater clarity. Cuts and ellipses have been made in such a way as not to affect the content, intent and tone of the original document. There has been no change of sequence except for the following pages, on which the order of paragraphs was reversed to avoid confusion in continuity: pp. 22, 240, 540.

AN INTRODUCTION

MARY McLEOD BETHUNE

It seems almost paradoxical, but nevertheless true, that the history of women and the history of Negroes are, in the essential features of their struggle for status, quite parallel. In the first place, they have both inherited from the long past a traditional status which has restricted not only their activities, but their thinking with reference to the rest of life and with reference to themselves. It is one of the peculiar accidents of our social life and of the mental and emotional relations between groups that are distinguished by any mark, that there should grow up around these differences certain imputations which depend for their advantage of statement upon the most articulate group. The arguments almost without change, used to prove that the position occupied by women through the years—a position of servility graduated from mildness to the harshest mental and physical slavery, is the only one for which they are satisfied by their nature, has been used, as you are aware, for Negroes through the years. There has been Biblical proof that this servile status was the wish of God: (1) "Servants obey your master," "Love, honor, and obey your husband" etc. (2) There has been proof from the evidence of anatomical differences between Negroes and whites. (3) There has been the proof offered that women have accomplished nothing in government, art, science or philosophy, just as it has been pointed out as evidence of Negro incapacity that they have failed in the government of Haiti and Liberia, that they have produced no great soldiers or statesmen, artists, or scientists.

But our more advanced thinkers now are beginning to point out that greatness is very largely a social accident, and almost always socially supported, and that the failure of one group to have shining representatives is more apt to be due to lack of opportunity in these fields from which they are barred by social pressure, than lack of capacity; that the measurements used for the anatomical differences are subject to severe strictures which disqualify them as scientific evidences; and that the revolution of thinking on the question has affected more startling changes in accomplishment than any revolution in physical structure could hope to bring about. In 1917, when women were granted suffrage, many of these problems were changed, for they took one step out of their traditional role. There has followed this much greater independence in thinking and in action, and for the first time there has been given promise of development, which heretofore has been considered hopeless on the basis of nature. What has happened in the case of women can happen in the case of Negroes, and not until this revolution of mind is completed will there be a fair chance for the full development of those principles of brotherhood and liberty which we hold as ideals.

Mary McLeod Bethune, "Notes for the Address Before the Women's Club," incomplete typescript, undated, Amistad Research Center, Dillard University, New Orleans, Louisiana.

BLACK WOMEN
IN
WHITE AMERICA

A DOCUMENTARY
HISTORY

CHAPTER ONE

SLAVERY

Ah done been in sorrow's kitchen and ah
licked de pots clean.

Gulla Proverb

SLAVERY

❦ The plantation slave system formed a separate and distinct culture which bound both master and slave in a complex and interdependent relationship. Although the race prejudices of whites, which antedated the institutionalization of slavery, shaped the system's form and character, its object was not genocide. American slavery was above all a labor system, designed to extract the maximum amount of profit from unwilling and dependent subjects. In practice, the production process and the objects of the system set some limits to its arbitrariness and cruelty. Self-interest of the master in the preservation of his property generally dictated the maintenance of minimum standards designed for survival of the slave, but it was the barest survival under the harshest conditions. On the other hand, the deeply ingrained racism of American culture, which designated Blacks not only as enslaved people but as inherently inferior because of their race, tended to worsen the conditions of American slaves as the system advanced in time. The mutually reinforcing interplay of racism and economic motivation made the slave system increasingly oppressive.

The essence of slavery was that the slave was legally a chattel, a piece of property to be bought and sold and disposed of at the master's will. He had no legal rights, could not testify in his own behalf nor bear witness against a white person. As a result of this feature of the slave system, which was peculiar to North American slavery, the slave was subject to the arbitrary will of his master in all matters. His treatment depended on the personality, circumstances and economic condition of his master.

The legal fiction of chattel slavery notwithstanding, the slave's humanity constantly and in a complex way affected his masters. Most slaves lived, not on large plantations, but in small isolated agricultural units where they were in close daily contact with their owners and often worked side by side with them. Far from being the passive objects which

racist historiography has made them out to be, slaves
exerted a constant active influence on their environment
and the whites with whom they came in contact. The selections in this chapter illustrate the rich variety of the slave's
self-assertion: the little child minding white babies, who
lets them drop out of her lap as soon as she is unobserved;
the slave woman shamming illness in order to avoid being
sold away from her husband; the effort of slave parents to
protect their children and families; the shamming, flattering,
negotiating, threatening and resisting that formed the daily
web of interaction between slaves and masters.

Although a certain amount of accommodation was necessary for survival, slaves, like all oppressed people, resisted
their oppression. Only the most severe system of terror
could keep this resistance from breaking into frequent and
large-scale rebellion. Thus, the harsh but tolerable labor
system was supplemented by a terroristic system of cruelty
and repression against all those slaves who dared to show any
sign of insubordination or rebellion. The hysterical and
tyrannical response to slave insubordination and the threat
of slave rebellion found expression in the often cruel punishment of the persons involved, in increasing restraints on
all slaves—such as the denial of schooling to black children
in the wake of the Denmark Vesey and Nat Turner
rebellions—and in restrictions on free Blacks.

PURCHASE AND SALE

❦ While slaveholders frowned upon the practice and
defenders of slavery denied its existence, the sale of slaves
away from their nearest relatives was a common practice.
It occurred with great frequency following the death of

a master and during periods of economic stress. The threat
of such a sale was also a common means of discipline, and
the actual sale was frequently a means of punishment of an
insubordinate slave.

BILL OF SALE OF ABRAHAM VAN VLEEK

Abm. Van Vleek purchased at Vandue of Barent Van Du-
pail October 28: 1811—

1 Faning Mill	$ 17.25
1 Red face Cow	13.25
1 Yearling Calf	4.25
1 Plough	1.6
1 Wench Nam. Eve & Child	156.00
8 Fancy Chairs	9.25
One Looking Glass. Ten Table Six Silver Table Spoons. Six So. Tea Spoons 10 China tea Saucers. 11 Wo. Cups 1 Tea Pot. Sugar and Milk Cups. 3 Plates Dish and tea Bord	35.12½
	——$236.18½

The Above Interest from the Date

Rcvd. December 26th 1811 of Abraham I. Van Vleek the
amount of the within amount in full———

Barent I. Goes (illeg.)

Slavery Manuscript, American Antiquarian Society, Worcester,
Massachusetts.

MRS. BLANKENSHIP WISHES
TO BUY A SLAVE GIRL

Nottoway Co. House March 29/63

Mr. E. H. Stokes

I am anxious to buy a small healthy negro girl—ten or twelve years old, and would like to know if you could let me have one—I will pay you cash in State money—and you allowing the per centage on it—I will take her on trial of a few weeks—please let me hear from you as soon as possible (—I would like a dark Mulatto)—describing the girl and stating the price—Address Mrs. B. L. Blankenship care A, D, Fargua —Nottoway Co. House Va.

Recd, and answered April 1/63

Lucy Chase Manuscript, American Antiquarian Society, Worcester, Massachusetts.

MOSES GRANDY'S WIFE IS SOLD

❦ *Moses Grandy, suspecting nothing, was standing in the street when the slave coffle passed with his wife in chains.*

Mr. Rogerson was with them on his horse, armed with pistols. I said to him, 'For God's sake, have you bought my wife?' He said he had; when I asked him what she had done, he said she had done nothing, but that her master wanted money. He drew out a pistol and said that if I went near the wagon on which she was, he would shoot me. I asked for leave to shake hands with her which he refused, but said I

might stand at a distance and talk with her. My heart was so
full that I could say very little. . . . I have never seen or heard
from her from that day to this. I loved her as I love my life.

Moses Grandy, *Narrative of the Life of Moses Grandy, Late a Slave
in the United States of America* (Boston: O. Johnson Publishing
Company, 1844), p. 11.

A SLAVE DEALER'S SALE RECEIPTS

Lucy Chase Manuscript. Photo courtesy of the American Antiquarian
Society, Worcester, Massachusetts.

A MOTHER IS SOLD AWAY
FROM HER CHILDREN

I remained in Williams' slave pen about two weeks. The night previous to my departure a woman was brought in, weeping bitterly, and leading by the hand a little child. They were Randall's mother and half-sister. On meeting them he was overjoyed, clinging to her dress, kissing the child. [Randall is a lad of about ten.]

Emily, the child, was seven or eight years old, of light complexion, and with a face of admirable beauty. . . . The woman also was arrayed in silk, with rings upon her fingers, and golden ornaments suspended from her ears. Her air and manners, the correctness and propriety of her language—all showed, evidently, that she had sometime stood above the common level of a slave. . . . Her name was Eliza, and this was the story of her life, as she afterwards related it.:

She was the slave of Elisha Berry, a rich man, living in the neighborhood of Washington. Years before he had . . . quarreled with his wife. In fact, soon after Randall was born, they separated. Leaving his wife and daughter in the house they had always occupied, he erected a new one near by, on the estate. Into this house he brought Eliza; and, on condition of her living with him, she and her children were to be emancipated. She resided with him there nine years, with servants to attend upon her, and provided with every comfort and luxury of life. Emily was his child. . . . At length, for some cause beyond Berry's control, a division of his property was made. She and her children fell to the share of Mr. Brooks [Berry's son-in-law]. During the nine years she had lived with Berry . . . she and Emily had become the object of Mrs. Berry's and her daughter's hatred and dislike. . . .

The day she was led into the pen, Brooks had brought her from the estate into the city, under pretence that the time had come when her free papers were to be executed, in fulfillment of her master's promise. Elated at the prospect of immediate liberty, she decked herself and little Emmy in their best apparel, and accompanied him with a joyful heart. On their arrival in the city . . . she was delivered to the trader Burch. The paper that was executed was a bill of sale. The hope of years was blasted in a moment. . . .

A planter of Baton Rouge . . . purchased Randall. . . . All the time the trade was going on, Eliza was crying aloud, and wringing her hands. She besought the man not to buy him, unless he also bought herself and Emily. She promised, in that case, to be the most faithful slave that ever lived. . . . Freeman turned round to her, savagely, with his whip in his uplifted hand, ordering her stop her noise, or he would flog her. He would not have such work—such snivelling; and unless she ceased that minute, he would take her to the yard and give her a hundred lashes. . . . She kept on begging and beseeching them, most piteously, not to separate the three. . . . But it was of no avail. . . . The bargain was agreed upon, and Randall must go alone. . . .

What has become of the lad, God knows. . . . I would have cried myself if I had dared. . . .

At length, one day . . . Freeman ordered us to our places, in the great room. A gentleman was waiting for us as we entered. After some further inspection . . . he finally offered Freeman one thousand dollars for me, nine hundred for Harry, and seven hundred for Eliza. . . . As soon as Eliza heard it she was in agony again. By this time she had become haggard and hollow-eyed with sickness and with sorrow. . . . She broke from her place in the line of women, and rushing down where Emily was standing, caught her in her arms. . . . Freeman sternly ordered her to be quiet, but she did not heed him. He caught her by the arm and pulled her rudely, but she only clung closer to the child. Then, with a volley of great oaths, he struck her such a heartless blow, that she staggered backward. . . . "Mercy, mercy, master!" she cried, falling on her knees. "Please, master, buy Emily. I can never work any if she is taken from me; I will die."

Finally . . . the purchaser of Eliza stepped forward, evidently affected, and said to Freeman he would buy Emily, and asked him what her price was. . . .

But to this human proposal Freeman was entirely deaf. He would not sell her then on any account whatever. There were heaps and piles of money to be made of her, he said, when she was a few years older. There were men enough in New Orleans who would give five thousand dollars for such an extra, handsome, fancy piece as Emily would be. . . . No, no, he would not sell her then. . . .

When Eliza heard Freeman's determination not to part with Emily, she became absolutely frantic. . . . We waited some time, when, finally, Freeman out of patience, tore Emily from her mother by main force. . . .

"Don't leave me, mama—don't leave me," screamed the child, as its mother was pushed harshly forward. . . . But she cried in vain. Out of the door and into the street we were quickly hurried. Still we could hear her calling to her mother, "Come back—don't leave me . . ." until her infant voice grew faint and still more faint . . . and finally was wholly lost.

Solomon Northup, *Narrative of Solomon Northup, Twelve Years a Slave* . . . (Auburn, New York: Derby and Miller, 1853), pp. 50–53, 81–82, 84–88.

A SLAVE MOTHER SUCCEEDS IN RETURNING TO HER FAMILY

Falmouth, Feb. 24, 1846

R. H. Dickerson & Brothers [Slavedealers]
Richmond, Va.
Gentlemen,

Your letter this moment came to hand and I hasten to reply. I fear you cannot sell Lucy, in her low spirited situation for more than four hundred and twenty five dollars, which sum I am not disposed to take. Therefore if you cannot get four hundred and fifty dollars twenty four hours after the receipt of this be so kind as to send her up and deliver her to Mr. Derricott and ask him to attend to her till she arrives in Fredbg. I apprehend from Frds. she will come home. Tell her to bring her child's clothes. . . .

I feel grateful to you . . . believing you have used your best exertions to sell but her hysterical, low spirited situation thwarted your best intentions. Be so good as to send her up Friday . . . and assure her I will keep her myself or sell her in Falmo. But my desire and that of the family is to keep her. . . .

In haste, with best wishes I subscribe myself your friend

Alex Fitzhugh

P.S. Your attention to seeing her safely conducted to the car will confer a favour, and write when you send her or the day before, if there no prospect of getting the 450.—

Lucy Chase Manuscript, American Antiquarian Society, Worcester, Massachusetts.

A SLAVE SHAMS ILLNESS TO STAY WITH HER HUSBAND

Feb. 7, 1847

R. H. Dickerson & Brothers
Richmond, Va.
Dear Sir

I saw Susan's master the day after I recd your note, and he requested me to say to you, that it is his wish that you would sell Susan the first opportunity, whatever you can get for her, as she is making so many complaints and as she says she is

not sound, he is not willing to warrant her sound for fear
that she may be returned in his hands or there may be some
difficulty about her, all of which he wishes to avoid, but war-
rants the right and title to be good. But I believe it is all pre-
tentious and false representations she is making with the
hope of returning to King Geo. to live with her husband
which she will never do. . . . Give me the prices and whether
you think they will be higher in the spring or not. I really
think that Susan is sound for I never heard any thing to the
contrary before I carried her to Richmond. . . .

R. V. Tiffey

Lucy Chase Manuscript, American Antiquarian Society, Worcester,
Massachusetts.

TELL IT LIKE IT WAS

❧ In contradiction to the popularly accepted myths
about slavery, the vast majority of slaves did not live on
large plantations. Most slaves lived on small, family-operated
farms, where their contacts with their masters were constant
and intimate. Unfortunately, there are very few sources
concerning the living conditions of these slaves. A considerable number of slaves lived in city households, where they
worked as servants, artisans, small tradesmen and where their
contacts with other slaves and with freedmen were frequent.

Source material concerning black women is much more
difficult to find than that pertaining to slaves in general.
Wherever possible, firsthand accounts of black women,
concerning themselves and others, have been assembled.
Where that was not possible, the eyewitness statements of
black men and of white abolitionists have been used. Some
descriptions of slave conditions, such as the routine of planta-

tion work, apply to both men and women and have been included.

In general, the lot of black women under slavery was in every respect more arduous, difficult and restricted than that of the men. Their work and duties were the same as that of the men, while childbearing and rearing fell upon them as as an added burden. Punishment was meted out to them regardless of motherhood, pregnancy or physical infirmity. Their affection for their children was used as a deliberate means of tying them to their masters, for children could always be held as hostages in case of the mother's attempted escape. The chances of escape for female slaves were fewer than those for males. Additionally, the sexual exploitation and abuse of black women by white men was a routine practice.

DAILY LIFE OF PLANTATION SLAVES

THEY WORKED, IN A MANNER OF SPEAKING, FROM CAN TO CAN'T, FROM THE TIME THEY COULD SEE UNTIL THE TIME THEY COULDN'T.

ABBIE LINDSAY, EX-SLAVE FROM LOUISIANA.

In the latter part of August begins the cotton picking season. At this time each slave is presented with a sack. . . . each one is also presented with a large basket that will hold about two barrels. This is to put the cotton in when the sack is filled. . . .

When a new hand . . . is sent for the first time into the field, he is whipped up smartly, and made for that day to pick as fast as he can possibly. At night it is weighed, so that his capability in cotton picking is known. He must bring in the same weight each night following. If it falls short, it is considered evidence that he has been laggard, and a greater or less number of lashes is the penalty. . . .

The hands are required to be in the cotton fields as soon as it is light in the morning, and, with the exception of ten or fifteen minutes, which is given them at noon to swallow their allowance of cold bacon, they are not permitted to be a moment idle until it is too dark to see. . . .

The day's work over in the field, the baskets are "toted" . . . to the gin-house, where the cotton is weighed. . . . A slave never approaches the gin-house with his basket of cotton but with fear. If it falls short in weight . . . he knows that he must suffer. And if he has exceeded it by ten or twenty pounds, in all probability his master will measure the next day's task, accordingly. . . . After weighing, follow the whippings; and then the baskets are carried to the cotton house, and their contents stored away like hay, all hands being sent in to tramp it down. . . .

This done, the labor of the day is not yet ended, by any means. Each one must then attend to his respective chores. One feeds the mules, another the swine—another cuts the wood, and so forth. . . . Finally, at a late hour, they reach the quarters, sleepy and overcome with the long day's toil. Then a fire must be kindled in the cabin, the corn ground in the small hand-mill, and supper, and dinner for the next day in the field, prepared. All that is allowed them is corn and bacon, which is given out at the corncrib and smoke-house every Sunday morning. Each one receives, as his weekly allowance, three and a half pounds of bacon, and corn enough to make a peck of meal. That is all. . . .

The same fear of punishment with which [the slaves] approach the gin-house, possesses them again on lying down to get a snatch of rest. It is the fear of oversleeping in the morning. Such an offence would certainly be attended with not less than twenty lashes. With a prayer that he may be on his feet and wide awake at the first sound of the horn, he sinks to his slumbers nightly.

Solomon Northup, *Narrative of Solomon Northup, Twelve Years A Slave* . . . (Auburn, New York: Derby and Miller, 1853), pp. 165–169.

THE SLAVES' GARDEN PLOT

On every plantation with which I ever had any acquaintance the people are allowed to make patches, as they are called— that is gardens, in some remote and unprofitable part of the estate, generally in the woods, in which they plant corn, potatoes, pumpkins, melons etc. for themselves. These patches they must cultivate on Sunday, or let them go uncultivated.

Charles Ball, *Slavery in the United States: A Narrative of the Life and Adventures of Charles Ball, a Black Man* (Lewistown, Pennsylvania: J. W. Shugert, 1836), p. 166.

A HOUSE SLAVE'S FAMILY LIFE

I have mentioned my great-aunt, who was a slave in Dr. Flint's family. . . . This aunt had been married at twenty years of age; that is, as far as slaves *can* marry. She had the consent of her master and mistress, and a clergyman performed the ceremony. . . . She had always slept on the floor in the entry, near Mrs. Flint's chamber door, that she might be within call. When she was married, she was told she might have the small room in an outhouse. Her mother and her husband furnished it. He was a seafaring man, and was allowed to sleep there when he was at home. But on the wedding evening, the bride was ordered to her old post on the entry floor.

Mrs. Flint, at that time, had no children; but she was expecting to be a mother, and if she should want a drink of water in the night, what could she do without her slave to bring it?

· · ·

❦ *The slave woman stayed at her post at night, even when she herself was pregnant. She gave birth to six children, all of whom died within the first few weeks of life.*

All the while she was employed as night-nurse to Mrs. Flint's children. Finally, toiling all day and being deprived of rest at night, completely broke down her constitution, and Dr. Flint declared it was impossible she could ever become the mother of a living child. After this, they allowed her to sleep in the little room in the outhouse, except when there was sickness in the family. She afterwards had two feeble babies, one of whom died in a few days, and the other in four weeks.

Harriet Brent Jacobs, Incidents in the Life of a Slave Girl, written by herself, edited by Lydia Maria Child (Boston: Author, 1861).

A SEAMSTRESS IS PUNISHED

A handsome mulatto woman, about 18 or 20 years of age, whose independent spirit could not brook the degradation of slavery, was in the habit of running away; for this offence she had been repeatedly sent by her master and mistress to be whipped by the keeper of the Charleston workhouse. This had been done with such inhuman severity, as to lacerate her back in a most shocking manner; a finger could not be laid between the cuts. But the love of liberty was too strong to be annihilated by torture; and, as a last resort, she was whipped at several different times, and kept a close prisoner. A heavy iron collar, with three prongs projecting from it, was placed round her neck, and a strong and sound front tooth was extracted, to serve as a mark to describe her, in case of escape.

Her sufferings at this time were agonizing; she could lie in no position but on her back, which was sore from scroung-ings, as I can testify from personal inspection, and her only place of rest was the floor, on a blanket. These outrages were committed in a family where the mistress daily read the scriptures, and assembled her children for family worship. She was accounted, and was really, so far as alms-giving was concerned, a charitable woman, and tender-hearted to the poor; and yet this suffering slave, who was the seamstress of the family was continually in her presence, sitting in her chamber to sew, or engaged in her other household work, with her lacerated and bleeding back, her mutilated mouth, and heavy iron collar without, so far as appeared, exciting any feelings of compassion.

Testimony of Sarah M. Grimké, abolitionist from South Carolina, in [Theodore D. Weld], *American Slavery As It Is: Testimony of a Thousand Witnesses* (New York: American Anti-Slavery Society, 1839).

THE DAILY LIFE OF HOUSE SLAVES

The utter disregard of the comfort on the slaves, in *little* things can scarcely be conceived of by those who have not been a *component part* of slaveholding communities. . . . In South Carolina musketoes [!] swarm in myriads, more than half the year—they are so excessively annoying at night that no family thinks of sleeping without nets . . . yet slaves are never provided with them . . . and yet these very masters and mistresses will be so kind to their *horses* as to provide them with *fly nets*. . . .

Only two meals a day are allowed the house slaves—the *first at twelve o'clock.* . . . They are often kept from their meals by way of punishment. No table is provided for them to eat from. . . . Each takes his plate or tin pan and iron spoon and holds it in the hand or on the lap. I *never* saw slaves seated round a *table* to partake of any meal.

As the general rule, no lights of any kind, no firewood—no

towels, basins, or soap, no tables, chairs or other furniture, are provided. . . . I have repeatedly known slave children kept the whole winter's evening, sitting on the stair-case in a cold entry, just to be at hand to snuff candles or hand a tumbler of water from the side-board, or go on errands from one room to another. It may be asked why they were not permitted to stay in the parlor, when they would be still more at hand. I answer, because waiters are not allowed to *sit* in the presence of their owners, and as children who were kept running all day, would of course get very tired of standing for two or three hours, they were allowed to go into the entry and sit on the staircase until rung for. Another reason is, that even slaveholders at times find the presence of slaves very annoying; they cannot exercise entire freedom of speech before them on all subjects.

I have also known instances where seamstresses were kept in cold entries to work by the staircase lamps for one or two hours, every evening in winter—they could not see without standing up all the time, though the work was often too large and heavy for them to sew upon it in that position without great inconvenience, and yet they were expected to do their work as *well* with their cold fingers, and standing up, as if they had been sitting by a comfortable fire and provided with the necessary light. House slaves suffer a great deal also from not being allowed to leave the house without permission. If they wish to go even for a draught of water, they must *ask leave*, and if they stay longer than the mistress thinks necessary, they are liable to be punished. . . .

It frequently happens that relatives, among slaves, are separated for weeks or months, by the husband or brother being taken by the master on a journey, to attend on his horses and himself.—When they return, the white husband seeks the wife of his love; but the black husband must wait to see *his* wife, until mistress pleases to let her chambermaid leave her room. . . .

The sufferings to which slaves are subjected by separations of various kinds, cannot be imagined by those unacquainted with the working out of the system behind the curtain. Take the following instances.

Chambermaids and seamstresses often sleep in their mistresses' apartments, but with no bedding at all. I know of an instance of a woman who has been married eleven years, and yet has never been allowed to sleep out of her mistress's chamber.—This is a *great* hardship to slaves. When we consider that house slaves are rarely allowed social intercourse during the *day*, as their work generally *separates* them; the barbarity of such an arrangement is obvious. It is peculiarly a hardship in the above case, as the husband of the women does not "belong" to her "owner" and because he is subject to dreadful attacks of illness, and can have but little attention from his wife in the *day*. And yet her mistress, who is an old lady, gives her the highest character as a faithful servant, and told a friend of mine, that she was "entirely dependent upon her for *all* her comforts; she dressed and undressed her, gave her all her food, and was so *necessary* to her that she could not do without her." I may add, that this couple are tenderly attached to each other. . . .*

Persons who own plantations and yet live in cities, often take children from their parents as soon as they are weaned, and send them into the country; because they do not want the time of the mother taken up by attendance upon her own children, it being too valuable to the mistress. As a *favor*, she is, in some cases, permitted to go to see them once a year. . . . Parents are almost never consulted as to the disposition to be made of their children; they have as little control over them, as have domestic animals over the disposal of their young. Every natural and social feeling and affection are violated with indifference; slaves are treated as though they did not possess them.

Another way in which the feelings of slaves are trifled with and often deeply wounded, is by changing their names; if, at the time they are brought into a family, there is another

---

* The case here referred to is that of Stephen and Juba. See pp. 42–45.

slave of the same name; or if the owner happens, for some other reason, not to like the name of the new comer. I have known slaves very much grieved at having the names of their children thus changed, when they had been called after a dear relation. . . .

The slave suffers also greatly from being continually *watched*. The system of espionage which is constantly kept up over slaves is the most worrying and intolerable that can be imagined. . . .

In the course of my testimony I have entered somewhat into the *minutiae* of slavery, because this is a part of the subject often overlooked, and cannot be appreciated by any but those who have been witnesses, and entered into sympathy with the slaves as human beings. Slaveholders think nothing of them, because they regard their slaves as *property*, the mere instruments of their convenience and pleasure. *One who is a slaveholder at heart never recognises a human being in a slave.*

> Testimony of Angelina Grimké Weld, in [Theodore D. Weld],
> *American Slavery As It Is: Testimony of a Thousand Witnesses*
> (New York: American Anti-Slavery Society, 1839).

I WASN'T CRYING 'BOUT MISTRESS, I WAS CRYING 'CAUSE THE WHITE BREAD WAS GONE

MARTHA HARRISON

❦ Martha Harrison was an old woman at the time of this interview; she did not know her age, but had vivid memories of the Civil War years when she was perhaps twelve years old. Her mother had twelve children, of whom she was the sole survivor.

Her account is interesting not only for its intimate details of a childhood in slavery, but for its vivid examples of slave resistance in its various forms. The interviewer provided the added information that Martha Harrison's father, who had been sold South as a punishment after killing the overseer, returned to his family some years later. As in so many other slave narratives, one encounters here once again a black couple struggling in every way open to them to defend themselves, their marriage, their children. Such primary evidence refutes the facile stereotypes of black "matriarchy" and "emasculated" black males, even under slavery.

They had cradles for the little nigger babies, and long before the War I was big enough to rock them babies, and old Cunningan would come in and tell ole Miss that they was gonna have a war to free the niggers, and I heard 'em talking, but I didn't know what they was talking 'bout. Mother come in with her steers, from hauling rails, and I told her what they said, and she made like it wasn't nothing, 'cause she was scared I'd tell them if she made like it was important. . . .

I didn't do nothing but play and pick up chips for old Aunt Fanny. She fed us. They had these round wooden bowls, and Aunt Fanny would take that and pour the licker in it, and put bread in it for the chillen to eat. It was a great big bowl, big as that dish pan there. That's what we had for dinner, and milk and bread for supper. Mistress would say, "Go pick up some chips for old Aunt Fan to put on the lid," and I would run and break out to get the chips first, 'cause I was crazy about white bread, and when we all got back with the chips, Mistress would give us some white bread, but she would make me wait till they all got there. I liked it 'cause mammy 'nem didn't get white bread but once a week —that was Sunday, and the rest of the time they had just corn bread or shorts. I was so foolish! When she died (Mistress) it liked to killed me; I just cried and cried, and mammy say, "What's the matter with you, gal?" I said, "Ole Miss is dead, and I won't get no more white bread." She said, "Shet your mouth, gal." I thought when she died she carried all the white bread with her. Folks was saying, "Look at that po little nigger crying 'bout her Mistress," but I wasn't crying 'bout mistress, I was crying 'cause the white bread was gone. . . .

I couldn't tell you how many niggers he [*her master*] did have; he had so many and his wife had so many. The place was full; times sho' was hard, sho' as you born. Chillen was just as lousy as pigs. They had these combs that was just like cards you "card" cotton with, and they would comb your head with them. That wouldn't get the lice out, but it would make it feel better. They had to use larkspur to get 'em out; that would always get lice out of your head. But there wasn't no chillen would get sick before the War. I reckon the lice musta kept 'em healthy. . . .

Lawd, the times we did have. I know that when the War got over and we got free they put me in the field to work. I never went to school a day in my life; what I learned to read, I learned myself. My children all went to school, though. . . .

[The] overseer . . . went to my father one morning and said, "Bob, I'm gonna whip you this morning." Daddy said, "I ain't done nothing," and he said, "I know it, I'm gonna whip you to keep you from doing nothing," and he hit him with that cowhide—you know it would cut the blood out of you with every lick if they hit you hard—and daddy was chopping cotton, so he just took up his hoe and chopped right down on that man's head and knocked his brains out. Yes'm, it killed him, but they didn't put colored folks in jail then, so when old Charlie Merrill, the nigger trader, come along they sold my daddy to him, and he carried him way down in Mississippi. Ole Merrill would buy all the time, buy and sell niggers just like hogs. They sold him Aunt Phoebe's little baby that was just toddling long, and Uncle Dick—that was my mammy's brother.

The way they would whip you was like they done my oldest sister. They tied her, and they had a place just like they're gonna barbecue a hog, and they would strip you and tie you and lay you down. . . . Old Aunt Fanny had told marster that my sister wouldn't keep her dress clean, and that's what they was whipping her 'bout. So they had her down in the cellar whipping her, and I was real little. I couldn't say "Big Sis," but I went and told Mammy, "Old Marster's got 'Big Jim' down there in the cellar beating her," and mammy got out of bed and went in there and throwed Aunt Fan out the kitchen door, and they had to stop whipping Big Sis and come and see about Aunt Fan. You see, she would tell things on the others, trying to keep from getting whipped herself. I seed mistress crack her many a time over the head with a broom, and I'd be so scared she was gonna crack me, but she never did hit me, 'cept slap me when I'd turn the babies over. I'd get tired and make like I was sleep, and would ease the cradle over and throw the baby out. I never would throw mammy's out, though. Old Miss would be setting there just knitting and watching the babies; they had a horn and every woman could tell when it was time to come and nurse her baby by the way they would blow the horn. The white folks was crazy 'bout their nigger babies, 'cause that's where they got their profit. . . . When I'd get tired, I would just ease that baby over and Mistress would slap me so hard; I didn't know a hand could hurt so bad, but I'd take the slap and get to go out to play. She would slap me hard and say, "Git on out of here and stay till you wake up," and that was just what I wanted, 'cause I'd play then. . . .

My husband never did like for me to work; he used to ask me how come I work when he was doing all he could to give me what I wanted. "Looks like you don't 'preciate what I'm trying to do for you." But I'd say, "Yes, I do, honey, I jest help you 'cause I don't want you to break down. If you put a load on one horse it will pull him down, but two horses can pull it jest as easy." . . .

[Ophelia Settle Egypt, J. Masuoka, Charles S. Johnson], "Unwritten History of Slaves; Autobiographical Accounts of Negro Ex-Slaves," Social Science Source Documents No. 1 (Nashville, Tennessee: Fisk University, Social Science Institute, 1946), bound typescript, pp. 113–117.

THE STRUGGLE FOR SURVIVAL—DAY-TO-DAY RESISTANCE

❦ While property relations assumed and legal fiction insisted that the slave was a chattel, the slaveholder knew very well that the slave was human. Because he was human, the slaveholder knew he would certainly respond as did other human beings to knowledge and enlightenment. While during the more patriarchal beginnings of the system, the slaveholder's conscience had prodded him into permitting the very minimal religious instruction of slaves, slave rebellions and the attacks upon the system from the North made the slaveholder's fearful for the safety of their human chattel. Thus, in the 1820's and 1830's all the slave states enacted more stringent laws, denying the slaves even the most rudimentary learning, restricting their contacts with fellow slaves, making manumission difficult or impossible and repressing the rights of freedom in every respect.

But the slave used his human resources to obstruct and thwart the slaveholder's best-laid plans. It was inevitable that in the daily, intimate contacts of plantation life there should be human ties formed between master and slaves, between slave and master's children. Often, the stringent laws were broken and circumvented with the tacit tolerance of indulgent masters. Mostly, slaves acquired knowledge by using their wits, by stealth, deceit and the most ingenious cooperation among themselves.

It was also inevitable that slaves, according to their individual characteristics, should succeed in influencing their masters, checking the masters' desires and, not infrequently, imposing their wills on their masters. Those looking only to slave rebellions as an indicator of the slave's desire for freedom are bound to see a distorted picture. The terror system against open rebellion was too cruel and overwhelming, the slave's isolation from supporting allies too complete to make rebellions anything but rare, sporadic outbursts, doomed to certain defeat. The real story of slave resistance must be sought in the buried record of daily sabotage, passive resistance and deliberate deceit.

In a system such as slavery, survival for the oppressed group was the greatest form of resistance. By role-playing and flattery, by cunning, intelligence and, often, passive resistance, the slave struggled to uphold his interests against those of his master. Carelessness and thievery, shamming illness and spoiling of produce and tools, mistreatment of the masters' cattle and property are the frequent complaints of slaveholders which indicate how widespread slave resistance was. Accounts of unexplained arson, poisonings, constant running away and numerous unsuccessful efforts at uprisings, culled from the press of the slaves states, indicate that more active forms of resistance were more frequent than historians usually recognized.

Slave women took part in all aspects of resistance, from slave rebellions to sabotage and passive resistance. The names of the many slave mothers who worked for years, or even decades, to buy their own freedom and that of their children have not been collected. Their stories lie buried in old newspapers and the memoirs of abolitionists. Their effort must certainly be reckoned in the struggle for survival of black people in this country.

SNEAKING AN EDUCATION: MEMORIES OF A CONTRABAND

SUSIE KING TAYLOR

I was born under the slave law in Georgia in 1848 and was brought up by my grandmother in Savannah. There were three of us with her, my younger sister and brother. My brother and I being the two eldest, we were sent to a friend of my grandmother, a Mrs. Woodhouse, a widow, to learn to read and write. She was a free woman and lived on Bay Lane between Habersham and Price Streets, about half a mile from my house. We went every day with our books wrapped in paper to prevent the police or white persons from seeing them. We went in, one at a time, through the gate into the yard to the kitchen, which was the school room. She had 25 or 30 children whom she taught, assisted by her daughter, Mary Jane. The neighbors would see us going in some time, but they supposed we were there learning trades, as it was the custom to give children a trade of some kind. After school, we left the same way we entered, one by one and we would go to a square about a block from the school and wait for each other. We would gather laurel leaves and pop them in our hands, on our way home. I remained at her school for two years or more, when I was sent to a Mrs. Mary Beasley, where I continued until May 1860, when she told my grandmother she had taught me all she knew, and grandmother had better get someone else who could teach me more, so I stopped my studies for a while.

I had a white playmate about this time, named Katie O'Connor, who lived on the next corner of the street from my house and who attended a convent. One day she told me, if I would promise not to tell her father, she would give me some lessons. On my promise not to do so, and gaining her mother's consent, she gave me lessons about four months every evening. At the end of this time she was put into the convent permanently, and I've never seen her since.

A month after this James Blouis, our landlord's son, was attending the high school and was very fond of grandmother, so she asked him to give me a few lessons which he did until the middle of 1861, when the Savannah Volunteer Guards, to which he and his brother belonged were ordered to the front under General Barton. In the first battle of Mannassas his brother Eugene was killed and James deserted over to the Union side and at the close of the war went to Washington, D.C., where he has since resided.

I often wrote passes for my grandmother, for all colored persons, free or slave were compelled to have a pass; free colored people having a guardian in place of a master. These passes were good until 10 or ten-thirty P.M. for one night or every night for one month. . . .

Susie King Taylor, Reminiscences of My Life in Camp with the 33rd United States Colored Troops (Boston: Author, 1902), pp. 5–6.

FOOLIN' MASSA: MEMORIES OF A CONTRABAND

Without any knowledge of newspapers, or books, or telegraphy, the slaves had their own way of gathering news from the whole country. They had secrets signs, an "Underground Telephone". . . . Intuitively they learned all the tricks of dramatic art. Their perceptions were quickened. When seemingly absorbed in work, they saw and heard all that was going on around them. They memorized with wonderful ease and correctness. . . .

Not long ago I heard some Negro women talking of old times over their sewing. One said,—

"My father and the other boys used to crawl under the house an' lie on the ground to hear massa read the newspaper to missis when they first began to talk about the war."

"See that big oak-tree there?" said another. "Our boys used to climb into that tree an' hide under the long moss while massa was at supper, so as to hear him an' his company talk about the war when they come out on the piazza to smoke."

"I couldn't read, but my uncle could," said a third. "I was waiting-maid, an' used to help missis to dress in the morning. If massa wanted to tell her something he didn't want me to know, he used to spell it out. I could remember the letters, an' as soon as I got away I ran to uncle an' spelled them over to him, an' he told me what they meant."

I was attracted by this, and asked if she could do this now. "Try me, missis; try me an' see!" she exclaimed. So I spelled a long sentence as rapidly as possible, without stopping between the words. She immediately repeated it after me, without missing a letter.

The children of this woman were amongst the first to enter a freedman's school during the war. They took to books as ducks take to water. The youngest, a boy, was really entered when a baby in his sister's arms, and was only allowed to remain because his nurse could not come without him. As soon as he could walk his mother complained he did not know anything. When he was three years old she was bitterly disappointed that he could not read.

"Why, if I had his chance," she exclaimed, rolling up her eyes and stretching out her hands, "do you think I would not learn!"

It goes without saying, that her children became good scholars. This youngest boy is now a leader amongst his own people.

Elizabeth Hyde Botume, *First Days Among the Contrabands*
(Boston: Lee & Shepard, 1893), pp. 6–7.

SHE FINALLY WENT TO SCHOOL THAT ONE NIGHT

JOSEPHINE ELIZABETH THOMAS WHITE

❦ *The following oral account concerning her mother was given in a tape-recorded interview by Mrs. Claudia White Harreld, seventy-six years old at the time of the recording. Her mother, Josephine White (1834–1902), was born a slave in Georgia and trained as a "sewing girl" by her mistress. When she was nine years old, she began to sit in the room with the white children and thus learned to read. She later married the Reverend William Jefferson White.*

She [Mama] devised a plan by which she could really acquire some knowledge. Her difficulty of course was pronouncing words the composition of which she knew, and she worked out a plan for that. Up on the top floor one of the aunts sat all day long blind, and Mama was very thoughtful of her. She finally decided to try Miss Ann out, so one night when she was sitting upstairs with Miss Ann, as she was doing frequently, she brought out her little blue-backed speller and began spelling the words and Miss Ann pronounced them for her. But she never asked Mama what she was doing or what she had in mind. Mama would ask her questions, Miss Ann would reply to them, but nothing more even passed between them about the matter. So that's how she learned to pronounce. She didn't have all the words straight, even with Miss Ann's help. . . . Then during her free time she had some hours that she could use and call her own. As she had charge of the linen—the household linen—she would slip into the linen closet and have a nook all ready, so that when she heard any footsteps she could slip the book under the things and they were safe. . . . She continued her education by reading everything she could put her hands on. . . . She heard of the great furor that was made when *Uncle Tom's Cabin*, came out. It was banned in the households and wasn't allowed to come into the house at all. . . . But a friend of hers told her that the book was in their household, that she had seen it and that she would steal it and bring it over. And she got about halfway through when somebody discovered it either in her hands or laid down carelessly somewhere, and of course they confiscated it at once. . . .

I was the tenth child in a family of eleven and I sat and listened on the day when I was a young girl when my mother told this story of *Uncle Tom*, that she had never been able to read, and how my brother, passing through the room heard the story that my mother was telling. He was a railway clerk and was one of the first to go in under Civil Service in [President] Grant's rule. When he got back from his next run he brought Mama an *Uncle Tom's Cabin* and she was able to finish the book. I must've been in my teens. . . .

My Papa and Mama married in 1853, I think. . . . My father was part Indian and part Caucasian. . . . She [Mama] claimed that she never went to school a day. And then we'd say, "But Mama, you went one night." And that story is that when my father established what is now Morehouse College, women were admitted at first as well as men, and Mama went to register there the first night. She told me that when she came from school, some work that she had taken in to do, some sewing—that's how she helped out the family budget—her sewing was right there on the bed just as she had left it, not a stitch taken in it, and she decided that she'd have to choose between the children—I guess she had about five or six or seven then—that she'd have to choose between the children's getting an education and her getting one, so she turned it over to them and never went back. But she did go that one night.

Mrs. Claudia White Harreld, taped interview, January, 1952, Schlesinger Library, Radcliffe College, Cambridge, Massachusetts. Used by permission.

A SLAVE WOMAN RUNS A MIDNIGHT SCHOOL

MILLA GRANSON

[In Natchez, Louisiana, there were] two schools taught by colored teachers. One of these was a slave woman who had taught a midnight school for a year. It was opened at eleven or twelve o'clock at night, and closed at two o'clock a.m. . . . Milla Granson, the teacher, learned to read and write from the children of her indulgent master in her old Kentucky home. Her number of scholars was twelve at a time, and when she had taught these to read and write she dismissed them, and again took her apostolic number and brought them up to the extent of her ability, until she had graduated hundreds. A number of them wrote their own passes and started for Canada. . . .

At length her night-school project leaked out, and was for a time suspended; but it was not known that seven of the twelve years subsequent to leaving Kentucky had been spent in this work. Much excitement over her night-school was produced. The subject was discussed in their legislature, and a bill was passed, that it should not be held illegal for a slave to teach a slave. . . . She not only [re]opened her night-school, but a Sabbath-school. . . . Milla Granson used as good language as any of the white people.

Laura S. Haviland, *A Woman's Life-Work, Labors and Experiences*
(Chicago: Publishing Association of Friends, 1889; copyright
1881), pp. 300–301.

A SLAVE MOTHER IN BUSINESS

My mother was a slave . . . owned by Mayor Harvey Griffin. . . . After my father was sold my master gave my mother permission to work for herself, provided she gave him one half she worked for which she agreed to do. She then obtained a situation as cook in the largest tavern in the village. . . . She did not stay there long because the mean brute threatened to whip her in one of his drunken sprees. . . .

My mother worked in the garrison [of Fort Washington, Maryland] a while and then she carried on a little business for herself by selling pies, hot coffee etc. to the Marines and exchanging the same for their rations. Her business increased and it became necessary that she should buy a horse and wagon to convey her goods to the fort, which she did. . . . My mother then got along very comfortably for about three years. . . .

My mother got many presents from the Marines in the shape of old clothes, shoes, caps, stockings etc. . . . Our business increased twofold then, because mother was running

a second hand clothing store on a small scale and made
quite a respectable living. The poor white surrounding us
became jealous in a body and waited on the Major and gave
vent to their feeling. The Major would have nothing to say
of any length but would only answer in monosyllables. . . .

Mother and I were freed in 1860 when the first regiment
of Union soldiers passed through Maryland on their way
to Washington . . . We marched with the soldiers.

J. E. Bruce, "A Sketch of My Life," Bruce Manuscripts, Schomburg
Collection, New York Public Library.

FIGHT, AND IF YOU CAN'T FIGHT, KICK

✦ *The following oral testimony of a former slave
provides a vivid character sketch of a type of slave frequently
depicted in slave narratives and primary sources—the black
mother and exemplary worker who was both feared and
respected by her masters, and who, by her courage and
militancy, imposed certain restrictions upon them.*

*The narrator was born and lived in a small town in
Tennessee. Her narrative is of great interest also because
it describes conditions on a small farm, where the master
and his family lived in close intimacy with four families of
slaves. In this account one catches fascinating glimpses of
the complex relationship of masters and slaves, and one can
get a sense of the daily interaction, affection, hatred and
conflict which must have characterized life under slavery
for both races. Historical accounts of slavery based on laws,
plantation overseers' records and the observations of travelers
fail to convey this lively reality.*

My mother was the smartest black woman in Eden. She was
as quick as a flash of lightning, and whatever she did could

not be done better. She could do anything. She cooked, washed, ironed, spun, nursed and labored in the field. She made as good a field hand as she did a cook. I have heard Master Jennings say to his wife, "Fannie has her faults, but she can outwork any nigger in the country. I'd bet my life on that."

My mother certainly had her faults as a slave. She was very different in nature from Aunt Caroline. Ma fussed, fought, and kicked all the time. I tell you, she was a demon. She said that she wouldn't be whipped, and when she fussed, all Eden must have known it. She was loud and boisterous, and it seemed to me that you could hear her a mile away. Father was often the prey of her high temper. With all her ability for work, she did not make a good slave. She was too high-spirited and independent. I tell you, she was a captain.

The one doctrine of my mother's teaching which was branded upon my senses was that I should never let anyone abuse me. "I'll kill you, gal, if you don't stand up for yourself," she would say. "Fight, and if you can't fight, kick; if you can't kick, then bite." Ma was generally willing to work, but if she didn't feel like doing something, none could make her do it. At least, the Jennings couldn't make, or didn't make her.

"Bob, I don't want no sorry nigger around me. I can't tolerate you if you ain't got no backbone." Such constant warning to my father had its effect. My mother's unrest and fear of abuse spread gradually to my father. He seemed to have been made after the timid kind. He would never fuss back at my mother, or if he did, he couldn't be heard above her shouting. Pa was also a sower of all seeds. He was a yardman, houseman, plowman, gardner, blacksmith, carpenter, keysmith, and anything else they chose him to be.

I was the oldest child. My mother had three other children by the time I was about six years old. It was at this age that I remember the almost daily talks of my mother on the cruelty of slavery. I would say nothing to her, but I was thinking all the time that slavery did not seem so cruel. Master and Mistress Jennings were not mean to my mother. It was she who was mean to them.

Master Jennings allowed his slaves to earn any money they could for their own use. My father had a garden of his own around his little cabin, and he also had some chickens. Mr. Dodge, who was my master's uncle, and who owned the hotel in Eden, was pa's regular customer. He would buy anything my pa brought to him; and many times he was buying his own stuff, or his nephew's stuff. I have seen pa go out at night with a big sack and come back with it full. He'd bring sweet potatoes, watermelons, chickens and turkeys. We were fond of pig roast and sweet potatoes, and the only way to have pig roast was for pa to go out on one of his hunting trips. Where he went, I cannot say, but he brought the booty home. The floor of our cabin was covered with planks. Pa had raised up two planks, and dug a hole. This was our storehouse. Every Sunday, Master Jennings would let pa take the wagon to carry watermelons, cider and ginger cookies to Spring Hill, where the Baptist church was located. The Jennings were Baptists. The white folks would buy from him as well as the free Negroes of Trenton, Tennessee. Sometimes these free Negroes would steal to our cabin at a specified time to buy a chicken or barbecue dinner. Mr. Dodge's slaves always had money and came to buy from us. Pa was allowed to keep the money he made at Spring Hill, and of course Master Jennings didn't know about the little restaurant we had in our cabin.

One day my mother's temper ran wild. For some reason Mistress Jennings struck her with a stick. Ma struck back and a fight followed. Mr. Jennings was not at home and the home and the children became frightened and ran upstairs. For half hour they wrestled in the kitchen. Mistress, seeing that she could not get the better of ma, ran out in the road, with ma right on her heels. In the road, my mother flew into her again. The thought seemed to race across my mother's mind to tear mistress' clothing off her body. She suddenly began to tear Mistress Jennings' clothes off. She caught hold, pulled, ripped and tore. Poor mistress was nearly naked when the storekeeper got to them and pulled ma off.

"Why, Fannie, what do you mean by that?" he asked.

"Why, I'll kill her, I'll kill her dead if she ever strikes me again."

I have never been able to find out the why of the whole thing. . . .

Pa heard Mr. Jennings say that Fannie would have to be whipped by law. He told ma. Two mornings afterward, two men came in at the big gate, one with a long lash in his hand. I was in the yard and I hoped they couldn't find ma. To my surprise, I saw her running around the house, straight in the direction of the men. She must have seen them coming. I should have known that she wouldn't hide. She knew what they were coming for, and she intended to meet them halfway. She swooped upon them like a hawk on chickens. I believe they were afraid of her or thought she was crazy. One man had a long beard which she grabbed with one hand, and the lash with the other. Her body was made strong with madness. She was a good match for them. Mr. Jennings came and pulled her away. I don't know what would have happened if he hadn't come at that moment, for one man had already pulled his gun out. Ma did not see the gun until Mr. Jennings came up. On catching sight of it, she said, "Use your gun, use it and blow my brains out if you will." . . .

That evening Mistress Jennings came down to the cabin.

"Well, Fannie," she said, "I'll have to send you away. You won't be whipped, and I'm afraid you'll get killed." . . .

"I'll go to hell or anywhere else, but I won't be whipped," ma answered.

"You can't take the baby, Fannie, Aunt Mary can keep it with the other children."

Mother said nothing at this. That night, ma and pa sat up late, talking over things, I guess. Pa loved ma, and I heard him say, "I'm going too, Fannie." About a week later, she called me and told me that she and pa were going to leave me the next day, that they were going to Memphis. She didn't know for how long.

"But don't be abused, Puss." She always called me Puss. My right name was Cornelia. I cannot tell in words the feelings I had at that time. My sorrow knew no bound. My very soul seemed to cry out, "Gone, gone, gone forever." I cried until my eyes looked like balls of fire. I felt for the first time in my life that I had been abused. How cruel it was to take my mother and father from me, I thought. My mother had been right. Slavery was cruel, so very cruel.

Thus my mother and father were hired to Tennessee. The next morning they were to leave. I saw ma working around with the baby under her arms as if it had been a bundle of some kind. Pa came up to the cabin with an old mare for ma to ride, and an old mule for himself. Mr. Jennings was with him.

"Fannie, leave the baby with Aunt Mary," said Mr. Jennings very quietly.

At this, ma took the baby by its feet, a foot in each hand, and with the baby's head swinging downward, she vowed to smash its brains out before she'd leave it. Tears were streaming down her face. It was seldom that ma cried, and everyone knew that she meant every word. Ma took her baby with her. . . .

An uneventful year passed. I was destined to be happily surprised by the return of my mother and father. They came one day, and found me sitting by the roadside in a sort of trance. . . .

"Puss, we've come back, me and pa, and we've come to stay." . . .

She and pa embraced and caressed me for a long time. We went to the cabin, and Master Jennings was there nearly as soon as we were.

"Hello, Fannie. How did you get along?" he asked.

"Why, Mr. Jennings, you know that I know how to get along," she answered.

"Well, I'm glad to hear that, Fannie."

Ma had on new clothes, and a pair of beautiful earrings. She told Aunt Mary that she stayed in Memphis one year without a whipping or a cross word.

Pa had learned to drink more liquor than ever, it seemed. At least, he was able to get more of it, for there were many disagreements between pa and ma about his drinking. Drinkers will drink together, and Mr. Jennings was no exception. Pa would have the excuse that Master Jennings offered him liquor, and of course he wouldn't take it from anybody else. It was common to see them together, half drunk, with arms locked, walking around and around the old barn. Then pa would put his hands behind him and let out a big whoop which could be heard all over Eden. . . .

Our family was increased by the arrival of a baby girl. Ma was very sick, and she never did get well after that. She was cooking for Mistress Jennings one day when she came home and went to bed. She never got up. I guess ma was sick about six months. During that time she never hit a tap of work. She said she had brought five children in the world for the Jennings, and that was enough; that she didn't intend to work when she felt bad.

On the day my mother died, she called pa and said . . . "Go tell Master Jennings to come in, and get all the slaves too."

Pa went and returned in five minutes with old master.

"Fannie, are you any worse?" said old master.

"No, no, Master Jennings, no worse. But I'm going to leave you at eight o'clock."

"Where are you going, Fannie," Master Jennings asked as if he didn't know that ma was talking about dying.

Ma shook her head slowly and answered, "I'm going where there ain't no fighting and cussing and damning."

"Is there anything that you want me to do for you, Fannie?"

Ma told him that she reckoned there wasn't much of anything that anybody could do for her now. "But I would like for you to take Puss and hire her out among ladies, so she can be raised right. She will never be any good here, Master Jennings."

A funny look came over Master Jennings' face, and he bowed his head up and down. All the hands had come in and were standing around with him.

My mother died at just about eight o'clock.

[Ophelia Settle Egypt, J. Masuoka, Charles S. Johnson], "Unwritten History of Slavery; Autobiographical Accounts of Negro Ex-Slaves," Social Science Documents No. 1 (Nashville, Tennessee: Fisk University, Social Science Institute, 1945), bound typescript, pp. 284–291.

A MOTHER PURCHASES
HER DAUGHTER

We solicited over seventy dollars for a poor woman by the name of Jackson, from Marseilles, Kentucky, who had bought herself by washing and ironing of nights, after her mistress' work was done. During seven long years she did not allow herself to undress except to change. Her sleep was little naps over the ironing board. Seven years of night work brought the money that procured her freedom. She had a son and daughter nearly grown, and to purchase their freedom she was now bending her day and night energies. . . . The master's indebtedness compelled him to sell one of them, and market was found for the girl of sixteen. Nine hundred dollars was offered, and the distressed mother had but four hundred dollars to pay. . . .

In her distress she went from house to house, to plead for a buyer who would advance the five hundred dollars, and take a mortgage on her until she could make it. At length she found a Baptist deacon who purchased her daughter, and she paid him the four hundred dollars. He was to keep her until the mortgage was redeemed by her mother. . . . After working very hard one year, she was able to pay but one hundred and fifty dollars toward the mortgage, when her health began to fail. The deacon told her . . . he could not wait longer than another year, before he would have to sell her. . . .

❦ *On the advice of a friendly merchant, the mother went to Cincinnati and contacted some abolitionists.*

Levi Coffin and lawyer John Joliffe . . . gave her letters of introduction to friends at Oberlin, and other places, and by the time she was sent to me, she had over two hundred dollars toward the release of the mortgage. . . .

A few weeks later the glad mother returned and redeemed the daughter. I saw them together at Levi Coffin's in Cincinnatti, happy in their freedom.

Laura S. Haviland, A *Woman's Life-Work*, *Labors and Experiences*
Chicago: Publishing Association of Friends, 1889),
pp. 234–236.

RANSOMING A WOMAN FROM SLAVERY

We have just received a call from Mrs. E. B. WELLS, a slightly colored lady, one who has experienced in her own person the evils inherent in slavery, a member of the Baptist Church in St. Louis, in good and regular standing, having any number of certificates of excellent character, and has given proof of the good qualities of her head and heart by having purchased her own freedom at the enormous price of sixteen hundred dollars, of which one thousand was raised by the citizens of St. Louis, and who had also purchased her mother and sister by the payment of one thousand five hundred dollars. This lady (for a lady she really is) is now in the city of Rochester for the purpose of raising money with which to purchase the freedom of her only remaining sister in slavery. This sister is owned by Mrs.

BRENT, of Boonville, Mo., and Mrs. BRENT is willing
to take one thousand dollars for this Christian chattel, of
which sum five hundred dollars have already been raised by
the indefatigable exertions of Mrs. WELLS.—Her case is
commended to the humane and benevolent portion of our
citizens, and we cannot but hope that at least a part of the
five hundred dollars still remaining to be raised for this
ransom may be obtained in the city of Rochester.

Frederick Douglass' Paper, Vol. 12, No. 7 (April 8, 1859).

STEPHEN AND JUBA

❦ The slave Stephen was owned by Mrs. Mary
Grimké who rented him out to Dr. Frost. Dr. Frost, apparently, sent him out to work on the Charleston waterfront.
It was hard work to which Stephen, formerly a house
servant, felt unsuited. He developed "fits," which neces-
sitated medical treatment. Stephen's wife, Juba, was owned
by an old lady, Mrs. Bizan, who depended on her entirely
for her care.

The ensuing correspondence between the abolitionists
Sarah and Angelina Grimké, then residing in New York
State, and their slaveholding mother, Mrs. Mary Grimké,
and sisters Elizabeth and Mary, residing in Charleston,
South Carolina, reveal intimate details of the slave-master
relationship. Sarah and Angelina had tried to prevail upon
their mother to free her slaves, but she had refused. However,
when Stephen's difficulties started, Mrs. Grimké was
willing to allow her daughters to take him North.

ELIZABETH GRIMKÉ TO HER SISTER ANGELINA GRIMKÉ WELD

May 2, 1838

. . . Stephen is now very sick with fits. . . . As you are now
all together would it not be best for you to make some ar-

rangement about him. You know he will not be recognized here as being free and there is no provision *even if he were* for free colored persons—no hospital, no lunatic asylum where they are received and owners are made to take care of them. I do think the best way would be to summon him to Philadelphia, where he might be placed where he would have proper attention. He has never stayed at Mrs. Bizans since he was so deranged—they are afraid to let him do so on account of his young children. I believe his wife sees but little of him, as during the day he is out at work. He has had fits several times lately. . . .

MARY S. GRIMKÉ TO THEODORE WELD AND HER DAUGHTERS
ANGELINA GRIMKÉ WELD AND SARAH GRIMKÉ

Nov. 16, 1838

[At their request, she has visited Stephen in the poorhouse.] Found him in good health and perfectly in his right mind and so rejoiced to see me that I was afraid the excitement would occasion a return of his malady. [She has spoken to the doctor who attended him while at the poorhouse.] He said he found him an intelligent, conscientious servant, saw no reason for keeping him confined, he had been greatly mismanaged while in the Medical College. . . . and that he was quite able to do light work. . . . I then sent to Mrs. Bizan who owns his Wife to know whether it would be agreeable to her to let him stay with her . . . she had no objections unless he was noisey and outrageous. [She has arranged for his release and will provide him with clothes which he needs badly.] He believes as I do that hard work was the cause of the violence of the fits, for he had several bad falls in loading vessels, while he was with me he was never unmanageable. He is desirous that I should take charge of him. . . . I have his book with Dr. Frosts receipts . . . the receipts in Dr. Frosts own handwriting after several deductions amounts to money received from him to $175.

❦ *The owner was very concerned about the expense of keeping Stephen at the poorhouse. The abolitionist daughters, horrified by such sentiment, began to send money for Stephen's expenses.*

MARY GRIMKÉ TO ANGELINA GRIMKÉ WELD

Jan. 10, 1839

[Stephen has been released from the poorhouse.] He is grateful for what has been done for him and is sensible of the great expense you have been at . . . he is willing to go to you and leave his wife. [But his wife, Juba, is very much attached to Stephen and does not want him to go. Her owner, Mrs. Bizan, to whom Angelina Grimké has applied with an offer to purchase Juba, refuses. She says she depends entirely on her services and will not free her until after her (the owner's) death.]

MARY GRIMKÉ TO A. G. WELD

April 1839

[Mrs. Bizan writes to Mrs. Grimké] "As long as Stephen behaved himself in an orderly and proper manner he was allowed to occupy the room of his wife and to pass freely in and out of the yard. Stephen has frequently been so disorderly and his conduct so improper; from madness or some other cause, that he is now *forbidden forever* to enter upon any part of the premises occupied by Mrs. Bizan . . . and should he be found thereon he will be so dealt with as the law directs." In consequence of this Stephen has made up his mind to leave his wife (as he says, she is of no service to him) and accept your offer [to come North]. . . .

❦ *Stephen returned to his owner's house and, although weak, earned enough to pay for his keep.*

MARY GRIMKÉ TO A. G. WELD

June 18, 1839

. . . Juba went to her mistress and told her that she could never be of the same service to her that she had ever been if she was the cause of separating her from her husband.

[As a consequence Mrs. Bizan has reconsidered and permitted Stephen to enter the yard during the day, but not at night.] Now that he can see his wife, Juba, during the day he wants to stay.

❦ *Stephen's owner died in July 1839. The heirs, much less sympathetic to the slave than their mother, placed him in the poorhouse when he had another fit. On August 30, 1839, one of the sisters writes about him:*

MARY GRIMKÉ TO ANGELINA GRIMKÉ WELD

Stephen . . . would not have been sent to the poorhouse, had he not become so deranged as to threaten the lives of those in the kitchen . . . he is at his wife's, last Sunday he was at Church, looking as usual. I have urged him to go out to you, but he says his wife is not willing.

❦ *Finally, Stephen, constantly beset by fits, which were probably epileptic, shuttled back and forth between the poorhouse and work which was too hard for him, decided to leave his wife and come North.*

ALL LETTERS:

Theodore Dwight Weld Collection, William L. Clements Library, University of Michigan, Ann Arbor, Michigan.

A WOMAN'S FATE

❦ *Under slavery, black women were savagely exploited as unpaid workers, as were black men; black women bred children to the master's profit and were sexually available to any white man who cared to use them. Mulattoes or especially beautiful black girls were sold at fancy prices as concubines.*

The sexual exploitation of black women by white men was so widespread as to be general. Some black women made the best of an inescapable necessity; others tried to strike an advantageous bargain. Many were assaulted not by their masters but by overseers, neighboring youth or the master's sons. The point here is that such exploitation was always possible and could in no way be fought or avoided—it was yet another way in which the total helplessness of the slave against arbitrary authority was institutionalized. It weakened the black family, robbed the black male of his role as support and protector of his wife and children, poisoned motherhood and created a class of mixed-bloods. The privileged house servants and artisans were usually selected from among the mulattoes, thus giving rise to a caste system within the slave group which served to divide and weaken the oppressed group. On the other hand, many of the leaders of slave rebellions and of resistance were mulattoes who had benefitted from their relatively more privileged position to become effective leaders.

Black women frequently fought tenaciously though unsuccessfully against the degrading and hated illicit relationship with their masters. In such cases, they suffered cruel punishment until they succumbed. Frequently this drew upon them the hatred and enmity of their mistresses. Yet such relationships were for slave women the one and only avenue toward some precarious improvement in their lot and that of their offspring. Promises of future emancipation for themselves and their children convinced some women when punishment did not. And there are sufficient cases on record of genuine human attachment between master and slave mistress to make all facile generalizations invalid; for in such cases it was the black woman who held the affection of the white man, while the mistress, the "chief slave in the harem," as one disenchanted plantation owner called her, had the empty shell of respectability as a substitute for a genuine marriage.

The sexual mores of slavery had far-reaching consequences for the adjustment of the races after slavery ended and to this day. The web of attraction and repulsion, guilt and hatred, intimacy and exploitation caught black and white in a complex dependency which impeded the acceptance of a multiracial society.

THE WAY WOMEN ARE TREATED

Women are generally shown some little indulgence for three or four weeks previous to childbirth; they are at such times not often punished if they do not finish the task assigned them. . . . They are generally allowed four weeks after the birth of a child, before they are compelled to go into the field. They then take the child with them, attended sometimes by a little girl or boy, from the age of four to six, to take care of it while the mother is at work. When there is no child that can be spared, or not young enough for this service, the mother, after nursing, lays it under a tree, or by the side of a fence, and goes to her task, returning at stated intervals to nurse it.

> Narrative of Nehemiah Caulkins of Waterford, Connecticut, in [Theodore D. Weld], *American Slavery As It Is: Testimony of a Thousand Witnesses* (New York: American Anti-Slavery Society, 1839), p. 12.

THE "BREEDER WOMAN"
MEMORIES OF SLAVERY BY AN 87-YEAR-OLD EX-SLAVE

"Lawdy, Lawdy, them was tribbolashuns! Wunner dese here womans was my Antie en she say dat she skacely call to min' he e'r whoppin' her, 'case she was er breeder woman

en' brought in chillum ev'y twelve mont's jes lak a cow
bringin' in a calf . . . He orders she can't be put to no strain
'casen uv dat."

Narrative of Martha Jackson, b. 1850, *Alabama Narratives*, Federal
Works Project, WPA for the State of Alabama, 1939.

THE NURSING MOTHERS

. . . As we went out in the morning, I observed several
women, who carried their young children in their arms to
the field. These mothers laid their children at the side of
the fence, or under the shade of the cotton plants, whilst
they were at work; and when the rest of us went to get
water, they would go to give suck to their children, requesting someone to bring them water in gourds, which they
were careful to carry to the field with them. One young
woman did not, like the others, leave her child at the end
of the row, but had contrived a sort of rude knapsack, made
of a piece of coarse linen cloth, in which she fastened her
child, which was very young, upon her back; and in this
way carried it all day, and performed her task at the hoe
with the other people.

Charles Ball, *Slavery in the United States: A Narrative of the
Life and Adventures of Charles Ball, a Black Man* (Lewistown,
Pennsylvania: J. W. Shugert, 1836), pp. 150–151.

A SLAVEHOLDER'S WIFE
LISTENS TO HER SLAVES

❦ *Frances Kemble, a distinguished British actress,
married Pierce Butler and, at her husband's insistence,
spent a season with him on his Georgia plantation. After*

five months' stay, she was oppressed by the innumerable
appeals addressed to her by the slave women, most of
which she was unable to fulfill. The biggest complaint was
that slave women on Mr. Butler's plantation were not
allowed the customary four weeks of rest after their con-
finement. Mrs. Butler never succeeded in getting this
favor for her slaves, despite her entreaties to her husband.

In considering the whole condition of the people on this
plantation, it appears to me that the principal hardships fall
to the lot of the women. . . .

[These were one day's petitioners:] Fanny has had six
children; all dead but one. She came to beg to have her
work in the field lightened. Nanny has had three children;
two of them are dead. . . . Leah has had six children; three
are dead. Sophy . . . came to beg for some old linen. She is
suffering fearfully; she had had ten children; five of them
are dead. Sally . . . has had two miscarriages and three
children born, one of whom is dead. She came complaining
of incessant pain and weakness in her back. Sarah . . . She
had had four miscarriages, had brought seven children into
the world, five of whom were dead, and was again with
child. She complained of dreadful pains in the back, and
an internal tumor which swells with the exertion of working
in the fields; probably, I think, she is ruptured. . . . Molly
. . . Hers was the best account I have yet received; she had
had nine children, and six of them were still alive. . . . There
was hardly one of these women . . . who might not have been
a candidate for a bed in a hospital, and they had come to
me after working all day in the fields. . . .

[One woman has a particularly dismal story to tell.] She
had had sixteen children, fourteen of whom were dead; she
had had four miscarriages: one had been caused with falling
down with a very heavy burden on her head, and one from
having her arms strained up to be lashed. . . . She said their
hands were first tied together . . . and they were then drawn

up to a tree or post . . . and then their clothes rolled round their waist, and a man with a cowhide stands and stripes them. I give you the woman's words. She did not speak of this as of anything strange, unusual, or especially horrid and abominable; and when I said: "Did they do that to you when you were with child?" she simply replied: "Yes, missis." And to all this I listen—I an Englishwoman, the wife of the man who owns these wretches, and I cannot say: "That thing shall not be done again . . ." I remained choking with indignation and grief long after they had all left me to my most bitter thoughts.

Frances Ann Kemble, *Journal of a Residence on a Georgian Plantation in 1838–1839*, John A. Scott, ed. (New York: Alfred A. Knopf, 1961), pp. 224–241.

THE SLAVEHOLDER'S MISTRESS

Patsey was slim and straight. . . . There was an air of loftiness in her movement, that neither labor, nor weariness, nor punishment could destroy . . . She was a skillful teamster. She turned as true a furrow as the best, and at splitting rails there were none that could excel her. . . . Such lightning-like motion was in her fingers . . . that in cotton picking time, Patsey was queen of the field. . . .

Naturally, she was a joyous creature, a laughing, light-hearted girl, rejoicing in the mere sense of existence. Yet Patsey wept oftener, and suffered more, than any of her companions. . . . Her back bore the scars of a thousand stripes . . . because it had fallen her lot to be the slave of a licentious master and a jealous mistress. . . . In the great house, for days together, there were high and angry words . . . whereof she was the innocent cause. Nothing delighted the mistress so much as to see her suffer. . . . Patsey walked under a cloud. If she uttered a word in opposition to her master's will, the lash was resorted to at once, to bring her to subjection; if she was not watchful while about her cabin, or when walking in the yard, a billet of wood, or a broken bottle perhaps, hurled from her mistress' hand, would smite her unexpectedly in the face. . . . Patsey had no comfort of her life. . . .

To be rid of Patsey—to place her beyond sight or reach, by sale, or death, or in any other manner, of late years, seemed to be the ruling thought and passion of my mistress.

☙ *Finally, for a trifling offense, Patsey was given a savage whipping, while her mistress and the master's children watched with obvious satisfaction. She almost died.*

From that time forward she was not what she had been . . . The bounding vigor, the sprightly . . . spirit of her youth was gone . . . She became more silent than she was, toiling all day in our midst, not uttering a word. A care-worn, pitiful expression settled on her face. . . . If ever there was a broken heart— . . . it was Patsey's.

Solomon Northup, *Narrative of Solomon Northup, Twelve Years A Slave* . . . (Auburn, New York: Derby and Miller, 1853), pp. 188–190, 198, 256–259.

A SLAVEHOLDER CONFIDES TO HER DIARY

Under slavery, we live surrounded by prostitutes, yet an abandoned woman is sent out of any decent house. Who thinks any worse of a negro or mulatto woman for being a thing we can't name? God forgive us, but ours is a monstrous system. . . . Like the patriarchs of old, our men live all in one house with their wives and their concubines; and the mulattoes one sees in every family partly resemble the

white children. Any lady is ready to tell you who is the
father of all the mulatto children in everybody's household
but her own. Those, she seems to think, drop from the
clouds.

Mary Boykin Chesnut, A *Diary from Dixie*, Ben Ames Williams,
ed. (Boston: Houghton Mifflin Company, 1961), pp. 21–22.
Copyright 1905, D. Appleton and Company; copyright 1949,
Houghton Mifflin Company.

THE STORY OF NANCY WESTON
AS TOLD BY HER SON

I am the son of Henry Grimké . . . he was a lawyer and
was married to a Miss Simons . . . and she died leaving
three children, viz. Henrietta, Montague and Thomas. After
her death he took my mother, who was his slave and his
children's nurse; her name is Nancy Weston. . . . By my
mother he had three children also, viz. Archibald, which is
my name, and Francis and John. He died about fifteen years
ago, leaving my mother with two children and in a pregnant
state, for John was born two mos. after he died, in the care
of his son, Mr. E.M. Grimké [Montague] in his own words,
as I heard, "I leave Nancy and her two children to be treated
as members of the family." . . .

My poor mother a defenceless woman, crippled in one
arm, with no one to care for her in the world, for Mr. G.
did not do as his father commanded, and three small children to provide for, was thrown upon the uncharitable
world. . . . By dint of hard labor working her fingernails
to the very quick she kept us from perishing by hunger and
on some bleak Dec. day from the cold and sat by and nursed
us when we were sick. . . . This she continued until 1860
when Mr. E.M. Grimké married a second time, his first
wife having died four years previous to this period, and he
wanted a boy to wait on him, he informed my mother that

he wanted me and that she should send me to his house. His mandate was irresistible; it was a severe shock to my mother. . . . But this was only the beginning of her sorrows, this he kept on until she was rendered childless . . . she thought of no one but her sons, who were groaning from the severity of their hard task masters, and when she remonstrated at their unjust treatment she was thrown into a loathsome cell and kept there for six days eating nothing during her stay there, until at last sickness prostrated her in the dungeon then he was compelled to remove her by the express request of the Physician. I afterwards fleed (*sic*) from my oppressor; Frank attempted to escape but was retaken and sold, my little bro. was next taken away . . . At last it [slavery] received its death blow, it was buried in the grave of dishonor never more to smite the land with a curse and *Freedom* was proclaimed to *all men*: and again the disjointed members of our little family were united and the quietude of the fireside returned.

Archibald Henry Grimké to Angelina Grimké Weld, February 20, 1868, Grimké Family Papers, Howard University, Washington, D.C.

ON THE ROAD TO FREEDOM

❦ *Most runaway slaves returned voluntarily, usually driven by hunger, from their brief escape to the woods, or they were hunted down and returned to their masters. Successful slave escapes were relatively rare, although attempted escapes were numerous. The absence of sheltered places of refuge, the vast distances to be covered, the slave's ignorance of geography, his illiteracy, isolation and general* lack of knowledge plus his high visibility were among the reasons why escapes were so difficult. All the more remarkable and heroic are the slaves who succeeded in escaping.

Most successful slave escapes started in the border states. The role of whites in the mythical "Underground Railroad" has been greatly exaggerated. Most slave escapes did, in fact, involve helping friends, but these were mostly black freedmen in Southern cities, sailors or persons across the river in the border states. In later years, the Vigilance Committees, often made up of black and white abolitionists in the Northern states, helped the successful escapee to continue toward the greater security of Canada. Spectacular slave rescue cases usually involved rescues taking place within free states, such as the cases of Jane Johnson and Margaret Garner. White Quakers and a few intrepid white foes of slavery within the Southern states helped individual slaves to escape. The largest number of escape cases known to history occurred in the years after the passage of the Fugitive Slave Act, when participation in such rescue operations became for many Northern and Western whites a means of expressing their political and moral abhorrence of the slave system.

It is obvious that slaves who escaped were the most resourceful, gifted and courageous of their kind.

THE RESCUE OF
JANE JOHNSON

❦ In July 1855, Colonel John H. Wheeler of North Carolina, the United States minister to Nicaragua, traveling by boat to New York with three of his slaves—one Jane Johnson and her two small children—was surprised to find a white man in the Philadelphia harbor engaging his slave in conversation. The man informed her that she was free by the laws of the state of Pennsylvania, if she wished to be free. Despite Colonel Wheeler's protestations, the slave and her two children followed the white abolitionist off the boat.

The rescue had been made possible by Jane Johnson herself, who had contacted the colored hotel porters during the stay in Philadelphia and asked for their help. The porters got in touch with members of the Vigilance Committee, who enlisted the help of one of their white members, and the rescue ensued.

The case came to court, and, in a most unusual move for a case of this kind, Jane Johnson was put on the stand to testify in her own behalf, despite the fact that federal marshals were ready to arrest her as a fugitive slave. To forestall this happening, members of the Female Antislavery Society surrounded her in the courtroom and kept a close watch over her.

She testified, substantially following the affidavit below. She won her case, her freedom and that of her children. Riot charges placed in reprisal against members of the Vigilance Committee resulted in a verdict of "not guilty." Two of the white abolitionists served short jail terms for "contempt of court."

AFFIDAVIT AND TESTIMONY OF JANE JOHNSON

STATE OF NEW YORK, CITY AND COUNTY OF NEW YORK.

Jane Johnson being sworn, makes oath and says—

My name is Jane—Jane Johnson: I was the slave of Mr. Wheeler of Washington; he bought me and my two children, about two years ago, from Mr. Cornelius Crew, of Richmond, Va.; my youngest child is between six and seven years old, the other between ten and eleven; I have one other child only, and he is in Richmond; I have not seen him for about two years; never expect to see him again; Mr. Wheeler brought me and my two children to Philadelphia, on the way to Nicaragua, to wait on his wife; I didn't want to go without my two children, and he consented to take them; we came to Philadelphia by the cars; stopped at Mr. Sully's, Mr. Wheeler's father-in-law, a few moments; then went to the steamboat for New York at 2 o'clock, but were too late; we went itno Bloodgood's Hotel; Mr. Wheeler went to dinner; Mr. Wheeler had told me in Washington to have nothing to say to colored persons, and if any of them spoke to me, to say I was a free woman traveling with a minister; we staid at Bloodgood's till 5 o'clock; Mr. Wheeler kept his eye on me all the time except when he was at dinner; he left his dinner to come and see if I was safe, and then went back again; while he was at dinner, I saw a colored woman and told her I was a slave woman, that my master had told me not to speak to colored people, and that if any of them spoke to me to say that I was free; but I am not free; but I want to be free; she said: 'poor thing, I pity you;' after that I saw a colored man and said the same thing to him, he said he would telegraph to New York, and two men would meet me at 9 o'clock and take me with them; after that we went on board the boat, Mr. Wheeler sat beside me on the deck; I saw a colored gentleman come on board, he beckoned to me; I nodded my head, and could not go; Mr. Wheeler was beside me and I was afraid; a white gentleman then came and said to Mr. Wheeler, 'I want to speak to your servant, and tell her of her rights;' Mr. Wheeler rose and said, 'If you have anything to say, say it to me— she knows her rights;' the white gentleman asked me if I wanted to be free; I said 'I do, but I belong to this gentleman and I can't have it;' he replied, 'Yes, you can, come with us, you are as free as your master, if you want your freedom come now; if you go back to Washington you may never get it;' I rose to go, Mr. Wheeler spoke, and said, 'I will give you your freedom,' but he had never promised it before, and I knew he would never give it to me; the white gentleman held out his hand and I went toward him; I was ready for the word before it was given me; I took the children by the hands, who both cried, for they were frightened, but both stopped when they got on shore; a colored man carried the little one, I led the other by the hand. We walked down the street till we got to a hack; nobody forced me away; nobody pulled me, and nobody led me; I went away of my own free will; I always wished to be free and meant to be free when I came North; I hardly expected it in Philadelphia, but I thought I should get free in New York; I have been comfortable and happy since I left Mr. Wheeler, and so are the children; I don't want to go back; I could have gone in Philadelphia if I had wanted to; I could go now; but I had rather die than go back. I wish to make this statement before a magistrate, because I understand that Mr. Williamson is in prison on my account, and I hope the truth may be of benefit to him.

her

Jane   X   Johnson

mark

William Still, *The Underground Railroad* (Philadelphia: Porter & Coates, 1872), pp. 86–97.

DRAMATIC SLAVE RESCUES

❦ *On Christmas Eve, 1855, six young slaves, availing themselves of a holiday and their master's horses and carriage, left Loudoun Co., Virginia, and traveling day and night through snow and cold, arrived in Columbia two days later. Barnaby Grigby was a twenty-six-year-old mulatto; his wife, Elizabeth, who had had a different owner than her husband, was twenty-four years old. Her sister, Ann Wood, was engaged to the leader of the group, Frank Wanzer. Ann was twenty-two, good-looking and smart. Frank was trying to escape from a particularly bad master. There were two more young men in the group.*

In Maryland the group was attacked by a posse of white men who demanded to know by what right they were traveling.

The *spokesman* amongst the fugitives, affecting no ordinary amount of dignity, told their assailants plainly, that "no gentleman would interfere with persons riding along civilly" —not allowing it to be supposed that they were slaves, of course. These "gentlemen," however, were not willing to accept this account of the travelers, as their very decided steps indicated. Having the law on their side, they were for compelling the fugitives to surrender without further parley.

At this juncture, the fugitives verily believing that the time had arrived for the practical use of their pistols and dirks, pulled them out of their concealment—the young women as well as the young men—and declared they would not be taken! One of the white men raised his gun, pointing the muzzle directly towards one of the young women, with the threat that he would "shoot," etc. "Shoot! shoot!! shoot!!!" she exclaimed, with a double barrelled pistol in one hand and a long dirk knife in the other, utterly unterrified and fully ready for a death struggle. The male leader of the fugitives by this time had pulled back the hammers of his pistols, and was about to fire! Their adversaries seeing the weapons, and the unflinching determination on the part of the *runaways* to stand their ground, "spill blood, kill, or die," rather than be taken, very prudently "sidled over to the other side of the road," leaving at least four of the victors to travel on their way.

At this moment the four in the carriage lost sight of the two on horseback. Soon after the separation they heard firing, but what the result was they knew not.

❦ *The others made their way to freedom. Fred Wanzer later left Canada "with twenty-two dollars and three pistols in his pockets" and returned South. He brought his sister, her husband and a friend out with him to freedom.*

In the winter of 1857 a young woman, who had just turned her majority, was boxed up in Baltimore by . . . a young man, who had the box conveyed as freight to the depot . . . consigned to Philadelphia. Nearly all one night it remained at the depot with the living agony in it, and after being turned upside down more than once, the next day about ten o'clock it reached Philadelphia. Her companion coming on in advance of the box, arranged with a hackman . . . having it brought from the depot to a designated house, Mrs. Myers . . . where the resurrection was to take place. . . .

The secret had been intrusted to Mrs. M by the young companion of the woman. A feeling of horror came over the aged woman. . . . A few doors from her lived an old friend . . . well known as a brave woman and a friend of the slave, Mrs. Ash, the undertaker or shrouder, whom everybody knew among the colored people. Mrs. Myers felt that it would not be wise to move in the matter of this resurrection without the presence of the undertaker. . . . They mustered courage and pried off the lid. A woman was discovered in the straw. . . . She could not speak, but being assisted, arose. She then went to bed. . . . The third day she began to come to herself and talk quite freely. . . . She had a pair of scissors with her, and in order to procure fresh air she had made a hole in the box, but it was very slight. How she ever managed to breathe and maintain her existence, being in the condition of becoming a mother, it was hard to comprehend. . . .

After spending some three or four days in Mrs. Myers' family she remained in the writer's family about the same length of time, and was then forwarded to Canada.

Both citations, William Still, *The Underground Railroad* (Philadelphia: Porter & Coates, 1872), pp. 124–125; 608–610.

THE CASE OF MARGARET GARNER

❦ *During the winter of 1856, seventeen slaves from Kentucky took a sled and two good horses belonging to their master and, late on Sunday night, drove to the frozen Ohio River. Leaving the sled on the Kentucky shore, they crossed the river on foot and arrived in Cincinnati in daylight. To be less conspicuous, the party separated.*

An old slave man named Simon, and his wife Mary, together with their son Robert and his wife Margaret Garner and four children, made their way to the house of a colored man named Kite, who had formerly lived in their neighborhood and had been purchased from slavery by his father, Joe Kite. They had to make several inquiries in order to find Kite's house, which was below Mill Creek, in the lower part of the city. This afterward led to their discovery; they had been seen by a number of persons on their way to Kite's, and were easily traced by pursuers. The other nine fugitives were more fortunate. They made their way up town and found friends who conducted them to safe hiding-places, where they remained until night. They were then put on the Underground Railroad, and went safely through to Canada.

Kite felt alarmed for the safety of the party that had arrived at his house, and as soon as breakfast was over, he came to my store, at the corner of Sixth and Elm Streets, to ask counsel regarding them. I told him that they were in a very unsafe place and must be removed at once. . . . I would make arrangements to forward them northward, that night, on the Underground Railroad. Kite returned to his house at once, according to my directions, but he was too late; in a few minutes after his return, the house was surrounded by pursuers—the masters of the fugitives, with officers and a posse of men. The door and windows were barred, and those inside refused to give admittance. The fugitives were determined to fight, and to die, rather than to be taken back to slavery. Margaret, the mother of the four children, declared that she would kill herself and her children before she would return to bondage. The slave men were armed and fought bravely. The window was first battered down with a stick of wood, and one of the deputy marshals attempted to enter, but a pistol shot from within made a flesh wound on his arm and caused him to abandon the attempt. The pursuers then battered down the door with some timber and rushed in. The husband of Margaret fired several shots, and wounded one of the officers, but was soon overpowered and dragged out of the house. At this moment, Margaret Garner, seeing that their hopes of freedom were vain, seized a butcher knife that lay on the table and with one stroke cut the throat of her little daughter. . . . She then attempted to take the life of the other children and to kill herself, but she was overpowered and hampered before she could complete her desperate work. The whole party was then arrested and lodged in jail. . . .

Margaret Garner, the chief actor in the tragedy which had occurred, naturally excited much attention. She was a mulatto, about five feet high. . . . On the left side of her forehead was an old scar, and on the cheek-bone, on the same side, another one. When asked what caused them, she said: "White man struck me." . . .

She appeared to be twenty-two or twenty-three years old. . . . The babe she held in her arms was a little girl, about nine months old, and was much lighter in color than herself. . . . The little boys, four and six years old, respectively . . . sat on the floor near their mother during the trial, playing together in happy innocence. . . . The murdered child was almost white, a little girl of rare beauty.

The case seemed to stir every heart that was alive to the emotions of humanity. . . .

A number of people who were deeply interested in the fugitives, visited them in prison and conversed with them.

Old Simon, his wife Mary, and their son Robert, while expressing their longing for freedom, said that they should not attempt to kill themselves if they were returned to slavery. Their trust in God seemed to have survived.

Levi Coffin, *Reminiscences* . . . (Cincinnati, Ohio: n.p., copyright 1876), pp. 558–560; 562–563.

❦ Not so Margaret Garner. She reiterated, according to the local newspapers, that "she had killed one and would like to kill the three others, rather than see them again reduced to slavery."

The case became complicated by conflicting claims of the federal and state authorities; with the federal marshals and attorneys working to enforce the Fugitive Slave Act while the state authorities wished first to try Margaret Garner for murder (in the hope of saving her life).

Governor Chase of Ohio requested the return of Margaret Garner to Ohio, but her owner, disregarding the request, had her shipped to Louisville aboard the Henry Lewis. The ship met with an accident.

REPORT FROM *The Cincinnati Commercial:*

When the accident occurred . . . the Negroes were . . . in the stern of the boat . . . ironed by couples. . . . They were heard calling for help and to be relieved of their handcuffs. . . . Margaret had her child in her arms; but by the shock of the boat that came to the assistance of the *Lewis* (as one story goes) she was thrown into the river with her child. . . . A black man, the cook on the *Lewis* sprang into the river, and saved Margaret who, it is said, displayed frantic joy when told that her child was drowned, and said she would never reach alive Gaines' Landing, in Arkansas, the point to which she was shipped—thus indicating her intention to drown herself.

Another report is that, as soon as she had an opportunity,

she threw her child into the river and jumped after it. . . .
It is only certain that she was in the river with her child,
and that it was drowned, while she was saved by the prompt
energy of the cook. . . . The last that was seen of Peggy, she
was on the *Hungarian* [the rescue ship], crouching like a wild
animal near the stove, with a blanket wrapped around her.

As cited in The Liberator, Vol. 26, No. 12 (March 21, 1856), p. 47.

❦ She *was sold South. Her husband later learned
that she was dead. He so informed Lucy Stone in a letter,
saying that "she had escaped at last."*

THEY CALLED HER "MOSES"

HARRIET TUBMAN

❦ *Harriet Ross Tubman* (c. 1823–1913) *was born to
slave parents in Maryland. Her childhood memories, like
those of other slave children, were mostly of hunger, mistreatment and hard work. At about fifteen years of age, she
intervened to protect another slave and was struck in the
head by a two-pound weight hurled by the overseer. The
injury caused her to suffer sleeping seizures and dizzy spells
for the rest of her life. In 1844 or 1845 she married John
Tubman, a freedman. Several years later, when she was
determined to escape to the North, her husband refused to
join her, and two brothers, who started out with her, lost
heart and returned. She went on alone and made her way
to freedom. For the next decade, all her amazing energies and
talents were devoted to rescuing her family, neighbors and
other slaves. In all, she made nineteen rescue trips to the
South—a legendary figure with a $40,000 reward on her
head. It was her pride that of the three hundred or more
slaves she rescued as a conductor on the Underground*

Railroad she "never lost a single passenger." She always carried a pistol, with which she spurred on laggard or despairing fugitives, telling them, "You'll be free or die."

Harriet Tubman was more than a brave abolitionist; she was a militant black leader, a revolutionist dedicated to winning black freedom. She was respected and befriended by black and white abolitionist leaders and was known for her exploits in Canada and Great Britain as well as throughout the North. She was unique among black women in her military role. She fully supported John Brown's plans for the raid on Harpers Ferry, but was prevented by illness from joining him as she had planned. During the Civil War she worked as a nurse, spy and scout (see p. 326). Her position was unique in that several times she commanded troops, both black and white, on scouting raids, on the most spectacular of which she rescued 756 slaves. After the war, she struggled for many years in poverty to support the needy freedmen who sought her aid. But she never ceased her activities, speaking, organizing, inspiring others. In her later years she attended several woman suffrage conventions and participated in the organization of the National Federation of Afro-American Women.

Harriet Tubman was belatedly granted a government pension, which helped her to support a home for aged freedmen in Auburn, New York, where she lived till her death.

The selection below describes one of her slave rescues.

MARTHA C. WRIGHT TO ELLEN WRIGHT

Auburn, Dec. 30, 1860

. . . We have been expending our sympathies, as well as congratulations, on seven newly arrived slaves that Harriet Tubman has just pioneered safely from the Southern Part of Maryland.—One woman carried a baby all the way and bro't [sic] two other chld'n that Harriet and the men helped along. They bro't a piece of old comfort and a blanket, in a basket with a little kindling, a little bread for the baby with some laudanum to keep it from crying during the day. They walked all night carrying the little ones, and spread the old comfort on the frozen ground, in some dense thicket where they all hid, while Harriet went out foraging, and sometimes cd not get back till dark, fearing she wd be followed. Then, if they had crept further in, and she couldn't find them, she wd whistle, or sing certain hymns and they wd answer.

William Lloyd Garrison Manuscripts, Sophia Smith Collection, Smith College, Northampton, Massachusetts.

HARRIET TUBMAN:

There was one of two things I had a *right* to, liberty, or death; if I could not have one, I would have the other; for no man should take me alive; I should fight for my liberty as long as my strength lasted, and when the time came for me to go, the Lord would let them take me.

Sarah Bradford, Harriet Tubman, The Moses of Her People (Auburn, New York: n.p., 1869); reprint ed., (New York: Corinth Books, 1961), p. 29.

AN INGENIOUS ESCAPE

WILLIAM AND ELLEN CRAFT

❧ William and Ellen Craft were slaves in Georgia, planning to escape. Ellen was fair enough to pass for white, and the couple decided to take advantage of that fact. They would escape by having Ellen act the part of the master while William posed as her servant.

Ellen cut her hair short, wore her real master's clothing, and, to disguise her beardless face, muffled it in a shawl, pretending to suffer from a severe toothache. They knew that in traveling they would have to register at hotels, but neither

of them could write. Anticipating this difficulty, they placed
Ellen's right hand in a sling. Their story was that William's
young master was terribly ill, traveling North in search of
medical care. The "young master" was provided with dark
glasses, a stout cane, a slight limp and was said to be almost
totally deaf—in that way avoiding all possibility of striking
up chance acquaintances with fellow passengers. "He"
relied entirely on his faithful servant to look after all his
needs.

With this ingenious plan, the two started out from Georgia
in December 1848.

We shooks hands, said farewell, and started in different directions for the railway station. I took the nearest possible way
to the train, for fear I should be recognized by someone, and
got into the Negro car in which I knew I should have to ride;
but my *master* (as I will now call my wife) took a longer way
round, and only arrived there with the bulk of the passengers.
He obtained a ticket for himself and one for his slave to
Savannah, the first port, which was about two hundred miles
off. My master then had the luggage stowed away, and
stepped into one of the best carriages. . . .

As soon as the train had left the platform, my master
looked round in the carriage, and was terror-stricken to find
a Mr. Cray—an old friend of my wife's master, who dined
with the family the day before, and knew my wife from childhood—sitting on the same seat. . . . My master's first impression, after seeing Mr. Cray, was, that he was there for the
purpose of securing him. However, my master thought it was
not wise to give any information respecting himself, and for
fear that Mr. Cray might draw him into conversation and
recognize his voice, my master resolved to feign deafness as
the only means of self-defense.

After a little while, Mr. Cray said to my master, "It is a
very fine morning, sir." The latter took no notice, but kept
looking out of the window. Mr. Cray soon repeated this re-

mark, in a little louder tone, but my master remained as before. This indifference attracted the attention of the passengers near, one of whom laughed out. This, I suppose, annoyed the old gentleman; so he said, "I will make him hear"; and in a loud tone of voice repeated, "It is a very fine morning, sir."

My master turned his head, and with a polite bow said, "Yes," and commenced looking out of the window again.

One of the gentlemen remarked that it was a very great deprivation to be deaf. "Yes," replied Mr. Cray, "and I shall not trouble that fellow any more." This enabled my master to breathe a little easier, and to feel that Mr. Cray was not his pursuer after all.

The gentlemen then turned the conversation upon the three great topics of discussion in first-class circles in Georgia, namely, Niggers, Cotton, and the Abolitionists.

My master had often heard of abolitionists, but in such a connection as to cause him to think that they were a fearful kind of wild animal. But he was highly delighted to learn, from the gentlemen's conversation, that the abolitionists were persons who were opposed to oppression; and therefore, in his opinion, not the lowest, but the very highest, of God's creatures. . . .

We arrived at Savannah early in the evening, and got into an omnibus. . . . Soon after going on board, my master turned in; and as the captain and some of the passengers seemed to think this strange, and also questioned me respecting him, my master thought I had better get out the flannels and opodeloc which we had prepared for the rheumatism, warm them quickly by the stove in the gentleman's saloon, and bring them to his berth. We did this as an excuse for my master's retiring to bed so early. . . .

There was no place provided for colored passengers, whether slave or free. So I paced the deck till a late hour, then mounted some cotton bags, in a warm place near the funnel, sat there till morning, and then went and assisted my master to get ready for breakfast. . . .

By this time we were near Charleston. . . . There were a large number of persons on the quay waiting the arrival of the steamer: but we were afraid to venture out for fear that someone might recognize me; or that they had heard that we were gone, and had telegraphed to have us stopped. . . . We had our luggage placed on a fly, and I took my master by the arm . . . he hobbled on shore, got in and drove off to the best hotel. . . .

On arriving at the house the landlord ran out and opened the door: but judging, from the poultices and green glasses, that my master was an invalid, he took him very tenderly by one arm and ordered his man to take the other. . . .

My master asked for a bedroom. The servant was ordered to show a good one, into which we helped him. . . . My master then handed me the bandages, I took them . . . and told the landlord my master wanted two hot poultices as quickly as possible. . . .

In a few minutes the smoking poultices were brought in. I placed them in white handkerchiefs, and hurried upstairs, went into my master's apartment, shut the door, and laid them on the mantlepiece. As he was alone for a little while, he thought he could rest a great deal better with the poultices off. However, it was necessary to have them to complete . . . the journey. . . .

When we left Macon, it was our intention to take a steamer at Charleston through to Philadelphia; but on arriving there we found that the vessels did not run during the winter, and I have no doubt it was well for us they did not; for on the very last voyage the steamer made that we intended to go by, a fugitive was discovered secreted on board, and sent back to slavery. However, as we had also heard of the Overland Mail Route, we were all right. I ordered a fly to the door, had the luggage placed on; we got in, and drove down to the Custom House Office, which was near the wharf where we had to obtain tickets, to take a steamer for Wilmington, North Carolina. When we reached the building, I helped my master into the office, which was crowded with passengers. He asked for a ticket for himself and one for his slave to Philadelphia. This caused the principal officer—a very mean-looking, cheese colored fellow, who was sitting there—to look up at us very suspiciously, and in a fierce tone of voice he said to me, "Boy, do you belong to that gentleman?" I quickly replied, "Yes, sir" (which was quite correct). The tickets were handed out, and as my master was paying for them the chief said to him, "I wish you to register your name here, sir, and also the name of your nigger, and pay a dollar duty on him."

My master paid the dollar, and pointing to the hand that was in the poultice, requested the officer to register his name for him. This seemed to offend the "high-bred" South Carolinian. He jumped up, shaking his head, and, cramming his hands almost through the bottom of his trousers pockets, with a slave-bullying air, said, "I shan't do it."

This attracted the attention of all the passengers. Just then the young military officer with whom my master travelled and conversed on the steamer from Savannah stepped in, somewhat the worse for brandy; he shook hands with my master, and pretended to know all about him. He said, "I know his kin (friends) like a book"; and as the officer was known in Charleston, and was going to stop there with friends, the recognition was very much in my master's favor.

The captain of the steamer, a good-looking jovial fellow, seeing that the gentleman appeared to know my master, and perhaps not wishing to lose us as passengers, said in an off-hand sailor-like manner, "I will register the gentleman's name, and take the responsibility upon myself." He asked my master's name. He said, "William Johnson." The names were put down, I think, "Mr. Johnson and slave". . . .

We left our cottage on Wednesday morning, the 21st of December, 1848, and arrived at Baltimore, Saturday evening, the 24th (Christmas Eve). Baltimore was the last slave port of any note at which we stopped. . . .

They are particularly watchful at Baltimore to prevent

slaves from escaping into Pennsylvania, which is a free
State. . . .

❦ To their horror the fugitives learned that they
would have to stop at an office, so that the master might give
proof that he properly owned the slave; otherwise they
would not be permitted to board the train.

On entering the room we found the principal man, to
whom my master said, "Do you wish to see me, sir?" "Yes,"
said this eagle-eyed officer; and he added, "It is against our
rules, sir, to allow any person to take a slave out of Baltimore
into Philadelphia, unless he can satisfy us that he has a right
to take him along." "Why is that?" asked my master, with
more firmness than could be expected. "Because, sir," continued he, in a voice and manner that almost chilled our
blood, "if we should suffer any gentleman to take a slave past
here into Philadelphia; and should the gentleman with whom
the slave might be travelling turn out not to be his rightful
owner, and should the proper master come and prove that his
slave escaped on our road, we shall have him to pay for; and,
therefore, we cannot let any slave pass here without receiving
security to show, and to satisfy us, that it is all right."

This conversation attracted the attention of the large
number of bustling passengers. After the officer had finished,
a few of them said, "Chit, chit, chit"; not because they
thought we were slaves endeavoring to escape, but merely
because they thought my master was a slaveholder and invalid gentleman, and therefore it was wrong to detain him.
The officer, observing that the passengers sympathized with
my master, asked him if he was not acquainted with some
gentleman in Baltimore that he could get to endorse for him,
to show that I was his property, and that he had a right to
take me off. He said, "No," and added, "I bought tickets in
Charleston to pass us through to Philadelphia, and therefore
you have no right to detain us here." "Well, sir," said the
man, indignantly, "right or no right, we shan't let you go."

These words fell upon our anxious hearts like the crack of doom and made us feel that hope smiles only to deceive. . . .

Just then the bell rang for the train to leave, and had it been the sudden shock of an earthquake it could not have given us a greater thrill. The sound of the bell caused every eye to flash with apparent interest, and to be more steadily fixed upon us than before. But, as God would have it, the officer all at once thrust his fingers through his hair, and in a state of great agitation said, "I really don't know what to do; I calculate it is all right." He then told the clerk to run and tell the conductor to "let this gentleman and slave pass," adding, "As he is not well, it is a pity to stop him here. We will let him go."

Narrative of the escape: Arna Bontemps, (ed.), *Great Slave Narratives*, reprint of the 1860 London edition of William Craft, *Running a Thousand Miles for Freedom* (Boston: Beacon Press, 1969), pp. 293–299; 301–302; 307–311.

❦ *The couple arrived safely in Philadelphia and at once became known all over the North for their bold escape. Slave hunters immediately took up their trail, but the Crafts were protected by the Vigilance Committee and later succeeded in making their way to England.*

There they went to school, started a new life in freedom and raised a family. But ugly rumors were being circulated about them in the United States. To these Ellen Craft replied with the following letter:

Ockham School, near Ripley, Surrey,
Oct. 26th, 1852

DEAR SIR,—I feel very much obliged to you for informing me of the erroneous report which has been so extensively circulated in the American newspapers: 'That I had placed myself in the hands of an American gentleman in London, on condition that he would take me back to the family who held me as a slave in Georgia.' So I write these few lines merely to say that the statement is entirely unfounded, for I have never had the slightest inclination whatever of returning to bondage; and God forbid that I should ever be so false to liberty as to prefer slavery in its stead. In fact, since my escape from slavery, I have got on much better in every respect than I could have possibly anticipated. Though, had it been to the contrary, my feelings in regard to this would have been just the same, for I had much rather starve in England, a free woman, then be slave for the best man that ever breathed upon the American continent.

Yours very truly,

ELLEN CRAFT

The *Liberator*, Dec. 17, 1852

❧ After the Civil War, the Crafts returned to Georgia, purchased a plantation and established an industrial school for black children.

CHAPTER TWO

THE STRUGGLE FOR EDUCATION

The drums of Africa still beat in my heart.
They will not let me rest while there is a
single Negro boy or girl without a chance to
prove his worth.

Mary McLeod Bethune

THE STRUGGLE FOR EDUCATION

❧ In the Negro's long struggle for survival, education was always a foremost goal, both as a tool for advancement and acceptance in the general society and as a means of uplifting and improving life in the black community.

Under slavery, whatever white benevolence was expended in efforts at amelioration found expression in providing religious instruction and some rudimentary education to a few privileged Blacks. Missionary groups, Manumission societies and the American Colonization Society sporadically engaged in efforts to educate slave children. In the North, such work continued after the abolition of slavery, when several religious denominations, notably the Society of Friends, established schools for black children. In the South, the slave rebellions of 1800 (Gabriel), 1822 (Denmark Vesey) and 1831 (Nat Turner) led to increasingly severe legislation forbidding the education of slaves and to stricter enforcement of laws already in the slave codes. The ingenious efforts of slaves to circumvent such laws and acquire some education have been illustrated by documents in the previous chapter. There is also evidence that some whites, especially women, continued to teach their slaves to read and write. One notable case is that of Mrs. Margaret Douglass, who with her daughter was found guilty in 1854 of keeping a Sunday school for slave children and who served one month in a Norfolk, Virginia, jail for the crime.

Separate schools for boys and girls, which were quite prevalent in the North in the early nineteenth century, were a luxury only few black communities could afford. Black girls and boys generally shared whatever inadequate educational facilities there were. This trend toward coeducational schools was also evident in the Reconstruction and post-Reconstruction South. The few separate schools for black girls before the Civil War were, like those for white girls, mostly designed to provide instruction in sewing, knitting and the household skills.

Black women teachers were few and far between in the early national period. The first such teacher known was Catherine Ferguson, a slave, who purchased her freedom and in 1793 took 48 children, 20 of whom were white, from the almshouse and opened "Katy Ferguson's Schools for the Poor" in New York City. In 1820, fifteen-year-old Maria Becraft opened the first boarding school for black girls in Washington, D.C. She taught until 1831, when she joined the order of the Sisters of Providence in Baltimore and, as a nun, continued her teaching.

By the 1830's, the number of black female graduates of schools run by whites had increased sufficiently to staff black schools in many communities. The Institute for Colored Youth in Philadelphia (see p. 76) became the training ground for a core of women teachers who significantly raised the educational level of black schools and whose training could match that of the female graduates of white seminaries. In 1851 Myrtilla Miner, a white woman, opened a teachers' training school for black girls in Washington, D.C. Despite fierce opposition, lack of funds, harassment and violence, she managed to maintain the school until 1859. It was on this foundation that her close associates continued, after the Civil War, to train teachers for the freedmen in Miners Teachers College (known today as District of Columbia Teachers College). Graduates of the Presbyterian Board of Missions' Scotia Seminary (founded 1867 in Concord, North Carolina) swelled the ranks of black teachers of the freedmen.

Despite the poverty of black communities and the severe discriminatory restrictions which dominated their lives, Blacks managed in the post–Civil War period to found and support schools and to raise the educational level of their children. "It is surprising to me to see the amount of suffering which many of the people endure for the sake of sending their children to school," wrote a white teacher of freedmen from Raleigh, North Carolina, in 1869. This effort was continuous and increasing, as can be seen from the documents concerning the school founders. The historical account of the great contributions made to Negro education by white individuals, benevolent societies and foundations has been frequently told. The story of the sustained self-sacrificing effort of the black community to educate its young has been less well documented and researched. The evidence, as recorded in some of the documents in this collection, suggests that black self-help community effort was far greater than is generally appreciated. In this effort black women played a significant role.

In considering the educational advancement of black women, it may be useful to compare their situation with that of white women, since both groups were denied access to equal educational opportunities due to their sex, and had to contend with discrimination in training, employment and upgrading. Advanced education was longer denied to black women than to white. As a result, black and white women moved into the professions at a different pace. Although Oberlin College accepted women and Blacks from its inception in 1833—the first academic institution to do so—only nine black women could take advantage of this opportunity before 1871 and of these four graduated in 1870. The few women's medical colleges early opened their doors to black women. Doctors Rebecca Lee, Rebecca Cole and Susan M. Smith McKenny Steward were the first black women doctors, graduating respectively in 1864 (Boston), 1867 (Philadelphia) and 1870 (New York). But they were pioneers whose entry into the medical profession remained a rarity until the twentieth century, when black women began to enter the field in greater numbers. Interestingly, the first female physicians in the South were black. Dr. Matilda Arabelle Evans, a graduate of Oberlin and Women's Medical College of Pennsylvania (1897), practiced in Columbia, South Carolina, where she is said to have founded two hospitals and a nurses' training institution. Dr. Hallie Tanner Johnson of Philadelphia was the first woman to practice medicine in the state of Alabama. By 1920, there were 65 black female physicians listed in the census.

A similar gap of several decades between the entry of a few pioneers and that of larger numbers of women occurred in the legal profession. Although there had been a few earlier women graduates of law schools, notably Charlotte Ray (Howard, 1872), Mary Ann Shadd Cary (Howard, 1883) and Ida Platt (Chicago), Lutie A. Lyttle of Topeka, Kansas, was the first black woman lawyer admitted to the bar. This was in 1897, twenty-five years later than the first white woman lawyers, Phoebe Couzins and Myra Bradwell. The black pioneer was not followed into the profession by a significant number of other women. In 1910, there were only two practicing black women lawyers.

Obviously, this slow advance into the professions was due to race discrimination, both in educational preparation and in access to institutions of higher learning. Perhaps the most notable achievement of the legal battles of earlier decades and the civil rights struggles of the 1950's has been in advancing educational opportunities for Blacks, which are reflected in employment statistics.

The 1960 census shows 487 black female physicians, representing 9.7 per cent of all black physicians, while the 14,031 white female physicians were only 6.4 per cent of all white physicians. The 222 black women lawyers and judges were 9.1 per cent of all Blacks in the profession, as against 6,898 white women lawyers and judges, representing 3.3 per cent of the profession. There were 94,606 black women teachers. Among these, female elementary school teachers were 84.5 per cent (86 per cent among whites) and secondary school teachers were 54.5 per cent (46.6 per cent among whites) of all Blacks in the profession. These figures show, above all, that women of both races are grossly underrepresented in the professions, but that black women are somewhat better represented than are white women. This is due to the fact that race-discrimination bars operate more rigidly against black men than against black women. The figures for elementary and high school teachers show that there is a higher percentage of black women than white in the more exalted ranks of the professions, while black and white women share the bulk of the lower-ranking jobs. The relatively greater "visibility" of females among black professionals may also be due to the fact that black women, whether married or not, are of necessity more likely to work than are white women. This reality is reflected in the way black families raise their daughters to accept work or career as a natural part of their lives. This may serve to actually make black women better equipped for the demands of a professional career than are most white women, in whom career demands often set up role conflicts and uncertainty as to their "femininity."

Notable among contemporary female physicians are Dr. Mildred Jefferson, who in 1951 was the first black woman to receive her doctorate from Harvard Medical School; Dr. Dorothy Brown, a graduate of Meharry Medical College, a practicing surgeon in Nashville, and the only woman member of the Tennessee House of Representatives (elected in 1966). Dr. Jane Wright, Associate Dean of New York Medical College, has been widely honored for her outstanding work as director of cancer chemotherapy research at New York University Medical Center.

The contributions of outstanding women lawyers are more fully discussed in Chapter Seven (see p. 359). Of these, Judge Constance Baker Motley, known for her brilliant work with the Legal Council of the NAACP, has reached the highest rank with her appointment to the federal bench in 1966. Sadie Tanner Mossell Alexander, the first black woman in the United States to receive a Ph.D. and a law degree, also broke race barriers when she was admitted to the Pennsylvania state bar in 1927. She is known for her outstanding civic and civil rights work. Marian Elizabeth Wright, a civil rights activist and graduate of Yale Law School in 1964, represents the new breed of young black lawyers. The first black woman to pass the Mississippi state bar exam, she became a director of the NAACP Legal Defense and Educational Fund, one of six black lawyers to serve the needs of over 900,000 Blacks in that state. She also shattered precedent with her 1971 appointment to the board of trustees of Yale University.

Many of the leading club women organized rudimentary social work services in their communities and their states. Their contributions are more fully discussed and documented in Chapter Eight. Jane Edna Hunter of South Carolina, later a lawyer, in 1911 founded the Working Girls' Home Association (renamed the Phillis Wheatley Association) in Cleveland. Originally, it served to provide shelter for black girls who were refused admission to the city's YWCA, but soon became a settlement house, offering a full range of social and educational activities, an employment agency and a summer camp. Under Jane Hunter's guidance the organization spread its idea and activities to several states. Social work as a profession did not begin to open to black women until the 1930's. Today black women make up 62.6 per cent of all black social workers.

Since black women for many decades were handicapped by racial restrictions on educational opportunities, it is not surprising that women of achievement first came to prominence in the cultural fields. Within the scope of this book it is impossible to do justice to their contributions. An arbitrary selection had to be made, and since cultural figures are somewhat better known to the general public than most of the women whose work is documented in this volume, it was decided not to do more than mention a few historical cultural figures. Their rich contribution and the specifically feminine aspects of their work certainly deserve more extended treatment.

In the cultural field, as in all others, lack of training opportunities undoubtedly stifled the development of much talent. During the earlier nineteenth century and well into the twentieth, art schools were virtually closed to black women. Still, Edmonia Lewis (1846–1890), who for a few years attended Oberlin and later studied privately, made a successful career as an artist and sculptor, working for years in a studio in Rome. Meta Warrick Fuller won recognition as a sculptor before World War I.

The black female literary tradition starts with the talented Phillis Wheatley (c. 1753–c. 1785), an African-born slave whose poetic achievements were celebrated on two continents. Carefully educated by her masters and later manumitted, Phillis Wheatley wrote religious and lyric poetry in the style of her day, published a book of verse which was widely admired in Europe and America, and died in poverty after the American Revolution. Almost a hundred years later, Frances Ellen Watkins Harper (see p. 243) was a widely read poet, who was able to make a living from her speeches and literary work. In this century the novelists Jessie Fauset, Zora Neale Hurston and Nella Larson were part of the Harlem Renaissance, the literary movement of the 1920's. Gwendolyn Brooks was the first Black to win a Pulitzer Prize for poetry in 1950. Lorraine Hansberry (1931–1965), at first an artist, had a tragically brief but distinguished career as a successful playwright. Today, the opening up of formerly closed opportunities to black writers has led to a veritable explosion of black literary talent.

Theatrical and musical careers were, like other professions, heavily restricted by race barriers. On stage and screen this was manifested in the absence of meaningful, dignified roles. Until very recently, talented black actresses were confined to playing stereotyped servant roles. An occasional run of Porgy and Bess or Carmen Jones and some musicals offered vehicles for a few singers and dancers. Still, a few black women managed to break through the barriers. Elizabeth Taylor Greenfield (1809–1876), known as the Black Swan, was a singer of astonishing range who made a successful career in America and England. Sisseretta Jones (1868–1933), known as the Black Patti, trained her great soprano voice at the New England Conservatory of Music and concertized extensively in this country and abroad, including a White House performance in 1892. She later formed her own troupe and toured for two decades in an all-black musical show.

Twentieth-century concert singers were severely hampered by racial restrictions and a number of them had to go to Europe to develop their talents and careers. Among these was Marian Anderson who, acclaimed in Europe as one of the greatest singers of the world, returned to a triumphant tour of her native land in 1935, only to be barred by the Daughters of the American Revolution from singing in Washington's Constitution Hall in 1939. The public outcry over this absurd indignity led to her singing, by invitation of the Secretary of the Interior, on the steps of the Lincoln Memorial on Easter Sunday of that year. This incident marked a turning point in breaking the color bar in music, although it took until 1955 for the Metropolitan Opera Company of New York to sign contracts with black singers Marian Anderson and, later, Mattiwilda Dobbs. Since then, the operatic triumphs of black singers have given them a predominant place in this country's musical life.

In no other cultural field has the black contribution been more pervasive and influential than in music. Through spirituals, the blues and jazz, black heritage has entered the mainstream American culture and transformed it. Women have played an integral part in this development which merits full and separate treatment. Among the many important artists, Billie Holiday and Bessie Smith are remarkable for having created a style uniquely their own which has inspired countless imitators. Mahalia Jackson (see p. 383) stands unequaled among gospel singers.

In the artistic and cultural fields, as in education and the professions, the lowering of race barriers has brought an explosion of talent and activity. Long repressed and stifled, black women are today a dynamic force in the creation of a uniquely expressive black culture in the United States.

TEACHING SCHOOL TO KEEP ALIVE
MARIA W. STEWART

❦ Maria W. Stewart (b. Miller, 1803–1879) is typical
of the nineteenth-century woman, white or black, who took
up teaching, not as an avocation, but because it was, for a
woman, the only respectable means of earning a living. Born
in Hartford, Connecticut, she was orphaned at the age of
five, then bound out to a clergyman's family with whom she
stayed until she was fifteen. Her education was minimal,
consisting mostly of attendance at Sabbath school. Married
to James W. Stewart in 1826, she lived in Boston and was
widowed in 1829. She was cheated out of her husband's
inheritance by unscrupulous lawyers and left impoverished.
She wrote a book of "devotional thoughts and various
essays," which William Lloyd Garrison printed as a tract
in 1832 and from which she derived a small income. It was
at this time that she gave four public lectures in Boston,
some of which were reprinted in The Liberator (see pp. 526,
563). She is the first American-born woman to have lectured
in public, preceded only by a British woman, Frances
Wright.*

Discouraged from speaking by unpleasant "notoriety,"
Maria Stewart moved to New York, attended school for
several years and then taught school herself. In 1852, she tried
organizing a school in Baltimore, an experience which is
described in the following selection. She moved to Washington in 1863, succeeded in starting and maintaining her
own school, taught Sabbath school and was active in church
work. She finally secured a job as matron in the Freedmen's
Hospital, which, together with the belated award to her
of her husband's pension as a soldier in the War of 1812,

---

* The first white American-born women to speak in public were Sarah and
Angelina Grimké, who undertook a New England lecture tour as agents of
the American Anti-Slavery Society in 1937.

afforded her some security. In 1871, she bought a building for $200 and opened a Sunday school for 75 children, enlisting the help of volunteers from Howard University. Deep religious convictions and missionary fervor sustained her through the hardships of her life.

When I saw the want of means for the advancement of the common English branches, with no literary resources for the improvement of the mind scarcely, I . . . wrote my programme, printed and issued my circulars, stating I would open school and would teach reading, writing, spelling, mental and practical arithmetic, and whatever other studies called for. Not knowing the prices, I found myself teaching every branch for 50 cents per month, until informed by another teacher that no writing was taught for less than $1 per month. Bought wit is the dearest wit. I have never been very shrewd in money matters; and being classed as a lady among my race all my life, and never exposed to any hardship, I did not know how to manage. I had been teaching in New York and Williamsburg, and had the means of always paying my way. But when I came to teach a pay school I found the difference. But God promised that my bread and water should be sure; and having food and raiment I was content. I would make enough just to supply my wants for the time being, but not a dollar over. I did not make any charge for wood and coal. And always had that refined sentiment of delicacy about me that I could not bear to charge for the worth of my labor. If any loss was to be sustained the loss was always on my side, and not on the side of the parent or the scholar. But toward the commencement of the war the times began to be hard, and I began to pay my rent; and, getting sick, became discouraged. I went to a colored gentleman (a man of influence) and to a lady friend and stated my condition, telling the amount of rent I owed; and they expressed their sympathy for me in strong terms, and said if I would be willing to have it put on the programme that I was poor, they would get up an entertainment for my benefit. I consented. They got up the festival with the help of others; made $300; gave me $30 to pay my rent; paid expenses, then divided the remainder among themselves, and then laughed ready to kill themselves to think what a fool they had made of me. I never noticed it, but quietly went on and did the best I could.

"Sufferings During the War," lecture by Maria W. Stewart, *Productions of Mrs. Maria W. Stewart* (Boston: W. Lloyd Garrison and Knapp, 1832), pp. 13–14.

ESTABLISHING A GIRLS' DEPARTMENT IN THE INSTITUTE FOR COLORED YOUTH

SARAH MAPPS DOUGLASS

❦ Sarah Mapps Douglass (1806–1882) was one of the outstanding teachers of her day. Born in Philadelphia into a prominent family of free Negroes and raised in comfortable circumstances, she was educated by private tutors. In 1820 she opened a private school, one of ten such schools then available to Philadelphia black children. The school was for several years subsidized by the Philadelphia Female Antislavery Society. Sarah Douglass was one of the founding members of this society, and held various offices in it until the Civil War. In 1853 she assumed responsibility for running the girls' department of the Institute for Colored Youth. In 1869, the enlarged girls' division was placed under the direction of Fannie Jackson Coppin (see pp. 88–92), but Sarah Douglass continued there as a teacher. She pioneered in introducing scientific subjects, such as physiology, into the curriculum. She continued to broaden her own education by reading and study, and between 1855 and 1858 took the medical course of the newly established Ladies' Institute of Pennsylvania Medical Uni-

versity. She gave up teaching in 1855, when she married
the Reverend William Douglass, rector of St. Thomas
Protestant Episcopal Church, but resumed her career after
she was widowed in 1861. Always active in community
affairs, she was vice-chairman of the Pennsylvania Freedmen's Aid Society after the Civil War. Her enduring
contribution is the training of two generations of Philadelphia
youths and of many of the city's black public school
teachers.

The earliest schools for black children were established in
Pennsylvania in 1774 under Quaker auspices. These and
the several other segregated schools run under the sponsorship of white benevolent organizations were later supplemented by private elementary schools run by Blacks. The
Institute for Colored Youth, established in 1852, was an
outstanding example of the successful effort of the black
community to provide higher education for its children.

AT A STATED MEETING OF THE MANAGERS OF THE INSTITUTE
HELD AT FRIENDS' BIBLE DEPOSITORY
4 MO. 18TH 1853.

The Committee appointed to make an agreement with
Sarah M. Douglass for a Girls' School, Report,

That they have made an agreement with her for one year
commencing 4th Mo. 4th, 1853, which is herewith presented
to the Board. The number of Free Scholars at that time was
20 and has since been increased to 25, the number contracted
for.

The School having been several times visited by members
of the Committee was found in satisfactory order—Books
and Stationery for the use of the Scholars sent at our expense,
being needed, an order was given for the required quantity
on U. Hunt & Son.

On behalf of the Committee

M. C. Cope.

AGREEMENT BETWEEN THE MANAGERS OF THE INSTITUTE
FOR COLORED YOUTH AND SARAH M. DOUGLASS

The said Managers agree to furnish to the said Sarah the
Front Room in the 3rd Story of their Building on Lombard
Street, for a School for girls, for one year, commencing
4th Month 4th 1853—to provide desks and Seats, Stove &
Coal for the said Room, to pay the said Sarah for the tuition
of 25 Scholars, to be admitted under the direction of the said
Managers, Two Hundred Dollars, per annum, and to furnish
for the use of said Scholars, suitable Books and stationery.
The said Sarah agrees to instruct the said Scholars to the
best of her ability in such Branches* of an English Education as she is qualified to teach, under such regulations as
the said Managers may from time to time adopt for the government of the School, and whenever any vacancies occur in
the said number of 25 scholars to inform the Managers, that
they may admit others to fill them.

It is further agreed that the said Sarah shall have the privilege of taking pay Scholars on her own account, provided the
whole number of Scholars in the School shall not exceed
thirty five.

In case either of the Parties to this Agreement are desirous
of discontinuing it at the expiration of the year above named,
three months notice of such intention shall be given.

Signed the second day of the fifth month 1853.

S. M. Douglass
M. C. Cope

Minutes, Meeting of the Board of Managers of the Institute for
Colored Youth, 1837–1855, Philadelphia Yearly Meeting of the
Religious Society of Friends, Philadelphia, Pennsylvania.

* The branches intended to be taught are spelling, reading, writing,
arithmetic and geography.

TRAINING TO BECOME
AN EDUCATOR

FANNIE JACKSON COPPIN

❧ Fannie Jackson Coppin (1837–1913) was born
a slave. Her aunt, herself a recently freed slave, went to work
at $6 a month and purchased the frail little girl's freedom for
$125, then sent her to another aunt in Bedford, Massachu-
setts. "She put me out to work," Fannie Jackson Coppin
writes in an autobiographical sketch, "at a place where I was
allowed to go to school when I was not at work. But I could
not go on wash day, nor ironing day, nor cleaning day, and this
interferred with my progress." She used her scanty spare time
and wages to get tutoring and the equivalent of an elementary
education. She attended the State Normal School for a brief
time. A $9 scholarship secured for her by Bishop Daniel A.
Payne of the African Methodist Episcopal (A.M.E.) Church,
and continuing aid from her aunt, made it possible for her
to enter Oberlin College in 1860. She graduated in 1865,
having made a distinguished record, went to work as a
teacher at the Institute for Colored Youth in Philadelphia
and in 1869 became the principal of its Female Department.

During her forty-one years in this office she made many
educational innovations, such as the addition to the curriculum of teachers' training courses and the establishment of a
school for industrial arts. This latter pioneering venture
antedated the establishment of Tuskegee Institute by some
years. She personally helped to raise $17,000 for this depart-
ment of the school. She married Reverend Levi J. Coppin
in 1881, and in 1901, upon her husband's promotion to
Bishop in the A.M.E. Church, went with him to a missionary
assignment in South Africa.

My aunt in Washington still helped me and I was able to pay
my way to Oberlin, the course of study there being the same

as that at Harvard. Oberlin was then the only College in the United States where colored students were permitted to study.

The faculty did not forbid a woman to take the gentlemen's course, but they did not advise it. There was plenty of Latin and Greek in it, and as much mathematics as one could shoulder. Now, I took a long breath and prepared for a delightful contest. . . . Then, one day, the Faculty sent for me. . . . It was custom in Oberlin that forty students from the junior and senior classes were employed to teach the preparatory classes. As it was now time for the juniors to begin their work, the Faculty informed me that it was their purpose to give me a class, but I was to distinctly understand that if the pupils rebelled against my teaching, they did not intend to force it. Fortunately for my training at the normal school, and my own dear love of teaching, tho there was a little surprise on the faces of some when they came into the class, and saw the teacher, there were no signs of rebellion. The class went on increasing in numbers until it had to be divided, and I was given both divisions. . . .

When I was within a year of graduation, an application came from a Friends' school in Philadelphia for a colored woman who could teach Greek, Latin and higher mathematics. The answer returned was: "We have the woman, but you must wait a year for her."

. . . I never rose to recite in my classes at Oberlin but I felt that I had the honor of the whole African race upon my shoulders. I felt that, should I fail, it would be ascribed to the fact that I was colored. . . .

When I came to the School [The Institute for Colored Youth], the Principal of the Institute was Ebenezer D. Bassett, who for fourteen years had charge of the work. He was a graduate of the State Normal School of Connecticut, and was a man of unusual natural and acquired ability. . . .

In the year 1869, Mr. Bassett was appointed United States Minister to Hayti by President Grant; leaving the principalship of the Institute vacant. Now, Octavius V. Catto, a professor in the school, and myself, had an opportunity to keep the school up to the same degree of proficiency that it attained under its former Principal and to carry it forward as much as possible. . . .

As our young people were now about to find a ready field in teaching, it was thought well to introduce some text books on school management, and methods of teaching, and thoroughly prepare our students for normal work [teaching]. . . .

I instituted a course in normal training, which at first consisted only of a review of English studies, with the theory of teaching, school management and methods. But the inadequacy of this course was so apparent that when it became necessary to reorganize the Preparatory Departments, it was decided to put this work into the hands of the normal students, who would thus have ample practice in teaching and governing under daily direction and correction. These students became so efficient in their work that they were sought for and engaged to teach long before they finished their course of study. . . .

In Philadelphia, the only place at the time where a colored boy could learn a trade, was in the House of Refuge, or the Penitentiary!

And now began an eager and intensely earnest crusade to supply this deficiency in the work of the Institute for Colored Youth.

Fannie Jackson Coppin, *Reminiscences of School Life*
(Philadelphia: African Methodist Episcopal Book Concern, 1913),
pp. 12, 15, 21–23.

METHODS OF INSTRUCTION

FANNIE JACKSON COPPIN

❦ *Fannie Jackson Coppin wrote a book of reminiscences, in which she included a section dealing with elementary education that gives us some clues to her success as an educator. In an age in which the usual schoolmistress ruled with a ruler and taught by rote, Mrs. Coppin's psycho-*

logical understanding and innovative approach to teaching are remarkable.

ELEMENTARY EDUCATION

Never let the word "dumb" be used in your class, or anything said disrespectful of parents or guardians who may have helped the child. . . .

Many a child called dull, would advance rapidly under a patient, wise, and skillful teacher, and the teacher should be as conscientious in the endeavor to improve himself as he is to improve the child. . . .

METHODS OF INSTRUCTION

I am always sorry to hear that such and such a person is going to school to be educated.

This is a great mistake. If the person is to get the benefit of what we call education, he must educate himself, under the direction of the teacher. . . .

OBJECT OF PUNISHMENT

To take a child's lunch from him is a great mistake. There is no use in attempting to teach a hungry child.

The ventilation of the school room may be responsible for what we call stupidity on the part of the child.

Let a stream of oxygen pass through the room and what a waking-up there will be! Sometimes if a child is naughty it will do him good to run out in the yard a minute.

Remember all the time you are dealing with a human being, whose needs are like your own.

HOW TO TEACH READING AND SPELLING

Words are more interesting than letters, and sentences are more interesting than words. So that as soon as possible the teacher wants to make a sentence. But it is not supposed that we should omit to teach the alphabet in order, for we know that this is necessary. But by no means allow this to be done mentally. Have the book or the chart with the letters large work as the teacher points to each letter and calls its name and distinctly made, and have the children's eyes follow the work as the teacher points to each letter and calls its name. . . .

I should have said, that as soon as possible, the child should be taught to write a letter. The words mother, father, sister, brother and teacher should be spelled and written for him so that the little letter beginning Dear mother can begin to be made the subject of instruction.

The child's interest is awakened and he will try his best to learn other words that he will write to his mother. If this begins in the first reader, before the third is finished the child will be quite a little scribe. But we must proceed very slowly with this work. One or two words at a time are all that can be taken, and for this reason, very careful training is necessary on the part of the teacher. If the child gets thoroughly interested in his lessons, it will certainly stop the truancies.

Fannie Jackson Coppin, *Reminiscences of School Life*
(Philadelphia: African Methodist Episcopal Book Concern, 1913),
pp. 41–69 *passim.*

TEACHING THE FREEDMEN

❦ In 1865, there were no school buildings, no teachers, no books, no money in the devastated South. But there were four million newly freed slaves, who sought education as eagerly as they sought land and who made untold sacrifices to acquire the rudiments of learning and establish schools for their children.

Before the Civil War, the South had no public school system, nor had there developed a system of taxation which alone could have financed public schooling and other municipal or rural services.

While the war was still raging, the Union forces were faced with the need of educating the slaves who had flocked behind the Union lines. An approach to the problem was first worked out in Port Royal, South Carolina, where the War Department, as early as 1862, encouraged Northern volunteers, selected, financed and supervised by voluntary relief organizations, to build a rudimentary school system for the freedmen. This set the pattern for Northern abolitionists or church-related groups to organize, finance and staff schools in the South. The Bureau of Refugees, Freedmen and Abandoned Lands, set up by Congress in March 1865, utilized and coordinated the efforts of the nearly three hundred groups operating schools in the South. The Freedmen's Bureau finally consolidated this vast volunteer effort and supplied money for school buildings and supplies, leaving the staffing and running of the schools to philanthropic groups, such as the American Missionary Association, the American Freedmen's and Union Commission and the Freedmen's Aid Societies of the various churches.

The story of this great social experiment, which saw nearly one quarter of a million black children regularly instructed in over 4,300 schools within five years of the end of the war, has never been adequately told. Undoubtedly, the success of the Freedmen's Bureau schools laid the foundation for the establishment of public schools and for the enactment of tax legislation to maintain them. Southern Reconstruction governments incorporated most of these schools into the newly established state public school systems. During the short reign of racially integrated governments, Southern public schools were open to children of both races. It is significant that these public school systems survived the overthrow of the Reconstruction governments although the schools were later strictly segregated by race, with the black schools receiving inferior facilities and inadequate budgets.

Teachers for the freedmen were at first recruited in the North, but their numbers were soon increased by volunteers from the South. By 1869, there were 9,000 teachers for the freedmen in the South. Over 45 per cent of these were women. Most of the white women came from the North, most of the black women from the South. Economic necessity forced many white Southern women to take up schoolteaching as a means of making a living, and quite a number of them chose to teach black children, often from the conviction that they were better qualified to do so than were Northern teachers.

There are no accurate figures available for the number of black women who taught the freedmen, but their number was great and increased rapidly after 1870. Except for the Northern-trained teachers, most of the teachers of the freedmen were only a little above the level of their students in education. The brightest students of every class soon took over classes, often while continuing their own education at night. The institutions for higher education founded by the American Missionary Association and the Freedmen's Bureau, such as Howard University, Hampton Institute, Atlanta University, Fisk University, Scotia Seminary and others, attempted to remedy this deficiency by yearly graduating a corps of black teachers who returned to their own home counties and staffed or founded schools of their own (see pp. 118–146).

The sources below give a sampling of the varied experiences of the black teachers of the freedmen, of their difficult living and working conditions and of the spirit that motivated them. These documents also offer a rare insight into the living conditions of the freedmen as seen by contemporaries.

A TEACHER FROM THE NORTH

CHARLOTTE FORTEN GRIMKÉ

❧ Charlotte Forten Grimké (1837–1914), daughter of Robert B. Forten, was a member of one of the leading

Negro families in Philadelphia. Her grandfather, James Forten, a Revolutionary War veteran, was a sailmaker whose invention and business skill netted him a fortune. A leader in rallying resistance to the American Colonization Society's aim of solving the race question by getting rid of free Negroes, he helped to organize the Philadelphia black comunity for abolition. Charlotte's uncle, Robert Purvis, was one of the founding members and later President of the American Anti-Slavery Society and in 1852 founder of the Vigilance Committee of Philadelphia, which helped hundreds of fugitive slaves to freedom. Charlotte Forten was educated by private tutors and later in the public schools of Salem, Massachusetts. There she graduated with honors from the Salem Normal School in 1856 and taught school for several years until illness forced her to stop working. For a few years she lived the cultured life of a young lady of leisure, attending lectures and antislavery meetings, writing poetry, enjoying friendships with leading black and white abolitionists and keeping a diary.

The outbreak of the Civil War found her, like most of the young women of her circle, eager for service. In 1862, the Union forces, having captured the islands off the coast of South Carolina, embarked on the experiment of military occupation. Over ten thousand freedmen were left destitute and hungry in this region; the War Department now pleaded for "suitable instructors" to help in their education. Charlotte Forten offered her services through the Philadelphia Port Royal Relief Association. From August 1862 to May 1864, she worked in Port Royal as a teacher, keeping a diary of her experiences. Her recollections are remarkable for the fact that she was one of the few Northern Negro teachers to have left a written account of her impressions. True to her upper-class background, she shared the values, even the prejudices, of her white counterparts to a remarkable degree and, although imbued with a missionary spirit and great idealism, viewed her new charges with patronizing amusement and wonder at their strange ways.

Wednesday, Nov. 5 [1862]. Had my first regular teaching experience, and to you and you only friend beloved, will I acknowledge that it was *not* a very pleasant one. Part of my scholars are very tiny,—babies, I call them—and it is hard to keep them quiet and interested while I am hearing the larger ones. They are too young even for the alphabet, it seems to me. I think I must write home and ask somebody to send me picture-books and toys to amuse them with. I fancied Miss T[owne] looked annoyed when, at one time the little ones were unusually restless. Perhaps it was only my fancy. Dear Miss M[urray] was kind and considerate as usual. She is very lovable. Well I *must* not be discouraged. Perhaps things will go on better to-morrow. . . .

We've established our household on—as we hope—a firm basis. We have *Rose* for our little maid-of-all-work, *Amaretta* for cook, washer, and ironer, and *Cupid*, yes Cupid himself, for clerk, oysterman and future coachman. I must also inform you dear A., that we have made ourselves a bed, whereon we hope to rest to-night, for rest *I* certainly did not last night, despite innumerable blankets designed to conceal and render inactive the bones of the bed. But said bones did so protrude that sleep was almost an impossibility to our poor little body.

Thursday, Nov. 13 . . . Talked to the children a little while to-day about the noble Toussaint [L'Ouverture]. They listened very attentively. It is well that they sh'ld know what one of their own color c'ld do for his race. I long to inspire them with courage and ambition (of a noble sort), and high purpose. . . .

This eve, Harry, one of the men on the place, came in for a lesson. He is most eager to learn, and is really a scholar to be proud of. He learns rapidly. I gave him his first lesson in writing to-night, and his progress was wonderful. He held the pen almost perfectly right the first time. He will very soon learn to write, I think. I must inquire if there are not more of the grown people who w'ld like to take lessons at night.

Whenever I am well enough it will be a real happiness to me to teach them . . . .

Monday, Nov. 17. Had a dreadfully wearying day in school, of which the less said the better. Afterward drove with the ladies to "The Corner," a colection of negro houses, whither Miss T[owne] went on a doctoring expedition. The people there are very pleasant. Saw a little baby, just borne [sic] today—and another—old Venus' great grandchild for whom I made the little pink frock. These people are very gratiful [sic]. The least kindness that you do them they insist on repaying in some way. We have had a quantity of eggs and potatoes brought us despite our remonstrances. Today one of the women gave me some Tanias. Tania is a queer looking root. After it is boiled it looks like a potato, but is much larger. I don't like the taste.

Tuesday, Nov. 18. After school went to The Corner again. Stopped at old Susy's house to see some sick children. Old Susy is a character. Miss T[owne] asked her if she wanted her old master to come back again. Most emphatically she answered. "No indeed, missus, no indeed dey treat we too bad. Dey tuk ebery one of my chilen away from me. When we sick and c'ldnt work dey tuk away all our food from us; gib us nutten to eat. Dey's orful hard Missis." When Miss T[owne] told her that some of the people said they wanted their old masters to come back, a look of supreme contempt came to old Susy's withered face. "Dat's 'cause dey's got no sense, den missus."

Sunday, Nov. 23. This eve. our boys and girls with others from across the creek came in and sang a long time for us. Of course we had the old favorites "Down in the Lonesome Valley," and "Roll, Jordan, Roll," and "No man can hender me," and beside those several shouting tunes that we had not heard before; they are very wild and strange. It was impossible for me to understand many of the words although I asked them to repeat them for me. I only know that one had something about "De Nell Am Ringing." I think that was the refrain; and of another, some of the words were "Christ build the church widout no hammer nor nail." "Jehovah Halleluhiah," which is a grand thing, and "Hold the light," an especial favorite of mine—they sang with great spirit. The leader of the singing was Prince, a large black boy, from Mr. R[uggles]'s place. He was full of the shouting spirit, and c'ld not possibly keep still. It was amusing to see his gymnastic performances. They were quite in the Ethiopian Methodists' style. He has really a very fine bass voice. I enjoyed their singing so much, and sh'ld have enjoyed it so much more if some dear ones who are far away c'ld have listened it to [sic] with me. How delighted they would have been. . . .

Jan. 31 [1863]. . . . In B[eaufort] we spent nearly all our time at Harriet Tubman's—otherwise "Moses." She is a wonderful woman—a real heroine. Has helped off a large number of slaves, after taking her own freedom. She told us that she used to hide them in the woods during the day and go around to get provisions for them. Once she had with her a man named Joe, for whom a reward of $1500 was offered. Frequently, in different places she found handbills exactly describing him, but at last they reached in safety the Suspension Bridge over the Falls and found themselves in Canada. Until then, she said, Joe had been very silent. In vain had she called his attention to the glory of the Falls. He sat perfectly still—moody, it seemed, and w'ld not even glance at them. But when she said. "Now we are in Can[ada]" he sprang to his feet with a great shout, and sang and clapped his hand [sic] in a perfect delirium of joy. So when they got out, and he first touched *free* soil, he shouted and hurrahed "as if he were crazy"—she said.

How exciting it was to hear her tell the story. And to hear her sing the very scraps of jubilant hymns that he sang. She said the ladies crowded around them, and some laughed and some cried. My own eyes were full as I listened to her—the heroic woman! A reward of $10000 was offered for her by the Southerners, and her friends deemed it best that she sh'ld, for a time find refuge in Can[ada]. And she did so, but only for a short time. She came back and was soon at the good brave work again. She is living in B[eaufort] now; keeping an eating house. But she wants to go North, and will probably do so ere long. I am glad I saw her—*very* glad . . .

The Journal of Charlotte Forten, Ray Allen Billington, ed. (New York: Collier Books, 1961), pp. 148–153, 180.

A FORMER SLAVE TEACHES BLACK SOLDIERS
SUSIE KING TAYLOR

❦ Susie (Baker) King Taylor (1848–?) was born a slave in Savannah, Georgia, and acquired some learning surreptitiously (see p. 27). During the war she served as laundress, teacher and nurse to the Union army, but received no compensation for her services. Her first husband, Sergeant King, died in 1866, shortly before the birth of their son. Mrs. King supported the child and herself by teaching school and later opened a night school for adults in Liberty County, Georgia. This paid so little that she was forced to enter domestic service. She married Russell L. Taylor in 1879 and moved to Boston. There she helped organize a Women's Auxiliary Corps of the Grand Army of the Republic and in 1896 compiled a roster of the surviving Union veterans in Massachusetts. Her memoirs offer vivid descriptions of life in a black army camp.

On April 1, 1862, about the time the Union soldiers were firing on Ft. Pulaski, I was sent out into the country to my mother. I remember what a roar and din the guns made, they jarred the earth for miles. The fort was at last taken by them. Two days after the taking of Ft. Pulaski my uncle took his family of seven and myself to St. Catherine Island. We landed under the protection of the Union fleet and remained there two weeks when about thirty of us were taken aboard the gunboat P—to be transferred to St. Simon's Island; at last, to my unbounded joy, I saw "the Yankee." . . .

After I had been on St. Simon's about three days Commodore Goldsborough heard of me and came to Gaston Bluff to see me. I found him very cordial. He said Capt. Woodborough had spoken to him of me and that he was pleased to hear of my being so capable etc. and wished me to take charge of the school for the children on the island. I told him I would gladly do so, if I could have some books. He said I should have them, and in a week or two I received two large boxes of books and testaments from the North. I had about forty children to teach, beside a number of adults who came to me nights, all of them so eager to learn to read above anything else. . . .

There were about 600 men and women and children on St. Simon's, the women and children being in the majority and we were afraid to go very far from our own quarters in the daytime, and at night even to go out of the house for a long time, although the men were on the watch all the time; for there were not any soldiers on the island, only the Marines, who were on the gunboats along the cost. The Rebels, knowing this, could steal by them under cover of the night, and getting on the island would capture any persons venturing out alone and carry them to the mainland. Several of the men disappeared. . . . [She was then transferred, with the other contrabands, to Beaufort, South Carolina.] I was enrolled as laundress. . . .

I taught a great many of the comrades in Company E to read and write when they were off duty, nearly all were anxious to learn. My husband taught some also when it was convenient for him. I was very happy to know my efforts were successful in camp also very grateful for the appreciation of my services. I gave my services willingly for four years and three months without receiving a dollar. I was glad, however, to be allowed to go with the regiment, to care for the sick and afflicted comrades.

[The regiment is ordered to fight in Florida, and she accompanies the men.] I learned to handle a musket very well while in the regiment and could shoot straight and often hit the target. I assisted in cleaning the guns and used to fire them off, to see if the cartridges were dry, before cleaning and re-loading, each day. I thought this was great fun. I was also able to take a gun all apart and put it together again. . . .

Fort Wagner being only a mile from our camp, I went there two or three times a week and would go up on the ramparts to watch the gunners send their shells into Charleston (which they did every fifteen minutes), and I had a full view of the city from that point. Outside of the Fort were many skulls lying about; I have often moved them one side out of the path. The comrades and I would have wondered a bit as to which side of the war the men fought on, some said they were the skulls of our boys; some said they were the enemies; but as there was no definite way to know, it was never decided which could lay claim to them. They were a gruesome sight, those fleshless heads and grinning jaws, but by this time I had become used to worse things and did not feel as I would have earlier in my camp life.

Susie King Taylor, *Reminiscences of My Life in Camp with the 33rd United States Colored Troops* (Boston: Author, 1902), pp. 5–9, 11–15, 26, 31–32.

TEACHERS WANTED, 1865

TEACHERS FOR THE SOUTH.—Several teachers, principals and assistants, male and female, are needed for the Government schools (white and colored) recently established in the District of Eastern Virginia by order of Major-Gen. Butler. The salary of male teachers is, principals $60 a month, assistants $45; female principals $30, assistants $20. Applications, stating qualifications with accompanying testimonials should be forwarded at once to the Superintendent of Public Education. Preference will in all cases be given to disabled soldiers and soldiers' widows and wives, if suitably qualified. The schools will be opened Jan. 1, 1865. Those wishing situations should address Charles A. Raymond, Chaplain U. S. A., and Superintendent of Public Education, District East Virginia, Chesapeake Hospital, Fortress Monroe, Va.

Ad in Boston newspapers, reprinted in
The Freedmen's Journal, Vol. 1, No. 1
(January 18, 1865).

REPORTS FROM THE FIELD

MISS M. A. PARKER

Raleigh, N. C., Feb. 22, 1869

It is surprising to me to see the amount of suffering which many of the people endure for the sake of sending their children to school. Men get very low ages here—from $2.50 to $8 per month usually, while a first rate hand may get $10, and a peck or two of meal per week for rations—and a great many men cannot get work at all. The women take in sewing and washing, go out by day to scour, etc. There is one woman who supports three children and keeps them at school; she says, "I don't care how hard I has to work, if I can only sen[d] Sallie and the boys to school looking respectable." Many of the girls have but one decent dress; it gets washed and ironed on Saturday, and then is worn until the next Saturday, provided they do not tear it or fall in the mud; when such an accident happens there is an absent mark on the register. . . . One may go into their cabins on cold, windy days, and see daylight between every two boards, or feel the rain dropping through the roof; but a word of complaint is rarely heard.

They are anxious to have the children "get on" in their books, and do not seem to feel impatient if they lack comforts themselves. A pile of books is seen in almost every cabin, though there be no furniture except a poor bed, a table and two or three broken chairs.

Miss M. A. Parker, *The American Freedman*, Vol. 3, No. 6
(April 1869).

MRS. ISABELLA GIBBINS

Charlottesville, Va., Oct. 17, 1866

Mrs. Gibbins (a colored native teacher) is very much liked by the colored people here. Her nature is so noble, that she is not so liable to stimulate petty jealousy among her people as many might under similar circumstances. . . . I think she is doing well in her new sphere of duty, especially in the matter of government. She has a kind of magnetism about her which is a good qualification for a teacher. She is really a fine reader of easy readings, and I should choose her to prepare scholars for me in that line, from among nine-tenths of those engaged in this work, so far as I have known her. She intends to pursue her studies in the evening with my help.

Anna Gardner, *The Freedmen's Record*, Vol. 2, No. 11
(November 1866).

Charleston, Va., Oct. 24, 1866

I have watched with considerable anxiety and interest the primary class taught by Mrs. Isabella Gibbins, her recent appointment as a teacher of her race an experiment as to how a colored woman, who had been a slave up to the time of the Surrender, would succeed in a vocation to her so novel, and one which, considering she was to lately grinding in the prison-house of slavery, seems almost a miracle. I am glad to be able to say that thus far she has quite equalled my sanguine expectations, especially in the matter of organizing her school, and governing it without resorting in any instance to severity of discipline. She has stimulated a good degree of self-respect among a class of scholars who were much more negligent in personal habits, etc. than those attending other schools. Her scholars appear very fond of her, and greatly pleased with a beginning which promises so much improvement.

Anna Gardner, *The Freedmen's Record*, Vol. 2, No. 12
(December 1866).

Charlottesville, Va., Oct. 15, 1866

I began my school on the 3rd of October with forty-two scholars. The sphere into which I have been put by your kindness is so different from slavery, I hardly knew what steps to take; but following Miss Gardner's exact rule, I read a chapter in the Bible, choosing the Eighty-third psalm, which I felt was suitable. . . . I then told them I wanted they should conduct themselves so as to reflect credit on the school and their race, in education, and by moral improvements. We had a meeting of the Freedman's Aid Society on the first of this month. I read Miss Anna's letter, and the compositions of Celia Woods and my son John West. I think it did great good. They seemed as though their eyes had just been opened to see what education would do for them. I believe all that were there joined the society. . . . I hope we may be successful in aiding the schools that are here. The schools are filled but the children still come to see if they can be admitted. I have sixty-three pupils.

Isabella Gibbins, *The Freedmen's Record*, Vol. 2, No. 11
(November 1866).

Charlottesville, Va., March 29, 1867

We have lived to see the fortieth Congress and to behold a change of affairs. The rebels begin to see the error of their way at last, and do all they can to better our race. They say, "the colored people are not only free but have a right to vote.

Now let us be kind to them; they have been our slaves, and we must do something for them. It will not do to leave them to the care of those hated yankees. They will build them up as a tower against us. We must not do as we would like, but as we must, in this time of trouble, because the time that the Garrisons, the Sumners, and Stevens' have been telling them about, has come, they will believe it if we do not take right steps in time. They are a good people, and so fond of their old masters, they will do what we want they should. Most of them love us, and have forgotten what happened while they were slaves. They know we are their friends."*

This is a grand story for them to tell, but let us answer them. Can we forget the crack of the whip, cowhide, whipping-post, the auction-block, the hand-cuffs, the spaniels, the iron collar, the negro-trader tearing the young child from its mother's breast as a whelp from the lioness? Have we forgotten that by those horrible cruelties, hundreds of our race have been killed? No, we have not, nor ever will.

If the Northern people who have given their life's blood for our liberty are not our friends, where can we find them? O, God help us to love these people.

Isabella Gibbins, The Freedmen's Record, Vol. 3, No. 6
(June 1867).

MISS J. HOSMER, MISS STONE

Gordonsville, Va., April 1, 1867

I write you this letter to return thanks for your kindness to me and my race. Our school prospers finely. They learn very fast. We have some grown scholars in the school and they work hard to learn all they can. Miss J. Hosmer teaches in the room with me, having as many as a hundred and fifteen scholars in our room. Miss Stone is in the next room. I think most of these children will become useful to their country. They all sing well and like their teachers, which is most important. It is true we have some do-nothings in our school as

---

* Quotation marks added by editor for greater clarity.

in all others; but there are but one or two of that family. I am thankful to say the colored people have the power to vote, and they are willing to put good men in office. The winter has been very hard here and prevented many from coming out during the bad weather. The colored people have been able to do but little for the school, but are willing to do all they can, I believe. I am thankful that I am blessed with this opportunity of learning. I thank God, and all my kind friends at the North for what I have learned. I want to make it known to them in every way I can. . . .

William P. Lucas, The Freedmen's Record, Vol. 3, No. 6
(June 1867).

MOTHER DRAYTON

Charleston, June 1, 1867

. . . There is an old woman in the city—Mother Drayton— who assembles about her every Sunday, and once besides during the week, all the children in the church to which she belongs. She calls them her good children, and I believe, at present, they number nearly a hundred. She has continued this for more than twenty years, and in the meantime children have grown up, and in their turn put their children in her care. She thought of it for ten years before putting it into operation. But, she says "It's not me, it was God that put it into my head." As might be expected, from the fact of her being a slave, she encountered many difficulties in the beginning. The children call her Godmother affectionately, and are proud of the honor of being among her number.

Ellen M. Patrick, The Freedmen's Record, Vol. 3, No. 7
(July 1867).

MISS J. J. R. RICHARDS

Jacksonville, Fla., March 11, 1867

We stopped at St. Mary's, Ga. and found a young colored woman, Miss J. J. R. Richards, who teaches about 70 day-scholars, a dozen adults in the evening, and nearly 100 children on Sundays. She has a wonderful history. Her mother was a white lady, and her father a mixture of the Cuban-Spaniard and negro. She was educated at Princeton, N. J., and went to Liberia as a teacher, where she remained about four years. On returning, she went to Richmond, and while appearing as a slave, was in the secret service of the U.S. . . . On the surrender of the city, she was engaged by the Baptist Home Missionary Society in its school in Dr. Ryland's old church. . . . Miss Richards is employed by the Bureau, but she has scarcely any books. . . . The colored people of St. Mary's are very poor and Miss Richards well worthy of support.

The Freedmen's Record, Vol. 2, No. 1 (April 1867).

MISS LAURA F. MOBLEY

Laura F. Mobley to Rev. E. M. Craveth, N. Y.
[American Missionary Association]

New Iberia, La., Dec. 3, 1874

. . . From appearances, I think we are going to have a very hard winter, and I fear there will be great suffering among our people. On account of political troubles a great many men (col) have been turned out of their situations. Large numbers of them joined in with the whites at the late election, which I consider a wise move on their part; for I tell you being an eye witness of the condition of both races, that this division politicaly [!] between the whites and blacks, if continued, will finally ruin the state. The prospects for the future are very discouraging indeed. As for making a living out of these people it is an impossibility. My father has a week day school of fifty five scholars, he having consolidated his and my schools, and then divided it into primary and grammar departments; in which he employs my sister and self, I having charge nominaly [!] of the whole school, principaly [!] of the grammar department; and the money we receive from it averages twelve dollars a month. The people did do somewhat better than this last year, but this year they are very poor. They promise to pay us some time or other, but as nearly every man that belongs to our church is out of work the prospects are very doubtful. Last year the church payed our house rent, but this year my father has it to pay himself; and as house rent is very high in this place it takes nearly half of what he receives from the A. M. A. to pay it; and if we did not live very close we would have nothing to eat part of the time. You may judge from these lines, somewhat, of our condition, and prospects for the future. . . .

American Missionary Association Archives, Dillard University,
New Orleans, Louisiana

ADMINISTRATION OF FREEDMEN'S SCHOOLS

✌ *The schools run under the sponsorship of the American Missionary Association were closely supervised. Monthly reports were required from every teacher. Notice that the accompanying report (see photo, p. 109) refers to a night school and the students' educational level ranges from second-grade readers to those studying English grammar and Latin. The number of assistants undoubtedly refers to unpaid students, who tutored other students on a lower educational level than themselves. The teacher signing this particular report is Mrs. Mary Ann Shadd Cary (see p. 324).*

AN EXAMPLE OF TEACHING MATERIALS USED IN FREEDMEN'S SCHOOLS IN VIRGINIA IN 1870

First stands the lofty Washington
That noble, great, immortal one!

13   101

[Ed. Form No. 3.]

TEACHER'S MONTHLY SCHOOL REPORT

For the Month of *April* 187*1*.

☞ To contain one entire calendar month, and to be forwarded as soon as possible after the close of the month.
☞ A School under the sole control of one Teacher, or a Teacher with one Assistant, is to be reported as one School.

[Answers placed here.]

Name of your School?	*Lincoln Miss* Location (town, county, or district)? *Washington D.C.*
Is it a Day or Night School?	*Night* Of what grade? *Mixed*
When did your present session commence?	*Feb. 1* When to close? *June*
Is your School supported by an Educational Society?	*Yes* What Society? *American Miss Association*
Is your School supported wholly by local School Board??	*No* Name of Board or Com.? *0* Am't p'd this month? *0*
Is your School supported in part by local School Board?	*Yes* Name of Board or Com.? *Miss Asso* Am't p'd this month?
Is your School supported wholly by Freedmen?	*No* Amount paid this month
Is your school supported in part by Freedmen?	*Yes* Amount paid this month? *$43.75*
Have you had Bureau transportation this term?	*No*
Who owns the School-building?	*Lincoln Miss Ass.*
Is rent paid by Freedmen's Bureau?	*No* How much per month? *0*
What number of Teachers and Assistants in your School?	*22* White? *1* Colored? *21*
Total enrolment for the month?	*181* Male? *85* Female? *98*
Number enrolled last report?	*209* { Number enrolled last report, by adding new scholars and subtracting those left school, must equal the present total enrolment. }
Number left School this month?	*39*
Number new Scholars this month?	*9*
What is the average attendance?	*123* { Schools are to be kept five days per week and six hours each day. }
Number of Pupils for whom tuition is paid?	How many hours have you taught per day?
Number of White Pupils?	*00* How many days have you taught this month?
Number always present?	*93* Give reasons for deficiency of time, (if any,) in teachi
Number always punctual?	*73*
Number over 16 years of age?	*133*
Number in Alphabet?	*00*
Number who spell, and read easy lessons?	*79* *Latin 1.*
Number in advanced Readers?	*108*
Number in Geography?	*70*
Number in Arithmetic?	*150*
Number in higher branches? *Grammar*	*33*
Number in Writing?	*92*
Number in needle-work?	*00*
Number free before the war?	*28*
Have you a Sabbath School?	*Yes* How many Teachers? How many Pupils?
Have you an Industrial School?	*0* How many Teachers? How many Pupils?
State the kind of work done?	*Needle & Machine work generally*

☞ To the following questions give exact or approximate answers, prefixing to the latter the word "about."

1. Do you know of any schools for Refugees or Freedmen not reported to the State Superintendent? How many?
2. Give (estimated) whole number of pupils in all such Schools? No. of Teachers, White, Colored
3. Do you know of Sabbath Schools not reported to the State Superintendent? How many?
4. Give (estimated) whole number of pupils in all such schools? No. of Teachers, White, Colored,
5. State the public sentiment towards Colored Schools.
6. How many pupils in your School are members of a Temperance Society: *19* Name of the Society? *Various*

Remarks:

(Sign.ed) *Mary A. S. Cary* Teacher.

*Or School Committee, School District, Town, City, County, or State?
†A pupil is not to be reckoned as enrolled until after five days' attendance.

The elder Adams next we see
And Jefferson counts number three
Then Madison is fourth you know
The fifth one on the list's Monroe
The sixth and Adams comes again
And Jackson seventh in the train
Van Buren eight upon the line
And Harrison makes number nine
The tenth is Taylor in his turn.
And Polk eleventh, as we learn.
Then comes Tyler for his term of four
The thirteenth on the list's Fillmore.
The fourteenth and Frank Pierce came
A drunkard whom we blush to name
Then came Buchanan to execute the law
Who plunged the country into civil war
Then Abraham Lincoln, the honored & brave
Who passed through the Red Sea his country to save
Then Johnson came in martyred Lincoln's place
The promised Moses of the colored race
(Two closing versions:)
A traitor he, a curse to our free land
Soon in his place brave Grant shall stand
or
A Pharoah (*sic*) he thank God his reign is over
Now Grant will take us to the promised shore!

As cited in Henry L. Swint, *Dear Ones at Home: Letters from Contraband Camps* (Nashville, Tennessee: Vanderbilt University, 1966), p. 253.

CATECHIZING FREEDMEN CHILDREN

❦ *The strongly missionary and paternalistic approach of many teachers to the freedmen is illustrated by the selections below. The first was recorded at a Richmond, Virginia, school; the second, at one in Louisville, Kentucky.*

I

TEACHER: Are you glad you are free?

STUDENTS: Yes, indeed.

TEACHER: Who gave you your freedom?

STUDENTS: God.

TEACHER: Through whom?

STUDENTS: Abraham Lincoln.

TEACHER: Is Mr. Lincoln dead?

STUDENTS: Yes.

TEACHER: Who is your president?

STUDENTS: Johnson.

TEACHER: Are you glad you have schools and teachers?

STUDENTS: Yes.

TEACHER: Do you want these friends who are here today to go North and send you more teachers?

STUDENTS: Yes, indeed.

II

TEACHER: Now children, you don't think white people are any better than you because they have straight hair and white faces?

STUDENTS: No, sir.

TEACHER: No, they are no better, but they are different, they possess great power, they formed this great government, they control this vast country. . . . Now what makes them different from you?

STUDENTS: MONEY. (Unanimous shout)

TEACHER: Yes, but what enabled them to obtain it? *How* did they get money?

STUDENTS: Got it off us, stole it off we all!

Both items cited in Henry L. Swint, *The Northern Teacher in the South; 1862–1870* (Nashville, Tennessee: Vanderbilt University Press, 1941), pp. 88–89.

THEY WOULD NOT LET US HAVE SCHOOLS

❦ *The violence which marked the overthrow of the Reconstruction governments fell with particular fury on teachers and supporters of black schools. The events described in the following testimony, given before a congressional committee investigating the Ku Klux Klan, typified what happened in many counties and states of the South.*

Atlanta, Georgia, October 21, 1871

WITNESS: Caroline Smith (age: 35)

QUESTION: What did you leave home for?

ANSWER: The Ku-Klux came there. . . .

QUESTION: How many were there?

ANSWER: A great many of them, twenty-five or thirty, perhaps more; but ten of them whipped me.

QUESTION: When was that?

ANSWER: Late in the night; I don't know what time. I sat up very late that night, for they had been there once before, and we never laid down early in the night all of us; some of us sat up the better part of the night. I was pretty nigh asleep when I heard them coming.

QUESTION: How were they dressed?

ANSWER: They had on pants like anybody else, but they were put on their body like they made children's clothes. They had on some kind of false face. . . . They caught my husband and beat him as much as they wanted to, and then they came in and said, "Who is this?" I said, "Caroline." He said, "H'm, h'm, come out of here." I went out and they made me get down on my knees. . . . Felker then said, "Take off this," pointing to my dress, "and fasten it around you." They then made me fasten it to my waist. He whipped me some; and then he made me take my body off, which I wore under my dress. He gave me fifty more, and then said, "Go and get some water, and don't let's hear any big talk from you, and don't sass any white ladies." I said, "I don't do that. . . ."

QUESTION: You say they made a general scattering of the darkies in March?

ANSWER: Yes, sir.

QUESTION: What reason did they give for that?

ANSWER: They said we should not have any schools; and that white people should not countenance us, and they intended to whip the last one; that is what they said.

QUESTION: Why did they not want you to have schools?

ANSWER: They would not let us have schools. They went to a colored man there, whose son had been teaching school, and they took every book they had and threw them into the fire; and they said they would dare any other nigger to have a book in his house. We allowed last fall that we would have a school-house in every district; and the colored men started them. But the Ku-Klux said they would whip every man who sent a scholar there. There is a school-house there, but no scholars. The colored people dare not dress up themselves and fix up, like they thought anything of themselves, for fear they would whip us. I have been humble and obedient to them, a heap more so than I was to my master, who raised me; and that is the way they serve us.

Report of the Joint Select Committee to Inquire into the Condition of Affairs in the Late Insurrectionary States. 42nd Congress, 2nd Session (Washington, D.C.: Government Printing Office, 1872), Vol. 6, pp. 400–403.

SCHOOLING IN THE JIM CROW SOUTH

SEPTIMA POINSETTA CLARK

❦ The schools for black children, which had been created and staffed by so much sacrifice and hard work, were eventually taken over by counties and states to become part of the Southern public school system. This system institutionalized racial segregation and the oppression of blacks by keeping the schools for black children underfinanced, poorly equipped and overcrowded. Comparative budgets and salary schedules for schools for black and white illustrate this pattern of white racism. The school experiences Septima Clark describes are typical of those of millions of black children. Little changed during the fifty years after the Civil War. It was only in the 1920's and 1930's that slight improvements, such as those described by Septima Clark, were won. In the post–World War II period, under the impact of the civil rights struggles, Southern school districts spent more money on new school buildings, equipment and salary equalization for black schools, in an effort to stave off school integration. But to this day, the segregated schools for black children are distinctly inferior in every regard to those for white children.

Septima Poinsetta Clark (1898–   ) worked as a schoolteacher on St. John's Island, South Carolina, before her marriage to Nerie Clark. Her husband's death three years later left her with a ten-month-old son to support. She continued teaching at Columbia, South Carolina, leaving her son to be raised by his grandmother, obtained an M.A. degree from Hampton Institute and then took a job in the Charleston, South Carolina, public school system. She was very active in civic work and pioneered in interracial work, which was considered so radical that, in 1956, she lost

her job and retirement pay. She became director of work-
shops, and later director of education, at the Highlander Folk
School, an interracial school with radical orientation. The
harassment of the school by Tennessee authorities once led
to her arrest on trumped-up charges. In recent years, she
has devoted her energies to voter registration work with the
Southern Christian Leadership Conference.

Here I was, a high-school graduate, eighteen years old, principal in a two-teacher school with 132 pupils ranging from
beginners to eighth graders, with no teaching experience,
a schoolhouse constructed of boards running up and down,
with no slats in the cracks, and a fireplace at one end of the
room that cooked the pupils immediately in front of it but
allowed those in the rear to shiver and freeze on their uncomfortable, hard, back-breaking benches. . . .

I had the older children, roughly the fifth, sixth, seventh
and eighth grades. The other teacher had those through the
fourth. But my pupils in the seventh and eighth grades . . .
were most erratic in their attendance, for they were old
enough to work in the fields. They didn't come in until the
cotton had been picked, and often it was Christmas and
sometimes even January before all the cotton was gleaned.
To add to this difficulty, most of these children had to stop
school in early spring to begin preparing the fields for the
new crop. Naturally, the attendance varied greatly from day
to day.

We tried as best we could to classify these children. But
it was difficult. Some subjects I was able to teach most of
them at the same time, and so was the other teacher; we
could make better time that way. But there were subjects
that required almost individual teaching. Another problem
was the lack of textbooks. There were so few, and what we
had were not uniform. In the spelling classes, I remember,
I often wrote out lists of words to be studied. . . .

In those days the state financed the schools, but

sometimes the counties provided small supplements and Charleston County was one of them. Soon I was getting a supplement of five dollars, which made my salary $35 a month. But right across from me—it happened that the white school and the Negro school in this community were not far apart—was the white teacher getting $85 a month and teaching three—yes, three—pupils.

It wasn't fair, of course; it was the rankest discrimination. That, however, was more than four decades ago. . . .

A Negro leader named T. E. Miller, who in the era of Reconstruction in the South had served as a representative in Congress and who both Negroes and whites considered a forceful and persuasive speaker, came to Charleston and held some meetings. He was then retired from the presidency of the State Colored Agricultural and Mechanical College at Orangeburg, South Carolina. Mr. Miller had decided, and the NAACP was in warm agreement, that the time had come in Charleston for Negro women to be employed as teachers in the Charleston public schools. As had been the case while I was a student at Avery, white teachers were still teaching the Negro children in the public schools and employment was available to Negro teachers only in private schools such as Avery.

These meetings and the speeches by Mr. Miller and others enraged some of the white citizens of Charleston and they shouted for all to hear that mulattoes—children of mixed blood—were the only ones who wanted Negro teachers for their children. The cooks and the laundresses, they declared, didn't want their children taught by Negro teachers. In recent years others in their desperate attempts to maintain segregation in the schools have echoed that declaration by saying that Negro parents do not want their children to attend public schools with white pupils.

Mr. Miller came to Principal Cox at Avery and asked him if he would ask his teachers to undertake a door-to-door

canvass to obtain signatures to a petition asking that Negro
teachers be employed to teach in Negro schools. That's when
I got into the fight. I volunteered to seek signatures and
started visiting the grass roots people. I worked Cannon
Street, a very long street, from Rutledge all the way to King.
Soon we brought in a tow sack—we called it a croaker sack,
I remember, back in those days—with more than 10,000
signatures to the petition. I remember the number because
of the fact that a white legislator known then as One-Eye
Tillman had declared Mr. Miller would never be able to get
10,000 signatures in all Charleston.

The law was passed. The next year, 1920, we had Negro
teachers in the public schools of Charleston and the year
following we had Negro principals. We had been victorious
in this my first effort to establish for Negro citizens what
I sincerely believed was no more than their God-given
rights. . . .

In Columbia I became interested and soon I was en-
thusiastically involved in the teachers' salaries equalization
campaign. . . . This equalization suit, in fact, had been started
in Charleston by a woman teacher. She had got married,
however, and for one reason or another the action had not
been pushed. But under the leadership of a teacher in
Columbia, J. Andrew Simmons, the action was resumed with
another teacher as the plaintiff in the test case.

We teachers, as I recall, did not have to raise one penny
to carry this case through the courts. The costs, I presume,
were borne entirely by the NAACP. . . .

Many of our Negro teachers, in fact, were opposed to
what we were doing. . . . I had attended a meeting . . . at
[which] a reporter was present and the proceedings appeared
in the newspapers. That frightened some of the teachers,
though others were completely unafraid. . . . .

And our efforts paid off, not only in the satisfaction of
having made a good fight, but also in actual cash. The courts

decided with us. When I went to Columbia, my salary was $65 a month. When I left I was getting almost $400 a month. Of course, I cannot rightfully argue that all the raise came from the action of the court. But a greater part did. And the decision of the court followed our institution of legal action.

All items: Septima Clark, *Echo in My Soul* (New York: E. P. Dutton & Co., 1962), pp. 38–39, 60–61, 81–83.

SCHOOL FOUNDERS

✿ Even before the Civil War there were, through the efforts of free Blacks, a few schools operating in the cities of the South, mostly in a clandestine fashion. With the end of the Civil War, these schools became schools for the freedmen and training grounds for teachers. This is exemplified by Mary S. Peake of Hampton, Virginia, a mulatto seamstress who in the 1850's kept school in her home. In 1861, under the sponsorship of the American Missionary Association, Mary Peake opened a day school for fifty pupils in Hampton, near Fortress Monroe. This school was one of the earliest of its kind in the South.

In the cities, free Blacks and freedmen were able to sustain a more elaborate network of schools for their children. In 1870, J. W. Alvord, the general superintendent of the Freedmen's Bureau, reported from an inspection tour in Charleston, South Carolina, that there were eight black schools in the city. "The Freedman's Pay School, 150 pupils with colored teachers, is a landmark, showing the progress of these people. All its expenses are met by the Freedmen."*

* *Letters from the South* (Washington, D.C.: Howard University Press, 1870). Pamphlet.

The freedmen's schools, briefly supported by the federal government, flourished during the Reconstruction period. In the decades following the defeat of the Reconstruction governments and the re-establishment of white supremacy rule, schools became resegregated, and before long, all pretense of educating black children to the same level as white children vanished. In a South now firmly dedicated to white supremacy, sharecropping and tenant farming, schooling for black children was considered an unnecessary luxury, if not a dangerous indulgence, by state and county governments. While the public education systems initiated by the Reconstruction governments survived after 1876, they did not include black children except on a bare-minimum level. In many rural counties, schools for black children were kept open only a few months of the year, expenditures for buildings and supplies and teacher's salaries were a fraction of that spent for the white schools and there was little pretense that higher education was being offered to black children. In 1910, one historian reports that there was not one eighth-grade school for Blacks in the rural South, no two-year high school, and that the average Negro school operated four months out of the year. Teachers in these schools usually had no more than eighth-grade training, and their salaries on the average were $150 a year.*

It took more than usual dedication to accept a teaching position in one of these rural schools. A young New Yorker, graduate of the Colored Orphan's Asylum in Riverdale, went to Butt's Road, Virginia, eager to be of service to her people. "I only cried once," she reported of her first impressions.

> I have some girls as large as myself and some
> larger. The people think I am too young to teach
> and manage the big boys. . . . The people tell
> me this Butt's Road is full of snakes; about the
> first of May one can't walk for black snakes. I

---

* Henry A. Bullock, A *History of Negro Education in the South: From 1619 to the Present* (Cambridge: Harvard University Press, 1967), p. 123.

don't know what I shall do; I'm sure I will be
afraid to walk across the yard.*

But she prevailed, and so did others like her, frightened,
poorly equipped, young, but full of faith in their objective—
education as a means of emancipation of black people.

The inadequacies of this segregated school system forced
Southern Blacks to build their own educational institutions.
In so doing, they had to overcome a variety of obstacles:
poverty, white hostility, their own lack of training and the
discouragement bred of repeated failures.

Black sharecroppers, scattered on widely separated plantations, living below subsistence level and without cash income,
were hardly in a position to found and fund schools for their
children. Thus it was usually the young man or woman with
exceptional leadership qualities and a missionary spirit who,
after obtaining an education at one of the Negro seminaries
or normal schools, returned to his home county to start a
school and support it with the help of white philanthropists.

Such schools were often of the most primitive sort. Emma
J. Wilson, a graduate of Scotia Seminary who had pledged to
go to Africa as a missionary, returned to her native Mayesville,
South Carolina, in 1892 and "found her Africa at her own
door." She opened school with ten pupils in an abandoned
cotton-gin house, accepted eggs, chickens and produce as
tuition, and persuaded the County Board of Education to
allot her $45 a year in aid. With this munificent sum she
hired an assistant, accepted more students and undertook to
build a schoolhouse. She made her way North by speaking
in black churches and camp meetings, collecting nickels
and dimes and, when necessary, working as a laundress to
support herself. After three years of such fund raising, she
won the support of Northern philanthropists, and with their
financial help, she founded Mayesville Institute. The school
was accredited in 1896, but received no more than $200

* Elizabeth Leonard, "History of the Riverdale Children's Association,
formerly the Colored Orphan's Asylum: 1836–1956," typescript, Schlesinger
Library, Radcliffe College, Cambridge, Massachusetts, p. 31.

annually from the state, although it had an enrollment of 500 students, including 50 orphans. The students raised their own food, built their own buildings and derived some income from a brickmaking establishment.

In the 1890's, Hampton and Tuskegee Institutes annually sent forth an idealistic group of young men and women who founded and staffed schools dedicated to self-help, uplift and industrial and agricultural training. Cornelia Bowen, a Tuskegee graduate who founded Mt. Meigs Institute in Alabama, was one such teacher. The work of these pioneers would have been impossible without the support of the black rural communities, the churches and white philanthropies. Starting in 1882, the Peabody and Slater Funds assisted in the training of black teachers and supported hundreds of agricultural and vocational country training schools. The Rockefeller Fund allocated millions of dollars to Southern private and public institutions for the training of Negro teachers. The Phelps-Stokes and Julius Rosenwald Funds supported black rural schools and colleges with building funds and grants for special projects. The Anna T. Jeanes Fund sponsored a network of rural agents and black teachers to do educational, social and vocational work. All of these private white philanthropies had the common goal of encouraging the upgrading of public education for Negroes, improving the segregated schools and, through the encouragement of self-help efforts and the promotion of vocational education, preparing a work force trained and willing to fill the needs of Southern industrialization. They encouraged the growth of black institutions, proved the feasibility and economy of upgrading black schools, and prodded local government into taking over some of the financial responsibilities for it. The motives for and long-range effects of this philanthropy are debatable, but there can be no question that the major educational institutions founded by Blacks, such as the ones discussed in the following documents, were largely dependent on it. The paternalistic attitudes of the white benefactors are vividly illustrated in some of the correspondence in this chapter. White boards of trustees, constant supervision and interference in school management by well-meaning white donors, innumerable indignities and snubs, not to speak of the indifference or hostility of local whites, were the price paid by the pioneering black women who raised the educational level of their communities by founding schools. Women such as Charlotte Hawkins Brown and Mary McLeod Bethune became accomplished diplomats and learned to accept much that was objectionable to them for the sake of their cause, yet they never stopped protesting against white paternalism in its various manifestations. A close reading of their correspondence will reveal this aspect of their personalities. It is also instructive to compare the tone of the correspondence in this chapter with the attitude toward whites of these two women, as expressed in discussions at interracial meetings (see Chapter Eight).

When the hard years were over and the schools well established, they were usually granted grudging—and partial—state support and accreditation. Some of the institutions built by black women have survived to the present day as private schools and seminaries. The tenacity, faith, talent and dedication of the founders deserves to be better known than it is.

A PROGRESS REPORT FROM THE FOUNDER OF THE HAINES SCHOOL

LUCY LANEY

❦ Lucy Laney (1854–1933) was born a slave in Macon, Georgia. She received her schooling with the help of her former master's sister, attended Atlanta University and graduated in 1886, after having taught public school for a number of years. In 1886, she founded Haines Normal Institute in Atlanta, Georgia, starting with 75 pupils. By the second year she had 234 students and was supported by the Presbyterian Board of Missions for Freedmen. A $10,000 donation from Mrs. F. E. Haines enabled her to enlarge the school, which in 1940 had over 1,000 students and was valued at $45,000.

In the *Southern States*, an illustrated magazine devoted to the South, among the advantages for higher education in Georgia the Haines School is very generously mentioned. Dr. Curry has also said very pleasant things of us. A very large number of Northern travellers passing have called upon us. Gen. Saylor, of Boston, was loud in his words of commendation. Among the many who have called on us in the past few months were a number of Southern women, some paying the second visit during the month, bringing other friends. None of these ladies were ever before in a colored school. They expressed themselves as well pleased, and have since showed their good will by little courtesies. I reasonably expect from this source in the future something of moral support. I have called your attention to the above things not without some pride, yet not with vain boasting, but rather that you may see what is expected of us, that you may know that your work in Georgia is beginning to be known. This section of the State is looking to you for teachers and leaders. Already in the public schools of this city, in sight of our building, four of our girls are employed as teachers. County School Commissioners send to us for teachers. We are through our students yearly reaching a large number of persons. Through our forty student teachers, with schools now under their care that average 35 scholars each, we are reaching indirectly 1400 children. The three or four hundred added to this that come directly under our care causes us to reach about 1800 young people; but, oh, large as this number seems, it is small when we think of the many hundreds to whom scarcely a ray of light has yet come!

Lucy Laney, *Church at Home and Abroad* (August 1893), p. 140.

FUND RAISING FOR PALMER MEMORIAL INSTITUTE

CHARLOTTE HAWKINS BROWN

❦ Charlotte Hawkins Brown (1882–1961) was born in North Carolina and raised in Boston by her mother, who had separated from her father. Her education was furthered and partially supported by Alice Freeman Palmer, the president of Wellesley College. Charlotte Hawkins attended Salem State Teachers College and took courses at Harvard, Simmons and Wellesley. After teaching briefly in a church-supported school in Sedalia, North Carolina, she opened her own school there in 1902. She raised the initial money by singing and speaking in Massachusetts summer resort hotels, sometimes giving three such programs a night for fifteen to twenty dollars. The school was built with the help of Northern and Southern whites, and supported by black and white sponsors and one large donation from the Rosenwald Fund. Charlotte Hawkins, who had married Edward S. Brown in 1911, conceived of the school as a finishing school for black girls. She named it the Palmer Memorial Institute and served as its president and moving force from 1904 to 1952, then as finance director until 1955. The institute, which stresses the arts, cultural subjects and the theater, is one of the leading Southern Negro schools. It has fourteen modern buildings and a plant valued at over one million dollars.

Charlotte Hawkins Brown was an outstanding educator and a national women's leader. She was vice-president of the National Association of Colored Women, president of the North Carolina Federation of Women's Clubs, president of the North Carolina Negro State Teachers Association and many other organizations. During World War II, she was the first woman of her race appointed to her state's Council of Defense, and served as consultant to the Secretary of War. In 1946 she went to the International Congress of Women as an American delegate. She was a distinguished speaker and organizer of interracial work and played an important role in the promotion of interracial work among club women. She won many honors, awards and honorary degrees.

Over the years Charlotte Hawkins Brown wrote hundreds of letters to beg, cajole, urge, plead for funds. One of her steady supporters and donors was Mr. Galen L. Stone, an attorney of Hayden, Stone and Co., Boston. These letters to him offer their own commentary on the kind of character, strength, resiliency and dedication it took to keep these institutions going year after year.

CHARLOTTE HAWKINS BROWN TO MR. AND MRS. GALEN STONE
June 19, 1920

My Dear Mr. Stone:

I have just gotten in from our State Teachers Association where the work of the Sedalia School and its influence in the state was lauded by the Superintendent of Education, County Superintendent and Supervisors. In the midst of discouragement I was made to feel that it was all worthwhile.

When I opened dear Mrs. Stone's letter I couldn't believe my eyes and it doesn't seem real yet that you folks have actually given me $10,000. I found myself beating my breast and ejaculating in quick succession saying with all my soul these words, "God, God, why have you done this for me?" The letter which accompanied the check is worth as much to me as the money. For if I did not keep my faith in God and the struggle I have everyday to keep my head above the waters of prejudice, above humiliation added to the financial struggle to keep Palmer Memorial Institute going, I would give up in despair. Then I turned to your letter, the letter of a practical businessman, the kind of a letter I should get and I want to thank you for it.

You make me think, think, think very seriously each year when you call my attention to what seems an absolute failure in finances. . . .

There never was a time Mr. Stone when the Boards, that are helping colored schools, were better pleased with Sedalia. The federal government has put its stamp of approval on the institution this year by giving three-fourths of the $1,300 a year salary to be paid the head of our Agricultural Department. This is the only school of its kind in the state that had been so recognized. The county authorities have agreed to give a per capita tax for all children, within the borders of the county, attending our school—boarding or others. This per capita isn't large, but it is an endorsement and points the way to permanent cooperation between county, state and federal government. Have my trustees done this? No, Mr. Stone, trustees of schools like this do not have time to enter into such details. I have had to do this and we have gone through every kind of inspection and their reports show that the institution is the most economically managed institution of its size, in the state. . . .

I suppose the next fact will startle you. In connection with the celebration of my 20th anniversary in this work which we hope to have next spring together with the dedication of Stone Hall, I propose the raising of dollars to $500,000, as an endowment to be placed in the hands of the county authorities for the upkeep of this institution, whether I live or die, leaving it to their wisdom, together with our board as to the nature of investment for large returns. This seems tremendous, I know, for me to undertake but folks don't seem to pay much attention nowadays to anything that's small and a fund like this places a sort of permanency to the thing.

Let me again thank you for this frank discussion for what seems a weakness in business affairs, although I expect there is a deficit on the books of most institution supported by charity, this year North and South. . . . My trip to Boston this spring counted less than $1,000. . . . God Bless you and

Mrs. Stone for this generous gift and may He help me to seek that knowledge, business efficiency and judgement that will direct more carefully the affairs of this school. Again thanking you for your letter.

I am yours, earnestly and gratefully . . .

❦ But these bright hopes were soon dashed by a fire which destroyed the barn and part of the new building. A series of disappointments followed in a period of business recession, while contributions fell off.

May 24, 1920

. . . You will be very much pleased to know of some of the wonderful things I have been able to do for the negro womanhood of North Carolina this year. I have been called upon to deliver addresses all through the state to white women, pleading for better consideration and justice at their hands for the negro woman. . . . I shall see you in June, when I am home and give you a recital of some of the forward moves that North Carolina has made along this line. . . .

Our own people here in the community have pledged another $1,000 towards the completion of the building, don't you think that it is wonderful. They are going to work their farms harder than ever this year to make that money good and when you realize that we have to have 25 or 30 families, it makes their gifts all the more remarkable. One man and his wife, who 19 years ago when I came here, did not have a penny in the bank, no home, was a tenant, is giving $100 altogether as his thank offering. He is one of my local trustees now, owns his own home, about 30 acres of valuable farm land and a nice little Ford car, which he has used for transportation purposes. As you know we are 10 miles from town. He is only one of several who has taken my advice and council and made themselves worthwhile assets to the community. It is very gratifying to me, friends, to be able to live and feel the appreciation of these people for whom I have poured out every atom of energy and devotion I have at my command. You who have helped me through the years should be equally gratified that you could share in the uplift of a community of this kind. . . .

March 10, 1921

My dear Mrs. Stone:

. . . People around Boston seem to have gotten discouraged about the building and I can't get any money to go ahead. It was a rather ambitious undertaking, I am afraid to admit but I didn't make one step, Mrs. Stone, about the building without the advice of the local Trustee. Our first plan, you will remember, was for $500,000 which would have covered everything under normal conditions. The need for the building was so great Mr. Wharton and Mr. Richardson, who has since died, voted to carry it on in spite of the rise, they promising to share equally the southern burden. Mr. Richardson had paid in only $500 of the $5,000 we had every reason to expect from his enthusiasm and expression of interest.

Mr. Wharton has failed us in nothing, he has carried notes, paid many bills from his personal account and has made many donations to the fund. For my last effort for current expenses I have been able to pay up the teachers for 2 months back salaries.

Surely I have labored against odds for many of my best friends have passed on since the building began, two of whose pledges I have been unable to collect.

I know not why, I am too much discouraged to think. I feel as Elijah felt and I'm saying almost daily, "it is enough —now take my life, I have no desire to go on." Perhaps with this foundation and less worn out from struggling those who will follow soon greet a new dawn. I am simply down and out, that is all. My nerves are just shattered, and I'm really unfit to plan anything. . . .

June 17, 1921

My dear Mr. Stone:—

For the last four years either you or Mrs. Stone has made us a contribution in June to help with the current expenses.

I didn't want to write you, but I've tried for three weeks to raise a little money, for one day, two weeks ago, we had overdrawn our accounts $35.00. I know that is bad business, but two or three local checks given us were returned.

This is the darkest hour I have ever known, last week we had neither meat or sugar, because deep in debt as we are, I don't want to go into debt for food. I had a little money ($135) saved up to assist me in the course of study I planned to take up this summer, but I've spent every dollar for the school. I know times are hard everywhere, I've just talked with Mrs. Bright—our trustees will meet next week.

May I tell you that plans are developing whereby we are going to ask The American Missionary Association of New York, that sent me here twenty years ago, to take us under that board. It will give a permanence to the work, and although like Fisk, we shall have to help look out for ourselves, it will give stability to the work—I am working to that end. The first step has been taken, my Uncle who has come to the work is soon to sign a contract with the Association to take charge of the community church (Congregational) joining school and church. A conference is arranged for August at which time I hope to present the plans of our Trustee Board to that effect.

Mr. Stone, I must try to raise some money to tide us over this summer, please don't turn me down, the dear Lord knows I've called on everybody and we are almost living from "hand to mouth," this summer. The fire put us so far behind for although the club raised $800, they had pledged toward current expenses, $500, that used up before it came.

It takes $500 a month to keep things going here. We have two men and two boys on the farm, three girls who help to do the work, the head of the Agricultural Department, and a Mechanic, the other place is being filled this summer by one of our boys at $35.00 per month.

Now is the time to buy coal. I haven't the first dollar to pay on it—I want to put in 50 tons—if I wait until fall it will cost one-third more. I can secure the amount by putting in $100. We can't even arrange to have the accountant put in the budget system until we have some money with which to pay him. I'm at my wit's end—everything looks dark, but I am bound to believe that help must soon.

I thank you for sending Mr. Totman. He was very interesting and instructive, we are following his suggestions to the letter. Mr. Stone if you good folks will help us now, it will tide us over the crisis while I busy myself to make plans for cooperation with the church agency herein mentioned. Let me hear from you please. . . .

Undated letter fragment

Now that things are turning and many are opening their eyes to what I've tried to do and desiring to have a share in the same, the question in my heart and mind, and God only knows how it hurts, is just what are they going to ask me to submit to as a negro woman to get their interest for there are some men who occupy high places who feel that no negro woman whether she be cook, criminal or principal of a school should ever be addressed as *Mrs.* I realize how trivial that sounds to you but there is a great principle back of it in the South and I have always resented it, because I was lucky enough to make friends who were above such littleness. My only point is, in my efforts to get money now, I don't want my friends in the North to tie my hands so I can't speak out when I am being crushed. Mr. Stone, I want to ask you to accept the place on our trustee board, please sir.

❦ *This crisis was weathered, as were many others, and by superhuman effort and sacrifice the institute continued to build.*

FROM AN AUTOBIOGRAPHICAL SKETCH BY
CHARLOTTE HAWKINS BROWN

In metropolitan New York I had an elevator ride that netted the school $75,000. In one of the "swanky" hotel lobbies, I attempted to enter the elevator and was told, "Around the other way!" But having traveled that way before, I had the cue. Another elevator started up. It was empty. I walked in. The starting porter said, "Carry her down to the cellar." With arms folded I smiled and said, "Young man, I am here for the rest of the day. I am not getting out here." Up and down, as people came and went, we rode. I impressed him that I wanted to go to the eleventh floor. I had a very important engagement with a trustee and large contributor to our school.

Family realizing that my friend was waiting, I got off at the tenth floor as some one else did and inquired of the hall clerk for the eleventh floor. "This way," said she, and to my surprise I found myself going up the back stairs.

However, I reached my destination, and in spite of the fight in my heart, I smiled. As a part of my argument for education for Negroes I used the incident as illustration that most white people looked upon every Negro, regardless of his appearance, modulated tones that reflected some culture and training, as a servant and happened to say, "If some person who had faith in the race would make a gift of 50 or 75 thousand dollars (and I needed just that amount then to carry out a building project) to some Negro woman, it would raise all Negro women hood in the estimation of people. My friends thought I was exaggerating that it could have any such appeal, but in less than 48 hours after consultation with other members of the family, there was flashed over the wires a gift of $75,000 to this Negro woman for a building project at the Palmer Memorial Institute at Sedalia, North Carolina and the Associated Press carried it to the remote places of America.

Letters from the Charlotte Hawkins Brown Papers; Autobiographical sketch from, Charlotte Hawkins Brown, "Some Incidents in the Life and Career of Charlotte Hawkins Brown Growing out of Racial Situations by the Request of Dr. Ralph Bunche," Typescript, Schlesinger Library, Radcliffe College, Cambridge, Massachusetts.

THE NATIONAL TRAINING SCHOOL FOR GIRLS APPEALS FOR FUNDS

❦ Nannie Helen Burroughs (1883–1961) was educated by her widowed mother in Washington, D.C. An honor student in high school, she absolved a business and a domestic science course, but did not get the teaching appointment in Washington for which she had hoped. After a year of doing office work, she joined the staff of the National Baptist Convention as a bookkeeper, but soon became assistant editor of its journal. She organized a Woman's Industrial Club which gave industrial training to working girls. In 1900, she became secretary of the Women's Auxiliary of the National Colored Baptist Convention and turned this organization, which had raised $15 the previous year, into a dynamic fund-raising group. She founded the National Training School for Girls with eight pupils, having raised the necessary funds herself. Under the motto "We specialize in the wholly impossible," the school trained over 2,500 girls. The Baptist Women's Auxiliary later assumed responsibility for partial financial support of the school. It was the founder's pride that hers was the only school entirely financed by contributions from the black community.

Nannie Burroughs was an active member in the National

Association of Colored Women's Clubs and the NAACP.
She was a prolific columnist in the Negro press.

The National Training School for women and girls at
Lincoln Heights, Washington, is the creation of Miss Burroughs. Twenty years ago she saw the need of a school for
the training of young colored women . . . She started on a
rugged clay hill that nobody else had ever dreamed of
beautifying. But Miss Burroughs has seen . . . her own school
grow from nothing to a plant with eight acres and eight
buildings, worth $225,000. There is a total of 102 students,
eight teachers and four assistants [and] business staff . . .
The last building erected was the new Trades Building,
which when completed, will cost $54,000. . . .

With this much done . . . one might think that Miss
Burroughs would be ready to rest for a while, but right now
she is planning the supreme struggle of her career. She will
soon launch a campaign for $225,000 to finance her program
for the next three years. This money will be used for the following: 1. Dormitory (to accommodate 150 girls); 2. Dining
room (seat 800); 3. Chapel, with pipe organ (to seat 1,000);
4. A fund of $10,000 for improvement of campus and
grounds. . . .

But to be more specific: "The aim of the National Training School is to give a training of head, hand and heart and
develop a definite and active social interest in the spiritual
and moral forces that make for human welfare. . . ."

The department of Negro History is of especial pride at
the National Training School. . . . Every student must take
the course in Negro History. Recitation every day for two
months is held in the subject, then an examination is held,
both written and oral. The students then write orations on
Negro achievements, and by a process of elimination the
two best orators from each class are selected. From these
winners an oratorical contest is held annually, at which
three awards in gold are made. The contests have created

wide interest and a healthy familiarity with Negro history and with current events among Negroes. . . .

And now comes the great new task of making the National Training School bigger and better. The foundation for a splendid school has been laid and Miss Burroughs is going out to ask both white and colored people to help enlarge . . . the only Christian institution for Negro girls north of Richmond, Va. . . .

Floyd Calvin, "That's Nannie Burroughs' Job, And She Does it," *Pittsburgh Courier*, June 8, 1929.

A COLLEGE ON A GARBAGE DUMP

MARY McLEOD BETHUNE

❦ *Mary McLeod Bethune (1875–1955) is one of the great women in American history and one of the great leaders of the black race. The autobiographical sketch below recounts her early childhood and her role as founder of Bethune-Cookman College. She was president of that institution from 1904 to 1942 and continued as one of its trustees to her death. She held leading offices in professional, civic and Negro organizations, was a founder and President of the National Association of Colored Women's Clubs, of numerous other women's organizations and later, founder and president of the National Council of Negro Women, an organization representing over one million Negro women.*

She was special adviser on minority affairs to President Franklin D. Roosevelt and in 1936 was appointed Director of the Division of Negro Affairs of the National Youth Administration, the first person of her race to hold such federal office. She served as special assistant to the Secretary of War during World War II and was appointed by President Truman to the twelve-member Committee for

National Defense. She also served as consultant at the
Conference to Draft a United Nations Charter. Her affili-
ations and the honors awarded her are too numerous to
mention. They include eleven honorary degrees and the
Spingarn Medal of the NAACP (1935). Despite the many
distinctions heaped upon her, she never lost her roots among
the black rural folk of the South. Her organizational genius,
indomitable energy and spirit, her considerable talent as a
speaker and writer were dedicated to one single aim—the
improvement of opportunities for every black child.

I was born in Maysville, South Carolina, a country town
in the midst of rice and cotton fields. My mother, father, and
older brothers and sisters had been slaves until the Emancipation Proclamation. . . . After Mother was freed she continued
in the McIntosh employ until she had earned enough to
buy five acres of her own from her former master. Then
my parents built our cabin, cutting and burning the logs
with their own hands. I was the last of seventeen children,
ten girls and seven boys. When I was born, the first free
child in their own home, my mother exulted, "Thank God,
Mary came under our own vine and fig tree."

Mother was of royal African blood, of a tribe ruled by
matriarchs. . . . Throughout all her bitter years of slavery
she had managed to preserve a queenlike dignity. She supervised all the business of the family. Over the course of years,
by the combined work and thrift of the family, and Mother's
foresight, Father was able to enlarge our home site to thirty-
five acres.

Most of my brothers and sisters had married and left home
when I was growing up—there were only seven or eight
children still around. Mother worked in the fields at Father's
side, cutting rice and cotton, and chopping fodder. Each
of us children had tasks to perform, according to our
aptitudes. Some milked the cows, others helped with the
washing, ironing, cooking, and house-cleaning. I was my

father's champion cotton picker. When I was only nine, I could pick 250 pounds of cotton a day. . . .

[In those days] it was almost impossible for a Negro child, especially in the South, to get education. There were hundreds of square miles, sometimes entire states, without a single Negro school, and colored chilren were not allowed in public schools with white children. Mr. Lincoln had told our race we were free, but mentally we were still enslaved.

A knock on our door changed my life over-night. There stood a young woman, a colored missionary sent by the Northern Presbyterian Church to start a school near by. She asked my parents to send me. Every morning I picked up a little pail of milk and bread, and walked five miles to school; every afternoon, five miles home. But I walked always on winged feet.

The whole world opened to me when I learned to read. As soon as I understood something, I rushed back and taught it to the others at home. My teacher had a box of Bibles and texts, and she gave me one of each for my very own. That same day the teacher opened the Bible to John 3:16, and read: "For God so loved the world, that He gave His only begotten Son, that whosoever believeth in Him should not perish, but have everlasting life."

With these words the scales fell from my eyes and the light came flooding in. My sense of inferiority, my fear of handicaps, dropped away. "Whosoever," it said. No Jew nor Gentile, no Catholic nor Protestant, no black nor white; just "whosoever." It meant that I, a humble Negro girl, had just as much chance as anybody in the sight and love of God. These words stored up a battery of faith and confidence and determination in my heart, which has not failed me to this day. . . .

By the time I was fifteen I had taken every subject taught at our little school and could go no farther. Dissatisfied, because this taste of learning had aroused my appetite, I was forced to stay at home. Father's mule died—a major calamity —and he had to mortgage the farm to buy another. In those days, when a Negro mortgaged his property they never let him get out of debt.

I used to kneel in the cotton fields and pray that the door of opportunity should be opened to me once more, so that I might give to others whatever I might attain.

My prayers were answered. A white dressmaker, way off in Denver, Colorado, had become interested in the work of our little neighborhood school and had offered to pay for the higher education of some worthy girl. My teacher selected me, and I was sent to Scotia Seminary in Concord, North Carolina. There I studied English, Latin, higher mathematics, and science, and after classes I worked in the Scotia laundry and kitchen to earn as much extra money as I could. . . .

When I was graduated, I offered myself eagerly for missionary service in Africa, but the church authorities felt I was not sufficiently mature. Instead, they gave me another scholarship, and I spent two years at the Moody Bible School, in Chicago. Again I offered myself for missionary service, and again I was refused. Cruelly disappointed, I got a position at Haines Institute, in Augusta, Georgia, presided over by dynamic Lucy C. Laney, a pioneer Negro educator. From her I got a new vision: my life work lay not in Africa but in my own country. And with the first money I earned I began to save in order to pay off Father's mortgage, which had hung over his head for ten years!

During my early teaching days I met my future husband. He too was then a teacher, but to him teaching was only a job. Following our marriage, he entered upon a business career. When our baby son was born, I gave up my work temporarily, so that I could be all mother for one precious year. After that I got restless again to be back at my beloved work, for having a child made me more than ever determined to build better lives for my people. . . .

In 1904 I heard . . . [that] Henry Flagler was building the Florida East Coast Railroad, and hundreds of Negroes had gathered in Florida for construction work. . . .

I [went to] Daytona Beach, a beautiful little village, shaded by great oaks and giant pines. . . . I found a shabby four-room cottage, for which the owner wanted a rental of eleven dollars a month. My total capital was a dollar and a half, but I talked him into trusting me until the end of the month for the rest. This was in September. A friend let me stay at her home, and I plunged into the job of creating something from nothing. I spoke at churches, and the ministers let me take up collections. I buttonholed every woman who would listen to me. . . .

On October 3, 1904, I opened the doors of my school, with an enrollment of five little girls, aged from eight to twelve, whose parents paid me fifty cents' weekly tuition. My own child was the only boy in the school. Though I hadn't a penny left, I considered cash money as the smallest part of my resources. I had faith in a living God, faith in myself, and a desire to serve. . . .

We burned logs and used the charred splinters as pencils, and mashed elderberries for ink. I begged strangers for a broom, a lamp, a bit of cretonne to put around the packing case which served as my desk. I haunted the city dump and the trash piles behind hotels, retrieving discarded linen and kitchenware, cracked dishes, broken chairs, pieces of old lumber. Everything was scoured and mended. This was part of the training to salvage, to reconstruct, to make bricks without straw. As parents began gradually to leave their children overnight, I had to provide sleeping accommodations. I took corn sacks for mattresses. Then I picked Spanish moss from trees, dried and cured it, and used it as a substitute for mattress hair.

The school expanded fast. In less than two years I had 250 pupils. In desperation I hired a large hall next to my original little cottage, and used it as a combined dormitory and classroom. I concentrated more and more on girls, as I felt that they especially were hampered by lack of educational opportunities. . . .

I had many volunteer workers and a few regular teachers,

who were paid from fifteen to twenty-five dollars a month and board. I was supposed to keep the balance of the funds for my own pocket, but there was never any balance—only a yawning hole. I wore old clothes sent me by mission boards, recut and redesigned for me in our dress-making classes. At last I saw that our only solution was to stop renting space, and to buy and build our own college.

Near by was a field, popularly called Hell's Hole, which was used as a dumping ground. I approached the owner, determined to buy it. The price was $250. In a daze, he finally agreed to take five dollars down, and the balance in two years. I promised to be back in a few days with the initial payment. He never knew it, but I didn't have five dollars. I raised this sum selling ice cream and sweet-potato pies to the workmen on construction jobs, and I took the owner his money in small change wrapped in my handkerchief.

That's how the Bethune-Cookman college campus started.

We at once discovered the need of an artesian well. The estimate was two hundred dollars. Here again we started with an insignificant payment, the balance remaining on trust. But what use was a plot without a building? I hung onto contractors' coat-tails, begging for loads of sand and second-hand bricks. I went to all the carpenters, mechanics, and plasterers in town, pleading with them to contribute a few hours' work in the evening in exchange for sandwiches and tuition for their children and themselves.

Slowly the building rose from its foundations. The name over the entrance still reads Faith Hall.

I had learned already that one of my most important jobs was to be a good beggar! I rang doorbells and tackled cold prospects without a lead. I wrote articles for whoever would print them, distributed leaflets, rode interminable miles of dusty roads on my old bicycle; invaded churches, clubs, lodges, chambers of commerce. . . .

Strongly interracial in my ideas, I looked forward to an advisory board of trustees composed of both white and colored people. I did my best missionary work among the prominent winter visitors to Florida. I would pick out names of "newly arrived guests," from the newspapers, and write letters asking whether I could call.

One of these letters went to James N. Gamble, of Procter & Gamble. He invited me to call at noon the next day. . . .

Mr. Gamble himself opened the door, and when I gave my name he looked at me in astonishment. "Are you the woman trying to build a school here? Why, I thought you were a white woman."

I laughed. "Well, you see how white I am." Then I told my story. "I'd like you to visit my school and, if it pleases you, to stand behind what I have in my mind," I finished.

He consented. . . . The next day . . . he made a careful tour of inspection, agreed to be a trustee, and gave me a check for $150—although I hadn't mentioned money. For many years he was one of our most generous friends.

Another experience with an unexpected ending was my first meeting with J. S. Peabody, of Columbia City, Indiana. After I had made an eloquent appeal for funds he gave me exactly twenty-five cents. I swallowed hard, thanked him smilingly, and later entered the contribution in my account book.

Two years later he reappeared. "Do you remember me?" he asked. "I'm one of your contributors." I greeted him cordially. He went on: "I wonder if you recall how much I gave you when I was here last?"

Not wishing to embarrass him, I told a white lie: "I'll have to look it up in my account book." Then after finding the entry, I said, "Oh, yes, Mr. Peabody, you gave us twenty-five cents."

Instead of being insulted, he was delighted that we kept account of such minute gifts. He immediately handed me a check for a hundred dollars and made arrangements to furnish the building. When he died, a few years later, he left the school $10,000. . . .

One evening I arranged a meeting at an exclusive hotel, expecting to talk to a large audience of wealthy people. But so many social functions were taking place that same night that I was greeted by an audience of exactly six. I was sick at heart—but I threw all my enthusiasm into my talk. At the end a gentleman dropped a twenty-dollar bill in the hat.

The next day he unexpectedly appeared at the school. He said his name was Thomas H. White, but it meant nothing to me. He looked around, asked where the shabby but immaculate straw matting on the floor came from. I said, "The city dump." He saw a large box of corn meal, and inquired what else there was to eat. I replied, "That's all we have at the moment." Then he walked about the grounds and saw an unfinished building, on which construction work had been temporarily abandoned for lack of funds. That was nothing new—there were always unfinished buildings cluttering up the landscape of our school. But I think the crowning touch was when he saw our dressmaking class working with a broken-down Singer sewing machine.

He turned to me, saying, "I believe you are on the right track. This is the most promising thing I've seen in Florida." He pressed a check in my hand, and left. The check was for $250. The following day he returned again, with a new sewing machine. Only then did I learn that Mr. White was the Singer people's principal competitor.

Mr. White brought plasterers, carpenters, and materials to finish our new building. Week after week he appeared, with blankets for the children, shoes and a coat for me, everything we had dreamed of getting. When I thanked him, with tears in my eyes, for his generosity, he waved me aside.

"I've never invested a dollar that has brought greater returns than the dollars I have given you," he told me. And when this great soul died, he left a trust of $67,000, the interest to be paid us "as long as there is a school."

Do you wonder I have faith?

I never stop to plan. I take things step by step. For thirty-five years we have never had to close our doors for lack of food or fuel, although often we had to live from day to day. . . .

As the school expanded, whenever I saw a need for some training or service we did not supply, I schemed to add it to our curriculum. Sometimes that took years. When I came to Florida, there were no hospitals where a Negro could go. A student became critically ill with appendicitis, so I went to a local hospital and begged a white physician to take her in and operate. My pleas were so desperate he finally agreed. A few days after the operation, I visited my pupil.

When I appeared at the front door of the hospital, the nurse ordered me around to the back way. I thrust her aside —and found my little girl segregated in a corner of the porch behind the kitchen. Even my toes clenched with rage.

That decided me. I called on three of my faithful friends, asking them to buy a little cottage behind our school as a hospital. They agreed, and we started with two beds.

From this humble start grew a fully equipped twenty-bed hospital—our college infirmary and a refuge for the needy throughout the state. It was staffed by white and black physicians and by our own student nurses. We ran this hospital for twenty years as part of our contribution to community life; but a short time ago, to ease our financial burden, the city took it over.

Gradually, as educational facilities expanded and there were other places where small children could go, we put the emphasis on high-school and junior-college training. In 1922, Cookman College, a men's school, the first in the state for the higher education of Negroes, amalgamated with us. The combined coeducational college, now run under the auspices of the Methodist Episcopal Church, is called Bethune-Cookman College. We have fourteen modern buildings, a beautiful campus of thirty-two acres, an enrollment in regular and summer sessions of 600 students, a faculty and staff of thirty-two, and 1,800 graduates. The college property, now valued at more than $800,000, is entirely unencumbered.

When I walk through the campus, with its stately palms and well-kept lawns, and think back to the dump-heap foundation, I rub my eyes and pinch myself. And I remember my childish visions in the cotton fields.

But values cannot be calculated in ledger figures and property. More than all else the college has fulfilled my ideals of distinctive training and service. Extending far beyond the immediate sphere of its graduates and students, it has already enriched the lives of 100,000 Negroes.

In 1934, President Franklin D. Roosevelt appointed me director of the division of Negro affairs of the National Youth Administration. My main task now is to supervise the training provided for 600,000 Negro children, and I have to run the college by remote control. Every few weeks, however, I snatch a day or so and return to my beloved home.

This is a strenuous program. The doctor shakes his head and says, "Mrs. Bethune, slow down a little. Relax! Take it just a little easier." I promise to reform, but in an hour the promise is forgotten.

For I am my mother's daughter, and the drums of Africa still beat in my heart. They will not let me rest while there is a single Negro boy or girl without a chance to prove his worth.

Mary McLeod Bethune, "Faith That Moved a Dump Heap," *Who, The Magazine about People*, Vol. 1, No. 3 (June 1941), pp. 31–35, 54.

ANOTHER "BEGGING" LETTER

MARY McLEOD BETHUNE

❦ The cheerful retrospective account above passes lightly over the hardships and tribulations of keeping the school going with insufficient endowments in the face of constantly pressing needs. The following letter, written well after the worst years had passed, offers some insight into the burdens borne by Mary McLeod Bethune and the other heroic school founders.

MARY MCLEOD BETHUNE TO GEORGE R. ARTHUR

November 1, 1930

My dear Mr. Arthur:

May I tell you again how grateful we are for your visit to Bethune-Cookman and for the opportunity you gave me to so fully converse with you, and the encouragement, light and information that came to me from this contact. I am thanking God for you and your interest and want to ask that you, possibly in a childlike way, adopt me as your big sister, and help to direct and guide me, and possibly take the unusual interest in the thing that I am trying so earnestly to do in Florida.

I do feel the need for some earthly stay; somebody to have pride in my efforts. I do feel, in my dreamings and yearnings, so undiscovered by those who are able to help me. I have been pulling along so long, fighting an unusual battle in an exceptionally difficult section of our country. But during these years, something has happened. A great change has come about and if at this critical moment, we can get the right shove-off, it will possibly save me for many more years of general service to humanity.

The burden is so heavy just now, the task is so great, that speedy reinforcement is needed. My mind is over-taxed. Brave and courageous as I am, I feel that creeping on of that inevitable thing, a break-down, if I cannot get some immediate relief. I need somebody to come and get me. The struggle has been long and courageous. I need help, not to tax me more, but help that will give me immediate relief. It is possible that my Maker permitted me to come into existence to serve in my way at just such a time as this. I feel I still have a larger contribution to make to the general masses. They are clamoring for the same inspirational counsel that I am permitted to give here, there and everywhere. Shall I be spared for this or shall I fall under the strain of this heavy burden-bearing? I think the time has come for my friends and philanthropic organizations to answer yes or no.

I spent two very interesting days of service in the White House conference last week. It seems necessary that I be one of the inter-racial group that will tour the southern schools early this month. A special invitation from President Hoover has just reached my desk for his final conference to be held November 19th to the 22nd. Organizations and groups are clamoring for me all over the country. With these opportunities for unique service and for making the contribution that the Negro womanhood of America needs to make today, if I am to fit into such a program, money worries for carrying on should be lifted from me. I believe there is relief. Will you help me find it?

Mr. Walton of the New York World called to see me yesterday. He is to run an article featuring me in one of his Sunday morning issues. I would like so such to have him go to Florida and study the surroundings of Bethune-Cookman, its actual functioning and give it to the world in magazine stories or newspapers with illustrations etc. I wish I had a fund with which to do that. Do you know any source from which I could get a fund for publicity purposes and the unfolding of the work I am doing so that the world can get it. My own life's story should be gotten together and sent out. I think this is the psychological time for it. I feel so helpless within myself without funds to get these things over. Will you think about it and tell me what you think of it?

I would like to have you consider the travelling scholarship for some of the heads of our departments, so that we might have this representation and be able to make contacts with different educational organizations and investigate schools so as to keep abreast with the best methods.

We shall use to the best of our knowledge any opportunity that may come to us through your foundation in making more thorough those who work in the commercial, musical and vocational departments. Please give me any definite instruction you may have on just what your organization may be in position to assist us in doing. I shall breathlessly await a reply from your board in answer to my application. Some immediate relief in the general running is my strongest plea just now.

I will not be able to get to Chicago until after the 22nd of November. You may communicate with me here until November 10th. I will possibly be away for ten days on the road with the Seminar and with Mr. Hoover's conference. I will be able to meet with them the last two days, missing two.

I have written you rather fully. I hope you understand my heart-pulse on the whole subject. No egotism is aimed at, at all, but I wanted to talk understandingly with you. I want you to feel free to write me and to suggest to me and to help me in any way you can.

Mary McLeod Bethune file, Julius Rosenwald Fund Papers,
Fisk University, Nashville, Tennessee.

CHAPTER THREE

A WOMAN'S LOT

I have seen very small white children
hang their black dolls. It is not
the child's fault, he is simply an apt pupil.

Anonymous, 1902

A WOMAN'S LOT

❦ The essence of black and white relations in United States history up to the present time has been the oppression of Blacks by whites, based entirely on arbitrary definitions of white superiority. Essential to the functioning and perpetuation of this racist system of oppression has been the special victimization of black women. This has taken several forms: (1) black women share in all aspects of the oppression of Blacks in general; (2) black women are objects of exploitative sex by white men; (3) the rape of black women is employed as a weapon of terror directed against the entire black community; (4) when black men are prevented, through social taboos and violence, from defending their own women, the oppression of all Blacks is heightened and institutionalized; (5) when black men are oppressed economically to the extent that they cannot secure steady employment at decent wages, many black women are deprived of the support of a male breadwinner and must take on added economic burdens. The psychological effects of the symbolic castration of black males is also borne by black women.

The sharing of women in the general oppression of Blacks in the United States is illustrated throughout this book.

BLACK WOMEN ARE SEX OBJECTS FOR WHITE MEN

❦ The pattern of exploitative sex relations was set during slavery when black women were used both as unpaid workers and as breeders of slaves. Their free avail-

ability as sex objects to any white man was enshrined
in tradition, upheld by the laws forbidding intermarriage,
enforced by terror against black men and women and, though
frowned upon by white community opinion, tolerated
both in its clandestine and open manifestations. Still, even
under slavery black women were not quite as defenseless as
has been generally assumed. They could and did use various
tactics of evasion, shamming, threats, refusal to work and
flight. Their men too, more frequently perhaps than has
hitherto been recognized, were able to assert themselves in
defense of their women, but it took heroic men and exceptional circumstances for them to prevail. It should be noted
here that the sexual exploitation of women of a subservient
class is as old as class society and that the sexual use of
slave women by their masters antedates class society and
can be found in every culture without regard to race. It is, in
fact, one of the very definitions of female enslavement.

THE MARRIED LIFE OF GEORGIA PEONS

❦ The following article, originally from The Independent (1901), is based on an interview with a Georgia
Negro. The narrator was born during the Civil War. He
describes his life, which is typical of that of thousands of
black men and women, living in the Southern states under
virtual peonage conditions in the last decade of the nineteenth and well into the twentieth century. The sharecropper, chronically indebted to the landlord, could easily be
turned into a forced laborer in a system in which the penalty
for even slight infractions was the chain gang. The effect
of such conditions on black family life is vividly illustrated
by the narrator's matter-of-fact account of his escape.

When I was about ten years old, my uncle hired me out to Captain ———. When I reached twenty-one the Captain told me I was a free man, but he urged me to stay with him. He said he would treat me right, and pay me as much as anybody else would. The Captain's son and I were about the same age, and the Captain said that, as he had owned my mother and uncle during slavery, and as his son didn't want me to leave them (since I had been with them so long), he wanted me to stay with the old family. And I stayed. I signed a contract—that is, I made my mark—for one year. The Captain was to give me $3.50 a week, and furnish me a little house on the plantation—a one-room log cabin similar to those used by his other laborers.

During that year I married Mandy. For several years Mandy had been the house-servant for the Captain, his wife, his son and his three daughters, and they all seemed to think a good deal of her. As an evidence of their regard they gave us a suit of furniture, which cost about $25, and we set up housekeeping in one of the Captain's two-room shanties. I thought I was the biggest man in Georgia. Mandy still kept her place in the "Big House" after our marriage. We did so well for the first year that I renewed my contract for the second year, and for the third, fourth and fifth year I did the same thing. Before the end of the fifth year the Captain had died, and his son, who had married some two or three years before, took charge of the plantation. . . . I think . . . [he] was in the Legislature or something of that sort—anyhow, all the people called him Senator. At the end of the fifth year the Senator suggested that I sign up a contract for ten years; then, he said, we wouldn't have to fix up papers every year. I asked my wife about it; she consented; and so I made a ten-year contract.

Not long afterward the Senator had a long, low shanty built on his place. A great big chimney, with a wide, open fireplace, was built at one end of it, and on each side of the house, running lengthwise, there was a row of frames or stalls just large enough to hold a single mattress. The places for these mattresses were fixed one above the other; so that there was a double row of these stalls or pens on each side. They looked for all the world like stalls for horses. . . . Nobody seemed to know what the Senator was fixing for. All doubts were put aside one bright day in April when about forty able-bodied negroes, bound in iron chains, and some of them handcuffed, were brought out to the Senator's farm in three big wagons. They were quartered in the long, low shanty, and it was afterward called the stockade. This was the beginning of the Senator's convict camp. These men were prisoners who had been leased by the Senator from the State of Georgia at about $200 each per year, the State agreeing to pay for guards and physicians, for necessary inspection, for inquests, all rewards for escaped convicts, the cost of litigation and all other incidental camp expenses. When I saw these men in shackles, and the guards with their guns, I was scared nearly to death. I felt like running away, but I didn't know where to go. And if there had been any place to go to, I would have had to leave my wife and child behind. We free laborers held a meeting. We all wanted to quit. We sent a man to tell the Senator about it. Word came back that we were all under contract for ten years and that the Senator would hold us to the letter of the contract, or put us in chains and lock us up—the same as the other prisoners. It was made plain to us by some white people we talked to that in the contracts we had signed we had all agreed to be locked up in a stockade at night or at any other time that our employer saw fit; further, we learned that we could not lawfully break our contract for any reason and go and hire ourselves to somebody else without the consent of our employer. . . . In other words, we had sold ourselves into slavery—and what could we do about it? The white folks had all the courts, all the guns, all the hounds, all the railroads, all the telegraph wires, all the newspapers, all the money, and nearly all the land—and we had only our ignorance, our poverty and our empty hands. We decided that the best thing to do was to shut our mouths, say nothing, and go back to work. And most of us worked side by side with those convicts during the remainder of the ten years.

But this first batch of convicts was only the beginning. Within six months another stockade was built, and twenty or thirty other convicts were brought to the plantation, among them six or eight women! The Senator had bought an additional thousand acres of land, and to his already large cotton plantation he added two great big saw-mills and went into the lumber business. Within two years the Senator had in all nearly 200 negroes working on his plantation—about half of them free laborers, so called, and about half of them convicts. The only difference between the free laborers and the others was that the free laborers could come and go as they pleased, at night—that is, they were not locked up at night, and were not, as a general thing, whipped for slight offenses. The troubles of the free laborers began at the close of the ten-year period. . . .

☞ *The men were made to sign written acknowledgements of their debts to the Commissary. They were then permitted to leave. But each owed well over $100. Once they had signed, they were informed that they had agreed to work off the debt.*

And from that day forward we were treated just like convicts. Really we had made ourselves lifetime slaves, or peons, as the laws called us. But, call it slavery, peonage, or what not, the truth is we lived in a hell on earth what time we spent in the Senator's peon camp.

I lived in that camp, as a peon, for nearly three years. My wife fared better than I did, as did the wives of some of the other negroes, because the white men about the camp used these unfortunate creatures as their mistresses. When I was first put in the stockade my wife was still kept for a while in the "Big House," but my little boy, who was only nine years old, was given away to a negro family across the river in

South Carolina, and I never saw or heard of him after that. When I left the camp my wife had had two children by some one of the white bosses, and she was living in fairly good shape in a little house off to herself. But the poor negro women who were not in the class with my wife fared about as bad as the helpless negro men. Most of the time the women who were peons or convicts were compelled to wear men's clothes. Sometimes, when I have seen them dressed like men, and plowing or hoeing or hauling logs or working at the blacksmith's trade, just the same as men, my heart would bleed and my blood would boil, but I was powerless to raise a hand. It would have meant death on the spot to have said a word. Of the first six women brought to the camp, two of them gave birth to children after they had been there more than twelve months—and the babies had white men for their fathers! . . .

Every year many convicts were brought to the Senator's camp down from a certain county in South Georgia. . . . The majority of these men were charged with adultery, which is an offense against the laws of the great and sovereign state of Georgia. . . . Down in that county a number of negro lewd women were employed by certain white men to entice negro men into their houses; and then . . . raids would be made by the officers upon these houses, and the men would be arrested and charged with living in adultery. Nine out of ten of these men, so arrested and so charged, would find their way ultimately to some convict camp, and, as I said, many of them found their way every year to the Senator's camp while I was there. The low-down women were never punished in any way. On the contrary, I was told that they always seemed to stand in high favor with the sheriffs, constables and other officers. There can be no room to doubt that they assisted very materially in furnishing laborers for the prison pens of Georgia, and the belief was general among the men that they were regularly paid for their work. I could tell more, but I've said enough to make anybody's heart sick. This great and terrible iniquity is, I know, widespread throughout Georgia and many other Southern States.

But I didn't tell you how I got out. I didn't get out—they put me out. When I had served as a peon for nearly three years—and you remember that they claimed that I owed them only $165—when I had served for nearly three years, one of the bosses came to me and said that my time was up. He happened to be the one who was said to be living with my wife. He gave me a new suit of overalls, which cost about seventy-five cents, took me in a buggy and carried me across the Broad River into South Carolina, set me down and told me to "git." I didn't have a cent of money, and I wasn't feeling well, but somehow I managed to get a move on me. I begged my way to Columbia. In two or three days I ran across a man looking for laborers to carry to Birmingham, and I joined his gang. I have been here in the Birmingham district since they released me, and I reckon I'll die either in a coal mine or an iron furnace. It don't make much difference which. Either is better than a Georgia peon camp. And a Georgia peon camp is hell itself!

> "The Life Story of a Negro Peon, Obtained from an Interview
> with a Georgia Negro,"
> in Hamilton Holt, *The Life Stories of Undistinguished Americans,*
> *As Told by Themselves* (New York: James Pott & Co., 1906).

WE ARE LITTLE MORE THAN SLAVES

ANONYMOUS

I remember very well the first and last work place from which I was dismissed. I lost my place because I refused to let the madam's husband kiss me. He must have been accustomed to undue familiarity with his servants, or else he took it as a matter of course, because without any love-making at all, soon after I was installed as cook, he walked up to me, threw his arms around me, and was in the act of kissing me, when I demanded to know what he meant, and shoved him away. I was young then, and newly married, and didn't know then what has been a burden to my mind and heart ever since; that a colored woman's virtue in this part of the country has no protection. I at once went home, and told my husband about it. When my husband went to the man who had insulted me, the man cursed him, and slapped him, and—had him arrested! The police judge fined my husband $25. I was present at the hearing, and testified on oath to the insult offered me. The white man, of course, denied the charge. The old judge looked up and said: "This court will never take the word of a nigger against the word of a white man." . . . I believe nearly all white men take, and expect to take, undue liberties with their colored female servants—not only the fathers, but in many cases the sons also. Those servants who rebel against such familiarity must either leave or expect a mighty hard time, if they stay. By comparison, those who tamely submit to these improper relations live in clover. They always have a little "spending change," wear better clothes, and are able to get off from work at least once a week—and sometimes oftener. This moral debasement is not at all times unknown to the white women in these homes. I know of more than one colored woman who was openly importuned by white women to become the mistresses of their white husbands, on the ground that they, the white wives, were afraid that, if their husbands did not associate with colored women, they would certainly do so with outside white women, and the white wives, for reasons which ought to be perfectly obvious, preferred to have their husbands do wrong with colored women in order to keep their husbands *straight!* And again, I know at least fifty places in my small town where white men are positively raising two families—a white family in the "Big House" in front, and a colored family in a "Little House" in the backyard. In most cases, to be sure, the colored women involved are the cooks or chambermaids or seamstresses, but it cannot be true that their real connection with the white men of the families is unknown to the white women of the families. The results of this concubinage can be seen in all of our colored churches and in all of our colored public schools in the South, for in most of our churches and schools the majority of the young men and women and boys and girls are light-skinned mulattoes. . . .

I have already told you that my youngest girl was a nurse. With scores of other colored girls who are nurses, she can be seen almost any afternoon, when the weather is fair, rolling the baby carriage or lolling about on some one of the chief boulevards of our town. The very first week that she started out on her work she was insulted by a white man, and many times since has been improperly approached by other white men. It is a favorite practice of young white sports about town—and they are not always young, either—to stop some colored nurse, inquire the name of the "sweet little baby," talk baby talk to the child, fondle it, kiss it, make love to it, etc., etc., and in nine of ten cases every such white man will wind up by making love to the colored nurse and seeking an appointment with her.

I confess that I believe it to be true that many of our colored girls are as eager as the white men are to encourage and maintain these improper relations; but where the girl is not willing, she has only herself to depend upon for protection. If their fathers, brothers or husbands seek to redress their wrongs, under our peculiar conditions, the guiltless negroes will be severely punished, if not killed, and the white blackleg will go scot-free!

We poor colored women wage-earners in the South are fighting a terrible battle . . . On the one hand, we are assailed by white men, and, on the other hand, we are assailed by black men, who should be our natural protectors; and, whether in the cook kitchen, at the washtub, over the sewing machine, behind the baby carriage, or at the ironing board, we are but little more than pack horses, beasts of burden, slaves! In the distant future, it may be, centuries and centuries hence, a monument of brass or stone will be erected to the Old Black Mammies of the South, but what we need is present help, present sympathy, better wages, better hours,

more protection, and a chance to breathe for once while alive
as free women.

"More Slavery at the South," by a Negro nurse,
The Independent, Vol. 72, No. 3295 (January 25, 1912), pp.
197–200.

NO PROTECTION FOR
BLACK GIRLS

❧ *The facts of the sexual exploitation of black women
by white men were well known to nineteenth-century
Southerners, but the subject was long taboo for public discussion. When the national magazine The Independent
opened its pages for a discussion of the race issue, the black
contributors to the discussion chose to remain anonymous,
since even carefully worded statements, such as the one
below, were considered explosive.*

It is commonly said that no girl or woman receives a certain
kind of insult unless she invites it. That does not apply to a
colored girl and woman in the South. The color of her face
alone is sufficient invitation to the Southern white man—
these same men who profess horror that a white gentleman
can entertain a colored one at his table. Out of sight of their
own women they are willing and anxious to entertain colored
women in various ways. Few colored girls reach the age of
sixteen without receiving advances from them—maybe from
a young "upstart," and often from a man old enough to be
their father, a white haired veteran of sin. Yes, and men high
in position, whose wives and daughters are leaders of society.
I have had a clerk in a store hold my hand as I gave him the
money for some purchase and utter some vile request; a
shoe man to take liberties, a man in a crowd to place his
hands on my person, others to follow me to my very door, a
school director to assure me a position if I did his bidding.

It is true these particular men never insulted me but once; but there are others. . . .

I dread to see my children grow. I know not their fate. Where the white girl has one temptation, mine will have many. Where the white boy has every opportunity and protection, mine will have few opportunities and no protection. It does not matter how good or wise my children may be, they are colored. When I have said that, all is said. Everything is forgiven in the South but color.

"The Race Problem—An Autobiography,"
by "A Southern Colored Woman,"
The Independent, Vol. 56, No. 2885 (March 17, 1904), pp. 587, 589.

THEIR RAGE WAS CHIEFLY
DIRECTED AGAINST MEN . . .

❦ *The events described below took place during the New York City Draft Riots of 1863 which were motivated largely by job competition between Irish immigrant laborers and free Blacks. The immediate cause of the outbreak was the resistance of striking longshoremen—who had been replaced by black strikebreakers—to being conscripted into the army. The smoldering resentment of the city's poor, who regarded the draft as unjust since the rich could buy their way out of serving, turned this incident into a major riot. The rage of the rioters focused on the city's black population, whom they regarded as the cause of the war and as a future threat to their jobs. After four days of lynchings of Blacks, burning of black homes and massive destruction, with hundreds killed and vast property destruction, four New York regiments were withdrawn from the front and succeeded in restoring order.*

In the aftermath of the riot private charitable organizations organized relief and collected the eyewitness testimony of some of the victims.

Mrs. Statts tells this story:—

... I had arrived from Philadelphia, the previous Monday evening, before any indications of the riots were known, and was temporarily stopping, on Wednesday, July 15th, at the house of my son, No. 147 East 28th Street.

At 3 o'clock of that day the mob arrived and immediately commenced an attack with terrific yells, and a shower of stones and bricks, upon the house. In the next room to where I was sitting was a poor woman, who had been confined with a child on Sunday, three days previous. Some of the rioters broke through the front door with pickaxes, and came rushing into the room where this poor woman lay, and commenced to pull the clothes from off her. Knowing that their rage was chiefly directed against men, I hid my son behind me and ran with him through the back door, down into the basement. In a little while I saw the innocent babe, of three days old, come crashing down into the yard; some of the rioters had dashed it out of the back window, killing it instantly. In a few minutes streams of water came pouring down into the basement, the mob had cut the Croton water-pipes with their axes. Fearing we should be drowned in the cellar (there were ten of us, mostly women and children, there), I took my boy and flew past the dead body of the babe, out to the rear of the yard, hoping to escape with him through an open lot into 29th street; but here, to our horror and dismay, we met the mob again; I, with my son, had climbed the fence, but the sight of those maddened demons so affected me that I fell back, fainting, into the yard; my son jumped down from the fence to pick me up, and a dozen of the rioters came leaping over the fence after him. As they surrounded us my son exclaimed, "save my mother, gentlemen, if you kill me." "Well, we will kill you," they answered; and with that two ruffians seized him, each taking hold of an arm, while a third, armed with a crow-bar, calling upon them to stand and hold his arms apart, deliberately struck him a heavy blow over the head, felling him, like a bullock, to the ground. (He died in the N.Y. hospital two days after.) I believe if I were to live a hundred years I would never forget that scene, or cease to hear the horrid voices of that demoniacal mob resounding in my ears.

They then drove me over the fence, and as I was passing over, one of the mob seized a pocket-book, which he saw in my bosom, and in his eagerness to get it tore the dress off my shoulders.

I, with several others, then ran to the 29th street Station House, but we were here refused admittance, and told by the Captain that we were frightened without cause. A gentleman who accompanied us told the Captain of the facts, but we were all turned away.

I then went down to my husband's, in Broome Street, and there I encountered another mob, who, before I could escape commenced stoning me. They beat me severely.

I reached the house but found my husband had left for Rahway. Scarcely knowing what I did, I then wandered, bewildered and sick, in the direction he had taken, and towards Philadelphia, and reached Jersey City, where a kind Christian gentleman, Mr. Arthur Lynch, found me, and took me to his house, where his good wife nursed me for over two weeks, while I was very sick.

I am a member of the Baptist Church, and if it were not for my trust in Christ I do not know how I could have endured it.

Report of the Merchants Committee for the Relief of Colored People Suffering from the Riots in the City of New York, July 1863 (New York: George A. Whitehorne, 1863).

THE FINAL SOLUTION

Oklahoma, 1911. At Okemah, Oklahoma, Laura Nelson, a colored woman, accused of murdering a deputy sheriff who had discovered stolen goods in her house, was lynched together with her son, a boy about fifteen. The woman and her son were taken from the jail, dragged about six miles to the Canadian River, and hanged from a bridge. The woman was raped by members of the mob before she was hanged.

Oklahoma, 1914. Marie Scott of Wagoner County, a seventeen-year-old Negro girl was lynched by a mob of white men because her brother killed one of two white men who had assaulted her. She was alone in the house when the men entered, but her screams brought her brother to the rescue. In the fight that ensued one of the white men was killed. The next day the mob came to lynch her brother, but as he had escaped, lynched the girl instead. No one has ever been indicted for this crime.

Mississippi, 1918. On Friday night, December 20, 1918, four Negroes, Andrew Clark, age 15; Major Clark, age 20; Maggie Howze, age 20; and Alma Howze, age 16, were taken from the little jail at Shubuta and lynched on a bridge over the Chickasawha River. They were suspected of having murdered a Dr. E. L. Johnston, a dentist.

An investigation disclosed the following facts: That Dr. Johnston was living in illicit relations with Maggie Howze and Alma Howze. That Major Clark, a youth working on Johnston's plantation wished to marry Maggie. That Dr. Johnston went to Clark and told him to leave his woman alone. That this led to a quarrel, made the more bitter when it was found that Maggie was to have a child by Dr. Johnston; and that the younger sister was also pregnant, said to be by Dr. Johnston.

Shortly after this Johnston was mysteriously murdered. There were two theories as to his death; one that he was killed by Clark, the other that he was killed by a white man who had accused him of seducing a white woman. It was generally admitted that Johnston was a loose character.

Alma Howze was so near to motherhood when lynched

that it was said by an eye-witness at her burial on the second day following, that the movements of her unborn child could be detected.

Investigation by the National Association for the Advancement of Colored People.

NAACP, 30 *Years of Lynching in the United States* (New York: NAACP, 1919).

THE MYTH OF THE "BAD" BLACK WOMAN

❦ *After slavery ended, the sexual exploitation of black women continued, in both the North and the South, although in different forms and with somewhat greater risk to the white man involved. To sustain it, in the face of the nominal freedom of black men, a complex system of supportive mechanisms and sustaining myths was created. One of these was the myth of the "bad" black woman. By assuming a different level of sexuality for all Blacks than that of whites and mythifying their greater sexual potency, the black woman could be made to personify sexual freedom and abandon. A myth was created that all black women were eager for sexual exploits, voluntarily "loose" in their morals and, therefore, deserved none of the consideration and respect granted to white women. Every black woman was, by definition, a slut according to this racist mythology; therefore, to assault her and exploit her sexually was not reprehensible and carried with it none of the normal communal sanctions against such behavior. A wide range of practices reinforced this myth: the laws against inter-marriage; the denial of the title "Miss" or "Mrs." to any* black woman; the taboos against respectable social mixing of the races; the refusal to let black women customers try on clothing in stores before making a purchase; the assigning of single toilet facilities to both sexes of Blacks; the different legal sanctions against rape, abuse of minors and other sex crimes when committed against white or black women. Black women were very much aware of the interrelatedness of these practices and fought constantly—individually and through their organizations—both the practices and the underlying myth.

THE ACCUSATIONS ARE FALSE

FANNIE BARRIER WILLIAMS

❦ Fannie Barrier Williams was born in Brockport, New York. She studied at the New England Conservatory of Music in Boston and at the School of Fine Arts in Washington, D.C. She taught school in the South until her marriage to S. Laing Williams, an attorney in Chicago. She was the first member of her race admitted to the Women's Club of Chicago and to the Chicago Library Board. She came into national prominence in 1892 when she convinced the board of the World's Columbian Exposition in Chicago to give official representation to Negroes. She lectured at the Columbian Exposition and at an international "Parliament of Religions." As a representative of her state, she participated in the National Colored Women's Congress, convened by the Negro Department of the Cotton States and International Exposition in Atlanta, Georgia, in 1895. The black women there assembled passed a set of resolutions protesting discrimination, the convict lease system and lynching and urging the establishment of a fully integrated woman's movement. Fannie Barrier Williams helped to organize the first training school for *black nurses in Chicago and worked with the Phillis Wheatley Home Association.*

I think it but just to say that we must look to America slavery as the source of every imperfection that mars the character of the colored American. It ought not to be necessary to remind a Southern woman that less than 50 years ago the ill-starred mothers of this ransomed race were not allowed to be modest . . . and there was no living man to whom they could cry for protection against the men who not only owned them, body and soul, but also the souls of their husbands, their brothers, and, alas, their sons. Slavery made her the only woman in America for whom virtue was not an ornament and a necessity. But in spite of this dark and painful past . . . I believe that the colored women are just as strong and just as weak as any other women with like education, training and environment.

It is a significant and shameful fact that I am constantly in receipt of letters from the still unprotected colored women of the South, begging me to find employment for their daughters according to their ability, as domestics or otherwise, to save them from going into the homes of the South as servants, as there is nothing to save them from dishonor and degradation. Many prominent white women and ministers will verify this statement. The heart-broken cry of some of of these helpless mothers bears no suggestion of the "flaunting pride of dishonor" so easily obtained, by simply allowing their daughters to enter the homes of the white women of the South. Their own mothers cannot protect them and white women will not, or do not. The moral feature of this problem has complications that it would seem better not to dwell on. From my own study of the question, the colored woman deserves greater credit for what she has done and is doing than blame for what she cannot so soon overcome. . . .

Prejudice is here and everywhere, but it may not manifest itself so brutally as in the South. The chief interest in the

North seems to be centered in business, and it is in business where race prejudice shows itself the strongest. The chief interest in the South is social supremacy, therefore prejudice manifests itself most strongly against even an imaginary approach to social contact. Here in the Northern States I find that a colored woman of character and intelligence will be recognized and respected, but the white woman who will recognize and associate with her in the same club or church would probably not tolerate her as a fellow clerk in office or [shop.]

The conclusion of the whole matter seems to be that whether I live in the North or the South, I cannot be counted for my full value, be that much or little. I dare not cease to hope and aspire and believe in human love and justice, but progress is painful and my faith is often strained to the breaking point.

Fannie Barrier Williams, "A Northern Negro's Autobiography,"
The Independent, Vol. 57, No. 2902 (July 14, 1904), p. 96.

A COLORED WOMAN, HOWEVER RESPECTABLE, IS LOWER THAN THE WHITE PROSTITUTE

ANONYMOUS

I am a colored woman, wife and mother. . . .

The Southerners say we negroes are a happy, laughing set of people, with no thought of to-morrow. How mistaken they are! . . . There is a feeling of unrest, insecurity, almost panic among the best class of negroes in the South. In our homes, in our churches, wherever two or three are gathered together, there is a discussion of what is best to do. Must we remain in the South or go elsewhere? Where can we go to feel that security which other people feel? Is it best to go in great numbers or only in several families? These and many other things are discussed over and over. . . .

A colored woman, however respectable, is lower than the white prostitute. The Southern white woman will declare that no negro women are virtuous, yet she places her innocent children in their care. . . . No amount of discussion will alter a fact, and it is a fact that a very great number of negro women are depraved. It is also a fact that . . . Christian men and women of the South sold wives away from their husbands and then compelled them to live with other men. Fathers sold their own children. Beautiful girls brought large sums to their owners when sold, especially for mistresses to the fathers and brothers of these same women who now marvel that the negro is not chaste. The negro woman's immorality shows more plainly than her white sister's because she is poor and ignorant.

A few years ago, within the memory of us all, a prominent white Senator was being tried for seducing a young white girl, and it was brought out at the trial that five hundred illegitimate white children were born in a particular infirmary in one city in one year. This would never have been known but for the accident of this trial. The negro girl is too poor to hide her shame. Since God created men and women there has been sin and it is confined to no particular race. . . .

The Southerner says the negro must "keep in his place." That means the particular place the white man says is his. . . .

Southern railway stations have three waiting rooms, and the very conspicuous signs tell the ignorant that this room is for "ladies," and this is for "gents" and that for the "colored" people. We are neither "ladies" nor "gents, but "colored."

There are aristocrats in crime, in poverty, and in misfortune in the South. The white criminal cannot think of eating or sleeping in the same part of the penitentiary with the negro criminal. The white pauper is just as exclusive; and altho the blind cannot see color, nor the insane care about it, they must be kept separate, at great extra expense. Lastly, the dead white man's bones must not be contaminated with the dead black man's. I know one of the "black mammies" that the Southerner speaks of, in tones low and soft, who is compelled to go to the authorities of a certain Southern city for a "pass" to visit the grave of a man she nursed at her breast and whose children she afterward reared. It does not matter that this old woman gave herself in slavery and out of slavery for this man and his children, she must have a "pass" to visit his grave.

Whenever a crime is committed in the South the policemen look for the negro in the case. A white man with face and hands blackened can commit any crime in the calendar. The first friendly stream soon washes away his guilt and he is ready to join in the hunt to lynch the "big, black burly brute." When a white man in the South does commit a crime, that is simply one white man gone wrong. If his crime is especially brutal he is a freak or temporarily insane. If one low, ignorant black wretch commits a crime, that is different. All of us must bear his guilt. A young white boy's badness is simply the overflowing of young animal spirits; the black boy's badness is badness, pure and simple.

Young colored boys, too small for other work, who need the work more than the white boys, are not allowed to sell newspapers on the streets in most of our Southern cities. . . .

This is the South's idea of justice. Is it surprising that feeling grows more bitter, when the white mother teaches her boy to hate my boy, not because he is mean, but because his skin is dark? I have seen very small white children hang their black dolls. It is not the child's fault, he is simply an apt pupil. No self-respecting negro fails to condemn the rapist; but all just men condemn a mob, and especially for killing a suspected thief or barn burner. A negro woman is killed because she had used "abusive language." Her provocation was great. Her brother had been almost killed by a mob because he had been suspected of taking a pocketbook that had been dropped in the public road. If one of New York's "Four Hundred" gives an especially unique ball in his palatial stable, it is telegraphed and cabled around the globe. Things past, present and future stir the people of the United States;

but its own citizens are butchered and burned alive and only a very mild wave of ever-lessening indignation sweeps by. Governors are vehement and determined (for a day) to discover the identity of the mobs of unmasked "best citizens."

When I think of these things, I exclaim, Why are we forgotten? Why does not the mistreatment of thousands of the citizens of our county call forth a strong, influential champion? It seems to me that the very weakness of the negro should cause at least a few of our great men to come to the rescue. Is it because an espousal of our cause would make any white man unpopular, or do most of our great men think that we are all worthless? Are there greater things to do than to "champion the rights of human beings and to mitigate human suffering?"

The way seems dark, and the future almost hopeless, but let us not despair. . . . Some one will at last arise who will champion our cause and compel the world to see that we deserve justice, as other heroes compelled it to see that we deserved freedom.

Anonymous article, The Independent, Vol. 54 No. 2807
(September 18, 1902), pp. 2221–2224.

IN DEFENSE OF BLACK WOMEN

ELSIE JOHNSON McDOUGALD

❦ *Elsie Johnson McDougald was a trained social worker and assistant principal of Public School 89 in Harlem.*

It is apparent . . . that even in New York City, Negro women are of a race which is free neither economically, socially nor spiritually. Like women in general, but more particularly like those of other oppressed minorities, the Negro woman has been forced to submit to over-powering conditions. Pressure has been exerted upon her, both from without and within her group. Her emotional and sex life is a reflex of her economic station. The women of the working class will react, emotionally and sexually, similarly to the working-class women of other races. The Negro woman does not maintain any moral standard which may be assigned chiefly to qualities of race, any more than a white woman does. Yet she has been singled out and advertised as having lower sex standards. Superficial critics who have had contact only with the lower grades of Negro women, claim that they are more immoral than other groups of women. This I deny. This is the sort of criticism which predicates of one race, to its detriment, that which is common to all races. Sex irregularities are not a matter or race, but of socio-economic conditions. Research shows that most of the African tribes from which the Negro sprang have strict codes for sex relations. There is no proof of inherent weakness in the ethnic group.

Gradually overcoming the habitual limits imposed upon her by slave masters, she increasingly seeks legal sanction for the consummation and dissolution of sex contracts. Contrary to popular belief, illegitimacy among Negroes is cause for shame and grief. When economic, social and biological forces combined bring about unwed motherhood, the reaction is much the same as in families of other racial groups. Secrecy is maintained if possible. Generally the married aunt, or even the mother, claims that the illegitimate child is her own. The foundling asylum is seldom sought. Schooled in this kind of suffering in the days of slavery, Negro women often temper scorn with sympathy for weakness. Stigma does fall upon the unmarried mother, but perhaps in this matter the Negroes' attitude is nearer the modern enlightened ideal for the social treatment of the unfortunate. May this not be considered another contribution to America?

With all these forces at work, true sex equality has not been approximated. The ratio of opportunity in the sex, social, economic and political spheres is about that which exists between white men and women. In the large, I would say that the Negro woman is the cultural equal of her man because she is generally kept in school longer. Negro boys, like white boys, are usually put to work to subsidize the family income. The growing economic independence of Negro working women is causing her to rebel against the domineering family attitude of the cruder working-class Negro man. The masses of Negro men are engaged in menial occupations throughout the working day. Their baffled and suppressed desires to determine their economic life are manifested in over-bearing domination at home. Working mothers are unable to instill different ideals in their sons. Conditions change slowly. Nevertheless, education and opportunity are modifying the spirit of the younger Negro men. Trained in modern schools of thought, they begin to show a wholesome attitude of fellowship and freedom for their women. The challenge to young Negro womanhood is to see clearly this trend and grasp the proferred comradeship with sincerity. In this matter of sex equality, Negro women have contributed few outstanding militants. Their feminist efforts are directed chiefly toward the realization of the equality of the races, the sex struggle assuming a subordinate place. . . .

We find the Negro woman, figuratively, struck in the face daily by contempt from the world about her. Within her soul, she knows little of peace and happiness. Through it all, she is courageously standing erect, developing within herself the moral strength to rise above and conquer false attitudes. She is maintaining her natural beauty and charm and improving her mind and opportunity. She is measuring up to the needs and demands of her family, community and race, and radiating from Harlem a hope that is cherished by her sisters in less propitious circumstances throughout the land. The wind of the race's destiny stirs more briskly because of her striving.

Elsie Johnson McDougald, "The Double Task: The Struggle of Negro Women for Sex and Race Emancipation," *Survey Graphic*, Vol. 6, No. 6 (March 1925), p. 691.

THE RAPE OF BLACK WOMEN AS A WEAPON OF TERROR

☞ The practice of raping the women of a defeated enemy is world-wide and is found in every culture. The occurrence of this practice during many race riots and during periods of terror against Blacks at various times in United States history merely affirms the colonial nature of the oppression of black people in the United States. It is the ultimate expression of contempt for a defeated foe since it symbolizes his helplessness more fully than any other conceivable act. As such, it functions as only lynching does as a weapon of terror for the whole community.

The historical record does not lend itself to interpretations explaining such events as the isolated acts of criminal individuals. The absence of punishment for white rapists of black women throughout most of our history and, lately, the great discrepancy in the punishment of white and black men for the same offense simply underscores the double standard of justice for the ruler and the ruled. It must also be understood that "individual acts of criminal behavior" on the part of white men toward black women arise out of and are reinforced by the prevalent cultural racist myths. The testimony presented in this chapter is a very small selection of pertinent historical data.

The sexual oppression of black women is not only an end in itself; it is also an instrument in the oppression of the entire race. When black men are prevented from defending their women and their children, they are symbolically castrated and assaulted in their essential dignity. Black women, in such a situation, are doubly instrumentalized— as objects of forcible rape and as instruments in the degradation of their men. In this sense, the sexual assaults on black

women are part of the reinforcing structure upholding a
system of racial and economic exploitation. Physical terror
against black men who defend their women is one aspect
of this reinforcing structure. The threat of death by lynching
against black men who have sexual contact with white
women is another. The possibility of love, friendship and
free human choice across racial lines must be prevented
and destroyed by rigid social taboos. Every black man must
learn two lessons, if the system of oppression is to survive.
"Defend black women—and die!" is one. "Touch white
women—and die!" is the other. In either case, women
become instruments to be manipulated by society for the
benefit of those in power.

THE MEMPHIS RIOT, 1865

❦ The existence of racially integrated and all black
militia units during Reconstruction was anathema to most
Southern whites. It became a symbol for "black rule" even
though these militia units functioned everywhere under the
orders and in defense of white-dominated state legislatures.
Conflicts between black militia and white police forces
have to be understood in this context. In Memphis, Tennessee, a jostling incident between black militia men and
white policemen became the excuse for a white mob attack
on the entire black community. Rioting lasted for three
days and was ended only by the intervention of federal
forces. During the mob action 46 Negro men, women and
children were killed, and more than 80 wounded. One white
man was injured. Four Negro churches, twelve schools and
innumerable homes were burned to the ground. The House
of Representatives appointed a three-man investigating
committee, which elicited the testimony from which the
following excerpts have been selected.

FRANCES THOMPSON (*colored*) *sworn and examined.*

By the CHAIRMAN:

2919. State what you know or saw of the rioting. [Witness] Between one and two o'clock Tuesday night seven men, two of whom were policemen, came to my house. I know they were policemen by their stars. They were all Irishmen. They said they must have some eggs, and ham, and biscuit. I made them some biscuit and some strong coffee, and they all sat down and ate. A girl lives with me; her name is Lucy Smith; she is about 16 years old. When they had eaten supper, they said they wanted some women to sleep with. I said we were not that sort of women, and they must go. They said "that didn't make a damned bit of difference." One of them then laid hold of me and hit me on the side of my face, and holding my throat, choked me. Lucy tried to get out of the window, when one of them knocked her down and choked her. They drew their pistols and said they would shoot us and fire the house if we did not let them have their way with us. All seven of the men violated us two. Four of them had to do with me, and the rest with Lucy.

2913. Were you injured? I was sick for two weeks. I lay for three days with a hot, burning fever.

LUCY SMITH (*colored*) *sworn and examined.*

By the CHAIRMAN:

2925. State what you know of the late riots. (Witness) On Tuesday, the first night of the riots, some men came to our house. We were in bed. They told us to get up and get some supper for them. We got up, and made a fire, and got them supper.

2926. What else took place? What was left of the sugar, and coffee, and ham they threw into the bayou.

2927. How many men were there? There were seven of them; but I was so scared I could not be certain.

2928. Did they rob you? We had two trunks. They did not unlock them, but just jerked them open. They took $100 belonging to Frances, and $200 belonging to a friend of Frances, given to her to take care of. They took all the money and clothes and carried them off.

2929. Did you know any of the men? There were two policemen with the men; I saw their stars.

2930. What else took place? They tried to take advantage of me, and did. I told them I did not do such things, and would not. One of them said he would make me, and choked me by the neck. My neck was swollen up next day, and for two weeks I could not talk to anyone. After the first man had connexion with me, another got hold of me and tried to violate me, but I was so bad he did not. He gave me a lick with his fist and said that I was so damned near dead he would not have anything to do with me.

2931. Were you injured? I bled from what the first man had done to me. The man said, "Oh, she is so near dead I won't have anything to do with her." I was injured right smart, and kept my bed for two weeks after.

LUCY TIBBS (colored) sworn and examined.
By the CHAIRMAN:

2151. How old are you? [Witness] I do not know exactly. I suppose about twenty-four.

2152. Have you a husband? Yes; my husband is on a steamboat. We came here from Jackson, Arkansas, when the rebellion broke out.

2153. Were you here during the riots? Yes, sir. . . .

2178. Did they come into your house? Yes; a crowd of men came in that night; I do not know who they were. They just broke the door open and asked me where was my husband; I replied he was gone; they said I was a liar; I said, "Please do not do anything to me; I am just here with two little children."

2179. Did they do anything to you? They done a very bad act.

2180. Did they ravish you? Yes, sir.

2181. How many of them? There was but one that did it. Another man said, "Let that woman alone—that she was not in any situation to be doing that." They went to my trunk, burst it open, and took this money that belonged to my brother.

2182. Did they violate your person against your consent? Yes, sir; I had just to give up to them. They said they would kill me if I did not. They put me on the bed, and the other men were plundering the house while this man was carrying on.

2183. Were any of them policemen? I do not know; I was so scared I could not tell whether they were policemen or not; I think there were folks that knew all about me, who knew that my brother had not been long out of the army and had money.

2184. Where were your children? In bed.

2185. Were you dressed or undressed when these men came to you? I was dressed.

2186. Did you make any resistance? No, sir; the house was full of men. I thought they would kill me; they had stabbed a woman near by the night before.

2187. How old are your children? One of them will soon be five, and the other will be two years old in August.

2188. What did they mean by saying you were not in a condition to be doing that? I have been in the family way ever since Christmas.

2189. Who was this woman stabbed the night before? I do not know. I heard a woman and a man who went over there and saw her talking about it.

2190. Was she violated too? I suppose she was; they said she was. The next night they burned all those shanties down. Where they went to I could not tell.

2191. How many houses did they burn down? Three or four.

2192. Would you know this man who committed violence upon you if you should see him? I do not think I would.

2193. What countryman was he? I could not tell.

2194. What countrymen did the crowd appear to be? They appeared to be like Irishmen.

2195. How many rooms were there in your house? Only one.
2196. And this took place in the presence of all these men?
Yes, sir. . . .

CYNTHIA TOWNSEND (*colored*) *sworn and examined.*
  By the CHAIRMAN:

2209. Have you been a slave? [Witness] Yes; but I worked
and bought myself. I finished paying for myself a few days
before they took this place. . . .
2215. Have you a husband? Yes. My husband and son are
about seven miles in the country at work. I sent word to
them not to come back until this fuss was over. . . .
2219. Did they rob your house? Yes; they took my clothes,
and fifty dollars in money, but I did not consider that
much. . . .
2220. Who did the money belong to? It belonged to my son
who was in the army, Frank King.
2221. Do you know of any violence being committed on the
women in your neighborhood? Yes, sir; I know of some very
bad acts. . . .
2223. State the circumstances? There is a woman who lives
near me by the name of Harriet; Merriweather was her name
before she married; I do not know what her husband's name
is. There were as many as three or four men at a time had
connexion with her; she was lying there by herself. They all
had connexion with her in turn around, and then one of
them tried to use her mouth.
2224. Was this during the riot? Yes, sir; it was on Monday
evening.
2225. Did you see these men go in the house? Yes; I saw
them going into the house and saw them coming out, and
afterwards she came out and said they made her do what I
told you they did; she has sometimes been a little deranged
since then, her husband left her for it. When he came out
of the fort, and found what had been done, he said he would
not have anything to do with her any more. They drew their
pistols before her and made her submit. There were white

people right there who knew what was going on. One woman called me to go and look in and see what they were doing; that was when this thing was going on. She is the woman who came and made a complaint to Charley Smith; she is a very nice woman. . . .

MARY JORDAN (*colored*) *sworn and examined.*

By the CHAIRMAN:

3861. How old are you? [Witness] I am thirty-three years old.

3862. Are you married? Yes, sir; but my husband is dead.

3863. Have you been a slave? Yes, sir.

3864. Were you here when the rioting took place? Yes, sir; I lived on Aiken street. . . .

3869. What else did you see? After they went away we thought it was all over; but they came back again and set the colored saloon on fire. It was kept by a man by the name of Robinson. When they set the saloon on fire I ran out. I was very much alarmed, as it was so near. My husband was just dead and buried, and I had a sick child in my arms, and they had begun shooting at the colored people.

3870. Did you see anyone shot? I saw one shot, but I don't know his name.

3871. Did they set fire to your house? After that I went back to my house. I was so afraid, expecting every minute I would be shot down or my house set on fire and burned. Then they set fire to it, when we were all there.

3872. How many of you were there in the house? There was my little babe, seven months old, my little girl, eight years old, and my eldest daughter, about sixteen. We were all in there when it was set on fire. . . .

3874. Did you go out when your house caught on fire? They would not let us out.

3875. How long did you remain in there? They would not let us out until the house was all in flames.

3876. What did you save? I saved my children. I took up my shoes, but I was so scared I could not put them on.

3877. Do you say they shot at you when you first went out of your house? Yes, sir. When they set fire to the saloon I ran out and they shot at me when I had my little babe in my arms. The bullets came all around me, and I would have been shot if I had not run round the corner.

3878. What else do you know of this rioting? When I was running away with my babe a man put a pistol to my breast, and said he, "What are you doing?" "I am trying to save my babe." "Sit down," said he, and I sat down, and they did not trouble me any more.

3879. Was your child injured? It rained, and my babe got wet and it afterwards died.

3880. Did you know any of these men? No, sir; I did not. Some of them had stars.

3881. What did you lose by the fire? I lost everything I had. I lost my clothes and my children's clothes, my bedstead and furniture.

3882. How much was it all worth? I had been working for three years, and trying to save, and my losses, I guess, would be $200.

3883. Had you any money? No, sir; I had no money.

3884. What else do you know about these troubles? When the flames were all around our house I told my children to follow me. My daughter said, "Mother, you will be shot." I said, "Better be shot than burned." It was raining, and I could get no shelter. We stayed out till they were all gone, and they did not disturb us any more. After a while I asked another colored woman to let me into her house, and she let me. Next day I had nothing to eat. After that I asked a white lady to give me some medicine for my babe; it was low and I could get nothing for it. They lady was kind; she gave me medicine for my babe, but it died and the lady buried it; I was not able to bury it. My babe lived nearly two weeks after that night, and then it died.

"Memphis Riot and Massacres," U.S. Document 1274, 39th Congress, 1st Session, 1865–66. House Reports, Vol. 3, No. 101.

KKK TERROR DURING
RECONSTRUCTION

❦ The Ku Klux Klan, a secret lodge describing itself
as dedicated to "chivalry, humanity, mercy and patriotism,"
had first been organized in Tennessee in 1865. It soon
spread to several Southern states and, together with a
number of other secret organizations of a similar nature,
became the instrument designed to defeat congressional
reconstruction by intimidation, violence, terror and murder.
Ostensibly "defensive" in nature, the KKK systematically
sought to destroy all efforts on the part of Radical Republicans and Negroes to assume and exercise political power.
The KKK's main thrust was directed against the black state
militias, against any Negro daring to vote or run for office,
against the Freedmen's Bureau and its agents and anyone
connected with the freedmen's schools. Intimidation and
terror were wielded with equal savagery against black and
white Republicans, but there are no records of the rape
and violation of white women whose husbands or male
relatives were associated with the Republican cause. Such
practices were confined to black women, as the following
testimony reveals.

In an effort to stem the tide of repression and terror
which amounted in many states to an undeclared civil war,
Republican state governments passed laws against the KKK.
The organization ostensibly dissolved itself in the spring
of 1869, but this was merely a tactical move to escape
prosecution. Due to the widespread support of the KKK
by the white population and to the weakness of state law
enforcement agencies, the state laws were unenforceable.
In a last-ditch effort to save congressional reconstruction,
the Congress passed the so-called Ku Klux Klan Act in
April 1871, in which it outlawed the organization and devised
heavy penalties against its activities. A joint congressional

committee, consisting of twenty-one members of both houses, was appointed and ordered to hold hearings to "inquire into the condition of the late insurrectionary states." The records of the committee hearings, which fill thirteen volumes, offer a graphic picture of a savage reign of terror directed against Blacks and their white allies. Witnesses came from every segment of the population, ranging from governors, state legislators, sheriffs and United States Army officers to ordinary people of both races. Committee members divided along party lines in their conclusion. The majority report (Republican) recommended continuing strong protective measures by the federal government and the continuing presence of federal troops to suppress the "widespread and dangerous conspiracy" against Reconstruction which the hearings had uncovered. But Republican power in the Southern states was already in a state of collapse. KKK terror was only part of the reason for the decline in Southern Republican power, yet the Klan's effect on the black community can be likened to the presence of an occupying army. Counter-Reconstruction returned white Democratic rule to the South and destroyed the basis of that incipient black and white alliance which had formed the revolutionary core of the Reconstruction governments. Another aspect of counter-Reconstruction was that it physically destroyed many of the black leaders and potential leaders of the post–Civil War generation of Blacks, repressed the schools and social institutions built with so much labor and effort in the preceding decade and denied to Negroes the economic advancement without which social reconstruction could not be secure. The Southern black community was, in fact, reduced to subsistence at the lowest economic level in a system of social oppression based on white racism.

TESTIMONY OF WITNESSES BEFORE THE JOINT CONGRESSIONAL COMMITTEE

Spartanburg, South Carolina

WITNESS: HARRIET HERNANDEZ

QUESTION: How old are you?

ANSWER: Going on thirty-four years.

QUESTION: Are you married or single?

ANSWER: Married.

QUESTION: Did the Ku-Klux ever come to your house at any time?

ANSWER: Yes, sir; twice.

QUESTION: Go on to the second time; you said it was two months afterwards?

ANSWER: Two months from Saturday night last. They came in; I was lying in bed. Says he, "Come out here, sir; Come out here, sir!" They took me out of bed; they would not let me get out, but they took me up in their arms and toted me out—me and my daughter Lucy. He struck me on the forehead with a pistol, and here is the scar above my eye now. Says he, "Damn you, fall!" I fell. Says he, "Damn you, get up!" I got up. Says he, "Damn you, get over this fence!" and he kicked me over when I went to get over; and then he went to a brush pile, and they laid us right down there, both together. They laid us down twenty yards apart, I reckon. They had dragged and beat us along. They struck me right on the top of my head, and I thought they had killed me; and I said, "Lord o' mercy, don't don't kill my child!" He gave me a lick on the head, and it liked to have killed me; I saw stars. He threw my arm over my head so I could not do anything with it for three weeks, and there are great knots on my wrist now.

QUESTION: What did they say this was for?

ANSWER: They said, "You can tell your husband that when we see him we are going to kill him."

QUESTION: Did they say why they wanted to kill him?

ANSWER: They said, "He voted the radical ticket, didn't he?" I said, "Yes, that very way."

QUESTION: When did your husband get back after this whipping? He was not at home, was he?

ANSWER: He was lying out; he couldn't stay at home, bless your soul! . . . He had been afraid ever since last October.

QUESTION: Is that the situation of the colored people down there to any extent?

ANSWER: That is the way they all have to do—men and women both.

QUESTION: What are they afraid of?

ANSWER: Of being killed or whipped to death.

QUESTION: What has made them afraid?

ANSWER: Because men that voted radical tickets they took the spite out on the women when they could get at them.

Columbia, S.C.

WITNESS: HARRIET SIMRIL

QUESTION: Who is your husband?

ANSWER: Sam Simmons.

QUESTION: Where do you live?

ANSWER: At Clay Hill in York County.

QUESTION: Has your husband lived there a good many years?

ANSWER: Yes, sir.

QUESTION: Do you know what politics he is?

ANSWER: He is a radical.

QUESTION: Did the Ku-Klux ever visit your house?

ANSWER: Yes, sir; they came on him three times. . . . The

first time they come my old man was at home.
They hollered out, "open the door," and he got
up and opened the door. . . . These young men
walked up and they took my old man out after
so long; and they wanted him to join this democratic ticket; and after that they went a piece
above the house and hit him about five cuts with
the cowhide.

QUESTION: Do you know whether he promised to be a democrat or not?

ANSWER: He told them he would rather quit all politics, if
that was the way they was going to do with him.

QUESTION: What did they do to you?

ANSWER: . . . They came back after the first time on Sunday
night after my old man again, and this second
time the crowd was bigger. . . . They called for
him, and I told them he wasn't here. . . . They
asked me where was my old man? I told them I
couldn't tell; when he went away he didn't tell
me where he was going. They searched about in
the house a long time, and staid with me an hour
that time. . . .

QUESTION: What did they do to you?

ANSWER: Well, they were spitting in my face and throwing
dirt in my eyes; and when they made me blind
they busted open my cupboard, and they eat all my
pies up, and they took two pieces of meat . . . and
after awhile they took me out of doors and told
me all they wanted was my old man to join the
democratic ticket; if he joined the democratic
ticket they would have no more to do with him;
and after they had got me out of doors, they
dragged me out into the big road, and they
ravished me out there.

QUESTION: How many of them?

ANSWER: There were three.

QUESTION: One right after the other?

ANSWER: Yes, sir.

QUESTION: Threw you down on the ground?

ANSWER: Yes, sir, they throwed me down.

QUESTION: Do you know who the men were who ravished you?

ANSWER: Yes, sir, I can tell who the men were; there was Ches McCollum, Tom McCollum, and this big Jim Harper. . . .

QUESTION: What was your condition when they left you?

ANSWER: After they had got done with me I had no sense for a long time. I laid there, I don't know how long. . . .

QUESTION: Have the Ku-Klux ever come to you again?

ANSWER: . . . They came back . . . but I was never inside the house.

QUESTION: Did your husband lay out at night?

ANSWER: Yes, sir; and I did too—took my children, and when it rained thunder and lightning. . . .

QUESTION: Did they burn your house down?

ANSWER: Yes, sir; I don't know who burnt it down, but the next morning I went to my house and it was in in ashes. . . .

Meridian, Miss.

WITNESS: ELLEN PARTON

I reside in Meridian; have resided here nine years; occupation, washing and ironing and scouring; Wednesday night was the last night they came to my house; by "they" I mean bodies or companies of men; they came on Monday, Tuesday and Wednesday; on Monday night they said they came to do us no harm; on Tuesday night they said they came for the arms; I told them there was none, and they said they would take my word for it; on Wednesday night they came and broke open the wardrobe and trunks, and committed rape upon me; there were eight of them in the house; I do not know how many there were outside; they were white men

. . . I called upon Mr. Mike Slamon, who was one of the crowd, for protection; I said to him, "Please protect me to-night, you have known me a long time;" this man covered up his head then; he had a hold of me at this time; Mr. Slamon had an oil-cloth and put it before his face, trying to conceal himself, and the man that had hold of me told me not to call Mr. Slamon's name anymore; he then took me in the dining room, and told me I had to do just what he said; I told him I could do nothing of that sort; that was not my way, and he replied, "by God, you have got to," and then threw me down; this man had a black eye, where someone had beaten him; he had a black velvet cap on; after he got through with me he came through the house and said he was after the Union Leagues; I yielded to him because he had a pistol drawn; when he took me down he hurt me of course; I yielded to him on that account; he . . . hurt me with his pistol. . . .

Columbia, S.C.

WITNESS: HARRIET POSTLE
EXAMINATION BY MR. CORBIN:

I live in the eastern part of York County . . . on Mr. James Smith's plantation; I am about thirty years old; my husband is a preacher; I have a family of six children; the oldest is about fourteen; the Ku-Klux visited me last spring . . . I was asleep when they came; they made a great noise and waked me up, and called out for Postle; my husband heard them and jumped up, and I thought he was putting on his clothes, but when I got up I found he was gone; they kept on halloo-ing for Postle and knocking at the door; I was trying to get on my clothes, but I was so frightened I did not get on my clothes at all . . . [they] began to come into the house, and my oldest child got out and ran under the bed; one of them saw him and said, "There he is; I see him;" and with that three of them pointed their pistols under the bed; I then cried out, "It is my child;" they told him to come out

. . . my child came out from under the bed . . . and . . . commenced hallooing and crying, and I begged them not to hurt my child . . . one of them ran the child back against the wall, and ground a piece of skin off as big as my hand. I then took a chair and sat it back upon a loose plank, and sat down upon it; one of the men stepped up; seeing the plank loose, he just jerked the chair and threw me over, while my babe was in my arms, and I fell with my babe to the floor, when one of them clapped his foot upon the child, and another had his foot on me; I begged him, for the Lord's sake, to save my child; I went and picked up my babe, and when I opened the door and looked I saw they had formed a line; they asked me if Postle was there; I said no; they told me to make up a light, but I was so frightened I could not do it well, and I asked my child to make it up for me; then they asked me where my husband was; I told him he was gone; they said, "He is here somewhere;" I told him he was gone for some meal; they said he was there somewhere, and they called me a damned liar; one of them said: "He is under the house;" then one of them comes to me and says: "I am going to have the truth to-night; you are a damned, lying bitch, and you are telling a lie;" and he had a line, and commenced putting it over my neck; said he; "you are telling a lie; I know it; he is here;" I told them again he was gone; when he had the rope round my head he said, "I want you to tell where your husband is;" . . . I commenced hallooing, and says he, "We are men of peace, but you are telling a damned lie . . . ;" and the one who had his foot on my body mashed me badly but not so badly as he might have done, for I was seven or eight months gone in travail; then I got outside of the house and sat down with my back against the house, and I called the little ones to me, after they were all dreadfully frightened; they said my husband was there, and that they would shoot into every crack; and they did shoot all over the place, and there are bullet-holes there and bullet-marks on the hearth yet; at this time there were some in the house and some outside, and says they to me: "We're going to have the truth out of you, you damned lying bitch; he is somewhere about here;" said I, "He is gone;" with that he clapped his hands on my neck, and with one hand put the line over my neck . . . and with that he beat my head against the side of the house till I had no sense hardly left; but I still had hold of my babe.

QUESTION: Did you recognize anybody?

ANSWER: Yes, sir; I did; I recognized the first man that came into the house; it was Dr. Avery (pointing to the accused). I recognized him by his performance, and when he was entangling the line round my neck; as I lifted my hand to keep the rope off my neck, I caught his lame hand; it was his left hand that I caught, his crippled hand; I felt it in my hand, and I said to myself right then, "I know you;" And I knew Joe Castle and James Matthews—the old man's son; I didn't know anyone else; I suppose there was about a dozen altogether there. . . . they said to me that they rode thirty-eight miles that night to see Old Abe Broomfield and preacher Postle; they said that they had heard that preacher Postle had been preaching up fire and corruption; they afterward found my husband under the house, but I had gone to the big house with my children to take them out of the cold, and I did not see them pull him out from the house.

K.K.K. Hearings, Vol. 5, South Carolina Court Proceedings, December 19 and 30, 1871; and Vol. 9, Testimony before the joint committee of Mississippi Legislature to investigate the Meridian riot, March 21, 1871.

DEFEND BLACK WOMEN— AND DIE! The Lynching of Berry Washington

FROM THE *Atlanta Constitution*, Georgia, July 25, 1919

An outrageous lynching occurred at Milan, Ga., May 24, 1919, Telfair County, Mr. John Williams, sheriff. On May

24 at 1 o'clock at night, John Dandy and Lewis Evans, white, went down into the colored people's section of the town and went to the home of a widow by the name of Emma McCollers, who had two daughters. They knocked: but the occupants refused to open the door, and Dandy shot through the door. The ball went through the organ and the machine. That frightened the girls and they ran out to another old lady's home. Her name was Emma Tisber and is a widow with two little children. The white men went after these colored girls; the girls ran under the porch and hid. These white men broke down the door and tore up the floor. The old widow lady got frightened, ran and jumped in the well, and the children screamed for help. Brother Berry Washington, colored, 72 years old, ran out with his shotgun in his hand. When he got near the hall he met both of the white men. John Dandy, 25 years old, with a wife and two children, asked the old man what he came out for. He said: "To see what was the matter with the women and children." Then John Dandy fired at him and said: "I will kill you, old man." The old man fired and killed him (John Dandy) first. He fell with his pistol in his right hand and a cigarette in the other, and a flask of—liquor fell out of his pocket. The other white fellow ran (Lewis Evans). A. Stricklin heard it.

Another colored man came out and advised Brother Washington to go up town and wake the chief of police and give himself up. The policeman's name is Mr. Stuckey. He sent Brother Washington to McCrae jail at 2 o'clock on the night of the 24th. He stayed in jail until Saturday night, the 25th, at 12 o'clock. A mob of 75 or 100 took Brother Washington out of jail and brought him back to Milan. They carried him to the same spot where he shot Dandy and lynched him. He was hanged to a post, his body shot into pieces and left hanging there until 2 o'clock Sunday morning, May 26. He was lynched because he protected his own women, in his part of the town. White boys came down there late hours of the night and disturbed the peace and happiness of the colored and white people.

They ordered every colored person to leave town Saturday
night. Poor old men, women and children left their homes
before dark. Not a colored person spent the night in their
homes Saturday night nor Sunday night. Up to the 27th of
May, this had not been published in any of the Georgia
papers, it was so disgraceful. . . .

> "A Lynching Uncovered by the NAACP," Pamphlet.
> (n.p., August 1919), pp. 3–4.

The Case of Mrs. Rosa
Lee Ingram and Her Two Sons

FROM THE *Atlanta Daily World*, February 3, 1948

Ellenville, Georgia: A Negro farm mother and two of her
youthful sons are awaiting death by electrocution at Reed-
ville State Prison as a result of their conviction last week
for the November, 1947 slaying of a white farmer.

The slain man is accused of attacking Mrs. Rosa Lee
Ingram, the doomed woman, with rifle in hand, when she
sought to stop him from shooting her farm animals. Judge
W. M. Harper sentenced 45 year old Mrs. Ingram and her
two sons, Wallace, 17 and Sammy, 14, to death in the electric
chair on February 27 in the slaying of John Ed Stratford, a
white farmer. Charlie Ingram, 18, another son, was acquitted
on the murder charge. A fourth son, Jackson, was sentenced
to serve twelve months in prison on the charge that he took
the farmer's purse, containing $133, from his pocket. The
purse was dug up behind a barn at the home of the Ingrams,
the State alleged.

The all-white jury disregarded the testimony of the Ingrams
that Stratford advanced on the mother with a rifle, and
engaged in a tussle with her, whereupon the sons intervened
and death blows resulted in their self-defense.

According to trial testimony, Stratford had found mules
and hogs belonging to the Ingram family in his corn field,

got his .32 caliber rifle to shoot them. With gun in hand, Stratford allegedly met Mrs. Ingram on the road about half-way between his house and the Ingrams' dwelling. A tussle reportedly ensued, according to the Sheriff, and the sons intervened when they saw their mother in danger of being killed. The farmer reportedly was so irate and determined that he was subdued only after he was struck a heavy blow across the head by one of the sons. Coroner R. M. Chapman said four heavy blows had been given the dead white man, and surmised that two of them had caused death. The State accused the mother and her sons of attacking the white farmer with Stratford's own rifle, a claw-hammer and a hoe. According to Sheriff Edgar Devain of Schley County, the fight over the livestock had been going on for weeks. The Ingrams lived on the M. Dellinger farm and the slaying occurred halfway between their farm and the Stratford house. At the time of the slaying and arrest Sheriff Devain placed the Ingrams in separate undisclosed jails as a precaution and guard against mob violence.

February 14, 1948

A citizen's defense committee has called a mass meeting for Monday night, February 16, in defense of the Ingrams. The committee has been investigating the case and feels that the families are being railroaded to death for a justified defense of their homes and persons. In southwest Georgia, Negroes have raised a small defense fund for the doomed mother and her family.

March 7, 1948

NAACP MAKES NATIONWIDE APPEAL FOR THE INGRAMS

An urgent appeal for funds for the defense of Mrs. Rosa Lee Ingram, widowed mother of twelve children and her two young sons . . . went out this week to the 1600 branches of the NAACP; calling the Ingram case one of the most shocking miscarriages of justice in the 39 years the NAACP has existed, Walter White, Secretary, urged the branches to arrange mass meetings and send appeals to churches, trade unions, and other organizations, in a concerted campaign to raise funds for the Ingrams. . . . The death sentence imposed on Mrs. Ingram, an impoverished sharecropper and her sons, originated in an argument last November with a neighboring white farmer, John Ed Stratford. Mrs. Ingram's pigs had rooted under the fence dividing Stratford's land from the farm on which she worked. Armed with a rifle, Stratford set out to shoot the animals. He encountered Mrs. Ingram and struck her with the butt of the firearm, inflicting a deep and bloody wound. She was struggling to prevent him from shooting her when two of her sons, Sammy Lee, 14 and Wallace, 17, rushed to her aid. Sammy Lee used a hammer with which he was repairing the fence, to strike the white assailant and save his mother's life. The blow was fatal. Mrs. Ingram and her sons were arrested and held without bail on trial for three months. In a one-day trial on February 3, with only court-appointed counsel to defend them, the mother and her sons were convicted and sentenced to death. . . . Meanwhile, Judge W. M. Harper, Southwest Judicial Circuit Judge, issued a stern rebuke to "Northern newspapers" for current agitation in the case. "This is an attack on the court," declared Judge Harper, "and when attacks are made upon the court, that is anarchy."

March 19, 1948

HEARING ON INGRAMS CASE POSTPONED AGAIN AS A RESULT OF REQUEST BY ATTORNEYS FOR MRS. INGRAM.

[Mrs. Rosa Lee Ingram] testified in court that the deceased had cursed her following words concerning her horse and livestock being in the white farmer's corn field, and denied that her sons had used anything but the farmer's gun in the beating. Mrs. Ingram has stated further that the white farmer tried to approach her on a matter of "meeting a man."

March 23, 1948
New Trial Hearing Set for Ingrams;
State NAACP Takes Over the Defense

March 26, 1948
Judge Ponders New Trial Pleas for the Ingrams

April 7, 1948
Judge Harper Commutes the Death Penalty to
Life Imprisonment

Counsel for the Ingrams indicated an appeal to the Georgia Supreme Court for a new trial. . . . Under Georgia law, a judge may, when a jury has convicted mainly under circumstantial evidence, order a lesser penalty of life imprisonment.

✧ Repeated appeals for parole were denied. After a world-wide amnesty campaign, the Ingrams were released from prison in 1959.

BLACK WOMEN ATTACK THE LYNCHING SYSTEM

✧ The myth of the black rapist of white women is the twin of the myth of the bad black woman—both designed to apologize for and facilitate the continued exploitation of black men and women. Black women perceived this connection very clearly and were early in the forefront of the fight against lynching. Their approach was to prove the falseness of the accusation, the disproportion between punishment and crime, the absence of legality, and lastly, to point to the different scales of justice meted out to the white and the black rapist. An often neglected aspect of this problem is judicial indifference to sexual crimes committed by black men upon black women.

LET THERE BE JUSTICE

FRANCES ELLEN WATKINS HARPER

A government which has power to tax a man in peace, draft him in war, should have power to defend his life in the hour of peril. A government which can protect and defend its citizens from wrong and outrage and does not is vicious. A government which would do it and cannot is weak; and where human life is insecure through either weakness or viciousness in the administration of law, there must be a lack of justice and where this is wanting, nothing can make up the deficiency.

Frances Ellen Watkins Harper, as cited in Rachel F. Avery, ed., *Transactions of the National Council of Women of the United States assembled in Washington, D.C. February 22, 1891* (Philadelphia: J. B. Lippincott Co., 1891), p. 29.

HOW TO STOP LYNCHING

In his very admirable and searching address delivered in this city, April 16th, Judge Albion W. Tourgee proposed as a remedy to prevent the lynching of colored people at the South, that the county where lynchings occur be compelled by law to pension the wife and children of the murdered man. This, he said would make murder costly and in self defense the local authorities would put a stop to it. At first blush, this is an attractive suggestion. But why not hang the murderers? Why make a distinction between the murderers of white men and the murderers of colored men? If the punishment for murder is hanging why hang the murderer in one case and in the other let the murderer go free and exact of the county a fine? If an eye for an eye and a tooth for a tooth is the rule in one case why should it not be the rule in the other case? No, the truth is this, nothing is to be expected from the South. The colored people must look to the general government. It had a right to their services and lives in time of war. They have a right to its protection certainly in time of peace. It is idle to say that it must leave to state governments the protection of the lives of its citizens. Why not leave to state governments the punishment of counterfeiters? If the United States government can protect money, the property of its citizens against destruction at the hands of the counterfeiter, it can protect the owners of the property against loss of life at the hands of the murderer. It is an astounding proposition that a great nation is powerful enough to stop white moonshiners from making whiskey but is unable to prevent the moonshiners or any one else from murdering its citizens. It can protect corn but cannot protect life. It can prevent the sale of tobacco unless the seller pays a revenue to the government but it cannot protect its citizens at any price. It can go to war, spend millions of dollars and sacrifice thousands of lives to avenge the death of a naturalized white citizen slain by a foreign government on foreign soil, but cannot spend a cent to protect a loyal, native-born colored American murdered without provocation by native or alien in Alabama. Shame on such a government! The administration in power is *particeps criminis* with the murderers. It can stop lynching, and until it does, it has on its hands the innocent blood of its murdered citizens.

"How to Stop Lynching," Editorial, *The Women's Era*, Vol. 1, No. 2 (1894), pp. 8–9.

A RED RECORD

IDA B. WELLS BARNETT

❦ Ida B. Wells Barnett (1862–1931) was born in
Holly Springs, Mississippi, the eldest child of slave parents.
She was educated at Rust College. When she was fifteen
years old, her parents and a brother died in a yellow
fever epidemic. She concealed her age, secured a position
teaching school, and became the support and substitute
parent for her five surviving brothers and sisters. In 1884 she
moved to Memphis, Tennessee, where she worked as a
schoolteacher and continued her education by attending
classes at Fisk University. During this time she began to
write articles for black newspapers under the pen name
"Iola." In retribution for her exposure of the inadequate
school facilities for black children, she was fired from her
job in 1891. She then began a full-time career in journalism
and soon became one of the two owners of the Memphis
Free Speech.

Her hard-hitting columns were marked by race pride and
urgent appeals to black resistance against discrimination.
In 1892, three black men, all personally known to her, were
lynched in Memphis. Ida Wells charged in her paper that
the motives for the lynching were purely economic—all
three men having been successful in business. She also urged
the black population of Memphis to emigrate to the West.

This case became a turning point in her life. While she
was on a business trip in the East, the offices of her paper
were destroyed and her life was threatened if she were to
return. She then began her one-woman crusade against
lynching—lecturing, writing and organizing. Her approach
was hard-hitting: she gathered the facts, using the services of
detectives, Pinkerton agents or informants, then exposed
them to all who would hear, laying bare the politics and
economics of lynching. Her contention was that lynching

was an integral part of the system of racial oppression, and that the motives for lynching usually had little to do with crime, but were either economic or political. She dared to bring out into the open what was the most taboo subject of all in Victorian America—the habitual sexual abuse of black women by white men and the myth that the only sexual contact between white women and black men must be based on rape.

Ida Wells toured Great Britain in 1893 and again in 1894. Her public speeches aroused British liberals against American lynching and led to the formation of a British Anti-Lynching Society. Her agitation in Britain aroused a great deal of displeasure and unfavorable comment in the American press and engendered a public controversy between Ida B. Wells and Frances Willard, the national President of the Women's Christian Temperance Union. Miss Willard was visiting in Britain at the same time as Miss Wells and the latter was repeatedly asked whether white reformers such as Miss Willard spoke out against lynchings. Miss Wells truthfully stated that Miss Willard not only had not spoken out against lynchings, but had returned from a Southern tour as an apologist of the white Southern attitude on the race question, an action for which the Negro press had universally condemned her. Stung by this charge, Miss Willard gave a published interview, disputing these facts. In the course of the interview she repeated the very apologetic statements for which Miss Wells had chided her. The incident is significant because Frances Willard was a lifelong abolitionist, suffragist and ardent reformer and had enormous influence over hundreds of thousands of women. She was, as Ida Wells acidly commented, "no better or worse than the great bulk of white Americans on the Negro question." Still, possibly as the result of this public debate, Frances Willard's name appeared as one of the subscribers to the British Anti-Lynching Society.

On her return to America, Ida B. Wells continued her solitary campaign against lynchings by pamphleteering and

lecturing on the subject. She later became chairman of the
Anti-Lynching Bureau of the National Afro-American
Council. The work of black club women and later the
NAACP on this issue is a direct outgrowth of Ida B. Wells'
persistent muckraking journalism, exposés, lectures and
organization.

She was also a very important force in the growth of the
women's club movement. She helped to organize the first
black women's club in Chicago, which took her name and
over which she presided. She kept in close touch with the
leading club women in the country. In 1895, she married
Ferdinand Lee Barnett, a prominent attorney in Chicago,
and, although announcing her "retirement," managed and
edited The Conservator, a newspaper her husband had
founded. "My duties as editor, as president of the Ida B.
Wells Woman's Club, and as speaker in many white
women's clubs in and around Chicago kept me pretty busy.
But I was not too busy to find time to give birth to a male
child the following March 25, 1896."* Four months later
she attended the first convention of the National Association
of Colored Women, bringing along her baby boy and a
nurse. A few months later she undertook a speaking tour all
over the state on behalf of the Republican Party, again
taking her nursing baby along.

In 1908, she organized the Negro Fellowship League
and became its President. The organization maintained a
settlement house in the slums and was instrumental in
organizing militant action around various local racial issues.
It was distinguished by its close ties to the poor and working-
class community which it served. Mrs. Barnett also was a
founding member of the NAACP, but later withdrew from
activity in the organization because she advocated more
militantly race-conscious leadership. All her life she was
critical of and in conflict with Negro leaders who accom-

* Alfreda M. Duster, ed., Crusade for Justice; The Autobiography of
Ida B. Wells (Chicago and London: University of Chicago Press, 1970),
p. 243.

modated themselves to whites, although at various times
in her career she worked well with some whites, such as
Jane Addams and Municipal Court Judge Harry Olsen. The
latter appointed her Adult Probation Officer, the first woman
in Chicago to hold this job.

Ida Wells Barnett was active in politics and always saw
woman suffrage as an instrument for achieving the emancipation of black people. She founded the first black women's
political club, the Alpha Suffrage Club of Chicago which
mobilized the women's vote in the 1914 mayoralty elections. During the years when she devoted most of her time
to raising her four children, she played a leading role in
mobilizing protest action in the wake of the post–World
War I lynchings and race riots. On several occasions she
was the first and only Black on the scene right after the
violence and on fact-finding commissions. Her persistent
militancy and courage gave her a position of undisputed
leadership in her own community and prominence on a
national level.

In addition to her journalistic work and anti-lynching
pamphlets, Ida B. Wells wrote an autobiography

Not all or nearly all of the murders done by white men,
during the past thirty years in the South, have come to light,
but the statistics as gathered and preserved by white men, and
which have not been questioned, show that during these
years more than ten thousand Negroes have been killed in
cold blood, without the formality of judicial trial and legal
execution. And yet, as evidence of the absolute impunity
with which the white man dares to kill a Negro, the same
record shows that during all these years, and for all these
murders only three white men have been tried, convicted,
and executed. As no white man has been lynched for the
murder of colored people, these three executions are the only
instances of the death penalty being visited upon white men
for murdering Negroes.

Naturally enough the commission of these crimes began to tell upon the public conscience, and the Southern white man, as a tribute to the nineteenth century civilization, was in a manner compelled to give excuses for his barbarism. His excuses have adapted themselves to the emergency, and are aptly outlined by that greatest of all Negroes, Frederick Douglass, in a article of recent date, in which he shows that there have been three distinct eras of Southern barbarism, to account for which three distinct excuses have been made.

The first excuse given to the civilized world for the murder of unoffending Negroes was the necessity of the white man to repress and stamp out alleged "race riots." For years immediately succeeding the war there was an appalling slaughter of colored people, and the wires usually conveyed to northern people and the world the intelligence, first, that an insurrection was being planned by Negroes, which, a few hours later, would prove to have been vigorously resisted by white men, and controlled with a resulting loss of several killed and wounded. It was always a remarkable feature in these insurrections and riots that only Negroes were killed during the rioting, and that all the white men escaped unharmed.

From 1865 to 1872, hundreds of colored men and women were mercilessly murdered and the almost invariable reason assigned was that they met their death by being alleged participants in an insurrection or riot. But this story at last wore itself out. No insurrection ever materialized; no Negro rioter was ever apprehended and proven guilty, and no dynamite ever recorded the black man's protest against oppression and wrong. . . .

Then came the second excuse, which had its birth during the turbulent times of reconstruction. By an amendment to the Constitution the Negro was given the right of franchise, and, theoretically at least, his ballot became his invaluable emblem of citizenship. . . . The southern white man would not consider that the Negro had any right which a white man was bound to respect, and the idea of a republican form of government in the southern states grew into general contempt. It was maintained that "This is a white man's government," and regardless of numbers white men should rule. "No Negro domination" became the new legend on the sanguinary banner of the sunny South, and under it rode the Ku Klux Klan, the Regulators, and the lawless mobs, which for any cause chose to murder one man or a dozen as suited their purpose best. It was a long, gory campaign. . . .

The government which had made the Negro a citizen found itself unable to protect him. It gave him the right to vote, but denied him the protection which should have maintained that right. Scourged from his home; hunted through the swamps; hung by midnight raiders, and openly murdered in the light of day, the Negro clung to his right of franchise with a heroism which would have wrung admiration from the hearts of savages. He believed that in the small white ballot there·was a subtle something which stood for manhood as well as citizenship, and thousands of brave black men went to their graves, exemplifying the one by dying for the other.

The white man's victory soon became complete by fraud, violence, intimidation and murder. The franchise vouchsafed to the Negro grew to be a "barren ideality," and regardless of numbers, the colored people found themselves voiceless in the councils of those whose duty it was to rule. . . . With the Southern governments all subverted and the Negro actually eliminated from all participation in state and national elections, there could be no longer an excuse for killing Negroes to prevent "Negro Domination."

Brutality still continued; Negroes were whipped, scourged, exiled, shot and hung whenever and wherever it pleased the white man so to treat them, and as the civilized world with increasing persistency held the white people of the South to account for its outlawry, the murderers invented the third excuse—that Negroes had to be killed to avenge their assaults upon women. . . .

Humanity abhors the assailant of womanhood, and this charge upon the Negro at once placed him beyond the pale of human sympathy. . . .

If the Southern people in defense of their lawlessness,

would tell the truth and admit that colored men and women are lynched for almost any offense, from murder to a misdemeanor, there would not now be the necessity for this defense. But when they intentionally, maliciously and constantly belie the record and bolster up these falsehoods by the words of legislators, preachers, governors and bishops, then the Negro must give to the world his side of the awful story.

A word as to the charge itself. In considering the third reason assigned by the Southern white people for the butchery of blacks, the question must be asked, what the white man means when he charges the black man with rape. Does he mean the crime which the statutes of the states describe as such? Not by any means. With the Southern white man, any mesalliance existing between a white woman and a colored man is a sufficient foundation for the charge of rape. The Southern white man says that it is impossible for a voluntary alliance to exist between a white woman and a colored man, and therefore, the fact of an alliance is a proof of force. In numerous instances where colored men have been lynched on the charge of rape, it was positively known at the time of lynching, and indisputably proven after the victim's death, that the relationship sustained between the man and the woman was voluntary and clandestine, and that in no court of law could even the charge of assault have been successfully maintained.

It was for the assertion of this fact, in the defense of her own race, that the writer hereof became an exile; her property destroyed and her return to her home forbidden under penalty of death, for writing the following editorial which was printed in her paper, the *Free Speech*, in Memphis, Tenn., May 21, 1892:

"Eight Negroes lynched since last issue of the *Free Speech* one at Little Rock, Ark., last Saturday morning where the citizens broke (?) into the penitentiary and got their man; three near Anniston, Ala., one near New Orleans; and three at Clarksville, Ga., the last three for killing a white man, and five on the same old racket—the new alarm about raping white women. The same programme of hanging, then shooting bullets into the lifeless bodies was carried out to the letter. Nobody in this section of the country believes the old threadbare lie that Negro men rape white women. If Southern white men are not careful, they will over-reach themselves and public sentiment will have a reaction; a conclusion will then be reached which will be very damaging to the moral reputation of their women."

But threats cannot suppress the truth, and while the Negro suffers the soul deformity, resultant from two and a half centuries of slavery, he is no more guilty of this vilest of all vile charges than the white man who would blacken his name.

During all the years of slavery, no such charge was ever made, not even during the dark days of the rebellion. . . . While the master was away fighting to forge the fetters upon the slave, he left his wife and children with no protectors save the Negroes themselves . . .

Likewise during the period of alleged "insurrection," and alarming "race riots," it never occurred to the white man, that his wife and children were in danger of assault. Nor in the Reconstruction era, when the hue and cry was against "Negro Domination," was there ever a thought that the domination would ever contaminate a fireside or strike to death the virtue of womanhood. . . .

It is not the purpose of this defense to say one word against the white women of the South. Such need not be said, but it is their misfortune that the . . . white men of that section . . . to justify their own barbarism . . . assume a chivalry which they do not possess. True chivalry respects all womanhood, and no one who reads the record, as it is written in the faces of the million mulattoes in the South, will for a minute conceive that the southern white man had a very chivalrous regard for the honor due the women of his race or respect for the womanhood which circumstances placed in his power. . . . Virtue knows no color line, and the chivalry which depends upon complexion of skin and texture of hair can command no honest respect.

When emancipation came to the Negroes . . . from every nook and corner of the North, brave young white women . . . left their cultured homes, their happy associations and their lives of ease, and with heroic determination went to the South to carry light and truth to the benighted blacks. . . . They became social outlaws in the South. The peculiar sensitiveness of the southern white men for women, never shed its protecting influence about them. No friendly word from their own race cheered them in their work; no hospitable doors gave them the companionship like that from which they had come. No chivalrous white man doffed his hat in honor or respect. They were "Nigger teachers"— unpardonable offenders in the social ethics of the South, and were insulted, persecuted and ostracised, not by Negroes, but by the white manhood which boasts of its chivalry toward women.

And yet these northern women worked on, year after year. . . . Threading their way through dense forests, working in schoolhouse, in the cabin and in the church, thrown at all times and in all places among the unfortunate and lowly Negroes, whom they had come to find and to serve, these northern women, thousands and thousands of them, have spent more than a quarter of a century in giving to the colored people their splendid lessons for home and heart and soul. Without protection, save that which innocence gives to every good woman, they went about their work, fearing no assault and suffering none. Their chivalrous protectors were hundreds of miles away in their northern homes, and yet they never feared any "great dark faced mobs." . . . They never complained of assaults, and no mob was ever called into existence to avenge crimes against them. Before the world adjudges the Negro a moral monster, a vicious assailant of womanhood and a menace to the sacred precincts of home, the colored people ask the consideration of the silent record of gratitude, respect, protection and devotion of the millions of the race in the South, to the thousands of northern white women who have served as teachers and missionaries since the war. . . .

These pages are written in no spirit of vindictiveness. . . . We plead not for the colored people alone, but for all victims of the terrible injustice which puts men and women to death without form of law. During the year 1894, there were 132 persons executed in the United States by due form of law, while in the same year, 197 persons were put to death by mobs who gave the victims no opportunity to make a lawful defense. No comment need be made upon a condition of public sentiment responsible for such alarming results.

Ida Wells Barnett, *A Red Record* (Chicago: Donohue & Henneberry, 1895), pp. 8–15.

LYNCHING FROM A NEGRO'S POINT OF VIEW

MARY CHURCH TERRELL

❦ *In the January 1904 issue of the North American Review, Thomas Nelson Page wrote an article entitled "The Lynching of Negroes—Its Cause and Its Prevention." He cited, as the cause of the increasing number of lynchings, increases in assault and rape of white women by Negroes, delay in meting out justice, and a desire to match the ferocity of attacks with ferocity of punishment. The increase in assaults was due to "racial antagonism and to the talk of social equality, from which it first sprang, that inflames the ignorant negro. . . . The negro does not generally believe in the virtue of women. It is beyond his experience . . . his passion, always his controlling force, is now, since the new teaching, for the white woman."*

How to stop lynching? The author considered emasculation a possibility. "The crime of lynching is not likely to cease until the crime of ravishing and murdering women and children is less frequent than it has been of late. And this crime, which is well-nigh wholly confined to the negro race, will not greatly diminish until the negroes themselves take it in hand and stamp it out."

This article was answered, at her request, by Mary Church Terrell.

Mary Church Terrell (1863–1954) was one of the few women of her race to win recognition and honors in the white world as well as the black during her lifetime. Raised in Tennessee, she enjoyed a good education and in 1884 graduated at the head of her class from Oberlin College. She taught at Wilberforce University and at the High School for Colored Youth in Washington, D.C., and studied for two years in European schools. In 1891, she married Robert H. Terrell, who later became a municipal judge in Washington, D.C. Mrs. Terrell was the first black woman appointed to the capital's Board of Education, on which she served for eleven years.

Mary Church Terrell was a leading club woman and suffragist. From 1896 to 1901 she was the first president of the National Association of Colored Women. A close friend of Susan B. Anthony and Jane Addams, she was a member of the National American Suffrage Association. She represented black women at international congresses in Berlin, Zurich and London. She was a charter member of the NAACP, a lecturer, writer and activist. Her lifelong resistance to discrimination was genteel in form by today's standards, but persistent and courageous. At the age of eighty-three, she rejoined the American Association of University Women, having allowed her earlier membership to lapse in 1900, in order to test the organization's more recent exclusion policy. Her action became the rallying point in the effort to end discrimination in the Washington branch and ended with the national AAUW establishing an "education only" qualification for membership and ousting the Washington chapter. That same year, the now eighty-five-year-old lady gave spirited leadership to a campaign to end discrimination in the capital's restaurants. She headed negotiating teams, walked on picket lines, addressed hundreds of meetings and was one of three plaintiffs in an important civil rights test case which ended with a Supreme Court decision upholding the right of all races to equal eating accommodations in Washington, D.C. Her many honors included honorary degrees and a listing as one of the hundred most famous alumni of Oberlin College.

Before 1904 was three months old, thirty-one negroes had been lynched. Of this number, fifteen were murdered within one week in Arkansas, and one was shot to death in Springfield, Ohio, by a mob composed of men who did not take the trouble to wear masks. Hanging, shooting and burning black men, women and children in the United States have become so common that such occurrences create but little sensation and evoke but slight comment now. . . . In the discussion of this subject, four mistakes are commonly made.

In the first place, it is a great mistake to suppose that rape is the real cause of lynching in the South. Beginning with the Ku Klux Klan the negro has been constantly subjected to some form of organized violence ever since he became free. It is easy to prove that rape is simply the pretext and not the cause of lynching. Statistics show that, out of every 100 negroes who are lynched, from 75–85 are not even accused of this crime, and many who are accused of it are innocent. . . .

In the second place, it is a mistake to suppose that the negro's desire for social equality sustains any relation whatsoever to the crime of rape. . . . It is safe to assert that, among the negroes who have been guilty of ravishing white women, not one had been taught that he was the equal of white people or had ever heard of social equality. . . . Negroes who have been educated in Northern institutions of learning with white men and women, and who for that reason might have learned the meaning of social equality and have acquired a taste for the same, neither assault white women nor commit other crimes, as a rule. . . . Strange as it may appear, illiterate negroes, who are the only ones contributing largely to the criminal class, are coddled and caressed by the South. To the educated, cultivated members of the race, they are held up as bright and shining examples of what a really good negro should be. The dictionary is searched in vain by Southern gentlemen and gentlewomen for words sufficiently ornate and strong to express their admiration for a dear old "mammy" or a faithful old "uncle," who can neither read nor write, and who assure their white friends they would not if they could.

On the other hand, no language is sufficiently caustic, bitter and severe, to express the disgust, hatred and scorn which Southern gentlemen feel for what is called the "New Issue," which, being interpreted, means negroes who aspire to knowledge and culture, and who have acquired a taste for the highest and best things in life. At the door of this "New Issue," the sins and shortcomings of the whole race are laid. This "New Issue" is beyond hope of redemption, we are told, because somebody, nobody knows who, has taught it to believe in social equality, something, nobody knows what. The alleged fear of social equality has always been used by the South to explain its unchristian treatment of the negro and to excuse its many crimes. . . . In the North, which is the only section that accords the negro the scrap of social equality enjoyed by him in the United States, he is rarely accused of rape. The only form of social equality ever attempted between the two races, and practised to any considerable extent, is that which was originated by the white masters of slave women, and which has been perpetuated by them and their descendants even unto the present day. . . . There is no more connection between social equality and lynching to-day than there was between social equality and slavery before the war, or than there is between social equality and the convict-lease system, or any other form of oppression to which the negro has uniformly been subjected in the South.

The third error on the subject of lynching consists of the widely circulated statement that the moral sensibilities of the best negroes in the United States are so stunted and dull, and the standard of morality among even the leaders of the race is so low, that they do not appreciate the enormity and heinousness of rape. . . . Only those who are densely ignorant of the standards and sentiments of the best negroes, or who wish wilfully [sic] to misrepresent and maliciously slander a race already resting under burdens greater than it can bear, would accuse its thousands of reputable men and women of sympathizing with rapists, either black or white, or of condoning their crime. . . .

What, then, is the cause of lynching? At the last analysis, it will be discovered that there are just two causes of lynching. In the first place, it is due to race hatred, the hatred of a stronger people toward a weaker who were once held as slaves. In the second place, it is due to the lawlessness so prevalent in the section where nine-tenths of the lynchings occur. . . .

Lynching is the aftermath of slavery. The white men who shoot negroes to death and flay them alive, and the white women who apply flaming torches to their oil-soaked bodies today, are the sons and daughters of women who had but little, if any, compassion on the race when it was enslaved. The men who lynch negroes to-day are, as a rule, the children of women who sat by their firesides happy and proud in the possession and affection of their own children, while they looked with unpitying eye and adamantine heart upon the anguish of slave mothers whose children had been sold away, when not overtaken by a sadder fate. . . . It is impossible to comprehend the cause of the ferocity and barbarity which attend the average lynching-bee without taking into account the brutalizing effect of slavery upon the people of the section where most of the lynchings occur. . . . It is too much to expect, perhaps, that the children of women who for generations looked upon the hardships and the degradation of their sisters of a darker hue with few if any protests, should have mercy and compassion upon the children of that oppressed race now. But what a tremendous influence for law and order, and what a mighty foe to mob violence Southern white women might be, if they would arise in the purity and power of their womanhood to implore their fathers, husbands and sons no longer to stain their hands with the black man's blood! . . .

Whenever Southern white people discuss lynching, they are prone to slander the whole negro race. Not long ago, a Southern writer of great repute declared without qualification or reservation that "the crime of rape is well-nigh wholly confined to the negro race," and insisted that "negroes furnish most of the ravishers." These assertions are as unjust to the negro as they are unfounded in fact. According to statistics recently published, only one colored male in 100,000 over five years of age was accused of assault upon a white woman in the South in 1902, whereas one male out of every 20,000 over five years of age was charged with rape in Chicago during the same year. If these figures prove anything at all, they show that the men and boys in Chicago are many times more addicted to rape than are the negroes in the South. . . .

But even if the negro's morals were as loose and as lax as some claim them to be, and if his belief in the virtue of women were as slight as we are told, the South has nobody to blame but itself. . . . Men do not gather grapes of thorns nor figs of thistles. Throughout their entire period of bondage colored women were debauched by their masters. From the day they were liberated to the present time, prepossessing young colored girls have been considered the rightful prey of white gentlemen in the South, and they have been protected neither by public sentiment nor by law. In the South, the negro's home is not considered sacred by the superior race. White men are neither punished for invading it, nor lynched for violating colored women and girls. . . .

How can lynching be extirpated in the United States? . . . Lynching can never be suppressed in the South, until the masses of ignorant white people in that section are educated and lifted to a higher moral plane. . . . Lynching cannot be suppressed in the South, until all classes of white people who dwell there . . . respect the rights of other human beings, no matter what may be the color of their skin . . . and learn a holy reverence for the law. . . .

Until there is a renaissance of popular belief in the principles of liberty and equality upon which this government was founded, lynching, the Convict Lease System, the Disfranchisement Acts, the Jim Crow Car Laws, unjust discriminations in the professions and trades and similar atrocities will continue to dishearten and degrade the negro, and stain the fair name of the United States. For there can be no doubt that the greatest obstacle in the way of extirpating lynching is the general attitude of the public mind toward this unspeakable crime. The whole country seems tired of hearing about the black man's woes. The wrongs of the Irish, of the Armenians, of the Roumanian and Russian Jews, of the exiles of Russia and of every other oppressed people upon the face of the globe, can arouse the sympathy and fire the indignation of the American public, while they seem to be all but indifferent to the murderous assaults upon the negroes in the South.

Mary Church Terrell, "Lynching from a Negro's Point of View,"
North American Review, Vol. 178, No. 571 (June 1904),
pp. 853–868.

THE ANTI-LYNCHING CRUSADERS

❦ *The public activities of black women against lynching dated back to 1895 and Ida Wells Barnett's one-woman crusade. The issue was of major concern to the national club movement of women and never disappeared from the agenda of their annual conventions although the approach was frequently tangential—a defense of black womanhood and the black home, instead of the exposé*

tactics Mrs. Barnett had favored. There were local and
regional protest meetings in response to particular outrages,
but the major attack on lynchings became a national issue
only with the formation of the National Association for the
Advancement of Colored People (NAACP) in 1910. This
national organization, equipped with funds and legal talent,
responded swiftly to every incident and coordinated a
national campaign against lynch terror. It publicized the facts
and issued annual statistics on lynching, lobbied for passage
of national anti-lynching legislation and, in a variety of
ways, focused the spotlight of publicity on this disgrace of
a nation. The Anti-Lynching Crusaders was formed in 1922
to rally women to the support of this NAACP campaign.
The following document should be read with the understanding that anti-lynching activities of Blacks had then
been going on for nearly thirty years and would continue
with greater intensity for another four and a half decades.

It was this issue above all which prompted black and white
women to seek interracial cooperation (see pp. 458–477),
with black women taking the leadership, and coaxing,
prodding and shaming white women into action. Only
with the establishment of the Association of Southern
Women for the Prevention of Lynching did white women
assume responsibility for combatting this particular form
of race hatred on their own.

The Executive Committee of the Anti-lynching Crusaders
held their third meeting in New York, with 5 states represented. The chairman, Mrs. M. B. Talbert, reported that the
movement was splendidly started, with over 700 key women
in 25 states hard at work. Ultimate success seemed assured.

The committee made the following statement in answer
to many inquiries:

a. The movement owes its origin to Mrs. Helen Curtis, who
was inspired by a public statement of Congressman L. C.
Dyer, made at the Annual Conference of the N.A.A.C.P. in

Newark, June, 1922, in which he said: "If 1,000,000 people were united in the demand from the Senate that the Dyer Bill be passed, there would be no question of its passage."

A small committee met immediately and organized a campaign.

b. The committee does not believe in duplicating organizations. We have enough and more organizations already for all the work there is to do. What we need is concentrated effort for specific objects. The committee, therefore, is organized to raise money for one object and then to disband.

c. The one object of the Anti-lynching Crusaders is to stop lynching and mob violence. There is no division of opinion on the imperative need of this among decent people, black and white.

d. The one clear and practical program so far outlined for the accomplishment of this end is that of the N.A.A.C.P., viz., to pass the Dyer Bill and enforce it. . . . .

e. The Anti-lynching Crusaders have, therefore, determined to raise 1,000,000 dollars, or as much thereof as is possible, by January 1st, and to turn this sum over to the Anti-lynching fund of the N.A.A.C.P. in trust to be used to pass and enforces the Dyer Anti-lynching Bill and to put down mob violence.

f. Some have doubted if such a sum is necessary. It is, and we have asked the executive office of the N.A.A.C.P. to outline roughly how it could be effectively and economically expanded. The statement follows:

An Anti-lynching program demands:

1. Publicity. The negro has never given his cause proper publicity. We propose, if we can obtain the funds, a campaign of newspaper publicity patterned after the Red Cross and Child Welfare campaigns. A campaign [to] . . . be repeated . . . until not a single person who reads the daily papers shall be ignorant of the fact that we are the only country that burns human beings at the stake, that 3,436 people have been lynched from 1888 to January 1, 1922, and that rape is not the primary cause of lynching. Such a campaign could

be started for $10,000 and would, to be complete, cost $1,000,000.

2. Pressure upon Congress. The country must be aroused by letters, telegrams and articles to pour in upon the Senate a stream of requests for immediate action. Such a campaign throughout the United States cannot be completely inaugurated for less than $25,000.

3. Pressure upon State Legislatures. Our efforts to strengthen state laws must not for a moment lag. . . . If the Dyer Bill fails of passage before March 1, the present bill must be reintroduced in the next Congress. If the Dyer Anti-lynching Bill is passed, the campaign against lynching, mob violence and legal defense has just begun, and we must immediately be ready for two things.

4. Investigation of every case of lynching and mob violence which occurs. . . . This will mean the use of detective agencies, local investigators, documentary research, etc. It is safe to say that in the next few years from $50,000 to $250,000 could be wisely and economically spent on such investigations.

5. Legal processes. Finally, there are actual law cases. . . . From $100,000 to $250,000 is a small estimate of the cost of preparing such cases. . . .

g. The Executive Committee of the Anti-lynching Crusaders accepts this program and will seek earnestly to raise the necessary funds. In the raising of these funds, no salaries are being paid and no commissions of any sort. The work of the Crusaders, both officers and others, is entirely voluntary and uncompensated in any way. . . .

> Mrs. Grace Nail Johnson
> Mrs. Alice Dunbar Nelson
> Mrs. William Alexander
> PUBLICITY COMMITTEE
> Mrs. Mary B. Talbert,
> NATIONAL DIRECTOR

❦ *The item above was followed by another endorsement.*

What will Mary B. Talbert do next? What next will the colored American woman do under her leadership?

An organization has been effected by colored women to get ONE MILLION WOMEN, of all kinds and colors, united by December 1, 1922, against lynching. These women are to be asked to put down at least one dollar each as a fighting fund against lynching.

Look out, Mr. Lyncher!

This class of women generally get what they go after.

The organization is to cover the whole United States. Mrs. Mary B. Talbert, 521 Michigan Avenue, Buffalo, N.Y., is the National Director of the movement. Miss Mary E. Jackson, of Providence, R.I., is National Organizer. Each State is to have its director, and each town or locality its "key women."

The women will begin with prayer at a sunrise, and end with prayer at a sunset—in between they will do a much more sweaty work than praying.

And this organization is not creating any positions or emoluments for anybody. It is to disband as soon as its campaign is over—and Mrs. Talbert is serving for NOTHING—absolutely nothing but to get the job done. And each State Director is to be paid in the same kind of thankless coin—the satisfaction of a noble deed well done.

Of course, there should not be a colored American woman from the washpot to the university who will not want to "count one" in this crusade. And every white woman, from Mrs. Woodrow Wilson and Mrs. Warren G. Harding down to those who watch Negroes burn in Texas, can afford to join it. They will all be publicly and many of them privately asked to be honored in this effort of womankind.

This idea originated with a group of women in New York. It is the greatest effort of Negro womanhood in a generation, and it if succeeds even by one-tenth, it will be also the greatest achievement.

WILLIAM PICKENS,
New York City.

Woman's Voice, Vol. 4, No. 3 (January 1923).

CHAPTER FOUR

MAKING
A
LIVING

There are two kinds of females in this country—colored women and white ladies. Colored women are maids, cooks, taxi drivers, crossing guards, schoolteachers, welfare recipients, bar maids and the only time they become ladies is when they are cleaning ladies.

> Louise D. Stone, "What It's
> Like to Be a Colored Woman,"
> **Washington Post**, November 13, 1966

MAKING A LIVING

❦ It has been customary to compare the economic status and educational attainments of black women with those of black men. A more useful comparison is that between white women and black women. Black women share with all women the employment discrimination patterns prevalent in our society. That is, more of them are in unskilled and service jobs than are men, they get paid less, work under worse conditions, advance less rapidly and are more likely to be poor. They are disproportionately few in professional and managerial positions.

The United States Department of Commerce census reported there were 6,273,000 black women eighteen years of age and over in this country in 1966. Of these 50 per cent were working, as against 39 per cent of white women of the same age group. Their unemployment rate was 9.3 per cent, as against 5 per cent of white women. Among women with children under eighteen years of age, 46 per cent of the nonwhite (34 per cent of the white) were in the labor force. In 1965, the median yearly earnings of nonwhite women who worked full-time the year round ($2,642) was 66 per cent of that of white women ($3,744).* This represents an improvement over 1939, when the median yearly earnings was only 38 per cent of that of white women. In other words: a greater percentage of black women than white women work after they are married and after they have children; they work more years of their lives than do white women; their earnings are lower, their unemployment rate greater.

---

* Median means half above and half below this figure. Census data traditionally refer to "whites" and "nonwhites." The latter category includes all racial groups but whites. Since Blacks are by far the largest group among these, "nonwhite" percentages are considered representative for Blacks. All figures based on: U.S. Department of Labor, Wage and Labor Standards Administration, and Women's Bureau, *Negro Women . . . in the Population and in the Labor Force* (Washington, D.C.: Government Printing Office, 1967).

Not surprisingly, black women are to be found in greatest numbers in the unskilled and semiskilled occupations. In 1966, 75.5 per cent of all black women workers were employed in service jobs, farm and factory work (for white women the figure was 37.9 per cent). Only 8.4 per cent of all black women were in professional occupations (13.7 per cent white women) and 11.8 per cent (34.1 per cent white women) were saleswomen.

This last set of figures is most important. The absence of opportunities for black women in the middle-range jobs, especially in sales and clerical work, make it necessary for black families to develop different employment expectations and educational goals than do white families. Until very recently—and for a majority of Blacks to this day—educational achievement for black men did not mean the opening up of economic opportunities. But it did mean that for black girls. Since black families could expect that their girls would have to work all or most of their lives and since there were few semiskilled or middle-range jobs available to them, the only hope for a girl to escape the unskilled, service job trap was in getting a professional education. This explains the incredible sacrifices made by generations of black families to give their daughters the best educational opportunity the family could afford. E. Wilbur Bock, in a perceptive article, has called this the "farmer's daughter effect," and has pointed out a parallel to the nineteenth-century white farmers who let their daughters rather than their sons stay in school through high school with the result that the daughters went into schoolteaching and were better equipped for upward mobility when migration from farm to urban areas occurred.* The farmers' sons moved into manual labor, the daughters into low-paying white-collar work. Without taking the parallel too far, one can observe that this represented in both cases a useful adaptation

* E. Wilbur Bock, "Farmer's Daughter Effect: The Case of the Negro Female Professionals," *Phylon*, Vol. 30, No. 1 (Spring 1969), pp. 17–26.

to economic realities and not a racially or culturally determined decision. Proof that we are here dealing with
functional adaptations to discriminatory patterns in the
mainstream culture can be found in the changing educational
levels of Blacks.

There has been a steady improvement in educational level
attained for the entire black population, with dramatic
improvement evident in the past twenty years. The median
years of school completed for nonwhite women and men
25–29 years of age in April 1940 were 7.5 years and 6.5 years
respectively. In March 1967, the figures were 12.1 years
(women) and 12.2 years (men). These figures and others
reveal that up until the 1950's, when job opportunities
for black men were severely restricted, black families tended
to keep their daughters in school somewhat longer than their
sons, possibly in the hope of equipping them for schoolteaching or another professional job. As educational opportunities for black men and increasing job opportunities
in the middle-range jobs for black women opened up, the
educational gap between black girls and boys closed. The
1967 figures show that black boys now stay in school somewhat longer than black girls. On the upper end of the
educational scale there are similar trends. In 1952, 2 per cent
of nonwhite men were college graduates (3 per cent of
nonwhite women). By 1967, the proportion changed to
5 per cent for both sexes. Thus, black boys made relatively
greater educational gains in the past two decades than did
black girls. Both, however, still lag far behind whites.

To summarize the implications of the statistical data:
Black women share in the economic discrimination patterns
based on sex which prevail in our society. They share in
race discrimination patterns imposed on all Blacks. But race
discrimination is enforced more strictly than sex discrimination. Black women rank lowest in any measurement of
economic and social status when compared with Blacks and
with white men and women. Only when it comes to educational attainment levels do black women enjoy a seeming

"advantage." Figures for 1966 for median years of school completed read as follows:

	White men	White women	Black men	Black women
Median years of school completed	12.0	12.2	9.4	10.1
4-year college completed	7.3	5.4	2.2	2.3

Thus it appears that black women stay in school somewhat longer than black men and that all whites stay in school longer than all Blacks. It also appears that white women drop off sharply in college attendance (i.e., more white men finish college than do white women), while black women maintain a slight lead in college attendance when compared to black men.

There is a "sex loophole" in race discrimination patterns. When employment and educational opportunities are opened up for Blacks, white society tends to favor awarding these opportunities to black women rather than to black men. This leads to a certain deviance from male-dominance patterns which United States society regards as "normal." Black men, being deprived by white society of most of the benefits enjoyed by dominant white men, are also deprived of the gap in status opportunity and economic advantage over black women, which white men take for granted in regard to white women.

Median years of school attendance figures do not, however, tell the full story. One has only to compare with the above figures the median yearly earnings of men and women workers to realize that school attendance and earning curves are positively correlated only in the case of white men.

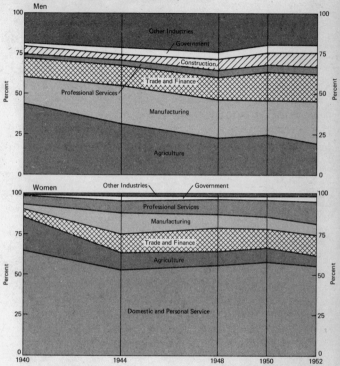

Percent Distribution of Negro Men and Women Workers Among Major Industries
Selected Years, 1940-1952

Other Industries Include for-
Men   Mining, Transportation, Communication and Public Utilities, and Domestic and Personal Service.
Women   Mining, Construction, and Transportation, Communication and Public Utilities.

United States Department of Labor
Bureau of Labor Statistics

Source: U.S. Bureau of the Census.

Percent of Negro and White Men and Women in the Labor Force, by Age, 1951

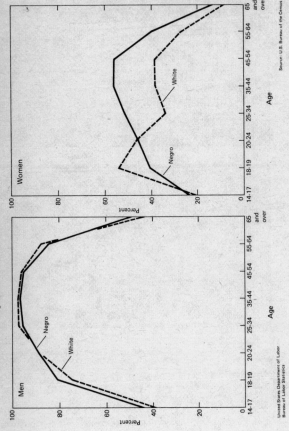

United States Department of Labor
Bureau of Labor Statistics

Source: U.S. Bureau of the Census

Median Earnings 1965 (in 1960 $)

White men	White women	Black men	Black women
6,289	3,744	4,012	2,642*

It is obvious that all women need more education to get the better-paying jobs than do men or, more likely, that they get less pay for the same work. Similarly, black women need more education to get the middle-range jobs than do white women and/or they get less pay for the same work. It is also well to remember that 75.5 per cent of all black working women are in the unskilled-work categories. Whatever slight "advantage" or "greater visibility" might accrue to the black professional woman, it only affects a minute segment of black womanhood.

Many people believe that black women have an "advantage" over black men in that they can more readily secure employment, even if only at the worst, menial jobs. Unemployment statistics disprove this commonly held belief. The unemployment rates for 1969 were.†

White men	1.9%
Black men	3.7%
White women	3.4%
Black women	6.0%

Unemployment rates usually err on the low side, in that many people who are actually unemployed have given up looking for work and are therefore not counted. It must be remembered that these are national figures. Male black unemployment is considerably higher in large cities, but this is probably offset by rural and small-town figures.

* Note that the figures on this page are for *all* men and women while median years of school attendance figures on page 222 are for the 25–29 years of age group only. Using the latter age group is more revealing of recent trends.

† U.S. Department of Labor (Bureau of Labor Statistics) and U.S. Department of Commerce (Bureau of the Census), *The Social and Economic Status of Negroes in the United States,* 1969 (Washington, D.C., Government Printing Office, 1970), p. 30.

However one interprets the causal factors, one thing is
clear: the vast majority of black women are at the bottom
of the earning-prestige-opportunity-status ladder in United
States society.

DOING DOMESTIC WORK

❦ There is always domestic work. The pattern has
changed very little since the days of slavery. Domestic service
is the occupation in which the largest number of American
women work. Of the nation's 2,275,000 domestic workers,
1,017,000 are black women. While 5.6 per cent of all employed white women are in domestic work, 30.3 per cent
of all black women are so employed.* Their hours are longer
than those of any other group of workers, their wages low,
their working conditions generally poor. As late as 1935, black
women did housework and laundry for $3 a week, and
washerwomen did a week's wash for 75¢. The substandard
wages and employment conditions of domestic workers
reflect not only the general vulnerability of female labor and
of workers in the service industries to exploitative practices,
but are a specific result of race prejudice. At various periods
in history when white immigrant labor was available, black
women were crowded out of domestic work or, at the least,
displaced from the better-paying servants' jobs. Enactment
of minimum wage legislation has had a similar effect, since
employers, when forced to pay more than substandard wages,
preferred to hire white workers. In order to compete at all,
black women had to underbid available white workers, thus,
in effect, lowering standards for all. Because of the marginal

* Figures based on 1960 census.

status of black men in the labor force due to race prejudice and outright discrimination, black women had to take the only jobs available to them, no matter how poor the conditions. As a result, the working conditions and wage standards of domestic workers have remained low.

While discriminatory wage patterns follow black women into industry, factory jobs are more easily unionized, and thereby upgraded, than is domestic work. Despite unionization, however, service workers remain in the lowest economic category.

I LIVE A TREADMILL LIFE

ANONYMOUS

I am a negro woman, and I was born and reared in the South. I am now past forty years of age and am the mother of three children. My husband died nearly fifteen years ago. . . . For more than thirty years—or since I was ten years old —I have been a servant . . . in white families. . . . During the last ten years I have been a nurse. . . .

More than two-thirds of the negroes of the town where I live are menial servants of one kind or another. . . . The condition . . . of poor colored people is just as bad as, if not worse than it was during the days of slavery. Tho' today we are enjoying nominal freedom, we are literally slaves. . . .

I frequently work from fourteen to sixteen hours a day. I am compelled . . . to sleep in the house. I am allowed to go home to my children, the oldest of whom is a girl of 18 years, only once in two weeks, every other Sunday afternoon—even then I'm not permitted to stay all night. I not only have to nurse a little white child, now eleven months old, but I have to act as playmate . . . to three other children in the home, the oldest of whom is only nine years of age. I wash and dress the baby two or three times each day; I give it its meals, mainly from a bottle; I have to put it to bed each night; and, in addition, I have to get up and attend to its every call between midnight and morning. If the baby falls to sleep during the day, as it has been trained to do every day about eleven o'clock, I am not permitted to rest. It's "Mammy, do this," or "Mammy, do that," or "Mammy, do the other," from my mistress all the time. So it is not strange to see "Mammy" watering the lawn in front with the garden hose, sweeping the sidewalk, mopping the porch and halls, dusting around the house, helping the cook, or darning stockings. Not only so, but I have to put the other three children to bed each night as well as the baby, and I have to wash them and dress them each morning. I don't know what it is to go to church; I don't know what it is to go to a lecture or entertainment or anything of the kind; I live a treadmill life and I see my own children only when they happen to see me on the streets when I am out with the children, or when my children come to the "yard" to see me, which isn't often, because my white folks don't like to see their servants' children hanging around their premises. You might as well say that I'm on duty all the time—from sunrise to sunrise, every day in the week. I am the slave, body and soul, of this family. And what do I get for this work . . . The pitiful sum of ten dollars a month! And what am I expected to do with these ten dollars? With this money I'm expected to pay my house rent, which is four dollars per month, for a little house of two rooms just big enough to turn round in; and I'm expected, also, to feed and clothe myself and three children. For two years my oldest child, it is true, has helped a little toward our support by taking in a little washing at home. She does the washing and ironing of two white families, with a total of five persons; one of these families pays her $1.00 per week, and the other 75 cents per week, and my daughter has to furnish her own soap and starch and wood. For six months my youngest child, a girl about thirteen years old, has been nursing and she receives $1.50 per week, but has no night work. . . .

You hear a good deal nowadays about the "service pan." The "service pan" is the general term applied to "left-over" food, which in many a Southern home is freely placed at the disposal of the cook, or, whether so placed or not, it is usually disposed of by the cook. In my town, I know, and I guess in many other towns also, every night when the cook starts for her home she takes with her a pan or a plate of cold victuals. The same is true on Sunday afternoons after dinner —and most cooks have nearly every Sunday afternoon off. Well, I'll be frank with you, if it were not for the service pan, I don't know what the majority of our Southern colored families would do. The service pan is the mainstay in many a home. Good cooks in the South receive on an average $8 per month. Porters, butlers, coachmen, janitors, "office boys" and the like receive on an average $16 per month. Few and far between are the colored men in the South who receive $1 or more per day. Some mechanics do; as, for example, carpenters, brick masons, wheelwrights, blacksmiths, and the like. The vast majority of negroes in my town are serving in menial capacities in homes, stores and offices. Now taking it for granted, for the sake of illustration, that the husband receives, $16 per month and the wife $8. That would be $24 between the two. The chances are that they will have anywhere from five to thirteen children between them. Now, how far will $24 go toward housing and feeding and clothing ten or twelve persons for thirty days? I tell you, with all of us poor people the service pan is a great institution.

"More Slavery at the South," by a Negro Nurse, *The Independent*, Vol. 72, No. 3295 (January 25, 1912), pp. 196–200.

SLAVE MARKETS IN NEW YORK CITY

Every morning, rain or shine, groups of women with brown paper bags or cheap suitcases stand on street corners in the

Bronx and Brooklyn waiting for a chance to get some work. Sometimes there are 15, sometimes 30, some are old, many are young and most of them are Negro women waiting for employers to come to the street corner auction blocks to bargain for their labor.

They come as early as 7 in the morning, wait as late as four in the afternoon with the hope that they will make enough to buy supper when they go home. Some have spent their last nickel to get to the corner and are in desperate need. When the hour grows late, they sit on boxes if any are around. In the afternoon their labor is worth only half as much as in the morning. If they are lucky, they get about 30 cents an hour scrubbing, cleaning, laundering, washing windows, waxing floors and woodwork all day long; in the afternoon, when most have already been employed, they are only worth the degrading sum of 20 cents an hour.

Once hired on the "slave market," the women often find after a days backbreaking toil, that they worked longer than was arranged, got less than was promised, were forced to accept clothing instead of cash and were exploited beyond human endurance. Only the urgent need for money makes them submit to this routine daily.

Throughout the country, more than two million women are engaged in domestic work, the largest occupational group for women. About half are Negro women. . . .

Though many Negro women work for as little as two dollars a week and as long as 80 hours a week . . . they have no social security, no workmen's compensation, no old age security. . . .

The Women's Bureau in Washington points out that women take domestic work only as a last resort. Largely unprotected by law they find themselves at the mercy of an individual employer. Only two states, Wisconsin and Washington, have wage or hour legislation. But enforcement is very slack. . . .

The tradition of street corner markets is no new institution in this city. As far back as 1834, the statute books show, a place was set aside on city streets where those seeking work could meet with those who wanted workers. This exchange also functions for male workers. . . . At present markets flourish in the Bronx and Brooklyn where middle-class families live. However, this method of employment is also instituted in Greenwhich Village, Richmond and Queens. . . .

The prosperity of the nation can only be judged by the living standards of its most oppressed group. State legislatures must pass laws to protect the health and work of the domestic. A world of education is still needed both for employees and employers.

Many civic and social organizations are now working toward improving conditions of domestics. Outstanding among these is the Bronx Citizens Committee for Improvement of Domestic Employees. The YWCA and many women's clubs are interested in the problem. Mayor LaGuardia . . . must be forced to end these horrible conditions of auction block hiring with the most equitable solution for the most oppressed section of the working class—Negro women.

Louise Mitchell, "Slave Markets Typify Exploitation of Domestics,"
The Daily Worker, May 5, 1940.

THE DOMESTIC WORKERS' UNION

❧ *Domestic workers have been one of the most difficult groups of workers to organize. The individual nature of the work, the isolation of the workers from one another, their low economic and social status and the intense competition among them are some of the factors explaining this difficulty. The historic indifference of organized labor toward unskilled women workers is certainly another factor. There have, over the years, been various attempts made at organizing domestic workers. In 1920, there were ten locals of domestic workers in Southern cities affiliated with the Hotel and*

Restaurant Employees Union, AFL. In 1936, a domestic Workers' Union started by seven women in Washington, D.C., had over a hundred members one year later and had succeeded in raising the prevailing wage from $3 to $10 a week.

A Domestic Workers' Association, sponsored by the National Negro Congress, began organizing in New York City in 1937. The YWCA and several other predominantly white women's organizations had at various times turned their attention to the problems of domestic workers and attempted to ameliorate their conditions. All these attempts were short-lived and only locally effective.

The most ambitious organizing effort was that headed by Dora Jones, the black executive secretary of the Domestic Workers' Union, which was founded in 1934 and was affiliated with the Building Service Union, Local 149, in New York City. Five years later the organization had 350 members, 75 per cent of them black women.

The work described by Dorothy Bolden (see p. 234) is an updated version of the same effort. The difficulties in organizing domestic workers remain. Enforcement of minimum wage standards by the United States Employment Service have had a slightly beneficial effect, which is, however, weakened by the policy of various welfare departments, which cut black women off the relief rolls unless they accept domestic work at "prevailing" wages, which are inevitably the lowest prevailing wages.

With a main office at 112 East Nineteenth street, where a framed charter hangs proudly on the wall, and a branch office at 2705 White Plains Road, the Domestic Workers' Union, which started as a mere suggestion in 1934, is part of the Building Service Union, and A.F. of L. affiliate, and boasts 350 members, seventy-five per cent of them Negroes.

The road has been rocky for the brave young women who have given unstintingly of their energy and time to capture the interest of the most difficult group of all, the domestic worker—difficult because of the long work hours, the area over which the industry extends, and the unfamiliarity of the girls, themselves, of trade unions.

Many of the women employed in domestic service still believe in widespread propaganda that all unions are rackets. Seeing no immediate gains, it has been a difficult task to make them see the ultimate goal.

"We are really handicapped because of lack of money," declared Miss Dora Jones, the union's vice-president, who heads up the work at the East Nineteenth street office. Miss Rosa Rayside, the acting president, works in the field.

"Because of this, we are not able to make a concerted appeal—but must appeal to the occasional worker who crosses our path. Our progress has been horribly slow. Maybe we are over-anxious; but it is so important that the condition of the domestic worker be improved, that sometimes we underestimate our progress."

Despite this complaint that the progress has been slow, the union after many months of study, has perfected a contract to protect the domestic worker on her job.

Some of the provisions in the contract, which will be tried out for the first time the end of this month, include the following:

Newly engaged employees shall be notified as to whether or not the job is permanent or temporary; there shall be a trial period of not less than two weeks; three good meals a day must be provided; there shall be a six-day sixty-hour week; wages must be paid weekly, or, if monthly, be computed as four-and-a-third weeks to a month; a two-weeks' notice or comparable pay; fifty cents an hour for overtime—thirty-five cents an hour when tending children.

And last, but not least, no window-washing!

Many of these provisions may seem foolish or unnecessary to the average person. But organizers in the Domestic Workers' Union feel that if they can make this contract stick, their fight to organize the thousands of black and white domestic workers throughout the metropolitan area will be greatly simplified.

Marvel Cooke, "Modern Slaves," *Amsterdam News*,
October 16, 1937.

ORGANIZING DOMESTIC WORKERS IN ATLANTA, GEORGIA
DOROTHY BOLDEN

I was born right here, and I lived in Atlanta all my life. I had trouble with my eyes when I was three years old, and I did gain my sight back when I was eight years old, and that was when I started going to school. In the eleventh grade I began to have more trouble with my eyes and I had to drop out. After I left school I got me a regular job with a Jew family. I only made three dollars per week. I would go at eight o'clock. I would get up about six. That's the times that I would bring a pan home. That is food that they would give you in a little pan. It would be enough for two or three people to eat. This was the only thing that we did have and we didn't resent it because you didn't make anything and you needed it.

Then I went to work at a laundry where I made a little bit more than $3. I went to work for the National Linen Service on Highland Avenue, where I made $7.11. But we wasn't making that much till our union came in. Then our wages went up and up. We got up to about $23. It made a great deal of difference. I stayed at Linen Supply for four years. Then I went to Sears and Roebucks and worked at the mail room.

That was a pretty good job. That was the first job that I had that really meant a lot to me. They paid a great deal, but that was right during the war and salaries went up. I made sometimes from sixty-five to seventy, even eighty dollars. They paid you overtime. Sears offered you a good opportunity

at the time cause that was the first time Negroes that was
employed at the store could really buy a little stock.

Then I decided I wanted to travel. I wanted to go somewhere, anyplace else, so I went over in Alabama and I looked
for work there and I ended up doing domestic. With the war
going on then, I couldn't find anything, so I left Alabama
and came back home, then I looked again and went to Chicago and I worked there for about a month in domestic—a
month and a half and I left and came back home and stayed
about a week, then I left again and I went to Detroit. I
stayed in school for about a year studying dress designing
and styling. When I came back my eyes was giving me a lot
of trouble. The doctor told me I couldn't make a profession
out of this on account of my eyes. So I went to New York,
and I didn't like the city of New York 'cause it was just a
hopped up city to me. I came back home a month later.

I got a job at the railway express. I was a trucker. You
push the freight around with a hand truck. We would make
real good money, sometimes a dollar seventy-some cents an
hour, and we would make overtime. I met my husband there.
He was working for the express company. And he asked me
to quit 'cause I would tear my body down. He explained to me
that it just wasn't healthy for me to work there. So I worked
for about six months and then I quit and I went back into
domestic. I made sometime eighteen dollars a week. It wasn't
anything much. But I liked it because I loved the children,
this was my most important thing. I never took a job lessen
they had children. I didn't work for any single people.

I would stay until I felt I wanted to roam again and I
would leave. I always fixed it where I could always go back
if I wanted to. They always knew that I was restless and I
was young. When I felt I was getting too attached to the family, was getting too attached to the children, I would break
off and go get me another job. I would change plenty of jobs.
I got to operate an elevator, I tried waitress, you name it, I
tried all of it. But I always went back to domestic. I love
children, I really love children. I should have been a teacher.

My ambition when I was going to school was to be a missionary. I love peoples.

I have six children in all. I stayed home while all my children was little. Then I went back into domestic. I wanted to go back in where the babies was.

I started organizing the maids in 1968. I had started three years ahead of time, thinking. I thought about how many times I would change jobs. I had been riding the bus to work. Every time we got off the bus I seen a different maid going to that same house. We knew that they had changed maids five or six times. And then I got to thinking about how it was a very poor communication established there somewhere, for maids to change jobs there that regularly and why the lady couldn't keep one maid. This began to worry me. Right away I worry about everybody's problems. And I said it's just that peoples don't communicate, and I knew that integration was here and I know that I had set down and discussed things in the community. I talked about civil rights and talked about integration and different other things.

The salary of the maids was very low. They were working in model homes, beautiful homes, and they had a great deal of responsibility. Where I was working was nothing but rich young people. The lady that I was working for was giving me a good salary. So I decided then that I was going to start communicating. I would go around in the bus and ask the maids how they would feel about joining if we would organize, and they would say, "Oh, I'm for that." One day I took three ladies, and made a radio announcement. Told how we was getting together in the National Domestic Workers Union of America. I picked up many members that time, which was beautiful.

I had to meet with the maids every week to keep them encouraged, to keep the strength up. I was talking, and they was responding to my talk. The Fleet Street Baptist Church Education Building was opened up for us. We meet there now. We used to meet every Thursday night for the union meeting, but now we meets only once a month.

You can't negotiate with private employers, private homes. You have to teach each maid how to negotiate. And this is the most important thing—communicating. I would tell them it was up to them to communicate. If I wanted a raise from you I wouldn't come in and hit you over your head and demand a raise—I would set out and talk to you and let you know how the living costs have gone up. We was asking for $13.50 a day and carfare, if a maid worked four to five days. And for working one day per week—the maid usually does more in one day than she does in three days—so we asked for $15 a day and carfare. We didn't want to frighten the employers, because that would cause a lot of peoples to lose jobs. And we know we couldn't replace those jobs. When the employers heard that we was unionizing, the wages went up to $12. The papers was trying to get news reporters in on our meetings. A lot of the maids got raises. They didn't get fired. Some of them quit because the lady wouldn't give them the money. When you unionize like this, on a private basis, and you're self-employed, your risk is that the one that *doesn't* join your union, she gets a good increase in salary. And this is the hardest part. And I told them we weren't going to be able to get in *all* the maids in Atlanta, but we could improve.

I was interviewed by all kinds of radio stations, and they would throw questions at me. I always understood that the employer was a human being too. You have to learn how to sit down and relax and talk to her. Maids was very valuable to a household. If you had a maid that's been with you for fifteen or twenty years, think about how she's been trying to scuffle and live, and she's honest, and she's dependable. If you get a dependable person, don't you think it's worth paying her more? And a lot of them would tell me, "Yes, you're right." I let the employer know their downfall, and I also let the maid know her weakness. You got to be dependable. You've got to go out and do your work. If I send you out, I'm not looking for you to cry on my shoulder.

We have our own employment service. The U.S. Employment Service only sends people from their office one day a week. Well, they said now that the maids are unionized, the wages gone up. They're getting vacation pay, too. We asked for all of that. We also asked for Social Security being deducted.

Now we meet the first Thursday of each month. We estimate about fifty attend the meetings. I send notices out every month. Some of them get a card, and all they want is the card. They pay $2.50 a month for dues. But you don't get them all. You're always going to have deadbeats.

I'm thinking on merging with the Laundry Workers Union. I want to establish a credit union because I'm against loan-sharks. Low-income people, and the majority of these people is women, are still in loan-shark offices. We need to educate these women on the level of their communities. I think women should have a voice in making decisions in their community for betterment. Because this woman in the slum is scuffling hard, and she's got a very good intelligent mind to do things, and she's been overlooked for so many years. I think she should have a voice.

Dorothy Bolden, taped interview with Gerda Lerner,
October 2, 1970. Used by permission.

FROM SERVICE JOBS TO THE FACTORY

❦ *Unlike white women, whose entry into the factories in the early nineteenth century coincided with industrialization, black women were denied access to factory employment until World War I. The only exceptions to this were the Southern tobacco and textile industries, where black women continued doing the unskilled factory work they had done ever since slavery. Until 1910, the majority of black work-*

ing women were farm laborers and domestic servants
while the next largest group (15 per cent) were employed
as laundresses. Between 1910 and 1920, more than
48,000 black women entered factory work. The largest group
of factory workers were employed in the steam laundries;
the others worked in various menial and undesirable occupations—sweepers, cleaners, ragpickers, pressers, in fruit peeling
and processing, labeling, stamping, etc. Few black women
worked on machines, and most of those who did worked
as press operators. The few sewing machine operators were
among the best skilled workers. Black women worked longer
hours and earned less than white women. The median
earnings of female black factory workers in 1920 were $6
a week.

Since black women were nearly always employed only in
those jobs for which white workers were not available, their
entry into new fields of employment usually occurred during
war periods. This was true for both World Wars. During
World War II, black women worked in the war industries, entered the automobile, textile, electrical and transportation industries in large numbers, and worked in hospitals, schools
and other institutional occupations. But the temporary
gains of the war periods were quickly eroded in the postwar
years, when black women were the first to be fired from
wartime jobs and through economic need were forced back
into domestic and other service jobs. Still, they retained
a sizable foothold in some of these industries and benefitted
by unionization, mostly in CIO unions, which organized
unskilled workers. Today, black women constitute a steady
component of the labor force in the following industries:
auto, meat packing, tobacco, textile, food processing. In all
these industries they are part of the organized labor movement. They are also organized in unions in the hotel and
restaurant industry, in hospitals and schools, in public
service and transportation. Racial barriers have only slowly
fallen in clerical and sales occupations, where sizable gains
were made only in the past two decades. In 1966, 13 per cent

of all black women workers were in clerical or sales jobs
and 10 per cent held other white-collar jobs. This was a
sizable gain over the previous decade, but falls far short of
the opportunities open to white women in these fields.

Unemployment is more severe among black women than
among any other group in the population.

1966 Unemployment Rate

Black men	Black women	White men	White women
6.6%	8.8%	2.9%	4.3%

Teenagers—14–19

21.2%	31.1%	9.9%	11.0%

Despite absolute improvement in job opportunities and
the erosion of some racial barriers in the middle-range jobs,
the economic gap between black women and other groups
in the population remains unchanged.

AN ARMY LAUNDRESS AT WAR
SUSIE KING TAYLOR

❦ Susie King Taylor was a "contraband," a fugitive
slave who followed the Union army in South Carolina,
attaching herself to one of the units and serving in whatever
capacity she could. Her husband, Sergeant King, was at the
front with his regiment.

I was enrolled as company laundress, but I did very little of
it, because I was always busy doing other things through
camp, and was employed all the time doing something for
the officers and comrades. . . .

The first colored troops did not receive any pay for eighteen months and the men had to depend wholly on what they received from the commissary, established by Gen. Saxton. A great many of these men had large families and as they had no money to give them their wives were obliged to support themselves and children by washing for the officers of the gunboats and the soldiers, and making cakes and pies, which they sold to the boys in camp. Finally, in 1863, the government decided to give them half pay, but the men would not accept this. They wanted "full pay or nothing." They preferred rather to give their services to the state, which they did until 1864, when the government granted them full pay with all the back pay due. . . .

I learned to handle a musket very well while in the regiment and could shoot straight and often hit the target. I assisted in cleaning the guns and used to fire them off, to see if the cartridges were dry, before cleaning and re-loading, each day. I thought this was great fun. I was also able to take a gun all apart and put it together again. . . .

We had fresh beef once in a while, and we would have soup and the vegetables they put in the soup were dried and pressed; they looked like hops. Salt beef was our standby. Sometimes the men would have what we called slap-jacks. This was flour made into bread and spread thin on the bottom of the mess-pan to cook; each man had one of them with a pint of tea for his supper, or a pint of tea and five or six hardtack. I often got my own meals and would fix some dishes for the noncommissioned officers also. . . .

About the first of June, 1864, the regiment was ordered to Folly Island, staying there until the latter part of the month, when it was ordered to Morris Island. We landed on Morris Island between June and July, 1864. This island was a narrow strip of sandy soil, nothing growing on it but a few bushes and shrubs. The camp was one mile from the boat landing, called Pawnell Landing, and the landing one mile from Fort Wagner. . . .

The regiment under Colonel Trowbridge did garrison duty, but they had troublesome times from Fort Gregg, on James

Island, for the rebels would throw a shell over on our island every now and then. Finally orders were received for the boys to prepare to take Fort Gregg, each man to take 150 rounds of cartridges, canteens of water, hardtack, and salt beef. This order was sent three days prior to starting, to allow them to be in readiness. I helped as many as I could to pack haversacks and cartridge boxes.

The fourth day, about five o'clock in the afternoon, the call was sounded, and I heard the first sergeant say, "Fall in, boys, fall in," and they were not long obeying the command. Each company marched out of its street, in front of their colonel's headquarters, where they rested for half an hour, as it was not dark enough, and they did not want the enemy to have a chance to spy their movements. At the end of this time the line was formed with the 103rd New York (white) in the rear, and off they started, eager to get to work. It was quite dark by the time they reached Pawnell Landing. I have never forgotten the goodbys of that day, as they left camp. Colonel Trowbridge said to me as he left, "Good-by, Mrs. King, take care of yourself if you don't see us again." I went with them as far as the landing, and watched them until they got out of sight, and then I returned to the camp. There was no one at camp but those left on picket and a few disabled soldiers, and one woman, a friend of mine, Mary Shaw, and it was lonesome and sad, now that the boys were gone, some never to return.

Mary Shaw shared my tent that night, and we went to bed, but not to sleep, for the fleas nearly ate us alive. We caught a few, but it did seem, now that the men were gone, that every flea in camp had located my tent, and caused us to vacate. Sleep being out of the question, we sat up the remainder of the night.

About four o'clock, July 2, the charge was made. The firing could be plainly heard in camp. I hastened down to the landing and remained there until eight o'clock that morning. When the wounded arrived, or rather began to arrive, the first one brought in was Samuel Anderson of our company. He was badly wounded. Then others of our boys, some with their legs off, arm gone, foot off, and wounds of all kinds imaginable. They had to wade through creeks and marshes, as they were discovered by the enemy and shelled very badly. A number of the men were lost, some got fastened in the mud and had to cut off the legs of their pants, to free themselves. The 103rd New York suffered the most, as their men were very badly wounded.

My work now began. I gave my assistance to try to alleviate their sufferings. I asked the doctor at the hospital what I could get for them to eat. They wanted soup, but that I could not get; but I had a few cans of condensed milk and some turtle eggs, so I thought I would try to make some custard. I had doubts as to my success, for cooking with turtle eggs was something new to me, but the adage has it, "Nothing ventured, nothing done," so I made a venture and the result was a very delicious custard. This I carried to the men, who enjoyed it very much. My services were given at all times for the comfort of these men. I was on hand to assist whenever needed.

> Susie King Taylor, *Reminiscences of My Life in Camp with the 33rd United States Colored Troops* (Boston: Author, 1902), pp. 15–16, 26–28, 32–35.

BLACK WOMEN IN THE RECONSTRUCTION SOUTH

FRANCES ELLEN WATKINS HARPER

❦ Frances Ellen Watkins (1825–1911), born in Baltimore of free parents, was orphaned at an early age and raised by an aunt. She had to be self-supporting from the age of thirteen. Working at first as a nursemaid, she was largely self-educated. At various times she took in sewing, taught needlecraft in school, wrote poems and novels and made a living as a traveling lecturer.

Frances Ellen Watkins Harper began her career as an antislavery lecturer before the Civil War and continued lecturing and reading from her poems in public for the rest of her life. She was equally famous as a writer, and in the later years of her life derived an adequate income from her literary activities. In 1856, she visited the Negro settlements in Canada and reported on them in articles and lectures. She published ten volumes of poetry, two before and eight after the Civil War, which reputedly sold remarkably well.

She married Fenton Harper in 1860 in Cincinnati, gave birth to a daughter, and was widowed four years later. After the Civil War she spent several years lecturing and working in the South. "I know of no other women, white or colored," wrote her contemporary William Still, the black editor of The Underground Railroad,

> who has come so intimately in contact with the colored people in the South as Mrs. Harper. Since emancipation she has labored in every Southern State in the Union, save two, Arkansas and Texas; in the colleges, schools, churches, and the cabins. . . . With her, it was no uncommon occurrence, in visiting cities and towns, to speak at two, three, and four meetings a day. . . . But the kind of meetings she took greatest interest in were meetings called exclusively for women. . . . She felt their needs were far more pressing than any other class.*

Her novel Iola Leroy or Shadows Uplifted, published in 1892, is the first book by a black writer dealing with the Reconstruction South, and is also the first novel published by an Afro-American woman. The story of an octoroon girl, it contains fascinating glimpses of black life among the freedmen. The heroine reflects her author's feminism, in that she aspires to work and tries her hand at a variety of occupations from nursing to saleswork.

* William Still, Introduction to Frances E. W. Harper, Iola Leroy or Shadows Uplifted, 2nd ed. (Boston: James H. Early, 1895).

Mrs. Harper had a sophisticated understanding of the social problems of Reconstruction. "While I am in favor of Universal Suffrage," she wrote in one of her letters from the South,

> yet I know that the colored man needs something more than a vote in his hand; he needs to know the value of a home life; to rightly appreciate and value the marriage relations; to know how to be incited to leave behind him the old shards and shells of slavery; to rise in the scale of character, worth and influence. . . . A man landless, ignorant and poor may use the vote against his interests; but with intelligence and land he holds in his hand the basis of power and elements of strength.*

Mrs. Harper was a leading club woman and concerned femininist. She spoke at the 1866 Women's Rights Convention, which indicates her interest in feminism, but her priority was always the race issue. In this she is typical of most black women, then and now. At the 1869 meeting of the Equal Rights Association, when white feminists and abolitionists came to a parting of the ways because of the latter's endorsement of the Fourteenth and Fifteenth Amendments, which did not give the vote to women as feminists had confidently expected it would, Frances Harper participated in the debate. She sided with the other black speaker, Frederick Douglass, who pleaded the greater urgency of the race issue and defended the position that now was "the Negro's hour," and that women's rights could wait. Frances Harper observed "that when it was a question of race she let the lesser question of sex go. But the white women all go for sex, letting race occupy a minor position."†

---

* George Bragg, "Frances E. Harper." *Men of Maryland* (Baltimore: Church Advocate Press, 1925).

† *The Revolution*, Vol. 3, No. 20 (May 20, 1869), p. 306; and Vol. 3, No. 21 (May 27, 1869), p. 322.

This accurate assessment was borne out by history.

Mrs. Harper's black feminism found expression in her participation in various women's clubs and in her leadership of the National Association of Colored Women, of which she was a founder and Vice-President until her death. She was also active as a temperance lecturer and held the office of Superintendent of colored work in the Woman's Christian Temperance Union for years. Her other civic interests included the promotion of Negro education and Sunday school teaching.

The article below is based on her impressions in the Reconstruction South, and the poem "Deliverance" is representative of her concern with social issues.

The women as a class are quite equal to the men in energy and executive ability. In fact I find by close observation, that the mothers are the levers which move in education. The men talk about it, especially about election time, if they want an office for self or their candidate, but the women work most for it. They labour in many ways to support the family, while the children attend school. They make great sacrifices to spare their own children during school hours. I know of girls from sixteen to twenty-two who iron till midnight that they may come to school in the day. Some of our scholars, aged about nineteen, living about thirty miles off, rented land, ploughed, planted, and then sold their cotton, in order to come to us. A woman near me, urged her husband to go in debt 500 dollars for a home, as the titles to the land they had built on were insecure, and she said to me, "We have five years to pay it in, and I shall begin to-day to do it, if life is spared. I will make a hundred dollars at washing, for I have done it." Yet they have seven little children to feed, clothe, and educate. In the field the women receive the same wages as the men, and are often preferred, clearing land, hoeing, or picking cotton, with equal ability.

In different departments of business, coloured women have

not only been enabled to keep the wolf from the door, but also to acquire property, and in some cases the coloured woman is the mainstay of the family, and when work fails the men in large cities, the money which the wife can obtain by washing, ironing, and other services, often keeps pauperism at bay. I do not suppose, considering the state of her industrial lore and her limited advantages, that there is among the poorer classes a more helpful woman than the coloured woman as a labourer. When I was in Mississippi, I stopped with Mr. Montgomery, a former slave of Jefferson Davis's brother. His wife was a woman capable of taking on her hands 130 acres of land, and raising one hundred and seven bales of cotton by the force which she could organise. Since then I have received a very interesting letter from her daughter, who for years has held the position of Assistant Postmistress. In her letter she says: 'There are many women around me who would serve as models of executiveness anywhere. They do double duty, a man's share in the field, and a woman's part at home. They do any kind of field work, even ploughing, and at home the cooking, washing, milking, and gardening. But these have husbands; let me tell you of some widows and unaided women:—

Mrs. Hill, a widow, has rented, cultivated, and solely managed a farm of five acres for five years. She makes her garden, raises poultry, and cultivates enough corn and cotton to live comfortably, and keep a surplus in the bank. She saves something every year, and this is much, considering the low price of cotton and unfavourable seasons. . . .

Mrs. Jane Brown and Mrs. Halsey formed a partnership about ten years ago, leased nine acres and a horse, and have cultivated the land all that time, just the same as men would have done. They have saved considerable money from year to year, and are living independently. They have never had any expenses for labour, making and gathering the crops themselves.

Mrs. Henry, by farming and peddling cakes, has the last seven years laid up seven hundred dollars. She is an invalid, and unable to work at all times. Since then she has been engaged in planting sweet potatoes and raising poultry and hogs. Last year she succeeded in raising 250 hogs, but lost two-thirds by disease. She furnished eggs and chickens enough for family use, and sold a surplus of chickens, say fifty dozen chickens. On nine acres she made 600 bushels of sweet potatoes. The present year she has planted ten acres of potatoes. She has 100 hogs, thirty dozen chickens, a small lot of ducks and turkeys, and also a few sheep and goats. She has also a large garden under her supervision, which is planted in cabbages. She has two women and a boy to assist. Miss Montgomery, a coloured lady, says: "I have constantly been engaged in bookkeeping for eight years, and for ten years as assistant post-mistress, doing all the work of the office. Now, instead of bookkeeping, I manage a school of 133 pupils, and I have an assistant, and I am still attending to the post-office." Of her sister she says, she is a better and swifter worker than herself; that she generally sews, but that last year she made 100 dozen jars of preserved fruit for sale. An acquaintance of mine, who lives in South Carolina, and has been engaged in mission work, reports that, in supporting the family, women are the mainstay; that two-thirds of the truck gardening is done by them in South Carolina; that in the city they are more industrious than the men; that when the men lose their work through their political affiliations, the women stand by them, and say, "stand by your principles." And I have been informed by the same person that a number of women have homes of their own, bought by their hard earnings since freedom. Mr. Stewart, who was employed in the Freedmen's bank, says he has seen scores of coloured women in the South working and managing plantations of from twenty to 100 acres. . . .

The coloured women have not been backward in promoting charities for their own sex and race. "One of the most efficient helpers is Mrs. Madison, who, although living in a humble and unpretending home, had succeeded in getting up a home for aged coloured women. By organized effort, coloured women have been enabled to help each other in sickness, and provide respectable funerals for the dead. . . ."

"Coloured Women of America," *Englishwoman's Review*,
January 15, 1878, pp. 10–15.

DELIVERANCE

And if any man should ask me
If I would sell my vote,
I'd tell him I was not the one
To change and turn my coat. . . .

But when John Thomas Reder brought
His wife some flour and meat,
And told her he had sold his vote,
For something good to eat,

You ought to see Aunt Kitty raise,
And heard her blaze away;
She gave the meat and flour a toss,
And said they should not stay. . . .

You'd laughed to seen Lucinda Grange
Upon her husband's track
When he sold his vote for rations
She made him take 'em back.

Day after day did Milly Green
Just follow after Joe,
And told him if he voted wrong
To take his rags and go.

I think that Curnel Johnson said
His side had won the day,
Had not we women radicals
Just got right in the way. . . .

Frances E. W. Harper, *Sketches of Southern Life* (Philadelphia:
Ferguson Brothers, 1893).

THE NEGRO WOMAN WORKER:
1860–1890
JEAN COLLIER BROWN

❦ *Jean Collier Brown worked for the Women's Bureau of the Department of Labor.*

In 1860, more than nine-tenths of the Negro population of the United States was to be found in the South, where a great majority were engaged in large-scale agriculture. It was estimated by the U.S. Census of 1850 that, of the 3,204,313 slaves in Southern States, 2,500,000 were devoted to the raising of certain staples—cotton, tobacco, sugar, rice, and hemp. The second largest group of Southern Negro workers found employment in domestic and personal service. The exact number so engaged will never be known, since no complete record of slaves in the various occupations has been preserved. It is apparent that large numbers of Negro women were found as maids, cooks, washerwomen, seamstresses, dressmakers, midwives, and parlor maids.

Previous to the Civil War, few Negroes of either sex were employed in mechanical and manufacturing pursuits in comparison with the numbers engaged as farm laborers. The explanation lies largely in the almost negligible industrial development of the South at that period. However, in the few textile mills in operation, Negroes were extensively employed. One coarse cotton mill in Alabama employed 100 slaves, three-fourths of whom were women. Similar mills were found in Georgia, North Carolina, Mississippi, and Florida. Tobacco factories, bagging factories, iron furnaces, charcoal plants, and the construction of railroads were among other industries utilizing Negro slave labor to some extent.

The small percentage of the total American Negro population found in the North prior to 1860 was restricted chiefly to the two occupations of agriculture and domestic service, the larger number finding employment in the latter field of work. The women again were for the most part maids, laundresses, cooks, seamstresses, nurse maids, hairdressers, or day laborers. In several Northern cities, a strong prejudice against the hiring of Negroes for any other than the most menial labor made it extremely difficult for men who were the heads of families to secure any kind of employment. Many families thus were forced to rely on the income of washerwomen mothers for bare subsistence.

Statistical records of the progress of Negro workers during the difficult transitional years following the Civil War up to the time of trade recovery in the nineties are scant. The war industries of the South which had used thousands of Negroes recruited from plantations were virtually in ruins at the close of the struggle. Accordingly, the large part of the freedmen gradually settled down to farming, either independently or, for the most part, as tenants working on shares for the landowner. The next largest group of Negroes through the transition period entered domestic and personal service, occupation in which at that time there was no competition from the whites.

Few Negroes were engaged in manufacturing during this period, even in industries which previous to the war had relied largely upon their labor. The rising class consciousness of the whites and the prevailing notion that Negroes were not fit for mill work were responsible for closing factory opportunities to this race. The Negroes found in cotton mills were engaged largely as common laborers in the yards, waste gatherers, and scrubbers of machinery. Among the few notable exceptions to the general rule of discrimination against the employment of Negroes in industrial pursuits was the successful use of hundreds of such workers in the large flour mills and tobacco factories of Richmond, the tobacco plants of Lynchburg, Va., and Durham, N.C., and the phosphate industry of South Carolina. In a handle factory of Greensboro, N.C., Negro operators turned out a useful product that was sent all over the world.

Just what numbers or percentages of Negroes were farm

laborers, servants, mechanics, and the like could not be ascertained with any degree of exactitude prior to 1890, at which time was taken the first United States Census making distinctions in race and color in compiling data on white and Negro laborers. These figures show that of 975,530 colored women gainfully employed at the beginning of the last decade of the nineteenth century—a figure which included Indians and a few Chinese and Japanese—38.74 per cent were agriculture, 30.83 per cent were "servants" (cooks, chambermaids, etc.), 15.59 per cent were laundresses, and 2.76 per cent were engaged in manufacturing and mechanical pursuits.

Jean Collier Brown, "The Economic Status of Negro Women,"
The Southern Workman, Vol. 60, No. 10 (October 1931),
pp. 430–431.

THE TOBACCO WORKERS

EMMA L. SHIELDS

❦ Emma L. Shields was a 1916 graduate of Fisk University in social work. She worked as a high school teacher in Wheeling, West Virginia, for one year and was then appointed by the Women's Bureau of the Department of Labor to study the condition of black women in industry. Her pamphlet, published by the Womens Bureau in 1922, was the first comprehensive study of the subject.

"Oh, yes, Negro women have been working here since 1875. Take Sally there—she and those older women you see there have been here between thirty and forty years. They feel that they belong to the firm, and to me—so much so that I think of them as my property."

Thus is the historical background of the Negro woman in the tobacco rehandling plants of the South well depicted by one employer. This process in the manufacture of tobacco has been conceded to be exclusively within the province of Negro women since the factory method of rehandling tobacco was evolved. . . .

A point of view is also indicated in the words quoted above. Not only do many old Negro women feel that they belong to the firms in which they are employed, but their implicit faith and confidence, on the one hand, and their servile fear and suspicion of their employers on the other, is both beautiful and pathetic. When it is realized that many of these older types began their employment in rehandling tobacco shortly after they were emancipated from slavery, it can be readily understood that there would be this blind submission to authority however kind or tyrannical. . . .

The employer who has grown old in his factory is also characteristic of the tobacco industry in the Southland. A few of these industrial veterans remain private owners of their plants, but a majority of them have placed their establishments under the control of those large tobacco corporations which are fast monopolizing the tobacco industry. However, these pioneers remain to a large extent as managers of factories; and their antiquity and ignorance of modern industrial standards are reflected in their management. . . .

Conditions of employment throughout the tobacco industry are deplorably wretched, and yet conditions for Negro women workers are very much worse than those for white women workers. . . . Negro women are employed exclusively in the rehandling of tobacco, preparatory to its actual manufacture. . . . Operations in the manufacture of cigars and cigarettes are performed exclusively by white women workers. Negro women workers are absolutely barred from any opportunity for employment on the manufacturing operations. The striking differences in working conditions which these occupational divisions provoke are further facilitated by the absolute isolation of Negro workers from white in separate parts of the factory buildings or else in separate buildings. . . .

It is not unusual to find the white women workers occupying the new modern sanitary parts of the factory, and the

Negro women workers in the old sections which the management had decided to be beyond the hope of any improvement. . . .

Tens of thousands of Negro women in the South are employed ten hours daily in old, unclean, malodorous buildings in which they are denied the most ordinary comforts of life. Either standing all day, in some occupations, or, in others, seated on makeshift stools or boxes with no back support, they toil incessantly throughout the long, tedious hours of the work day, except for a half-hour lunch period at noon. During the intermission there is no means of securing a hot meal or of resting, and there is no alternative except to spend this short period in the workroom or on the streets. The air in the workroom is so heavily laden with fumes and dust that it is nauseating. It is not unusual to see women with handkerchiefs tied over their nostrils to prevent inhaling the stifling, strangling air.

This condition is further accentuated by the bad sanitation in the workroom, which is often unclean, and has a small space partially partitioned off which serves as the toilet room, whose only ventilation comes from the workroom. With conditions such as these a washroom or dressing room becomes a humane and paramount necessity, and yet this facility was entirely lacking in the typical tobacco factory of the South. . . . The barrel of water to which a common drinking cup is attached by a chain is also typical of the tobacco rehandling plants. . . .

The majority of women earn on an average of twelve dollars a week during the working season, which extends from September to May. This inadequacy of wages and the seasonal aspect of the work, existing simultaneously, present a vital problem to the many Negro women workers who are responsible for the support of others besides themselves. . . .

Race prejudice . . . is the underlying cause of many of her industrial deprivations. It has denied her any chance for promotion to those better paying, skilled occupations in the manufacture of tobacco products. . . .

Her efforts at labor organization as a source of protection and strength in certain tobacco centers are noteworthy, even though it will be a long time before she can do any successful collective bargaining. Employers in some centers have given evidence of their feeling that their Negro women workers are their "property," in the methods used by them to obstruct any effort at labor organization within their plants. In other tobacco centers, employers resent organization, but they tolerate it because they know that conditions of the labor market will prevent any labor organization from functioning in the tobacco rehandling plants of the South.

Emma L. Shields, "Negro Women and the Tobacco Industry,"
Life and Labor, May 1921, pp. 142–144.

TWO MILLION WOMEN AT WORK

ELIZABETH ROSS HAYNES

❦ Elizabeth Ross Haynes is one of the pioneer social workers. The daughter of former slaves, she was born in Alabama. She graduated from that state's normal school in 1898, earned a B.A. at Fisk in 1903, studied for several summers at the University of Chicago while teaching school in Alabama and Missouri and in 1923 earned an M.A. at Columbia University. In 1910, she married George Edmund Haynes, a sociologist and later a founder of the National Urban League. The couple lived in New York City and had one son.

After working for two years for the national board of the YWCA, Mrs. Haynes became a volunteer worker for that organization in 1910. In 1924, she became the first black woman elected to the YWCA national board, on which she remained until 1934. From 1920 to 1922, she was Domestic Service Secretary of the United States Employment Service and later became Secretary of the board of management of the Adam Clayton Powell Home for the Aged. Her civic activities included interracial work for the Federated Council of Churches and membership on the New York City Planning Commission.

Two million Negro women in the United States [work in] three types of occupations: (1) domestic and personal service, (2) agriculture, (3) manufacturing and mechanical industries.

To-day they are found in domestic service, nearly a million strong, . . . with all of the shortcomings of ordinary domestic service; namely, basement living quarters, poor working conditions, too long hours, no Sundays off, no standards of efficiency, and the servant "brand." In spite of migration during the World War they are found on the farms, with all of the inconveniences and health hazards of Southern plantation life, in larger numbers than in domestic service. Before the World War there were over 67,000 of them in the unskilled processes of the manufacturing and mechanical industries and 3000 in the semi-skilled processes. These numbers were greatly increased during the war. In 152 plants visited in 1918–19, by Department of Labor representatives, more than 20,000 were found employed.

DOMESTIC SERVICE

During the past twelve months some decided changes affecting Negro women have taken place in domestic and personal service. For instance, in Detroit, Michigan, to-day, from eighty to ninety per cent of the calls for domestic workers are for white girls. The average wage in that city for general houseworkers is from $8 to $12 a week as against $15 to $20 a year ago. Women working by the day receive from $.40 to $.50 an hour as against $.60 to $.70 one year ago. The calls for office, elevator, and stock girls are no longer for Negro girls.

In Washington, D.C., with the fixing of the minimun

wage in the hotels, restaurants, etc., at $16.50 for a forty-eight hour week, and the increasing number of available white women, Negro women were to a very large extent displaced. Wages for domestic service for the rank and file have fallen in the past twelve months from $10 a week without any laundry work to $7 and $8 with laundry work. In the parlance of the women, "general housework" now means "cook, wash, and ine (iron)." The numbers driven into domestic work are very large. At one employment agency in this city there are often as many as 200 Negro women a day applying for work. A large majority of them are untrained, inefficient, and poorly equipped with the one thing needful—a good reference.

Only two of the Washington laundries are to-day paying the minimum wage. The average wage in the other laundries is $9 per week, and a few workers get as little as $6. Ninety percent of these laundry workers are Negro women. As soon as some of the laundries began to fear that they would be forced to pay the minimum wage they began to ask the employment bureaus about the possibility of obtaining white girls. Now that they are not paying the minimum wage they are perfectly satisfied with Negro women. A few of these have been in the laundries from fourteen to thirty-eight years, working through from the flat-work department until they are now "finishing" shirt-bosoms—which one who understands must term really artistic work. In Los Angeles, California, Negro women cooks get from $60 to $100 per month, . . . nurses from $50 to $75, mothers' helpers from $20 to $40. Day workers receive from $.45 to $.50 an hour. These women are, however, through the unions, excluded from even the laundries. . . .

MANUFACTURING AND MECHANICAL PURSUITS

There were and are still some thousands of Negro women in the cigar and tobacco factories of the country. They are poorly paid, of course, their wages ranging from $6 to $10 for a sixty-hour week. The work is dirty, and most of the

factories are poorly ventilated, being without an air shaft for
the expulsion of the dust; the result is that the tobacco fumes
and dust almost suffocate new workers. Then, the work being
more or less seasonal, women are sometimes out of employment for weeks at a time. In most tobacco factories the only
seats for the women are boxes or stools without backs; and
in a few factories women stemming tobacco sit flat on the
floor, humming a tune while they work. Even fairly respectable lunch rooms and decent toilet facilities are lacking.

Before the World War unskilled Negro women workers
in small numbers were in the clothing, food, and metal industries. They were to be found especially in slaughtering
and meat-packing houses, crab and peanut factories, and iron,
steel and automobile industries. They were also working in
furniture and shoe factories, printing and publishing establishments, and in cotton and silk mills. There were semiskilled workers in electrical-supply, paper-box, and rubber
factories, and in the textile industries. Finally there were a
few skilled tailoresses, tinsmiths, coppersmiths, and uphol-
sterers. The story of their entrance into industry in large numbers during the World War is too familiar to warrant
repetition here. The part they played in winning the war
will probably not be told for many years to come.

Just before the beginning of the unemploymer.t crisis the
Women's Bureau of the Department of Labor made a survey
of Negro women employed in 150 plants in 17 localities of
9 States. In those plants, covering food, furniture, glass,
leather, metal, and paper products, tobacco, and textiles,
there were 11,812 Negro women employed. Some of these
were even making and decorating lamp-shades; some were
making cores in foundries; and others were competing successfully (according to their employers) with girls of many
years' experience in the textile industries. Still others were
serving as stenographers, typists, etc., in two large mail-order
houses in the Middle West.

The questions in the minds of us all are these: How many
of these industries still employ Negro women in appreciable

number in the skilled and unskilled processes? Are there many Negro women in other industries? And how will Negro women bread-winners, unused to domestic service, weather the storm of the unemployment depression? Information to date from industrial plants in the East, West, North, and South indicates. . . . that many have lost their places. . . . A Southern mill that used some Negro women before the war says, "We use Negro women only occasionally now for odd jobs."

In spite of such reports, at least some Negro women are still employed in factories. For instance, the Virginia and Maryland crab factories employ 5000 to 8000 of these women. Some of them now forty or fifty years old have been in the same factory since they were twelve years old. Crabs are brought in barrels placed in large, iron, crate-like kettles, . . . [which are] run on tracks into a steam chest, which cooks the crabs in a few minutes. When they are cold each woman receives a certain number of shovelfuls at a long wooden table, or, in a more up-to-date factory, at a better arranged table for two workers. The woman sits on a box, or a "backless" stool, strikes a crab one blow with the handle of a small knife with curved blade, taking off a part of the shell, and often without even looking at the crab, cuts out what is called "the dead man" and then the white meat, which falls into a pan, and the dark meat, which falls into another. The work is done so rapidly that women pick from forty to seventy-five pounds a day, thus earning $3 or more a day. The crab factories are built over the water, many of them having cement floors. A woman who has worked in such a factory for many years, upon being asked about the healthfulness of such an arrangement, said, "Yes, ma'am, the floors gen'ally fills you full o' rheumatism. Some mo'nin's I kin hardly get out o' bed, I'se so stiff and painful." . . .

Women who have never worked out and whose husbands have lost their jobs after ten or twenty years' service on the railroads or in other places, and others who have worked out but have not been inside of an employment agency for twenty-five or more years, are now trying, through such agencies or through friends, to find a day's work—cleaning or washing or sewing; hair-dressing or manicuring; acting as agents for selling goods; assisting undertakers; or doing anything else whereby they can earn a living. Struggling against lack of training and against inefficiency, restricted in opportunities to get and hold jobs, more than two million Negro women and girls are to-day laboring in domestic service, in argriculture, and in manufacturing pursuits with the hope of an economic independence that will some day enable them to take their places in the ranks with other working women.

Elizabeth Ross Haynes, "Two Million Negro Women at Work,"
The Southern Workman, Vol. 51, No. 2 (February 1922),
pp. 64–72.

WOMEN OF THE STEEL TOWNS

MOLLIE V. LEWIS

I know these women of the steel towns . . . these women living dreary lives under the domination of powerful and impersonal corporations. I have been one of them. The conditions under which they live, the excessive rents demanded for cramped and inadequate shelter, the uncertainty of employment for their men folk and the disruptive inconvenience of the mill shifts all combine to make life a hard and uneven road for them. It is because of such conditions, faced by the women of every mill worker's family, that the Steel Workers' Organizing Committee, of the Committee for Industrial Organization, has sponsored the formation of women's auxiliaries in the campaign for the unionization of the industry.

Last summer I revisited Gary, that hard and unbeautiful metropolis of steel upon the banks of Lake Michigan. In the mills which line the lake shore, furnaces were going full blast, twenty-four hours a day. Steel was pouring from them in molten streams. Thousands of men of both races and many nationalities, sweaty and grimy, were tending the furnaces and conducting the ore through its processes to the finished product.

Something new had come into the lives of these men. Thousands of them had joined the union. For the first time it was possible for them openly to be union men in the mills of the United States Steel Corporation. For the first time this vast corporation for which they worked had recognized their union and entered into an agreement with it.

Only a few miles distant, however, in Indiana Harbor and South Chicago, Little Steel had taken a bitter stand against the union and against the spirit of the New Deal and had engaged in a costly fight which was climaxed by the Memorial Day Massacre. The strike was now over and the men were returning to work without the recognition which had been negotiated with Big Steel.

Hand in hand with the campaign to organize the mill workers went the drive to bring the women folk of these men into active participation in the labor movement. The agency for organizing the women was the Women's Auxiliary of the Amalgamated Association of Iron, Steel and Tin Workers of North America. The objectives of the campaign were to organize the women "to lend aid to the union in all possible ways," to help them to maintain the morale of the steel workers, to educate them in the principles of trade unionism, and to weld them into a force for social betterment.

In the matter of race relations, Gary and the adjacent steel towns are by no means utopian. From time to time bitter racial animosities have flared, not only between Negroes and whites, but also between native citizens and foreign born. In addition many of the foreign born brought with them to this country nationalistic enmities rooted in Old World conflicts. To induce the women of such diverse groups to join the same organization, even for their own benefit, has been no easy task. . . .

In Indiana Harbor where Inland Steel had forced its workers into a long and bitter strike rather than grant their demand for recognition, a number of Negro women had been drawn into the auxiliary. In Gary, however, Negro women seemed more reluctant to join and the campaign had been less successful among them. Along with the women of other groups, Negro women were represented on the picket lines of the struck plants.

During the strike they cooperated with others behind the lines in the preparation and serving of hot meals to the strikers. They were members of the various committees which sought contributions of money and food to keep the strike going. . . .

There is not one auxiliary where the staying power of these courageous women has not carried the organization over some critical period, especially in the first days of unseen and unsung organizing drudgery before the body took form. They were undaunted and gave great moral strength with their persistence. . . .

While the municipal government of Gary continues to keep the children apart in a system of separate schools, their parents are getting together in the union and in the auxiliary. . . . The only public eating place in Gary where both races may be freely served is a cooperative restaurant largely patronized by members of the union and auxiliary.

These, it may be true, are of minor importance. But they represent steps toward inter-racial cooperation on a mass basis. When the black and white workers and members of their families are convinced that their basic economic interests are the same, they may be expected to make common cause for the advancement of these interests. . . .

Mollie V. Lewis, "Negro Women in Steel," *The Crisis*, Vol. 45,
No. 2 (February 1938), p. 54.

A BLACK UNION ORGANIZER

SABINA MARTINEZ, ORGANIZER,
AMALGAMATED CLOTHING WORKERS OF AMERICA

Organized labor has rescued the Negro woman from her obscure position in basic industry, where she once toiled and labored from ten to twelve hours a day under most inhuman conditions and at a starvation wage. Some women have come timidly, others very sure of their convictions, and some with mental reservations. But all have secured better wages, in many cases as much as 60 per cent increase. All their hours have been reduced to eight hours a day, and all their positions have been rendered more secure. The bosses, who formerly subjected them to their whims and fancies, through their participation in unions, have learned to respect them.

In bringing this about organized labor found it no easy task; not because women did not appreciate unions, but because of the false anti-union propaganda that had been handed out to our women by the bosses . . . and because of the definitely Jim-Crow policy of the high executives of the A. F. of L., which ignored Negro people. . . . This policy, along with corrupt Negro leadership, has made it difficult for progressive labor . . . to win the confidence of the Negro people, especially that of the Negro women. However, this mass movement seeking to improve social and economic conditions can no longer be ignored. . . .

Negro women workers welcomed the birth of the C.I.O. and the partially open door of the A. F. of L. and are now a part of such unions as: Laundry, Cleaners and Dyers, Textiles, Teachers, Domestic and others. Negro women helped to lay the basis for these unions and in many instances were on the first committees that helped to formulate the policies of these unions. . . .

The Laundry workers were unorganized for thirty years in the city of New York. In six months the C.I.O. has organized this industry into a compact body of some 27,000 Laundry workers, the great majority of whom are Negro women. Negro women helped lay the foundation, formulate the policies and now hold executive offices in this union, which is an affiliate of the Amalgamated Clothing Workers of America. Some of those who serve on the executive staff of this group are Charlotte Almond, Phoebe Symond, Roberta Randolph, and Sabina Martinez.

The Cleaners and Dyers Union which is only four years old was given its first impetus toward C.I.O. by Ida J. Dudley, a Negro woman. Seeing the need for organization in this field, she started to round up the clerks, being able to organize a vast number of them. The Textile and Domestic workers, who are only partially organized, have brought into the ranks of organized labor hoards of miserable, exploited workers who are denied protection under Social Security or State Labor laws.

Dora Jones, backed by many progressive labor groups, is preparing an extensive drive for the organization of Domestic workers. . . .

In 1930, 3 out of every 5 Negro women employed were in the field of domestic or personal service. Many Negro women have started upon their careers in business as domestic workers, and should be willing to help gain some protection for those who, because of circumstances, are forced to remain in this field.

The Sharecroppers Union, the Tenant League, and many of the newly organized unions owe their existence to the unselfish contributions of Negro women. . . . Organized labor owes women as a class more than a union book. It must rid itself of the old idea that women must be subordinate to men, or that women do not provide as good leadership as men. Organized labor must make a sincere effort to increase the women personnel of its membership. . . . Once a woman has entered her field of industry, she must join that union. She must become a part of the union just as she is a part of her shop. She must attend meetings, participate in discussions and be ever eager to improve the position of herself and her fellow workers. She must consider herself a worker, and be conscious of all political and economic struggles that affect the working group to which she belongs. She must never pass a picket line or buy anything that labor has requested boycotted. She must seriously question herself on the wise use of her vote. . . . Most of all she [the black woman] must have complete confidence in herself and . . . in the principles of organized labor, or she will never be able to convince any fellow workers. . . . She must continue to contribute to the cause of organized labor as a laborer and as a leader.

"Negro Women in Organization—Labor," *The Aframerican*, Vol. 2, Nos. 1 and 2 (Summer and Fall, 1941), p. 17.

ORGANIZING AT WINSTON-SALEM, NORTH CAROLINA

❦ In 1930, there were 34,000 black tobacco workers, representing 23 per cent of those employed. Working conditions in the Southern tobacco industry had remained virtually unchanged since the late nineteenth century. The industry had, since slavery days, employed large numbers of black workers. The tobacco industry preserved a rigidly race-segregated occupational pattern. All skilled and supervisory jobs were held by white men. Machine shredding and other machine operations were done by white men; boxing and packing were jobs for white men and women; cigarette machines were operated by white women, who also did weighing and counting. Black men did the cleaning and sweeping, made containers, lifted and handled shipments. Hand stemming, shredding and blending was work done by black women—all of these operations were carried out in separate buildings. As late as 1944, low wage-scales prevailed: white women earned 57¢ an hour, black women 44¢ an hour. There were other patterns of race discrimination which worked to the disadvantage of black workers. The large stemmeries, which offered year-round employment, hired mostly white help. The small independent stemmeries, which often were located in isolated towns and offered only seasonal employment, hired black women at half the hourly rates earned in the large stemmeries. While white workers could count on being employed two-thirds of the year, black workers would find employment for only one-third of the year. Black women working in the tobacco industry frequently had to supplement their earnings by doing domestic work in the off seasons.

The tobacco industry had been organized since 1890 by the Tobacco Workers International Union, AFL. This weak, undemocratically run union did little to organize black workers and kept those it did organize in race-segregated locals. The National Labor Relations Act of 1937 and competition from several CIO unions put new life into the union and resulted in the inclusion of a number of black men into union leadership. Several CIO unions entered the field in the late 1930's. The Food, Tobacco, Agricultural and Allied Workers of America, CIO (FTA) organized the North Carolina tobacco industry in 1943. It brought black workers into local and regional leadership and claimed to have approximately 50,000 members in 1947. It was a left-wing CIO union, cited in HUAC hearings in 1947 as Communist-dominated, and later purged by the national CIO. Local 22 of the FTA-CIO struck R. J. Reynolds Tobacco Company in May 1947, when 10,000 workers walked off the job, asking for a 15¢-an-hour raise. The R. J. Reynolds Company "Camel" strike was marked by violence, the eviction of strikers, some Communist influence, the intervention of the House Un-American Activities Committee and a militant rank-and-file movement of black women.

Why I Need A Pay Raise
ESTELLE FLOWERS

Sister Estelle Flowers works at the Piedmont Leaf Tobacco Company in North Carolina and makes $21 a week. Mrs. Flowers has four children and is their sole support. "Food takes about all of my wages," she says. "What do we eat? Beans, collards, cornbread. I can't afford milk for the children. My six months old baby has to have milk—one can of evaporated milk—15¢ a can a day. It takes $2 a week for coal and that doesn't keep the home warm. What would I do with more wages? Buy the clothes the children need— more food and I could give more to the church."

FTA News, January 15, 1947.

A Rank-and-File Unionist Speaks
LUANNA COOPER

☞ *Luanna Cooper attended a Progressive Party conference in Cleveland as a delegate from Winston-Salem, North Carolina. She told her story in the following brief interview.*

I'm 49, born in Williamsberg, South Carolina. My mother was afflicted. I never got education. I had to work. I had to get the groceries and sometimes they wouldn't sell to us. I don't understand reading but I know what people need. I've been in service most of my life.

[She went to work for the Winston Leaf Tobacco Storage Company in 1936. Six years later, the CIO Food, Tobacco and Agricultural Workers came to Winston-Salem.] A drink-

ing girl told me about it one day when we left the plant. I
didn't like her but I knew it was right. The bosses are always
telling you some day you'll get to be a big boss but you'll be
dead and all your children be dead before you get to be a
boss. [She became a steward in the local, which was made up
mostly of black women. The local was being raided by another union.] They're trying to have jimcrow unions. But I'm
telling you jimcrow unions aren't good. They wanted me to
join. I told them: "I get jimcrow free. I won't pay for that."

[In December 1948, Luanna Cooper was fired. She has not
had a job since.] I could've got a job as domestic. But I didn't
want to leave the union. But I guess I got to take it now.
Women are being pushed around, back into the kitchen.
During the war domestics got $25 a week. Now they get them
cheap.

In our community today, women can't send their kids to
school. Some of them go without food themselves to get
shoes so the kids can go to school. And they won't give you
relief in Winston-Salem unless you tell them where you were
born, where you're going to die and who your pallbearers
are going to be.

*Her brief speech at the convention had the delegates cheer-
ing. It exemplified the militancy of rank-and-file black
workers.*

I go to conferences and conferences and every place I get
armfuls of papers and resolutions. Sometimes the same resolutions and the same papers.

But resolutions on paper won't solve people's problems.
We got to send men and women out to organize. These
people want to live and if the bosses don't like having you
around bullets will hit you in the head. But we have to send
men and women to organize the people, to tell the people
the truth.

This nation won't ever be free unless people learn the

truth. Speeches is all right but you might as well be asleep if you have just speeches. I tell you, black and white, we can't survive without the other. We got to organize.

"Listen to the story of Luanna Cooper," *National Guardian*, Vol. 1, No. 50 (September 26, 1949), p. 3.

After a 39-day strike, the 8,000 workers won a 12¢-an-hour wage increase. They could also boast of having helped to elect two labor candidates as aldermen of Winston-Salem, one of them the first black man ever in this office.

Black Workers and Unions

MORANDA SMITH

❦ *In November 1947, Moranda Smith (1915–1950), the local's dynamic educational director, attended the national CIO convention. There she spoke in opposition to the Taft-Hartley Bill which was then being debated in the Congress and which the CIO convention opposed.*

I work for the R. J. Reynolds Tobacco Company in Winston-Salem North Carolina. I want to say a few words on this resolution for the reason that I come from the South and I live in the South. I live where men are lynched, and the people that lynch them are still free.

The Taft-Hartley Bill to Local 22 in Winston-Salem is an old, old story. The Taft-Hartley Bill was put before the workers in Winston-Salem about four years ago when the CIO came to Winston-Salem to organize the unorganized workers in the R. J. Reynolds Tobacco plant. We were faced at that time with a lot of court actions. They tried to put fear into the hearts of the workingmen in Winston-Salem.

One of the things in the Constitution of the United States is a guarantee to a human being, regardless of his race, creed or color, of freedom from fear. I say the Taft-Hartley Bill is nothing new to us. When men are lynched, and when men try to strike and walk the picket line, the only weapons that the workers in America, especially in the South, have to protect themselves is action. When they are put in jail, they must protect themselves. If that is the protection of democracy in the United States of America I say it is not enough.

I want to emphasize a few of the things that you have in this resolution. Too long have the Negro people of the South and other workers in America heard a lot of words read to them. It is time for action, and I am now wondering if the CIO is going to stop and do some of the things by action. You talk about political action and you talk about politics. How can there be any action when the Negroes in the South are not allowed to vote? Too long have the workers in the South stopped and looked to Congress for protection. We no longer look to the government in Washington for protection. It has failed. Today we are looking for an organization that says they are organized to fight for the freedom of all men regardless of race, creed or color, and that is the CIO.

I will tell you this and perhaps it will interest you. To the Negro workers in Winston-Salem it means a great deal. They told us, "You cannot vote for this and you cannot vote for that." But last May in the city of Winston-Salem the Negro and white workers, based on a program of unity, were able to put in their city government two labor men. I am proud to say one of those was a Negro. The other was a white labor leader. (Applause.) Yes. We are faced today with this word that they call "democracy." I want to say to this convention let us stop playing around. Each and every one of you here today represents thousands and thousands of the rank and file workers in the plants who today are looking for you to come back to them and give them something to look forward to: not words, but action.

We want to stop lynching in the South. We want people to walk the picket lines free and unafraid and know that they are working for their freedom and their liberty. When you speak about this protection of democracy, it is more than just words. If you have got to go back to your home town and call a meeting of the rank and file workers and say, "This is what we adopted in the convention, now we want to put it into action," if you don't know now how to put it into action, ask the rank and file workers. Ask the people who are suffering, and together you will come out with a good program where civil rights will be something to be proud of. When you say "protection of democracy" in your last convention, along with it you can say we have done this or that. The people that lynch Negroes in the South, the people that burn crosses in the South, the people who put men in jail because they wanted 15 or 20 cents an hour wage increase will learn that the workers can walk as free men, because we have done something in action.

One thing more. I have looked over this delegation, and I wonder if you cherish the word "democracy." I say to you it means something to be free. It means a great deal. I do not think you have ever read or have ever heard of a Negro man or a Negro woman that has ever been a traitor to the United States of America. . . .

They can lynch us. They can beat us. They can do anything they want to, but the Negroes of America who have always been true to the American flag, will always march forward. We are just asking your help. We are not asking for charity. We do not want charity. We belong to America.

Our forefathers fought and bled and died for this country and we are proud to be a part of it just as you are. When the civil liberties of Negroes in the South are interfered with [and] you do nothing about it, I say to you you are untrue to the traditions of America. You have got to get up and do something in action, as I have said before and not by mere words. So we are looking forward to your help and we call on you, because we have called on you before and you have given us aid. We will call on you again, and we ask you not to fail us.

Final Proceedings of the 9th Constitutional Convention of the CIO,
October 15, 1947. Pamphlet.

Tobacco Workers Honor
Fighting Union Leader

On June 3, 1951, thousands of workers, Negro and white together . . . paused to pay tribute to the memory of Sister Moranda Smith.

Moranda Smith was a young Negro woman who had moved as a child with her family from their sharecropper's farm in South Carolina to the tobacco center of Winston-Salem, North Carolina. She was a striking spark of the union spirit that set thousands of workers into militant motion for labor's cause.

She died . . . on April 13, 1950, a casualty of the southern workers' fierce struggle, though she was still in the very prime of life and in the midst of her great work. Born June 3, 1915, she died at the age of 34. Her work as International Representative for FTA took her into contact with many thousands of workers throughout the South Atlantic States.

She was the first woman to serve as Regional Director for an International Union in the South.

In 1943, when an elderly Negro worker fell dead from overwork in a Reynolds plant in Winston-Salem, N.C., after the foreman had refused to let him go home, thousands of Negro women in the plant staged a spontaneous sit-down.

10,000 Walked. This soon spread into a walkout covering some 10,000 workers which forced all the Reynolds Camels-Prince Albert plants to shut down for several days until the company agreed to meet with a workers' committee.

Thousands of workers joined the union to form Local 22, later winning elections and bargaining rights, with contracts won from 1944 through 1947.

In the course of the long union struggle with the R. J. Reynolds Tobacco Company, the workers, led in the main by Negro women workers like Sister Smith, helped to end what amounted to almost slave working conditions and low pay. Many of the workers who joined up were not acquainted with labor unions; but, once members, they were its best supporters.

Memories of Misery. Others could remember 1919 and 1929, when the Reynolds Company ruthlessly crushed attempts by the workers to organize in hopes of gaining a fairer share of the tremendous wealth they were creating by their long hours of drudgery in the tobacco plants.

With the advent of Local 22, these workers won $1,250,000 retroactive pay in the leafhouses and stemmeries. Though before the union they received as little as 40–53 cents an hour, today—because of the local's fight—they receive a minimum of 93 cents. This was made possible because of many great workers who became union leaders—such as Moranda Smith.

Working to build and to keep unity among the workers in the R. J. Reynolds plants, Sister Smith would visit workers at night, and even at lunchtime she would devote the few minutes to persuading workers to join or to become more active in the Local.

Demanded Respect. Because Sister Smith was determined and militant, she was chosen to serve on the union's negotiating committee. The white bossmen who had heaped abuse and poor wages on Negro women now had to deal with them in a respectful manner.

At first, they tried to ignore her presence on the negotiating committee, but she would stand up and forcefully present her arguments. When the bossmen would speak only to the men leaders of the union, the men rejected this attempt to snub her and said: "Address your remarks to Sister Moranda Smith, she is a member of this committee."

And then, much against their wishes, the bosses would have to recognize her. This was a new day and a new way, and Moranda Smith was one of those greatly responsible for making it come about. . . .

Before Local 22 was organized, there were only 163 Negro voters registered in Winston-Salem. After the Union's campaign to register more voters, more than 8,000 new names were placed on the books. The first Negro Alderman to be elected in the South since the turn of the century was elected on the strength of these newly won rights.

Sister Smith held many classes to give instructions on the "know how" of registration and led many workers groups to the courthouse to demand the right to vote.

While Sister Smith was in Apopka, Florida, Klan members seized a Negro worker and tried to force him to tell her whereabouts. He refused to tell. They beat him, threatened to kill him, ground his face into the Florida soil. Still he refused to tell. They gave up and left him lying there, still keeping the secret of her whereabouts.

Defying the Klan. When Sister Smith heard of the Klan attack, she walked, as a friend relates, "down the middle of the street just to show the bosses that union members would not be intimidated."

Meanwhile, the white and Negro workers saw to it that Sister Smith was protected and could leave town after her visit, with no harm.

To Moranda Smith, the union was one of the most important things in her life. She read and studied so she could pass the information on to her fellow-workers. She would travel all night by bus, and the next day—without any sleep —would participate in a meeting or picket line.

It was the terrible strain of [working and organizing] . . . which finally proved too great for this working class heroine. But when she died, she left an inspiring example for all workers to follow. . . .

Today, many Negro women in the South are carrying on in the spirit of Moranda Smith. . . .

Article by a group of Winston-Salem workers and close friends of
Moranda Smith, Union Voice, June 3, 1951.

IT TAKES A WHILE
TO REALIZE THAT IT IS
DISCRIMINATION

FLORENCE RICE

❦ *Florence Rice is a resident of Harlem and a leading activist in tenant and consumer organization.*

I know the Bronx slave market. We used to stand there and people would come and give you any kind of work. At that time it was at 174th street and Sedgwick Avenue. We used to go up there for domestic work. You were competing against each other, because you went out there and you was looking for a dollar a day.

Many times you got a dollar and a half. I always remember my domestic days. Some of the women, when they didn't want to pay, they'd accuse you of stealing. I remember a couple of times the woman said that I had stole something, which I know I hadn't—I just walked out and left that money. It was like intimidation. In those days a white woman says something about a black person, that was it. And what you were subjected to if you'd go in domestic work, the men —I encountered it one time. This man picked me up and said his wife was ill and then when I got there his wife wasn't there and he wanted to have an affair. It seems like I just had enough sense not to let myself get involved with anything like that and I started crying and he didn't force me and I was able to get out. When maids would get together, they'd talk of it. Some of them was very attractive and good-looking. They always had to fight off the woman's husband.

I got out of domestic and went into the laundry. In fact, it was quite interesting. I got my first laundry job on the slave market. This man came to recruit. If you got there early enough they were recruiting for the laundry. They'd pick you up for a day's work or they'd just pick you up for regular work. I think I got regular work from that time on. I went to work in the Bonn Laundry, which is at 175th street. It was better than domestic work, certainly. You were getting twelve dollars and whatever the change was at that time. This was in '36, I think. I was in the laundry before the unions were organizing there. Twelve dollars—oh God, you had to be there at seven and I know you didn't get off at five. I think you got off at six and you were forced to work Saturdays. I wasn't in there too long before the unions came about. The Laundry Workers Union. It was like the salvation. It certainly got better after the union came in. We got better wages, worked a certain amount of hours.

During the war I worked for Wright Aeronautical. They claim that people can't be trained, that you've got to go through seven, eight weeks of training, when during the war we trained in two weeks. I was an internal grinder. You grind with a great big machine and use a micrometer. And we knew how to use a micrometer and we read blueprints and we read the outline. I think I was making anywhere eighty-five, ninety-five dollars a week, which was utopia. I don't think I belonged to the union. There was a lot of black people in the plant. One of the things, there was no black personnel that I can remember. Our heads was white.

At the end of the war we were turned out in the street. The factory didn't close at that time. The factory continued on. They laid us off. This is no more than I think mostly all of us expected.

I had made up my mind that I wasn't going back into the laundry. I didn't go back to the employment service. What the employment agencies did to the blacks was always direct you back into all the servitude jobs. They never tried to encourage you to get something better. And I had a daughter, but I was just determined I wasn't going to the laundry. At that time in the black community the factory was much better than the laundry, like the laundry was better than domestic work.

It was the same with welfare. I always remember when I went to apply for welfare one time, and the woman said, well she needed someone to clean up her house—the welfare investigator, the intake woman, when they sent me to the investigator. She wanted me to do domestic work, and because I refused to do domestic work, I didn't get welfare at that time.

At that time you found lots of black women coming into the garment area. In the cheap shops you found all black women, black and Puerto Rican. A friend of mine heard of a job that was available in her shop. I never saw the kind of a machine I was supposed to work on, and I lied and I said that I knew that machine. She showed me how, she taught me that machine. She said, "All you have to do is sit down and run the machine, if anything happens I'll come up and thread it."

I worked on leggings as a piece worker in Feldman's shop. It was Local 105, International Ladies Garment Workers Union (ILGWU). It was an integrated local. One of the things, they took care of the whites, you didn't have to worry about that. In other words, the white women, white Jewish women, they did always get the work there. Yet I must say with Feldman, he was a pretty fair guy. You would automatically assume this. He was a pretty good boss compared to many of the other bosses. When I say he was fair, I remember that he wanted me to work two machines. When you finished one you got on another machine, and I refused to do it. And I brought the complaint to the union, and the union man came in there, and was very nasty to me, and told me if I didn't want to do it he would get someone else. Well, the union wasn't for us blacks, that's one of the things you recognize. What happened, instead of the union fighting for me, what I did, I got up, put on my clothes, and left. And Feldman, he came to the door and said, "Florence, you and I can talk this out." He said, "I'll tell you what I'll do. I'll

guarantee you a salary, that you'll never make less than that."
And we worked it out. But as far as the union, the union
never stood up for us.

I was a chairlady for five years, I think, from the bottom of
'57 up until '61. When I went in the union, I found myself
thinking that the union was the greatest thing. I even believe
in unions now. I could never say I'm against them—I'm just
against the way that the unions have discriminated against
minority people.

I had some illusions at first. Then all of a sudden you begin
to recognize that all this that glitters is not gold. Underneath
the whole damn thing it's ugliness, because you begin to see,
whites are in control. You're not in control yourself. Many
of the black workers never felt that the union really represented them. What you always found out was that the union
man would say something in front of your face and he would
go back to the boss and it would be completely different. So
the union members began to learn that it was always a sweetheart arrangement with the manufacturer.

For a time I was what you'd call a "good nigger." Because
when you are making like I was anywhere from $135 to $145
a week, then you have reached your utopia, and you were so
very happy to be making that that whatever the boss did you
never could see it. I was a zipper setter, and zipper setters was
paid very well. And I came in the shop first. That was at
Melino's. I was a zipper setter, and there was a black guy
knew the job was going to be open, the place was opening,
and he told me that it was a good job and he wanted to see
me with it. But while I was there, there was another white
girl came in, she came in as a sample maker. But when work
was short, well, she would get all the work. In other words,
they kept her working. And generally it was the black girls
who did not, and this is I think recognized. Because what
you begin to see is that there was discrimination rampant in
the ILGWU. I called the union a country club, because there
is no black people in the leadership at all. None at all. The
union men told me one day they had gotten a colored fellow

to come to a meeting, and he sat up and slept. So there was no use bringing in colored fellows—that was the idea. But what was the most interesting thing, they never brought in people who wouldn't sleep. They never brought in an aggressive person, they always liked somebody who was docile. And they found out that I was very resentful, and I was always making trouble, to which they would say, "Well, you're making a good salary." So the idea in the garment area is, "If you're making a good salary, then you be happy and you keep your mouth shut."

I always remember a girl named Maddy. And Maddy had been there almost as long as I was, she came in after I did. And poor Maddy worked for $40 a week for so long, and yet they brought in white girls right off the street and them girls rose to $80 just like that. They'd bring Italian girls from overseas, they'd train them, they would work, but not the black girls.

I felt very guilty of making good money, and I knew that Maddy wasn't making but $40, and other girls weren't making but a bit of money, until I really begin to act like I was them. I would be fighting to bring up their wage scale and trying to get their pay raised. And when you would do that, you found a business agent would tell you one thing but then he'd go back to the boss and tell another thing. It's done very subtly, and you begin to know. And then afterwards everyone begins to dislike you and you're the enemy. They would tell you that I was a troublemaker.

A group of people I later joined, they were white, Jewish, and they were called the rank and file. But to humiliate them at a union meeting they'd call them Communists. So naturally I was known as a Communist. That was a way of putting you down. I generally continued working with them.

One of the things about the union, especially in piece work, they could always see that you never got that work again. They could cut you down. Many people were afraid to really venture out. The way it works is like this: The boss calls to tell you to come in to work. But what he did, he would call in all the white help first. Then we found out this was a pattern. I would say that all the white girls was making exceptionally good pay. Regardless. It was seen that they made good pay. White folks was always supposed to make more money than black folks. It was done in mostly all the shops. It takes a while to recognize that it is discrimination.

Blacks and Puerto Ricans, I would say, are treated the same way, but what they do, they use a Black against a Puerto Rican and a Puerto Rican against a Black. Because if you have a shop where there's all Blacks in it, who are making good money, then they'll bring in a Puerto Rican at a cheaper price. Then the Puerto Ricans will bring in their people, and they'll all come in at a cheaper wage, so the boss steps down the salary scale. It's divide and conquer.

I brought it to the attention of some of the other black chairladies, didn't they realize they were being discriminated against, and could we do something about it together, and one of the ladies said, well, she had children and she could not get involved, she would rather have a little bit than none at all. To organize working people, that's the hardest work of all, because you must remember they have to make a living. Working women do not have the time to organize. They can't allow themselves to get involved in discussions. Because their first duty is to their family. Most of them were married women with children and families—and so therefore it gave them little time. Of course you did have the lucky women, the single women, but those women were really after good homes and good cars, things like that, so they weren't that aggressive. The black workers had a feeling that if you fought the union you automatically lost your job. You found out, that you eventually would be just knocked off, the next year they wouldn't call you back or they'd find a way of eliminating your work. They always found a way of hitting you financially. It was done on me.

At Malena, that was another company, I was the first to be laid off. I had been the first hired, but when work came in

I was never the first to get called. Our work always started up early in the season, so you had sample work, but up until that year June I had not been called. My daughter was graduating. I couldn't get no welfare help, I wasn't called in to work. As a result of it, that morning I got up and I played this number 617. This is the way my daughter got her graduation dress, playing that number that day. One hundred thirty-five dollars.

At Malena is where they started giving me very bad work, and half the time they wouldn't call me in, and it just took a toll on my income. I was slowly pushed out. My God, from a hundred and some dollars a week, I had dropped down to sixty, sixty-five. There was never no work for me. So I couldn't stay there. Then I started going elsewhere, I started going into non-union shops. If I went for a job and I'd say, "I'm Florence Rice," which I didn't try to hide, even if they wanted somebody, then they didn't need anybody. I was blacklisted, that's what I was, blackballed. I would say the union did it, it's very easy to do. You never have no kind of proof. Those of us who know what the whole thing is all about, know its quietly done.

The union was running my life and the whites were in control of black people and we could never be able to do anything as long as it was set up like it is now. I see hopes for unions as long as they practice true democracy. The fact is, the democracy that they talk about has never been practiced in this country in anything. And as long as this continues on you're always going to have the frustrations that's in this country now. The unions as they are, they're just a dictatorial power that has power over people's lives.

❦ *Florence Rice testified concerning discrimination in the ILGWU at hearings held in 1962 by the House Committee on Labor, Education and Welfare. The committee was then headed by Congressman Adam Clayton Powell.*

In 1962, as I was sitting in the outer office, where they were interviewing for the people who was going to testify, everyone who had promised Odell [Odell Clark, the committee representative] they were going on the stand that next morning was all calling up or stopped in and said that they would not do it, and this was whites and Blacks. They would not testify on what they had said before, because they were afraid of losing their jobs. And so as I sat there I felt that I had nothing to lose. I was still working for Malena, but I felt that I did not have nothing to lose, and that I would go on and make a statement. I told them that I would go on record that what many of them had said about discrimination in the union was true, and that I had witnessed it. The next day people was just withdrawing. Helen Green and I was the only person who came in, and what we had said in closed doors we were willing to say to the public. This is what I testified:

I have been a member of the ILGWU for approximately 16 years, having become a member in 1946 when I started work in the garment industry as an operator.

For the last 8 years I have been a member of local 155, ILGWU, a local in which I alone along with the other Negro and Puerto Rican members of the local have been subject to discrimination in many subtle forms.

The business agents of the ILGWU are well aware of what is taking place as regards to discrimination in the shops. They either condone it or overlook it. That during the time I was employed at Malena's Sportswear at 191 Chrystie Street in New York City as an operator, when the Negro and Puerto Rican girls complained that they could not make out, produce enough work for a minimum day's pay, no attempt to adjust the work was ever made for our group.

The Puerto Rican girls always get the cheaper work,

or the prices are set so low that it is impossible for them to make out. The white employees, however, are given a better price for the same jobs given to the Negro and Puerto Rican employee.

Whenever a new type machine was brought into the shop the white employee was always taught how to operate it first. They were given preference. Though I was employed for 8 years at Malena's Sportswear, I was never given the opportunity to work on any other machine which might enable me to earn added income even though I was second in seniority.

I attribute this to the discriminatory pattern used against the Negro and Puerto Rican employees in the shops, because even though our business agent was informed of this situation and advised us that he would look into the matter, nothing was ever done.

When it is slow and employees are laid off, the first ones to be laid off are the minority groups and when the season starts again, the minority groups are the last ones to be called back.

I have learned that the workers have been intimidated by union officials with threat of losing their jobs if they so much as appear at the hearing which not one has at this time.

Later, the union had a hearing on us. They had us there up on stage at a local meeting. They wanted us to say in front of union members that we had lied on the stand, and stuff like that. And Helen Green and I, we just stood up. They never expelled you, but when you go through that, it's like a gentleman agreement. I didn't work in the shops after that. A friend of mine gave me my first job in the white collar workers, and that's where I've sort of been ever since.

Since I left, I think it's gotten worse, from what I hear. The wages are down, the garment industry is moving out, and it's a really cut-throat business now. It's worse.

The young kids ask me why don't I wear an Afro. Well, I

don't have to prove nothing. I got scars all over my body
from all the struggles I been in.

Florence Rice, taped interview with Gerda Lerner, September 23,
1970. Used by permission.
Hearing testimony: Ad Hoc Subcommittee on Investigation of the
Garment Industry of the Committee on Education and Labor,
House of Representatives, 87th Congress, 2nd Session, Adam C.
Powell, Chairman; Hearings held in New York, New York,
August 17, 18, 23, 24; Washington, D.C., September 21, 1962
(Washington, D.C.: Government Printing Office, 1962).

CHAPTER FIVE

SURVIVAL IS A FORM OF RESISTANCE

Neber 'spise a bridge dat carries
you safely ober.

Gulla Proverb

SURVIVAL
IS A FORM OF
RESISTANCE

❦ Over and over again, in their 350 years of history, black people in white America have had to struggle for sheer survival. Not only physical and economic survival, but spiritual survival was at stake as generation after generation sought to come to terms with an impeccably hostile and exploitative environment. Black women played their part: bearing and rearing children, often working to support them, educating them for their dual roles in white and black society and transmitting the traditions and heritage of black culture as best as they could. Black women endured for the sake of their children; black folk survived despite all odds. Survival meant scrounging for food and curing sickness with home remedies, building schools and hospitals and orphanages out of pennies and nickels saved, scrubbing white people's floors and laundry to send the children to school and college. It meant daily living in danger and hardship, swallowing anger and suppressing rage, and yet somehow raising children with enough hope and courage to survive on their own.

The black family established its own form of existence in response to the environment. Theirs was not the small and vulnerable nuclear family of white America, but the extended kinship system of rural folk and of the poor who cooperate that each child may live and survive, no matter what befalls its own father and mother. The black family endured. Black women stood beside and with their men, doing their share and more, taking over when there was a need, seeing to it that the race survived.

SOMETHING TOLD ME NOT TO BE AFRAID

CHARLOTTE ANN JACKSON

When i was liveing with White People i was tide down
hand and foot and they tide me to the Post and whip me till
i Could not stand up and they tide my Close over my head
and whip me much as they want and they took my Brother
and sent him to Richmond to stay one year And sent my
Aunt my Sister my farther away too and said if he did not
go away they would kill him they said they was Goin to Put
me in Prisens But the light has come the Rebles is put down
and Slavry is dead God Bless the union Forever more and
they was puting people in tubs and they stead me to Death
and i hope slavry shall be no more and they said that the
yankees had horns and said that the yankees was Goin to kill
us and something told me not to Believe them and som-
thing told me not to Be afraid and when they Come hare
they would not let me Come out to see them and when i
was out in the Street they was Stead i would go away from
them and they said I Better stay whith them for the yankees
would kill me I would Better stay

Lucy Chase Manuscript, American Antiquarian Society,
Worcester, Massachusetts. Reprinted in Henry L. Swint,
Dear Ones at Home: Letters from Contraband Camps
(Nashville, Tennessee: Vanderbilt University Press, 1966), p. 252.

THREE TIMES THREE CHEERS FOR THE GUNBOAT BOYS

❦ *A freedwoman speaks of her experiences.*

In one cabin there were two quite intelligent mulatto
women, better clad than any I had met in the camp, one of
whom was the mother of three fine-looking children. I . . .
inquired how long they had been within our lines.

One of them answered, "Only ten days. Thar was thirty-three when we left our plantation seven miles below Memphis, 'bout three weeks ago, but some of our people stopped at Memphis when we came up the river."

As I was interested in her recital, she became more excited in giving details, and said:

"Mistress got mighty feared of black smoke, an'watched boats mighty close. One day as she was settin' on the sofa she say, "Mill, I reckon that's a gunboat comin'; see de black smoke; an' if they do come, I reckon they won't fin' that trunk o' money, an'ches' of silver plate you put up in the lof' t'other day.' Lookin' out for the boat, 'Yes that's a gunboat sure. Now, if the Yankees do stop, you all run and hide, won't you?' I looked too, but didn't answer till I see the big rope flung on the bank. An' mistress got wild-like. 'Yes, they are stoppin'. Mill an' Jule run, tell all the niggers in the quarters to run to the woods an' hide; quick, for they kills niggers. Mill, why don't you go?' I said, ' I ain't feared the Yankees.' 'Jule, you run and tell all the niggers to run to the woods, quick. Yes, here they are coming, right up to the house. Now, Mill, you won't go with them, will you?' As the men had started for the house I felt safe, and said, 'I'll go if I have a chance.' 'Jule, you won't go, will you?' 'I shall go if Mill goes.' She began to wring her hands and cry. 'Now, 'member I brought you up. You won't take your children away from me, will you, Mill?' 'Mistress, I shall take what children I've got lef'. 'If they fine that trunk o' money or silver plate you'll say it's your'n, won't you?' 'Mistress, I can't lie over that; you bo't that silver plate when you sole my three children.' 'Now, Jule, you'll say it's yourn, won't you?' 'I can't lie over that either.' An' she was cryin' an' wringin' her han's, an' weavin' to an' fro as she set thar. 'Yes, here they come, an' they'll rob me of every thing. Now, 'member I brought you up.' Here come in four sojers with swords hangin' to their sides, an' never looked at mistress, but said to me, 'Auntie, you want to go with us?' 'Yes, sir,' I said, an' they look to Jule an' say, 'You want to go?' 'Yes, sir.' 'Well, you can all go; an' hurry, for we shall stay but a little while.'

An' Jule jus' flew to the quarters, an' they all tied up beds an' every thing, an' tote 'em down to the gunboats in a hurry. An two sojers went up-stairs an' wa'n't gone but a few minutes, an' don't you think here they come, with that tin trunk o' money an' ches' of silver plate, an' broke 'em open an' tuck out a big platter an' water-pitcher an' a few other pieces an' say, 'See here, Tom, haven't we foun' a prize of solid silver for gov'ment,' an' he put it all back. . . . Then they broke open the meal-room, an' rolled out barrels of meal and flour, saved for secesh sojers, an' rolled 'em down to the gunboat. An', last of all, they went to the smoke house, an' broke it open an' got a lot of bacon. 'Now, auntie, you all ready,' they say? 'Yes, sir,' I tell 'em. 'Here's a roll of linsey for our cloze, shall we take it?' 'Certainly, an' any thing else you'r a mine to.' As we started for the door mistess followed us cryin' an' wringin' her han's. 'Now, Mill an' Jule, I know you'll suffer when you leave me.' One o' the sojers turn to her and said, 'They won't suffer again as they have done with you.' An' this was the firs' words she spoke after they come in, an' the firs' they said to her. An' we all got on the boat in a hurry; an' when we's fairly out in the middle of the river, we all give three times three cheers for the gunboat boys, and three times three cheers for big Yankee sojers, an' three times three cheers for gov'ment; an' I tell you every one of us, big and little, cheered loud and long and strong, an' made the old river just ring ag'in."

Laura S. Haviland, A Woman's Life-Work, Labors and Experiences (Chicago: Publishing Association of Friends, 1889), pp. 273–275.

A BLACK WOMAN REMEMBERS HER FATHER

ANONYMOUS

My father was slave in name only, his father and master being the same. He lived on a large plantation and knew many useful things. The blacksmith shop was the place he liked best, and he was allowed to go there and make little tools as a child. He became an expert blacksmith before he was grown. Before the war closed he had married and was the father of one child. When his father wanted him to remain on the plantation after the war, he refused because the wages offered were too small. The old man would not even promise an increase later; so my father left in a wagon he had made with his own hands, drawn by a horse he had bought from a passing horse drover with his own money.

He had in his wagon his wife and baby, some blacksmith tools he had made from time to time, bedding, their clothing, some food, and twenty dollars in his pocket. As he drove by the house he got out of the wagon to bid his father good-by. The old man came down the steps and, pointing in the direction of the gate, said: "Joseph, when you get on the outside of that gate—stay." Turning to my mother, he said: "When you get hungry and need clothes for yourself and the baby, as you are sure to do, come to me," and he pitched a bag of silver in her lap, which my father immediately took and placed at his father's feet on the steps and said, "I am going to feed and clothe them and I can do it on a bare rock." My father drove twenty-five miles to the largest town in the State, where he succeeded in renting a small house.

The next day he went out to buy something to eat. On his way home a lady offered him fifty cents for a string of fish for which he had only paid twenty cents. That gave him an idea. Why not buy fish every day and sell them? He had thought to get work at his trade, but here was money to be made and quickly. So from buying a few strings of fish he soon saved enough to buy a wagon load of fish.

My mother was very helpless, never having done anything in her life except needlework. She was unfitted for the hard work, and most of this my father did. He taught my mother to cook, and he would wash and iron himself at night.

Many discouraging things happened to them—often sales were slow and fish would spoil; many would not buy of him

because he was colored; another baby was born and died, and
my father came very near losing his life for whipping a white
man who insulted my mother. He got out of the affair finally,
but had to take on a heavy debt, besides giving up all of his
hard earned savings.

My father said after the war his ambition was first to
educate himself and family, then to own a white house with
green blinds, as much like his father's as possible, and to
support his family by his own efforts; never to allow his wife
and daughters to be thrown in contact with Southern white
men in their homes. He succeeded.

"The Race Problem—An Autobiography," by "A Southern Colored
Woman," *The Independent*, Vol. 56, No. 2885 (March 17, 1904),
p. 586.

A FAMILY STRUGGLES
TO KEEP GOING

MRS. FRANCES A. JOSEPH GAUDET

❦ *Mrs. Frances A. Joseph Gaudet here recalls her
childhood in Mississippi during the Reconstruction. After the
death of her father during the Civil War, her grandparents
took over the care of the two children. Her grandfather
helped to build the first church for Negroes in the town
of Summit and organized the first school there. The struggles
of the small family for survival and for an education for
the children are quite typical of the self-help efforts of the
freedmen.*

How I loved the big meeting days, when on the first Sunday
of the month, people came from one to thirty miles to hear
the gospel from some poor, earnest, struggling black preacher.
We children sat on the floor around the altar, glad to be

there, sometimes falling asleep and bumping our heads. When preaching was over we would eat dinner that had been prepared on Saturday, water our stock and start for home. As we only lived two miles from church my grandparents walked. Brother Eugene and I ran on in front through the woods taking off our shoes and wading the creek, while the old folks walked the log further down. Our parents were very poor. We had to go barefooted all the summer, so as to save our shoes for winter. They were russets with brass tips and brother and I would try to see which could shine those tips the brightest. Then when all work was done we rushed away to the clay pile to make mud pies, men, houses, etc. Sometimes grandfather came out, and while watching us made some useful suggestions, that we always prized.

We had no toys and sometimes amused ourselves catching butterflies. Grandfather would tell us the names of the pretty colors on their wings, then we would let them go; often I watched them as far as I could, then would ask where they had gone; was there another town like ours? He would answer, yes, and tell of the large city far away where he hoped to go some day.

His hopes were realized sooner then he expected. My oldest uncle lived on a plantation with his wife and two children. The overseer had forced my uncle's wife to come to his room while uncle was away. When he returned he took his gun and killed the overseer, and this made my uncle a fugitive from his town. Grandfather was so troubled by this he couldn't live in peace at his home. I was eight years old and brother was ten when they moved to the city of New Orleans and sent us to a private school near our home. Four years later found me in the fourth grade in Mrs. Ludwig's room in the public school on Clio street, near Prytania. My grandparents both died, leaving us with mother, who had married a sailor. She moved downtown and sent me to Straight University a while. My stepfather died and mother had to take me from school. Brother and I had to help her earn money to support the other three children. My

heart ached and many nights my pillow was wet with tears
because I could not finish school. I loved poetry and every
spare penny I got went for books which I read at night.

Autobiography of Mrs. Frances A. Joseph Gaudet,
as cited in Elizabeth L. Davis, *Lifting As They Climb*
(Washington, D.C.: National Association of Colored Women,
1933), pp. 229–230.

A NIGHT WATCH

MARIA L. BALDWIN

✓ Maria Louise Baldwin (1856–1922) was born in
Cambridge, Massachusetts. After graduating from Cambridge
High School in 1874, she took a one-year teacher training
course and accepted her first teaching assignment in Ches-
tertown, Maryland. In 1881, she started teaching in the
Cambridge public school system at the Agassiz Grammar
School. In 1899, she became the school's principal and held
that position until her death. In 1916, when a new building was erected for the school, her title was changed to
"Master." All the teachers she supervised and most of the
students in the school were white.

Maria Baldwin was one of the founders of the Women's
Era Club, President and member of the Boston Ethical
Society and the League for Community Service, and a
member of the 20th Century Club. She was an excellent and
popular lecturer. One of her activities was the sponsorship
of a kindergarten in Atlanta, Georgia.

The following is a childhood reminiscence.

One evening during the latter part of the Civil War the town
of Bainbridge was filled with suppressed excitement. News
had been brought from a neighboring city that the mob
which a few days before had fallen upon New York, burning

houses, killing helpless women and children—the mob that had left New York streets one mass of trampled human bodies—was coming to Bainbridge to continue its murderous work. Men gathered in groups on the street and talked in grave low tones, then separated to make ready their guns and pistols. A neighbor came in to tell my mother the worst that was expected. For answer she gave him a look pitiable in its helplessness; then she stretched out her hand toward us children and looked about wildly as if for some way of escape.

Nothing happened that night, and with returning day hearts grew stronger. But at evening the men came home again with faces full of foreboding and that night no man in the town slept. The twilight deepened, darkness settled down unrelieved by a single gleam of light from the houses. A dreadful stillness pervaded the streets, and in one window of each of these darkened homes sat a silent watcher.

My mother tremblingly put together a few things in a bundle; I closely followed her. I think my child's heart recognized that her fright was as great as my own. Our house was surrounded by a low paling fence over which any school-boy might easily have vaulted, but the little gate of this fence my mother tied with yards of clothes line. Against the front door she pulled our heavy mahogany sofa. But, after all, how defenceless we were. Oh the happy children who were protected by a "big man with a gun."

When everything was done, my mother laid us children, fully dressed, upon the bed and sat down beside it at the open window. I took fast hold of her dress and lay straining my eyes in the darkness to keep her outlines. I was in an agony of fear lest somehow I should lose her, and kept fastening my slipping fingers nearer to the gathers of her dress. I think I must have fallen asleep and then wakened—wakened to the awful darkness—wakened to find that I had lost her. I screamed in terror. I felt her almost spring upon me to silence me; then she gathered me close up to her and again took up her watch.

Suddenly the stillness became full of a commotion that I

felt, rather than saw or heard. My mother grasped the bundle beside her, dragged us both to our feet, then stood listening.

From the direction in which the men had been watching came a sound like that of horses' feet. There was noiseless running and husky whispering in the streets. The clattering noise grew clearer. I was leaning from the window now beside my mother, and in a moment more we saw the twinkle of lights carried by men on horseback with tall plumes upon their heads. Then men came tearing through the streets, the frantic joy of their voices breaking the terrible silence. "The soldiers! The soldiers! They've come to protect us!"

> Maria L. Baldwin, "A Night Watch," *The Women's Era*,
> Vol. 1, No. 6 (September 1894).

I WAS A NEGRO COME OF AGE

ELLEN TARRY

❦ *Ellen Tarry was born in Birmingham, Alabama, in 1906, the child of mulatto parents who were highly respected in the white community. Blond, blue-eyed and white-skinned, she had been raised to think of herself as superior to most Negroes by virtue of her family's gentility, respectability and good education. She attended a Catholic school and, despite her family's strong opposition, converted to Catholicism. After taking writing courses at Alabama State College, she worked as a feature writer on the black weekly Birmingham Truth from 1926 to 1929.*

In 1929, she moved to New York City. Because of her difficult struggle for subsistence during the Depression, she had to abandon her plan to study journalism at Columbia University. Instead she was on the WPA Federal Writers' Project, wrote several children's books and later did free-lance writing for black newspapers and Catholic magazines. She became part of the sophisticated literary set which

clustered around Claude McKay and other writers of the
Harlem Renaissance group. Ellen Tarry also worked with
a group of Catholic activists who sought to offset Communist
influence in Harlem. In 1942 she moved to Chicago, where
she helped to organize Friendship House, an international
center.

Her autobiography, The Third Door: The Autobiography
of an American Negro Woman, describes life in Jim Crow
America from the point of view of a black woman who at
any time could pass for white. In the pages below she
describes her first contact with the realities of black life. The
incident takes place in the 1920's.

I felt like a real grown-up lady when I finally won consent
to go to a party without a chaperon. I was more than a little
excited when one of the boys who took me out borrowed an
automobile and called for me. Mama was giving my escort
her final instructions on what time I should come home
when a car drove up. A light was flashed on our porch, then
on the house next door before the driver stopped alongside
a parked car that belonged to a man I had heard our new
neighbors call "Shorty." Anxious to be on our way, we
promised to be home "early" and started down the steps.

"Wait!" my mother screamed as two white policemen
jumped out of the automobile with drawn guns and moved
toward Shorty's car.

"Get out of there!" we heard one of them call to the two
Negro men sitting in the parked automobile.

"And get out with your hands in the air!" yelled the other.
"You boys got corn in this car and we gonna find it tonight!"

"Well, what you standing there like dummies for?" the
first officer continued. "You *have* got whisky, haven't you?"

"No, sir!" the Negroes cried, their arms high in the air.

"We'll see," the officer said as he and his partner started
searching the car.

Watching from our vine-covered porch, it looked as if the

policemen were trying to turn the automobile into something for a junk dealer's yard. Cushions were thrown in the street, tools were scattered about and we could hear boards being ripped from the floor, although it was already evident that the zealous enforcers of Birmingham's dry law were laboring in vain.

"We didn't get you tonight," one of them said, wiping the sweat from his face. "But we've had a tip on you boys and we'll catch you yet!"

The rare sight of two white men working so hard—and in vain—must have amused Shorty, the smaller of the two Negroes, and he giggled.

"So it tickles you, eh?" shouted one of the officers. "Well, laugh this off!"

There was a succession of thuds as the butt of the officer's revolver cracked against the little Negro's skull again and again. He raised his arms to ward off the blows, but they came too fast and with too much force. He fell and his body lay crumpled and still on the pavement as his friend stood helpless, his black hands high above his head.

"Guess that'll teach him not to be so smart the next time," laughed the other policeman as he walked over to the prostrate form and gave it a kick. The Negro groaned and the white men laughed louder.

I suddenly realized this was not a bad dream. Shorty was real and so were the two men standing over him, especially the one who had raised his foot again.

"You dirty dog!" I screamed, "you're kicking a man who's flat on his back!"

A hand was clasped over my mouth. "Shut up, you little simpleton!" Mama muttered. "Don't you know they could do the same thing to you and I couldn't do a thing about it?"

Shorty groaned again before I could grasp the full meaning of what my mother had said to me. She tried to block me but I ran around her, down the steps, and into the street where Shorty lay with his attackers towering over him. I could hear words coming out of my mouth but I was past fear. The officers peered at me for a second, then ordered Shorty's friend to "get" and he ran up the street.

The men were still laughing when they drove away. Suddenly, I saw that the street was in darkness except for the corner light. The porches were empty, front shades were drawn. Mama was behind the vines and my escort was leaning over the fence retching as he vomited out his fear. There was nobody in the street but Shorty and me.

At that moment words and phrases which had lurked in the nether regions of my consciousness took on meaning. I knew that Shorty and I were alone; nobody wanted anything to do with us at the moment. They would say we were "hotheaded," that we didn't "know our place." Shorty was only half-conscious, but for the first time in my life I knew who and what I was. . . . I was a Negro come of age! All my life I must have looked at things which I had refused to *see*. Now I both saw and understood.

My legs felt weak and I sat on the curb. I remembered the boy whom I had first heard whisper "race riot." Soon after, I remembered, I saw Papa put a gun in the drawer of a table in the parlor. Then came the parade in the middle of the night. A Ku Klux Klan parade, they said.

I remembered how Mama took me out of bed and carried me to the parlor where I saw Papa, in his old-fashioned night shirt, standing by the front window. He was as still as a statue and his fists were clenched. There had been the clatter of horses' hooves as the light from a fiery cross held high by white-robed men on horseback flashed a warning of destruction to all Jews, Catholics, and Negroes. Papa had opened the table drawer. As the reflection from the burning cross lighted up our room, it glistened against the steel of the revolver in his hand. Mama tightened her grip on my arm but I broke away and pressed my nose against the windowpane, the better to see the men who rode white horses and carried fiery crosses. After the last clop-clop died away there was a long stillness.

As I sat there . . . I closed my eyes and saw again the

frightened faces of Negro mothers when white men stalked through our neighborhood, jingling money in their pockets. Now I knew why schoolchildren shouted, "Yaller is roguish, but black is honest." . . .

Shorty stirred, then dragged himself to the curb where he sat with his head between his knees. We had never spoken in our lives. Tonight there was no need for words.

"Why," I asked myself, "did I ever think I was needed in Africa? Alabama was my Africa. Catholic or Protestant, white, black, or yellow, whatever I was, was wrong. I wanted to hide. But there was no hiding place and nobody to tell me why. The world—it could not be God's world. It was the white man's world and I was not white. . . ."

Ellen Tarry, The Third Door: The Autobiography of an American Negro Woman (New York: David McKay Co., 1955), pp. 60–64.

WE WANT TO LIVE, NOT MERELY EXIST

MRS. HENRY WEDDINGTON

Chicago, Illinois
Feb. 16, 1941

Dear President Roosevelt:

I really don't know exactly how to begin this letter to you. Perhaps I should first tell you who I am. I am a young married woman. I am a Negro. . . . I believe that you are familiar with the labor situation among the Negroes, but I want you to know how I and many of us feel about it and what we expect of you.

My husband is working for the W.P.A. doing skilled labor. Before he started on this we were on relief for three months. We were three months trying to get relief. While trying to obtain relief I lost my unborn child. I believe if I had sufficient food this would not have happened. My husband was perfectly willing to work but could not find it. Now I am pregnant again. He is working at Tilden Tech. School where there are more white than colored. Every month more than one hundred persons are given private employment and not one of them are colored. It isn't that the colored men are not as skilled as the white, it is the fact that they are *black* and therefore *must not* get ahead.

We are citizens just as much or more than the majority of this country. . . . We are just as intelligent as they. This is suppose to be a free country regardless of color, creed or race but still *we* are slaves. . . . Won't you help us? I'm sure you can. I admire you and have very much confidence in you. I believe you are a real Christian and non-prejudice. I have never doubted that you would be elected again. I believe you can and must do something about the labor conditions of the Negro.

Why must our men fight and die for their country when it won't even give them a job that they are fitted for? They would much rather fight and die for their families or race. Before it is over many of them might. We did not ask to be brought here as slaves, nor did we ask to be born black. We are real citizens of this land and must and *will* be recognized as such! . . . If you are a real Christian you can not stand by and let these conditions exist.

My husband is young, intelligent and very depressed over this situation. We want to live, not merely exist from day to day, but to live as you or *any* human being desires to do. We want our unborn children to have an equal chance as the white. We don't want them to suffer as we are doing now because of race prejudice. My husband is 22 and I am 18 years of age. We want to own just a comfortable home by the time he reaches his early thirties. Is that asking too much? But how can we do that when the $26 he makes every two weeks don't hardly last the two weeks it should. I can manage money rather well but still we don't have the sufficient amount of food or clothes to keep us warm. . . .

I would appreciate it very much if you would give this letter some consideration and give me an answer. I realize that you are a very busy person and have many problems but please give this problem a little thought also.

I will close thanking you in advance.

Sincerely and hopefully yours
Mrs. Henry Weddington

WPA Box, Howard University, Washington, D.C.

BLUE FORK IS THE WORST PLACE I KNOW ...
SARAH TUCK

❖ *Sarah Tuck is thirteen years old. Her mother died about a year before this interview. Sarah lives with her father, a cotton sampler who earns $13 per week, and her three sisters and one brother in a shabby little house which they own in Blue Fork, Sandy Run, North Carolina.*

I get up at six o'clock every morning. In the winter time I don't have to cook, wash, or clean up. Papa pays a lady from Woodson to come here and do it. She gets here every morning about six-thirty, cooks breakfast for us and cleans the house. She looks after everything. All us children help, though, when she tells us to. Papa says it's too much for me to try to go to school and look after everything, too. In the summer I do everything—all the washing, cooking and minding the children. I don't mind. Mama taught us all to work before she died. I think I ought to see after my sisters and brothers. . . .

Light brown is the best color of all. It's just pretty. . . . I'd rather be any color but black. . . . It is nasty looking. . . . My own color is the one I like most. It would make me mad if I was black and somebody called me that. Papa is my color. He's so tall you have to look way up to see him.

I just hate white people. Don't like them at all. I'm just like my auntie. She hates them, too. They call colored people black and nigger and smut black, and I hate them. I wouldn't play with white children—never have and won't if I never have no children to play with. I only see them in stores and I act just as hateful as they do. They throw the money down at you and I throw it down to them. I just can't stand Mr. Josh—that's the white man where my father works. If you cough around his baby he gets mad. So does his wife. One day a colored boy coughed near his baby and he was so mad he wanted to whip the colored boy—said, 'Don't you never dare cough 'round this child.' His wife kept on turning her head around like this to see if anyone was going to touch the baby. They don't want no colored people touching their baby 'cause they think colored will give the baby germs. . . . Wanted me to quit school and stay and help his wife wash dishes. He thinks colored don't need to go to school. That's the way he is. Well, I wouldn't do it. 'Spec I'd cry myself to death if I couldn't go to school. White people look bad to me. Most of them are red white people with all them red wrinkles 'round their neck. Well, it looks rusty and nasty to me. They like to make believe they are so much better than the colored people but they ain't really as good. They are too mean and low. I ain't never had a fight with any, but I wouldn't be afraid to fight them if I had to. There ain't many whites here in Blue Fork—just a few and they are so poor and low. They drink whiskey and act somethin' terrible. When they ain't drunk they get on all right with the colored, but when they are drunk and the colored are drunk too it's terrible. They fight and cuss and carry on. Soon's they sober up they get back friends again. I don't like 'em—them what do can have my share.

Blue Fork is the worst place I know. I'd a heap rather live out there in Littleton near my grandmother. We been here eleven years and Papa keeps saying we going to move but we haven't moved nowhere. People here are rough and bad. . . . 'Bout all the men-folks round here don't do nothin' but sell whiskey and beat their wives. That woman what was fighting so yesterday out in the road, well her husband beats her somethin' terrible, but she sho loves him. She won't leave him for nothin'. I wouldn't stand for no man to beat me if I was grown. I don't even like to say I live at Blue Fork. It's got a bad name. Everyone knows what rough and bad people live here and I feel shameful to have anybody come out here to visit me. They think all the people out here are so bad, so they think you must be, too, if you live out here. . . . Well, I try to be good and do what is right. Papa, he does, too. He ain't round here drinking and selling whiskey. He's a good man. He goes to the Israel Baptist church and walks every Sunday, but the rest of us go to Rev. Goons' church in Woodson. It's Baptist, too, and ain't so far to walk. . . .

I don't go over to the recreation center much during the summer. It's so far and if I went I'd have to take all these other children along, too. What I like to do most of all is go to the movies. About once a month Papa gives me money to go and take all the children. That's the most fun I have. I don't like those western movies, though. The boys go to see them and come home and try to act just like the wild people act in them. I like Jane Withers and Shirley Temple and pictures like that. I don't go to parties. I don't think I'd like a party—I've never been to one. They are too dangerous. People always fighting and killing at parties and we don't go. I play games and read books for fun. The kind of books I read are my school books.

I like school. I failed this year because I had so much to do at home. I felt bad about failing my grade but they are going to give me a chance to take the tests over when school opens. I try to study my lessons a little every day now, but the children always run in and want something and I never get back to studying. They're always out in the road singing and dancing and that takes my attention. I like to dance, too, so I put my books up and go out with them. Miss Benson is my favorite teacher. I like the way she explains things. She's about thirty or thirty-five, been out of school a long time, but she don't act real old just the same. She is light brown and nice looking. Geography is my favorite subject. You learn all about parts of the world. . . . Arithmetic is the subject I hate. It is so hard. I can't ever do the problems or know what the teacher means—that's one thing that held me back. Papa went to school to ask the teacher why I failed and she said I did the best work I could, but I just couldn't get it. . . .

What I want to do when I've grown is to be a show girl and sing and dance. I can sing pretty good—sometimes I sing in the road in front of folk's houses and they give me nickels. I know how to tap dance, Susie Q, and do the check and double check. I can do any dance I see in the movies. I don't need lessons—it just comes natural. . . . If I can't be a dancer or a show girl, I'd be a piano teacher. I never had lessons, but Papa's going to begin me in the fall. My auntie lives in Woodson and she's got a piano so she will let me come to her house for music lessons. Miss Wells is a music teacher and is going to teach me. Other than them I don't want to do nothin'. I like school, but I wouldn't want to be no school teacher. I got all the children right here I want to see after and I don't never want to look after no more. That's why I'd never have no children when I marry. I don't never want to have to look after no more children. . . .

I'll get married some day when I'm older, but not for a long time. I'd like to marry a man has an orchestra so I could do the singing and dancing in the orchestra. I wouldn't want him to drink whiskey or stay out late at night, he'd sho have to treat me nice, I wouldn't stand for no bad treatment. . . .

Charles S. Johnson, "The Social World of Negro Youth" Social Science Source Documents, No. 5 (Nashville, Tennessee: Fisk University, Social Science Institute, 1946), bound typescript, pp. 138, 142–148.

I DID NOT REALLY UNDERSTAND WHAT IT MEANT TO BE A NEGRO

DAISY LEE BATES

❦ *Daisy Lee Bates (1920–   ) was educated in Little Rock, Arkansas, where, in 1941, she married Christopher Bates. She and her husband founded and edited the Arkansas State Press, a weekly newspaper. They were both convicted of contempt of court in 1946 for criticizing a circuit court trial, but the conviction was later reversed. Mrs. Bates, who is a member of the national board of the NAACP, was president of the Arkansas branch from 1953 on. Her leadership during the 1957 Little Rock school integration crisis and during subsequent integration struggles led to the loss of her newspaper and her livelihood.*
In 1960, in Bates vs. Little Rock, the Supreme Court reversed her conviction for refusal to furnish NAACP membership lists to city officials. Mrs. Bates was honored by being awarded the Spingarn Medal of the NAACP in 1958. Her autobiographical work, The Long Shadow of Little Rock, from which the selection below is taken, appeared in 1962.

I was born Daisy Lee Gatson in the little sawmill town of Huttig, in southern Arkansas. . . . As I grew up in this town, I knew I was a Negro, but I did not really understand what that meant until I was seven years old. My parents, as do most Negro parents, protected me as long as possible from the inevitable insult and humiliation that is, in the South, part of being "colored." . . .

One afternoon, shortly after my seventh birthday, my mother called me in from play.

"I'm not feeling well," she said. "You'll have to go to the market to get the meat for dinner."

I was thrilled with such an important errand. I put on one of my prettiest dresses and my mother brushed my hair. She gave me a dollar and instructions to get a pound of center-cut pork chops. I skipped happily all the way to the market.

When I entered the market, there were several white adults waiting to be served. When the butcher had finished with them, I gave him my order. More white adults entered. The butcher turned from me and took their orders. I was a little annoyed but felt since they were grownups it was all right. While he was waiting on the adults, a little white girl came in and we talked while we waited.

The butcher finished with the adults, looked down at us and asked, "What do you want, little girl?" I smiled and said, "I told you before, a pound of center-cut pork shops." He snarled, "I'm not talking to you," and again asked the white girl what she wanted. She also wanted a pound of center-cut pork chops.

"Please may I have my meat?" I said, as the little girl left. The butcher took my dollar from the counter, reached into the showcase, got a handful of fat chops and wrapped them up. Thrusting the package at me, he said, "Niggers have to wait 'til I wait on the white people. Now take your meat and get out of here!" I ran all the way home crying.

When I reached the house, my mother asked what had happened. I started pulling her toward the door, telling her what the butcher had said. I opened the meat and showed it to her. "It's fat, Mother. Let's take it back."

"Oh, Lord, I knew I shouldn't have sent her. Stop crying now, the meat isn't so bad."

"But it is. Why can't we take it back?"

"Go on out on the porch and wait for Daddy." As she turned from me, her eyes were filling with tears.

When I saw Daddy approaching, I ran to him, crying. He lifted me in his arms and smiled. "Now, what's wrong?" When I told him, his smile faded.

"And if we don't hurry, the market will be closed," I finished.

"We'll talk about it after dinner, sweetheart." I could feel his muscles tighten as he carried me into the house.

Dinner was distressingly silent. Afterwards my parents went into the bedroom and talked. My mother came out and told me my father wanted to see me. I ran into the bedroom. Daddy sat there, looking at me for a long time. Several times he tried to speak, but the words just wouldn't come. I stood there, looking at him and wondering why he was acting so strangely. Finally he stood up and the words began tumbling from him. Much of what he said I did not understand. To my seven-year-old mind he explained as best he could that a Negro had no rights that a white man respected.

He dropped to his knees in front of me, placed his hands on my shoulders, and began shaking me and shouting.

"Can't you understand what I've been saying?" he demanded. "There's nothing I can do! If I went down to the market I would only cause trouble for my family."

As I looked at my daddy sitting by me with tears in his eyes, I blurted out innocently, "Daddy, are you afraid?"

He sprang to his feet in an anger I had never seen before. "Hell, no! I'm not afraid for myself, I'm not afraid to die. I could go down to that market and tear him limb from limb with my bare hands, but I am afraid for you and your mother."

That night when I knelt to pray, instead of my usual prayers, I found myself praying that the butcher would die. After that night we never mentioned him again. . . .

Daisy Bates, *The Long Shadow of Little Rock: A Memoir*
(New York: David McKay Co., 1962), pp. 8–9.

HELPING OUT DADDY

LOUISE MERIWETHER

I spent most of my free time reading fairy tales from the library on the fire escape, trying to avoid Sukie. Then, hallelu, five-fourteen played. Daddy's dollar had dwindled to a quarter, but Mother also caught it for ten cents straight and thirty cents combination. Together they collected two hundred and fifteen dollars. A fortune.

"Where else can a poor man get such odds?" Daddy asked. "Six Hundred dollars for a buck. If only I hadn't cut that number down to a quarter." But he had dreamed about his mother and had switched the dollar to nine-oh-nine which played for the dead.

That night Mother and Daddy sat at the dining room table counting that money over and over. There was something different about them, some soft way they looked at each other with their eyes and smiled. I went to bed and didn't even bother to pull the couch away from the wall, I was that happy. Let the bedbugs bite. Everybody, even those bloodsucking bugs, had to have something sometime.

We ate high off the hog for about a week. It sure was good to get away from that callie ham which you had to soak all night to kill the salt and then save the juice and skin to flavor beans and greens. I think the reason why I was so skinny was that I just didn't like the poor mouth collards and salt pork. . . .

Daddy paid up the back rent and Mother bought us all winter coats and shoes. But before long we were back to fried cabbage and ham hocks and it was just as if the big hit had never been. It wasn't long before the explosion came.

That Saturday Mother was at work and Daddy had already left on his rounds. I was in the kitchen scorching the rice for dinner when the two plainclothes cops pushed past that rotten lock Daddy had never fixed and walked right in. By the time I got to the dining room they were poking around as if they had been invited in. I knew instantly they were cops. The oldest one was huge with purple, loose, jaws like a bulldog. The other one was younger and nervous.

"Where does your old man hide his numbers?" Bulldog asked me, pulling open the buffet drawers.

I was so scared I couldn't speak, so I just shook my head.

Bulldog pulled out the drawer and placed it on the table.

The young one sorted through it, pushing aside Mother's sewing bag and the old rags she was saving to sell to the rag man. He replaced the drawer and it jammed. I almost cried out loud. Then he gave it a shove and it closed.

They went through the other drawers in the same manner, then Bulldog went into the kitchen and began banging the pots and pans around in the cupboard.

I heard Daddy coming up the stairs and I ran towards the door yelling: "Don't come in, Daddy! It's the cops!"

Bulldog hollered, "Grab her!"

The young cop swung me off my feet. I screamed and kicked, aiming for his private parts like Mother had told me to do if a man ever bothered me.

Daddy came through the door. With one long stride he was at the young cop's side. He grabbed me, at the same time pushing the cop backwards.

"You all right?" Daddy asked.

I nodded. He put me down and straightened up.

"Hold it right there," Bulldog said. He was pointing his gun at Daddy's chest.

"You all got a warrant to mess up my house like this?" Daddy asked. "And stop waving that gun around. I ain't going nowhere. You're scaring my little girl to death."

Bulldog put the gun back inside his shoulder holster. "Don't need no warrant," he said. "Now hand over your numbers and come along quietly."

"You ain't got no warrant," Daddy repeated.

"Search him," Bulldog ordered the young one, who approached Daddy with hesitation and went through his pocket. He pulled out an envelope. Lord, I thought, they're gonna put Daddy underneath the jail. The cop opened the envelope and pulled out an unpaid gas bill.

"The only house where we can't find a number slip," Bulldog said, "is a number runner's house. Nobody else is that careful." He reared back on his heels. "Tell you what I'm gonna do, though. I'm gonna run you in for assault and battery for pushing my partner like you did. Let's go."

I was crying loudly by this time. "Hush," Daddy said. "You're a big girl now and you know what to do."

I nodded. He meant that after he was gone I was to take the numbers downstairs to Frenchy and tell him Daddy had been arrested. And that's exactly what I did do after the police had driven Daddy away in an unmarked blue car, and I cried every step of the way. . . .

"Goddamn," I whispered, waiting for the lightning to strike me dead. "Goddamn them all to hell." But I was not chastised for my blasphemy. Even the Lord didn't care.

I walked to the corner and, turning my face away from home, I made my way aimlessly down Fifth Avenue.

Louise Meriwether, "Daddy Was a Number Runner,"
Antioch Review, Fall 1967.

"AM I MY BROTHER'S KEEPER?"

HELEN HOWARD

Am I my brother's keeper? I have to be. The poor people, who live just above the welfare and relief, have to live by that old saying, "I can see farther over the mountain than the man who is standing atop of it." We know and see the problems, because we *have* to live so close to them. We know that we have a sense of responsibility, and we (some of us) have tried to instill some of the ambitions we could not realize into our children. . . .

Am I my brother's keeper? I have to be. Have you ever tried to send two children to college? At the same time? Well, I have, and most of the time I prayed during the day as I worked, and cried and prayed at night when I went to bed. . . .

We (the poor) know what the "nitty-gritty" poor is like. The "nitty-gritty" poor is the hopeless and bleakness we have to face night and day. You, the so-called middle class, and the rich, cannot begin to know how much harder we have to work, and still not accomplish a thing. . . .

Am I my brother's keeper? I have to be. When we apply for aid from the relief or the welfare, we get turned down. Why? Because we make *too much money*, so they say, or our husbands haven't been gone three months, or we haven't starved to death or been put outdoors yet. When we try to better ourselves, and apply for government jobs like the E.O.A., we get turned down because of our "poor credit ratings," or "our previous jail records." They expect us to have lived a spotless life, but how can we, living in places like these? We have to rob Peter to pay Paul, then we get undesirable credit ratings. We have to steal sometimes to keep the family from starving to death. We make the same mistakes other people make, but ours are held against us. You, who have never had to experience this, cannot begin to imagine what this hell is really like. You, middle class or rich people, can't know how hard it is to have to accept this fate; you can't imagine what we people who are just above the welfare and relief have to do just to try to meet some (not all) of our daily obligations. We try to make it, honestly we do; it's not a case of being "lazy" or not wanting things for ourselves, no matter what you have heard or what you may think. We do have dreams. We do have ambitions.

Am I my brother's keeper? I have to be. You wonder who sells the liquor, and who writes the numbers? We do! The poor people who can't find jobs that pay enough to feed us, we, the poor people, who have ambitions and refuse to be pushed down any farther than we already are, we, the poor people, who have ambitions for our children, and are trying every way we know how, even by "Hook or crook" to make it. . . .

Middle class and rich people take things for granted, things that we would call heaven, your nice painted walls, for instance, while we, as I heard a little boy say, "Lay down in bed at night, look through the ceiling and see shooting stars." You have your nice wall to wall carpets, while we have our little 9 by 12 linoleums, that will not cover half of the floor, and will wear out before long because of the awful floors that they cover.

Am I my brother's keeper? I have to be. I see all these things going on around me, things like selling liquor, writing numbers, boys gambling on the street corners, and transient houses. No . . . I don't and I won't call the police to these people, because the people who are doing these things are the people with ambitions, the people who are making a better life for themselves, and their family. These are the people who will be able to send their children to colleges, who will be able to pay their bills, buy their homes and move to a higher economical, as well as social status. These are the people who want to and will get a little respect. This is why I am, why I have to be my brother's keeper.

Southern Regional Council Magazine, November 1965, pp. 11, 12.

HAVING A BABY INSIDE ME IS THE ONLY TIME I'M REALLY ALIVE

ANONYMOUS

❦ *A Georgia woman who recently migrated to Boston tells how she feels about family planning.*

They came telling us not to have children, and not to have children, and sweep up, and all that. There isn't anything they don't want to do to you, or tell you to do. They tell you you're bad, and worse than others, and you're lazy, and you don't know how to get along like others do. Well, for so long they told us we couldn't ever go near anyone else, I suppose we should be grateful for being told we're not going to get near enough if we don't behave in the right way—which is the sermon I get all the time now.

Then they say we should look different, and eat different—
use more of the protein. I tell them about the prices, but
they reply about "planning"—planning, planning, that's all
they tell you. The worst of it is that they try to get you to
plan your kids, by the year; except they mean by the ten-year
plan, one every ten years. The truth is, they don't want you
to have any, if they could help it.

To me, having a baby inside me is the only time I'm really
alive. I know I can make something, do something, no matter
what color my skin is, and what names people call me. When
the baby gets born I see him, and he's full of life, or she is;
and I think to myself that it doesn't make any difference
what happens later, at least now we've got a chance, or the
baby does. You can see the little one grow and get larger and
start doing things, and you feel there must be some hope,
some chance that things will get better; because there it is,
right before you, a real, live, growing baby. The children and
their father feel it, too, just like I do. They feel the baby is a
good sign, or at least he's *some* sign. If we didn't have that,
what would be the difference from death? Even without children my life would still be bad—they're not going to give us
what *they* have, the birth control people. They just want us
to be a poor version of them, only without our children and
our faith in God and our tasty fried food, or anything.

They'll tell you we are "neglectful"; we don't take proper
care of the children. But that's a lie, because we do, until we
can't any longer, because the time has come for the street to
claim them, to take them away and teach them what a poor
nigger's life is like. I don't care what anyone says: I take the
best care of my children. I scream the ten commandments at
them every day, until one by one they learn them by heart—
and believe me they don't forget them. (You can ask my
minister if I'm not telling the truth.) It's when they leave
for school, and start seeing the streets and everything, that's
when there's the change; and by the time they're ten or so,
it's all I can do to say anything, because I don't even believe
my own words, to be honest. I tell them, please to be good;

but I know it's no use, not when they can't get a fair break, and there are the sheriffs down South and up here the police-men, ready to kick you for so much as breathing your feel-ings. So I turn my eyes on the little children, and keep on praying that one of them will grow up at the right second, when the schoolteachers have time to say hello and give him the lessons he needs, and when they get rid of the building here and let us have a place you can breathe in and not get bitten all the time, and when the men can find work—be-cause *they* can't have children, and so they have to drink or get on drugs to find some happy moments, and some hope about things.

As cited in Robert Coles, *Children of Crisis*
(Boston: Little Brown and Company, 1964), pp. 368–369.

CHAPTER SIX

IN GOVERNMENT SERVICE AND POLITICAL LIFE

What we need is more women in politics . . . and not just to stuff envelopes, but to run for office. It is women who can bring empathy, tolerance, insight, patience, and persistence to government—the qualities we naturally have or have had to develop because of our suppression by men. . . . At present, our country needs women's idealism and determination, perhaps more in politics than anywhere else.

Representative Shirley Chisholm

IN GOVERNMENT
SERVICE AND
POLITICAL LIFE

❦ The chief professional and skilled occupations in which American women are employed are (in the order of numbers employed) clerical work, teaching (on the elementary and high school level), nursing and health services and sales work. Fifty-one per cent of all women workers were to be found in these occupations in 1962.

But the story is quite different for black women, who until very recently were excluded from clerical work, nursing and sales work, except for the relatively few openings in segregated institutions. In 1969, there were 3,601,000 black women in the labor force.

A comparison of their distribution in the better-paying, more highly skilled job categories shows the following:*

Per Cent Distribution of Employment by
Occupation and Sex

	1966		1970	
	Black Women	White Women	Black Women	White Women
Total Employment	100	100	100	100
Professional and technical occupations	8.4	13.7	12	19
Clerical occupations	13.8	42.3	22	44

* The Socio-Economic Status of Negroes in the United States, 1969," U.S. Department of Labor, Bureau of Labor Statistics (Washington, D.C.: Government Printing Office, 1970), p. 42.

These figures reveal that in the last five years, job opportunities in the professional and skilled categories have greatly improved for black women, but that the opportunity gap earlier noted between white and black women still persists.

Nursing, earlier carried on by women in peacetime and war as an extension of their domestic services, was professionalized after the Civil War with the founding of nurses' training institutions and the gradual recognition of the Registered Nurse degree. The first black nurse, Mary Eliza Mahoney, graduated from the New England Hospital for Women and Children in 1879. The majority of the black graduate nurses following in her footsteps were trained and employed in Negro hospitals and were for forty-two years denied admission to the National Association of Graduate Nurses. They organized their own national association in 1908 and worked ceaselessly, under the leadership of Mabel K. Staupers, R.N., for an end to discrimination and for job opportunities. Prior to World War II, only 34 of the 1,200 schools of nursing in the United States admitted black students. During World War I, a small band of black nurses served in the army under segregated conditions. During World War II, the army relaxed its quota restrictions, and 343 black women served in the Army Nurse Corps. Still, in January 1945 there were only four black nurses in the navy. Full integration of black nurses into the armed forces came with President Truman's 1948 Executive Order. The National Association of Colored Graduate Nurses disbanded in 1950 after its members had been accepted into membership of the American Nurses Association in 1948.

Until the post–World War II period, the majority of black women professionals were teachers. Their status and contributions have been discussed elsewhere. Social work did not begin to open up as a profession to black women until the 1930's.

Race discrimination was most seriously felt in terms of employment opportunities in the skilled and semiskilled trades, particularly in clerical and sales work. White women entered these fields in large numbers during the Civil War and retained their hold on them during the postwar period. Their mass entry into the business world came with the development of the typewriter. The availability of these middle-range occupations dramatically improved the lives of millions of working girls and provided them with a chance for upward mobility. Not so for black women, to whom these occupations were virtually closed until the 1960's. White women entered government service during the Civil War, but black women, who were first and most grudgingly admitted to such jobs during World War I, suffered quotas, discrimination and segregation even in the very limited number of jobs offered to them. It should be noted that until very recently a particularly insidious form of discrimination consisted in reserving what few jobs were given to black women for only the most light-skinned applicants. (See Mary Church Terrell's account on p. 333) Integration of government hiring was legislated only with passage of the Civil Rights Act of 1964.

Similarly, the entry of black women into political life was delayed and restrained by race discrimination. While a few club women such as Josephine St. Pierre Ruffin, Mary Church Terrell, Ida Wells Barnett and Mary McLeod Bethune were suffragists, the majority of black women did not primarily concern themselves with voting rights or even women's rights. There were a few black women's suffrage clubs, and these participated in the national woman suffrage campaigns, although frequently on a segregated basis. The white women's suffrage movement, as a whole, was far more concerned with its "Southern strategy," its effort to win votes for the woman suffrage amendment in the South, than it was with the problems and interests of black women. After passage of the Nineteenth Amendment, there was some direct political activity by black women, especially in the Republican Party. Mrs. E. Howard Harper, appointed in 1927 to succeed her deceased husband in the West Virginia legislature, as the first black woman to hold such a position. In the same year Mrs. Mary C. Booze of Mound Bayou, Mississippi, and Mrs. George S. Williams of Savannah, Georgia, gained membership on the Republican National Committee.

The Democrats appointed several black women to lesser administrative posts in the federal government after President Franklin D. Roosevelt had broken precedent by his 1936 appointment of Mary McLeod Bethune as director of the Division of Negro Affairs, National Youth Administration. He also appointed Crystal Bird Fauset, who in 1938 became the first black woman elected to the Pennsylvania State Assembly, to the Office of Civilian Defense.

In 1946, two black women were appointed Assistant District Attorney of their states: Eunice Carter in New York and Pauli Murray in California. The same year Sadie M. Alexander won a presidential appointment to the United States Commission on Civil Rights.

In the 1950's, only a few black women won elective office in the states. Suzie Monroe and Sarah Anderson became Assemblywomen in Pennsylvania in 1948 and 1954. Cora M. Brown was the first black State Senator in Michigan in 1952, and Verda Welcome, who served in the Maryland Assembly from 1958 to 1962, won a place in the State Senate in 1962. Twelve other black women won elective state offices in the 1960's. Of these, four were Southerners: Lena K. Lee and Victorina Adams, both to the State Assembly of Maryland in 1966; Grace Hamilton, State Assembly, Georgia, 1966 and Barbara Jordan, the first woman elected to the Texas Senate, 1966.

In 1964, President Johnson appointed Mrs. Franklin Muse Freeman, a former Assistant Attorney General of Missouri, to the Civil Rights Commission, and in 1966 chose Municipal Court Judge Marjorie M. Lawson for United States representative on the United Nations Economic and Social Commission. He also made Patricia Roberts Harris Ambassador to Luxembourg and elevated several other black women to high federal posts. New York State Senator (1964)

Constance Baker Motley, who had broken precedent by her election to the presidency of the Borough of Manhattan in 1965, was the first woman of her race to be elevated to the federal bench in 1966. Mrs. Edith Sampson served on the United States delegation to the United Nations from 1950 to 1954.

Another racial barrier fell before the talent and perseverance of black women with the election of Shirley Chisholm to the House of Representatives in 1967.

A PIONEER NEWSPAPER WOMAN
MARY ANN SHADD CARY

✌ Mary Ann Shadd Cary (1823–1893) was born in Wilmington, Delaware, and educated in a Quaker boarding school in West Chester, Pennsylvania. She taught school in Delaware, Pennsylvania and New York. After passage of the Fugitive Slave Law, she and her brother Isaac emigrated to Canada. They settled in Windsor, West Canada, and Mary Ann Shadd at once became deeply involved in the political and educational life of the small colony of black refugees from the United States who had settled there and in nearby Chatham. She established a school and taught for over a decade, seeking first to make the school self-sustaining, then accepting support from the American Missionary Association. She wrote a pamphlet, Notes on Canada West, designed to encourage emigration of Blacks to the province. Mary Ann Shadd helped to found, finance and write the first antislavery weekly newspaper in the region, The Provincial Freeman, and between 1854 and 1856 was the paper's editor. She was the first black woman newspaper editor and suffered criticism and attacks, some of which were due to her unique status. Much of the opposition she encountered was, however, based on political differences she had with the leaders of Chatham colony and especially with the Reverend Josiah Henson and his supporters. Mary Ann Shadd had very strong convictions, which she did not hesitate to defend with vigor and considerable asperity, concerning the uselessness and ill effects of the Refugee Home Society, a United States–based fund-raising organization in support of the refugee colonists. She considered them a mere "begging society" designed to enrich individual leaders and make the refugees dependent instead of self-sustaining. The feud between her and Reverend Henson, Henry Bibb, editor of a rival newspaper, and their supporters, filled many issues of The Provincial Freeman and was carried on by way of correspondence, political meetings, resolutions and pungent editorial comment. It marked Miss Shadd as a political force in her community.

She married Thomas F. Cary of Toronto in 1856 and had one daughter. After resigning from the newspaper, which sustained itself for another two years, Mrs. Cary continued teaching school and lecturing. She returned to the United States during the Civil War, was appointed recruiting army officer by Governor Levi Morton of Indiana, and helped to assemble a regiment of black soldiers. After the war she settled in Washington, D.C., where she headed an American Missionary Association school (see p. 108). In her late forties, she entered the newly founded law school of Howard University and received her law degree in 1870. She practiced private law in Washington, D.C., and was, presumably, the first black woman lawyer. A Miss Platt of Chicago earned a law degree a few years later, but did not practice. Full accreditation for a black woman lawyer was not achieved until 1897 when Lutie Lytle of Topeka, Kansas, was admitted to the bar of the state of Tennessee.

The following is illustrative of the response Mary Ann Shadd elicited in her pioneering newspaper career.

About two years ago a few colored men and women established in Canada a newspaper called *The Provincial Freeman*. . . . The press became a necessity and was bravely supplied by Miss Mary Ann Shadd. This lady, with very little assistance from others has sustained *The Provincial Freeman* for more than two years. She has had to contend with lukewarmness, false friends, open enemies, ignorance and small pecuniary means. The tone of her paper has been at times harsh and complaining and whatever may be thought or felt of this we are bound to bear testimony to the unceasing industry, the unconquerable zeal and commendable ability which she has shown. We do not know her equal among the colored ladies of the United States. . . .

The Freeman is not well supported and owing to the hard work to which its editor is subjected to obtain the means of support for the paper it is not very well edited. Mr. Hezekia Ford Douglass, a young man of excellent natural abilities, has been secured as editor of *The Freeman* and with the united labors of the two editors we hope the character and prospects of the paper will materially improve.

Editorial, "Canada," *The North Star; Frederick Douglass' Paper,*
Vol. 9, No. 29 (July 4, 1856).

❦ *The following illustrates the kind of political activity in which Mary Ann Shadd engaged:*

A meeting of the colored citizens of Windsor, Canada West was held on September 27. Mary A. Shadd was appointed Secretary. [Among the resolutions passed was the following:] Resolved, that we do not regard the Refugees' Home Society as a benevolent institution designed to benefit a formerly downtrodden people, but as an exceedingly cunning land scheme the continuance of which, by giving fresh impulse and a specious character to the begging system, will materially compromise our manhood by representing us as objects of charity, injure seriously the character of this country and tend to the pecuniary advantage of its agents and theirs only.

The North Star; Frederick Douglass' Paper,
Vol. 5, No. 45 (October 29, 1852).

NURSE, SPY AND SCOUT

HARRIET TUBMAN

❦ Harriet Tubman capped her remarkable career as antislavery leader and conductor of the Underground Railroad by three years of outstanding war service. She earned the honorary title "General Tubman," which John Brown earlier had bestowed upon her and by which her black countrymen referred to her, as a spy, scout and guerrilla leader for the Union army. She served in South Carolina from May 1862 till the end of the war, when she returned to Auburn, New York, to take care of her aged parents. Among her various scouting exploits, the most spectacular was the engagement on the Combahee River, in which she piloted Colonel James Montgomery and his black troops up the river, lifting torpedoes and rescuing 756 slaves without the loss of a single Union soldier. During her three years of service, she received only $200 from the government which she used to build a washhouse for freedwomen in Florida. She was, at some times, allowed to draw soldier's rations; at other times she supported herself by baking pies and making root beer, which she sold to the soldiers. Like other black women, she also performed nursing services whenever needed.

> Head Qrs 3d Military District
> Chief QMasters Office
> Atlanta Ga. March 21st 1868

Dear Madam

I have just recd your letter in regard to Harriet Tubman. I can bear witness to the value of her services rendered in the Union Army during the late war in South Carolina & Florida. She was employed in the Hospitals and as a spy. She made many a raid inside the enemy's lines displaying remarkable courage, zeal and fidelity.

She was employed by Genl Hunter and I think both by Generals Stevens and Sherman—and is as deserving of a pension from the Government for her services as any other of its faithful servants.

> Signed very truly yours
> Rufus Saxton
> Brt-Brig General
> U.S.A.

> Washington, July 25, 1865.

Major Gen'l Hunter—My Dear Sir:

Harriet Tubman, a colored woman, has been nursing our soldiers during nearly all the war. She believes she has claims for faithful services to the command in South Carolina, which you are connected, and she thinks that you would be disposed to see her claim justly settled.

I have known her long as a noble, high spirit, as true as seldom dwells in the human form. I commend her therefore to your kind attention.

> Faithfully your friend,
> Wm. H. Seward.

Major Gen. Hunter.

HARRIET TUBMAN'S PETITION, 1898

I am about 75 years of age. I was born and reared in Dorchester County, Md. My maiden name was Araminta Ross. [S]ometime prior to the late War of the Rebellion I married John Tubman who died in the State of Maryland on the 30th day of September, 1867. I married Nelson Davis, a soldier of the late war, on the 18th day of March, 1869, at Auburn, N.Y.

I furnished the original papers in my claim to one Charles P. Wood, then of Auburn, N.Y., who died several years ago.

Said Wood made copies of said original papers which are hereunto annexed. I was informed by said Wood that he sent said original papers to one James Barrett, an attorney on 4½ Street, Washington, D.C., and I was told by the wife of said Barrett that she handed the original papers to the Hon. C. D. MacDougall, then a member of the House of Representatives.

My claim against the U.S. is for three years' service as nurse and cook in hospitals, and as commander of Several men (eight or nine) as scouts during the late war of the Rebellion, under directions and orders of Edwin M. Stanton, Secretary of War, and of several Generals.

I claim for my services above named the sum of Eighteen hundred dollars. The annexed copies have recently been read over to me and are true to the best of my knowledge information and belief.

I further declare that I have interest in said case and am concerned in it's prosecution and allowance.

her
Harriet × Davis
mark
late Harriet Tubman

All three items:
Charles P. Wood Manuscript, Bill H.R. 4982, Papers of the House of Representatives, 55th Congress, National Archives.

❦ *Her application for a government pension, from which the documents above are taken, was not approved until 1897 and was even then opposed by Southern congressmen, who cut $5 a month from the award. The $20 monthly pension she was finally granted eased her financial burden. However, since she had turned her little house into a Home for Aged Freemen, she continued to labor into advanced old age in order to supply the needs of her charges. The letter reprinted below deals with her efforts to raise funds through selling reprints of her biography*

HARRIET TUBMAN (DICTATED LETTER) TO MARY WRIGHT

Syracuse, N.Y.
May 29, 1896

Mrs. Mary Wright,

I received the trunk and package which you sent me and I am very thankful to you for them. I have been appointed by the pastors of the first M.E. and the A.M.E. Churches of Auburn, to collect clothes for the destitute colored children and the things which you sent are very acceptable. . . .

I would like for you to see Miss Edna Cheny [sic] for me. I would like to get out another edition of books. The editor says he can publish five hundred books for $100. before he destroyed the plates. I would like to have another set of books published to take to the Methodists Centennial at New York this fall. I can raise fifty dollars and if Miss Cheny can see Mr. Sanburn [sic] and some of those anti-slavery friends and have them raise fifty dollars more that will enable me to get the books out before the editor destroys the plate. If they will help me raise the money they can hold the books until I can sell enough to pay them back. I would like to come and see you but my brother is sick and I cannot very well leave him at this time. I am not doing anything now as I am not able.

Miss Cheny has done very well by me and I do not wish to ask for money by [but] if through her influence I can get the friends to help me I shall be very thankful. My home is incorperated [sic] for an asylum for aged colored people that will hold the mortage and I wont be troubled now. Remember me in your prayers as your father did before you. If I never see you again I hope to see you in the kingdom. Good by, God bless you all, from your friend who loves you all,

Harriet Tubman

Edna D. Cheney Papers, Manuscript Division, Boston Public Library.

OPPORTUNITIES FOR THE
EDUCATED COLORED WOMAN

EVA D. BOWLES
ADMINISTRATOR, COLORED WORK, Y.W.C.A.

❦ *Eva Bowles was the first black woman on the staff of the YWCA when she was employed by the Harlem branch in 1905. A social worker, she subsequently did case work in Columbus, Ohio. In 1913, she joined the national staff of the YWCA, first as secretary with the War Work Council, then as secretary for Colored Work. In 1932, she left the organization after twenty-seven years of service to take a position in private industry.*

It is perfectly reasonable to assume that the educated Negro woman seeks a career as naturally as any of her sex. She, perhaps, labors under the handicap of her race and thru the past years prescribed limitations have been placed upon her, especially in pursuits other than teaching. During the past few years because of the changing world, barriers have been breaking away, and by degrees she has achieved success in avenues of life where formerly she dared not approach. She has not been wanted, especially, but she was needed.

The profession of teaching was perhaps the first one open to the Negro woman. The last available census reported 22,528 Negro women teachers. The range in standards is vast—from the untrained country school teacher in a four months' Negro school, to the position in cities like New York and Chicago, where they are accepted as teachers rather than Negro teachers. There are schools of high standing such as Baltimore, Washington, St. Louis, Kansas City where Negroes are taught separately. . . . One of these cities has 396 Negro women teachers in their public schools, less than one-fourth are products of the local school system. The greatest number of teaching positions are open in the elementary grades where too often the poorly equipped woman is placed and where experience and character are needed in moulding the youth of the race. The positions in the Kindergarten are becoming more numerous as the school systems grow better. A number of our Negro schools are taking forward steps and providing for the mentally defective. There is a need for teachers to qualify in a specific way to occupy these positions. . . . Grade school principalships have in several instances been filled by women and after apprenticeship there is no reason why Negro women, as well as Negro men, should not hold the position of a High School principal. As registrar of a school, college or university women have been successful. Standing in the highest ranks of educational leadership is the Dean of Women in our universities. We are glad that Howard University and a few other good schools have created this position and we look forward to other universities for the education of Negro youth as an inspiration in the developing of Negro womanhood.

Turning from the well trodden paths of the pedagogue, let us consider opportunities opening in Social Work. In the year 1900, the City of New York produced the first accredited Negro Social Worker, Miss Jessie Sleet, who was employed by the Charity Organization Society as Case Worker until 1909; and in 1906, Negro nurses were employed in the San Juan Hill District, West 63rd Street. During the past few years the Urban League has been foremost in creating opportunities for social workers. . . . Since leadership is one of the greatest needs of the Negro race the Young Women's Christian Association has given particular attention to the training of Negro women. No different standards apply to the Negro candidates desirous of making the secretaryship of the Young Women's Christian Association their profession than to candidates of the white race.

On January 1st, 1923, there were 107 Negro women holding secretaryships in the Young Women's Christian Association. . . . The field of Social Work has tremendously expanded. In Boston, New York, Pittsburgh, Philadelphia,

Chicago and many other large cities, Negro women are successfully filling positions with the Associated Charities, Juvenile and Women's courts, Day Nurseries, Community Service, Child Welfare organizations, Travelers' Aid Societies, Playground Associations and as school visitors, visiting nurses, parish visitors, etc. Information has just been received concerning a new opening in a middle west city to the effect that this city is planning to open a psychiatric clinic. . . . While the social consciousness has developed more rapidly in Northern cities, our Southern communities are fertile fields for well equipped and conscientious women social workers. Perhaps, the outstanding Negro woman social worker in the Southland is Mrs. Janie Barrett, who is superintendent of the Industrial Home for Wayward Girls, Peaks, Virginia.

Altho most of the 30,074 Negro women in the professional world are teachers, there is an ever increasing group entering the world of law, medicine, nursing and business. In 1910 we had two women lawyers. There is an increasing number of practising physicians and pharmacists. There are a few Negro women in our Northern medical colleges and several in our medical institutions in the southland. There is a possibility of a career in combining the profession of medicine with the technical aspect of social work, child welfare, community health, and positive health measures particularly. Too much encouragement cannot be given to the nursing profession. . . . There are now approximately 50,000 Negro business establishments with an annual volume of business amounting to $1,500,000,000 operated by Negroes and in which women are beginning to share. Of course these establishments are small and are dealing to a large extent with personal service but they are growing. Of the larger business offering a future for employment, the insurance companies possess perhaps the best opportunities. There are about 60 of these writing over about $75,000,000 in insurance a year. Dr. Sadie Mossell was taken over by the North Carolina Mutual as their statistician as soon as they learned of her preparation. The late Madam C. J. Walker and Mrs. Malone of the Poro Institute have demonstrated the fact that Negro women can not only create business, but manage large establishments. A visit to Poro College, St. Louis, can bring to the most skeptical person the knowledge and confirmation that in spite of traditional and present day handicaps the Negro woman can take her rightful place in business. Mrs. Maggie L. Walker of Richmond, Va., holds the distinction of being the first Negro woman president of a bank.

The World War bridged over many years in woman's economic development and along with all women the Negro woman was given a chance and she made good. This fact has given her courage and strength to take no backward steps, but go on thru the doors already open and with the creative power with which she is so richly endowed, press on into other realms. . . .

Opportunity, Vol. 1, No. 3 (March 1923), pp. 8–10.

GOVERNMENT WORK IN WORLD WAR I

MARY CHURCH TERRELL

During the World War almost everybody in Washington who knew how to write and spell was taking an examination of some kind, so as to get a job in one of the Government departments. The officials were calling loudly for assistance. . . . Accordingly, I decided to take an examination as a typist. . . .

Shortly after that I was summoned to the War Risk Insurance Bureau and appointed to a clerkship. The man before whom I then appeared did not consume enough time in giving me the "once over" to note any peculiarity in my complexion which would suggest to him that I was "different from the rest." That little oversight on his part undoubtedly accounts for the fact that I was placed in the room with white women. After I had been appointed and assigned to this room, I learned that the women who were known to be colored had been placed in a section to themselves.

In the division to which I was assigned it was the duty of the clerks to send in the records of the soldiers who were ill or insane. . . .

I had been working about two months in this section when, suddenly, I received a letter saying I had been suspended from duty from October 15 up to and including October 20, during which time I was requested to prepare my defense in answer to the following charges preferred against me: "It has been reported that you have taken action on cases contrary to the rules and regulations of the Bureau and contrary to the regulations of the chief medical adviser. It has been found that you have made numerous mistakes, and when these mistakes were called to your attention you cause considerable disturbance and tend to deny responsibility. You do not want to understand or can not understand the requests of your superiors in the matter of properly performing duties assigned to you."

There was not a scintilla of truth in any of these charges. It was a case of "framing" a colored woman, so as to remove her from a room in which she had been placed by mistake where they did not want one of her race to work. If I had really "taken action contrary to the rules and regulations of the Bureau and of the chief medical adviser," those responsible for the proper conduct of the office would have called me to account the very first time they learned I was guilty of the infraction of the rules. . . .

But I had never seen any rules and regulations in print, nor had anybody stated any to me which I had violated in any way, shape or form. As careful as any colored woman would be in an office in which she knew her slightest mistake or dereliction of duty would be greatly exaggerated and summarily punished, it is inconceivable that she would fail to obey to the letter every rule or regulation enforced. I realized that I was treading on thin ice all the time, and I was very careful to do the work exactly as I was instructed. . . .

Nobody who understands conditions in the National Capital would believe that a colored woman working in one of the Government departments in a room with white women "would cause considerable disturbance" when mistakes were called to her attention if she were sane and wished to retain her job. Colored women know all too well if they make themselves conspicuous or objectionable, either to their fellow clerks or to their superior officers, they are courting disaster and ruin. The few colored women who are assigned to rooms in which white women work are constantly in a state of suspense and apprehension, not knowing the day or the hour when the awful summons of removal or dismissal will come. . . .

Young women with only a high school education were able to perform the duties in the room to which I was assigned. It could scarcely be possible, therefore, that a woman who had graduated with a good record from a reputable college, who had studied all her life and had taught school, could not surmount the difficulties which these girls could master with ease. . . .

The truth of the matter is that when some of the superior officers of the Bureau saw that a colored woman was working in that particular room, they decided to remove her at all hazards. The easiest way to do this was to prefer charges against the colored woman, and they decided to resort to this method to get rid of me. . . .

Colonel Wainer, who wrote the letter containing the charges, was a Jew. When I urged him to give me a square deal, presented facts to show that the charges were trumped up, and requested him to get my record directly from the woman in charge of the room, he turned a deaf ear to my appeal. I did not want to allow myself to be dismissed from that clerkship without waging a hard fight against such cruel injustice. It was one of the most galling experiences of my life. If my husband had not occupied such a prominent position in the city, I should never have submitted to that outrage without waging a righteous war against it. I knew that any contest on my part would embarrass him and might easily hurt his standing as a judge in the Municipal Court. I have always believed that a wife has no right to injure her husband's career by what she says or does.

Shortly after this experience I was appointed by the Census Bureau. Here I was placed in a section, one portion of which was set aside exclusively for colored clerks, although white clerks sat in another part of the same large room. From the building on Pennsylvania Avenue, which was once occupied by the Census Bureau and in which I worked when I was first appointed, all of the colored clerks were transferred to one of the temporary structures erected in another section of the National Capital during the World War. Here they were herded together in a room with a colored man as director who was very efficient and whom it was a pleasure to assist.

One day a clerk sitting near me wrote me a note telling me to stop work a second and look ahead. Then I saw a woman, who I knew had been working in another section of the Bureau, come into our large room carrying her hat, her umbrella, and her purse. The white man who accompanied her then left and she was given a seat by the colored director of our division. In a few minutes another woman was ushered into our room and given a seat. And this was repeated half a dozen times. Then it suddenly dawned upon me what the advent of these newcomers signified.

They were colored women so fair that they had been assigned to sections set aside exclusively for white women. By fair means or foul their racial identity had been disclosed to somebody "higher up," who was opposed to allowing the women of two races to work in the same room together. . . .

A short while after that drastic separation of the two races occurred, one of the young women came to tell me that an order had been promulgated whereby the colored women clerks in our section would no longer be allowed to enter the lavatory which they had used up to that time because it had just been set aside for the women of the other group. Then and there I made up my mind I would do everything in my power to prevent that order from being executed. . . .

❦ *She protested to the supervisor, to no avail.*

Then I decided to resign and sent in my resignation immediately. As my reason, I stated that I was unwilling to remain in a Government department in which colored women were subjected to such an indignity as we had been.

A few minutes after the author of the order had received my resignation he sent for me to come to see him immediately. . . . After a long conference with him . . . I agreed to modify the reason of my resignation if he would rescind the objectionable order which he had issued. This he agreed to do. . . . I felt it would be foolish to stick to the original statement when, by making a slight compromise, I could relieve the women of my group from embarrassment and humiliation without sacrificing my self-respect.

The head of the division in which I worked urged me to remain in the Bureau, but I decided to resign. . . . The idea of remaining in a section over which were placed men who had no regard whatever for the feelings of colored women was abhorrent to me. I simply could not stay even for the sake of the salary which would have filled a long felt want.

Mary Church Terrell, *A Colored Woman in a White World*
(Washington, D.C.: Ransdell Inc. Publishing Co.,
1940), pp. 250–259.

"ELECTION DAY"

ELIZABETH PIPER ENSLEY

❦ *The Denver, Colorado, columnist of* The Woman's Era *describes the first election (1894) in Colorado in which women voted. The Republicans won the election.*

Lessons learned from the election and the campaign preceding it:

1. Women will study politics. This was proven by the great number of political study clubs formed during the past year. A populist woman, who stumped the state, says, "Politics was the theme of discussion morning, noon and night. The women talked politics over the dishwashing, and during their social calls. Politics has made them read and think more, and in new and different lines. . . .

2. Women will vote. The women of Colorado have demonstrated that conclusively.

3. They will generally vote straight. This fact was shown by the Republican women, though it may be that in this instance they believed it necessary to do so in the interest of law and order.

4. There should be thorough and systematic organization of the women of all parties.

The good government committee will now take steps to strengthen its force and organize more thoroughly for the municipal election in the spring.

The first important work of the women will be to see that the party emblem in the Australian ballot is done away with, thus insuring a truly secret ballot, and therefore more independent voting.

The readers of the ERA will be interested to know what special part the colored women have taken in the election. Most of them have done admirable work in the interest of the Republican party. They also formed clubs of their own and heroically helped their brothers to elect a representative to the legislature, although the majority of those brothers voted against woman's enfranchisement.

They made good campaign speeches.

Mrs. Olden is deserving of especial mention. She was one of fourteen delegates sent from the colored Republican club to the county convention held last summer. She suggested that they ask for representation in the state convention, but was discouraged by her too-timid brothers, on the ground that there was no use asking for what they would not get. But this courageous little woman persisted. The outcome of it all was that Mrs. Olden was unanimously elected third Vice-President of the Republican State League of Colorado. She has done most excellent work for the party.

Mrs. Olden is a graduate of Fisk University. On the eve of election in November, '93, she came to Denver from Tennessee at the head of a small colony of people who longed for the free air of the mountains. They sought a dwelling place where free speech would not be denied them.

The colored women of Denver have recognized the worth of Mrs. Olden by making her president of their league lately organized, and about which I will tell you later.

The Woman's Era, Vol. 1, No. 3 (June 9, 1894), pp. 17–18.

THE NEGRO WOMAN IN POLITICS

MRS. ROBERT M. PATTERSON

Never was there a time in which there was greater need for sane and sober thought on the part of Negro Women. . . .

A new system must be installed. If we study the history of the Negro men in politics, we will learn some valuable lessons. We will learn, first, that, so far as the Negro is concerned, the Republican Party is the same as the Democratic Party; we will learn that the primary step in the systematic disfranchisement of the Negro in the South was taken when the Republicans betrayed and handed them over to the "White League" of the South in lieu of the acquiescence on the part of the Southern Democrats, in the fraudulent seating of President Hayes. They will learn that lynchings, burning at the stake goes on apace with a Republican President, Congress and Supreme Court. They will learn that the good old Republican Congress cannot or will not pass an anti-lynching bill. They will learn that it was Taft who started kicking them out of appointive positions at Washington. They will note that the Republican Party of Pennsylvania refused to pass a "Civil Rights Bill." They will learn that your husbands, fathers, brothers and sweethearts have consistently supported by their votes this abominable condition for a half a hundred years.

All of the phenomena above mentioned have a well-defined and fundamental cause. The Republican Party has not, cannot and will not remedy them because they are not interested in "humanity," they are interested in "property." . . . They represent the owning class in society. The owning class must divide and sub-divide the non-owning class. The poor whites and blacks are the non-owning class in America; this non-owning class has been divided on racial lines and sub-divided along economic, industrial, social and political lines. In doing this, capitalistic society is performing its historic mission. The average Negro's lot in life is one long dreary night of the hardest and dirtiest work with the smallest amount of pay; there is not a faint star of glimmering hope in our present social firmament to relieve the monotony of his cheerless watches. He is doubly cursed by a capitalist system which is a savage jungle—a system which forces millions of human beings, black and white, to dwell in poverty—millions of unfortunate women, black and white, to be driven to the bitter bargain of their bodies. A system where few hold sway over body and soul of the many. . . .

The Socialist Party is organizing workers, black and white, on the political field with the aim of putting an end to exploitation. . . . One of the most encouraging signs of the time, to my mind, has been the open-mindedness exhibited by quite a few young women on this momentous question. I have in mind that part of the platform endorsed by the Colored Women Political League, sponsored by Mrs. Somerville Fauntleroy, inviting all parties to present their platforms to the League. . . .

Now the time is ripe for the women to step in and take hold of conditions. . . . The women should form clubs, explain the correct use of the ballot, consult among ourselves the best way this particular principle or policy will benefit society, then make a demand and see to it that it is carried out by those whom you have elected into office. Let us not waste any time talking about voting "good men and women" into office into the various parties when our object is rather to put "good policies" into action. The best man or woman in the world could not possibly do the Negro any good if his or her party's policies and principles were at variance with the Negroes' best interest. . . .

In these times of unrest we need women of the type of Harriet Tubman and Sojourner Truth. Women of mental ripeness, courage and clearness of purpose and a burning spirit to dare and to do. We need women who are not content to trail along in foolish political paths of the Negro men. We need women who will not sell their rights for a mess of pottage. We need women who will not follow blindly a party because of its name, women who will break away from any party that does not stand for absolute equality of opportunity for each and every human being. We should insist that the Negro women get their rightful share of all public offices, and that a common test should be applied to all aspirants.

We should agitate and insist that a larger number of our young women be allowed to qualify as social workers, inspectors and investigators in welfare work, etc.; we should set our faces against the vile and insidious propaganda of separate schools. We must not permit the fight for equal civil rights to cease until it will be possible for every citizen, without regard to race, to have complete civil rights guaranteed to him or her. We should insist that there should be an extended education for all, compulsory education for youth. We should insist upon a system of education where our youths will have every advantage and opportunity to bring out the finer qualities in them. Oh! where are you women of courage? Step out into the battle. Those of you who want

the best things in life for all human-kind—you who yearn for
that social justice without which the advent of the brotherhood of man is a myth—step out! . . . Vote for Socialism!

> Mrs. Robert M. Patterson, Socialist candidate for General Assembly,
> Twentieth Ward, Twenty-eighth Division, Philadelphia, Pennsyl-
> vania, in *Women's Voice*, Vol. 3, No. 9 (September 1922).

I ACCEPT THIS CALL

CHARLOTTA BASS
CANDIDATE FOR VICE-PRESIDENT OF THE UNITED STATES
PROGRESSIVE PARTY CONVENTION, APRIL 1952

❦ *Charlotta A. Bass (1890–   ) was born in Little
Compton, Rhode Island. She studied journalism at Brown
University and took courses at Columbia and UCLA. Residing in Los Angeles, California, she edited and published the
California Eagle for over forty years. A longtime member
of the Republican Party, she was Western regional director
of the Wendell Willkie presidential campaign in 1940. She
broke with the party in 1948 over the civil rights and peace
issues and became a founding member of the Progressive
Party and national co-Chairman of Women for Wallace.
In 1950, she ran for Congress on the Progressive Party ticket
in the Fourteenth Congressional District and in 1952 was
candidate for Vice-President of the United States on the
ticket with Vincent Hallinan. Charlotta Bass was a militant
leader in community affairs and a member of many black
organizations, including the Pan-African Congress.*

For the first time in the history of this nation a political party
has chosen a Negro woman for the second highest office in
the land.

It is a great honor to be chosen as a pioneer, and a great
responsibility. . . .

I shall tell you how I came to stand here. I am a Negro woman. My people came before the Mayflower. I am more concerned with what is happening to my people in my country than war. We have lived through two wars and seen their promises turn to bitter ashes.

For forty years I have been a working editor and publisher of the oldest Negro newspaper in the West. During those forty years I stood on a watch tower watching the tide of racial hatred and bigotry rising against my people and against all people who believe the Constitution is something more than a piece of yellowed paper to be shut off in a glass cage in the archives.

I have stood watch over a home to protect a Negro family against the outrages of the Ku Klux Klan. And I have fought the brazen attempts to drive Negroes from their home under restrictive covenants. I have challenged the great corporations which extort huge profits from my people, and forced them to employ Negroes in their plants. I have stormed city councils and state legislatures and the halls of Congress demanding real representation for my people. . . .

I cannot help but hark back to the thirty years I spent in the Republican Party as an active member. . . . As a member of the great elephant party, I could not see the light of hope shining in the distance, until one day the news flashed across the nation that a new party was born.

Here in this party was the political home for me and for my people. Here no one handed me a ready-made program from the back door. Here I could sit at the head of the table as a founding member, write my own program, a program for me and my people, that came from us. In that great founding convention in Philadelphia in 1948 we had crossed the Jordan. . . . Now perhaps I could retire. . . . I looked forward to a rest after forty years of struggle.

But could I retire when I saw that slavery had been abolished but not destroyed; that democracy had been won in World War I, but not for my people; that fascism had been wiped out in World War II, only to take roots in my own country where it blossomed and bloomed and sent forth its fruits to poison the land my people had fought to preserve!

. . . Where were the leaders of my nation—yes, my nation, for God knows my whole ambition is to see and make my nation the best in the world—where were these great leaders when these things happened?

To retire meant to leave this world to these people who carried oppression to Africa, to Asia, who made profits from oppression in my own land. To retire meant to leave the field to evil.

This is what we fight against. We fight to live. We want the $65 billion that goes for death to go to build a new life. Those billions could lift the wages of my people, give them jobs, give education and training and new hope to our youth, free our sharecroppers, build new hospitals and medical centers. The $8 billion being spent to rearm Europe and crush Asia could rehouse all my people living in the ghettos of Chicago and New York and every large city in the nation.

We fight that all people shall live. We fight to send our money to end colonialism for the colored peoples of the world, not to perpetuate it in Malan's South Africa, Churchill's Malaya, French Indo-China and the Middle East.

Can you conceive of the party of Taft and Eisenhower and MacArthur and McArthy and the big corporatioɪs calling a Negro woman to lead the good fight in 1952? Can you see the party of Truman, of Russell of Georgia, of Rankin of Mississippi, of Byrnes of South Carolina, of Acheson, naming a Negro woman to lead the fight against enslavement?

I am stirred by the responsibility that you have put upon me. I am proud that I am the choice of the leaders of my own people and leaders of all those who understand how deeply the fight for peace is one and indivisible with the fight for Negro equality.

And I am impelled to accept this call, for it is the call of all my people and call to my people. Frederick Douglass would rejoice, for he fought not only slavery but the oppression of women.

I make this pledge to my people, the dead and the living—to all Americans, black and white. I will not retire nor will I retreat, not one inch, so long as God gives me vision to see what is happening and strength to fight for the things I know are right. For I know that my kingdom, my people's kingdom, and the kingdom of all the peoples of all the world, is not beyond the skies, the moon and the stars, but right here at our feet.

I accept this great honor. I give you as my slogan in this campaign—"Let my people go."

National Guardian, Vol. 4, No. 24 (April 2, 1952), p. 3.

DEVELOPING COMMUNITY LEADERSHIP

ELLA BAKER

❦ Ella Baker, a veteran of five decades of work in the freedom movement, is one of the foremost organizers of our time. A woman of dynamic strength, quiet persistence and great conviction, she works out of the limelight, providing the essential skill and experience which sustain dynamic mass movements.

Born in Norfolk, Virginia, she grew up in a small town in North Carolina, and received her formal education, through the college level, in that state. Upon graduation from Shaw University in Raleigh, she came to New York just before the Depression of 1929. In the 1930's she identified with movements in the area of workers' education, consumer cooperatives, consumer protection and community organizing.

Early in the 1940's she began to work with the NAACP as an assistant field secretary. Later she became the national director of branches of the NAACP. As President of the New York Branch NAACP, she helped to initiate community action against de facto segregation in the New York public schools.

Following her two years of work with the Southern Christian Leadership Conference (SCLC) she was a founder, advisor and active participant of the Student Non-violent Coordinating Committee (SNCC) through its lifetime. In 1964, Miss Baker helped to found the Mississippi Freedom Democratic Party (MFDP), gave the keynote address at its founding convention and helped organize its challenge to the National Democratic Party in Atlantic City.

Through the years, there has been a procession of men and women whose commitments were deepened because they knew Miss Baker at a crucial point in their development. Among these are Mrs. Rosa Parks, who started the Montgomery bus protest in 1955, but who long before that worked with Miss Baker in the NAACP in Alabama; James Forman, who led SNCC through its most crucial years; Stokely Carmichael; H. Rap Brown; and many more, both black and white.

Miss Baker now serves as a consultant to a number of human rights groups in both the South and other parts of the country.

In my organizational work, I have never thought in terms of my "making a contribution." I just thought of myself as functioning where there was a need. And if I have made a contribution I think it may be that I had some influence on a large number of people.

As assistant field secretary of the branches of the NAACP, much of my work was in the South. At that time the NAACP was the leader on the cutting edge of social change. I remember when NAACP membership in the South was the basis for getting beaten up or even killed.

I used to leave New York about the 15th of February and travel through the South for four to five months. I would go to, say, Birmingham, Alabama and help to organize membership campaigns. And in the process of helping to organize membership campaigns, there was opportunity for developing community reaction. You would go into areas where people were not yet organized in the NAACP and try to get them more involved. Maybe you would start with some simple thing like the fact that they had no street lights, or the fact that in the given area somebody had been arrested or had been jailed in a manner that was considered illegal and unfair, and the like. You would deal with whatever the local problem was, and on the basis of the needs of the people you would try to organize them in the NAACP.

Black people who were living in the South were constantly living with violence. Part of the job was to help them to understand what that violence was and how they in an organized fashion could help to stem it. The major job was getting people to understand that they had something within their power that they could use, and it could only be used if they understood what was happening and how group action could counter violence even when it was perpetrated by the police or, in some instances, the state. My basic sense of it has always been to get people to understand that in the long run they themselves are the only protection they have against violence or injustice. If they only had ten members in the NAACP at a given point, those ten members could be in touch with twenty-five members in the next little town, with fifty in the next and throughout the state as a result of the organization of state conferences, and they, of course, could be linked up with the national. People have to be made to understand that they cannot look for salvation anywhere but to themselves.

I left the NAACP and then worked at fund-raising with the National Urban League Service Fund and with several national health organizations. However, I continued my work with the NAACP on the local level. I became the advisor for the Youth Council. Then I served as President of the New York branch at a point where it had sunk to a low level in membership and otherwise. And in the process of serving as

President we tried to bring the NAACP back, as I called it, to the people. We moved the branch out of an office building and located it where it would be more visible to the Harlem community. We started developing an active branch. It became one of the largest branches. I was President for a couple of years. It was strictly volunteer work which lasted until four o'clock in the morning, sometimes.

When the 1954 Supreme Court decision on school desegregation came, I was serving as chairman of the Educational Committee of the New York branch. We began to deal with the problems of *de facto* segregation, and the results of the *de facto* segregation which were evidenced largely in the achievement levels of black children, going down instead of going up after they entered public school. We had called the first committee meeting and Kenneth Clark became the chairman of that committee. During that period, I served on the Mayor's Commission on School Integration, with the subdivision on zoning. In the summer of 1957, I gave time to organizing what we called Parents in Action for Quality Education.

I've never believed that the people who control things really were willing and able to pay the price of integration. From a practical standpoint, anyone who looked at the Harlem area knew that the potential for integration *per se* was basically impossible unless there were some radically innovative things done. And those innovative things would not be acceptable to those who ran the school system, nor to communities, nor even to the people who call themselves supporters of integration. I did a good deal of speaking, and I went to Queens, I went to the upper West side, and the people very eagerly said they wanted school integration. But when you raised the question of whether they would permit or would welcome Blacks to live in the same houses with them, which was the only practical way at that stage to achieve integration, they squirmed. Integration certainly had to be pushed concurrently with changing the quality of education that the black children were getting, and changing the attitudes of the educational establishment toward the black community.

I don't think we achieved too much with the committee except to pinpoint certain issues and to have survived some very sharp confrontations with the Superintendent and others on the board of Education. But out of it came increased fervor on the part of the black communities to make some changes. One of the gratifying things to me is the fact that even as late as this year I have met people who were in that group and who have been continuously active in the struggle for quality education in the black communities ever since.

There certainly has been progress in the direction of the capacity of people to face this issue. And to me, when people themselves know what they are looking for and recognize that they can exercise some influence by action, that's progress.

Come 1957, I went down South a couple of times in connection with the formation of the Southern Christian Leadership Conference. At the end of '57 there was the need for someone to go down to set up the office of SCLC in Atlanta and to coordinate what it considered its first South-wide project, which was the holding of simultaneous meetings on February 12th in twenty different cities. I went down with the idea of not spending more than six weeks there, giving myself a month to get the thing going, and then two weeks to clean it up. I stayed with SCLC for two and a half years, because they didn't have anybody. My official capacity was varied. When I first went down, I didn't insist on a title, which is nothing new or unusual for me; it didn't bother me. I was just there in person. And then they were looking for a minister, a man, and I helped to find a minister and a man, and he stayed a while, and when he came I decided that since I was doing what I was doing, he was the director and I became, I think, co-director. And then there was nobody, and of course there was no money in those days, so I kept on until the summer of 1960. And prior to that, of course, the sit-ins had started, and I was able to get the SCLC to at least sponsor the conference in Raleigh. We had hoped to call together about 100 or 125 of the young leaders who had emerged in the sit-ins in the South. But of course the sit-ins had been so dynamic in the field that when we got to the meeting we had two hundred and some people, including some from the North. And out of that conference of the Easter weekend of 1960, which I coordinated and organized, we had a committee that came out of it, and out of that committee SNCC was born.

And after SNCC came into existence, of course, it opened up a new era of struggle. I felt the urge to stay close by. Because if I had done anything anywhere, it had been largely in the role of supporting things, and in the background of things that needed to be done for the organizations that were supposedly out front. So I felt if I had done it for the elders, I could do it for young people.

I had no difficulty relating to the young people. I spoke their language in terms of the meaning of what they had to say. I didn't change my speech pattern and they didn't have to change their speech pattern. But we were able to communicate.

I never had any income or paid relationship with SNCC. In order to be available to do things with SNCC, I first found a two-year project with the Southern Region of the National Student YWCA in a special Human Relations Program. Then I took up a relationship with the Southern Conference Educational Fund (SCEF). I still am on their staff in a consultative role, and I stayed in Atlanta until the summer of '64, spring and summer of '64. I was asked to come up and help organize the challenge of the Mississippi Freedom Democratic Party at the Democratic Convention. So offices were set up in Washington and I functioned there until after the convention, closed up the office, and then moved back to New York from Atlanta.

There are those, some of the young people especially, who have said to me that if I had not been a woman I would have been well known in certain places, and perhaps held certain kinds of positions.

I have always felt it was a handicap for oppressed peoples to depend so largely upon a leader, because unfortunately in our culture, the charismatic leader usually becomes a leader because he has found a spot in the public limelight. It usually means he has been touted through the public media, which means that the media made him, and the media may undo him. There is also the danger in our culture that, because a person is called upon to give public statements and is acclaimed by the establishment, such a person gets to the point of believing that he *is* the movement. Such people get so involved with playing the game of being important that they exhaust themselves and their time, and they don't do the work of actually organizing people.

For myself, circumstances frequently dictated what had to be done as I saw it. For example, I had no plans to go down and set up the office of SCLC. But it seemed unless something were done whatever impetus had been gained would be lost, and nobody else was available who was willing or able to do it. So I went because to me it was more important to see what was a potential for all of us than it was to do what I might have done for myself. I knew from the beginning that as a woman, an older woman, in a group of ministers who are accustomed to having women largely as supporters, there was no place for me to have come into a leadership role. The competition wasn't worth it.

The movement of the '50's and '60's was carried largely by women, since it came out of church groups. It was sort of second nature to women to play a supportive role. How many made a conscious decision on the basis of the larger goals, how many on the basis of habit pattern, I don't know. But it's true that the number of women who carried the movement is much larger than that of men. Black women have had to carry this role, and I think the younger women are insisting on an equal footing.

I don't advocate anybody following the pattern I followed, unless they find themselves in a situation where they think that the larger goals will be shortchanged if they don't. From the standpoint of the historical pattern of the society, which seems to assume that this is the best role for women, I think that certainly the young people who are challenging this ought to be challenging it, and it ought to be changed. But I also think you have to have a certain sense of your own value, and a sense of security on your part, to be able to forgo the glamor of what the leadership role offers. From the standpoint of my work and my own self-concepts, I don't think I have thought of myself largely as a woman. I thought of myself as an individual with a certain amount of sense of the need of people to participate in the movement. I have always thought what is needed is the development of people who are interested not in being leaders as much as in developing leadership among other people. Every time I see a young person who has come through the system to a stage where he could profit from the system and identify with it, but who identifies more with the struggle of black people who have not had his chance, every time I find such a person I take new hope. I feel a new life as a result of it.

Ella Baker, taped interview with Gerda Lerner,
December 1970. Used by permission.

THE 51% MINORITY

**REPRESENTATIVE SHIRLEY CHISHOLM
(DEMOCRAT, NEW YORK)**

❦ *Shirley Chisholm (1924–   ), born Shirley St. Hill in Brooklyn, was raised and educated until the age of seven by her grandmother in Barbados while her parents struggled for an economic foothold in New York City. Reunited with her parents in New York in 1934, she went to Brooklyn public schools and graduated from Brooklyn College with a cum laude B.A. in 1946. After obtaining an M.A. at Columbia University, she began teaching nursery school and became a nursery school director, a position she held for* twenty years. She married Conrad Chisholm, a detective, in 1949.

Shirley Chisholm entered Brooklyn Democratic Party politics on the club level in the early 1950's and did many years of routine party work in the lowest echelons. Her election as a New York State assemblywoman in 1964 climaxed a decade of struggle for black representation for her district. In 1967, she emerged victorious in a three-way primary race for the Brooklyn House seat vacated by Representative Edna Kelly and proceeded to win the election against James R. Farmer, the Republican candidate. Congresswoman Chisholm is the first black woman ever elected to the House of Representatives. She broke precedent by successfully fighting her assignment to the House Agricultural Committee, winning an assignment more closely related to her interests and the needs of her constituents. Shirley Chisholm has won many awards and honors and has published an autobiography, Unbought and Unbossed (Boston: Houghton Mifflin Company, 1970).

. . . I am, as it is obvious, both black and a woman. And that is a good vantage point from which to view at least two elements of what is becoming a social revolution: the American black revolution and the women's liberation movement. But it is also a horrible disadvantage. It is a disadvantage because America as a nation is both racist and anti-feminist. Racism and anti-feminism are two of the prime traditions of this country. For any individual, breaking with social tradition is a giant step—a giant step because there are no social traditions which do not have corresponding social sanctions— the sole purpose of which are to protect the sanctity of those traditions.

That's when we ask the question, "Do women dare?" We're not asking whether women are capable of a break with tradition so much as we're asking whether they are capable of bearing the sanctions that will be placed upon them. . . .

Each—black male and black female, white male and white female—must escape first from their own intolerable trap before they can be fully effective in helping others to free themselves. Therein lies one of the major reasons that there are not more involved in the women's liberation movement. Women cannot, for the most part, operate independently of men because they often do not have sufficient economic freedom.

In 1966, the median earnings of women who worked full time for the whole year was less than the median income for males who worked full time for the whole year. In fact, white women workers made less than black male workers, and of course, black women workers made the least of all. Whether it is intentional or not, women are paid less than men for the same work, no matter what their chosen field of work. Whether it is intentional or not, employment for women is regulated more in terms of the jobs that are available to them. This is almost as true for white women as it is for black women. Whether it is intentional or not, when it becomes time for a high school girl to think about preparing for her career, her counselors, whether they be male or female, will think first of her so-called natural career—housewife and mother—and begin to program her for a field with which children and marriage will not unduly interfere.

That's exactly the same as the situation of the young black students who the racist counselor advises to prepare for service-oriented occupations, because he does not even think of them entering the professions. And the response of the average young female is precisely the same as the response of the average young black or Puerto Rican—tacit agreement—because the odds seem to be stacked against them.

This is not happening as much as it once did to young minority group people. It is not happening because they have been radicalized, and the country is becoming sensitized to its racist attitudes. Women must learn a lesson from that experience. They must rebel. . . .

The law cannot do it for us. *We must do it for ourselves*. Women in this country must become revolutionaries. We must refuse to accept the old, the traditional roles and stereotypes. . . . We must replace the old, negative thoughts about our femininity with positive thoughts and positive action affirming it, and more. But we must also remember that we will be breaking with tradition, and so we must prepare ourselves educationally, economically, and psychologically in order that we will be able to accept and bear with the sanctions that society will immediately impose upon us.

I'm a politician. . . . I have been in politics for 20 years, and in that time I have learned a few things about the role of women in power. And the major thing that I have learned is that women are the backbone of America's political organizations. They are the letter writers, the envelope stuffers, the telephone answerers; they're the campaign workers and the organizers. Perhaps it is in America, more than any other country, that the inherent proof of the old bromide, "The power behind the throne is a woman" is most readily apparent.

Let me remind you once again of the relatively few women standard bearers on the American political scene. There are only 10 United States Representatives; one Senator; no cabinet members who are women; no women on the Supreme Court and only a small percentage of lady judges at the federal court level who might be candidates.

It is true that at the state level the picture is somewhat brighter, just as it is true that the North presents a service that is somewhat more appealing to the black American when compared to the South. But even though in 1967 there were 318 women who were in the state legislatures, the percentage is not good when compared with the fact that in almost all 50 states, there are more women of voting age than there are men and that in each state, the number of women of voting age is increasing at a greater rate than the number of men. Nor is it an encouraging figure when compared with the fact that in 1966 there were not 318 women in the state legislatures, as now, but there were 328, which shows that there has been a decline. . . .

I have pointed out time and time again that the harshest

discrimination that I have encountered in the political arena is anti-feminism, both from males and brain-washed, Uncle Tom females. When I first announced that I was running for the United States Congress, both males and females advised me, as they had when I ran for the New York State legislature, to go back to teaching—a woman's vocation— and leave the politics to the men.

And one of the major reasons that I will not leave the American scene—that is, voluntarily—is because the number of women in politics is declining. There are at least 2,000,000 more women than men of voting age, but the fact is that while we get out the vote, we also do not get out *to* vote. In 1964, for example, 72% of registered males voted, while only 67% of the registered females voted. We seem to want to become a political minority by choice. I believe that women have a special contribution to make to help bring order out of chaos in our nation today because they have special qualities of leadership which are greatly needed today. And these qualities are the patience, tolerance, and perseverance which have developed in many women because of suppression. And if we can add to these qualities a reservoir of information about the techniques of community action, we can indeed become effective harbingers for change.

Women must participate more in the legislative process, because even of the contributions that I have just mentioned, the single greatest contribution that women could bring to American politics would be a spirit of moral fervor, which is sorely needed in this nation today. But unfortunately, women's participation in politics is declining, as I have noted. . . .

Your time is now, my sisters. . . . New goals and new priorities, not only for this country, but for all of mankind must be set. Formal education will not help us do that. We must therefore depend upon informal learning. We can do that by confronting people with their humanity and their own inhumanity—confronting them wherever we meet them: in the church, in the classroom, on the floor of the Congress and the state legislatures, in the bars, and on the streets. We must reject not only the stereotypes that others hold of us, but also the stereotypes that we hold of ourselves.

In a speech made a few weeks ago to an audience that was predominately white and all female, I suggested the following, if they wanted to create change. You must start in your own homes, your own schools, and your own churches. I don't want you to go home and talk about integrated schools, churches, or marriages if the kind of integration you're talking about is black and white. I want you to go home and work for, fight for, the integration of male and female—human and human. . . .

Speech delivered at the Conference on Women's Employment. Hearings before the Special Subcommittee on Education of the Committee on Education and Labor, House of Representatives, Ninety-First Congress, Second Sesssion (Washington, D.C.: Government Printing Office, 1970), pp. 909–915.

CHAPTER SEVEN

THE MONSTER PREJUDICE

We meet the monster prejudice everywhere.
We have not power to contend with it, we
are so down-trodden. We cannot elevate
ourselves. . . . We want light; we ask it, and
it is denied us. Why are we thus treated?
Prejudice is the cause. . . .

Statement by Clarissa Lawrence,
Proceedings, Anti-Slavery Convention of
American Women, held in Philadelphia,
May 15, 16, 17, and 28, 1838
(Philadelphia: Merrirew & Gunn, 1838), p. 8.

IN THE GRIP OF
THE MONSTER

❦ Throughout United States history race prejudice
has been a devastating, inescapable and recurrent experience
in the life of each black man, woman and child. The following
selections represent only a small sampling of the bitter
experiences recounted by black women of different historical
periods. The overwhelming impression one gets from reading
the many available autobiographies, letters and manuscripts
is how little change there has been, over time, in the daily
indignities, humiliations and acts of violence imposed by
white society upon Blacks.

MARTYR FOR FREEDOM
AMY SPAIN

One of the martyrs of the cause which gave freedom to her
race was that of a colored woman named Amy Spain, who
was a resident of the town of Darlington, situated in a rich
cotton-growing district of South Carolina. At the time a portion of the Union army occupied the town of Darlington she
expressed her satisfatcion by clasping her hands and exclaim-
ing, "Bless the Lord the Yankees have come!" She could not
restrain her emotions. The long night of darkness which had
bound her in slavery was about to break away. It was impossible to repress the exuberance of her feelings; and although
powerless to aid the advancing deliverers of her caste, or to
injure her oppressors, the simple expression of satisfaction at
the event sealed her doom. Amy Spain died in the cause of
freedom. A section of Sherman's cavalry occupied the town,
and without doing any damage passed through. Not an insult
nor an unkind word was said to any of the women in that
town. The men had, with guilty consciences, fled; but on
their return, with their traditional chivalry, they seized upon

poor Amy, and ignominiously hung her to a sycamore-tree standing in front of the court-house, underneath which stood the block from which was monthly exhibited the slave chattels that were struck down by the auctioneer's hammer to the highest bidder.

Amy Spain heroically heard her sentence, and from her prison bars declared she was prepared to die. She defied her persecutors; and as she ascended the scaffold declared she was going to a place where she would receive a crown of glory. She was rudely interrupted by an oath from one of her executioners. To the eternal disgrace of Darlington her execution was acquiesced in and witnessed by most of the citizens of the town. Amy was launched into eternity, and the "chivalric Southern gentlemen" of Darlington had fully established their bravery by making war upon a defenseless African woman. She sleeps quietly, with others of her race, near the beautiful village. No memorial marks her grave, but after-ages will remember this martyr of liberty. Her persecutors will pass away and be forgotten, but Amy Spain's name is now hallowed among the Africans, who, emancipated and free, dare, with the starry folds of the flag of the free floating over them, speak her name with holy reverence.

Harper's Weekly, September 30, 1865.

I BELIEVE THEY DESPISE US FOR OUR COLOR . . .

SARAH M. DOUGLASS

❧ Sarah M. Douglass (see p. 85), although brought up in a sheltered environment, experienced subtle forms of race discrimination which she protested throughout her life. The letter below was written to the abolitionist Quaker William Bassett of Lynn, Massachusetts, at the request of the white abolitionist Sarah Grimké. Bassett cited Sarah Douglass' complaint in his protest against race discrimination

by the Society of Friends, for which he was later disowned.
He and Sarah Grimké tried to enlist the support of British
Quakers by publicizing the complaints of Sarah Douglass
and others in a pamphlet published in Britain. In this
pamphlet the facts were cited, but names were omitted. One
of the complaints in this pamphlet concerned the time Sarah
Douglass had stayed in New York City and found herself
ostracized by white Quakers. Only one woman ever spoke to
her. In her own words: "I had been attending one month,
when a friend accosted me thus—'Does thee go out a house
cleaning?' I looked at her with astonishment,—my eyes
filled with tears, and I answered no. 'What does thee do
then?' 'I teach a school'—'oh, then thee's better off'. . . . I
wept during the whole of that meeting. . . ."

SARAH DOUGLASS TO WILLIAM BASSETT

Philadelphia, December 1837

Esteemed Friend.

. . . The questions you ask me, make me feel my weakness,
and in view of the great responsibility that rests upon me in
answering them, my flesh trembles; yet will I cast my burden
on Him, who is strength in weakness and resolve to do my
duty; to tell the truth and leave the consequences to God.
. . . And as you request to know particularly about Arch
Street Meeting, I may say that the experience of years has
made me wise in this fact, that there is a bench set apart at
that meeting for our people, whether *officially* appointed or
not I cannot say; but this I am free to say that my mother
and myself were told to sit there, and that a friend sat at each
end of the bench to prevent white persons from sitting there.
And even when a child my soul was made sad with hearing
five or six times during the course of one meeting this language of remonstrance addressed to those who were willing
to sit by us. "This bench is for the black people." "This
bench is for the people of color." And oftentimes I wept, at
other times I felt indignant and queried in my own mind

are these people Christians. Now it seems clear to me that had not this bench been set apart for oppressed Americans, there would have been no necessity for the oft-repeated and galling remonstrance, galling indeed, because I *believe they despise us for our color*. I have not been in Arch Street meeting for four years; but my mother goes once a week and frequently she has a *whole long bench* to herself. The assertion that our people who attend their meetings prefer sitting by themselves, is not true. A very near friend of ours, that fears God and who has been a constant attender of Friends meeting from his childhood, says ". . . Several years ago a friend came to me and told me that 'Friends' had appointed a back bench for us. I told him with some warmth that I had just as lief sit on the floor as sit there. I do not care about it, Friends do not do the thing that is right." Judge now, I pray you, whether this man preferred sitting by himself. Two sons of the person I have just mentioned, have left attending Friends meetings within the last few months, because they could no longer endure the "scorning of those that are at ease, and the contempt of the proud." Conversing with one of them today, I asked, why did you leave Friends. "Because they do not know how to treat me, I do not like to sit on a back bench and be treated with contempt, so I go where I am better treated." . . . In reply to your question "whether there appears to be a diminution of prejudice towards you among Friends," I unhesitatingly answer, no. I have heard it frequently remarked and have observed it myself, that in proportion as we become intellectual and respectable, so in proportion does their disgust and prejudice increase.

Yet while I speak this of Friends as a body, I am happy to say that there is in this city a "noble few", who have cleansed their garments from the foul stain of prejudice, and are doing all their hands find to do in promoting the moral and mental elevation of oppressed Americans.

Some of these are members of Anti-Slavery Societies and others belong to the old abolition School. . . .

Did all the members of Friends society feel for us, as the sisters Grimké do, how soon, how very soon would the fetters be stricken from the captive and cruel prejudice be driven from the bosoms of the professed followers of Christ.

Theodore Dwight Weld Collection, William L. Clements Library,
University of Michigan, Ann Arbor, Michigan.

WHEN, OH! WHEN SHALL THIS CEASE?

CHARLOTTE FORTEN GRIMKÉ

❦ Reared in a comfortable, loving home, Charlotte Forten had enjoyed a sheltered middle-class upbringing. Her family's abolitionist activities, the runaway slaves sheltered in her uncle Robert Purvis' home, the frequent visits of leading abolitionists who made the Forten home their headquarters, all served to make the growing girl strongly conscious of her race. Pride in her people, a desire to excel in the white world, empathy for the victims of slavery were part of her upbringing. But her own contact with race prejudice was long delayed.

When she was denied admission to the white schools of Philadelphia, her father had her instructed by tutors. At the age of sixteen she was sent to the home of a family friend, the Negro abolitionist Charles Lenox Remond, in Salem, Massachusetts, to enter the nonsegregated public schools there. Here, Charlotte Forten personally experienced prejudice, and recorded her feelings in her diary.

Wednesday, Sept. 12, [1855]. To-day school commenced— Most happy am I to return to the companionship of my studies,—ever my most valued friends. It is pleasant to meet the scholars again; most of them greeted me cordially, and were it not for the thought that *will* intrude, of the want of *entire sympathy* even of those I know and like best, I should greatly enjoy their society. There is one young girl and only one—Miss [Sarah] B[rown] who I believe thoroughly and heartily appreciates anti-slavery,—*racial* anti-slavery, and has no prejudice against color. I wonder that every colored person is not a misanthrope. Surely we have everything to make us hate mankind. I have met girls in the schoolroom[—] they have been thoroughly kind and cordial to me,—perhaps the next day met them in the street—they feared to recognize me; these I can but regard now with scorn and contempt,— once I liked them, believing them incapable of such meanness. Others give the most distant recognition possible,—I, of course, acknowledge no such recognitions, and they soon cease entirely. These are but trifles, certainly, to the great, public wrongs which we as a people are obliged to endure. But to those who experience them, these apparent trifles are most wearing and discouraging; even to the child's mind they reveal volumes of deceit and heartlessness, and early teach a lesson of suspicion and distrust. Oh! it is hard to go through life meeting contempt with contempt, hatred with hatred, fearing, with too good reason, to love and trust hardly any one whose skin is white—however lovable, attractive and congenial in seeming. In the bitter, passionate feelings of my soul again and again there rises the questions "When oh! when shall this cease?" "Is there no help?" "How long oh! how long must we continue to suffer—to endure?" Conscience answers it is wrong, it is ignoble to despair; let us labor earnestly and faithfully to acquire knowledge, to break down the barriers of prejudice and oppression. Let us take courage; never ceasing to work—hoping and believing that if not for us, for another generation there is a better, brighter day in store—when slavery and prejudice shall vanish before the glorious light of Liberty and Truth; when the rights of every colored man shall everywhere be acknowledged and respected, and he shall be treated as a *man* and a *brother!*

The Journal of Charlotte Forten, Ray Allen Billington, ed. (New York. Collier Books, 1961), pp. 74-75.

❧Thirty-four years later, Charlotte Forten Grimké, now the wife of the Reverend Francis J. Grimké in Washington, D.C., recalled the long and bitter struggle against race prejudice in the New England of her youth.

Washington, D.C. Oct. 10, 1889

TO THE EDITOR OF *The Evangelist*:

Dear Sir:—In your letter of Sept. 26th, entitled "Relations of Whites and Blacks in the South as compared with the North—Is there a Color Line in New England?" there are some erroneous statements, which I should like to correct. I think you will willingly accord me this privilege, as you say that you should be glad to be corrected if you have made mistakes. As I am identified with the people of whom you write, I am naturally anxious that no statements in regard to them should be published which are not strictly in accordance with the facts; especially at this time, when the tendency all over the country is to depreciate them.

First, in regard to the colored people in New England, you say "In half the country there was no effort to keep them down; for slavery was abolished a century ago . . ." But in fact, it is less than half a century since colored people, even in free Massachusetts, were denied the privilege of attending the public schools, and of riding in the public conveyances. Frederick Douglass was forcibly ejected from a stage coach running from Salem to Lynn, and there were other instances of the kind. You are doubtless familiar with the story of Prudence Crandall, who for attempting to establish a boarding school for colored girls in Canterbury, Conn., was most outrageously persecuted and insulted by the citizens of the place, and finally imprisoned and her schoolhouse set on fire. Through the influence of these citizens upon the Legislature, a "Black Law" was enacted, forbidding any person to establish in the State any school, academy, or literary institution for the instruction or education of colored persons who are not inhabitants of the State, "without the consent in writing first obtained of a majority of the civil authority, and also of the select men of the town, in which such school, academy, or literary institution is situated," etc. We are told that, "on the receipt of the tidings that the Legislature had passed the law, joy and exultation ran wild in Canterbury. The bells were rung and a cannon fired until all the inhabitants for miles around were informed of the triumph."

In another New England town, a schoolhouse was fired into and afterward destroyed, because Henry Highland Garnett and other colored young men were admitted as students. In view of such facts . . . is it quite fair to say that for a century in New England "the black man has had every right that belongs to his white neighbor," and that "with such advantages, a race that had natural genius ought to have made great progress in a hundred years?"

Now as to the present condition of the colored people in New England, you say "I look about me here in New England and I see a few colored men; but what are they doing? They work in the fields, they hoe the corn; they dig potatoes; the women take in washing. I find colored barbers and white-washers, shoeblack and chimney-sweeps; but not a colored man who has grown to be a merchant or a banker, a judge or a lawyer to practice even in the petty courts, a member of the Legislature or a justice of the peace, or even a selectman of the town. In all of these respects they remain where they were in the days of our fathers."

In answer to this I send you the following facts, which have been forwarded to me by my brother-in-law, A. H. Grimké, a lawyer, who has been long a resident of Massachusetts: "There are about a dozen colored lawyers in Massachusetts, a majority of whom are justices of the peace. There has been a colored man in the Legislature every year since 1882. Prior to that period, there was a colored member of the Legislature every second or third year since the close of the war. Twice during these periods, two colored men were members at the same time. Every year there are three or four colored members of the Republican State Convention, and this year there was a colored member of the Democratic

State Convention as well. Mr. J. C. Chappelle is at present a member of the Republican State Central Committee. In my own town of Hyde Park, a colored man is Sealer of Weights and Measures. If you will allow a personal reference, I am one of the trustees of a public institution (The Westborough Insane Hospital), recognized as one of the most important in the State, and I am, in addition, Secretary of the Board. The expenditures of this hospital are about $100,000 a year. Judge Ruffin was appointed Judge of the Charlestown Municipal Court in 1883, and filled the position with credit to himself and the community until his death about three years afterwards. Dr. Grant is one of the best dentists in Boston, and has a large practice among both races. He is a man of inventive skill in his profession. His invention in relation to cleft palates is well known here and elsewhere. Besides, he has been for years an instructor in the Dental College connected with Harvard University—mechanical dentistry being his department. John H. Lewis has a merchant tailoring establishment in Washington Street, Boston, and does the second largest business in New England. His transactions annually exceed $100,000; he has just started a branch store in Providence, R.I. Mr. Joseph Lee is owner and proprietor of one of the first-class hotels of the East. The richest people of the State are guests at the Woodland Park Hotel, at Auburndale. His business is rapidly increasing, he has already enlarged the original building, and is about to enlarge a second time to meet the increasing demands of the public. The property is valued at about $120,000. Besides Mr. Lewis above mentioned, there are three colored merchant tailors doing a handsome business in Boston.

"In New Bedford, one of the largest and finest drug stores is owned and conducted by a young colored man. In that city the colored people are butchers, fruiterers, grocers, master shipbuilders, etc. Colored young women have taught in the public schools of Boston within the past few years, and one, Miss Baldwin, has been for some years one of the most popular teachers in the public schools of Cambridge."

What is true of the condition of the colored people in New

England, is true of their condition in the Northern States generally and in many of the Southern states. Among them you will find numbers of lawyers, doctors, teachers, professors in colleges, merchants, etc.

Here in the city of Washington there are not a few colored men who are engaged in real estate business. There are also brokers, bankers, successful lawyers and physicians, besides scores of teachers. . . .

In spite of seemingly overwhelming obstacles, in spite of the weight of oppression and prejudice, leaders, in one sense, did arise among the colored people. Such men as Frederick Douglass, Henry Highland Garnett, Samuel R. Ward, and others—men who were born slaves—did much by their energy, eloquence, and ability to create that public sentiment which led ultimately to the overthrow of slavery.

As to the colored soldiers in the late war, you say "though they were brave enough in the ranks, yet no one had the natural capacity to command." May I ask what authority you have for this statement? There were colored officers who acquitted themselves honorably . . . the fact that there were no colored colonels or generals, may readily be accounted for by the strong prejudice, which prevented the Government from employing colored troops at all, until it was forced to do so from sheer necessity. Many of them displayed distinguished bravery; there may have been many a Toussaint among them, but no matter how great their capacity to command, there was no chance for promotion in the face of the cruel and unjust prejudice which they had to encounter. . . .

Anna J. Cooper, *The Life and Writings of the Grimké Family* (n.p., n.d., copyright 1951).

FIGHTING JIM CROW

SOJOURNER TRUTH

❦ *Sojourner Truth (c. 1797–1883) was born a slave in Ulster County, New York. Her Dutch master named her*

Isabella Baumfree, but called her "Bell." She saw her brothers and sisters sold off and was herself sold with some sheep to a Yankee farmer who beat her for not understanding English. Bell was sold twice more before she was twelve years old. Her master John Dumont raped her and later married her to an older slave, Thomas, by whom she had five children. Although slavery was ended by law in New York, her master delayed her emancipation and sold her five-year-old boy Peter, despite his earlier promise to free him. Bell ran away with her baby and contracted to serve another master for a year. He freed her in 1827.

She then set about retrieving her boy Peter, who had been sold South. She sued for his freedom in Kingston, New York, won the case and was reunited with her child. For a number of years, she worked in New York City as a domestic. Then she became involved with a group of religious fanatics under the "prophet" Mathias and lived and worked in their religious commune. One of the members of the group was murdered and Bell, with the others, was forced to stand trial. But she was freed of any implication in the murder and, somewhat disillusioned with the city, considered leaving it.

An earlier religious vision had imbued her with a strong sense of mission. She felt that God talked to her and that she must obey. In June 1843, she left the city on foot, leaving all her possessions behind her, lodging wherever she could find hospitality and preaching her own unique gospel. It was as this time that she changed her name. She later explained this decision:

"When I left the house of bondage I left everything behind. I wa'n't goin' to keep nothin' of Egypt on me, an' so I went to the Lord an' asked him to give me a new name. And the Lord gave me Sojourner because I was to travel up an' down the land showin' the people their sins an' bein' a sign unto them. Afterward I told the Lord I wanted another name 'cause everybody else had two names; and the Lord gave me Truth, because I was to declare the truth to the people."

It was as an itinerant preacher that Sojourner Truth reached fame and prominence in the North. She had a strong, almost mystical effect on audiences and frequently tamed hostile crowds by her fearless attitude and pithy comments. This illiterate woman spoke in metaphors of Biblical richness, commenting shrewdly on politics, manners, mores and prevalent values. She advocated abolition, women's rights, the protection of the poor and her own brand of Christianity and brotherly love. She dictated her autobiography to a white friend and lived by selling it at her lectures. She bought a little house in Battle Creek, Michigan, where she made her home in her old age.

During the Civil War she visited the Union troops, distributed gifts to the soldiers and entertained them by singing spirituals, many of her own composition.

In 1864, she traveled to Washington to see President Lincoln. She stayed on to work for a year in the Freedmen's Village at Arlington Heights. She conceived the idea of resettling groups of freedmen in the West, lobbied and petitioned for this scheme and continued to work for freedmen's relief. She died at her home in Battle Creek, Michigan, in 1883.

The episodes described below took place in post–Civil War Washington.

While Sojourner was engaged in the hospital, she . . . would sometimes be obliged to walk a long distance. . . . She would gladly have availed herself of the street cars; but although there was on each track one car called the Jim Crow car, nominally for the accommodation of colored people, yet should they succeed in getting on at all they would seldom have more than the privilege of standing, as the seats were usually filled with white folks. Unwilling to submit to this state of things, she complained to the president of the street railroad, who ordered the Jim Crow car to be taken off. A law was now passed giving the colored people equal car privileges with the white.

Not long after this, Sojourner, having occasion to ride, signaled the car, but neither conductor nor driver noticed her. Soon another followed . . . but they also turned away. She then gave three tremendous yelps, "I want to ride! *I want to ride!!* I WANT TO RIDE!!! . . ." People, carriages, go-carts of every description stood still. The car was effectually blocked up, and before it could move on, Sojourner had jumped aboard. Then there arose a great shout from the crowd, "Ha! ha! ha!! She has beaten him," &c. The angry conductor told her to go forward where the horses were or he would put her out. Quietly seating herself, she informed him that she was a passenger . . . neither a Marylander nor a Virginian to fear his threats; but was from the Empire State of New York, and knew the laws as well as he did. . . .

Sojourner rode farther than she needed to go; for a ride was so rare a privilege that she determined to make the most of it. She left the car feeling very happy, and said, "Bless God! I have had a ride."

Returning one day from the Orphan's Home at Georgetown, she hastened to reach a car; but they paid no attention . . . and kept ringing a bell that they might not hear her. She ran after it . . . succeeded in overtaking it and, getting in, said to the conductor, "It is a shame to make a lady run so." He told her if she said another word, he would put her off the car, and came forward as if to execute his threat. She replied, "If you attempt that, it will cost you more than your car and horses are worth." . . .

At another time, she was sent to Georgetown to obtain a nurse. . . . They went to the station and took seats in an empty car, but had not proceeded far before two ladies came in, and seating themselves opposite the colored woman began a whispered conversation, frequently casting scornful glances at the latter. At length one of the ladies called out . . . "Conductor, conductor, does niggers ride in these cars?" He hesitatingly answered, "Ye yea-yes," to which she responded, ". . . They ought to have a nigger car on the track." Sojourner remarked, "Of course colored people ride in the cars. Street cars are designed for poor white, and colored folks. Carriages are for ladies and gentlemen. There are carriages . . . standing ready to take you three or four miles for sixpence, and then you talk of a nigger car!!!" Promptly acting upon this hint, they arose to leave. "Ah!" said Sojourner, "now they are going to take a carriage. Good by, ladies."

Mrs. Laura Haviland, a widely known philanthropist . . . sometimes went about the city with Sojourner to procure necessaries for the invalids. Returning one day . . . Mrs. Haviland proposed to take a car although she was well aware that a white person was seldom allowed to ride if accompanied by a black one. "As Mrs. Haviland signaled the car," says Sojourner, "I stepped one side as if to continue my walk and when it stopped I ran and jumped aboard. The conductor pushed me back, saying, 'Get out of the way and let this lady come in.' Whoop! said I, I am a lady too. We met with no further opposition till we were obliged to change cars. A man coming out as we were going into the next car, asked the conductor if 'niggers were allowed to ride.' The conductor grabbed me by the shoulder and jerking me around, ordered me to get out. I told him I would not. Mrs. Haviland took hold of my other arm and said, 'Don't put her out.' The conductor asked if I belonged to her. 'No,' replied Mrs. Haviland, 'She belongs to humanity.' 'Then take her and go,' said he, and giving me another push slammed me against the door. I told him I would let him know whether he could shove me about like a dog, and said to Mrs. Haviland, Take the number of this car.

"At this, the man looked alarmed, and gave us no more trouble. When we arrived at the hospital, the surgeons were called in to examine my shoulder and found that a bone was misplaced. I complained to the president of the road, who advised me to arrest the man for assault and battery. The Bureau furnished me a lawyer, and the fellow lost his situation. It created a great sensation, and before the trial was ended, the inside of the cars looked like pepper and salt; and I felt, like Poll Parrot, 'Jack, I am riding.' A little circumstance will show how great a change a few weeks had produced: A lady saw some colored women looking wistfully toward a car, when the conductor, halting, said, 'Walk in, ladies.' Now they who had so lately cursed me for wanting to ride, could stop for black as well as white, and could even condescend to say, 'Walk in, ladies.' "

Olive Gilbert, Narrative of Sojourner Truth . . . (Battle Creek,
Michigan: Review and Herald Office, 1884), pp. 184–187.

SUING FOR HER RIGHTS

CHARLOTTE HAWKINS BROWN

❦ *Charlotte Hawkins Brown made it a practice, whenever insulted in a train or forced to leave a pullman coach and enter the Jim Crow car, to bring suit. She did this out of principle, since the small sums she collected were hardly worth the effort. The following concerns one such lawsuit.*

Her attorney had been corresponding with the Pullman Company in regard to her claim for damages for mistreatment accorded her while a passenger. He suggested a damage settlement of $3,000. The Company offered to pay $200. He advised the company that "the sum is too small to merit further negotiations." However, he wrote to his client as follows:

F. P. HOBGOOD, JR., ATTORNEY AT LAW, TO CHARLOTTE HAWKINS BROWN:

Greensborough, N.C., October 4, 1921

The foregoing letter expressed my real sentiments, however in view of the expensive litigation and the vexatious questions which would be raised, to say nothing to the expense to you of getting your witnesses here, I am wondering if we had not better make a very much more liberal offer than the one heretofor made. . . ."

✌ He suggested that they offer to settle for $1,000 and be prepared to accept $500. He expressed himself as willing to accept a 50 per cent fee.

RESPONSE TO THIS LETTER BY CHARLOTTE HAWKINS BROWN

October 19, 1921

Dear Sir:

. . . I feel that the time has come when absolute justice for Negroes who are not seeking social equality ought to at least be tested in the Courts. . . . I do not want to bring this Pullman matter into the Courts, if I get what I think is even partial justice, but I certainly do not think you ought to ask for less than $1,500 . . .

As for me, a Negro woman, I feel so intently the insults that are heaped upon me by the Railroad Company that I am willing to become a martyr for Negro womanhood in this instance and give up my chance of holding, as friends, people who would withdraw because of my attitude. . . . A few of us must be sacrificed perhaps in order to get a step further.

Charlotte Hawkins Brown Manuscript, Schlesinger Library,
Radcliffe College, Cambridge, Massachusetts.

THE SMALL HORRORS
OF CHILDHOOD

ANONYMOUS

The very first humiliation I received I remember very distinctly to this day. It was when I was very young. A little girl playmate said to me: "I like to come over to your house to play, we have such good times, and your ma has such good preserves; but don't you tell my ma I eat over here. My ma says you all are nice, clean folks and she'd rather live by you than the white people we moved away from; for you don't borrow things. I know she would whip me if I ate with you, tho, because you are colored, you know."

I was very angry and forgot she was my guest, but told her to go home and bring my ma's sugar home her ma borrowed, and the rice they were always wanting a cup of.

After she had gone home I threw myself upon the ground and cried, for I liked the little girl, and until then I did not know that being "colored" made a difference. I am not sure I knew anything about "colored." I was very young and I know now I had been shielded from all unpleasantness.

My mother found me in tears and I asked her why was I colored, and couldn't little girls eat with me and let their mothers know it.

My mother got the whole story from me, but she couldn't satisfy me with her explanation—or, rather, lack of explanation. The little girl came often to play with me after that and we were little friends again, but we never had any more play dinners. I could not reconcile the fact that she and her people could borrow and eat our rice in their own house and not sit at my table and eat my mother's good, sweet preserves.

The second shock I received was horrible to me at the time. I had not gotten used to real horrible things then. . . . I was only a child, but I remember to this day what a shock I received. A young colored woman of a lovely disposition and character had just died. She was a teacher in the Sunday school I attended—a self-sacrificing, noble young woman who had been loved by many. Her coffin, room, hall, and even the porch of her house were filled with flowers sent by her friends. There were lovely designs sent by the more prosperous and simple bouquets made by untrained, childish hands. I was on my way with my own last offering of love, when I was met by quite a number of white boys and girls. A girl of about fifteen years said to me, "More flowers for that dead nigger? I never saw such a to-do made over a dead nigger before. Why, there must be thousands of roses alone in that house. I've been standing out here for hours and there has been a continual stream of niggers carrying flowers, and beautiful ones, too, and what makes me madder than anything else, those Yankee teachers carried flowers, too!" I, a little girl, with my heart full of sadness for the death of my friend, could make no answer to these big, heartless boys and girls, who threw stones after me as I ran from them.

When I reached home I could not talk for emotion. My mother was astonished when I found voice to tell her I was not crying because of the death of Miss W., but because I could not do something, anything, to avenge the insult to her dead body. I remember the strongest feeling I had was one of revenge. I wanted even to kill that particular girl or do something to hurt her. I was unhappy for days. I was told that they were heartless, but that I was even worse, and that Miss W. would be the first to condemn me could she speak.

That one encounter made a deep impression on my childish heart; it has been with me throughout the years. I have known real horrors since, but none left a greater impression on me.

"The Race Problem—An Autobiography" by
"A Southern Colored Woman," *The Independent*,
Vol. 56, No. 2885 (March 17, 1904), pp. 588–589.

WHAT IT MEANS TO BE COLORED IN THE CAPITAL OF THE UNITED STATES

MARY CHURCH TERRELL

❦ Mary Church Terrell published her autobiography, A Colored Woman in a White World, in 1940. The article "What It Means to Be Colored in the Capital of the United States," which became one of the chapters of the book, had been published much earlier, in 1907, in the popular maga-

zine The Independent. The discriminatory practices it
describes remained virtually unchanged until 1949, when,
following upon a two-year protest campaign, a suit brought by
Mrs. Terrell as one of the plaintiffs resulted in the outlawing
of discrimination in eating places in the nation's capital.
Other segregationist practices continued unchanged until
the civil rights struggles of the 1950's and 1960's.

For fifteen years I have resided in Washington, and while
it was far from being a paradise for colored people when I
first touched these shores it has been doing its level best ever
since to make conditions for us intolerable. As a colored
woman I might enter Washington any night, a stranger in
a strange land, and walk miles without finding a place to lay
my head. Unless I happened to know colored people who live
here or ran across a chance acquaintance who could recommend a colored boarding-house to me, I should be obliged to
spend the entire night wandering about. Indians, Chinamen,
Filipinos, Japanese and representatives of any other dark race
can find hotel accommodations, if they can pay for them.
The colored man alone is thrust out of the hotels of the
national capital like a leper.

As a colored woman I may walk from the Capitol to the
White House, ravenously hungry and abundantly supplied
with money with which to purchase a meal, without finding
a single restaurant in which I would be permitted to take a
morsel of food, if it was patronized by white people, unless I
were willing to sit behind a screen. As a colored woman I
cannot visit the tomb of the Father of this country, which
owes its very existence to the love of freedom in the human
heart and which stands for equal opportunity to all, without
being forced to sit in the Jim Crow section of an electric
car which starts from the very heart of the city—midway
between the Capitol and the White House. If I refuse thus
to be humiliated, I am cast into jail and forced to pay a fine
for violating the Viginia laws. . . .

As a colored woman I may enter more than one white church in Washington without receiving that welcome which as a human being I have the right to expect in the sanctuary of God. . . .

Unless I am willing to engage in a few menial occupations, in which the pay for my services would be very poor, there is no way for me to earn an honest living, if I am not a trained nurse or a dressmaker or can secure a position as teacher in the public schools, which is exceedingly difficult to do. It matters not what my intellectual attainments may be or how great is the need of the services of a competent person, if I try to enter many of the numerous vocations in which my white sisters are allowed to engage, the door is shut in my face.

From one Washington theater I am excluded altogether. In the remainder certain seats are set aside for colored people, and it is almost impossible to secure others. . . .

With the exception of the Catholic University, there is not a single white college in the national capital to which colored people are admitted. . . . A few years ago the Columbian Law School admitted colored students, but in deference to the Southern white students the authorities have decided to exclude them altogether.

Some time ago a young woman who had already attracted some attention in the literary world by her volume of short stories answered an advertisement which appeared in a Washington newspaper, which called for the services of a skilled stenographer and expert typewriter. . . . The applicants were requested to send specimens of their work and answer certain questions concerning their experience and their speed before they called in person. In reply to her application the young colored woman . . . received a letter from the firm stating that her references and experience were the most satisfactory that had been sent and requesting her to call. When she presented herself there was some doubt in the mind of the man to whom she was directed concerning her racial pedigree, so he asked her point-blank whether she was colored or white. When she confessed the truth the merchant expressed . . . deep regret that he could not avail himself of the services of so competent a person, but frankly admitted that employing a colored woman in his establishment in any except a menial position was simply out of the question. . . .

Not only can colored women secure no employment in the Washington stores, department and otherwise, except as menials, and such positions, of course, are few, but even as customers they are not infrequently treated with discourtesy both by the clerks and the proprietor himself. . . .

Altho white and colored teachers are under the same Board of Education and the system for the children of both races is said to be uniform, prejudice against the colored teachers in the public schools is manifested in a variety of ways. From 1870 to 1900 there was a colored superintendent at the head of the colored schools. During all that time the directors of the cooking, sewing, physical culture, manual training, music and art departments were colored people. Six years ago a change was inaugurated. The colored superintendent was legislated out of office and the directorships, without a single exception, were taken from colored teachers and given to the whites. . . . Now, no matter how competent or superior the colored teachers in our public schools may be, they know that they can never rise to the height of a directorship, can never hope to be more than an assistant and receive the meager salary therefor, unless the present regime is radically changed. . . .

Strenuous efforts are being made to run Jim Crow cars in the national capital. . . . Representative Heflin, of Alabama, who introduced a bill providing for Jim Crow street cars in the District of Columbia last winter, has just received a letter from the president of the East Brookland Citizens' Association "indorsing the movement for separate street cars and sincerely hoping that you will be successful in getting this enacted into a law as soon as possible." Brookland is a suburb of Washington.

The colored laborer's path to a decent livelihood is by no means smooth. Into some of the trades unions here he is admitted, while from others he is excluded altogether. By the union men this is denied, altho I am personally acquainted with skilled workmen who tell me they are not admitted into the unions because they are colored. But even when they are allowed to join the unions they frequently derive little benefit, owing to certain tricks of the trade. When the word passes round that help is needed and colored laborers apply, they are often told by the union officials that they have secured all the men they needed, because the places are reserved for white men, until they have been provided with jobs, and colored men must remain idle, unless the supply of white men is too small. . . .

And so I might go on citing instance after instance to show the variety of ways in which our people are sacrificed on the altar of prejudice in the Capital of the United States and how almost insurmountable are the obstacles which block his path to success. . . .

It is impossible for any white person in the United States, no matter how sympathetic and broad, to realize what life would mean to him if his incentive to effort were suddenly snatched away. To the lack of incentive to effort, which is the awful shadow under which we live, may be traced the wreck and ruin of scores of colored youth. And surely nowhere in the world do oppression and persecution based solely on the color of the skin appear more hateful and hideous than in the capital of the United States, because the chasm between the principles upon which this Government was founded, in which it still professes to believe, and those which are daily practiced under the protection of the flag, yawn so wide and deep.

"What It Means to Be Colored in the Capital of the United States,"
The Independent, Vol. 62, No. 3034
(January 24, 1907), pp. 181–186.

TRAVELING JIM CROW

MAHALIA JACKSON

❧ Mahalia Jackson (1911–   ) was born and raised
in New Orleans, Louisiana. She moved to Chicago at the
age of sixteen, worked there as a maid and later opened her
own beauty shop. She sang in the Salem Baptist Choir and
made her first record in 1934. Fame came with the record
"Move On Up a Little Higher," which sold over one million
copies. She concertized in Europe and won wide acclaim
there. In 1950, she gave a highly successful concert at
Carnegie Hall and has since continued her career as a concert
and record artist. Her fame as the "world's greatest gospel
singer" is undisputed.

Until my singing made me famous, I'd lived so far inside
the colored people's world that I didn't have to pay attention
every day to the way some white people in this country act
toward a person with a darker skin. I could go for long
stretches and not be made angry or hurt by them. . . .

A little while back I made a concert tour through the
South from Virginia to Florida. There were lots of white
people at those concerts and they sat side by side with colored
folks because my instruction to the ushers is to say, "Come
right in. Pick a seat and sit right down—anywhere." Because
if you come to hear religious music, you're not supposed to
feel any bigger than anybody else. Those white people—and
a lot of them were ministers—applauded just as hard as
anybody in the audience, and afterward some of them came
around to tell me how much they had enjoyed the evening.

But the minute I left the concert hall I felt as if I had
stepped back into the jungle. My accompanist, Mildred Falls,
and I were traveling in my car, a Cadillac. My cousin, John
Stevens, a young actor and drama teacher from Chicago, was
doing the driving. From Virginia to Florida it was a night-

mare. There was no place for us to eat or sleep on the main
highways. Restaurants wouldn't serve us. Teen-age white
girls who were serving as car hops would come bouncing out
to the car and stop dead when they saw we were Negroes,
spin around without a word and walk away. Some gasoline
stations didn't want to sell us gas and oil. Some told us that
no rest rooms were available. The looks of anger at the sight
of us colored folks sitting in a nice car were frightening to
see.

To turn off the main highway and find a place to eat and
sleep in a colored neighborhood meant losing so much time
that we finally were driving hundreds of extra miles each day
to get to the next city in which I was to sing so that we
could get a place to eat and sleep. It got so we were living on
bags of fresh fruit during the day and driving half the night
and I was so exhausted by the time I was supposed to sing I
was almost dizzy.

When the white people came crowding around us after
the concerts—ministers, teachers, educated people—I
thanked them for their praise but I felt like saying, "How big
does a person have to grow down in this part of the country
before he's going to stand up and say, 'Let us stop treating
other men and women and children with such cruelty just
because they are born colored!' "

Mahalia Jackson with E. M. Wylie, *Movin' On Up*
(New York: Hawthorne Books, 1966), pp. 96–97.

THE LIFE AND DEATH
OF JULIETTE DERRICOTTE

AN INTERPRETATION

Tall, well-built, attractive, Miss Derricotte had an expression
of keen intelligence lighted and softened in turn by a radiant
wit and an unusual capacity for sympathy and for a sense
of the tragic. . . .

She grew up in a middle-sized Georgia town, carefully

reared in a strict and religious home. She often recounted the incidents of her childhood with laughing tenderness for her parents to whom she acknowledged a debt of which she never lost sight. Particularly was she conscious of the claims of her parents and of the young members of her family. She was never too busy to send fresh reading matter to her mother, nor too occupied to help with family plans. Her perspective, her rare sense of humor and her ability to be objective grew with the years. She did not fail people who needed her or trusted her. She never missed the psychological moment for action. She did not forsake her deepest purposes.

Miss Derricotte came to the National Student Council of the Y.W.C.A. at a time of great importance for the movement and for the country so far as inter-racial development was concerned. To her must be given credit for pioneering in the methods of work and organizational structure which made the council an interracial fellowship in the year 1922 and since. Up to 1922, there had been Negro secretaries on the staff of the student division of the Y.W.C.A.; but interracial divisions of council made up of faculty and students, fraternal delegates at summer conferences, student forums, interracial weekend conferences, etc., became an integral part of the structure and program of the student council during her leadership. The foresight and conviction of Miss Derricotte and her colleagues both colored and white made possible the beginnings of an interracial procedure which, although far from ideal, has contained essential and rudimentary elements for an interracial movement. . . .

How did this come to be? How did a young colored woman, born and reared in the middle-sized Georgia town, of fine and simple home background, where rigid religious traditions were tempered by kind and sensible parents, emerge at thirty into positions of trusted leadership? How does a freshman at Talladega College, shy, fun-loving, sit twelve years later on the Board of Trustees of that same college and return to it as visiting student pastor to help the students of her alma mater with their religious perplexities?

The purpose of these paragraphs is not analytical. Juliette

Derricotte became within her short life a trusted member of the staff of the National Student Council of the Y.W.C.A. which she served for eleven years; a regular advisor to the Women's Home Missions Council of the church; a member of the General Committee of the World's Student Christian Federation which she served from 1924–31; a recent non-resident member of the National Board of the Young Woman's Christian Association; a member of the Interracial Commission and one of the faculty at Fisk University. . . .

She loved her race passionately. Her life was dedicated to justice and mutuality for America's tenth citizen. She resigned from the National Student Council of the Y.W.C.A. because she felt that she had a particular call to participate in Negro education in the South. At no time in her life did she mitigate her sense of loyalty, responsibility and joy as an American Negro. Never did she compromise with her un-deviating devotion to a just future for her own people. At the same time, Miss Derricotte saw people as people. Her white friends who were innumerable were not members of another race, but persons. . . . In Europe, in Asia, wherever she went, she saw the full implications of the events about her. Equipped with a master's degree from Columbia University, and with that more potent intellectual tool, a keen mind, she brought to bear upon her work with Negro and white students, among whom she was very popular, logic, accurate data and fine feeling.

Winifred Wygal in *The Crisis*, Vol. 39,
No. 3 (March 1932), pp. 84–85.

HER UNFINISHED WORK

Here is Juliette Derricotte's own story of how she stopped being a colored girl and became an interpreter. "Five years ago something happened that made my whole life over, and I've been a different person ever since. A Western woman told us how bitter the feeling was between white and colored students in some of the Mid-West universities. From the

South there had been a large influx of white students and also of Negroes; and they simply did not know how to get on together when they met in Kansas or Missouri or Oklahoma. It just happened that I was the person who was free to go out to see what ought to be done. A white secretary went with me. I didn't know her, though we had been working in the same building, but we liked each other as soon as we got acquainted on this trip.

"When we got to our university, the colored girls wouldn't talk to me when Miss ——— was around. And the white girls wouldn't talk to her when I was there. So we talked with them in separate corners till we understood. Then we chose ten white girls and ten Negro girls and brought them together to work this thing out.

"'How can you call yourselves Christians?' we asked. 'How can you say that you want to bring freedom to all people when there are on your own campus people that you won't speak to?' We made them face it, first the white Y.W.C.A. girls, and then both together. They did. After we left they wanted to go on, and we gave them a simple outline of some questions that neither group had thought about before. For example, How did the Negro get here in the United States? What has slavery done for him, and for the white people? (That was hard for both of them.) What contribution has the Negro made in art, in music, in religion? Is it possible that he has something that the white man needs for complete living?

"Our group worked hard on these questions for a year. All the time I kept answering their letters about it. The next year, they had learned so much together that they went out to teach their university. Programs of Negro music or Negro poetry were put on. Bars were taken down. Colored girls were sought out and invited to the Y.W.C.A., welcomed when they got there, and urged to work on committees. The next year, the whole Y.W.C.A. dropped the interracial issue and together, white and colored, went out to clean up on that campus the things that were not Christian! So I learned that the most worth while thing to do is to be yourself and do your own work, not to attack just the interracial question."

In discovering what these students could do together Juliette Derricotte had begun to discover herself. From this time on she came to work easily with students of any race. Part of her job was still the planning of student conferences in colored colleges. One friend pictures such a conference in a tiny college in Mississippi, seven miles from a half-dead town. Here the men and women, nearly all of them working their way, would invite thirty or forty colored students from other colleges south to New Orleans and north to Tennessee. Everyone was poor but could manage fifty cents for registration and the dollar guest fee for a week-end conference. To these isolated students, most of them off the farm, Miss Derricotte would bring the best ideas she had to offer out of her experience and wide contacts, and the best college leadership that she could command. She herself would come, radiant and sure, fairly breathing confidence into some of those shy, awkward students whose morale had collapsed because they felt themselves already beaten in a struggle too great for them. They would remember her all their lives as one who had put new heart into them.

> Mary Jenness, *Twelve Negro Americans* (New York:
> Friendship Press, 1936), pp. 166–169.

JULIETTE DERRICOTTE:

Off to my left sat a Britisher and an Indian whom I happened to know had talked hard and fast in a discussion on England in India. Only a few weeks before, upon entering a church, the young Indian woman had been told that all the whites must be seated before they could give her a seat. In another direction sat my little Korean tent-mate who had kept me awake till two in the morning telling me that I knew nothing of prejudice, segregation and discrimination, that to know the real meaning of those words I'd have to be a Korean under a Japanese government; and not far from her was my newly made friend from Japan who had asked me a few questions about our immigration laws. And the white South Africans had just told of the real spiritual experience which was theirs when they could shake hands with Max Yergan, a Negro. My eyes roamed to those of us in that big meeting tent from the United States, those of us who were white, those of us who were brown, and I remembered that we did not represent the masses in the United States.

Something jerked me back and I thought, "Under the double roof of this tent your committee is prophetic in the sense that this is what can happen to all the world. With all the differences and difficulties, with all the entanglements of international attitudes and policies, with all the bitterness and prejudice and hatred that are true between any two or more of these countries, you are here friends working, thinking, playing, living together in the finest sort of fellowship, fulfilling the dream of the World's Student Christian Federation 'That All May be One.'"

Written by Juliette Derricotte after attending a World's Student Christian Federation meeting in India and read at the Memorial Service held for her on November 12, 1931, 600 Lexington Avenue, New York City.

DALTON, GEORGIA

Juliette Derricotte was fatally injured in Dalton, Georgia. Dalton is the county seat of Whitfield County and is forty miles southeast of Chattanooga. Dalton is a shipping point for cotton, cattle, grain and fruit, and has cotton mills . . . canning factories, flour mills, foundries and machine shops. . . . It is, of course, a religious town. There are 5 white churches and 6 Negro. It figured for a time as a health resort; it is the seat of Dalton Female College. There are public schools and weekly newspapers and a national bank.

In particular, for our purpose, there is the Hamilton Memorial Hospital, with a complete modern equipment, supported by public taxation.

Miss Derricotte, with three other passengers, was traveling

to her home in Athens, Ga., to settle certain business matters for her family. She had with her Nina Johnson, a senior at Fisk, Edward Davis, a student who lives in Athens, and Marian Price, another student who lives in Atlanta. They were traveling by automobile in order to avoid the "Jim-crow" cars of the South, and the difficulty in getting meals and other transportation.

"We left Chattanooga about three o'clock. Miss Derricotte was driving. I was in the front seat with her; Miss Johnson and Miss Price were in the rumble seat. We had been driving along at a fair rate of speed and were about a mile and a half out of Dalton. I was talking to Miss Johnson and Miss Price when I suddenly turned around and noticed another car very close to us. A second later the two cars hit each other. Miss Derricotte snatched the steering wheel to the right, turned it loose and called to me. When I reached for the steering wheel the car was beginning to turn and by the time I got hold of it the car was turning over. I then turned the wheel loose and threw up my hands in an effort to save myself. The last I remember then was hearing the crash.

"The next thing I remember, I was lying in a field. Miss Derricotte was lying near me groaning."

There immediately began a series of investigations. Mrs. Ethel B. Gilbert, an official at Fisk University, heard of the accident, telephoned and rushed to Chattanooga. Thence, she wrote various private letters. Other officials came from Fisk University, including Dr. Elmer S. Imes and Warner Lawson. The President of Fisk University later began an investigation; the Secretary of the N. A. A. C. P. stopped in Chattanooga and inquired into the facts; finally, the Commission on Interracial Co-operation of Atlanta made an investigation "at the request of Fisk University and other organizations interested in ascertaining the facts of the situation." After that, the participants in the accident were requested to make no further statements and the Y.W.C.A., so far as we know, did nothing. . . .

W. E. B. DuBois in *The Crisis*, Vol. 39 No. 3 (March 1932), p. 85.

REPORT OF THE COMMISSION ON INTERRACIAL COOPERATION
REGARDING THE AUTOMOBILE ACCIDENT IN DALTON, GEORGIA,
NOVEMBER 6, 1931

. . . Mr. and Mrs. Halton, unhurt, climbed out through the broken windshield of their car and went immediately to Miss Derricotte's car. Miss Derricotte and Mr. Davis had been thrown into the field several feet in front of their car. . . . Miss Johnson was unconscious, Miss Derricotte intermittently conscious, while Miss Price and Mr. Davis, though shocked and injured, were in possession of their faculties. Immediately after the crash, Miss Price went to Miss Johnson, and Mr. Davis tried to help Miss Derricotte to a standing position. Mr. Halton stated that he hurried someone off to call for an ambulance. (No ambulance came.)

Mrs. Gordon Mann, white, who lives near-by . . . saw the collision and ran immediately for her car, and went directly to the scene of the accident where she was joined by her husband, who was near-by at a home he is having built, and upon hearing the crash had hurried to the scene. Miss Johnson, who seemed to be the worst injured of the four, was put into the Mann car. . . . Mr. and Mrs. Mann report that they were away from the scene of the accident within five minutes after the crash, and that a couple of minutes later were in Dr. Steed's office on King Street in Dalton. . . . Mr. Mann is of small built; severely injured Miss Johnson was rather stout. In the rush against time, Mr. Penn, white, of the Carter Funeral Offices, carried Miss Johnson on his shoulder up the narrow stairs and placed her on Dr. Steed's operating table.

Upon placing Miss Johnson in Dr. Steed's care, the Manns started back toward the scene of the accident to get others of the injured persons. Before they had gotten out of town they met a car bringing in Miss Derricotte, and on the edge of town they met Miss Price and Mr. Davis in another car.

Mr. and Mrs. Mann stated that all of the injured persons were in town within about twenty minutes after the accident. . . .

Miss Johnson was taken to the office of Dr. J. H. Steed, a physician with a record of many years' service in Dalton. Miss Derricotte was taken to the office of Dr. O. E. Shellhorse. Miss Price and Mr. Davis were taken to the office of Dr. G. L. Broaddrick. These three doctors, all white, have offices within two blocks of each other on King Street. . . .

Mrs. Mann, who brought Miss Johnson in, stated that she inquired where Negroes could get treatment, and was told to go to a doctor's office, which she did.

Dr. Steed states that Miss Johnson was unconscious when brought to his office and never regained consciousness, and it was evident from the first that she was seriously wounded. Observing her condition, he called to assist him Dr. Woods, of six years' interne experience in a New York hospital and one of the most competent surgeons of the town. Dr. Steed and Dr. Woods worked with Miss Johnson for over an hour. They were afraid from the outset that she was dying. . . . Either or both Dr. Steed or Dr. Woods was in constant attendance upon Miss Johnson in Dr. Steed's office for approximately an hour and a half.

Miss Derricotte was taken to Dr. O. E. Shellhorse's office and placed on his operating table. She was in a semi-conscious condition, being in possession of her faculties a part of the time, and indicating that she had severe pains in her chest and hip. Dr. Shellhorse states that he examined her thoroughly, saw the seriousness of her condition and called in for consultation Dr. Ault, who has an office next door, and that they agreed she should be kept warm and perfectly quiet and given stimulants and other treatment to enable her to recuperate from her condition of profound shock. She was in his office under his care for something like an hour and a half. . . .

When Miss Derricotte had been treated by Dr. Shellhorse, he called the local Negro undertaker, Mr. Johnson, and asked him to build a fire and prepare a room for Miss Derricotte in the home of Mrs. Alice Wilson, colored, 3 Emory Street, where the white physicians placed their colored patients who require local hospital treatment.

Mrs. Wilson's home is a five or six-room one-story cottage, and is in somewhat better condition than the typical Negro home of this size. The physicians of Dalton have been taking patients to Mrs. Wilson's home for a number of years, and major operations have been successfully performed there. Except in emergency cases, however, most of the Dalton Negroes who can afford it are treated in Chattanooga and Atlanta hospitals. Doctors Shellhorse, Steed, and Broaddrick stated that a colored ward was needed at the Hamilton Memorial Hospital, and that some work has been done to that end during the past two years. . . .

Upon arrival at the Wilson home, Miss Derricotte and Miss Johnson were placed on a bed and a couch respectively, and Doctors Wood and Shellhorse came to see them shortly. In the meantime the Trimble car and ambulance from Chattanooga had reported at Dr. Broaddrick's office for Miss Price and Mr. Davis and had taken them, too, to the Wilson home.

Miss Price hâd a semi-confidential conference with Dr. Shellhorse with regard to the condition of Miss Derricotte. Dr. Shellhorse told her that Miss Derricotte was suffering from a severe shock and should be kept warm and allowed to remain quiet in order to give her an opportunity to recuperate. Miss Price asked Dr. Shellhorse, according to Dr. Shellhorse's statements, if Miss Derricotte could be moved to Chattanooga. He advised against this in the presence of one of the men from Chattanooga who had come with the Trimble car and ambulance, and there was an understanding that Miss Derricotte would remain at the Wilson home. . . . Dr. Shellhorse, upon leaving the Wilson home, gave instructions to Mrs. Wilson and asked her to call him if Miss Derricotte got worse, saying he would come back early next morning if he had no call in the meantime. When he went to the Wilson home early next morning he was surprised to find that Miss Derricotte had been taken to Chattanooga. . . .

Just here it is pertinent to state . . . that the Trimbles of Chattanooga were personal friends of Miss Derricotte, and that she and the three Fisk students had lunched there shortly before the accident; that Miss Price called the Trimbles and asked for an ambulance; and that Mr. Trimble asked Dr. Patton to accompany him to Dalton. Upon their arrival Miss Price naturally assumed that they would take charge of the situation. It is understood that Miss Derricotte, although at first evincing a preference to remain at Mrs. Wilson's home, later expressed a willingness to follow whatever procedure was advised by Mr. Trimble, Dr. Patton, Dr. Woods, and others present. Accordingly, Miss Derricotte was placed in the ambulance and taken to Chattanooga; Miss Price and Mr. Davis shortly afterward left for Chattanooga in the Trimble car; and Dr. Patton remained at the Wilson home with Miss Johnson, who had been placed in his charge by Dr. Steed and Dr. Woods. Without regaining consciousness, Miss Johnson was placed in the ambulance upon its return and died before reaching Chattanooga. Miss Derricotte, who was placed at the Walden Hospital in Chattanooga, died about six o'clock the following evening (Saturday, November 7).

. . . Miss Duke, resident nurse in charge of the Hamilton Memorial Hospital, stated that no one of the Negroes in the accident had been brought there. When asked whether Miss Derricotte and Miss Johnson would have been treated had they been brought to the Hamilton Memorial Hospital, Miss Duke hesitated and said: "I do not see that we could have done otherwise." She stated that there are no precedents for the answer to this question in that no Negro had even been brought to the hospital for care, stating that it was generally understood that Negroes were not treated there, and that Negro patients were cared for either in the offices of doctors or in the home of a Negro woman, Mrs. Alice Wilson, who had beds available for the care of Negro patients. . . .

It is not amiss to point out that of Whitfield County's 20,808 inhabitants in 1930, only 1,371, or 6.6 per cent, were Negroes, and that there is no Negro physician in this north Georgia county.

THE COST OF RACE PREJUDICE

Significant factors in the Dalton case are:

1. That no one even thought of asking admission of the patients to the well equipped hospital in Dalton.
2. That the system is so rigid that it could not be broken even in an emergency as serious as this one.
3. That the doctors were kind according to the social pattern of Dalton, a pattern which takes for granted that Negroes cannot be accorded the same treatment as is given to white people.
4. That public opinion sanctions social institutions built on principles of unreasoning and heartless race discriminations.
5. That the final responsibility for this inhuman treatment which caused Miss Derricotte undue suffering and possibly caused her death, must rest upon every one of us, North and South, whether we belong to that class which is unaware that such conditions exist or are indifferent to them, or to that class which will be terribly crushed by this specific tragedy but have no clearcut program of action that can cope with the fundamental problem.

Sophia Smith Collection, YWCA Papers,
Smith College, Northhampton, Massachusetts.

A LETTER TO THE EDITOR OF THE NEW YORK HERALD TRIBUNE

At this season of the year it may not be amiss to make a plea for simple humanity. We make it on the basis of a text furnished by the death, in Chattanooga, of a distinguished colored woman, Miss Juliette Derricotte, dean of women at Fisk University, Nashville, Tennessee, a member of the national board of the Y.W.C.A.; a leader in the field of race relations and community work, and one revered alike by white and colored people.

Miss Derricotte, with three other colored persons, students at Fisk University, was the victim of an automobile crash last November 9, in Dalton, Ga. One of her companions was fatally injured, so that she died a few hours later. Miss Derricotte was injured in such a way that immediate and skilled hospital attention was imperative.

The white doctors of Dalton with the greatest kindness received these colored people and treated them in their offices. Yet, although there is a well-equipped hospital in Dalton, no one even thought of procuring their admission there for the treatment so urgently needed. Miss Derricotte, dangerously injured, with probable fractures of her pelvic bones, had to be transported for a distance of fifty miles by automobile to Chattanooga, Tenn., and was even then placed in a colored institution which lacked X-ray apparatus.

This valuable life was snuffed out on the following morning, after she had endured agonies of pain. Perhaps Miss Derricotte might not have lived even had quick and adequate hospitalization been forthcoming. But the fact is that the hospital in Dalton "does not receive" colored patients. And the long automobile ride, with the patient in extreme pain and shock, undoubtedly hastened her death.

The doctors did what they could. It is not to them that this appeal goes. It is to the hearts of humane people throughout the South, in behalf of the colored men and women who are denied elementary care in dangerous illness or emergency. The National Association for the Advancement of Colored People is appealing to humane and human sentiments against the rigors of a segregation policy which in cases like the one instanced inflict upon colored people a cruelty which most people would not wish to be guilty of inflicting upon a dumb animal.

Walter White
Secretary, National Association for the
Advancement of Colored People

New York Herald Tribune, December 31, 1931.

THERE IS NO PREJUDICE
IN ARKANSAS

❦ *The Federal Writers' Project of the WPA undertook the compilation of state guidebooks. Under the heading
"Negro Studies," black writers were assigned the compilation
of data concerning racial practices in the various states. As
part of such an assignment, questionnaires were sent to
hundreds of Arkansas communities to survey accommodations available to Negro tourists. The following are two
representative replies.*

Cotter, Arkansas, July 3rd, 1936.

Dear Mrs. Haag:

Replying to letter next attached wish to advise that there is
no prejudice or discrimination against the negro tourists in
this section of the State. All garages and service stations give
to the negro the same courteous treatment as to whites.

Hotels and tourist camps up to this time have made no
provision as to sleeping quarters for negroes, but cafes and
hotels do furnish meals. Negro drivers for white tourists are
furnished with sleeping quarters. I do not know of any negro
tourists having applied for and been refused sleeping quarters,
but they might have difficulty in securing same. However,
they would be politely refused and not mistreated.

Baxter County does not have a negro within its bounds,
and the negro tourist trade is not sufficient to justify preparation for same, or the furnishing of accommodations. Vacant
lots and city park are available to the Negro, for camping
purposes, without cost.

The "Gypsy" is about the only one against whom a prejudice exists in Baxter County.

Yours very truly,
(Signed) H. J. Denton,
Sec'y. Chamber of Commerce.

Newport, Arkansas, July 6, 1936

Dear Madam:—

In regard to your letter of June 26th, 1936, please pardon the delay. Will try and give you the information you request. I do not think that there is any section in the state of Arkansas that the negro would be discriminated against as long as he knows his place and most of our southern negroes do. However, the negroes from the north and east are not familiar with the conditions and laws in the south especially, in Arkansas, and would possibly have a right to feel that they are being discriminated against. For reason they are not allowed certain privileges of the white people. Namely, eating at the same table, rooms at the same hotel, riding in the same sections on trains. Divisions are made of the passengers in buses, trolley cars and other conveyances. These are laws our state enforces very rigidly.

However, I assure you that in the negro tourist traffic through Arkansas he must resort to negro tourist camps or colored quarters. I am sure you will find the same conditions in all southern states.

There is no feeling against the colored race as far as his being a tourist is concerned. He has the same road protection that any other person would have.

Hoping this is the information you desire.

> Yours very truly,
> (Signed) Marion Dickens,
> President, Chamber of Commerce

Both items: Works Projects Administration Manuscript, Federal Writers' Project, Negro Studies, National Archives.

DISCRIMINATION ON WPA

BLACK WOMEN APPEAL TO FDR

❦ *Racist practices were so thoroughly ingrained in every aspect of American life that it was little wonder that*

New Deal relief and welfare expenditures were allocated on a discriminatory basis in many states. Administrators, investigators and welfare workers on a state and local level were usually white and followed "local practice," which was inevitably racist. Black people, whose needs were usually greater, whose families were larger and whose chances for employment were worse than those of whites, were the last to receive relief, the first to be cut off, the last to be hired for work relief. The following selections are personal appeals by desperate women who had tried all the regular channels for help and had been turned down. Their faith in the all-powerful benevolence of the President is as pathetic as is their need. Yet these letters also reveal a strong self-assertion, an insistence on being given their rights, an attitude of exasperation with unfulfilled promises.

> Millen, Ga.
> R 1, Box 31
> February 4, 1935

United States Department of Agriculture
Extension Service
Office of Cooperative Work
Washington, D.C.
Dear Friends:

I am a widow woman with seven head of children, and I live on my place with a plenty of help. All are good workers and I wants to farm. I has no mule, no wagon, no feed, no grocery, and these women and men that is controlling the Civil Work for the Goverment won't help me.

Because I am a woman. I wants to ask you all to please help me to make a crop this year and let me hear from you on return mail. Yours for business.

> Mosel Brinson
> Please answer me on return mail.

P.S. These poor white people that lives around me wants the colored people to work for them for nothing and if you won't do that they goes down to the relief office and tell the women,—"don't help the colored people, we will give them plenty of work to do, but they won't work." That is the reason the poor colored people can't get any help, these poor white people going down to the relief office telling lies. Now I am living on my own land and I am got a plenty of children to make a farm, and all I wants is a chance, and I am not in debt. I wants a mule and feed, and gear and plows, and a little groceries and guano. Please help a poor widow woman one year. Please help me to get a start, I will try to keep it.

Fort Valley, Ga.
March 11, 1935

Mr. Harry Hopkins
Dear Sir:

I am asking you to please help me and my poor husband, we are old and well on in years. I am 60 years old and my husband is 85 or older, *he was a plough boy in slavery time.* He been sick here almost four years down helpless as a baby and these relief people will not give me any help. I wrote Mrs. Gay B. Shepperson of Atlanta and she wrote these people here and sent them the letter I wrote her and they disliked it very much and talked very hard to me because I am in my own house. It just a 3 room house me and my husband worked and paid for when we could work and every time we ask for help they tell me we have our own house and they can't help us, and they say they don't help old people nohow, they help young people who is able to work, but there are plenty of people who is much better off than I will ever be. I thought I would apply to you all for help. My husband is bare for clothes and also for food. I have only one child, she is grown and married but her husband is dead and she do all she can for me and my husband but she only make $3.00 per week cooking at a boarding house 3 meals a day but she cannot keep us all on that. My husband work for the city of Fort Valley 22 years and they give him a little money for a few weeks and stop that and I can't get him on the county or get help any way. When I go to them for help they talk to me like I was a dog. My husband have a stroke of paralysis was brought home three times from the streets where he worked. I have high blood pressure. Looking to hear from you at once,

Sarah Young

117 Ash St.
Greenwood, Miss.
Dec. 23, 1936

President Roosevelt
Dear Sir:

We are wondering what is going to become of this large number of widow women with and without children. These white women at the head of the PWA is still letting we colored women when we go to the office to be certified for work to go hunt washings. . . .

I was in the office a few days ago. A woman was there she had five children and a husband not able to work. They told her to go hunt washings. . . . The white people dont pay anything for their washing. She cant do enough washing to feed her family. I was reading an article in the paper enquiring why colored men did not show up on WPA projects in some places. You all are not down here. So you has to take these white people word. . . .

I know we have had men here in Greenwood to walk [to the relief office] several weeks then white women and men would tell them come back tomorrow come back Monday. Finally they would say what are you Nigers [sic] keep on coming up here for. We cant take on any more go hunt you some work. Then they will write you all our men and women cant be found. Good many of our men have told me they would eat grass like a cow and drink water before they would go back to any of the relief offices, let them white people dog them again. We have old people cant get any help. If the old people go they will say go to your children if the children go to the relief they will tell them we cant take on any more. Like my father is old. Last week he came to me for help. He is on relief but cant get nothing. He lives in Carroll County.

. . . I cant get work. I could not help him and he cant help me. I was at the coat house last week said to be colored people day to get cloth. They had about a dozen gowins at the coat house in a little draw they give the real old men and women one gown. I saw that with my own eyes if you all keep on sending cloth here these white people will have anough to last the next century. They are making themselves whole.

Now about a month ago they employed two white women, one to sit at the coat house then employed another under her to come visit the colored people. The money you all pay out for poor white women visiting the colored people you could throw it in the river or in the fire for what it do us. . . .

I visit my sick people because I feel like it is my duty. The white woman got mad with me because she thought I was taking note of how they was being treated. Come to my house to raise a fuss. Told me I better not take any note of the sick people she visit, if I did, what she was going to do.

That why many of our people are gone to untimely graves. Poor white people is nothing but Negro haters. If you all would please let the colored people look after the colored people old sick and the white look after white that will keep down confusion and save many of our lives if we cant have colored home visators we dont want any. We have been slaves for them all our lives and dont need them standing around over us telling us how to sweep the floor, writeing down how many people visit the sick room and what they brought.

Respectifully
/s/ Pinkie Pilcher

New Orleans, Louisiana
April 18, 1941

Mrs. F.D.Roosevelt
Dear Mrs.

I'm a Negro girl of 25 yrs. I'm sick. I been sick 4 months. I'm in need of food and closes. I don't have any relative at all so help me. I hop I'm not asking so much of you, but I hop you would help me, Mrs. Roosevelt. I'm righting you this morning I dont have food for the day. I gose to the hospital. The dr say all my sickes is from not haveing food.

I was working on the NYA [National Youth Administration]. . . . I work there 10 month. They lad me off because I was sick and diden give me nothing to live off after tune me off. . . . They was so hard every time I get a job I get sick but I try to keep them anyway but after all I lose them. Mrs. Roosevelt I'm rooming with a old lade she dont have a husban. She give me food when she have it but she dont have it all the time. I own her 5 month rent right now. She have to pay rent her silf. She was asking me when I was going to pay her. If I dont be able to pay her in 2 week she going to put me out. I dont have nobody to go to for help and no where to go what I going to do if she put me out.

Could you do something for me help me to fine something. Tell me what to do if you could give me some to do in the hospitial or in a hotel or any where I will do it. I will take a day job are a night job anything. Please help me. You can see I'm in need of help Mrs. Roosevelt. Will you please help me I can live much longer without food.—have lot of micine to take I do take it but it wont do me any good without food and if the lady put me out I just no I will die because I dont have no where to go. . . . Mrs. Roosevelt if you can get me a job in the post office anywhere it will do. Please wright at once as soon as you can. I be looking for a letter from you.

Please do what every you can for me. I'm in need of help bad. . . . Thank you. Your kindes will never be foregoting. Yours sincerely.

Mabel Gilvert
1225 Poydres St. New Orleans, La.

Please do some thing for me at once any thing. Pleasanywhere pleas.

Mt. Pleasant, Texas
4/25–41

Mr. Theodore Roosevelt[!]
Dear Sir

I am writing you and askin you is it fair or not for the white woman to do all this WPA work in titus county. Mr. Roosevelt I am a poor Negro widow woman and have 3 children to take care of and I dont have nothing to go upon. They told me that they diden no if they wood work enymore Negro woman on this WPA work. That is why I am writing you about this.

I wood like to no please sir Mr. Roosevelt is that right or not. Mr. Roosevelt they is your and we poor Negro is yours to. Cause when you says come or go we have to do what you says do. So please turn us a helping hand by put us Negro woman to work on these WPA work project. I am in needst condition. Please give this consideration as soon as possible.

Answer by help your a Negro woman here in Mt. Pleasant, Texas. I am afraid to put my name on this letter.

Woodland Park Biteley, Mich.
April 23, 1941

President Roosevelt
Dear Sir:

We are the colored women Democrat club. We are sending in a plea for help for our people of our community. Our men are out of work and have ben for sometimes.

We can't get any Welfare help unless we sign our homes over to the welfare. We do not want to be beggers. Our men would work if they could only get work to do. We have helped in every way we could to help make your third election a success. We had some hard things to undergo during the time we were campaigning but the victory was well worth the pain. Our club were and are still for you and all of your supporters, one hundred percent. . . .

We here in this community are having a tuff way to go just now. There were a lay off just after Jan. and our men were laid off. Any time anything happens like this our group are always the first ones to get the first blow. We have tried to get work. We are sending our plea to you feeling sure you will and can help us in our needy condition. We aren't getting a fair deal. Some of our boys are being drafted for service for our country and here we are in a free land are not aloud to work and make a living for their wives and childrens. You are the Father of this country and a Father are suppose to look out for all of his children so we are depending on you.

From the Colored Womens Democrat Club. We are hoping to hear from you soon.

Yours truly
Lutensia Dillard

All items: WPA Box, Howard University, Washington, D.C.

FREEDOM—NOW!

❦ As the previous selections in this chapter have illustrated, black resistance to "the monster prejudice" goes back deep into the historic past and forms a constant theme in Black history. Of necessity, throughout much of the American past, this resistance was individual and sporadic, localized and in response to white provocation. In the 1950's, this pattern changed in such a way as to put the race issue into the center of public consciousness and confront white Americans with what many regarded, erroneously, as a black "revolution." It was far from being a revolution, since the aims of the civil rights movement were simply the winning of full equality for Blacks in the existing society and within the existing system of laws, and the means used by the movement were nonviolent.

Historically, the civil rights movement was rather the last phase of that legal and social reform movement begun with the passage of the Civil War amendments to the Constitution—a massive effort to complete the unfinished task of the Reconstruction which had been abandoned and nullified by Southern white resistance and Northern indifference. This attempt at a second Reconstruction was characterized by massive and well-organized black resistance to discrimination on a national scale, the forming of a coalition with whites and the support of the federal courts and government and the deliberate challenge by Blacks of every aspect of the race oppression system. The failure of the civil rights movement to achieve its objectives laid the basis on which more radical and revolutionary movements have sprung up in the 1960's and 1970's.

THE CAUSES OF THE HARLEM RIOT

NANNIE H. BURROUGHS

❧ The tradition of local boycott movements of the past (see pp. 196–205) was revived in the 1930's in the cities of the North. The great migration of the post–World War I period had brought hundreds of thousands of impoverished rural migrants into the already overcrowded black slums of Detroit, Cleveland, Chicago and New York. White hostility and competition for scarce jobs led, in 1918 and 1919, to a wave of race riots, which were remarkable for their intensity and for the effectiveness with which Blacks fought openly and in great numbers against their attackers. For the next decade an uneasy peace prevailed. White political machines began to give token recognition to the fact that, in the cities of the North, a "new Negro" was emerging who would have to be reckoned with as a political force. Meanwhile, the ghetto community sought improvement for its chronic poverty and unemployment by various self-help schemes. One of these, the Colored Merchants' Association drive to establish Black-owned businesses on a cooperative basis in Harlem in order to provide jobs for Blacks, failed during the 1929 depression. It was followed by a nation-wide "Jobs for Negroes" movement, led in New York City by the Citizens' League for Fair Play.

An intensive campaign of picketing white-owned Harlem businesses sought to persuade these stores to hire black workers. Under the slogan "Don't buy where you can't work," intense educational and political work was carried on and a large-scale boycott movement developed. Eventually, the campaign resulted in a change of employment practices by some Harlem businesses and by public utilities, such as the telephone, electric and bus companies.

In March of 1935 the anger of Harlemites against white businessmen and landlords exploded over a relatively minor

*incident. In the selection below, Nannie Burroughs puts
the background and meaning of these events into sharp
focus.*

Harlem did not have a "race" riot. It had a "human" revolt.

Communistic propaganda, Red agitation and unemployment are not the causes. Nor did a colored boy, a nickel pen-knife and a screaming woman cause the uprising. Hush the voice that tells you so. . . .

This nation openly endorses, tolerates and legalizes the very abuses against which she originally waged a bloody revolution.

A colored boy, a nickel pen-knife and a screaming woman were no more the cause of the Harlem uprising in 1935, than was a shipload of tea in the Boston harbor, in 1773, the cause of the Revolutionary War. The tea party episode was only the manifestation. "A long train of abuses" created the cause.

Samuel Adams feared that colonists were being lulled into indifference to their rights. He was mistaken. The Boston tea party convinced him.

The causes of the Harlem riot are not far to seek. They lie buried beneath mountains of injustices done the colored man in every state and in every relationship, through years of "patient sufferance" on his part. In dealing with colored people, America makes "void the law through custom"— that's the deep-seated cause of the Harlem riot.

A few years ago there was a gigantic explosion of dynamite on the New Jersey side of New York Bay. It shattered thousands of windows in Manhattan and even broke dishes in Brooklyn, fifteen miles away. All the fire engines in the lower part of New York came out and raced helplessly up and down the streets looking for the cause of the damage. They found plenty of manifestation of the explosion, but did not discover the cause, for that was miles out of their reach.

The framers of the Declaration of Independence prophesied that uprisings would occur "in the course of human events," if people are denied those inalienable rights to which the "laws of nature and of nature's God entitle them."

Re-read their prophecy—their justification for such natural, human resentment after such patient sufferance. It is written in every American history. They declared that "when a long train of abuses and usurpations pursuing, invariably the same object, evinces a design to reduce them under absolute despotism, it is their right, it is their duty to throw off such government, and to provide new guards for their future security."

If that's Red, then the writers of the Declaration of Independence were very Red. They told Americans not to stand injustice after "patient sufferance."

The colored man has reached the endurance limit—the point where the Declaration of Independence says, it is time to revolt when the "invasion on the rights of the people seem most likely to effect their safety and happiness and obstruct the administration of justice." Yes, a long train of abuses caused the Harlem uprising. . . .

Day after day, year after year, decade after decade, black people have been robbed of their inalienable rights. They have been goaded, hounded, driven around, herded, held down, kicked around and roasted alive, by America's home-made Reds. In Harlem the cornered rats fought back. The worms turned over and turned around.

The majority of the colored people of Harlem came from mob-ruled sections, or are the victims of persecutions of various kinds. They came to Harlem seeking opportunity to enjoy life, liberty, labor and happiness. They are beginning to feel cramped and handicapped. Their hearts are hurt. They find themselves apparently pursued by the very evils from which they fled.

America's age-old attitude on the race question is the cause of the Harlem riot. That "long train of abuses" is a magazine of powder. An unknown boy was simply the match—a frightened woman's screams lighted it and threw it into the magazine of powder, and Harlem blew up.

Colored folks feel that Harlem is their last stand.

"Declaration of 1776 Is Cause of Harlem Riot,"
The Afro-American, April 13, 1935.

BREAKING RESTRICTIVE COVENANTS

❦ After World War II, increased black militancy was manifested in more frequent challenges of established segregation patterns. One of the most pervasive of these patterns, especially in the North, was housing segregation which confined Blacks to squalid, overcrowded slums by the simple expedient of denying them housing elsewhere. Banks and mortgage companies refused to give mortgages to black home purchasers except in ghetto areas. Federal housing policy was to ignore and tacitly support such practices. To enforce compliance in racist exclusion policies, neighbors banded together to sign restrictive covenants, i.e., agreements not to sell to persons of another race or creed. These covenants were treated as though they had the force of law. By such devices, housing segregation—and with it, de facto school segregation—was institutionalized.

Black veterans, returning from fighting for democracy abroad and seeking to take advantage of their low-cost federal mortgage rights under the G.I. Bill, came into inevitable conflict with restrictive covenants. An increasing number of challenges finally reached the Supreme Court, and, in 1948, enforcement of restrictive covenants was outlawed. It is an interesting commentary on United States society that one-third of the court had to disqualify itself from sitting on the case, presumably because the three justices themselves lived in covenanted areas.

Housing segregation was further challenged in privately

owned housing developments such as Stuyvesant Town apartments in New York City, Levittown housing developments in Pennsylvania and New York State and, later, in the lily-white suburbs surrounding Chicago, Cleveland and most major United States cities.

One of the most widely publicized cases in the fight against restrictive covenants was that of the Laws family of Los Angeles, California.

The recent decision of the United States Supreme court that restrictive covenants are unconstitutional, and cannot be enforced by the courts of the land, affects favorably one of the most famous, possibly the most famous case on restrictive covenants in America today.

It is the case of the Laws family. The family in the house on 92nd street. . . .

Henry and Anna Laws had bought a lot in 1933 at what is now 1235 East 92nd street, and nine years later they had built their little home there—a neat, comfortable . . . house, with green grass and flowers around it.

They lived there very happily for almost three years. Then suddenly out of a clear blue sky they were notified that the place was restricted. That a Negro family was not allowed to live there.

Two real estate men, G. Freers and a man by the name of Boyer, who did not live in that district, had nevertheless dug up an old restrictive covenant made on that property, and entered a suit to restrain the Laws family from living in their own home.

The Laws family fought back. But they were advised by their lawyer to vacate their home, in a letter dated as early as May 29, 1944, "Your occupancy of the premises at this time may be deemed contempt of court, if the plaintiffs in the case were to secure an order citing you for contempt."

It was then that Mrs. Charlotta A. Bass, editor and publisher of The California EAGLE, called for a meeting of citizens opposed to such legal highway robbery to meet in the office of the EAGLE, and devise means to fight the nefarious restrictive covenants.

The meeting was held. And true Americans, black and white, pledged themselves to continue to oppose putting Negro families out of their homes, simply because they are Negroes. At first the organization was known as the Home Owners Protective Association. Mrs. Bass was elected president, and it was decided to appoint a committee to go to Messrs. Freers and Boyer . . . [to] "appeal to their reason and fairness."

Might as well have appealed to the reason and sense of fair play of a hungry, man-eating tiger. . . .

In a letter dated June 19, 1944, the lawyer for the Laws family advised his clients that he had been notified that "unless your premises are vacated by the 20th of this month, he will commence proceedings to restrain your further occupancy of your property. . . . You may desire to dipose of your property, and if so, Mr. Boyer or Mr. Freers could be of assistance in finding you buyers."

What a letter to receive, telling you to get out of your own home, or else!

Well, the Laws family didn't take the advise of their lawyer. They decided to stay put. And the Home Protective Association, organized at first to fight restrictive covenants everywhere, concentrated now on this one case especially.

"We'll fight until hell freezes over," declared Mrs. Bass, "before we'll let you be put out of your own home."

The HPA fought. The case was taken to court. It was postponed again and again. Meetings were held in churches, in halls, wherever people could gather. . . .

The case was taken to the municipal court. It was postponed from one time to another. Finally, November 22, 1945, . . . in a crushing decision . . . by Judge Allen W. Ashburn, Department 14 Superior Court, Henry and Anna Laws, victims of a restrictive covenant clause, were ordered to vacate their home by Friday, November 30. . . .

The Laws family didn't comply with this order. They were cited for contempt of court, and ordered to jail.

This aroused the entire community. A committee of prominent members of all races waited upon Judge Ashburn, asking him to reverse his decision. He refused bluntly. "I would not even if I could," he said.

So Mr. and Mrs. Henry Laws and their daughter, Mrs. Pauletta Fears, were dragged off to jail. Two sons of Mr. and Mrs. Laws and Mrs. Fears' husband, Antoine Fears, who had been fighting in the Pacific area, were even then on their way home.

They came home to find their family in jail. For daring to live in their own home.

But the aroused community did not rest with a mere appeal to Judge Asburn. They went to other courts and other judges, and finally the Laws were released by a writ from the State Supreme court.

The case was not settled, however. And ever since that time the Laws family had been living in their home on East 92nd street with a cloud hanging over their heads. The case was taken through the municipal courts, the county courts, and finally to the State Supreme Court. It was resting there for nearly two years. And now at long last it has finally been decided, as have the cases of thousands of other families threatened with eviction because their skins are not lily white.

The Supreme Court of the United States of America has declared restrictive covenants are unconstitutional, that they cannot be enforced by any court in America.

And so the Laws family and every other family in the United States may now live in peace wherever they may choose to buy or build.

It was a long fight. But it was worth it.

"Famed Laws Case Reviewed from Eagle Files,"
California Eagle, May 20, 1948.

THE ORDEAL OF THE CHILDREN

DAISY BATES

❦The long struggle for the lowering of racial bars in
education reached a new level when the NAACP mounted
a concerted challenge of school segregation in a series of cases
which reached the Supreme Court under the designation
Brown vs. Board of Education of Topeka, Kansas. In May
1954, the Court ruled in a unanimous decision that segregated
schools were inherently unequal, deprived black children of
equal protection of the laws and had a detrimental effect
upon them. Segregated schools were declared unconstitutional under the Fourteenth Amendment, and in 1955, the
states were ordered by the Court to abolish school segregation
"with all deliberate speed."

While a few large Southern cities quietly complied, massive
white resistance to the Supreme Court decision was
mobilized under the leadership of state governments, utilizing
every legal device and a seemingly endless variety of extra-
legal procedures to thwart the Court's ruling and intent.
Rioting and violence occurred in Clinton, Tennessee, in
1956 and 1958, at the University of Alabama in 1956 over the
admission of Autherine Lucy and later in a number of other
cities.

The events at Little Rock, Arkansas, which the following
document describes, marked a new turn in racial confrontations. School authorities in the city had decided peacefully
to comply and had selected nine black student volunteers
to integrate Central High School. Governor Orville Faubus,
in a delicate act of defiance of the federal government, called
out the National Guard to bar the students' entrance,
thereby precipitating a crisis in federal-state relations of a
kind unknown since 1877. President Eisenhower met the
challenge by using federal troops to insure the safety of the
black students as they entered the high school. Although

the students were daily harassed and threatened, the segregationist mobs failed in their purpose owing to the fact that, for the first time since Reconstruction, the federal government was throwing the weight of its power and authority behind enforcement of school desegregation.

After Little Rock, segregationist tactics changed from open defiance to the covert encouragement of mobs, harassment and every conceivable stalling device. In 1959, Governor Faubus closed all Little Rock high schools rather than accept desegregation. Similarly, Prince Edward County in Virginia closed all its schools in the same year to avoid integrating them. In 1962, serious rioting erupted at the University of Mississippi over the admission of James Meredith, leading again to the intervention of federal troops. Violence marked school desegregation in a large number of Southern and Northern cities. While the official resistance of Southern state governments relaxed somewhat after 1959, the progress of desegregation was disappointingly slow. In many of the cities of the South, the Northern pattern of de facto segregation (based on gerrymandered districts and segregated housing) replaced the de jure (legally sanctioned) segregation patterns of the past. Today, in the South, 38.1 per cent of all black children attend desegregated schools.* In the North, school integration has failed dramatically, with more black children attending segregated schools now than in 1954.

---

* The Health, Education and Welfare Department preliminary (estimated) figures for the extent of desegregation in 1970 show that 38.1 per cent of all black children in the South are enrolled in predominantly white schools, with another 20.4 per cent enrolled in schools which are 50–79.9 per cent black. These figures have to be seen in light of the fact that, according to latest estimates, one half million white Southern children attend segregated private schools. Much of Southern desegregation has been achieved by closing down black schools, dismissing or downgrading black teachers and busing black children long distances to white schools where they are then placed in virtually segregated classrooms as the result of "tracking."

Figures from HEW News (January 14, 1971) as cited in Paul M. Gaston, "The Region in Perspective," The South and Her Children: School Desegregation 1970–1971 (Atlanta, Georgia: Southern Regional Council, 1971), p. 16.

In her autobiography, Daisy Bates chronicles the crisis at Little Rock, in which she played a decisive role. As president of the Arkansas NAACP, she initiated the integration campaign, guided and supported the students in their long ordeal and herself braved bombings, threats and the loss of her own and her husband's life work, the weekly State Press.

On September 4, 1957, Central High School was surrounded by National Guard troops as fifteen-year-old Elizabeth Eckford attempted to enter alone. She was turned away by the guardsmen's bayonets and suddenly faced a white mob. There were shouts: "Get her! Drag her over to this tree! Lynch her!" With the help of two white people, Elizabeth escaped. The hideous incident, flashed by television and news media around the world, deeply shocked public opinion. The scene is movingly described by Daisy Bates in her book and has been frequently reprinted. Elizabeth's bravery was even more evident in her continued attendance at Central High than it was in the dignity and resolve with which she faced the mob that day. The following selections describe the harrowing ordeal of several of the other girl students during that year when they attended high school under the protection of federal troops. Their quiet courage inspired hundreds of youths to become civil rights activists.

MINNIJEAN BROWN

Minnijean Brown, sixteen years old and in the eleventh grade, was tall, attractive, and outgoing. Her manner was friendly and good-natured. She sang well, was good at sports, and liked dancing. She was the oldest of four children and lived with her parents, Mr. and Mrs. W. B. Brown. Minnijean's feelings were quickly mirrored in her face. At school she was subjected to no greater pressure than were the other Negro pupils. However, the incidents in which she was involved were certainly more dramatic, if not spectacular.

The first of these incidents took place on October 2, 1957. Minnijean and Melba Pattillo were roughed up by several unidentified boys and girls in the corridors as they left their second class for the day. One girl deliberately ran into Minnijean, and a group of boys formed a line to block her entrance to her classroom. Then followed an incredible catalogue of violence:

Minnijean was kicked by a boy as she was going to her seat at "pep" assembly, prior to a football game.

She was threatened by a pupil who said, "I will chase you down the hall and kick all your teeth out the next time you do what you did yesterday afternoon." The boy alleged that she had made insulting gestures at him. Minnijean insisted she did not remember ever seeing him before. The boy was taken to the principal's office and reprimanded.

By the middle of December Minnijean had had enough. After repeated provocation by white pupils blocking her path as she attempted to reach a table in the cafeteria, she warned her persecutors that they might get something on their heads. On December 17, when chairs had been shoved in her way, she emptied her tray on the heads of two boys. These boys excused her, saying that she had been annoyed so frequently they "didn't blame her for getting mad." The boys were sent home to change their clothing. But Minnijean was suspended for six days because of the incident.

Soon after she returned to her classes, a pupil emptied a bowl of hot soup on Minnijean. The reason he gave was that he remembered she had earlier spilled chili on two white boys. He was suspended for three days. . . .

One of the many unprovoked attacks was witnessed by Mrs. Brown. Toward the end of January, she was waiting for Minnijean at the Fourteenth Street exit. At about 3:30 P.M., Minnijean came out of school and saw that her mother was parked at the curb. Minnijean quickened her steps as she made her way to the car. Just before she reached her mother, a pupil, Richard Boehler, came up in back of Minnijean and gave her a vicious kick. Mrs. Brown, seeing this cruel attack on her daughter, screamed and jumped from the car. She started toward the boy but a teacher, who had also seen the incident, apprehended the boy and took him to the office of the Vice-Principal for boys. Boehler, who had been suspended from school earlier that same day, stated that he kicked Minnijean because he "was dared to." He also claimed that Minnijean had stamped on his leg in French class, but he couldn't remember the day. During the subsequent investigation, one of the soldiers reported that Boehler had previously threatened Minnijean with a knife.

Mrs. Brown attempted to file charges against Boehler, but the prosecuting attorney, J. Frank Holt, refused to issue a warrant for his arrest. He said that it was a matter for the school authorities. The school officials, in turn, did not take any action because of Boehler's suspension earlier that day. Poor Minnijean remained at home for a few days until she could sit without pain.

On February 6 Minnijean was suspended for the second time. She walked into my house that afternoon. "They did it to me again," she began. "I just lost my temper. I know it will make it harder for the other kids, but I just couldn't take it any longer."

Pacing the floor, she told me how a girl had been pestering her for days. "When I entered the building this morning," she related, "this girl followed me from the first floor to the third floor, kicking me on the back of my legs and calling me names. As we were entering our homeroom, she called out, 'black bitch.'

"I turned and screamed, 'White trash! Why don't you leave me alone? If you weren't white trash, you wouldn't bother with me!' The girl looked startled for a moment. I started for my seat. She threw her pocketbook at me and hit me on the head with it. I picked up the bag. My first impulse was to knock the devil out of her with it."

"I'm glad you were able to restrain yourself," I said.

"Yes, I am, too," she acknowledged. "I threw the bag on the floor and walked away in disgust. Then, while I was eating

my lunch in the cafeteria, during first lunch period, a character walked over to the table and deliberately dumped a hot
bowl of soup on me. A national guardsman came over and
took us to Mr. Powell's office. He told the Vice-Principal he
had dumped the soup on me because he remembered I had
poured chili on some white boys."

The other Negro students later told me they had reported
this same student several times to school authorities for
harassing them.

The Principal, Jess W. Mathews, suspended both Minnijean and the boy. The suspension notice he sent to her
parents stated:

> Reinstated on probation January 13, 1958, with the
> agreement that she would not retaliate, verbally or
> physically, to any harassment but would leave the
> matter to the school authorities to handle.
>
> After provocation of girl student, she called the girl
> "white trash" after which the girl threw her purse at
> Minnijean.

Upon recommendation of Superintendant of Schools
Virgil Blossom, the Board of Education expelled Minnijean
for the remainder of the school term.

After Minnijean's expulsion the small group of students
who began tormenting the Negro children began wearing
printed cards that read: "One down and eight to go." . . .

❦ *Through the intervention of Robert Carter,
NAACP attorney, and Dr. Kenneth B. Clark of the College
of the City of New York, Minnijean was enrolled for the
spring term at the private New Lincoln School in New York
City. She was later granted a scholarship and graduated from
New Lincoln on June 5, 1959.*

Next to Minnijean, Jefferson [Thomas] was the one singled
out for the segregationists' wrath. . . . Early in October, 1957,

a small but well-organized group of segregationist students gained complete control inside the school. Significantly, it was about this time that the 101st Airborne troops were withdrawn from inside Central. They were replaced by the Arkansas federalized national guardsmen. The segregationist students were quick to note that, unlike the Army paratroopers, many of the guardsmen looked the other way when the Negro pupils were attacked.

The hoodlums used different methods of torture for each of the nine pupils. . . .

♥ *In a locker-room incident several boys ganged up on Jefferson Thomas, one hitting him such a severe blow on the head he was rendered unconscious. Still, he returned to school the next day.*

The students . . . told me what happened to them that day. Carlotta had been kicked, Melba had dropped her books in the hall and was kicked over on her face as she bent to pick them up; Ernest upon entering the shower room after gym class found the room so full of steam that he couldn't see and several boys threw hot, wet towels in his face; Elizabeth had signed out of school about three o'clock after girls in her gym class had hit her repeatedly with basketballs and the teacher had made no attempt to stop them; and the boys in Jeff's gym class had tried to push him into the hot steam pipes and had also deliberately knocked him down a number of times. . . .

♥ *Mrs. Bates had for several days been trying to persuade School Superintendent Blossom that the nine students needed protection inside the school. Her efforts were fruitless. She was finally able to contact General Walker, the officer in command of United States troops at the school, and was promised he would take care of the situation.*

Around nine thirty the next morning, Minnijean called me from the office of the Vice-Principal for Girls, saying, "Come and get us. We can't take it any longer. Melba and I are in Mrs. Huckaby's office. The junior mob has taken over the school. Jeff and Terry were attacked by a group of boys. They're in the office of the Vice-Principal for Boys. When we entered school this morning a boy wearing boots with steel taps on the toe kicked me. About five boys knocked Melba into her locker. We haven't seen the other kids since this morning."

I told Minnijean that they should remain in the office until I called. Evidently the news reached the Superintendent that the Negro pupils were planning to walk out because of lack of protection. For immediately after my telephone talk with Minnijean, Mr. Blossom called and said, "Try to encourage the students to remain. Additional guards are enroute to the school to provide adequate protection to the students."

At around 11:30 A.M., Carlotta called and said that two guards from the 101th Airborne had been assigned to each student. It was now quiet at the school.

CARLOTTA WALLS

. . . Carlotta was fourteen. She was a tall, angular girl who liked swimming and bowling, and was one of the best baseball players in her neighborhood. . . . [She] was subjected to much the same type of physical and psychological tortures as the other students.

Each day after school I sat with the embattled nine in the quiet basement of my home, away from the probing eyes of the reporters and the hysterical charges by the segregationists that the pupils were hirelings of the NAACP, imported from the North to integrate "our" schools.

These meetings were not unlike group therapy. In relating the day's experiences, all the suppressed emotions within these children came tumbling out.

Carlotta would pace the floor, saying, "If only I could sock her!" She was referring to one of her classmates who followed her constantly in the halls, stepping on her heels and calling her names. After school one day, Carlotta was delivered to my house as usual under escort of a guardsman. She stopped off at my kitchen to fix herself a ham sandwich before joining the other children in the basement for our daily session. . . .

"I'm sorry to hold up the meeting," she announced, sheepishly. "I didn't have any lunch." Then she explained. "When I left my classroom before lunch, *that* girl was waiting for me. One of my teachers joined me and walked to the cafeteria with me. Just as I started to eat my lunch, the girl passed my table and dropped a handful of milk bottle tops and soiled paper napkins in my food. I almost hit her!" She pointed her finger at me and added emotionally, "I don't care what you say. One of these days I'm going to knock the hell out of her!"

A few days later Carlotta related another incident. "Today I was walking down the hall. In fact I was nearly running. *That* girl was trying to keep up with me. I turned suddenly and stepped on her foot. But hard! I smiled at her and called her a few choice names, and I told her what I'd do to her if she didn't leave me alone. And each time I saw her after that, I smiled, pretty like. And you know what? She didn't come near me anymore today."

Carlotta ended her story thus: "You know, today was rather a nice day at school.". . .

GLORIA RAY

Gloria Ray had just turned fifteen when she entered Central High School. . . . Although Gloria was subjected to a certain amount of physical abuse, the attacks on her were mostly of a psychological nature. A few days before the Christmas holidays, a girl sitting next to her in her homeroom told her that she had heard that some of the boys had guns in school that day. Later, Gloria was walking down the corridor of the second floor when torpedoes—a type of firecracker—started exploding around her. . . .

The next day a boy attempted to lasso Gloria with a rope fashioned into a hangman's noose. The threat to hang Gloria was followed up by a phone call to her mother that evening. The unidentified caller told Mrs. Ray, "If Gloria comes to school tomorrow there will be a lynching."

The psychological and physical attacks continued in the vain effort to break the spirit of the students. . . .

Just before the spring vacation in 1958, as the children were leaving Central, the segregationists spread a rumor around the campus that some of the boys were going to bring water pistols filled with acid to school the next day and spray the liquid on the Negro students. Gloria was informed about this by a so-called "friend" and advised that it would probably be better if she stayed home the next day.

Gloria did not tell me or her parents about the threat. . . .

[The next day] as Gloria was leaving her locker, she saw a group of boys blocking the hall. She recognized them to be among the troublemakers. She turned and walked in the opposite direction. Just as she turned a corner in the corridor, she came face to face with a boy holding a water pistol. He aimed it at her face.

She told me later. "If I live forever I don't think I'll ever be as frightened as I was at that moment. I just stood there, petrified with fear. I shut my eyes tight. After liquid hit me in the face, I could hear the boy running down the hall. I dropped my books and grabbed the hem of my dress and wiped my face. It took a moment or so before I could convince myself that it was only water." As Gloria was relating this horrifying experience, tears came rolling down her cheeks, but she was apparently unaware that she was crying.

In spite of the mounting attacks, the incessant humiliations, the degradations, and the harrassments inflicted on the Negro students, the courageous youngsters were not to be deterred from their single-minded goal. When school reconvened after spring vacation, all of them returned to their classes, at Central. And when they did, the harassments resumed. . . .

❧ On May 27, 1958, protected by 125 federalized national guardsmen, Ernest Green graduated with his class; he was the first Negro in the history of Central High School to do so. The following fall, rather than comply with the Supreme Court's desegregation order, Arkansas Governor Faubus ordered Central High School and three other Little Rock high schools closed.

In the ensuing weeks and months the families of the Negro pupils were also constantly under attack from the segregationists. Gloria's mother was forced to resign her job in the Welfare Department because of a series of unpleasantnesses which followed when her fellow employees learned that her daughter was "one of the nine."

Carlotta's father was forced to seek employment out of the state because building contractors in Little Rock refused to employ him.

The strain was too much for Terrance Roberts' family and they moved to California.

Elizabeth's mother was fired from her job at the State School for the Blind where she was a teacher.

Of the original nine pupils, only five remained in Little Rock. They were: Carlotta Walls, Jefferson Thomas, Thelma Mothershed, Elizabeth Eckford, and Melba Patillo. Barred from school, they took correspondence courses offered to high school pupils by the University of Arkansas.

Daisy Bates, *The Long Shadow of Little Rock: A Memoir* (New York: David McKay Co., 1962), pp. 116–124, 128–132, 139, 141–144, 159–160.

ALL I COULD
THINK OF WAS HOW SICK
MISSISSIPPI WHITES WERE

ANNE MOODY

❦ *The violence of the racial confrontations engendered by the Supreme Court's desegregation decision
and the scenes of black children set upon by mobs, spurred
Blacks to a new level of militancy. The "sit-in" movement
began in February 1960 in Greensboro, North Carolina, when
four black students, challenging Jim Crow eating facilities,
sat down at the local Woolworth lunch counter until they
were arrested. The technique, which had been developed
by pacifists during World War II and by the Congress of
Racial Equality (CORE) in the 1930's, caught on. Massive
nonviolent direct action campaigns erupted all over the South,
led and organized mostly by black youths. Violence and
mass arrests of demonstrators became the order of the day.
The movement inspired considerable white support and
galvanized students into action in militant pursuit of social
change. Thousands of young men and women found a spiritual home and a new life style in the civil rights movement.
In 1960, a conference of student activists formed the Student
Non-violent Coordinating Committee (SNCC), which led
the movement, basing itself on the philosophy of nonviolent
mass resistance to evil as exemplified by the Reverend Martin
Luther King, Jr.*

*The "Freedom Summer" of 1964, when hundreds of white
and black students went into Mississippi to promote voter
registration and to focus national attention on the denial of
citizenship rights to Blacks, was the final thrust of that phase
of the civil rights movement. It led to the creation of the
Mississippi Freedom Democratic Party (MFDP), which
challenged the official lily-white state delegation at the
Democratic National Convention in 1964. That challenge*

was turned away in favor of a compromise, worked out under the leadership of vice-presidential hopeful Senator Hubert Humphrey which the MFDP delegation refused to ratify.

Disenchantment of Blacks over such liberal tactics, over the limited gains achieved by the civil rights movement and over the wave of killings and violence against Blacks, led to disillusionment with the goal of integration and the methods of nonviolence. Many Blacks, especially the young, now turned away from cooperation with whites and returned to the tradition of self-help, black nationalism and reliance on their own resources. The slogan "Black Power" expressed the new emphasis on autonomy and self-determination gained through struggle. Whether the goal would mean incorporation into the existing political and economic system, separatist nationalism or a revolutionary reordering of society would depend largely on the speed and the manner in which white society would respond to black needs. There was every indication that there could be no going back to accustomed modes of relations between the races. A new phase of Black history in the United States had begun.

Anne Moody's autobiographical novel describes her childhood in a small Mississippi town, her gradual awakening to militancy and her involvement with the civil rights movement which begins after she enters Tougaloo College. The following excerpt describes the Woolworth sit-in in Jackson, Mississippi, in the aftermath of which Medgar Evers, the Mississippi NAACP leader, was murdered. Anne Moody continued as an activist with SNCC, taking part in demonstrations, and was repeatedly jailed, harassed and threatened.

During my senior year at Tougaloo . . . I had found something outside myself that gave meaning to my life.

I had become very friendly with my social science professor, John Salter, who was in charge of NAACP activities on campus. All during the year, while the NAACP conducted a boycott of the downtown stores in Jackson, I had been one of Salter's most faithful canvassers and church speakers. During the last week of school, he told me that sit-in demonstrations were about to start in Jackson and that he wanted me to be the spokesman for a team that would sit-in at Woolworth's lunch counter. The two other demonstrators would be classmates of mine, Memphis and Pearlena. Pearlena was a dedicated NAACP worker, but Memphis had not been very involved in the movement on campus. It seemed that the organization had had a rough time finding students who were in a position to go to jail. I had nothing to lose one way or the other. Around ten o'clock the morning of the demonstration, NAACP headquarters alerted the news services. As a result, the police department was also informed, but neither the policemen nor the newsmen knew exactly where or when the demonstrations would start. They stationed themselves along Capitol Street and waited.

To divert attention from the sit-in at Woolworth's, the picketing started at J. C. Penney's a good fifteen minutes before. The pickets were allowed to walk up and down in front of the store three or four times before they were arrested. At exactly 11 A.M., Pearlena, Memphis, and I entered Woolworth's from the rear entrance. We separated as soon as we stepped into the store, and made small purchases from various counters. Pearlena had given Memphis her watch. He was to let us know when it was 11:14. At 11:14 we were to join him near the lunch counter and at exactly 11:15 we were to take seats at it.

Seconds before 11:15 we were occupying three seats at the previously segregated Woolworth's lunch counter. In the beginning the waitresses seemed to ignore us, as if they really didn't know what was going on. Our waitress walked past us a couple of times before she noticed we had started to write our own orders down and realized we wanted service. She asked us what we wanted. We began to read to her from our order slips. She told us that we would be served at the back counter, which was for Negroes.

"We would like to be served here," I said.

The waitress started to repeat what she had said, then stopped in the middle of the sentence. She turned the lights out behind the counter, and she and the other waitresses almost ran to the back of the store, deserting all their white customers. I guess they thought that violence would start immediately after the whites at the counter realized what was going on. There were five or six other people at the counter. A couple of them just got up and walked away. A girl sitting next to me finished her banana split before leaving. A middle-aged white woman who had not yet been served rose from her seat and came over to us. "I'd like to stay here with you," she said, "but my husband is waiting."

The newsmen came in just as she was leaving. They must have discovered what was going on shortly after some of the people began to leave the store. One of the newsmen ran behind the woman who spoke to us and asked her to identify herself. She refused to give her name, but said she was a native of Vicksburg and a former resident of California. When asked why she had said what she had said to us, she replied, "I am in sympathy with the Negro movement." By this time a crowd of cameramen and reporters had gathered around us taking pictures and asking questions, such as Where were we from? Why did we sit-in? What organization sponsored it? Were we students? From what school? How were we classified?

I told them that we were all students at Tougaloo College, that we were represented by no particular organization, and that we planned to stay there even after the store closed. "All we want is service," was my reply to one of them. After they had finished probing for about twenty minutes, they were almost ready to leave.

At noon, students from a nearby white high school started pouring in to Woolworth's. When they first saw us they were sort of surprised. They didn't know how to react. A few started to heckle and the newsmen became interested again. Then the white students started chanting all kinds of anti-Negro slogans. We were called a little bit of everything.

The rest of the seats except the three we were occupying had been roped off to prevent others from sitting down. A couple of the boys took one end of the rope and made it into a hangman's noose. Several attempts were made to put it around our necks. The crowds grew as more students and adults came in for lunch.

We kept our eyes straight forward and did not look at the crowd except for occasional glances to see what was going on. All of a sudden I saw a face I remembered—the drunkard from the bus station sit-in. My eyes lingered on him just long enough for us to recognize each other. Today he was drunk too, so I don't think he remembered where he had seen me before. He took out a knife, opened it, put it in his pocket, and then began to pace the floor. At this point, I told Memphis and Pearlena what was going on. Memphis suggested that we pray. We bowed our heads, and all hell broke loose. A man rushed forward, threw Memphis from his seat, and slapped my face. Then another man who worked in the store threw me against an adjoining counter.

Down on my knees on the floor, I saw Memphis lying near the lunch counter with blood running out of the corners of his mouth. As he tried to protect his face, the man who'd thrown him down kept kicking him against the head. If he had worn hard-soled shoes instead of sneakers, the first kick probably would have killed Memphis. Finally a man dressed in plain clothes identified himself as a police officer and arrested Memphis and his attacker.

Pearlena had been thrown to the floor. She and I got back on our stools after Memphis was arrested. There were some white Tougaloo teachers in the crowd. They asked Pearlena and me if we wanted to leave. They said that things were getting too rough. We didn't know what to do. While we were trying to make up our minds, we were joined by Joan Trumpauer. Now there were three of us and we were integrated. The crowd began to chant, "Communists, Communists, Communists." Some old man in the crowd ordered the students to take us off the stools.

"Which one should I get first?" a big husky boy said.

"That white nigger," the old man said.

The boy lifted Joan from the counter by her waist and carried her out of the store. Simultaneously, I was snatched from my stool by two high school students. I was dragged about thirty feet toward the door by my hair when someone made them turn me loose. As I was getting up off the floor, I saw Joan coming back inside. We started back to the center of the counter to join Pearlena. Lois Chaffee, a white Tougaloo faculty member, was now sitting next to her. So Joan and I just climbed across the rope at the front end of the counter and sat down. There were now four of us, two whites and two Negroes, all women. The mob started smearing us with ketchup, mustard, sugar, pies, and everything on the counter. Soon Joan and I were joined by John Salter, but the moment he sat down he was hit on the jaw with what appeared to be brass knuckles. Blood gushed from his face and someone threw salt into the open wound. Ed King, Tougaloo's chaplain, rushed to him.

At the other end of the counter, Lois and Pearlena were joined by George Raymond, a CORE field worker and a student from Jackson State College. Then a Negro high school boy sat down next to me. The mob took spray paint from the counter and sprayed it on the new demonstrators. The high school student had on a white shirt; the word "nigger" was written on his back with red spray paint.

We sat there for three hours taking a beating when the manager decided to close the store because the mob had begun to go wild with stuff from other counters. He begged and begged everyone to leave. But even after fifteen minutes of begging, no one budged. They would not leave until we did. Then Dr. Beittel, the president of Tougaloo College, came running in. He said he had just heard what was happening.

About ninety policemen were standing outside the store; they had been watching the whole thing through the windows, but had not come in to stop the mob or do anything. President Beittel went outside and asked Captain Ray to come and escort us out. The captain refused, stating the manager had to invite him in before he could enter the premises, so Dr. Beittel himself brought us out. He had told the police that they had better protect us after we were outside the store. When we got outside, the policemen formed a single line that blocked the mob from us. However, they were allowed to throw at us everything they had collected. Within ten minutes, we were picked up by Reverend King in his station wagon and taken to the NAACP headquarters on Lynch Street.

After the sit-in, all I could think of was how sick Mississippi whites were. They believed so much in the segregated Southern way of life, they would kill to preserve it. I sat there in the NAACP office and thought of how many times they had killed when this way of life was threatened. I knew that the killing had just begun. "Many more will die before it is over with," I thought. Before the sit-in, I had always hated the whites in Mississippi. Now I knew it was impossible for me to hate sickness. The whites had a disease, an incurable disease in its final stage. What were our chances against such a disease? I thought of the students, the young Negroes who had just begun to protest, as young interns. When these young interns got older, I thought, they would be the best doctors in the world for social problems.

Anne Moody, *Coming of Age in Mississippi*
(New York: Dial Press, 1968), pp. 235–239.

CHAPTER EIGHT

"LIFTING AS WE CLIMB"*

We need to feel the cheer and inspiration
of meeting each other, we need to gain the
courage and fresh life that comes from the
mingling of congenial souls, of those
working for the same ends. . . . We need to
talk over . . . the things that are of especial
interest to us as **colored** women. . . .

Josephine St. Pierre Ruffin,
First National Conference of Colored Women

* The motto of the National Association of Colored Women.

FROM BENEVOLENT SOCIETIES TO NATIONAL CLUB MOVEMENT

❦ Black women organized, at first on a local level, small groups meeting monthly or weekly to undertake educational, philanthropic and, at times, welfare activities. Women frequently joined together to support a church, a school, an orphanage or an old people's home. Such societies existed among free Negroes, both North and South, but there is evidence that benevolent, burial and secret societies existed even under slavery. The number and size of these groups grew in the Northern cities in the 1830's. Their importance can be judged when it is considered that the nearly sixty benevolent associations of colored people in Philadelphia spent $10,000 yearly in that period for poor relief.

In the two decades before the Civil War, abolition societies proliferated; many of these were female societies whose major activity was the distribution of literature, the collection of signatures to antislavery petitions and the financing of the movement through annual fund-raising affairs. Some of these societies were interracial; the Philadelphia Female Antislavery Society is notable for maintaining a racially integrated membership and leadership throughout its existence. Black men took the lead in Vigilance Committees which engaged in the rescue of fugitive slaves and later operated an underground railroad in defiance of the Fugitive Slave Act. Black women performed many daring feats in this rescue work and were always ready to provide refuge within their homes for some of the escaped slaves.

During the Civil War, supplying relief to the black regiments and to the freedmen was a natural extension of the work of abolition societies. Women played an important role both in relief and teaching (see Chapter Two) and continued the work of maintaining schools, churches and orphanages in their own communities. The growth of black urban communities due to migration from the South, the presence of several generations of educated women with some leisure, and the urgent social needs of the poor who depended on private relief gave rise to a national black women's club movement, which harnessed the force of women to national, political and economic goals.

Women's clubs sprang up in a number of cities, usually centered around some local welfare or education project. Following a pattern not unlike that of white women, these local clubs began to exchange information and delegates and to form large federations. But the spur for a permanent national organization came from the outside.

In 1895, lynchings in America had begun to arouse censure and protest from abroad. This was largely the result of the untiring campaign of an Afro-American woman, Mrs. Ida Wells Barnett, whose speaking tour in Great Britain aroused an international debate over lynching and resulted in the formation of a British anti-lynching society. Rising to the defense of the white South, James Jacks, president of the Missouri Press Association, wrote to the British society in a widely publicized statement that "the Negroes in this country were wholly devoid of morality, the women were prostitutes and all were natural thieves and liars." This statement was the last straw for black club women, who had endured similar slanders in silence. It prompted the convening of the first national conference of colored women, which led to the formation of the National Association of Colored Women (NACW) in 1896 (see pp. 440–447).

The NACW united the National League of Colored Women, the National Federation of Afro-American Women (both short-lived earlier attempts at federation), and over a hundred local women's organizations. After some rivalry between leaders of the major organizations, it became a unifying force, an authoritative voice in defense of black womanhood. It greatly spurred local and regional organization.

At the ninth biennial meeting in 1914, the NACW represented over 50,000 black women in 28 state federations and over a thousand clubs. Its 1968 membership was 850,000. It may be that the rapid proliferation of women's clubs after the formation of the National Association of Colored Women is more apparent than real and due simply to the fact that the NACW kept minutes and records. There is reason to believe that there was an uninterrupted continuity of organization, certainly since the Civil War. But the national federation movement provided encouragement, direction, expert leadership and example. Like the club movement of white women, this movement was led by middle-class women, but unlike white club women, the members of black women's clubs were often working women, tenant farmwives or poor women. Thus, while the Negro women's clubs were equally concerned with education, self-improvement and community improvement, there was always a strong emphasis on race pride, on the defense of the black community and home, and on race advancement. The leadership exerted by black women in the fight against lynching, for equal accommodations on railroads and for integration in community and national organizations is particularly important.

THE AFRIC-AMERICAN FEMALE INTELLIGENCE SOCIETY OF BOSTON

❦ The Afric-American Female Intelligence Society is typical of early nineteenth century benevolent organizations.

We are glad to find that Associations, benevolent and literary appear to be multiplying among our colored sisters. We learn by the Liberator that one has recently been established at Boston, under the name of The Afric-American Female Intelligence Society. A literary association was also some months since organized by some of the colored females of Philadelphia. We wish them both success and a long career of usefulness.—We hail with delight every intimation that our Afric American sisters are becoming more sensible of the value of mental cultivation, and are exerting themselves to procure it. We have copied the Preamble and such articles of the Constitution of the Boston Society as will best explain their objects and be most useful to those who may wish to imitate them.

CONSTITUTION

Of the Afric-American Female Intelligence Society of Boston

PREAMBLE

Whereas the subscribers, women of color of the Commonwealth of Massachusetts, actuated by a natural feeling for the welfare of our friends, have thought fit to associate for the diffusion of knowledge, the suppression of vice and immorality, and for cherishing such virtues as will render us happy and useful to society, sensible of the gross ignorance under which we have too long labored, but trusting, by the blessing of God, we shall be able to accomplish the object of our union—we have therefore associated ourselves under the name of the Afric-American Female Intelligence Society, and have adopted the following Constitution.

Art. 1st. The officers of this society shall be a President, Vice-President, Treasurer, Secretary, and a Board of Directors of five—all of whom shall be annually elected.

Art. 2d. Regular meetings of the Society shall be held on the first Thursday of every month, at which each member shall pay twenty-five cents, and pay twelve and a half cents at every monthly meeting thenceforth.

Art. 3d. The money thus collected shall be appropriated for the purchasing of books, the hiring of a room and other contingencies. . . .

Art. 11th. All candidates for membership shall be of a good moral character, and shall be elected by a majority of the votes of the Society.

Art. 12th. All members who shall be absent at the regular monthly meetings, shall be fined six and a quarter cents, unless a satisfactory apology can be offered to the Society.

Art. 15th. Any member of this Society, of one year's standing, having regularly paid up her dues, who may be taken sick, shall receive one dollar per week out of the funds of the Society as long as consistent with the means of the institution.

Art. 18th. In case any unforeseen and afflictive event should happen to any of the members, it shall be the duty of the Society to aid them as far as in their power. . . .

BY-LAWS

Art. 1st. Each member who wishes to speak shall rise and address the chair.

Art. 2d. While any member addresses the chair there shall be no interruption.

Art. 3d. If any member becomes sick, it shall be made known to the President, who will instruct the Directors to visit the sick person, and devise means for her relief.

Art. 4th. Twelve members shall constitute a quorum to transact business.

Art. 5th. Any person or persons who shall rashly sacrifice their own health, shall not be entitled to any aid or sympathy from the Society.

Art. 6th. Each meeting of this Society shall begin and end with prayer.

Art. 7th. The Treasurer shall make quarterly reports of the state of the funds.

Art. 8th. The Secretary shall read the proceedings of the last
meeting at each succeeding one.

Genius of Universal Emancipation, Vol. 2, No. 10,
3rd. Ser. (March 1832), pp. 162–163.

THE BEGINNINGS OF THE
NATIONAL CLUB MOVEMENT

ADDRESS OF JOSEPHINE ST. PIERRE RUFFIN
TO THE FIRST NATIONAL CONFERENCE
OF COLORED WOMEN (1895)

☙ Josephine St. Pierre Ruffin (1842–1924) was born
in Boston and was educated in public schools. In 1858, she
married St. Pierre Ruffin, a Harvard graduate who later
became the first colored judge in Massachusetts. The couple
lived for a few years in England and had five children. She
was active in war relief work during and after the Civil War
and was a member of the New England Women's Club,
founded by Julia Ward Howe. Growing out of her association
with this club of white women, she began to perceive the
need for organizing black women which she proceeded to
do in the New Era Club of which she was the president.
The club issued a newspaper, The Women's Era, which
Mrs. Ruffin edited. She was a moving force in promoting a
national organization of black women.

The First National Conference of Colored Women, which
convened under her leadership in Boston in 1895, resolved
to form such a national organization and to make The
Women's Era its official organ. The National Federation
of Afro-American Women was founded the same year with
Mrs. Margaret Murray Washington as president. It united
36 women's clubs in twelve states, including the New Era
Club. Meanwhile a similar movement toward national unity
had taken place under the leadership of the Washington
Women's Club and led to the formation of the National

League of Colored Women under Mrs. Mary Church Terrell's leadership. There ensued a brief rivalry for leadership of the national organization, which was resolved when the two groups united in 1896 and drew large numbers of new affiliates into the National Association of Colored Women. Mrs. Terrell was the first national president of the NACW, with the seven vice-presidents (Josephine St. Pierre Ruffin, Massachusetts; Fannie Jackson Coppin, Pennsylvania; Frances Ellen Watkins Harper, Illinois; Josephine Silone Yates, Missouri; Sylvanie Williams, Louisiana; Jennie Chase Williams, South Carolina; Lucy Thurman, Missouri) representing regional strength. Virginia E. Matthews from New York was appointed national organizer. Mrs. Ruffin's journal became the official organ of the new federation, and she continued to be active in club work until her death.

The reasons why we should confer are so apparent that it would seem hardly necessary to enumerate them, and yet there is none of them but demand our serious consideration. In the first place we need to feel the cheer and inspiration of meeting each other, we need to gain the courage and fresh life that comes from the mingling of congenial souls, of those working for the same ends. Next, we need to talk over not only those things which are of vital importance to us as women, but also the things that are of especial interest to us as *colored* women, the training of our children, openings for our boys and girls, how they can be prepared for occupations and occupations may be found or opened for them, what *we* especially can do in the moral education of the race with which we are identified, our mental elevation and physical development, the home training it is necessary to give our children in order to prepare them to meet the peculiar conditions in which they shall find themselves, how to make the most of our own, to some extent, limited opportunities, these are some of our own peculiar questions to be discussed. Besides these are the general questions of the day, which we cannot afford to be indifferent to: temperance, morality, the higher education, hygienic and domestic questions. . . .

I have left the strongest reason for our conferring together until the last. All over America there is to be found a large and growing class of earnest, intelligent, progressive colored women, women who, if not leading full useful lives, are only waiting for the opportunity to do so, many of them warped and cramped for lack of opportunity, not only to do more but to *be* more; and yet, if an estimate of the colored women of America is called for, the inevitable reply, glibly given, is, "For the most part ignorant and immoral, some exceptions, of course, but these don't count."

Now for the same of the thousands of self-sacrificing young women teaching and preaching in lonely southern backwoods for the noble army of mothers who have given birth to these girls, mothers whose intelligence is only limited by their opportunity to get at books, for the sake of the fine cultured women who have carried off the honors in school here and often abroad, for the sake of our own dignity, the dignity of our race, and the future good name of our children, it is "mete, right and our bounden duty" to stand forth and declare ourselves and principles, to teach an ignorant and suspicious world that our aims and interests are identical with those of all good aspiring women. Too long have we been silent under unjust and unholy charges; we cannot expect to have them removed until we disprove them through *ourselves*. It is not enough to try to disprove unjust charges through individual effort, that never goes any further. Year after year southern women have protested against the admission of colored women into any national organization on the ground of the immorality of these women, and because all refutation has only been tried by individual work the charge has never been crushed, as it could and should have been at the first. Now with an army of organized women standing for purity and mental worth, we in ourselves deny the charge and open the eyes of the world to a state of affairs to which they have been blind, often willfully so, and the very fact that the charges, audaciously and flippantly made, as they often are, are of so humiliating and delicate a nature, serves to protect the accuser by driving the helpless accused into mortified silence. It is to break this silence, not by noisy protestations of what we are not, but by a dignified showing of what we are and hope to become that we are impelled to take this step, to make of this gathering an object lesson to the world. For many and apparent reasons it is especially fitting that the *women* of the race take the lead in this movement, but for all this we recognize the necessity of the sympathy of our husbands, brothers and fathers.

Our woman's movement is woman's movement in that it is led and directed by women for the good of women and men, for the benefit of *all* humanity, which is more than any one branch or section of it. We want, we ask the active interest of our men, and, too, we are not drawing the color line; we are women, American women, as intensely interested in all that pertains to us as such as all other American women; we are not alienating or withdrawing, we are only coming to the front, willing to join any others in the same work and cordially inviting and welcoming any others to join us.

If there is any one thing I would especially enjoin upon this conference, it is unity and earnestness . . .

First National Conference of Colored Women, held July 29, 30, 31, 1895 at Boston. The Women's Era, Vol. 2, No. 5 (September 1895), p. 14.

THE BEGINNINGS OF THE NATIONAL CLUB MOVEMENT: CLUB WORK AMONG NEGRO WOMEN
MARGARET MURRAY WASHINGTON

❦ *Margaret Murray Washington (1865–1925) was born and raised in Macon, Georgia, one of ten children in a poverty-stricken household. At the age of seven, following* the death of her father, she moved into the household of her Quaker teachers. She began teaching school at the age of fourteen, then entered Fisk University as a part-time student. She graduated from Fisk in 1889 and accepted a position as "Lady Principal" of Tuskegee Institute. She married the recently widowed Booker T. Washington in 1893 and collaborated with him in building Tuskegee, first as Director of Girls' Industries, later as Dean of women. She was president of the Tuskegee Women's Club from its inception and played a leading role in the national women's club movement. As President of the Afro-American Federation of Colored Women (founded in 1895), she moved this federation into the National Association of Colored Women (founded 1896). This move unified black women and provided the base for the spectacular growth of the club movement. Margaret Murray Washington was President of the NACW from 1914 to 1918 and for many years editor of National Notes, the organization's official newspaper. At the time of her death she was President of the Alabama State Federation of Colored Women's Clubs. She helped to organize many local welfare institutions, among these the Reform School at Mt. Meigs, Alabama and a home for delinquent colored girls. She served as trustee of the National Frederick Douglass Memorial and Historical Association. As a lecturer, teacher and journalist she worked to promote interracial cooperation, to improve the condition of black women, and to carry the philosophy of Booker T. Washington on to the national scene.

The First National Meeting.—In 1895, in the city of Boston, Mass., was called the First National Body of Colored Women. The call was made by Mrs. Josephine Saint Pierre Ruffin, who had for many years been associated with Mrs. Julia Ward Howe, Susan B. Anthony, Elizabeth Cody Stanton, and other forward moving women, and from whom she had received the inspiration which led her to know and to feel that what one group of organized women could do another with equal chance could also do. For this equal chance Mrs. Ruffin knew all too well that the colored women would have to fight, not separately, but together. . . .

. . . So [in 1896] came into shape the National Association of Colored Women's Clubs, which now has a membership of over 300,000 women located in every State in the country, including Canada, Liberia, Hayti and Cuba. . . .

Works Through Departments.—The national association does its work through departments, and these carry on the work through individual clubs. The leading departments are: Woman Suffrage, Patriotism, Education, Conditions in Rural Life, Music, Literature and Art, Gainful Occupation and Business, Better Railroad Conditions, Mothers' Meetings and Night Schools, Health Conditions, Child Welfare and Public Speaking, etc.

The School Question.—How many people realize that even today in many parts of the country the school term for the colored child is not more than four months in a year? How many people in making up their opinion as to the colored woman and her people stop to consider in their comparison that the children with whom the study is made are in school often ten months in the year, and that such conditions are unfair and un-American, and sooner or later colored children, not being given a square deal for growth and all around citizenship, will become a menace and a burden to the community in which they live? No question today is of so vital an interest to the colored woman's club as this one which deals with the schools and the general educational advantages for their children and those of their sister club workers. . . .

The National Association.—. . . Our National Association of Colored Woman's Clubs . . . is to us what the general federation of white women's clubs is to them. . . .

A large group of women stand out . . . as leaders in this forward and progressive field of the colored woman's organized efforts in her own behalf—Mrs. Josephine St. Pierre

Ruffin, of Boston, Mass., who called the first national gathering of colored women; Mrs. Mary Church Terrell, of Washington, D.C.; the late Mrs. J. Siloame Yates, of Kansas City, Mo.; Miss Elizabeth Carter, of New Bedford, Mass.; the late Mrs. Lucy Thurman, of Jackson, Mich.; Mrs. Mary B. Talbert, of Buffalo, N.Y., our present leader; Mrs. Nettie Langston Napier, of Nashville, Tenn.; Mrs. Mary E. Steward, of Louisville, Ky.; Mrs. Mary Josenberger, of Fort Smith, Ark.; Mrs. Mary Bethune, of Daytona, Fla.; and hundreds of others whose names cannot be mentioned in a short article of this nature. . . .

Suffrage.—Colored women, quite as much as colored men, realize that if there is ever to be equal justice and fair play in the protection in the courts everywhere for all races, then there must be an equal chance for all women as well as men to express their preference through their votes. There are certain things so sure to come our way that time in arguing them is not well spent. It is simply the cause of right which in the end always conquers, no matter how fierce the opposition. Personally, woman suffrage has never kept me awake at night, but I am sure before this country is able to take its place amongst the great democratic nations of the earth it has got to come to the place where it is willing to trust its citizens, black as well as white, women as well as men, to be loyal to their Government, to be willing to leave the carrying out of governmental offices to the intelligent part of the citizenship. Our Department of Suffrage conducts training classes in the Constitution of the country, and has given time to the study of all governmental affairs, so that women may be prepared to handle the vote intelligently and wisely when it comes to them. Thousands of our women vote in the Northern States where they live, and in no instance have they shown any disposition to assume control of affairs, nor have they presumed anything more than a desire to be counted as a citizen of a country where they are giving the best of themselves in building better homes, better schools, better churches, and finally better citizenship.

"Anti Lynching."—Our club women work incessantly to help mould sentiment against lynching, and although it is a slow process, there is a strong and growing feeling against this form of punishment for any cause whatsoever.

The Georgia State Federation of White Women's Clubs in their last convention came out strongly in favor of law and order as against mob violence and lynching. When the Women's State Federation of other Southern States take a stand against this evil, the men in authority in these States will see that lynching is put down and not until then will it be done. It is woman's work now as always. . . .

Nothing has so changed the whole life and personnel [!] of the colored woman and so surely brought her into her own as has the club life to which she has lent herself, inspired by the national association which has for its aim the development of its women, mentally, morally and industrially, as well as along civic lines, and whose motto is, "Lifting as we climb." . . .

Margaret Murray Washington, "Club Work Among Negro Women," in J. L. Nichols and William Crogman, eds., *Progress of a Race*, rev. ed. (Naperville, Illinois: J. L. Nichols Co., 1929), pp. 178, 182, 192–195, 209.

THE RUFFIN INCIDENT—1900

FANNIE BARRIER WILLIAMS

❦ *The national club movement of white women had preceded that of black women by six years, with the organization of the General Federation of Women's Clubs, (GFWC) founded in 1890. Inevitably, the existence of a national movement of colored women precipitated a debate over racial integration of the GFWC. This issue had first presented itself on a local level when, in 1894, Fannie Barrier Williams was rejected from membership in the Chicago Women's Club because of her race. After fourteen months of debate and agitation, the decision was reversed. The next*

*incident, reported in the document below, occurred at the
1900 biennial convention of the GFWC in Milwaukee.*

The following is a condensed statement of the Woman's Era
Club (colored) of Boston, concerning the "Ruffin incident."

"The Woman's Era Club . . . became a member of the
Massachusetts State Federation, and no club in that body
had a deeper pride in it and the women it represents than we.
Our association with Massachusetts club women had been
such that the possibility of color discrimination had been lost
sight of. Our delegates had been received at meetings, recep-
tions and conventions with that courtesy invariably extended
by ladies toward all with whom they come in contact; nothing less was expected; certainly nothing less was received.

[The Women's Era Club was invited to join the
G.F.W.C., accepted and was handed a certificate of membership in May 1900.]

"Acting upon this situation, the Women's Era Club sent
Mrs. Ruffin as its delegate to the biennial convention held
at Milwaukee, Wisconsin. She was also elected a delegate by
the Massachusetts State Federation, and also an alternate
from the N. E. W. [New England Women's] Press Association.

Upon arriving at Milwaukee, Mrs. Ruffin was forced into
a humiliating position for which she was wholly unprepared.
The Massachusetts delegation was immediately notified that
the Board had met and would not receive an application for
membership of the Woman's Era Club. Mrs. Ruffin was informed that she could not enter the convention representing a 'colored club' but would be received as a delegate from
a 'white club,' and to enforce this ruling an attempt was
made to snatch from her breast the badge which had been
handed her on the passing of her credentials.

Mrs. Ruffin refused to enter the convention under the
conditions offered her. . . ."

The whole country was aroused over this Milwaukee incident. As in the case cited, the newspapers of the country

made much of the case and were generally on the side of the strong and womanly stand taken by Mrs. Ruffin. . . .

Protest of White Clubs.—Among the first clubs to take a decided stand against such injustice was the Catholic Woman's League of Chicago. . . . It is notable that the Catholic woman's clubs throughout the country are uncompromising in their stand for an equality of opportunity.

The Chicago Women's Club again fought out this question against fierce opposition from some of its members, but under the leadership of its best women, including many cultured women of Southern birth and with the assistance of their one colored member, they once more triumphed over their prejudices.

These discussions in many clubs are creating much bitterness, and there are heard on every side threats of the withdrawal of Southern clubs, and some Northern clubs that sympathize with the Southern woman. It is also curious to observe how slight has been the advance in thought and argument over the same arguments of ante-bellum days. The women are still haunted by the old phantoms "Do you want your daughter to marry a Negro?" "Do you want social equality?" "White supremacy?" These are all used in the same manner and with the same assurances of effectiveness as they were fifty years ago against the abolitionists. It is the same old fight of light against darkness and progress against caste. Prejudice resists all that tends to soften the heart and enlighten the mind. It defies logic. It has no part with charity. . . . The colored women of the country have borne the burden of more misery than has ever been imposed upon womankind by a Christian nation. She knows herself and asks for the assistance and encouragement of those who are more or less responsible for this burden. Yet there are thousands of free strong women in this country who would refuse her appeal.

Friends of the Colored Woman.—There is, however, a brighter side to this question. The women who are committed to a more liberal view on the admission of colored clubs to the National Federation are equally tenacious of their position. They insist the great Federation shall not commit itself to any policy of exclusion, by which the deserving woman of any race or color shall be kept from its benefits and inspirations.

There are thousands of such women, and they prefer that the Federation should go to pieces and cease to be rather than to make vital in their work the prejudices and principles of fifty years ago. . . . They believe that the white women of the country should not be unwilling to aid in every way colored women who are struggling to work out their own salvation. They are not disturbed by the cry of social equality. They stand for progress and for the broadest sympathy and for womankind. This seems to be the sentiment of the majority of the noble women in the country, and they have no doubt of saving the Federation from committing itself to the meaner policy of exclusion.

The Attitude of Colored Women in the Controversy.— The colored women have kept themselves serene while this color-line controversy has been raging around them. They have taken a keen and intelligent interest in all that has been said for and against them, but through it all they have lost neither their patience nor their hope in the ultimate triumph of right principles.

✌ *The GFWC maintained its segregationist policy for several decades after this incident.*

Fannie Barrier Williams, "Club Movement Among Negro Women," in J. W. Gibson and W. H. Crogman, eds., *Progress of a Race*, (Atlanta, Georgia: J. L. Nichols Co., 1903), pp. 220–226.

(Note: In the 1929 edition of this book, the article on this same topic was written by Margaret Murray Washington.)

CLUB ACTIVITIES

✌ *The following accounts of club activity, as reported to the 1906 convention of the NACW, are fairly representative. It is noteworthy how much energy was devoted to* supplying needed welfare services and building community institutions. In fact, black initiative, effort and organizational talent supplied what white racism sought to deny the black community. Reports such as these, coming in year after year from virtually every area in which Blacks lived, are convincing proof of the internal strength of the black community against all odds. The leadership contributions and sustaining efforts of black women are remarkable and can be fully appreciated only when measured against the general impoverishment of the communities in which they lived and worked.

COLORED WOMAN'S LEAGUE

The Colored Woman's League was organized in June, 1892. Its central idea was National Union. It appealed to the Colored Women of the country to form similar organizations and to co-operate with them for the accomplishment of the objects set forth in its constitution. As a result of the appeal the First National organization of Colored Women was formed and was finally admitted into the National Council of Women at the Triennial meeting held in Washington, February, 1895. After a brilliant and successful convention held in 1896, The National League agreed to unite with another organization of colored women. The Washington League then turned with increased ardor to its local work. It established a training school for kindergarten teachers, October, 1896, and for two years after maintained seven free kindergartens. Later the kindergarten system was introduced into the public schools of Washington. The credit is due the League for furnishing to the public schools from their training classes seven of the eight teachers appointed. . . .

The women of the League are at present engaged in carrying on a Day Nursery to provide a place where poor mothers who work out may leave their little ones during the day, knowing that they will be kindly cared for. . . .

Annual membership dues, $1.00. Regular monthly meeting held last Monday in each month at 1505 M street, 7:30 p.m. . . .

Andrew F. Hilyer, ed., *The 20th Century Union League Directory: A Historical, Biographical and Statistical Study of Colored Washington* (Washington, D.C.: Union League, 1901), p. 155.

WOMEN'S CHRISTIAN, SOCIAL AND LITERARY CLUB
OF PEORIA, ILL.

We, the Women's Christian, Social and Literary Club of Peoria, Ill. beg leave to submit the following report for 1905–1906: We have a membership of 15 active members and 7 honorary members. . . . Our motto is "For God and Humanity." . . . Last year we had a good school for the little ones, and did much good and realized $5.50 from their work. . . . We have seventeen pupils. We have donated to the Baptist Church $15 and to the A.M.E. Church $17. . . . Assisted 44 different persons. We meet every Monday afternoon. . . .

On June 28, 1906, we made arrangements to purchase 5½ acres of land on which we will erect an industrial home and school for all ages of our people. This piece of land cost us $6000. It is a handsome place, and it is now laid out in 36 lots, thirty by one hundred twenty-five feet. After paying all expenses and $150 on the place, we will have left in the bank $25. Respectfully submitted, Mrs. Anna R. Fields, Founder and President.

PHILLIS WHEATLEY HOME ASSOCIATION OF DETROIT

The Phillis Wheatley Home Association of Detroit, Michigan was organized in 1897, the object being the establishment of a home for our aged colored women. In 1897 a few earnest women met . . . and they were without funds but each one contributed her might and the Committee rented a building. Furnishings were solicited . . . applications were received and on our opening day seven old ladies were received in the Phillis Wheatley Home. In 1901 the Phillis Wheatley Home Association was incorporated under the state laws, and seeing the necessity of having a permanent building, we purchased the property at 176 East Elizabeth Street at a cost of $4000, paying $1300 cash. We had [!] at present 12 inmates. . . . We have 24 members, regular meetings are held every Tuesday evening. Cash receipts (from donations for the past two years, 1904–1906) includes $1847. Respectfully submitted, Eliza Wilson, President.

SOJOURNER TRUTH CLUB OF MONTGOMERY, ALA.

The Sojourner Truth Club of Montgomery, Alabama furnished a reading room, this being the only one of its kind available for colored people in our city. It has six tables, two bookcases, three sets of bookshelves, one and a half dozen chairs, stove pictures, floor coverings of linoleum, rugs, twelve to fifteen current periodicals, 300 or more books. The room is lighted by shaded incandescent lights. The librarian is hired and the hours are from 3 p.m. to 9 p.m. Back of the reading room we have recently furnished a club room with a small table, two dozen chairs, matting, rugs, curtains, stove and pictures. It makes quite a cozy appearance. A third room we hope to furnish is a kitchen. Here we hope to have cooking lessons given for the benefit of the public. All this is paid for by 25¢-per-month membership dues and fund-raising affairs held by the club. They have also invited guest speakers, such as Dr. Booker T. Washington, W. E. B. Du-Bois and Kelly Miller.

The membership is 29.

Above three items: Margaret Murray Washington Papers, Tuskegee Archives, Tuskegee Institute. Used by permission.

TUSKEGEE WOMAN'S CLUB

The Tuskegee Woman's Club closes the tenth year of its work in sober retrospection of the days that have closed in upon it since its organization in March 1895. . . . The first club year ended with a membership of thirty-five. This tenth year closes with a . . . membership of seventy-four. . . .

The literary calender of the Tuskegee Woman's Club has ended for the year 1904–05. Among the various topics discussed in the semi-monthly meetings have been the works of leading colored musicians, the value of the X Ray, Wireless Telegraphy, Famous Women of the Hour, The Christ Child in Art, The Use of Electricity in Medical Science. These, with reviews of current articles, debates, musical numbers and readings, have formed the literary programs for the year. . . .

Of the work accomplished during the year, the heads of the divisions, with two exceptions, report the following:

Jail Work.—Thirty visits have been made to the prisoners in the jail of the town of Tuskegee. Religious services have been held at each visit. Fruit and clean clothing have been given to the prisoners who have expressed their gratitude, and made successful efforts to present a tidy appearance during our visits. Four small boys, imprisoned for theft, were with four men who could not read or write. All were given their first lessons by a fellow prisoner who had better advantages. . . . Four Bible students and several teachers have given much time to help better the work for these unfortunates. . . .

Elizabeth A. Russell Settlement Work.—The work at the Settlement has been carried on as formerly, by the resident worker, Miss Annie Davis, who for the first time in the seven years' history of the Settlement, has received recognition from the county authorities. The cooking, sewing classes, and Mothers' Organization have been conducted by Miss Davis; the pupils of the day school have put in the crops on the ten acre lot of the settlement. . . . The school cottage and the home cottage with their twenty acres comprise the E. A. Russell Settlement, but the workers are encouraged because their efforts for the year have been fruitful. The year ends with an average attendance of fifty-three children in the school; fifteen girls in the sewing and cooking classes; thirty-four women in the Mothers Meetings, and one hundred thirty-eight men, women and children in the Sunday school.

Thompson's Quarters Out-of-Door Sunday School.—After more than three years' work in Thompson's Quarters we find the interest increasing in the Sunday school and a larger attendance during the winter and spring months. The average attendance has been thirty-five, mostly children, occasionally four or five adults have been present. . . .

Along with the Bible teaching, we have given a helping hand wherever it has been needed, by visiting the sick and adding somewhat to the comfort of the afflicted. . . .

Temperance Work.—Vigorous efforts have been made during this year, as has been true in past years, to keep the work of the temperance cause fresh in the minds of the students and the children of the neighboring vicinity. . . .

Mothers' Meetings.—For a number of years we have carried on the Mothers' Meetings in the town of Tuskegee. Our object has been to create an interest among the women for self improvement; for the betterment of their homes and the development of their children. . . . We have held twenty-eight meetings beginning at two o'clock on Saturdays and closing at five. There has been an average attendance of fifty. Often there have been seventy-five present.

We have no president of the meeting and no treasurer. In fact we have had no officers. It has been a gathering of women who wanted to be helped and who wanted to help. We have always opened the meetings with devotional exercises. We have discussed helpful subjects freely. Among them have been: "The part a woman should take in buying land and building a house," "The care of children . . . ," "The boy's place in the home," "The importance of close confidence between mother and daughter; father and son," "How to teach children respect for parents and sacred relations," "The kind of a teacher to have in a community."

The mothers have also been urged to plant and raise all kinds of vegetables that they may improve the physical condition of themselves and families.

Once during the year the mothers evinced great interest in bringing together a creditable exhibit of turnips, peas, beans, potatoes, butter, eggs, and chickens.

The mothers have been glad to learn how and what to buy, not only for their tables but for their wearing apperal [*sic*]. . . .

Many of the women belonging to these Mothers' Meetings are engaged themselves in other meetings throughout the country. At Little Texas, Sweet Gum, Howard Chapel, and Shady Grove they have opened subdivisions. . . .

Woman's Suffrage Division.—There has been greater interest in the study of the suffrage movement during the year past than ever before in the history of the club. . . . Ten minutes of each club meeting have been devoted to this study under the leader, Mrs. Logan, whose excellent library on the subject has been placed at the service of all interested members of the club.

Report of the Tuskegee Women's Club 1904–1905
(n.p., 1906). Pamphlet.

THE ST. LOUIS COLORED ORPHAN HOME

St. Louis, July 8, 1906

To the President and Members of the National Association of Colored Women here assembled.

Dear Sisters and Co-workers for God and the promotion of the welfare of our race. In submitting to you a report of our work we do not intend to weary you with a lengthy report. . . . Today we give you the report of three months labor, which resulted in the hearty cooperation of our people. "Orphans Home Day" free will offerings represent the churches, Sunday schools, secret, benevolent, and social organizations of St. Louis and vicinity. . . . We gave two Day Excursions just one week apart, 25th of June and 2nd of July, and of course we feel very proud to submit the financial report of this effort. Especially because it truly represents race effort, for there is not in this over fifty Dollars contributed by our white friends. We would not have you think they are not generous to our work they are. *But these* are our special Days.

Orphans May Day Collections	$529.95	
Refreshments	203.35	
Total	$733.30	
Expense	177.05	
	$556.25	

Appropriated to Building Fund $278.00

June excursion	$1129.00	
Expense	349.00	
Balance	$780.00	

July Excursion	$767.00	
Expense	309.00	
Balance	$458.00	

Bro't Forward		$278.00
″ ″		780.00
		458.00
From interest Note Club on Interest		60.00
Total		$1576.00

Paid on Principal	$1000.00	
For carpentry, painting & roofing	164.00	
Special Sewer tax	200.00	
Total	$1364.00	$1364.00
Balance		$ 212.00
Paid by the Interest Note Club on Interest	60.00	

Summary of five years.

Dec. 1901 we came in possession of property by paying $1200 cash. Have raised and paid during five years on principal $4500. Paid on Interest $930.00. Improvements and repairs $1200.00. Making a total on property $7830. Besides meeting the current expenses of the Home *this* Represents the co-operation of *our* people in St. Louis. . . . Yours Sincerely Interest Note Club, Wardrobe Club and Nursery Club Board of Managers, Mrs. M. L. Harrison Pres.

> Mary Margaret Washington Papers, Tuskegee Archives,
> Tuskegee Institute. Used by permission.

INTERRACIAL WORK

❦ Even during the worst periods of repression of Blacks, cooperative efforts between white and black Southern women occurred sporadically, usually on a community basis. Temperance societies sometimes cooperated, churches joined in a common charity, and, for the relief of a particular need, club women cooperated across racial lines. Outside the field of education, such contacts were the exception. Parallel but race-segregated endeavors of women's clubs were the rule. Only in the YWCA were there some steps taken toward interracial contacts, but these were faltering and insignificant until the 1920's (see pp. 480–483).

As a result of the democratic hopes raised by World War I and the shocking polarization of the races at the end of the war which found expression in race riots, lynchings and terror, women of both races felt impelled to make stronger efforts than before to bridge the gap. Eva Bowles, the first YWCA Secretary in charge of "colored work," and Mrs. Lugenia Hope, wife of the President of Atlanta University, led the move among black women. In July 1919, the Women's Missionary Council Committee on Race Relations sent two white delegates, Mrs. Luke Johnson and Mrs. Haskins, as observers to a Tuskegee conference of the National Association of Colored Women. In a small meeting after the public gathering, the black women sought to enlist the aid of white club women in order to stop lynchings and the white women promised to bring the issue before their own organizations. The black women later prepared a statement of their major needs and grievances (pp. 461–467) which was presented to the white women's clubs. In 1920, through the efforts of the Commission on Interracial Cooperation (CIC) under the leadership of Dr. Will Alexander, four black guest speakers were invited to a conference of white Southern women to describe the needs of their people. While the first three speakers confined themselves to conventional statements of appreciation and good will, Charlotte Hawkins Brown electrified the meeting with her frank account of what it was like to suffer discrimination in trains and public conveyances (see pp. 467–472). The emotion-filled meeting ended with the 105 representatives of church and secular woman's organizations constituting themselves the Women's Council of the CIC and pledging themselves to grass-roots interracial work. The Women's Council, gradually growing in stature and importance, spearheaded this effort with a variety of organizational and educational activities. By 1929, 805 interracial county committees were functioning in the Southern states.

In 1930, at the initiative of the Women's Council, the Association of Southern Women for the Prevention of Lynching (ASWPL) was formed under the leadership of Jesse Daniel Ames, a businesswoman and suffragist from Texas (see pp. 472–477). Interracial conferences, local committees and the slow integration of state and national community organizations continued for several decades. Black and white women were in this respect ahead of their communities and their men, possibly because the common concerns of women for their homes and their children prevailed over prejudice and vested interests.

COOPERATION ON A COMMUNITY LEVEL

Athens, Ga., accredits its name by the fact that it is the seat of the University of Georgia, of the State Normal School and of the Lucy Cobb Seminary for girls. The latter was long under the charge of Mrs. M. A. Lipscomb, and Dr. Lipscomb was president of the University of Georgia. Mrs. Lipscomb is president of the Georgia State Federation of Women's Clubs and in a letter to the Athens *Banner* . . . she tells the story of a new and simple and beautiful effort on the part of the white and colored women of Athens to join in an act of sweet charity. . . .

A colored seamstress, Martha Holsey, was troubled because she could find no home where three colored orphans could be placed. There was not a charity that would undertake their care. She wanted a home for them in Athens, a place, also, where mothers, compelled to work out all day could leave their children protected and kept from the evil of the street. She talked it over with her own people, and then, timidly, she asked the counsel of several white women for whom she had sewed. Mrs. Lipscomb asked her if there was not a colored woman's club that could undertake to establish such a home. There was such a club, but they were too poor. She was told to go to the president of the Athens Woman's Club and present the case. She did so and made a good plea, and was told to look up a house for the purpose. The Woman's Club met and agreed to help. It is now provided for by their subscriptions, and the club is responsible. A nice, clean cottage is rented for a home, and a competent colored woman is put in charge. Mothers will leave their children there all day, and they will be given two good meals, kept from the streets, taught to "do things," and at night they will be taken to their homes. The mothers will pay a small sum monthly, and this will be supplemented by the Athens Woman's Club. Martha Holsey was happy, and a request came that some of the club women would speak at a mass meeting of the colored women interested in the work. So they went to the colored Baptist Church Sunday afternoon, told the story of the plan, promised their sympathy and help; and then the two colored ministers and Martha Holsey assured their cooperation and thanks. It is a simple story and touchingly sweet and Christian. How much better as a solution of the so-called race problem than grandfather clauses and disfranchisement, which only stir race hatred on both sides. May the movement grow!

Editorial, *The Independent*, Vol. 63, No. 3082
(December 26, 1907), pp. 1582–1583.

THE COLORED WOMEN'S STATEMENT TO THE WOMEN'S MISSIONARY COUNCIL, AMERICAN MISSIONARY ASSOCIATION

First of all, we wish to express our sincere gratification in the fact that race relations in the South have advanced to the place where the white women of the South are conscious of the part which colored women must play in any successful effort to adjust the unhappy conditions which have distressed the hearts of all lovers of right and justice, and dangerously threatened the common welfare and the safety of the Nation.

We are also keenly alive to the growing tendency to give a larger place to the influence of womanhood in the affairs of the Nation and to the increasing number of Southern white women whose vision includes the welfare of women of every race and condition; who desire to secure equal opportunities for development to all womanhood, and are determined to face the truth without flinching, and to give themselves to creating an enlightened sentiment among their own people, and establishing a new and better foundation for relations between white and colored women in the South.

We have for a long time been painfully conscious of the many unjust and humiliating practices of which colored women in the South have been the victims. There is not one of us who has not at various times and places been called upon to face experiences which are common to the women of our race. We, therefore, take this opportunity to call to the attention of white women certain conditions which affect colored women in their relations with white people, and which, if corrected, will go far toward decreasing friction, removing distrust and suspicion, and creating a better atmosphere in which to adjust the difficulties which always accompany human contacts.

I. CONDITIONS IN DOMESTIC SERVICE.

The most frequent and intimate contact of white and colored women is in domestic service. We, therefore, direct attention to—

1. Protection in white homes against
   (a) Unnecessary and preventable physical hardship incurred by working hours
   (b) Exposure to moral temptations
   (c) Undesirable housing conditions
2. We recommend
   (a) Definite regulation for hours and conditions of work
   (b) Sanitary, attractive, and wholesome rooming facilities
   (c) Closer attention to personal appearance,
   (d) Provision for and investigation of character of recreation

II. CHILD WELFARE.

The large burden of economic responsibility which falls upon many colored women results in their prolonged absence from home and the consequent neglect of the children of the homes. We direct your attention to—

1. Child Welfare.
   (a) Neglected homes (irregularity in food, clothing, conduct, training)
   (b) Truancy
   (c) Juvenile delinquency

We recommend

2. Welfare Activities
   (a) In Day Nurseries, Playgrounds and recreation centers
   (b) Home and school visitation
   (c) Probation Officers and Reform Schools

III. CONDITIONS OF TRAVEL.

Conditions under which Negroes travel at present are uncomfortable, at times hazardous, and unjust, and inevitably create race friction. To reduce this friction, and remove causes for just complaints from colored passengers, we call your attention to—

1. Seating accommodations on street cars
2. Unsanitary surroundings
   (a) at stations
   (b) on trains
3. Toilet facilities
   (a) at stations
   (b) on trains
4. Difficulties in securing
   (a) Tickets (waiting at ticket windows until all white passengers are served)
   (b) Pullman accommodations
   (c) Meals
5. Abuse of rights of colored passengers by train crew and white passengers
   (a) Occupying seats while passengers stand
   (b) Smoking

(c) Use of profane language

(d) Overcrowding

CORRECTIVE MEASURES

1. Steps be taken to secure equal accommodation in all public carriers and courteous treatment at the hands of street car and railway officials, for all passengers.

IV. EDUCATION

1. Better Educational Facilities

(a) Adequate accommodations for all Negro children of school age

(b) Vocational Training in all secondary schools.

(c) Improved rural schools—longer terms, suitable buildings

(d) Training Schools for teachers

(e) City and Rural High Schools

(f) Standard Colleges and Universities

(g) Adequate salaries for teachers

V. LYNCHING

1. We deplore lynching for any crime whatever, no matter by whom committed.

2. We believe that any person who commits a crime should have punishment meted out to him, but not without thorough investigation and trial by the courts. We further believe that the present safety of the country depends upon a just and fair trial for all persons, white and colored alike.

3. CORRECTIVE MEASURES

(a) We therefore urge such courage and foresight on the part of the officers of the law as will guarantee trials which will insure punishment of the guilty, and acquittal of the innocent.

(b) Further, we appeal to the white women

(i) To raise their voices in immediate protest when lynching or mob violence is threatened.

(ii) To encourage every effort to detect and punish the leaders and participants in mobs and riots.

> (iii) To encourage the white pulpit and press in creating a sentiment among the law-abiding citizens and outspoken condemnation of these forms of lawlessness.

VI. SUFFRAGE.

We believe that the ballot is the safe-guard of the Nation, and that every qualified citizen in the Nation should have the right to use it.

We believe that if there is ever to be any justice before the law, the Negro must have the right to exercise the franchise.

RECOMMENDATION

1. We ask therefore, that white women, for the protection of their homes as well as ours, sanction the ballot for all citizens.

PRESS

In the great majority of cases the white press of the South gives undue prominence to crime and the criminal element among Negroes to the neglect of the worthy and constructive efforts of law-abiding citizens. We feel that a large part of the friction and misunderstanding between the races is due to unjust, inflammatory, and misleading headlines in articles appearing in the daily papers.

RECOMMENDATION

We earnestly urge that white women include in their local community program a united effort to correct this evil and to secure greater attention to worthy efforts of Negro citizens.

In these articles, we are stating frankly and soberly what in our judgement, white women may do to correct the ills from which our race has so long suffered, and of which we as a race are perhaps more conscious than ever.

We recall how in the recent days of our nations's peril so many of us worked side by side for the safety of this land and the defense of the flag which is ours as it is yours. In that spirit of unselfishness and sacrifice we offer ourselves to serve again with you in any and every way that a courageous facing of duty may require as you undertake heroically this self-appointed task. We deeply appreciate the difficulties that lie before you, but as you undertake these things which are destined to bless us all, we pledge you our faith and loyalty in consecration to God, home, and country.

SIGNED:

Mrs. Charlotte Hawkins Brown
President of North Carolina Federation
of Colored Women.

Mrs. Marion B. Wilkinson
President South Carolina Federation
of Colored Women.

Miss Lucy C. Laney
Principal Haines Institute, Augusta, Ga.
President of City Federation of Colored
Women's Clubs, Augusta, Ga.

Mrs. Mary J. McCrorey
Chmn. Com. of Management,
Charlotte Branch, Y.W.C.A.

Mrs. Janie P. Barrett
President of Va. Federation
of Colored Women's Clubs

Mrs. Booker T. Washington
Honorary President, National Association of
Colored Women's Clubs

Mrs. R. R. Moton
Tuskegee Institute, Ala.

Mrs. John Hope
Dept. Neighborhood Works,
National Fed. C. W. Clubs

Mrs. M. L. Crosthwait
Registrar, Fisk University, Nashville, Tenn.

Mrs. Mary McLeod Bethune,
Principal Daytona N. & I. School for Negro Girls
President of the Southeastern Federation of
Colored Women's Clubs

Trevor Arnett Library, Atlanta University, Atlanta, Georgia.

SPEAKING UP FOR THE RACE AT MEMPHIS, TENNESSEE, OCTOBER 8, 1920

CHARLOTTE HAWKINS BROWN

❦ *There was apprehension among the white organizers of this precedent-shattering interracial meeting, lest the black visitors be embarrassed or insulted. Although the audience was seated in segregated sections, four seats in front of the auditorium had been reserved for the invited guests. When the four women—Mrs. Booker T. Washington, Mrs. Charlotte Hawkins Brown, Mrs. Russa R. Moton and Mrs. George E. Haynes—walked into the auditorium, all the white women rose in a spontaneous gesture of greeting. Then all joined in singing a hymn. Eyewitnesses later recalled that this small courtesy across the wide chasm of race hatred had occasioned deep emotion among the participants. It is typical of her consistent militancy that Charlotte Hawkins Brown saw it as her function to move from gestures to substance and prod her audience into a realization of what the reality of segregation meant to Blacks.*

I am very grateful for this opportunity. At Tuskegee when we met . . . I believe Mrs. Johnson and Mrs. Haskins both discovered that I was a little bit radical but at the least sincere. The things I uttered were the things I believed. You heard from Mrs. Washington yesterday afternoon, who represents the most conservative type of our Negro women in this country. And then you heard from Mrs. Moton directly and we all know what Dr. Moton stands for, and now you have heard from Mrs. Haynes. I, perhaps, represent a little different type than those in this particular. . . . I grew up in the City of Cambridge. It gave me an opportunity to study the white race in a way that I could never have studied them if I had remained in the South. . . . Having gone back into my native state and meeting what any colored woman meets, it took time to convince the white people in that particular section . . . that what I wanted for the boys and girls of my race was just a fair chance, not what they termed social equality. I did want those boys and girls trained in the right way. Having an opportunity to know the white people, I do not believe that today in North Carolina there is a single colored woman who has more friends than I have been able to get in Guilford County, where my school work is located. I think, my friends, that that one instance in itself proves that if we can find some point of contact, simply get close enough together to know each other, that it makes no difference from what section of the country we are, we can work out amicable relations.

I came to Memphis crushed and humiliated. I had been very optimistic. . . . But on my way to this conference, I went into the station at Greensboro and I told the man I was coming to this conference and that I had to be on the train overnight. I had just opened school that day, had been working hard all day and I needed a night's sleep. I wasn't going into that sleeper because I wanted to be with white people. Nine times out of ten, in taking a sleeper, I don't go anywhere near the dressing room. And so I took a sleeper just as I had taken one before and I said to the agent "Do you think it is all right to go on to Birmingham." He said, "Yes." I stayed in the sleeper, until I thought we were perhaps a few hours away from Birmingham. I had a premonition of trouble and I got out of my berth. I saw a young colored girl sitting in the car and I said, "We won't occupy two seats, I am going to sit beside you," so as I sat there, as we rode into Anniston, Ala. and while backing out, three or four young men began to walk up and down the aisle and by and by they gathered more and they began to stand at one corner and then at another and my heart began to fill up with fear. . . . Finally the group of three or four young men grew into eight and ten, then I counted twelve men. . . . One or two in the group were older men; they went first to the conductor and then to the porter. These twelve men came to look after two poor, colored women. Will you just put yourself in my place. Just be colored for a few moments, and see yourself sitting down in a seat, helpless, with twelve young white men sitting around. A young man leaned over and said, "We have wired ahead to have you taken off this train. Now, we give you your choice, to get off this car right away and go into the day coach, or be taken off." I said, "I don't want any trouble." He said, "You must get up and go or we will take you." I said, "Let me see the conductor for a moment." They said, "No." So, friends, not wishing to create a scene, wishing to get here, I said, "I want to get to that meeting, I want to tell those women that are gathered there that the woman whom you had asked to come here and talk on race relations had to go through such an experience." The leader of the crowd said, "Let's march" and these young men got in front of us and two or three behind and we were ushered in the colored day coach. Friends, I came here with a feeling of humiliation and I was so glad Mrs. Johnson didn't call on me yesterday. Last night I prayed and poured out my soul to my God, and I want to tell you that it was a struggle. . . .

And now, my friends, I want you to know that I do not think for a moment that those young men are in the majority. There is another thing, I don't know whether or not there are any women who were on that train, but the thing that grieved me most was that there were women in the car and there wasn't a dissenting voice. I want to tell you that I grew up without any prejudice. I am going to tell you something right now. Mrs. Haynes referred to it. The greatest struggle on the part of Dr. Washington and other leaders of the negro race in the South today was to keep prejudice away from our own souls. That is the very thing we are trying to fight. The younger people in our schools are getting to the place where they don't want to hear a member of your race preach. You hear the young people say, "I don't want any white man to preach to me." That is unfortunate for you, for us all. . . .

Friends. . . . I told you to begin with, that we have become a little bit discouraged. We have begun to feel that you are not, after all, interested in us and I am going still further. The negro women of the South lay everything that happens to the members of her race at the door of the Southern white woman. Just why I don't know but we all feel that you can control your men. We feel that so far as lynching is concerned that, if the white women would take hold of the situation, that lynching would be stopped. . . . I want to say to you, when you read in the paper where a colored man has insulted a white woman, just multiply that by one thousand and you have some idea of the number of colored women insulted by white men. . . .

There is nothing fast looking about me. And yet I can tell you that more than a hundred times in twenty years I have had to speak up and say, "Mister, you have missed your woman." I want to ask, my friends, that while you want to see the criminal who sets upon you punished, won't you help us, friends, to bring to justice the criminal in your race who is just as much criminal when he tramps on the womanhood of my race. I want you to know, my friends, that we are anxious to work with you to bring about a better citizenship.

The term "Mister" and "Mistress" has been referred to here. I do not want to give any more time to it. Two years ago, one of the editors in Greensboro said several nice things about the school and in an editorial he refrred to Mrs. Brown. He told me afterwards that numbers of white women called him up and censured him for referring to a negro women as "Mrs." The next time there was an article about Charlotte Hawkins Brown, and right on that page it said Louise McWhorter, bootlegging, and I said to the man, "Don't you think you should make a little difference between me and Louise McWhorter." He said, "Yes, but it is the policy of our paper not to put Mr. or Mrs. before the name of any colored person." So I said, "Will you make a compromise for the sake of the Negroes that are interested in the school?" I finally said, "If you will keep my name in the paper, won't you please put 'Principal' before it, so the negroes who are selling whisky will feel that you at least look upon those of us who are struggling with higher respect than those who are doing nothing at all."

I tell you that the fault of a great many of us, is with all the advancements of these past fifty years, you are still thinking of the negro in the terms of 1860. I have some idea of what bitter times the reconstruction days were. But we do not tell to our children the horrible stories of slavery that come down to us. I know that slavery in the U.S. may have been far more beneficient than in any other place but yet I know too that there were some horrible crimes committed against our people. But I say, you and I are not particularly concerned with reconstruction days. I should not have hatred or feeling against you because of things that happened in slavery, neither should you have things against me because of the days of reconstruction. If I refuse to tell the things my grandmother told me, aren't you willing to forget those horrible things of reconstruction and not pass them on to your children? You are not going to let me be bigger than you? We are trying to put back of us all of the things that have happened to us. We are trying to keep these things away from our children. . . .

The thing I want to ask you, the white women all over this country . . . is to put yourself in my place, and then . . . I want you as Christian women, to ask yourself, "What would Jesus do if he were in my place?" . . .

As Christian women, in the final analysis you are going to have to reach out for the same hand that I am reaching out for, but I know that the dear Lord will not receive it, if you are crushing me beneath your feet.

Commission on Interracial Cooperation Papers,
Trevor Arnett Library, Atlanta University.

HOW TO STOP LYNCHINGS: A DISCUSSION

✿ Black women had been fighting lynching for over forty years through organized effort (see pp. 205–215) when in 1930 the Association of Southern Women for the Prevention of Lynching was formed by white women. Five years later, when the meeting at Atlanta University took place, that organization had not yet reached its full stride. Its major contribution was the repudiation of the myth that lynchings were done in the defense of white womanhood. "We declare lynching an indefensible crime . . . hateful and hostile to every ideal of religion and humanity, debasing and degrading to every person involved. . . . We believe . . . public opinion has accepted too easily the claim of lynchers and mobsters that they were acting solely in defense of womanhood. In the light of facts, we dare no longer permit this claim to pass unchallenged. . . . We solemnly pledge ourselves to create a new public opinion in the South, which will not condone, for any reason whatever, acts of mobs or lynchers. . . ." So read their statement, to which they would eventually secure 40,000 signatures of white women in practically every county of the South. They also acted repeatedly and effectively on a local level to stop actual lynchings.

The debate below is a rare instance in which the behind-the-scenes efforts of black leaders in educating and influencing white leadership is recorded and preserved. It is of special interest also in revealing the militancy and astute tactics of well-known leaders whose formal and written statements and speeches often fail to reveal the very qualities which marked their leadership.

Participants in the discussion were Mrs. Mary McLeod Bethune; Mrs. Daisy Lampkin, NAACP field secretary; Mrs. Charlotte Hawkins Brown; Miss Nannie Burroughs and Mrs. Lugenia Hope. The white women were Mrs. Jesse D. Ames, Secretary of the ASWPL, Mrs. Lawrence and Mrs. Long.

FRIDAY, JANUARY 11, 1935, ATLANTA UNIVERSITY, MINUTES OF MEETING

Mrs. Ames reported on the meeting of the ASWPL which was held on January tenth.

Mrs. Bethune: I might express this on the part of the Negro people of the country. We think one of the most significant and outstanding things that have been done toward our redemption, for the thing we have been working toward, has been the work of this group of Southern women who have made this very fine bold and Christian declaration to the world as to their stand in regard to the situation. We feel that you have gone a long distance. I have been interpreting your expressions as you have been giving them. I have common sense enough to know that we have got to go step by step in order to get what we want. I think your organization has come a long distance to do what it has done. . . . When I was in New York they asked me to use my influence to get the Southern women to wholeheartedly get behind the endorsement of this anti-lynching bill.* I know

---

* In 1933, Senator Robert F. Wagner of New York and Senator Edward Costigan of Colorado co-sponsored a bill to make lynching a federal crime. Campaign efforts on behalf of the bill included petitions from state legislatures, professional people, 2800 white Southern college students and hundreds of thousands of ordinary citizens. A companion bill passed the House of Representatives, but a six-week-long filibuster by Southern Senators effectively killed the Wagner-Costigan bill. A similar effort had met with the same fate in 1922.

how happy they would have been if you had said in the papers this morning that you had given your full endorsement to this bill. But I think you have been cautious and wisely so. I do not want to throw overboard the good we have accomplished. I think it is going to take some time yet before our legislators and men in Congress can get the full interpretation of what we are trying to do down here in the South. I, for one, come again with my heart full, as full of appreciation as I can be for the step you have taken and the awakening you have given to the courageous, because of the daring stand taken by this group of women. I have only gratitude for what you have done.

Mrs. Lampkin: I can quite understand all you have said, and appreciate it. However, I do feel that the fact that 24,000 women who have signed a resolution would have had a great effect and I do believe it is true that you are not sufficiently organized to be able to defeat these senators from the Southern states if you ask them to vote for the Costigan-Wagner bill, but I do happen to know that they take new courage and they use it to their advantage when they can stand on the floor and say that the two strongest organizations of Southern white women did not endorse the Costigan-Wagner bill and the thing you have done in not endorsing it will do more to retard the passage of that bill than anything you might have done.

Mrs. Brown: I was born in the South and I have spent thirty-four years of my life here. I am just as appreciative as I can be. I endorse all Mrs. Bethune has said. I know you have gone along cautiously, and I know you have had to go cautiously, and I think you have done the thing you think is wisest and best, but on the other hand if we are ever to be free—I know the North—the step must be taken by Southern people. Southern women, you can do more with 24,000 signatures to bring about that freedom for the Negro race than a million from the North. . . . Congress is controlled by Southerners. . . . I would not have expected you to have done it if the South was not in the saddle, but I feel you women could have taken the step. I think you did what you think wisest and best, but in my own soul I think you missed a step.

Mrs. Lawrence: I represent one of those constituencies where some of those signatures have come from. Those signatures have come to the first proposition. It is not what we want. We simply face some facts. Those signatures are not a constituency we could swing behind legislation.

Mrs. Hope: Honestly, my heart is so sick and so weak over it that I don't know whether I can say anything. I do think the stand that the Southern women took will retard everything. You may not think so, but it will hold back our interracial work and everything else in the South. Because we have just banked so much on it. . . . it is going to be so difficult for us to help you explain.

Mrs. Ames: One thing we have felt is that after we take the position we do, after discussion and consideration, we don't defend our position because we feel it is as far as we could go. I am sure the white women will agree with me when I say, don't try to defend us.

Miss Burroughs: We are going to have the bill passed against lynching. All of us are going to settle that in our minds. I am sure there will be a great many people seriously disappointed that perhaps a very definite stand was not taken on the present bill. There is that disappointment. There is nothing we can do to help in that matter, in this matter of disappointment at this time. There is left, however, just a ray of hope: that the women did leave the door open and that there is every indication that they are going to do what should be done about it. When we are not a part of an organization, I don't know how much influence we can have after a position has been taken. We can express ourselves—disappointment or satisfaction—but here is a group of people in an organization proceeding as they think they can proceed, as they think wisest and best for them to proceed. Now that is the privilege of an organization. You see we will have to accept things as they are and not as we would have them. We would like to have Heaven here, but I am glad it is a long way off so we can have some thrill in getting there. We would like to have this thing but I am going to be very frank with you. I am sorry, but I am not disappointed. I did not think it was going to be done. I did not think this organization was going to endorse this Costigan-Wagner bill. . . . There isn't any use in my telling you in tears that I am so disappointed, because I did not expect you to do it.

I come back to my first statement and that is they are going to pass a bill against lynching in the United States. That is if we are going to build a civilized nation. The people in this generation who are working at it are going to help pass that bill. Women who live in the midst of these trials and tribulations are going to have a great deal of influence and direct responsibility for having passed that bill. If I did not think that I would take my hat and walk out this morning. But I do know that in organization work like this and in building a civilization like the one we are building you take the long-range view of everything, and in passing laws now, particularly in the United States when we have passed so many rotten laws, they won't be worth the paper on which they are written. . . . The words, "superiority" and "supremacy" . . . are the only words that express what will be understood by the rank and file of people who live where lynchings take place. Something will have to be done . . . we still have to carry on campaigns of education. We cannot do it in any possible other way. Anything that is as old as that, you cannot do anything with it. It is in the blood of the nation. It is not any superficial thing—that attitude is in the blood of the nation and we have got to educate it out. . . . It is very difficult and it is very long. That is what will have to take place. As long as those campaigns of education are going on there is hope. . . . Somebody spoke of the Negro voting the democratic ticket in the hope that these things would be changed. I don't think any Negro outside of the asylum voted that ticket thinking the democratic party was going to bring the millenium. They did not vote it because they thought the bill against lynching would be passed. It was an economic question with the colored people just as it was with the white people. They thought they were going to get more to eat. They were not thinking of getting killed, but rather of getting filled. The thing that I leave as a final statement for all this rambling is that I think now—I am not a member of that Association. I am going to be a member of it some of these days. But I think for the campaign of education—while we are carrying it on—it would not be a bad idea for the organization to . . . prepare the kind of bill which might be passed and give us a sample of what this bill should contain to make it lynch-proof so far as it is humanly possible. . . . That would be a tremendous service rendered to us in this country. . . .

Mrs. Long: You have been doing your very best to educate the group. . . . We further realize that our women can go so far until they have converted the men and then they can go no further. . . . I believe if you move and make yourself a little more courageous, . . . having the men to understand the necessity of making our country Christian and the only way we can do it is to wipe out this dreadful taking of human life.

Papers of the Association of Southern Women to Prevent Lynching,
Trevor Arnett Library, Atlanta University.

INSIDE A WHITE ORGANIZATION: YOUNG WOMEN'S CHRISTIAN ASSOCIATION

❦ *In 1893, the first segregated colored YWCA branch was chartered in Dayton, Ohio. Segregated locals flourished in other Northern cities and, in the North and the South, Negro women joined the "Y" as individuals.*

In 1906, when the national YWCA was organized, there

were no Negro branches in the South. Through the initiative of the white reformer, Grace Dodge, the race issue was brought before an Asheville, North Carolina, student conference. The National Board, accommodating to the prejudices of its Southern members and hoping to avoid the attendance of Negro delegates from Southern locals at national conventions, set up segregated Negro branches which were considered "subsidiaries" to the local white branch (see protest of Negro leaders, p. 480). In 1913, Eva Bowles was appointed as the first colored YWCA Secretary. This "experimental appointment" was followed in 1915 by the first interracial conference ever held in the South. This conference set up a biracial committee to help promote organization among colored women and launched a leadership training program. This effort was spurred during World War I, when YWCA work in military camps was extended to colored soldiers. Black women entered YWCA work on a large scale, leading to an increase in colored branches from 16 in 1915 to 49 in 1920, with a corresponding rise in staff—from 9 paid local workers to 86, from one national Secretary to 12.

The first interracial clubs were organized among working girls in 1919. Shortly thereafter, due to the patient but persistent work of Eva Bowles and the grass-roots leadership of Southern women like Lugenia Hope and Charlotte Hawkins Brown, the demand that black women be integrated into the YWCA on the basis of full equality was raised publicly (pp. 479–484). Eva Bowles' Annual Reports (pp. 484–488) offer an unusual insight into the painstaking, pioneering work done by black women inside this predominantly white organization to combat white racism, to advance understanding of the needs and aspirations of Blacks and to assert their right to control over their own branches and activities. The slow but distinct progress of the YWCA on the racial issue is marked by the organization's growing emphasis on interracial work. During the Depression years the "Y" worked for anti-lynching legislation. After World

War II, it endorsed the establishment of the Fair Employment Practices Commission (FEPC), full integration in the armed forces and in industry and housing. It took until 1946 for the national convention to vote an "interracial charter" and to commit the organization to full integration of black women into the "mainstream of association life." This resolution was implemented by carefully planned educational work, leadership training and staff policy. This advance toward sisterhood at a snail's pace can be better evaluated by reading the personal account of Anna Arnold Hedgeman's experiences (pp. 489–497). It must also be seen in the perspective of comparing it with the much less successful efforts of other women's and community organizations.

EVA BOWLES CALLS FOR ACTION

EVA BOWLES TO [MRS. JOHN HOPE OF ATLANTA, GEORGIA]
Brooklyn, January 25, 1920

'My dear good friend'
Just a little personal note to tell you how deeply grateful I am to you and the other leading colored women of the country for your loyalty to the movement and your personal loyalty to me. It was a great balm at just the right time and meant *everything*.

I waited until I had it from the proper sources not by way of spoken word but *written* that there would be no white women appointed as secretary for the colored student work. In the process of finding out these facts I found out to my disappointment that our white women do not properly appreciate the strength of our colored women throughout the country. We must face this job of letting them understand it better. It will take time of course but what is the use of a few of us paid workers to do things. We want our own colored women to be able to help make policies.* It is our job to let our colored women more clearly see the intricate situations and let them think from actual knowledge of facts.

Am hoping to arrange a conference soon in order to set forth the association principles as they are. Hope the strongest women will attend.

Another thing—our colored secretaries from headquarters must not be longer excluded from Southern soil. We have no desire of pushing things any faster than communities will allow but we do have resources and knowledge of things that will be helpful and that are necessary to ideal growth.

We have no fair way of being interpreted unless the women themselves know us.

Let it be known far and wide, I have no thought but the understanding of the movement for us as well as others and personally can never bring this to pass without unqualified loyalty of our colored women and staff of workers. It will be thwarted if we allow personal things to enter. We must eliminate the personal.

I am with faith in God and my colored women willing to help bring about the real association spirit in action as well as words.

With love to you & Mr. H.

Eva D. Bowles

Neighborhood Union Papers of the Negro Collection,
Trevor Arnett Library, Atlanta University.

WHAT THE COLORED WOMEN ARE ASKING OF THE Y. W. C. A.

The Colored Woman is asking for representation on the National Board of the Y. W. C. A.

* The writer here refers to the situation within the YWCA, in which a handful of paid organizers carried responsibility for "colored work" and maintained contact with the white organization while the majority of black members was isolated in segregated branches.

(a) Because the Colored woman has no representation except the employed worker who can not represent us as a volunteer worker could.

(b) Because the time has come when no person can interpret the needs and desires of Colored people as well as a Colored person. The following organizations similarly planned and operating have already realized this point and met it. The International Committee of the Y. M. C. A. which has two Colored members and the National Urban League. In fact the National Board of the Y. W. C. A. is the only National organization working among Negroes that does not recognize this principle.

We are asking that in all work affecting Colored people, full recognition of leadership be given Colored women because we wish to develop initiative and leadership in our own group.

We are asking that the supervision of Colored work be from National headquarters rather than from Field headquarters.

(a) Because all of the Y. W. C. A. work that we have known has been directed from the National Headquarters, and there is no question as to its success. There was a group of strong Colored women at Headquarters who so wonderfully developed the work during the war and [are] sure they could carry this work on a few more years until we can recover from that terrible period of unrest. The country is not settled and we have not had time to think out very carefully the future.

(b) There is an awakening to the responsibility that rests on the womanhood of both races, in this section of our country. A very small group of white women have taken a forward step and these women will find it very difficult to bring their people to the point where they are willing to regard the Colored group as a group among groups (and the Colored women know that our group is much more skeptical about white women than the world knows anything about). Now under these conditions we desire this interracial relationship to grow normally and not to be forced. For while we believe in cooperation between the races we do know that it is impracticable and unwise for our white women to select our leaders or direct our activities. For they know only the individual Colored woman and must depend absolutely on her to do the thinking and directing; and this is too much power for any one person and can only cause friction and upset the interracial cooperation for which we are now working so earnestly.

We are asking to be permitted to form independent organizations whenever the Branch relationship is not desirable for any reason whatever, or where there is no Central Association.—

Because we feel that it is not fair to the Colored group to refer to the historical fact "that the Y. W. C. A. never in any place or in any part of its work can go faster than the people of the community will permit." And at present this means to the Colored womanhood of this country—you can have no Association but you may become a branch if the white women in your community will permit. This is true in Little Rock. The Colored women there are waiting for the white women to have a change of heart. The Colored women . . . could not be recognized by the Association until the white women organized. Is this fair—is this Christian? Is this as Christ would have it? . . .

We recommend that the policy of the Association with reference to Colored work be reversed and Colored committees appoint their own representatives as secretaries and other officers since white women north or south are not acquainted with the Colored woman and her problems.

We recommend two probable working plans for the Y. M. C. A.:

1. (a) Supervision from Headquarters in New York
   (b) Colored Advisory committee
   (c) Local interracial advisory committee
   (d) For direction of student work from Colored Bureau in New York

(e) Central Association's responsibility for salary of secretary of Colored work be entirely optional, then there would grow up between the races a very much more healthy and lasting relationship

2. If Field supervision is to obtain we ask:
   (a) For Colored representation on the Field Committee which is the lawmaking body
   (b) Colored committee from within the Field
   (c) Colored representation on the Local Board of Directors
   (d) If our work is to be directed from the Field we recommend that we have Colored secretaries in all of the Departments at Field Headquarters in order that our secretaries be trained to do the Association work
   (e) For the privilege of organizing Y. W. C. A. work where the Central Association for any reason is unable or refuses to take our work on, or where there is no Central Association
   (f) That Colored Secretaries be selected by Colored Committee subject to approval of the Board of Directors of Local Association
   (g) For direction of student work from Colored Bureau in New York

We see nothing for the Y. W. C. A. as a Christian organization in this age of progress to do but to accept either one of these two policies.

YWCA Manuscript, Neighborhood Union Papers,
Trevor Arnett Library, Atlanta University.

TOO MUCH PATERNALISM IN "Y's"

There is more than a remote possibility that the good which Colored branches of the Y.M.C.A. and of the Y.W.C.A. may be in position to achieve will be interfered with by a too strict and too objectionable supervision over activities that ought to be directed by Colored workers.

Much as we would like to disguise the fact that the Y.M.C.A. and Y.W.C.A. movement among Colored people is a form of segregation, we are forced to admit that the funds contributed by white philanthropists to aid in maintaining Colored branches are contributed to preclude the possibility of Colored men and women desiring to gain admission and membership in the white branches.

If the Colored branches are to be, as they are, in the final analysis, segregated institutions, then Colored men and women should direct and control them, something they do not now do.

It is true that all boards of managers for Colored branches are composed of Colored men, and of Colored women, but these have their limitations. They function only up to the point the whites permit them to function. They may engage a secretary, and they may, theoretically, have the power of removing a secretary, if he fails, in their estimation, to make good, but . . . the people who must first be consulted before a Colored board of managers can act, is their white overseers associated with the white branches.

Editorial, The Cleveland, Ohio *Advocate*, May 1, 1920.

REPORTS BY THE SECRETARY FOR COLORED WORK

EVA BOWLES

ANNUAL REPORT—1922

. . . Our Committees on Colored Work are just developing . . . I believe that the Y.W.C.A. has a great share in proving that democracy is not a failure and that Christianity is not mockery. Much will depend upon our national white and Colored leadership. This year has proven the futility of an understanding if white people interpret colored people to white people. *Colored people are their own best interpreters.* It has been my experience . . . that if things don't go well inevitably the blame is placed on the attitude of the colored worker. I grant that she is not free from blame, but the white worker concerned should bear her share of the responsibility in this as in everything else. As we look back over the past, our greatest strength as colored women has been our patient endurance, even though at times it has almost been worn threadbare. As an individual I have emerged from an almost overwhelming pressure with determination to think only the best, to work only for the best and to *expect* only the best. I shall endeavor to try and develop this spirit in our colored leadership. We cannot fail—we can only be retarded by an unwillingness to be an association which in the true sense is interracial.

JANUARY 1924—ARTICLE IN *The Woman's Press*

For some years the City Department of the National Board has been experimenting and practically working out a plan whereby the Y.W.C.A. in cities could function as an interracial movement. It has endeavored to develop a Y.W.C.A. among colored women and girls and not a colored Y.W.C.A. These years have been years of caution and patience. . . .

The management of the branches is vested in colored women who qualify for the Committee of Management. In ideal relationship each committee of the branch develops a working relationship with the corresponding committee of the Central Association. . . . Whether we like to acknowledge it or not we realize that there is racial prejudice. We like to express it with regard to a Christian nation as lack of understanding. The fact that there is prejudice often causes natural relationships to be strained and in some instances to be impossible. Where there is understanding and where the situation is more normal, the Chairman of the Committee of Management is a member of the Board of Directors. This condition exists in 8 of our Northern cities. Of course this is an impossibility in those sections of the country where great barriers arise between the race and where tradition and custom will not permit this. We have attempted to form an extra committee which we believe can help to bring about happy relationships and also help the growth of racial understanding. . . . This is the Committee on Colored Work.

❦ *This interracial committee in fact became a buffer between the colored branch and the white leadership. It coordinated the work of colored branches and interpreted it to the white leadership.*

ANNUAL REPORT—DECEMBER 1924

The Committee on Colored Work needs to be given considerable attention. As it appears now . . . it either does not function at all or it takes upon itself the managing of the branch, thus stunting the initiative of the colored women.

I still feel that there should be a colored and white group that learn together things that are of an inter-racial significance, but there is a possibility that the time may come when it would be differently placed in our whole organizational scheme. . . .

Because of the slowly awakening social activities within each community were there is a large population of Negroes *can* we successfully organize a woman's movement which is an inter-racial one until some inter-racial consciousness is already working on the whole situation?

ANNUAL REPORT—1925

. . . Although we theorize as to working principles in our cities, we find three stages of developments: In some we still find the colored group being patronized and subsidized by the white association; in other Associations there is a conscious attempt at inter-racial cooperation; while in a few there are natural contacts of women and girls without race consciousness. In some associations all three degrees of development may be observed. . . .

As a movement we have pioneered in inter-racial committees; they of course must continue, for much good has already come because of them and much more will necessarily follow. At the same time we cannot afford to keep snugly within the realm of discussion; there must be some actual and practical means of working together. The group discussion is good, but actual contact in a project is better.

I am more than ever convinced that emphasis must be placed on co-responsibility of white and colored workers. . . .

ANNUAL REPORT—1926

. . . Three months of the past year have been devoted to the only real vacation that I have enjoyed since becoming a member of the National staff. Most positions and work within our movement have their natural setting, adequate salaries, vacations and so forth which come in the general course of affairs. The work that it has been my privilege to attempt in this respect has been different until quite recently. Few can realize what it means to live a racial life at the same time to be "forevermore" realizing you are an inter-racial problem, at the same time being committed to promote the Association movement and still be just a human being. Thanks to an inherited health and a will to succeed I was carried over to a vacation of escape and relief from all these things without a collapse. I'm glad that it will not be necessary for another colored woman to have such an experience, for we are apparently now at a place where to return to such inequalities as have existed would be taking backward steps. I'm glad to be renewed not only in health, but spirit. . . .

Out of our experience I feel that we can authoritatively announce that *organization of work among colored people depends on inter-racial readiness*. It is astonishing when we realize that practically none of the cities which have been organized on this basis have been lost. We do have concrete illustrations that where this is not done we have no real basis for existence and there is little help that can be given. . . .

Having gone thus far we now face the need for searching for next best. In my opinion we must continue the philosophy of *finding the way together*. There is a question in my mind on how far we can go together until we individually have arrived . . . to the place of individual responsibility. . . .

Our real inter-racial progress is the byproduct of working together with women on something other than race. Not until then can we arrive into a natural state of living together. We are encouraged that this is happening in spots and we feel sure that time and patience will work wonders.

ANNUAL REPORT—1930

. . . The Y.W.C.A. was a pioneer in race relations between American Negro women and other women in America. The fact that the women took the initiative in this nebulous realm so early has been a stimulus for others to band together along this line. The Y.W.C.A. began to be articulate with a simple slogan . . . "We want the same things for the colored girl that we want for the white girl." This carried us to the war period when opportunity was given to demonstrate it through the blessings of the War Work Fund. Out of this period we emerged into the annunciation of our first principles: "We go as far as both the Negroes and whites are agreed to go together", which by the way was our only basic principles found up to the present time. This is a simple statement. Like other simple, fundamental statements, individuals attempt to evade its real significance. . . .

The American Negro wants nothing more or less than to be included for what he really is and not to be excluded upon the artificial basis of so-called race inferiority. He desires that no opportunity be denied him because of his color.

YWCA Manuscripts, Sophia Smith Collection,
Smith College, Northhampton, Massachusetts.

REMINISCENCES OF A YWCA WORKER

ANNA ARNOLD HEDGEMAN

❦ Anna Arnold Hedgeman was born in Marshall-town, Iowa. She earned her B.A. at Hamline University (St. Paul, Minnesota) in 1922 and was awarded the L.H.D. from the same institution in 1948. She also studied at the University of Minnesota and the New School for Social Research. After teaching school in Mississippi, she did YWCA work from 1924 to 1941. She married Merritt A. Hedgeman in 1933. She was executive director of the National Council for a Permanent Fair Employment Practices Committee (1944–1948) and Dean of women at Howard University (1946). Her distinguished career as a federal and local administrator includes the following: assistant to Oscar R. Ewing, administrator of the Federal Security Agency (1949–1953); member of Mayor Robert F. Wagner's cabinet in New York City in charge of liaison of eight city departments (1954–1958); member of the National Advisory Council of the Department of Health, Education and Welfare. She also served as editor and columnist of the New York Age from 1958–1961 and was and continues to be active in numerous political, civic and religious organizations.

During my college days I had worked as a volunteer with the YWCA. A white friend who knew this suggested that I . . . apply for work with the Association. . . . I was offered a number of opportunities in the North and finally accepted a position with the YWCA in Springfield, Ohio. Here I met the sugar-coated segregated pattern of social work and housing in the North. I would, if hired, service a "neighborhood" and, of course, it was important that the facilities of the YWCA be close to the people it serviced. In the North we didn't call this separate branch the "Negro" branch publicly.

We named the branch for the street on which it was located. The branch did not have a gymnasium, swimming pool, or cafeteria, nor an adequate staff. The Negro executive would be expected to service young people, industrial and business workers, adult committees, and membership. She would, also, raise funds and interpret the Christian fellowship to the Negro community. (In fairness to the history of the YWCA, it must be said that the organization was in the forefront by even hiring Negro executives.)

The first week of my employment in such a Negro branch in the fall of 1924 was one of appalled discovery of Northern segregation. I found, for example, that even as a professional worker, I could not eat in the cafeteria of the Central Association. The young people I supervised could not use the swimming pool or the gymnasium in the Central building. (During that first week a Negro minister walked into a drug store of this mid-western city, bought some aspirin, and then asked the clerk at the soda fountain for a glass of water with which to take the tablet. The clerk handed him the water, watched him drink it with the pill, and then, in the minister's presence, broke the glass.)

The Negro youngsters who came for activities were bitter about the restrictions within the Association and within the town. I was expected to build a fellowship of women and girls committed to the development of a Christian community, yet there were no tools of the spirit in the relationships beween Negro and white youth. Only a few individuals in the white and Negro community believed in each other or were honest with each other.

By this time I was grateful for my Mississippi experience and for all that I had learned from the teachers there of how to give Negro children faith and confidence in themselves in spite of discrimination and segregation. . . .

As executive of the YWCA Negro branch in Springfield, I was much in demand for lectures on race relations, but I found such lectures difficult, for there WERE no relations. The adults to whom I spoke were usually good Christian white people, who thought of themselves as "liberal" if they invited a Negro speaker to their meetings. It was difficult for me to know how and where to begin for it was obvious that they did not understand this Jesus whom they quoted so lavishly in the prayers preceding my speech. Their image of the Negro always emerged clearly in the question period following my speech and their questions gave me nightmares. The first was always "What do Negroes want?" It did not occur to them that the question itself was an insult. I lashed out at them with the bitterness and venom born of Mississippi and, now, the Midwest and they loved it, in a way, for it relieved them of their shame for a moment, even as it purged me.

It was in this community that I recognized fully that "separate" meant inferior, despised and unequal. . . . Our Negro committee went to the Central board of directors and put the issues squarely: "As a part of the fellowship of the Young Women's Christian Association, we request that all facilities be open to all members of the fellowship. We believe that it is not sound spiritually for the fellowship to be separated on the basis of color." . . .

The Board reviewed our request and reported: "The Community Chest will not give us funds for capital investment. The community itself is not ready yet to open up the facilities of the Central Association. We are, however, making progress in understanding and we ask for the patience of the branch leadership as they interpret this to the Negro community."

Springfield's Negro women leaders were furious but helpless. Should we withdraw from the Association? Was it wrong to accept the unequal facilities offered our young people? . . . I was reminded of the teachers of Mississippi and of the young people there whom I had assured of opportunity in the North. Were there no allies anywhere? . . .

I contacted the national YWCA and requested an opportunity to work in the East. . . .

My new job was the executive directorship of a Negro "Y" branch in Jersey City. The patterns in this New Jersey community were slightly different, for Negroes were represented on all the committees of the YWCA and there were a few Negro teachers in the public schools.

Soon after I arrived the Central Association decided to construct an expensive new building to meet the "Y's" growing needs. Our Negro branch board members realized that this might be the time to press for a merger of our "neighborhood" fellowship with the total Association. Several white staff and board members joined us in urging consideration of the idea, but the white board members as a whole decided that the community was not ready for such a "drastic" step. To salve their own consciences, they asked "Don't you really think Negro young people are happier among themselves?" "How could any intelligent young Negro be happy?" I asked. No one answered me. . . .

When the whole Association moved into the new building, matters finally came to a head, for there was no excuse for a separate Negro branch a few blocks away from this new, modern, and well-equipped building. To add insult to injury, the separate branch now offered to Negroes was the old building which the Association found inadequate for the white fellowship. Again came the same old question. Should we take the old building since it was larger than our former one or should we pull out of the Association and establish our own Christian community center? The realities were brutal. Middle-class Negroes in Jersey City could not financially support such an enterprise and the rank and file Negroes were barely existing on the low wages paid them in domestic and laundry service. The husbands and boyfriends of many of these Negro women, regardless of their educational qualifications, were carrying bags in Pennsylvania Station or running on the road as Pullman porters. . . .

More and more I was conscious of the continued pattern of segregation and discrimination. The difference between the North and South was not a difference in basic philosophy. In the South the weapon was a meat axe; in the North, a stiletto. Both are lethal weapons. It was a long time before

I knew that they are as lethal to the wielders as to the victims. . . .

I felt that I had no choice but to reject all white people. Even my hometown church no longer belonged to me. Beyond this personal reflection was the knowledge, born out of experience, that no Negro could expect any white person to love, respect and honor any people except white people. . . .

❦ *After several years as a staff worker in the Harlem YWCA, Anna Hedgeman began to work in Brooklyn in 1938.*

The Central YWCA of Brooklyn was located in a large, well-equipped building, while the Negro Club, Ashland Place Branch, was in an unattractive, poorly maintained clubroom-residence operation in a former brownstone residence. Approximately four blocks separated these two buildings. There was no Negro neighborhood in the immediate vicinity of the Negro branch. It reminded me sharply of the big houses of Southern white folks and the shacks of Southern Negroes. . . .

The white women of Brooklyn had "inherited" the association from their mothers and grandmothers. Most of them were "Old Brooklyn," with the same overtones as "Old Philadelphia," and I knew what to expect. They were well trained and many of them were wealthy. They were kindly in intent but were disturbed by all of the "newcomers," whether immigrants from abroad or Negroes from Harlem or the South. They were class conscious, and even the white professional help was treated more like maids than professional people. . . .

The Negro members of the branch Board were "Old Brooklyn" too. Some had been born in Brooklyn; others had been born in New England but had lived in Brooklyn long before the "influx" of Southern Negroes. These white and Negro women of "Old Brooklyn" had worked together for nearly twenty-five years, and shared a common gentility and determination to maintain the status quo.

As the new executive I faced two other difficult elements. The first was the newcomer. He came from anywhere and saw in Brooklyn a chance for more living space, better schools and lower rent. . . . Job and educational discrimination had previously kept him from preparing for many fields, and roomers were the main source of additional income.

The other difficult element in the Brooklyn situation were the young Negro women, the most articulate of whom were in the Business and Professional Women's Club. Actually these girls were for the most part college students, for business opportunities were rare. . . . Very few worked even in city government. . . .

They developed one project because the local ten-cent store refused to hire any Negro clerks. . . . We tried to negotiate the matter with the manager and were told that he would not be in for a couple of weeks. At the end of the two-week period the manager refused to talk with us unless we explained in detail to his secretary the purpose of such a meeting. We finally suggested to the secretary that we would like to talk about work opportunities for Negroes. We were promised an answer two days later and were not surprised when the management again refused to see us.

The young women were discouraged and after some discussion we decided that we would form a picket line in front of the store. This meant that I had to be present each day in order to be sure that the girls were protected if any negative reaction developed. The older Negro Board members of the YWCA were as disturbed as the whites were over this development, for the sight of their Executive Director leading a picket line was not their idea of suitable leadership for the young people of the community. In any case, our picket line did not achieve the desired results. We still could not secure an appointment with the manager . . .

Shortly after this experience, some of the college students came to our club meeting with an announcement which had appeared on the bulletin board at Brooklyn College. The announcement read, "College students may secure clerkships in local department stores during the Christmas holidays."

When I asked, "Have you applied?" one student answered cynically, "Mrs. H., be your age, you know they won't take us." Again I asked, "Have you applied?" After much discussion we agreed that personnel officers of the stores must be given an opportunity to meet personable, qualified Negroes who could easily serve as clerks. Reluctantly, the students agreed to apply to the personnel divisions of several Brooklyn department stores. We held a rehearsal and planned the interviews. I knew that these young people would probably be informed that they could expect notification when vacancies for maids occurred in the establishments and I asked the girls what their responses would be if they were so informed. As I had expected, one of the girls flared immediately and said, "I will tell him at once that we are not interested in menial jobs." "No you won't," I replied, "those maid jobs are important. Many Negroes have not had your educational opportunity and those jobs have been much better for some women than the domestic jobs open to them." We rehearsed that they would say something like this to the personnel director: "Mr. ——, we have heard that maids' jobs here are excellent, but we would like to be clerks." . . .

When the girls returned from their first interview they reported the amazement, embarrassment and confusion of the manager. They also said, "We told you we wouldn't get the job."

Shortly after this series of interviews with department store personnel, Mrs. Allen Knight Chalmers, the white chairman of the Race Relations Committee of the Federation of Protestant Churches, called with Mrs. Nora Jiles Hill, the Negro vice chairman, to ask me to speak to the Committee about white-collar opportunities for young Negroes. It occurred to me that our young college students could report their department store experience to these women and be much more impressive than any speech I could make. Three of the girls reported their experiences to this very powerful group of New York City Church women. When they had finished their account of their visits to the personnel managers of some of the most influential department stores in Brooklyn, there wasn't a dry eye in the room. One member of the Committee commented to me, "They are so young and so poised, and I found myself thinking of my own children who are about their ages."

The church women were so impressed that they worked out a plan of action and decided to visit the same personnel managers and others in the city. They asked me whether they should take a mixed delegation of Negro and white women or whether the delegation should be all white. I explained that the managers of these stores needed to see white and Negro women coming together to discuss the problem of fair employment opportunity for all people. Their visits, too, were unsuccessful and the resultant indignation prompted another strategy conference. The women decided that since negotiation had not proved fruitful, economic pressure might be useful. They wrote on their monthly bills, "We expect to see Negro clerks among the other clerks in our stores. As Christians we must patronize those stores which respect all human beings." Many of these church women had large charge accounts and the stores began to take notice.

As a result of this campaign, which we augmented by the work of Robert J. Elzy, director of the Brooklyn Urban League, Fred Turner of the local NAACP and other organizations, Negro clerks were employed by many of the department stores in the city. . . .

Our Negro branch of the YWCA was also concerned about practices within the Association itself. . . . A study of our general election practices revealed that many of the Board members were older women and the voice of youth was seldom heard. In addition, the membership had no opportunity to propose names for the slate of officers at each annual election. . . .

Growing expressions of interest on the part of the membership, finally, made it necessary for the nominating committee to present a ballot which included representation from the variety of groups within the Negro branch. Encouraged by this representation on the ballot, the young business and industrial workers electioneered vigorously for their own nominees and for women whom they believed were sympathetic to changes in committee personnel and branch policy. Some of the Negro Board members disapproved of such activity, calling it undignified, but the majority of the members were thrilled with the new democratic approach. When it seemed likely that the branch chairman of seventeen years might lose the election, my executive sent for me.

I was reminded again of the ways in which Negro leadership is so often selected by white people outside of the Negro community, for my executive said, "The president of the General Board does not wish a change in Negro branch leadership this year." I answered, "Branch members have been discussing this election for months. They are determined to choose their own leadership. The president cannot make a decision about their free election or in any way determine the results." My executive answered, "I am sorry you feel this way."

When the election was over, and a combination of old and new leadership installed, I wrote my resignation as executive director of the Negro branch. A majority of the Negro Board members asked me to reconsider, but after reflection I wrote my "white paper" and presented it to the Board, explaining that my leadership could not bring "wholeness" to the branch because I had become a symbol of revolt.

Anna Arnold Hedgeman, *The Trumpet Sounds: A Memoir of Negro Leadership* (New York: Holt, Rinehart and Winston, 1964). Copyright A.A. Hedgeman, pp. 30–35, 38–39, 43, 72–79.

GRASS-ROOTS WORK

❦ *The partial record of the organizing work of black women in Atlanta in the following selections provides evidence of the continuity and strength of grass-roots or-*

ganization in the black community. In its way The Neighborhood Union is as atypical as is Hull House in Chicago of the organizational work of white women: both represent an unusual achievement under the leadership of an unusual woman. Yet in a sense, the Neighborhood Union is quite representative. Mrs. Lugenia Hope of Atlanta has a counterpart in Janie Edna Hunter and her settlement house in Cleveland, Janie Porter Barret and her school for delinquent girls in Virginia, Victoria Earle Matthews and her White Rose Mission in New York. What is particularly interesting about the Atlanta material is that it records continuous social service effort from 1908 to the present day.

While the presence of a group of educated, middle-class black women centered in the college community undoubtedly contributed to sustaining this organizational effort and to the professional quality of much of the work, it is noteworthy that the large number of block leaders and volunteer campaign captains represent the general community. The Neighborhood Union started out with the concept of "servicing the poor," but turned into an instrument for self-help and a training ground for grass-roots leadership. The Vine City Foundation is entirely made up of and led by working-class and poor people living in the slum ghetto.

It should be remembered that this record of grass-roots organization could be duplicated for most urban black communities and for many rural areas.

PLAN OF WORK
ATLANTA COLORED WOMEN'S WAR COUNCIL

1. Division of city into nine zones, covering colored districts of Atlanta.
2. Zones sub-divided into Neighborhood units.
3. Each Neighborhood unit to organize for community bet-

terment. The following are some of the committees to be thoroughly worked out in each Zone.

1. Educational Department
2. Protection of our Girls
   (a) To organize Patriotic Leagues
   (b) To inject into every girls' club the spirit of the Patriotic League
3. Conservation of food—with the garden feature
4. Industrial Department
5. Sanitation. Police Protection. Street Lights
6. Suppression of Liquor
7. Community Entertainment   Including list of social and church entertainments to which the soldiers might be invited.
8. Camp Entertainment   Co-operation with the Men's Committee in supplying entertainers at the Camp.
9. The Saturday and Sunday Dinner Committee
10. Boarding and Lodging Houses for the visiting friends and relatives of soldiers
11. Committee to assist at the Hostess House

WORK DONE

A written report was made on the need of lights and police protection and a definite request made. But we have secured no relief as yet in either particular.

We divided the city into nine Zones, and organized some of the Zones. As a result of this organization, when we called for workers for the Y.M.C.A. rally, we had a committee of over five hundred women. These people went through their zones from house to house collecting the pennies, nickels, and dimes, so that when the day's work was over $1800.00 had been collected. It may be well to explain why this War Committee worked for the Y.M.C.A. We are a home loving people, we therefore have almost no first class restaurants and club houses, we have no place for our soldiers to go when off duty and the colored Y.M.C.A. building for which we have struggled so hard has not been completed. So the Woman's War Council as its first War Work effort raised this money to help furnish the building in order that soldiers might have a wholesome place to go. Hence, this $1800.00 was turned over to the Y.M.C.A. . . .

OUR IMMEDIATE NEEDS

The first very urgent need is a Hostess House [near the Army Camp] to contain a cafeteria with its equipment where the soldiers may have a place to go for a meal with visiting friends.

Two trained workers (Travelers Aid) at the two railroad stations.

One Y.W.C.A. worker for girls.

We wish an automobile put at our disposal that we may do a more effective, constructive work at the Cantonment and in the Neighborhood.

Neighborhood Union Papers, Trevor Arnett Library,
Atlanta University.

THE NEIGHBORHOOD UNION, ATLANTA, GEORGIA: A Black Settlement House

Organized 1908 Incorporated 1911 An Organization for the Moral, Economic and Social Advancement of Negroes.

The Neighborhood Union is an outgrowth of an organized effort of a number of Negro women to improve the social conditions of the city—particularly of their neighborhood.

ITS AIM

1. To unite for their advancement of the people of each section of the city into an organization, which shall

be a branch of the Neighborhood Union; and to effect similar Neighbor Unions in other cities.

2. To develop a spirit of helpfulness among the neighbors and to co-operate with one another in their respective neighborhoods for the best interests of the community, city and race.

3. To provide playgrounds, clubs, good literature, and Neighborhood centers for the moral, physical, and intellectual development of the young.

4. To establish lecture courses, classes, and clubs for adults, for the purpose of encouraging habits of cleanliness and industry, promoting child welfare, and of bringing about culture and efficiency in general home-making.

5. To improve the sanitation of homes and streets, and to bring to the attention of the city the need of lights and of other improvements.

6. To abolish slums and houses of immorality; to investigate dance halls, pool rooms, and vaudeville shows; and generally to co-operate with city officials in suppressing vice and crime.

7. To co-operate with the Associated Charities and the Juvenile Court.

8. To make surveys of small communities showing the operation of factors and forces at work therein; and, at intervals, to take a census of the neighborhoods in Atlanta showing the status of each family and individual therein as well as to prepare maps of the sections inhabited by Negroes.

9. To bring about a better understanding between the races.

PLANS OF THE ORGANIZATION

Neighborhoods are organized in certain sections of the city. Each neighborhood is divided into districts. The work of a district is supervised by a director and the work of a neighborhood by a president. The directors of the districts are organized into a BOARD OF DIRECTORS of which the president of the neighborhood is chairman. The work of the city as a whole is supervised by the BOARD OF MANAGERS of the Neighborhood Union of which board the presidents of the neighborhoods must be members. This board is the governing body and has power to appoint committees which conduct various parts of the Union's work, to elect a general director, etc. It must make annual reports to the members of the Neighborhood Union.

WHAT THE ORGANIZATION HAS ACCOMPLISHED

1. A playground has been provided for children.
2. Fourth of July Carnivals have been held for the amusement of the children, several hundred boys and girls being annually reached.
3. Clubs have been conducted for the physical and social improvement of children.
4. Domestic science classes have been conducted.
5. Many helpful lectures have been delivered to mothers of children.
6. The services of four trained nurses have been secured for those who are not able to pay for treatment.
7. Dives of immorality have been broken up.
8. Needy families have been given aid, some cases being turned over to the Associated Charities.
9. The people have been urged to keep their back yards and store premises sanitary.
10. Lights have been secured and holes and other defects in streets have been remedied through the effort of the organization.
11. Investigations have been made to aid other organizations in promoting their work.
12. Children placed in homes, orphan asylums, and reformatories.
13. The use of the public school buildings has been obtained and recreation schools conducted in them during the vacation.
14. A settlement house has been purchased on Lee Street.
15. Five neighborhoods are now organized in Atlanta.

IMMEDIATE PURPOSES

The Neighborhood Union purposes to organize neighborhoods in each section of the city as speedily as possible. It is our desire to have a settlement house in each neighborhood where the people can gather for their meetings, clubs and classes and feel that it is their very own. Then the work outlined above can be done more systematically and effectively. You can help us to aid you by cooperating with us and calling our attention to the need of clubs and organizations in your particular community.

Address all inquiries to:

> Mrs. L. B. Hope,
> Neighborhood Union,
> Care of Morehouse College,
> Atlanta, Ga.

> "But I turn not away from their smiles nor their tears
> Both are parts of an infinite plan;
> Let me live in my house by the side of the road,
> And be a friend to man."

> Neighborhood Union Papers, Trevor Arnett Library,
> Atlanta University. Pamphlet (*n.d.*, *n.p.*).

THE NEIGHBORHOOD UNION:
Survey of Colored Public Schools (1913–1914)

Under the auspices of the Neighborhood Union some of the leading Negro women of the city were organized into a Social Improvement Committee, whose object was to work for better conditions of the Negro public schools of Atlanta. They met regularly and promptly every week about six months regardless of the severe heat or cold. Upon the close of the investigation and inspection of every colored school in Atlanta, it was found that the condition was very deplorable. In most instances it was found:

I. That sanitary conditions were very unhealthful.
II. Light and ventilation in the majority of cases unusually poor so that many children suffered from eye strain, or were made sick because of the impure air.
III. The schools were congested with children.
IV. Double sessions existed in all the public schools and in most of them through the sixth grade, with the same teacher teaching both sessions.

Every influential white woman in the city that could be reached was visited and her interest sought. Some of these women met with us and pledged their co-operation. They could scarcely believe the facts we presented to them, but they visited these schools themselves and saw conditions just as we had pictured. We did not stop with the white women, but the members of the Social Committee went in twos and threes and interviewed every member of the city council, pleading with them for better conditions for the colored children. Some of the influential white pastors of the city were visited and their aid sought. The mayor of the city was not omitted. Several mass meetings were held and one lecture with slides showing conditions of the schools was given. Placards were posted everywhere and the colored ministers urged to interest their congregations and get them together on the subject. Petition after petition was carried before the board of education asking them for better conditions, especially to abolish double sessions, the greatest evil of the children of Atlanta, and their homes. For the year 1913–1914 there was a seating capacity in the Negro schools of 4,102, while the enrollment was 6,163, making the number of pupils affected by double sessions 2,061. As a direct result of the work of the committee, the teachers' salaries were raised and a makeshift of a school established in South Atlanta. The men joined in with the women to have better schools. The committee agreed not to cease work until better schools prevailed for colored children.

Neighborhood Union Papers, Trevor Arnett Library,
Atlanta University.

THE NEIGHBORHOOD UNION:
Summary of Activities*

1908   Organized by neighbors and wives of faculty members of Spelman and Morehouse Colleges, Atlanta, Ga. Since there was not a single public park or playground for black children, the women persuaded the administration of Morehouse College to allow the use of part of its grounds for a playground and provided volunteers to supervise the children. The Neighborhood Union soon expanded this activity and maintained it until the city took over and provided public play space.

Yearly activities of the Neighborhood Union: Carnival and Fourth of July celebrations for the children; neighborhood improvement campaigns; organized gardening and clean-up campaigns. Summer vacation Bible schools for children. Participation in Associated Charities, anti-TB campaigns and Red Cross.

1912–13 Survey of Public Schools (see pp. 503–504) and follow-up political pressure campaign to get school improvements.

1915   Established a Health Center which offers a clinic, some nursing services and advice on sanitation.

---

* This summary was made by the editor on the basis of the annual reports of the Neighborhood Union in the organization's manuscript files. Quoted sections are excerpted from these reports.

1916   Ran 35 clubs for girls, 10 for boys.

1917–21 A Home Investigation Committee undertook a housing survey and improvement campaign. The work was done by volunteer block captains, each assigned a specific area and a certain number of homes. Each volunteer kept a careful record of conditions found and of subsequent improvements. The survey revealed appalling housing conditions: no street lights or pavements; insufficient trash removal; in half of the houses surveyed the water connection was bad or contaminated; most homes lacked adequate toilet facilities. "Out of 180 places reported as unsanitary, 42% or 76, lacked toilets or plumbing. 5513 homes were visited during the 1921 campaign. The result of that campaign was 40 houses repaired, two streets paved, lights put on one street, improvements made in twelve streets, plumbing repaired in one house, sewers put on two streets, toilets repaired in one house, and street improvements made in twenty streets."

1922   The Neighborhood Union purchased a clubhouse at 41 Leonard Street. It employed two social workers and ran classes for children.

1923   Report on community work listed the following committees: "A relief committee; the publicity committee and investigation committee to look into situations of housing, health, etc. The District committee to run classes and instruct people how to demand the required wages. A fund-raising committee; a cooperation committee to teach people the value of mixing and mingling together; a health and sanitation committee to teach people to burn, bury and beautify. A literature and music committee to teach the community the importance of reading and the joy gained from music; teach them how to read our own literature and buy our own music. A Child welfare committee. A citizenship committee: teach them the right to be a citizen, to vote, register, be within the law at all times. Religion: see that everyone has a chance to go to the church of his choice. Recreation: teach the people the advantages of recreation, plan something for their leisure time."

A letter to the Mayor of Atlanta and to the City Council, September 29, 1923, summarizing a survey of the schools for Negro children:

"The city has 17,750 Negro children, 34% of the school population. For the instruction of these children, there are twelve public school buildings. These have a total seating capacity of 4,877. The total enrollment is 11,469. Therefore, the seating capacity is only 42% of the total enrollment. The children are on triple session, and many children are on 2½-hour school sessions. Including the half-day teachers, there are 159 teachers for these 11,469 pupils, or an average of 72 children for each teacher employed. Only 203 pupils in the entire system are getting adequate school work, or less than 2% of the total." A school-by-school detailed fact-finding survey is appended.

1924   The report of one Committee on Health for five months' work:

"196 visits were made to homes, clubs, churches and individuals. A baby center was organized, where babies are weighed, measured, treated and seen by doctors. Three locations for playgrounds secured. Instructions on home care and home economics given at 12 different meetings. Arranged clinics to treat out-patients. In March there were 217 visits made, 14 cases investigated and helped, six meetings held in the office, 132 pieces of mail sent out, and 51 visitors were taken care of. 32,000 pieces of clean-up literature distributed. 16,000 persons reached by various activities of this one committee."

1927   "999 children were examined in health clinics
        (36 of them), 82 mothers are enrolled in Moth-
        ers' Clubs, two new Boys' Clubs have been organ-
        ized."

1928   "27 medical clinics were held, in which more than
        800 school children were examined and treated.
        Three health classes were organized for 78 women
        in the community, two new Boys' Clubs were or-
        ganized with an enrollment of 112; two Girls' Clubs
        were organized; and almost 3000 pieces of literature
        were distributed."

1929   "280 patients examined in health clinics; 782 follow-
        up visits made to home of patients; 14 women
        received training in home hygiene and care of the
        sick; and National Negro Health Week was spon-
        sored in all of the schools, social agencies, and
        businesses."

1931–32 During the depression all efforts were concentrated
        on providing relief. Mrs. L. B. Shivery, Secretary of
        the Unemployment Relief Committee reported on
        a survey of neighborhood needs. "59 families were
        destitute, subsisting on $4 per week for a family of
        six or seven. Work was found for a small number of
        families. The Committee concentrated on helping
        to keep the children in school. More than 400 chil-
        dren helped to return to school; . . . parents in
        more than 1684 families were helped to stay out of
        the bread line; money was raised by holding a circus,
        a fair, some sponsored movies, tea parties, getting
        cheap clothing from Sears & Roebuck at wholesale
        prices. The Health Clinic at the Neighborhood
        Union House was enlarged to include medical and
        dental clinics and mothers' clinics for home care of
        the sick. A registered nurse, a doctor and a dentist
        were in attendance. Over 4000 people used the
        services of the Health center. 684 pre-school-age

children were treated, 176 families were supplied with milk, and 432 children were supplied with cod liver oil."

Summary based on manuscript reports and W. Walter Chivers', "Survey of the Work of the Neighborhood Union," typescript, Neighborhood Union Papers, Trevor Arnett Library, Atlanta University.

THE STORY OF THE GATE CITY FREE KINDERGARTEN ASSOCIATION

More than twenty years ago, in the chapel of Atlanta University, of Atlanta, Georgia, Dr. W. E. B. DuBois, who was then a teacher there, had for the subject of his Annual Conference, "The Welfare of the Negro Child." Miss Gertrude Ware, the Kindergarten-Training-School-Teacher at the University, led a discussion concerning the care of children whose mothers went out to work daily, leaving them locked in their homes or locked out to rove the streets of the city. A few interested young colored mothers at this meeting decided that they would attempt to establish free kindergartens in widely separated parts of the city convenient to such mothers who might leave their children of pre-school age at least one-half day of each school day. Gertrude Ware was approached by Dr. DuBois and was asked to call the women together and effect the organization.

Fired with enthusiasm, and willing to sacrifice time and means, these women went into organization and established a kindergarten Association. They employed and paid a strong Christian kindergarten teacher to take charge. From this one kindergarten, in one of the poorest parts of the city, the work grew in three years to five kindergartens, all in the slums, where they were most needed, with an average of thirty children in attendance in each daily.

How the money was raised to take care of the work was a

mystery even to the members of the association. Many times the promoters wondered themselves how they would carry on, but a way always was provided.

The association never had more than twenty members with about twelve always active. Concerts, Fairs, Track-Meets, Contests and other entertainments of various kinds were used to raise funds. Of course, it meant hard work for those "faithful few." However, at the end of the twentieth year the association had raised and used over thirty thousand ($30,000) dollars in cash to carry on the work.

The kindergartens were at this time giving great help to the children of working mothers, but it was seen more and more plainly that the need for nurseries was great. For the children needed to be cared for all day rather than for just a part of the time, while their mothers were at work. God heard the prayers of the women and opened a way for the first Nursery to be established in the fall of 1918. The late Mr. A. F. Herndon, the colored millionaire of Atlanta gave to the Gate City Kindergarten Association a large stone building located at White's Alley; the salary for the Head Matron; and two gallons of milk per day for several years. This house cost Mr. Herndon ten thousand dollars ($10,-000) and the matron's salary four hundred and eighty dollars a year ($480.00). There is now supported by the Association a Day Nursery in West Atlanta and one in East Atlanta with four regular workers at each nursery. The annual expenditure is about ten thousand dollars which amount is supplied by the community chest of Atlanta. No member of the association has received so much as a penny for this work. All has been given to the children of the less fortunate mothers who would have become the wayward and criminal element of our city had it not been for the assistance the organization was privileged to give them.

The organization was very particular to give them the services of well-educated Christian teachers to teach in the kindergartens as well as competent women as matrons and helpers in the nurseries who would see to the comfort and training of the children. Each child was given plenty of milk.

They also served wholesome meals on time with strict attention to the dietary needs of the children. Each child was given its bath and, under six years of age they were given a quiet hour each day. All children over six were sent to the nearest public school dressed neatly and clean. They had a study period to prepare lessons under the supervision of the matron. The purpose was to furnish as far as possible a mother and home life for the underprivileged children whose mothers were away earning a support for them. Thus the organization aided in producing future citizens for the race.

The history of the methods of securing the buildings and the funds, amounting to more than $30,000 in twenty years is very interesting.

The people in the communities where the schools are located show their appreciation by helping with small donations of coal or small contributions toward rent. The rent and fuel for kindergartens 4 and 5, are given by the Leonard St. Orphanage, and by the Presbyterian Mission where these schools are taught. Even with this help there is a monthly rent bill of $17, and the annual coal bill is a very big item. The Association is able to rent only the poorest houses which have numerous openings, simplifying the ventilation problem, but making it very hard to keep the children warm.

For two years a good friend has given two gallons of buttermilk a day in one of the kindergartens, and one of the bakeries of the city supplies bread each day. In another kindergarten, members of one of the working circles have sent soup from time to time. It is our earnest hope that some one else will become interested enough to do the same thing for other kindergartens, because that is what they all need. In many cases the children come from homes where they are improperly fed, and a nutritious lunch of bread and milk or bread and soup, would do a great deal towards helping them physically and morally.

During the cold weather the Association is constantly called upon to provide clothes for these little ones. On the bleakest day some of them come to school barefoot, some with very poor shoes and no stockings, and to many of them underwear of any kind is unknown.

Each year at Christmas the Association receives gifts of new clothes from the sewing guild to be distributed among the children, and at all times the teachers are glad to receive children's clothing and shoes. In some cases the parents are encouraged to buy the clothes for a small sum, and often the teacher has been able to have the children who needed shoes to bring their pennies which would have been spent for candy or knick-knacks until enough had been saved to pay for repairing shoes which the teacher had. In this way she has taught thrift and self-respect.

The aim of the teachers in their schools is to make them social centers for the communities, and thru their unselfish devotion to the work and thru the combined and untiring efforts of members of the Association, during the past twelve years, 3000 children have been started on lives of decency and usefulness in Atlanta; 3000 children who would otherwise have been on the streets and a growing menace instead of an asset to the city. We believe that the work which we are doing for these children is second to none in the city, and we need the interest and sympathy of every humanity-loving man and woman. We need money for salaries, coal, rents, material for the children to work with, lunches for the children, clothes for them, and in behalf of thousands of little people who need our help, we ask for your cooperation. . . .

Flyer, typescript, Neighborhood Union Papers,
Trevor Arnett Library, Atlanta University.

THE POOR HELP THEMSELVES: THE VINE CITY FOUNDATION, ATLANTA, GEORGIA

A charge frequently made about slum dwellers—particularly when they are Negro—is that they won't do anything to help themselves. It is said that they sit around and wait for the government to give them everything.

This is not true of a group of Atlanta Negroes who have banded together to improve their neighborhood, one of the worst slums in the city. They are doing an enormous amount of good in an area which has pitifully little other social-service help. What financing they have comes from private sources. . . .

The group goes by the name of Vine City Foundation. It had its genesis a little over three years ago in a survey college students took of the community, called Vine City. The students asked several residents to help them. After the survey eight of the residents decided to band together and do something about the terrible problems they had just seen throughout the neighborhood.

The foundation began by offering an emergency service—helping anyone with whatever his problem was. It got some people out of jail, helped others get on welfare, loaned money to those in greatest need, looked up birth certificates for people needing social security, and so on. These services are still among the foundation's main efforts.

It paid for all these activities through the slim proceeds of a thrift shop, where the area's 8,000 residents could buy donated old clothes for less the $1—and generally between 5 cents and 15 cents. The thrift shop still exists.

Several other services have been added in three years: a nursery, a medical clinic, a craft and candle shop, Boy and Girl Scout groups, monthly family suppers, the beginnings of a hoped-for food cooperative, a monthly newspaper, and a family-counseling service.

Members of the foundation have demonstrated—successfully—to obtain a city playground on a vacant lot; they have conducted a rent strike (unsuccessfully) against absentee landlords who own 95 percent of the area's housing. Most homes are dilapidated, single-story, and wooden. "We came here in 1928," says Mrs. Helen Howard, "and some of them was old then." She is the foundation's director and one of the eight founding members.

She says of the way new activities were added: ". . . It's

just that a need was there, and we said, 'O.K., let's try to do something about it.' "

Started a year ago, the nursery this summer had 49 children in two sessions, crammed in a small basement of an uncompleted church nearby. The youngsters were between three and five; all were carefully chosen as children who most needed nursery-school experienc. Some now have entered the public kindergartens. There now are 22 nursery-school children.

A new place must be found for the nursery; the church basement has no central heating and is always damp. It rents for $70 monthly.

Four evenings a week the foundation provides a free medical clinic. It is held in the one-story wooden converted home that is the foundation's main building. One physician is present each evening; 16 physicians all told donate their services. Between them they obtain many needed supplies free. The foundation buys whatever else is needed. Each night an average of 15 people are seen.

Each Friday evening the local arm of the federal anti-poverty programs conducts a planned-parenthood clinic at the foundation.

Next door is the craft and candle shop. There a paid neighborhood resident works with teen-age girls and older women, teaching them to make ceramics and to sew. Most ceramics are sold on premises.

"There isn't much profit," says the perceptive Mrs. Howard, "but there is involvement of people of the neighborhood. They're learning how to do things. The ladies make enough to supplement, to do some things they couldn't do otherwise." Except for the teacher, workers are paid only from the profits of what is sold.

The Scout groups have been in operation about seven months. So has the family-counseling service, in which 12 residents meet weekly to discuss their problems in a group. Also present is a representative of the state counseling service.

The food co-op concept grew from the present "bread club." Mrs. Howard heard a nearby supermarket threw out all its old bread; in response to her request they said they'd give it to the foundation. They deliver it thrice weekly. Residents pay 25¢ a week to belong to the bread club, which entitles them to bread three times a week. With those 25¢ charges the group has been buying canned goods, and selling them at lower prices than commercial markets.

The house next door is being remodeled for use as a thrift shop, coop (with meat and fresh vegetables), arts and candle shop, and office space. The foundation is trying to find the money to buy it.

The foundation has seven paid staff members "and a slew of volunteers," says Mrs. Howard. "That's the way we run—on volunteers."

It has two special activities designed both to raise money and to develop a close-knit community. (One of the area's problems is that there is little community spirit, unlike some other slum areas.) One activity is the monthly community supper, served in the main building.

Another is the occasional—about every other week—selling on Saturday of hot dogs and soda. "Two weeks ago we raised $150 this way," Mrs. Howard says. "And then it gives people something to do together. People just don't like to come to meetings per se, especially in low-income communities. You have to get them together some way, any way you can."

But most of these activities require money. And lack of it is the foundation's biggest problem.

In June of this year it received a $30,000 grant from the Episcopal Church. This helped—but it already has used up $14,000 of this and the pinch remains.

Later Trinity Presbyterian Church began giving $450 a month—$300 for the nursery, and $150 for the foundation to use as it saw fit. This church is in an upper income white area of Atlanta. It is one of the most progressive, socially conscious churches in the city.

Many individuals have sent donations, Mrs. Howard says, and she expresses much gratitude for them. Most are small.

Assuming she can come up with the money somehow, what are her eventual plans for her neighborhood?

"Maybe I'm too ambitious, but I think this whole block should be took up by a supermarket, a beauty shop—the whole works—and be controlled by the poor people in the community. That's where I want to go. But I don't know where I'm going to get the money."

Robert P. Hey, "Atlanta Self-help," *Christian Science Monitor*, October 19, 1968, pp. 1, 10.

HELEN HOWARD:

We have about 10,000 people in Vine city. Most of them work as domestic and in service kind of jobs. And construction, that's what they're hiring now—laborers. I know of one family has a couple of teachers in it and my kids were in college—but it's just a few. As soon as they can afford it, they move. They run like hell.

I lived in Vine City all my life, but I managed to buy a little house, my husband did. You tend to forget how bad it really is. You live right here and still you don't realize it. I organized this neighborhood organization, two men and six ladies started it. That was a hard pull. A lot of people joined in later. For about five months we had meetings pretty near every night. We learned how to work with other people. You know, poor people—this is a new thing for them, they just don't know how to organize things. We had to learn how even to communicate with each other. A white man, a Quaker, he live in the community, he was the kind to say, "Don't be afraid, go ahead and do it." A lot of people were afraid to really do anything. You were afraid to go to the city hall or ask for anything. You didn't even ask the landlord anything, you were afraid of him. Then we had meetings and then we weren't afraid so much anymore. First we tried to go down to city hall and tell them how bad things is and how people is suffering around here and the lawyers they didn't do anything about it. Then we have a press conference out in the street. We got a lot of publicity on that. And then people could see that you *can* make somebody listen to you.

And so we really got brave and people started demanding their rights.

The way we got this playground: we blocked off the street, wouldn't let anything come through. We wouldn't let the trolley bus come through. The whole neighborhood was in it. Took record players and danced; it went on for a week. We didn't get arrested, they was too many of us. So then the city put up this playground for the kids and they maintaining it, too. To a degree.

I think our support is less now. People tend to get tired. When we first started it was kind we were doing it together. Now it seems to be, you do it for us. Still, I think the biggest thing we did is that we learned to mobilize. People now know their rights and they know where to get the services and stop being so damn afraid of everybody. That really happened. I think it's the most sophisticated poor neighborhood in the United State, because people really know how to gripe. We have a lot of people on relief. Now if people aren't getting a good deal, we just go down there and work it out.

Helen Howard, taped interview, Atlanta,
Georgia. Used by permission.

OPERATION DAILY BREAD:
THE NATIONAL COUNCIL
OF NEGRO WOMEN

❦ *This coordinating council of 20 national organizations and 95 local councils was formed in 1935 with Mary McLeod Bethune as its first President. It represents nearly 850,000 organized black women. It has embraced every kind of club activity carried out by its affiliated organizations. In recent years the NCCW has increasingly turned its attention to helping the poorest segments of black society, selecting Sunflower County, Mississippi, for the several pilot projects described below.*

The Honorable Orville Freeman
Secretary
U.S. Department of Agriculture
Washington, D.C.
Dear Mr. Secretary:

"This is an application on behalf of the needy children and low-income persons of Sunflower County, Miss., for relief from hunger as a result of a lack of sufficient food through no fault of their own. Sunflower County, which is described in detail below, has a food stamp program; but that program is a failure in Sunflower County, and many of the county's residents are still hungry—still without food—and continue to be malnourished. Some of the citizens of Sunflower County have organized a project to combat the hunger which is a part of their every day. And now they seek through this application to you, their rightful share of additional food from your Department. . . .

Sunflower County, Miss., is one of the poorest counties in the Nation. It is in miserable condition. Out of a total population of about 46,000 (of which 39,000 live in rural areas), 33,000 comprise the "poor" who earn less than $3,000 per year. Of the 33,000 poor people in the county, 26,000 are classified as "hardcore poor," people who earn less than $2,000 per year. Moreover, public assistance is only reaching about 4,211 persons and the Food Stamp Program—as a not much better supplement—is estimated to be serving around 9,300 people. The result is that while approximately 13,700 persons now receive some form of public assistance, there are from 12,000 to 16,000 mainly "hardcore poor" who receive no benefits whatsoever. There are approximately 9,115 families in Sunflower County with a medium income of $1,790. Over 68.1% of these families earn less than $3,000.

What all these figures mean is that this county is very poor; that its citizens are trapped in a "cycle to nowhere." If one takes this over-whelming poverty and combines it with the fact that 68% of the county is black, then one comes to the inescapable and well-known proposition that for anyone poor and black in Mississippi, "food is the one thing always on his mind—and rarely in his stomach." Food is scarce for most black people in this county, and when there is food, such as fatback, grits, dried beans, pork neckbone, it has rarely had the protein to keep even the dogs healthy. And there are a substantial number of white people in this county who face the same conditions, and who face the same hunger. The more substantial and nutritional foods are lacking; i.e. meat, milk, fish and eggs, and so forth. . . .

To further compound the poor problem, about half of those eligible for food stamps do not have the money with which to buy them. The food stamp program in Sunflower County is a failure. It simply does not reach the hungry. Welfare, difficult to come by, is no better. At best the assistance payments are a sub low; $34.55 per month vs. $277.20 per month in New York for a family of four. In summary, poor people are suffering from hunger caused by no fault of their own, except that they were cursed to be born in Sunflower County.

Recently, the National Council of Negro Women organized about forty families in the county into a project called Operation Daily Bread. The purpose of this co-operative is to help alleviate the food shortage by encouraging members to grow food in large garden plots. The project supplies seeds to the members who in turn plant, tend and harvest the crops. All of the harvest crops are then placed in sort of a "food bank," and it is finally distributed to member families according to need. A similar community type of plan is a livestock program which has begun a "pig bank," which in turn gives these pigs to another family. . . . The project is the beginning of a self-help approach to the problem of hunger. The poor people have the sole responsibility for operating this project under the direction of a staff who is trained in the areas of agricultural crops and livestock. . . . In summary, the applicants are pointing to the existence of an institution that is able and prepared to distribute needed food. . . .

The applicants believe an emergency situation exists which is caused by a disaster. In plain language, it is a disaster in the form of many poor people suffering from hunger due to lack of sufficient and adequate food. . . .

The 1969 appropriations for the Department of Agriculture expressly provide for Section 32 of the Act of August 24, 1935, (7 U.S.C. 612C) funds to be made available for direct distribution without regard to whether such areas have a food stamp program. Section 32 of the Act provides for the distribution of food for an adequate diet in the immediate vicinity of the places where the people live. . . .

Therefore, the applicants make direct application to the Secretary of Agriculture for $123,500 of Section 32 funds to provide for the direct distribution of food to those needy persons in the county who are suffering, through no fault of their own, from general and continued hunger.

Respectfully submitted by:
NATIONAL COUNCIL OF NEGRO WOMEN, INC.
By: Miss Dorothy I. Height
National President
OPERATION DAILY BREAD
By: Miss Ruby L. Doss, Ruleville, Miss.

❦ *The Department of Agriculture, through Howard P. Davis, Deputy Administrator of the Consumer Food Program, answered this appeal with the following explanations: The department was authorized to distribute food stamps directly only in "situations arising from natural disasters or civil disorders"; needy children were receiving school lunches and needy expectant mothers were receiving supplemental food packages; recent food-stamp program changes had reduced purchase requirements for the very low income group; and the President considered hunger and malnutrition "one of the highest priorities in this administration."*

Progress Report, National Council of Negro Women, June 1969.

CHAPTER NINE

RACE PRIDE

We will teach the children to be proud.
Nothing you know is worth anything if
you don't first know how to be proud of
yourself.

Community Committee member, Child
Development Group of Mississippi,
as cited by Polly Greenberg, **The
Devil Has Slippery Shoes** (London:
Macmillan Company, 1969), p. 65.

RACE PRIDE

❦ Throughout the history of black people in the United States race pride has manifested itself in a variety of attitudes and ideas. These have included: racial solidarity, pride and assertion of a separate black cultural heritage, black nationalism as expressed through emigrationism or territorial separatism, organizational and economic separatism as a tactic or as an end in itself. Race pride has meant self-assertion, self-help and the transmission of a viable, separate black culture.

A militant assertion of race pride runs like a constant thread through the recorded expression of well-known and anonymous black women of the past. Some, like Maria Stewart and Sojourner Truth, were sufficiently moved by the urgent need for arousing militant resistance among Blacks, to overcome the cultural strictures against women lecturing and preaching. In their speeches they stressed the urgent need for race solidarity in order to overcome repression and prejudice. Both sensed the need for building black pride upon the cultural heritage of the race. Maria Stewart, in evoking the revolutionary American past as a model for Blacks, thereby asserted their right to revolution. While she rejected the concept of colonization, as advocated by the American Colonization Society, as a form of enforced deportation, she coupled this with a militant assertion of the right of black people to an equal share in American society. Her speeches urged the establishment of separate black institutions and self-help organizations. She predicted a racial civil war in apocalyptic terms, if other measures should fail to win long-overdue rights.

Sojourner Truth, essentially a preacher and charismatic leader, asserted black pride by her indomitable dignity and self-confidence and by her use of poetic metaphors from the black experience in her parables and exhortations. Her homely, pungent language illuminated the most complex political questions with the sharp insight of folk wisdom.

> You think your talk does any good, old woman? Why,
> I don't care any more for it than for a fleabite.—
> Maybe not. But the Lord willing, I'll keep you
> scratching.

Or, comparing the Constitution to a sick ear of wheat:

> I hear talking about the Constitution and the rights
> of man. I comes up and I takes hold of this Constitu-
> tion. It looks mighty big, and I feels for my rights,
> but there aren't any there. Then I say, "God, what
> ails this Constitution?" He says to me, "Sojourner,
> there is a little weasel in it."

Her poetic language spoke of an African culture rooted in
the American soil, a black interpretation of the Christian
Bible, a black religion which sounded "quaint" to her white
contemporaries, but which was perfectly comprehensible
to her black audiences. Black solidarity meant acceptance of
all kinds, all classes of Blacks within the black community.
Sojourner Truth asserted over and over again, in speech
and action, the right of lower-class Blacks to speak for
themselves and to be themselves. It also meant that black
spokesmen among whites should represent themselves or
their people and not be selected or appointed by whites.
Sojourner Truth would demand her right to be heard in
abolitionist and women's rights meetings, as well as in
hostile, proslavery crowds, thus making herself a model and
symbol of race pride.

The theme of racial solidarity recurs persistently in the
historical record. Even such genteelly raised women as
Charlotte Forten and Frances Harper recognized the necessity of accepting the uneducated and the poor as part of the
black folk. Charlotte Forten's often naive astonishment at
the potential and achievements of the ignorant ex-slaves,
like Frances Harper's more self-conscious expressions of
solidarity, is a recognition of this racial unity.

Owing to the savage repression and the mounting indignities of Jim Crow legislation and practice in the 1890's, the defensive-assertive aspects of race pride had to come to the fore. Black women in clubs and community organizations considered it necessary, even essential, to persuade white women of the respectability, decency and morality of black women. It took courage and political conviction for women like Mary Church Terrell, Amanda Smith Jemand and Mary McLeod Bethune to answer in patient articles, arguments and speeches the slanders and racist insults spread over the pages of national magazines. Unfortunately, their educational effort was met with rebuff, indifference and apathy on the part of white women. The more militant self-assertion expressed in the work and writings of Ida B. Wells Barnett was more effective as an irritant to white complacency. This was also the tone and stance taken by Nannie Burroughs, whose race pride and sharp argument sound amazingly modern. The celebration of blackness, pride in race achievement and the fostering of a sense of community are recurrent themes in the writings of Barnett, Burroughs and Bethune. That such an attitude was not at all incompatible with a conciliatory, accommodating and integrationist one taken toward whites is evident in the writings and letters of Charlotte Hawkins Brown and Mary McLeod Bethune. The contrast between Mrs. Bethune's articles (see pp. 134–146) and her attitude as revealed in the minutes of interracial meetings is particularly striking. Other manuscript sources not included here also bear out this point. Like many leaders of her generation, Mrs. Bethune struck a fine balance between her "official" posture as a leader who knew how to deal with whites on their terms and the militant prodding and confrontation approach which she used in her actual work with whites.

Race pride could take many forms and political directions —it could encompass a fervent plea for asserting and winning a place within white society, a place of equality and dignity as an American citizen (Stewart); it could take the

form of advocating emigration, voluntary resettlement and
the building up of a new community in a freer climate
(Item 2; also see selections by Ida B. Wells Barnett and the
arguments of Mary Shadd Cary); it could finally take the
nationalist cast expressed by Dara Abubakari—the right of
self-determination of a black nation on American soil.

Race pride always, throughout Black history, demanded
transmission of the black cultural and historical heritage.
Document after document reveals the patient efforts of
black women to celebrate black heroes, such as Crispus
Attucks, Toussaint L'Ouverture, David Walker and Nat
Turner. From the earliest literary societies to the women's
clubs, there was a conscious effort made to keep the historic
black heritage alive and to fill the minds of young people
with concepts designed to counteract the daily poison of
racist indoctrination. In the worst period of oppression,
small groups of women, such as the Tuskegee Women's
Club or the New York Enquiry Club, studied Black history
and literature, kept the oral tradition alive and honored
the surviving veterans of abolitionist struggles. The scholarly
work of men such as W. E. B. DuBois, Carter Woodson
and Charles S. Johnson rested on the solid foundation of
a black popular culture transmitted from generation to
generation and kept alive by anonymous black men and
women.

THROW OFF YOUR FEARFULNESS AND COME FORTH!

MARIA W. STEWART

My beloved brethren. . . . It is upon you that woman depends; she can do little beside using her influence; and it is
for her sake and yours that I have come forward and made
myself a hissing and a reproach among the people; for I am
also one of the wretched and miserable daughters of the

descendants of Africa. Do you ask: "Why are you wretched and miserable?" I reply: Look at many of the most worthy and interesting of us doomed to spend our lives in gentlemen's kitchens. Look at our young men—smart, active and energetic, with souls filled with ambitious fire; if they look forward, alas! what are their prospects? They can be nothing but the humblest laborer, on account of their dark complexion; hence many of them lose their ambition, and become worthless. Look at our middle-aged men, clad in their rusty plaids and coats. In winter, every cent they earn goes to buy their wood and pay their rent; their poor wives also toil beyond their strength, to help support their families. Look at our aged sires, whose heads are whitened with the frosts of seventy winters, with their old wood-saws on their backs. Alas, what keeps us so? Prejudice, ignorance, and poverty. . . . Did the pilgrims, when they first landed on these shores, quietly compose themselves, and say: "The Britons have all the money and all the power, and we must continue their servants forever?" Did they sluggishly sigh, and say, "Our lot is hard; the Indians own the soil, and we cannot cultivate it?" No; they first made powerful efforts to raise themselves, and then God raised up those illustrious patriots, WASHINGTON and LAFAYETTE, to assist and defend them. And, my brethren, have you made a powerful effort? . . . .

*　　　　*　　　　*

I would ask, is it blindness of mind or stupidity of soul or the want of education that has caused our men . . . never to let their voices be heard nor their hands be raised in behalf of their color? Or has it been for fear of offending the whites? If it has, O ye fearful ones, throw off your fearfulness and come forth, in the name of the Lord and in the strength of the God of Justice, and make yourselves useful and active members in society . . . If you are men, convince them that you possess the spirit of men; and as your day so shall your strength be. . . . Where can we find among ourselves the man of science, or a philosopher, or an able statesman, or a counsellor at law? Show me our fearless and brave, our noble and gallant ones. Where are our lecturers on natural history and our critics in useful knowledge? There may be a few such men among us, but they are rare. It is true, our fathers bled and died in the revolutionary war, and others fought bravely, under the command of Jackson, in defense of liberty. But where is the man that has distinguished himself in these modern days by acting wholly in the defense of African rights and liberty? There was one; although he sleeps, his memory lives. . . .

Talk, without effort, is nothing. You are abundantly capable, gentlemen, of making yourselves men of distinction; and this gross neglect on your part causes my blood to boil within me. Here is the grand cause which hinders the rise and progress of the people of color. It is the want of laudable ambition and requisite courage. . . .

History informs us that we sprung from one of the most learned nations of the whole earth; from the seat, if not the parent of science; yes, poor, despised Africa was once the resort of sages and legislators of other nations, was esteemed the school of learning, and the most illustrious men of Greece flocked thither for instruction. . . .

But it is no use for us to boast that we sprung from this learned and enlightened nation, for this day a thick mist of moral gloom hangs over millions of our race. . . . Most of our color have been taught to stand in fear of the white man from their earliest infancy, to work as soon as they could walk, and to call "master" before they scarce could lisp the name of *mother*. Continual fear and laborious servitude have in some degree lessened in us that natural force and energy which belong to man; or else, in defiance of opposition, our men, before this, would have nobly and boldly contended for their rights. But give the man of color an equal opportunity with the white man from the cradle to manhood, and from manhood to the grave, and you would discover the dignified statesman, the man of science, and the philosopher. But there is no such opportunity for the sons of Africa, and I fear that our powerful ones are fully determined that there never shall be. Forbid, ye Powers on high, that it should any longer be said that our men possess no force. O ye sons of Africa, when will your voices be heard in our legislative hall, in defiance of your enemies, contending for equal rights and liberty? . . . Cast your eyes about, look as far as you can see; all, all is owned by the lordly white, except here and there a lowly dwelling which the man of color, midst deprivations, fraud and opposition has been scarce able to procure. Like King Solomon, who put neither nail nor hammer to the temple, yet received the praise; so also have the white Americans gained themselves a name, like the names of the great men that are in the earth, while in reality we have been their principal foundation and support. We have pursued the shadow, they have obtained the substance; we have performed the labor, they have received the profits; we have planted the vines, they have eaten the fruits of them. . . .

Let our money, instead of being thrown away as heretofore, be appropriated for schools and seminaries of learning for our children and youth. We ought to follow the example of the whites in this respect. . . . The rays of light and knowledge have been hid from our view; we have been taught to consider ourselves as scarce superior to the brute creation; and have performed the most laborious part of American drudgery. Had we as a people received one half the early advantages the whites have received, I would defy the government of these United States to deprive us any longer of our rights. . . .

It is of no use to wait any longer for a generation of well educated men to arise. We have slumbered and slept too long already; the day is far spent; the night of death approaches. . . Let every man of color throughout the United States, who possesses the spirit and principles of a man, sign a petition to Congress to abolish slavery in the District of Columbia, and grant you the rights and privileges of common free citizens; for, if you had had faith as a grain of mustard seed, long before this the mountains of prejudice might have been removed. . . .

It appears to me that America has become like the great city of Babylon. . . . She is indeed a seller of slaves and the souls of men; she has made the Africans drunk with the wine of her fornication; she has put them completely beneath her feet, and she means to keep them there; her right hand supports the reins of government, and her left hand the wheel of power, and she is determined not to let go her grasp. But many powerful sons and daughters of Africa will shortly arise, who will put down vice and immortality among us, and declare . . . that they will have their rights; and if refused, I am afraid they will spread horror and devastation around. I believe that the oppression of injured Africa has come up before the majesty of Heaven. . . .

The unfriendly whites first drove the native American from his much loved home. Then they stole our fathers from their peaceful and quiet dwellings, and brought them hither and made bond men and bond women out of them and their little ones; they have obliged our brethren to labor, kept them in utter ignorance . . . and now that we have enriched their soil, and filled their coffers, they say that we are not capable of becoming like white men, and that we can never rise to respectability in this country. They would drive us to a strange land. But before I go, the bayonet shall pierce me through. African rights and liberty is a subject that ought to fire the breast of every free man of color in these United States, and excite in his bosom a lively, deep, decided and heart-felt interest.

Lecture delivered in the African Masonic Hall in Boston, Massachusetts, February 27, 1833, as cited in Meditations from the Pen of Mrs. Maria W. Stewart, 2nd edition (Washington, D.C.: n.p., 1879), pp. 58–59; 66–73.

EMIGRATION TO MEXICO

❦ *Throughout the nineteenth century Blacks expressed their resistance to prejudice and oppression by* demanding their full rights as citizens in a democracy. Although this was the majority position, there was a significant minority who persistently advocated emigration but specified that such emigration must be voluntary, based on the Negro's own choice and, if possible, carried out through black community effort. Various destinations for emigration were proposed, among them Africa, the Caribbean, Canada and South America. Over 50,000 United States Negroes actually emigrated to Canada before the Civil War. The document below is interesting not only for its eloquent argument, but because of its early advocacy of emigration to a country which attracted the author of the letter because its population was colored.

Philadelphia, January 2, 1832

MR. EDITOR,—I am happy to learn that the sentiments of some of my Trenton brethren are in accordance with my own, in regard to our locating in Mexico and Upper Canada; for, in my humble opinion, one thing is needful for us as a people, even emigration; but not to Africa; nor to place ourselves as a distinct people any where; but to attach ourselves to a nation already established—. The government of these United States is not the only one in this hemisphere that offers equal rights to men; but there are others, under whose protection we may safely reside, where it is no disgrace to wear a sable complexion, and where our rights will not be continually trampled upon on that account. We profess to be republicans, and such I hope we are, but wherein do we show our republican spirit, by sitting still and sighing for that liberty our white brethren tell us we never shall obtain; or in hoping that in some fifty or a hundred years hence, our children's children will be made free? I think we do not evince republicanism by this conduct, but verily believe that the time has arrived, when we too ought to manifest that spirit of independence which shines so conspicuously in the character of the Europeans, by leaving the land of oppression, and emigrating where we may be received and treated as brothers; where our worth will be felt and acknowledged; and where we may acquire education, wealth, and respectability, together with a knowledge of the arts and sciences; all of which may be in our power—of the enjoyment of which, the government of the separate states in the union is adopting means to deprive us . . .

Some of your readers may inquire, where is that country to which we may remove, and thus become free and equal? I believe that country to be Mexico.—There is an independent nation, where indeed 'all men are born free and equal,' possessing those inalienable rights which our constitution guarantees. The climate is healthy and warm, and of course adapted to our nature; the soil is rich and fertile, which will contribute to our wealth; and there we may become a people of worth and respectability; whereas in this country we are kept poor, and of course cannot aspire to any thing more than what we always have been. I have been waiting to hear of some way being pointed out, that will tend to better the present generation; but, as yet, have heard of nothing that appears to be permanent. I would not wish to be thought pleading the cause of colonization, for no one detests it more than I do. I would not be taken to Africa, were the society to make me queen of the country; and were I to move to Canada, I would not settle in the colony, but take up my abode in some of the cities where a distinction is not known; for I do not aprove of our drawing off into a separate body any where. But I confess, I can see no just reason why we should not cultivate the spirit of enterprise as well as the whites. They are found in every quarter of the globe, in search of situations to better their condition; and why may we not 'go and do likewise.'

I am informed that the population of Mexico is eight millions of colored, and one million of whites; and by the rapid growth of amalgamation amongst them, there is every probability that it will ere long become one entire colored nation. I am of opinion that Mexico would afford us a large field for speculation, were we to remove thither; and who can say that the day will not soon arrive, when the flag of our colored American merchants' ships from the Mexican ports shall be seen proudly waving in the breeze of the American harbors? And shall not our sons feel proud to enlist under the Mexican banner, and support her government? Surely they will . . .

> "A Colored Female of Philadelphia," *Genius of Universal Emancipation*, Vol. 3, No. 3 (January 1833). Reprinted from *The Liberator*.

I BELONG TO THIS RACE
FRANCES ELLEN WATKINS HARPER

❧ *Frances Harper, who had for some years earned her living as a lecturer in the North, spent several years in the Reconstruction South. Her eyewitness reports of conditions among the freedmen are of particular interest because of her literary background.*

Athens, Ga., Feb. 1, 1870

. . . As far as the colored people are concerned, they are beginning to get homes for themselves and depositing money in [the] Bank. They have hundreds of homes in Kentucky. There is progress in Tennessee, and even in this State while a number have been leaving, some who stay seem to be getting along prosperously. In Augusta colored persons are in the Revenue Office and Post Office. I have just been having some good meetings there. Some of my meetings pay me poorly; but I have a chance to instruct and visit among the people and talk to their Sunday-schools and day-schools also. Of course I do not pretend that all are saving money or getting homes. I rather think from what I hear that the interest of the grown-up people in getting education has somewhat subsided, owing, perhaps, in a measure, to the novelty having worn off and the absorption or rather direction of the mind to other matters. Still I don't think that I have visited scarcely a place since last August where there was no desire for a teacher. . . . There has been quite an amount of violence and trouble in the State; but we have the military here, and if they can keep Georgia out of the Union about a year or two longer, and the colored people continue to live as they have been doing, from what I hear, perhaps these rebels will learn a little more sense. I have been in Atlanta for some time, but did not stay until the Legislature was organized; but I was there when colored members returned and took their seats. It was rather a stormy time in the House; but no blood was shed. Since then there has been some "sticking;" but I don't think any of the colored ones were in it.

Eufaula, Ala., December 9, 1870

Last evening I visited one of the plantations, and had an interesting time. Oh, how warm was the welcome! I went out near dark, and between that time and attending my lecture, I was out to supper in two homes. The people are living in the old cabins of slavery; some of them have no windows at all, that I see; in fact, I don't remember of having seen a pane of window-glass in the settlement. But, humble as their homes were, I was kindly treated, and well received. . . . I had quite a little gathering, after less, perhaps, than a day's notice; the minister did not know that I was coming, till he met me in the afternoon. There was no fire in the church, and so they lit fires outside, and we gathered. . . around the fire. To-night I am going over to Georgia to lecture. In consequence of the low price of cotton, the people may not be able to pay much, and I am giving all my lectures free. . . .

It is remarkable, however, in spite of circumstances, how some of these people are getting along. Here is a woman who, with her husband, at the surrender, had a single dollar; and now they have a home of their own, and several acres attached—five altogether; but, as that was rather small, her husband has contracted for two hundred and forty acres more, and has now gone out and commenced operations. . . .

Greenville, Georgia, March 29, 1870

But really my hands are almost constantly full of work; sometimes I speak twice a day. Part of my lectures are given privately to women, and for them I never make any charge, or take up any collection. . . . I am now going to have a private meeting with the women of this place if they will come out. I am going to talk with them about their daughters, and about things connected with the welfare of the race. Now is the time for our women to begin to try to lift up their heads and plant the roots of progress under the hearthstone. Last night I spoke in a school-house, where there was not, to my knowledge, a single window-glass; to-day I write to you in a lowly cabin, where the windows in the room are formed by two apertures in the wall. There is a wide-spread and almost universal appearance of poverty in this State where I have been, but thus far I have seen no, or scarcely any, pauperism. . . . The climate is so fine, so little cold that poor people can live off of less than they can in the North. Last night my table was adorned with roses, although I did not get one cent for my lecture. . . .

The political heavens are getting somewhat overcast. Some of this old rebel element, I think, are in favor of taking away the colored man's vote, and if he loses it now it may be generations before he gets it again. Well, after all perhaps the colored man generally is not really developed enough to value his vote and equality with other races, so he gets enough to eat and drink, and be comfortable; perhaps the loss of his vote would not be a serious grievance to many; but his children differently educated and trained by circumstances might feel political inferiority rather a bitter cup.

After all whether they encourage or discourage me, I belong

to this race, and when it is down I belong to a down race; when it is up I belong to a risen race.

Demopolis, Ala., March [1], 1871

Oh, what a field there is here in this region! Let me give you a short account of this week's work. Sunday I addressed a Sunday-school in Taladega; on Monday afternoon a day-school. On Monday I rode several miles to a meeting; addressed it, and came back the same night. Got back about or after twelve o'clock. The next day I had a meeting of women and addressed them, and then lectured in the evening in the Court-House to both colored and white. Last night I spoke again, about ten miles from where I am now stopping and returned the same night, and to-morrow evening probably I shall speak again. I grow quite tired part of the time. . . . And now let me give you an anecdote or two of some of our new citizens. While in Taladega I was entertained and well entertained, at the house of one of our new citizens. He is living in the house of his former master. He is a brick-maker by trade, and I rather think mason also. He was worth to his owner, it was reckoned, fifteen hundred or about that a year. He worked with him seven years, and in that seven years he remembers receiving from him fifty cents. Now mark the contrast! That man is now free, owns the home of his former master, has I think more than sixty acres of land, and his master is in the poor-house. I heard of another such case not long since: A woman was cruelly treated once, or more than once. She escaped and ran naked into town. The villian in whose clutch she found herself was trying to drag her downward to his own low level of impurity, and at last she fell. She was poorly fed, so that she was tempted to sell her person. Even scraps thrown to the dog she was hunger-bitten enough to aim for. Poor thing, was there anything in the future for her? Had not hunger and cruelty and prostitution done their work, and left her an entire wreck for life? It seems not. Freedom came, and with it dawned a new era upon that poor, overshadowed, and sin-darkened life. Freedom brought opportunity for work and wages combined. She went to work, and got ten dollars a month. She has contrived to get some education, and has since been teaching school. While her former mistress has been to her for help.

Do not the mills of God grind exceedingly fine? And she has helped that mistress, and so has the colored man given money, from what I heard, to his former master. After all, friend, do we not belong to one of the best branches of the human race? And yet, how have our people been murdered in the South, and their bones scattered at the grave's mouth! Oh, when will we have a government strong enough to make human life safe? Only yesterday I heard of a murder committed on a man for an old grudge of several years' standing. I had visited the place, but had just got away. Last summer a Mr. Luke was hung, and several other men also, I heard. . . .

Oh, if some more of our young women would only consecrate their lives to the work of upbuilding the race! Oh, if I could only see our young men and women aiming to build up a future for themselves, which would grandly contrast with the past—with its pains, ignorance and low social condition.

> Frances E. W. Harper's letters, as cited in William Still, *The Underground Railroad* (Philadelphia: Porter & Coates, 1872), pp. 770–778.

LET THE AFRO-AMERICAN DEPEND BUT ON HIMSELF

IDA B. WELLS BARNETT

❦ In 1892, *following a dispute between black and white children, a white mob attacked a Negro-owned grocery store in Memphis, Tennessee. The owners and some of their friends defended themselves and beat off the attackers. Three black men were arrested, charged with murder and a few* days later, taken from the jail and lynched. A reign of terror against the black community followed upon this outrage. Ida B. Wells, then owner and editor of the Memphis Free Speech, exposed the lynching as having been caused by economic rivalry and white resentment over the patronage of Negro business by Blacks. She commented:

> There is nothing we can do about the lynching now, as we are out-numbered and without arms. . . . There is therefore only one thing left that we can do; save our money and leave a town which will neither protect our lives and property, nor give us a fair trial in the courts, but takes us out and murders us in cold blood when accussed by white persons.

She continued writing in this vein in her paper and was threatened with violence. "I had bought a pistol the first thing after Tom Moses was lynched," she wrote,

> because I expected some cowardly retaliation from the lynchers. I felt that one had better die fighting against injustice than to die like a dog or a rat in a trap. I had already determined to sell my life as dearly as possible if attacked. I felt if I could take one lyncher with me, this would even up the score a little bit.*

She never got the chance, for her office was mobbed and her press destroyed while she was out of town. Now herself a forced migrant from the South, Ida B. Wells continued agitating for self-defense, migration and organized resistance to discrimination in her column in The New York Age. She always stressed the need for unity within the black community. When, in response to discrimination and abuses on the Jim Crow streetcars of Atlanta, the Blacks of that city organized a boycott movement, she saw in this an exemplary combina-

* Both citations: Alfreda M. Duster, ed., *The Autobiography of Ida B. Wells* (Chicago and London: University of Chicago Press, 1970), pp. 52, 62.

tion of resistance to race oppression and the exercise of economic power. The Atlanta streetcar boycott was one of the earliest manifestations of a method of struggle which the NAACP and Urban League later perfected in the "Don't buy where you can't work" campaigns of the 1940's. The same tactic has been successfully used by the civil rights movement in the 1960's and in the present day.

The people of Atlanta are helping themselves right along in the street car matter. The ministers have taken hold of it. Elder L. Thomas, the pastor of Big Bethel, one of the largest churches in Atlanta and one other have put it to vote to their congregations whether they would ride in the cars or stay on the ground. Both voted to stay on the ground. The Atlanta *Journal* announces that the street car company lost $700 during the month of October because the colored people refused to ride and now that the white man's pocket is feeling it, this paper condemns the unjust treatment of colored passengers. It never did so before, and if they keep on losing money, the whites will be the first to petition the legislature for the repeal of any such law. Let the good work go on. A colored lady who determined to ride any way was thrown off the car two weeks ago, her head bruised, arm broken and other injuries inflicted because she would not sit in the colored people's part of the street car. I only hope this action will make others who refuse to unite with their race for a principle determine to stay off the street cars and keep their nickels to themselves.

Let the Afro-American depend on no party, but on himself for his salvation. Let him continue to education, character, and above all, put money in his purse. When he has a dollar in his pocket and many more in the bank, he can move from injustice and oppression and no one to say him nay. When he has money, and plenty of it, parties and races will become his servants. The Afro-American for the next four years should bank every five cent piece which does not have to go for the necessaries of life, and at the end of that time he will be far more independent than any party can make him. The dimes which go for car rides, for cigars, for drinks, for bootblacks, for foolishness of all sorts, make others rich and keep us poor. A wasteful and spendthrift race or individual is always poor, is always the slave of the man who has money and will never be in a position to dictate to parties, or demand race rights. Let each one of us try saving a part of every day's earnings, for the next four years and see how much better off we will be.

The Southern Emigration Association of Chicago was organized for the purpose of finding work for and locating colored people who wanted to leave the South. The association has no funds to pay the fare of those desiring to move. It only undertakes to find homes for those who are able to pay their own way. Yet many write for money to get away on, and because they do not receive it, express their belief that the Emigration Association is a humbug. It is an organization to aid those in finding work who are enterprising enough to get away from the South.

> All three items taken from "Iola's Southern Field,"
> *The New York Age*, November 19, 1892.

THE SOUTH IS OUR HOME

AMANDA SMITH JEMAND

The Southerner boasts this is a white man's country. I deny it; it is my country as well as his. The South, especially, is as much the black man's as the white man's; for every plantation, town and city shows the work of his hands.

A goodly share of the South was bought and cultivated with the proceeds from the sale of his body.

Tell me, white man, North and South, for whose country

did the black soldiers fight in the Revolutionary War? Half the Rhode Island soldiers were negroes. For whose country did they fight in the Civil War? For whose country did the black men fight and die on fair Cuba's soil? Did they fight for a white man's country or their own? If they fought for a white man's country, then they did not learn their generosity from their white brothers. . . .

Why cannot I ride in a first class car when every Southern white woman is allowed to carry her black nurse or maid into a first-class car if she chooses?

No honest man will say we get equal if separate cars. In the drug stores we can buy poison but not a five-cent glass of soda water. We can mix bread with our hands; it is good enough to go into their stomachs, but not a penny roll can we eat in their restaurants. We can sleep in their houses, in their beds, by their sides as long as we are servants; but go into some public hostelry with money to buy our lodging in a separate room and bed, immediately we have developed a case of leprosy. We should be elevated, oh yes; but our clean, respectable boys dare not darken the doors of the Young Men's Christian Association. Public libraries are for the white public. Preachers' alliances are for white preachers. . . .

We ask no social rights. I think it is time these people knew the difference between social and civil rights. If their brains could be relieved of that phantom, I am sure they would think clearer on other subjects. . . .

The Southerner would say, then if the negro would not come to us in our churches, theaters, etc., why all this? I answer, because we are human beings, because we are humiliated to know we are discriminated against. And when the Southerner says if we do not like the South let us leave it, I answer him, we do like the South, it is our home, and we shall stay here and continue to ask for civil, not social, equality.

Amanda Smith Jemand, "A Southern Woman's Appeal for Justice," *The Independent*, Vol. 52, No. 2725 (February 21, 1901), pp. 438–439.

BLACK HISTORY BUILDS RACE PRIDE

VICTORIA EARLE MATTHEWS,
MARY M. WASHINGTON,
MARY McLEOD BETHUNE

❦ Victoria Earle Matthews (1861–1898), born in Georgia, was a reformer and social worker. In 1873, she came to New York where she later married William Matthews. She had one son, who died at the age of sixteen. Mrs. Matthews was the founder and president of a New York and Brooklyn women's club, The Woman's Loyal Union. She also was one of the seven vice-presidents of the National Association of Colored Women in 1896 and one of the corresponding editors of The Woman's Era, a Boston journal. Mrs. Matthews saw the need for social work among black girls recently arrived from the South. She founded the White Rose Mission in 1897 as a shelter and rescue home and set up branches in various cities.

Her organization was a black women's counterpart of the Travelers Aid Society. Agents met the boats and trains on which black girls arrived in town, assured them of a safe place to sleep, helped them and counseled them in finding employment, and provided them with companionship, training and education at the "Home for Colored Working Girls."

Victoria Earle Matthews always had a strong interest in Black history and once planned to write a series of textbooks for black children. The selection below discusses her pioneering educational and organizational work. Later, the White Rose Mission Home was furnished with a large library of books on Black history and classes on race history were regularly held.

J. E. BRUCE, "NOTED RACE WOMEN I HAVE KNOWN AND MET"

Cambridge, Mass. Monday, Sept. 23

. . . I was well acquainted with Miss Matthews and when on a visit to New York City to visit some relatives in 1882 I called to pay my respects on this popular young woman who was then quite actively engaged in laying the foundation of the great work which had linked her name with remedial and reforming work among Negroes in New York City. Before my visit was over we had formulated a plan for the organization of a literary club for the study and discussion of racial questions to be known as the Enquiry Club. Our people at that period were not so keen about Negro history as some of us are now. They were studying Shakespeare's immortal tragedies, etc. . . . So the Enquiry Club under her presidency got very busy and soon began to find out a few things and to discover that after all we who call ourselves Negroes are really somebody, that our forebears had done some things for which they have not been given full credit. It kept up its work for over two years when interest in it waned because its members were scattered in various parts of the country and could not function as a club of this kind showed that it had planted the seeds, awakened and aroused the social consciousness thanks to this lone woman and now we have historical societies and journals of Negro history.

J. E. Bruce Manuscript, Schomburg Collection,
New York Public Library.

MRS. BOOKER T. WASHINGTON TO MRS. LUGENIA HOPE

September 15, 1922

. . . The first thing we are doing is trying to get into every school, private, public, or otherwise, Negro literature and history. We are not trying to displace any other literature or history, but trying to get all children of the country acquainted with the Negro. We feel that we can do this if we all pull together. . . . I think you will be surprised to know how many schools, North and South, even our own schools where our children are taught nothing except literature of the Caucasian race. We are not fighting any race, we are simply looking for our own. The first law of nature is Self-preservation.

We have appointed a committee, Mrs. Dickerson, Miss Bowles and Mrs. Terrell to make out such course of study for the original eighteen for one year, as they see fit to do. We will let you have this course in a little while. . . . We can secure help from men like Mr. W.B.T. Williams, Dr. Dillard and others who are traveling and visiting schools. Any suggestion, criticism, etc., you care to make, feel free to speak out. . . .

Neighborhood Union Papers, Trevor Arnett Library,
Atlanta University, Atlanta, Georgia.

MARY MCLEOD BETHUNE

If our people are to fight their way up out of bondage we must arm them with the sword and the shield and the buckler of pride—belief in themselves and their possibilities, based upon a sure knowledge of the achievements of the past. That knowledge and that pride we must give them "if it breaks every back in the kingdom."

Through the scientific investigation and objective presentation of the facts of our history and our achievement to ourselves and to all men, our Association for the Study of Negro Life and History serves to tear the veil from our eyes and allow us to see clearly and in true perspective our rightful place among all men. Through accurate research and investigation, we serve so to supplement, correct, re-orient, and annotate the story of world progress as to enhance the standing of our group in the eyes of all men. In the one hand, we bring pride to our own; in the other, we bear respect from the others.

We must tell the story with continually accruing detail from the cradle to the grave. From the mother's knee and the fireside of the home through the nursery, the kindergarten and the grade school, high school, college and university,—through the technical journals, studies and bulletins of the Association,—through newspaper, story-book and pictures, we must tell the thrilling story. When they learn the fairy tales of mythical king and queen and princess, we must let them hear, too, of the Pharoahs and African kings and the brilliant pageantry of the Valley of the Nile; when they learn of

Caesar and his legions, we must teach them of Hannibal and his Africans; when they learn of Shakespeare and Goethe, we must teach them of Pushkin and Dumas. When they read of Columbus, we must introduce the Africans who touched the shores of America before Europeans emerged from savagery; when they are thrilled by Nathan Hale, baring his breast and crying: "I have but one life to give for my country," we must make their hearts leap to see Crispus Attucks stand and fall for liberty on Boston Common with the red blood of freedom streaming down his breast. With the *Tragic Era* we give them *Black Reconstruction*; with Edison, we give them Jan Matzeliger; with John Dewey, we place Booker T. Washington; above the folk-music of the cowboy and the hill-billy, we place the spiritual and the "blues"; when they boast of Maxfield Parrish, we show them E. Simms Campbell. Whatever man has done, we have done—and often, better. As we tell this story, as we present to the world our facts, our pride in racial achievement grows, and our respect in the eyes of all men heightens.

Certainly, too, it is our task to make plain to ourselves the great story of our rise in America from "less than the dust" to the heights of sound achievement. We must recount in accurate detail the story of how the Negro population has grown from a million in 1800 to almost 12 million in 1930. The Negro worker is today an indispensible part of American agriculture and industry. His labor has built the economic empires of cotton, sugar cane and tobacco; he furnishes nearly 12 per cent of all American bread-winners, one-third of all servants, one-fifth of all farmers. In 1930, we operated one million farms and owned 750,000 homes. Negroes operate today over 22,000 business establishments with over 27 million dollars in yearly receipts and payrolls of more than five million dollars. Negroes manufacture more than 60 different commodities. They spend annually for groceries over two billion dollars, a billion more for clothes, with total purchasing power in excess of 4½ billion dollars. Negro churches have more than five million members in 42,500 organizations, owning 206 million dollars' worth of property and spending 43 million dollars a year. Some 360,000 Negroes served in the World War, with 150,000 of them going to France. Negroes are members of legislatures in 12 states; three or more states have black judges on the bench and a federal judge has recently been appointed to the Virgin Islands. Twenty-three Negroes have sat in Congress, and there is one member of the House at present. Under the "New Deal," a number of well qualified Negroes hold administrative posts.

Illiteracy has decreased from about 95 per cent in 1865 to only 16.3 per cent in 1930. In the very states that during the dark days of Reconstruction prohibited the education of Negroes by law, there are today over 2 million pupils in 25,000 elementary schools, 150,000 high school pupils in 2,000 high schools and 25,000 students in the more than 100 Negro colleges and universities. Some 116 Negroes have been elected to Phi Beta Kappa in white Northern colleges; over 60 have received the degree of Doctor of Philosophy from leading American universities and 97 Negroes are mentioned in *Who's Who in America*. It is the duty of our Association to tell the glorious story of our past and of our marvelous achievement in American life over almost insuperable obstacles.

From this history, our youth will gain confidence, self-reliance and courage. We shall thereby raise their mental horizon and give them a base from which to reach out higher and higher into the realm of achievement. And as we look about us today, we know that they must have this courage and self-reliance. We are beset on every side with heart-rending and fearsome difficulties.

Recently, in outlining to the President of the United States the position of the Negro in America, I saw fit to put it this way: "The great masses of Negro workers are depressed and unprotected in the lowest levels of agriculture and domestic service while black workers in industry are generally barred from the unions and grossly discriminated against. The housing and living conditions of the Negro masses are sordid and unhealthy; they live in a constant terror of the mob, generally shorn of their constitutionally guaranteed right of suffrage, and humiliated by the denial of civil liberties. The great masses of Negro youth are offered only one fifteenth the educational opportunity of the average American child."

These things also we must tell them, accurately, realistically and factually. The situation we face must be defined, reflected and evaluated. Then, armed with the pride and courage of his glorious tradition, conscious of his positive contribution to American life, and enabled to face clear-eyed and unabashed the situation before him, the Negro may gird his loins and go forth to battle to return "with their shields or on them." And so today I charge our Association for the Study of Negro Life and History to carry forward its great mission to arm us with the facts so that we may face the future with clear eyes and a sure vision. Our Association may say again with Emperor Jean Christophe: "While I live I shall try to build that pride we need, and build in terms white men as well as black can understand! I am thinking of the future, not of now. I will teach pride if my teaching breaks every back in my Kingdom."

Mary McLeod Bethune, "Clarifying Our Vision with the Facts," *Journal of Negro History*, Vol. 23, No. 1 (January 1938), pp. 12–15.

PLEASE STOP USING THE WORD "NEGRO"

MARY CHURCH TERRELL

TO THE EDITOR OF THE *Washington Post*   May 14, 1949

Dear Sir:

Please stop using the word "Negro". Several days ago "BAN ON WORD ASKED" was the Post's title of an appeal made by a leper who stood before a congressional committee urging that the Federal Government ban the use of the word "leper." He said the word "leper" should be removed from the dictionary because of its unjust and shameful stigma which hurts its victims and efforts to control and wipe the disease out. He wants the affliction to be called "Hanson's Disease," because lepers are treated unfairly owing to "public misunderstanding."

For a reason similar to the one given by the leper I am urging the Post and others willing to advance our interests and deal justly with our group to stop using the word "Negro". The word is a misnomer from every point of view. It does not represent a country or anything else except one single, solitary color. And no one color can describe the various and varied complexions in our group. In complexion we range from deep black to the fairest white with all the colors of the rainbow thrown in for good measure. When twenty or thirty of us are meeting together it would be as hard to find three or four of us with the same complexion as it would be to catch greased lightning in a bottle. We are the only human beings in the world with fifty seven variety of complexions who are classed together as a single racial unit. Therefore, we are really, truly colored people, and that is the only name in the English language which accurately describes us.

To be sure the complexion of the Chinese and Japanese is yellow. But nobody refers to an individual in either group as a colored man . . . They say he is Chinese. . . . When I studied abroad and was introduced as an "American," (generally speaking, everybody from the United States used to be called an "American" in Europe) occasionally somebody would say "you are rather dark to be an American, aren't you?" "Yes" I would reply, "I am dark, because some of my ancestors were Africans." I was proud of having the continent of Africa part of my ancestral background. "I am an African-American," I would explain. I am not ashamed of my African descent. Africa had great universities before there were any in England and the African was the first man industrious and skillful enough to work in iron. If our group must have a special name setting it apart, the sensible way to settle it would be to refer to our ancestors, the Africans, from whom our swarthy complexions come.

There are at least two strong reasons why I object to designating our group as Negroes. If a man is a Negro, it follows as the night the day that a woman is a Negress. "Negress" is an ugly, repulsive word—virtually a term of degradation and reproach which colored women of this country can not live down in a thousand years. I have questioned scores of men who call themselves "Negroes", and each and every one of them strenuously objected to having his wife, or daughter or mother or any woman in his family called a "Negress".

In the second place, I object to . . . Negro because our meanest detractors and most cruel persecutors insist that we shall be called by that name, so that they can humiliate us by referring contemptuously to us as "niggers", or "Negras" as Bilbo used to do. Some of our group say they will continue to classify us as Negroes, until an individual re-ferred to as such will be proud of that name. But that is a case of wishful thinking and nothing else. For the moment one hears the word Negro in this country, instantly, auto-matically, in his mind's eye he sees a human being who is ignorant, segregated, discriminated against, considered in-ferior and objectionable on general principles from every point of view. God alone knows how long it will take our minority group under prevailing conditions in this country to reach such heights that a representative of it will be proud to be called a Negro. That would be a double, back action, super-duper miracle indeed! . . .

It is a great pity the word "Negro" was not outlawed in the Emancipation Proclamation as it certainly should have been. After people have been freed, it is a cruel injustice to call them by the same name they bore as slaves. It is painful and shocking indeed that those in our group who have en-joyed educational opportunities; that officials in the National Association for the Advancement of Colored People, founded forty years ago which repudiated the word "Negro" should continue to use the slave term and thereby increase the difficulties of their group in their effort to reach the worthy goal toward which they strive.

The founders of the N.A.A.C.P. which has been and still is waging such a holy warfare against disfranchisement, segregation and discrimination of all kinds certainly deserves our gratitude for not naming that wonderful, powerful instrument for good "The National Association for the Advancement of Negroes".

Mary Church Terrell Manuscript,
Library of Congress, Washington, D.C.

GLORIFY BLACKNESS

NANNIE H. BURROUGHS

Where is the Negro going and what is he going to do when he gets there? That's the question.

Despite the fact that the race is traveling at high speed materially, it cannot get within hailing distance of the race that has a thousand years lead of him in material things. . . . In fact, America will destroy herself and revert to barbarism if she continues to cultivate the things of the flesh and neglect the higher virtues. The Negro must not, therefore, contribute to her doom, but must ransom her. Furthermore it will profit the Negro nothing to enter into ungodly competition for material possessions when he has gifts of greater value. The most valuable contribution which he can make to American civilization must be made out of his spiritual endowment. . . . The Negro has helped save America physically several times. He must make a larger contribution for her spiritual salvation. . . .

The tragedy in this problem-solving enterprise is that the Negro is not being taught the tremendous achieving power of his virtues. He is not being taught to glorify what he is. . . .

When the Negro learns what manner of man he is spiritually, he will wake up all over. He will stop playing white even on the stage. He will rise in the majesty of his own soul.

He will glorify the beauty of his own brown skin. He will stop thinking white and go to thinking straight and living right. He will realize that wrong-reaching, wrong-bleaching and wrong-mixing have "most nigh ruin't him" and he will redeem his body and rescue his soul from the bondage of that death . . . I believe it is the Negro's sacred duty to spiritualize American life and popularize his color instead of worshipping the color (or lack of color) of another race. . . . No race is richer in soul quality and color than the Negro. Someday he will realize and glorify them, he will popularize black.

. . . Preachers, teachers, leaders, welfare workers are to address themselves to the supreme task of teaching the entire race to glorify what it has—its face (its color); its place (its homes and communities); its grace (its spiritual endowment). If the Negro does it there is no earthly force that can stay him.

"With All They Getting," *The Southern Workman*,
Vol. 56, No. 7 (July 1927), pp. 299–301.

UNLOAD YOUR UNCLE TOMS

NANNIE H. BURROUGHS

"Chloroform your 'Uncle Toms'," said Miss Nannie H. Burroughs, president of the National Training School for Girls, Washington, D.C., to an applauding crowd of 2,500 that overflowed the City-wide Young Peoples' Forum, at Bethel A. M. E. church, Friday night, [December 20].

Speaking on the subject, "What Must the Negro Do To Be Saved?" Miss Burroughs said:

Chloroform your "Uncle Toms." The Negro must unload the leeches and parasitic leaders who are absolutely eating the life out of the struggling, desiring mass of people.

Negroes like that went out of style seventy years ago. They are relics and good for museums. I don't care whether they are in the church as the preacher, in the school as the teacher, in the ward as politicians—the quickest way to get rid of them is the best way, and the sooner the better. They are luxurious, expensive, unworthy. . . .

They have sold us for a mess of pottage. We got the mess, but not the pottage. The question, "What am I going to get out of it?" must get out of our thinking. This race would have been one hundred years advanced if it had not been for this thought uppermost in the minds of our so-called leaders.

Don't wait for deliverers. . . . I like that quotation, "Moses, my servant, is dead. Therefore, arise and go over Jordan." There are no deliverers. They're all dead. We must arise and go over Jordan. We can take the promised land.

The Negro must serve notice on the world that he is ready to die for justice. To struggle and battle and overcome and absolutely defeat every force designed against us is the only way to achieve. Men must have life, the opportunity to learn, to labor, to love. Without these fundamental virtues we cannot achieve. We must not give up the struggle until this is obtained.

More than this, the Negro must glorify the things of the spirit and keep the things of the flesh under control. We must get a correct sense of values. When we've accomplished this—Shiloh will be here.

Human beings are equipped with divinely planted yearnings and longings. That's what the constitution meant by— "certain inalienable rights"!

There must be no substitute for them in the form of charity, philanthropy, or any man-made institution. There must be no compromise.

The Negro is oppressed not because he is a Negro—but because he'll take it. Negroes forget your color. Stop apologizing for not being white and rank you race.

Organize yourself inside. Teach your children the internals and eternals, rather than the externals. Be more concerned with "putting in" than "getting on." We have been too bothered about the externals—clothes, money. What we need are mental and spiritual giants who are aflame with a purpose.

The Anglo-Saxon has four great loves. Love of liberty, love of home, love of women, and love of life. He'll wade through blood for these. When we make up our minds to not take substitutes for them, we'll get them.

But we're not going to get them as individuals. The day of individualism is past. We'll get them as a great race or group.

We're a race ready for crusade, for we've recognized that we're a race on this continent that can work out its own salvation. A race must build for nobility of character, for a conquest not on things, but on spirit.

We must have a glorified womanhood that can look any man in the face—white, red, yellow, brown, or black, and tell of the nobility of character within black womanhood.

Stop making slaves and servants of our women. We've got to stop singing—"Nobody works but father." The Negro mother is doing it all. The women are carrying the burden.

The main reason is that the men lack manhood and energy. They sing too much, "I Can't Give You Anything But Love, Baby." The women can't build homes, rear families off of love alone. The men ought to get down on their knees to Negro women. They've made possible all we have around us —church, home, school, business.

Aspire to be, and all that we are not, God will give us credit for trying.

The Louisiana Weekly, December 23, 1933.

THE ONLY THING YOU CAN ASPIRE TO IS NATIONHOOD

DARA ABUBAKARI (VIRGINIA E. Y. COLLINS)
VICE-PRESIDENT, SOUTH; REPUBLIC OF NEW AFRICA

❦ Virginia Collins is a frail, dynamic grandmother, who has lived most of her life in New Orleans, Louisiana.

The youngest of her ten children is sixteen years old, and she has twenty-three grandchildren. She is a registered nurse; her husband is employed in New Orleans. One of her sons, Walter, is now in jail as a draft resister.

Mrs. Collins is the oldest of fifteen children. Her father was a Baptist minister, her mother a missionary. Both had been active in community leadership, NAACP and the church, and Virginia Collins followed in the family tradition by her civil rights activity. As a PTA president, she was working for integrated education in the period following the Supreme Court school desegregation decision. She worked for the Public Education Association, an interracial educational group concerned with improvements in the curriculum. Later she helped organize and became the President of Citizens for Quality Education, a city-wide citizen's organization. She was active in the campaign to get over a hundred black paraprofessionals in the schools upgraded in their jobs. This was one of the few victories she can count in her decades of community work. She is bitterly disappointed in the results of her twenty years of work for school integration. Not one of her children has gone to an integrated school, and she feels that de facto segregation still prevails, due mostly to the gerrymandering of school districts. "Negro education has not improved. Period," she says.

From 1960 to 1964 she devoted all her time to voter registration work. She organized a voter registration project which ran day and evening schools for black voters and a series of demonstrations against discrimination in voter registration. Of 400 high school students mobilized for this campaign, 184, including several of Mrs. Collins' children —and herself—were arrested, some as many as seven times during the campaign. After passage of the Civil Rights Act of 1964 all the charges against the demonstrators were dropped. This militant campaign resulted in bringing the federal registrars into the state and winning a sizable increase in the number of black registered voters. But the ensuing small gain in representation for black people in the govern-

ment has been disappointing to Mrs. Collins. She has kept
up her work with the Coordinating Council through several
political campaigns in which black candidates for office were
defeated. She has also kept her membership on the National
Board of the Women's International League for Peace and
Freedom, a liberal women's organization. But she has given
up hope that working from within the establishment can
benefit black people. After nearly thirty years of steady
grass-roots leadership in the black community, working for
democratic social change, Virginia Collins has become a
black nationalist.

Way back in '53 I used to think that there was hope, that
maybe black and white people together could solve all the
problems. But in the recent years I learned it is not true.
I'm a separatist now. I think that black people now have to
go back to what I call the Reconstruction days in order that
black people will be able to stand in dignity and freedom.
Because there is no way for the son of a slave to stand up
to the son of a master and be two people together—because
the psychological position of both parties is still that one is
slave and one is master. And it does not change. Black people
have to get freedom for themselves; it cannot be given to
them.

The only thing you can aspire to is nationhood. We are a
nation within a nation. A territory—a five-state area, because
without land you have no nation. First I think we have to
have what the U.N. calls a plebiscite—the vote of the people.
This is what we call a negotiated settlement. We have not
been paid any indemnity for our free labor here. The Jewish
people were paid indemnity . . . We have not been paid
anything. We have built this country with our free labor. So
now we go back and ask for indemnity, for reparations.

We don't intend to force it on the government. We intend
to internationalize our problems by carrying them to the rest
of the oppressed world, which is also black. We plan to bring

our case before the World Court. Since the United States is trying to be a world power, then other pepole have to examine the condition of black people in this country.

Our movement is the Republic of New Africa. I am the Vice President, South. We held elections all over the country and I got elected. Brother Imari from Detroit became President. We have four Vice Presidents, one for each region in the country. The South is a subjugated territory; others are foreign territory. We have organizations in more than twenty cities.

We are not religious nationalists like the Muslims. They are buying land—but you cannot buy freedom. We are talking about a plebiscite conducted by the United Nations—a negotiated settlement by vote. People have to give consent to be governed. The idea is something like the Irish Republic, or like the Jews. When the Jewish people went into Palestine, and established for themselves a nation, only then did the world begin to respect the Jews as a people. They knew the Jewish people had a certain togetherness before, but their togetherness did not make them a political nation. The Jews were scattered all over. But then they got land. Now wherever Jews are they consider themselves a nation. They don't intend to go back over there, but they consider themselves a part of the nation, and their money goes over there. Why can't we do this?

What we have in mind is the states of Mississippi, Louisiana, Alabama, Georgia and South Carolina. The Black Belt area. We constitute there the attributes that make a nation by international law.

I think these states can exist by themselves because they're rich. We don't base our economic struggle on the same kinds of economics as the United States: profit. We're not talking about profit. We are talking about a collective struggle, and we're also talking about collective economics.

My whole analysis is that whites consider these to be the five poorest states, by their standards. The five poorest states in the United States. We consider them the five richest states. And we intend that the United States will say, when we present our case to them, that we could have these five states.

We feel that the land is rich. We talk about black genuis. Black people have inhibited their genius, they have not been able to use it. So with the power of creativity, which black people will use collectively, and with land and labor, we intend to create for ourselves an economy which we call collective government for the people. We have what we call inhibited talents. For ourselves we will be able to create the kind of wealth we need, not just agriculture. We will live in a technical society. With land and labor we can create wealth.

The white people who live in those states—some will stay, some will leave. If white people want to stay under black rule, we have nothing against that. And we feel that some will stay. All nations have immigrants. We will have white people that want to enter our nation.

We are different from the Panthers. The Panthers are talking about revolutionary change. We know that if a revolution would come today, the black man would still be in the same way he is. A revolution cannot change your status, even though you change hands for government. You still retain the same status that you had previously because you have not done anything about your liberation. Black people must liberate themselves before they can talk about revolution.

We get a very good response from the grass roots people. It's hard to get people to register to vote and that kind of stuff, but it's not hard to talk to people about black liberation. They respond, and even some of the more affluent Blacks respond, because they too have seen that if you're black, you're black. It doesn't matter whether you are a doctor or a lawyer, the establishment doesn't differentiate. You're black.

We feel black people have to be prepared. The police will come to your house now—they got the no-knock law—if they come here, they just knock this door open. If I resist, they'll shoot me. Not only that, but the police force down here is teaching white women to use guns. They call them rifle clubs. Black people can't have a rifle club—they can have a gun, because you can hunt, but you can't organize yourself a club. Only whites can do that. So we feel that for us, we need self-defense.

I'm very optimistic. For one reason: this is the age of revolution. Black and white, the young people question their fathers and mothers. The world is in revolution. There are going to be some changes made.

Dara Abubakari (Virginia E. Y. Collins), taped interview with Gerda Lerner, New Orleans, Louisiana, October 11, 1970.
Used by permission.

CHAPTER TEN

BLACK WOMEN SPEAK OF WOMANHOOD

For above all, in behalf of an ailing
world which sorely needs our defiance,
may we, as Negroes or women, never
accept the notion of—"our place."

Lorraine Hansberry

BLACK WOMEN SPEAK OF WOMANHOOD

❧ "What if I am a woman?" Maria Stewart asked in 1833, trying to defend herself against critics who censured her for speaking in public. "Did not Queen Esther save the lives of the Jews?. . . Did St. Paul but know of our wrongs and deprivations, I presume he would make no objection to our pleading in public for our rights. . . ." But her contemporaries were not as tolerant as she assumed St. Paul would have been. Only the urgency of her people's need had driven her to fly in the face of custom and propriety, and she had met with so much adverse criticism that she gave up after lecturing four times. "I find it is no use for me, as an individual, to try to make myself useful among my color in this city," she conceded with some bitterness. The two white women who followed in her footsteps five years later were motivated by the same concern and met the same prejudice and abuse. The Grimké sisters, like Maria Stewart, attempted to speak in public for the rights of black people and were attacked, as she had been, not as abolitionists, but as women. The difference was that five years of organizing effort had laid the groundwork for a network of female abolition societies which could sustain the speaking tour of the Grimké sisters, while Maria Stewart's lonely effort had been cut short. One hundred thirty years later, the first black woman to sit in the House of Representatives would state flatly: "Of my two 'handicaps,' being female put many more obstacles in my path than being black."*

Other women leaders at various times in history would draw attention to the special needs and concerns of black women. Sojourner Truth and Anna J. Cooper offered a distinctly feminist argument and asserted, with great convic-

* Shirley Chisholm, *Unbought and Unbossed* (Boston: Houghton Mifflin Company, 1970), p. xxi.

tion, that the needs of black women were different and
distinct from those of black men. The feminism of Fannie
Barrier Williams, Mary McLeod Bethune, Josephine St.
Pierre Ruffin and Mary Church Terrell was of a different kind.
They saw the separate organization of women as an expedient,
a means for elevating not only women but the race. Female
suffrage was similarly viewed pragmatically as a necessary
tool for winning black rights. Their feminism was also
inspired by the hope that it would be easier for black and
white women to find some common ground for cooperation
than it would be for men. In the struggle for upgrading the
educational opportunities and social services available to the
black community, such interracial cooperation of women
was, at times, effective. But, as can be seen from the YWCA
documents and the records of the Neighborhood Union
(see p. 500), such cooperation was achieved only at the price
of constant watchfulness, prodding, educational effort and
persistent militancy of black women.

The "defense of black women" argument, which appears in
a number of documents (see pp. 166, 169, 205), was similarly
a pragmatic appeal for the understanding and support of
white women. This was especially crucial in the fight against
lynchings. Black women early perceived that lynchings could
be tolerated by white communities because of the rape
charges against black men and the belief of whites in the
inherent immorality of black women. They therefore attacked
lynching by exposing the falsity of the rape charge, case by
case, and by trying to convince white women, by argument
and direct personal contacts, that black women had the same
moral standards, religious beliefs and ambitions as white
women. How effective this appeal was can be judged from
the record, but there is no doubt that women of both races
played an important role in the promotion of interracial
contact and organization.

Undoubtedly, the organization of black women in female
clubs also sprang from the recognition that women are most
readily organized by women and that they have separate and

specific interests. The effectiveness of the women's club movement has never yet been fully explored, but even the few samples in this volume should offer convincing proof that its significant role in community development and political life should not be underestimated.

It is no accident that the black women who advance the strongest feminist argument have been active on the political scene. It is in this field that sex discrimination is most obvious and explicit. The response to economic discrimination is not infrequently the organization of women into trade union locals run by women, as in the case of the Tobacco Workers' and the Domestic Workers' unions (see pp. 231, 234, 252).

Nevertheless, it appears from the record that most black women see race discrimination as a much more serious problem than sex discrimination. Black women, speaking with many voices, have been near unanimous in their insistence that their own emancipation cannot be separated from that of their men. Their liberation depends on that of the race and on the improvement of the life of the black community. Their main concern is with their families and their children. Their history has given them a strong sense of their own worth. Black womanhood speaks with dignity, pride and a strong sense of community.

WHAT IF I AM A WOMAN?
MARIA W. STEWART

❦ Maria W. Stewart was the first American-born woman to speak in public. She lectured in Boston in 1832–1833. The selection below is from her farewell address, delivered September 21, 1833.

On my arrival here, not finding scarce an individual who felt interested in these subjects, and but few of the whites, except Mr. Garrison and his friend, Mr. Knapp; and hearing that those gentlemen had observed that female influence was powerful, my soul became fired with a holy zeal for your cause; every nerve and muscle in me was engaged in your behalf. I felt that I had a great work to perform, and was in haste to make a profession of my faith in Christ that I might be about my Father's business. Soon after I made this profession the Spirit of God came before me, and I spake before many. When going home, reflecting on what I had said, I felt ashamed, and knew not where I should hide myself. A something said within my breast, "press forward, I will be with thee." And my heart made this reply: "Lord, if thou wilt be with me, then will I speak for thee so long as I live." . . .

What if I am a woman; is not the God of ancient times the God of these modern days? Did he not raise up Deborah to be a mother and a judge in Israel? Did not Queen Esther save the lives of the Jews? And Mary Magdalene first declare the resurrection of Christ from the dead? Come, said the woman of Samaria, and see a man that hath told me all things that ever I did; is not this the Christ? St. Paul declared that it was a shame for a woman to speak in public, yet our great High Priest and Advocate did not condemn the woman for a more notorious offense than this; neither will he condemn this worthless worm. . . . Did St. Paul but know of our wrongs and deprivations, I presume he would make no objection to our pleading in public for our rights. . . .

Among the Greeks, women delivered the oracles. The respect the Romans paid to the Sybils is well known. The Jews had their prophetesses. The prediction of the Egyptian women obtained much credit at Rome, even unto the emperors. And in most barbarous nations all things that have the appearance of being supernatural, the mysteries of religion, the secrets of physic, and the rights of magic, were in the possession of women.

If such women as are here described have once existed, be no longer astonished, then, my brethren and friends, that

God at this eventful period should raise up your own females to strive by their example, both in public and private, to assist those who are endeavoring to stop the strong current of prejudice that flows so profusely against us at present. No longer ridicule their efforts, it will be counted for sin. For God makes use of feeble means sometimes to bring about his most exalted purposes.

In the fifteenth century, the general spirit of this period is worthy of observation. We might then have seen women preaching and mixing themselves in controversies. Women occupying the chairs of Philosophy and Justice; women haranguing in Latin before the Pope; women writing in Greek and studying in Hebrew; nuns were poetesses and women of quality divines; and young girls who had studied eloquence would, with the sweetest countenances and the most plaintiff voices, pathetically exhort the Pope and the Christian princes to declare war against the Turks. Women in those days devoted their leisure hours to contemplation and study. The religious spirit which has animated women in all ages showed itself at this time. It has made them, by turns, martyrs, apostles, warriors, and concluded in making them divines and scholars. . . .

What if such women as are here described should rise among our sable race? And it is not impossible; for it is not the color of the skin that makes the man or the woman, but the principle formed in the soul. Brilliant wit will shine, come from whence it will; and genius and talent will not hide the brightness of its lustre.

But to return to my subject. The mighty work of reformation has begun among this people. The d'rk clouds of ignorance are dispersing. The light of science is bursting forth. Knowledge is beginning to flow; nor will its moral influence be extinguished till its refulgent rays have spread over us from East to West and from North to South. Thus far is this mighty work begun, but not as yet accomplished. . . .

Yet; notwithstanding your prospects are thus fair and bright, I am about to leave you, perhaps never more to return; for I find it is no use for me, as an individual, to try to make myself useful among my color in this city. It was contempt for my moral and religious opinions in private that drove me thus before a public. Had experience more plainly shown me that it was the nature of man to crush his fellow, I should not have thought it so hard. Wherefore, my respected friends, let us no longer talk of prejudice till prejudice becomes extinct at home. Let us no longer talk of opposition till we cease to oppose our own. . . . Men of eminence have mostly risen from obscurity; nor will I, although a female of a darker hue, and far more obscure than they, bend my head or hang my harp upon willows; for though poor, I will virtuous prove. And if it is the will of my Heavenly Father to reduce me to penury and want, I am ready to say: Amen; even so be it;

> "Mrs. Stewart's Farewell Address to Her Friends in the City of Boston. Delivered September 21, 1833," *Productions of Mrs. Maria W. Stewart* (Boston: W. Lloyd Garrison and Knapp, 1832), pp. 76–79.

I SUPPOSE I AM ABOUT THE ONLY COLORED WOMAN THAT GOES ABOUT TO SPEAK FOR THE RIGHTS OF COLORED WOMEN....

SOJOURNER TRUTH

FOURTH NATIONAL WOMAN'S RIGHTS CONVENTION, NEW YORK CITY, 1853:

Sojourner Truth, a tall colored woman, well-known in anti-slavery circles . . . made her appearance on the platform. This was the signal for a fresh outburst from the mob . . . Sojourner combined in herself . . . the two most hated elements of humanity. She was black, and she was a woman, and all the insults that could be cast upon color and sex were together hurled at her; but there she stood, calm and dignified, a grand, wise woman, who could neither read nor write, and yet with deep insight could penetrate the very soul of the universe about her. As soon as the terrible turmoil was in a measure quelled she said:

Is it not good for me to come and draw forth a spirit, to see what kind of spirit people are of? I see that some of you have got the spirit of a goose, and some have got the spirit of a snake. I feel at home here. I come to you, citizens of New York, as I suppose you ought to be. I am a citizen of the state of New York; I was born in it, and I was a slave in the state of New York; and now I am a good citizen of this State. I was born here, and I can tell you I feel at home here. I've been lookin'round and watchin' things, and I know a little mite 'bout Woman's Rights, too. I come forth to speak 'bout Woman's Rights, and want to throw in my little mite, to keep the scales a-movin'. I know that it feels a kind o' hissin' and ticklin' like to see a colored woman get up and tell you about things, and Woman's Rights. We have all been thrown down so low that nobody thought we'd ever get up again; but we have been long enough trodden now; we will come up again, and now I am here.

I was a-thinkin', when I see women contendin' for their rights, I was a-thinkin' what a difference there is now, and what there was in old times. I have only a few minutes to speak; but in the old times the kings of the earth would hear a woman. There was a king in the Scriptures; and then it was the kings of the earth would kill a woman if she come into their presence; but Queen Esther come forth, for she was oppressed, and felt there was a great wrong, and she said I will die or I will bring my complaint before the king. Should the king of the United States be greater, or more crueler, or more harder? But the king, he raised up his sceptre and said: "Thy request shall be granted unto thee—

to the half of my kingdom will I grant it to thee!" Then he said he would hang Haman on the gallows he had made up high. But that is not what women come forward to contend. The women want their rights as Esther. She only wanted to explain her rights. And he was so liberal that he said, "the half of my kingdom shall be granted to thee," and he did not wait for her to ask, he was so liberal with her.

Now, women do not ask half of a kingdom, but their rights, and they don't get 'em. When she comes to demand 'em, don't you hear how sons hiss their mothers like snakes, because they ask for their rights; and can they ask for anything less? The king ordered Haman to be hung on the gallows which he prepared to hang others; but I do not want any man to be killed, but I am sorry to see them so short-minded. But we'll have our rights; see if we don't; and you can't stop us from them; see if you can. You may hiss as much as you like, but it is comin'. Women don't get half as much rights as they ought to; we want more, and we will have it. Jesus says: "What I say to one, I say to all—watch!" I'm a-watchin'. God says: "Honor your father and your mother." Sons and daughters ought to behave themselves before their mothers, but they do not. I can see them a-laughin' and pointin' at their mothers up here on the stage. They hiss when an aged woman comes forth. If they'd been brought up proper they'd have known better than hissing like snakes and geese. I'm 'round watchin' these things, and I wanted to come up and say these few things to you, and I'm glad of the hearin' you give me. I wanted to tell you a mite about Woman's Rights, and so I came out and said so. I am sittin' among you to watch; and every once and awhile I will come out and tell you what time of night it is.

CONVENTION OF THE AMERICAN EQUAL RIGHTS ASSOCIATION, NEW YORK CITY, 1867:

❦ *The movements for the abolition of slavery and for the rights of women had for nearly thirty years been* closely linked. During the Civil War feminists had subordinated their own interests to an all-out effort on behalf of "the Negro's cause," agitating and petitioning for passage of the Thirteenth Amendment, which they expected would include women. They were bitterly disappointed when abolitionists, struggling to get controversial Negro suffrage legislation passed, were unwilling to saddle their cause with the even less popular one of female suffrage. The issue precipitated a serious rift between abolitionists and feminists and would later cause a split within the women's rights movement. Even so staunch a defender of women's rights as Frederick Douglass declared that this was "the Negro's Hour" and that the desperate plight of the freedmen and the terrible prejudice prevailing against them made their cause more urgent that that of women. But no one, except Sojourner Truth, spoke for those doubly oppressed by race and sex.

My friends, I am rejoiced that you are glad, but I don't know how you will feel when I get through. I come from another field—the country of the slave. They have got their liberty— so much good luck to have slavery partly destroyed; not entirely. I want it root and branch destroyed. Then we will all be free indeed. I feel that if I have to answer for the deeds done in my body just as much as a man, I have a right to have just as much as a man. There is a great stir about colored men getting their rights, but not a word about the colored women; and if colored men get their rights, and not colored women theirs, you see the colored men will be masters over the women, and it will be just as bad as it was before. So I am for keeping the thing going while things are stirring; because if we wait till it is still, it will take a great while to get it going again. White women are a great deal smarter, and know more than colored women, while colored women do not know scarcely anything. They go out washing, which is about as high as a colored woman gets, and their men go about idle, strutting up and down; and when the women come home, they ask for their money and take it all, and then scold because there is no food. I want you to consider on that, chil'n. I call you chil'n; you are somebody's chil'n, and I am old enough to be mother of all that is here. I want women to have their rights. In the courts women have no right, no voice; nobody speaks for them. I wish woman to have her voice there among the pettifoggers. If it is not a fit place for women, it is unfit for men to be there.

I am above eighty years old; it is about time for me to be going. I have been forty years a slave and forty years free, and would be here forty years more to have equal rights for all. I suppose I am kept here because something remains for me to do; I suppose I am yet to help to break the chain. I have done a great deal of work; as much as a man, but did not get so much pay. I used to work in the field and bind grain, keeping up with the cradler; but men doing no more, got twice as much pay. . . . We do as much, we eat as much, we want as much. I suppose I am about the only colored woman that goes about to speak for the rights of the colored women. I want to keep the thing stirring, now that the ice is cracked. What we want is a little money. You men know that you get as much again as women, when you write, or for what you do. When we get our rights, we shall not have to come to you for money, for then we shall have money enough in our own pockets; and maybe you will ask us for money. But help us now until we get it. It is a good consolation to know that when we have got this battle once fought we shall not be coming to you any more. . . .

I am glad to see that men are getting their rights, but I want women to get theirs, and while the water is stirring I will step into the pool. Now that there is a great stir about colored men's getting their rights is the time for women to step in and have theirs. I am sometimes told that "Women aint fit to vote. Why, don't you know that a woman had seven devils in her: and do you suppose a woman is fit to rule the nation?" Seven devils aint no account; a man had a legion in him. The devils didn't know where to go; and so they asked that they might go into the swine. They thought that was as good a place as they came out from. They didn't ask to go into the sheep—no, into the hog; that was the selfish beast; and man is so selfish that he has got women's rights and his own too, and yet he won't give women their rights. He keeps them all to himself. . . .

❦ *Later on, during the evening session, Sojourner spoke once again. Introducing her, Susan Anthony remarked that Sojourner was forty years a slave in the state of New York. She was a product of the barbarism of New York, and one of her fingers was chopped off by her cruel master in a moment of anger.*

I have lived on through all that has taken place these forty years in the anti-slavery cause, and I have plead with all the force I had that the day might come that the colored people might own their soul and body. Well, the day has come, although it came through blood. It makes no difference how it came—it did come. I am sorry it came in that way. We are now trying for liberty that requires no blood—that women shall have their rights—not rights from you. Give them what belongs to them; they ask it kindly too. I ask it kindly. Now, I want it done very quick. It can be done in a few years. How good it would be. I would like to go up to the polls myself. I own a little house in Battle Creek, Michigan. Well, every year I got a tax to pay. Taxes, you see, be taxes. Well, a road tax sounds large. . . . There was women there that had a house as well as I. They taxed them to build a road, and they went on the road and worked. It took 'em a good while to get a stump up. Now, that shows that women can work. If they can dig up stumps they can vote. It is easier to vote than dig stumps. It doesn't seem hard work to vote, though I have seen some men that had a hard time of it. . . . I don't want to take up your time, but I calculate to live.

Now, if you want me to get out of the world, you had better get the women votin' soon. I shan't go till I can do that.

Both items: E. C. Stanton *et al.*, *History of Woman Suffrage*, 6 vols. (New York: Fowler and Wells, 1881–1922): Vol. 1, pp. 567–568, Vol. 2, pp. 193–194, 222, 224–225.

THE COLORED WOMAN SHOULD NOT BE IGNORED

ANNA J. COOPER

❦ Anna Julia Cooper (1858–1964) was born into slavery in Raleigh, North Carolina. She graduated from St. Augustine Normal School in that city in 1869, began teaching at an early age and married the Reverend George A. C. Cooper in 1877. She was left a widow two years later. She completed her education at Oberlin College, obtaining an M.A. degree in 1884. She spent most of her life as an educator. Her service as a teacher in the Washington, D.C., public schools began in 1887. In 1901, she became the second female school principal in Washington, D.C., holding that office at "M" Street High School for Negroes. A a crusader for higher education, she secured scholarships and admissions for black students at Harvard, Yale and Brown Universities. Near retirement age, she earned a Ph.D. in Latin at the Sorbonne in Paris and published two historical works in French. In her later years, she established Frelinghuysen University in Washington, D.C., an evening college for employed adults, and served as the institution's President from 1929 to 1941. The excerpt below is from her book, *A Voice from the South,* a collection of her essays and speeches.

The colored woman of to-day occupies, one may say, a unique position in this country. In a period of itself transitional and unsettled, her status seems one of the least ascertainable and definitive of all the forces which make for our civilization. She is confronted by both a woman question and a race problem, and is as yet an unknown or an unacknowledged factor in both. While the women of the white race can with calm assurance enter upon the work they feel by nature appointed to do, while their men give loyal support and appreciative countenance to their efforts . . . the colored woman too often finds herself hampered and shamed by a less liberal sentiment and a more conservative attitude on the part of those for whose opinion she cares most. That this is not universally true I am glad to admit. There are to be found both intensely conservative white men and exceedingly liberal colored men. But as far as my experience goes the average man of our race is less frequently ready to admit the actual need among the sturdier forces of the world for woman's help or influence. . . .

Fifty years ago woman's activity according to orthodox definitions was on a pretty clearly cut "sphere," including primarily the kitchen and the nursery, and rescued from the barrenness of prison bars by the womanly mania for adorning every discoverable bit of china or canvass with forlorn looking cranes balanced idiotically on one foot. The woman of to-day finds herself in the presence of responsibilities which ramify through the profoundest and most varied interests of her country and race. . . . No plan for renovating society, no scheme for purifying politics, no reform in church or in state, no moral, social, or economic question, no movement upward or downward in the human plane is lost on her. A man once said when told his house was afire: "Go tell my wife; I never meddle with household affairs." But no woman can possibly put herself or her sex outside any of the interests that affect humanity. All departments in the new era are to be hers, in the sense that her interests are in all and through all; and it is incumbent on her to keep intelligently and sympathetically *en rapport* with all the great movements of her time, that she may know on which side to throw the weight of her influence. She stands now at the gateway of this new era of American civilization. In her hands must be moulded the strength, the wit, the statesmanship, the morality, all the psychic force, the social and economic intercourse of that era. To be alive at such an epoch is a privilege, to be a woman then is sublime. . . .

But to be a woman of the Negro race in America, and to be able to grasp the deep significance of the possibilities of the crisis, is to have a heritage, it seems to me, unique in the ages. In the first place, the race is young and full of the elasticity and hopefulness of youth. All its achievements are before it. It does not look on the masterly triumphs of nineteenth century civilization with that *blasé* world-weary look which characterizes the old washed out and worn out races which have already, so to speak, seen their best days.

Said a European writer recently: "Except the Slavonic, the Negro is the only original and distinctive genius which has yet to come to growth—and the feeling is to cherish and develop it."

Everything to this race is new and strange and inspiring. There is a quickening of its pulses and a glowing of its self-consciousness. Aha, I can rival that! I can aspire to that! I can honor my name and vindicate my race! Something like this, it strikes me, is the enthusiasm which stirs the genius of a young Africa in America; and the memory of past oppression and the fact of present attempted repression only serve to gather momentum for its irrepressible powers. Then again, a race in such a stage of growth is peculiarly sensitive to impressions. . . .

What a responsibility then to have the sole management of the primal lights and shadows! Such is the colored woman's office. She must stamp weal or woe on the coming history of this people. May she see her opportunity and vindicate her high prerogative.

Anna J. Cooper, A *Voice from the South by A Black Woman of the South* (Xenia, Ohio: The Aldine Printing House, 1892), pp. 134, 135, 142–145.

THE NEW BLACK WOMAN

FANNIE BARRIER WILLIAMS

Afro-American women of the United States have never had the benefit of a discriminating judgment concerning their worth as women made up of the good and bad of human nature. . . . These women have been left to grope their way unassisted toward a realization of those . . . standards of family and social life that are the badges of race respectability. They have had no special teachers to instruct them. No conventions of distinguished women of the more favored race have met to consider their peculiar needs. There has been no fixed public opinion to which they could appeal; no protection against the libelous attacks upon their characters, and no chivalry generous enough to guarantee their safety against man's inhumanity to woman. Certain it is that colored women have been the least known, and the most ill-favored class of women in this country.

Thirty-five years ago they were unsocialized, unclassed and unrecognized as either maids or matrons. They were simply women whose character and personality excited no interest. If within thirty-five years they have become sufficiently important to be studied apart from the general race problem and have come to be recognized as an integral part of the general womanhood of American civilization, that fact is a gratifying evidence of real progress.

In considering the social advancement of these women, it is important to keep in mind the point from which progress began, and the fact that they have been mainly self-taught in all those precious things that make for social order, purity and character. They have gradually become conscious of the fact that progress includes a great deal more than what is generally meant by the terms culture, education and contact.

The club movement among colored women reaches into the sub-social condition of the entire race. Among white women clubs mean the forward movement of the best women in the interest of the best womanhood. Among colored women the club is the effort of the few competent in behalf of the many incompetent; that is to say that the club is only one of many means for the social uplift of a race. Among white women the club is the onward movement of the already uplifted.

The consciousness of being fully free has not yet come to the great masses of the colored women in this country. The emancipation of the mind and spirit of the race could not be accomplished by legislation. More time, more patience, more suffering and more charity are still needed to complete the work of emancipation. . . .

Colored women organized have succeeded in touching the heart of the race, and for the first time the thrill of unity has been felt. They have set in motion moral forces that are beginning to socialize interests that have been kept apart by ignorance and the spirit of dependence.

They have begun to make the virtues as well as the wants of the colored women known to the American people. They are striving to put a new social value on themselves. Yet their work has just begun. It takes more than five or ten years to effect the social uplift of a whole race of people.

The club movement is well purposed . . . It is not a fad . . . It is rather the force of a new intelligence against the old ignorance. The struggle of an enlightened conscience against the whole brood of social miseries, born out of the stress and pain of a hated past.

"Club Movement Among Colored Women of America," [J. E. MacBrady, ed.], A *New Negro for a New Century* (Chicago: American Publishing House, n.d. [1900]), pp. 381–383, 427–428.

WOMEN AS LEADERS

AMY-JACQUES GARVEY

❧ *Amy-Jacques Garvey is the widow of Marcus Garvey, the West Indian–born founder of the Universal*

Negro Improvement Association (UNIA), a powerful "Back
to Africa" movement which at its peak in the early 1920's
embraced a world-wide membership of two million, with an
estimated four million sympathizers. A strong advocate of
race consciousness and black nationalism, Garvey was opposed
by white authorities and the established Negro leadership,
but had a magnetic effect on the black masses. Convicted on
a dubious charge of mail fraud, he was jailed in 1925 and
deported in 1927. Amy-Jacques Garvey was her husband's
secretary and co-worker. For four years she edited a women's
page in Negro World, the popular newspaper published
by the UNIA from 1918 to 1933. In 1925, she edited and
published The Philosophy and Opinions of Marcus Garvey
and Garveyism (New York: Universal Publishers), a two-
volume compilation of her husband's ideas. Since Garvey's
death in London in 1940, she has remained active in black
nationalist work, written a biography, Garvey and Garveyism
(New York: University Place, 1963), and a book of articles
(1966). She resides in Jamaica, West Indies.

The exigencies of this present age require that women take
their places beside their men. White women are rallying all
their forces and uniting regardless of national boundaries to
save their race from destruction, and preserve its ideals for
posterity. . . . White men have begun to realize that as
women are the backbone of the home, so can they, by their
economic experience and their aptitude for details participate effectively in guiding the destiny of nation and race.

No line of endeavor remains closed for long to the modern
woman. She agitates for equal opportunities and gets them;
she makes good on the job and gains the respect of men
who heretofore opposed her. She prefers to be a bread-winner
than a half-starved wife at home. She is not afraid of hard
work, and by being independent she gets more out of the
present-day husband than her grandmother did in the good
old days.

The women of the East, both yellow and black, are slowly,

but surely imitating the women of the Western world, and as the white women are bolstering up a decaying white civilization, even so women of the darker races are sallying forth to help their men establish a civilization according to their own standards, and to strive for world leadership.

Women of all climes and races have as great a part to play in the development of their particular group as the men. Some readers may not agree with us on this issue, but do they not mould the minds of their children the future men and women? Even before birth a mother can so direct her thoughts and conduct as to bring into the world either a genius or an idiot. Imagine the early years of contact between mother and child, when she directs his form of speech, and is responsible for his conduct and deportment. Many a man has risen from the depths of poverty and obscurity and made his mark in life because of the advices and councils of a good mother whose influence guided his footsteps throughout his life.

Women therefore are extending this holy influence outside the realms of the home, softening the ills of the world by their gracious and kindly contact.

Some men may argue that the home will be broken up and women will become coarse and lose their gentle appeal. We do not think so, because everything can be done with moderation. . . . The doll-baby type of woman is a thing of the past, and the wide-awake woman is forging ahead prepared for all emergencies, and ready to answer any call, even if it be to face the cannons on the battlefield.

New York has a woman Secretary of State. Two States have women Governors, and we would not be surprised if within the next ten years a woman graces the White House in Washington D.C. Women are also filling diplomatic positions, and from time immemorial women have been used as spies to get information for their country.

White women have greater opportunities to display their ability because of the standing of both races, and due to the fact that black men are less appreciative of their women than white men. The former will more readily sing the praises of white women than their own; yet who is more deserving of admiration than the black woman, she who has borne the rigors of slavery, the deprivations consequent on a pauperized race, and the indignities heaped upon a weak and defenseless people? Yet she has suffered all with fortitude, and stands ever ready to help in the onward march to freedom and power.

Be not discouraged black women of the world, but push forward, regardless of the lack of appreciation shown you. A race must be saved, a country must be redeemed, and unless you strengthen the leadership of vacillating Negro men, we will remain marking time until the Yellow race gains leadership of the world, and we be forced to subserviency under them, or extermination.

We are tired of hearing Negro men say, "There is a better day coming," while they do nothing to usher in the day. We are becoming so impatient that we are getting in the front ranks, and serve notice on the world that we will brush aside the halting, cowardly Negro men, and with prayer on our lips and arms prepared for any fray, we will press on and on until victory is ours.

Africa must be for Africans, and Negroes everywhere must be independent, God being our guide. Mr. Black man, watch your step! Ethiopia's queens will reign again, and her Amazons protect her shores and people. Strengthen your shaking knees, and move forward, or we will displace you and lead on to victory and to glory.

Editorial, The *Negro World*, October 24, 1925.

A CENTURY OF PROGRESS
OF NEGRO WOMEN

MARY McLEOD BETHUNE

To Frederick Douglass is credited the plea that, "the Negro be not judged by the heights to which he is risen, but by the depths from which he has climbed." Judged on that basis, the Negro woman embodies one of the modern miracles of the New World.

One hundred years ago she was the most pathetic figure on the American continent. She was not a person, in the opinion of many, but a thing—a thing whose personality had no claim to the respect of mankind. She was a house-hold drudge,—a means for getting distasteful work done; she was an animated agricultural implement to augment the service of mules and plows in cultivating and harvesting the cotton crop. Then she was an automatic incubator, a producer of human live stock, beneath whose heart and lungs more potential laborers could be bred and nurtured and brought to the light of toilsome day.

Today she stands side by side with the finest manhood the race has been able to produce. Whatever the achievements of the Negro man in letters, business, art, pulpit, civic progress and moral reform, he cannot but share them with his sister of darker hue. Whatever glory belongs to the race for a development unprecedented in history for the given length of time, a full share belongs to the womanhood of the race. . . .

By the very force of circumstances, the part she has played in the progress of the race has been of necessity, to a certain extent, subtle and indirect. She has not always been permitted a place in the front ranks where she could show her face and make her voice heard with effect. . . . [But] she has been quick to seize every opportunity which presented itself to come more and more into the open and strive directly for the uplift of the race and nation. In that direction, her achievements have been amazing. . . .

Negro women have made outstanding contributions in the arts. Meta V. W. Fuller and May Howard Jackson are significant figures in Fine Arts development. Angelina Grimké,*

---

* Angelina Weld Grimké (1880–1958), poet and teacher, was the daughter of Archibald Henry Grimké, a lawyer and distinguished race leader. Her father was the son of slaveholder Henry Grimké and his slave, Nancy

Georgia Douglass Johnson and Alice Dunbar Nelson are poets of note. Jessie Fausett has become famous as a novelist. In the field of Music Anita Patti Brown, Lillian Evanti, Elizabeth Greenfield, Florence Cole-Talbert, Marion Anderson and Marie Selika stand out pre-eminently.

Very early in the post-emancipation period women began to show signs of ability to contribute to the business progress of the Race. Maggie L. Walker, who is outstanding as the guiding spirit of the Order of Saint Luke . . . in 1902 . . . went before her Grand Council with a plan for a Saint Luke Penny Savings Bank. This organization started with a deposit of about eight thousand dollars and twenty-five thousand in paid-up capital, with Maggie L. Walker as the first Woman Bank President in America. For twenty-seven years she has held this place. Her bank has paid dividends to its stockholders; has served as a depository for gas and water accounts of the city of Richmond and has given employment to hundreds of Negro clerks, bookkeepers and office workers. . . .

With America's great emphasis on the physical appearance, a Negro woman left her wash-tub and ventured into the field of facial beautification. From a humble beginning Madame C. J. Walker built a substantial institution that is a credit to American business in every way.

Mrs. Annie M. Malone is another pioneer in this field of successful business. The C. J. Walker Manufacturing Company and the Poro College do not confine their activities in the field of beautification, to race. They serve both races and give employment to both. . . .

When the ballot was made available to the Womanhood of America, the sister of darker hue was not slow to seize the advantage. In sections where the Negro could gain access to the voting booth, the intelligent, forward-looking element

Weston (see pp. 52–53). Angelina Weld Grimké was named after her white great-aunt, the abolitionist Angelina Grimké Weld, who after the Civil War learned of the existence of her three mulatto nephews, accepted them as family members and paid for their education.

of the Race's women have taken hold of political issues with an enthusiasm and mental acumen that might well set worthy examples for other groups. Oftimes she has led the struggle toward moral improvement and political record, and has compelled her reluctant brother to follow her determined lead. . . .

In time of war as in time of peace, the Negro woman has ever been ready to . . . [serve] . . . for her people's and the nation's good. . . . During the recent World War . . . she . . . pleaded to go in the uniform of the Red Cross nurse and was denied the opportunity only on the basis of racial distinction.

Addie W. Hunton and Kathryn M. Johnson gave yeoman service with the American Expeditionary Forces . . . with the Y. M. C. A. group. . . .

Negro women have thrown themselves whole-heartedly into the organization of groups to direct the social uplift of their fellowmen . . . one of the greatest achievements of the race.

Perhaps the most outstanding individual social worker of our group today is Jane E. Hunter, founder and executive secretary of the Phillis Wheatley Association, Cleveland, Ohio.

In November, 1911, Miss Hunter, who had been a nurse in Cleveland for only a short time, recognizing the need for a Working Girls' Home, organized the Association and prepared to establish the work. Today the Association is housed in a magnificent structure of nine stories, containing one hundred thirty-five rooms, offices, parlours, a cafeteria and beauty parlour. It is not only a home for working girls but a recreational center and ideal hospice for the Young Negro woman who is living away from home. It maintains an employment department and a fine, up-to-date camp. Branches of the activities of the main Phillis Wheatley are located in other sections of Cleveland, special emphasis being given to the recreational facilities for children and young women of the vicinities in which the branches are located.

In no field of modern social relationship has the hand of

service and the influence of the Negro woman been felt more distinctly than in the Negro orthodox church. . . . It may be safely said that the chief sustaining force in support of the pulpit and the various phases of missionary enterprise has been the feminine element of the membership. The development of the Negro church since the Civil War has been another of the modern miracles. Throughout its growth the untiring effort, the unflagging enthusiasm, the sacrificial contribution of time, effort and cash earnings of the black woman have been the most significant factors, without which the modern Negro church would have no history worth the writing. . . .

Both before and since emancipation, by some rare gift, she has been able . . . to hold onto the fibres of family unity and keep the home one unimpaired whole. In recent years it has become increasingly the case where in many instances, the mother is the sole dependence of the home, and single-handed, fights the wolf from the door, while the father submits unwillingly to enforced idleness and unavoidable unemployment. Yet in myriads of instances she controls home discipline with a tight rein and exerts a unifying influence that is the miracle of the century. . . .

The true worth of a race must be measured by the character of its womanhood. . . .

As the years have gone on the Negro woman has touched the most vital fields in the civilization of today. Wherever she has contributed she has left the mark of a strong character. The educational institutions she has established and directed have met the needs of her young people; her cultural development has concentrated itself into artistic presentation accepted and acclaimed by meritorious critics; she is successful as a poet and a novelist; she is shrewd in business and capable in politics; she recognizes the importance of uplifting her people through social, civic and religious activities; starting at the time when as a "mammy" she nursed the infants of the other race and taught him her meagre store of truth, she has been a contributing factor of note to interracial relations.

Finally, through the past century she has made and kept her home intact—humble though it may have been in many instances. She has made and is making history.

"A Century of Progress of Negro Women," an address delivered before the Chicago Women's Federation, June 30, 1933. Typescript, Amistad Research Center, Dillard University, New Orleans, Louisiana.

THE STRENGTH OF THE NEGRO MOTHER

MAHALIA JACKSON

As far as socializing goes, we colored people have . . . got our own social life and family life and it can be rich and satisfying. And I wouldn't be surprised if a lot of the time it's even happier than white folks'!

Negroes make a mistake in believing they're going to be in paradise if they have more money and less discrimination. It will be nice to have the clean homes to live in and education for the children and other opportunities, but for a long time the Negro hasn't needed money to be happy. Colored people are used to being happy with less. In New Orleans they lived freely. They didn't work on Saturday, and Blue Monday nobody worked either. They had dances and house rent parties and socials, and lived slowly.

Here and there you find colored men who marry white, but I think they are going the long way around to find happiness. I have nothing against intermarriage except that it means a Negro man leaving behind the Negro woman who has worked and suffered with him since slavery times.

I say to him, "What is going to happen to the Negro woman if when you're successful you marry out of your race? Who's going to make her feel she's an important lady?"

Ever since slavery times it's been the Negro woman in the South who has had to shoulder the burden of strength and dignity in the colored family. Even when she let the white man have his way with her—and it must have happened often because many, many Negroes in this country are not black like myself—I believe she went with the plantation master or the field overseer or his sons so they would be easier on the colored men on her plantation. She had some control over the white men and could make them act more kindly toward her people.

Down in the South the white man has never given the Negro man a job he could be very proud of. He has always called him "Boy" or by some nickname. It was hard for colored children to be proud of fathers who were treated like that and it was usually the Negro mother who had to keep a certain dignity in the family to offset the inferiority the white man inflicted on her husband. She held her head up high and she showed the way to her children.

I believe that right now down South behind most of those brave colored school children and college students you'll find there still is a Negro mother telling them to hold their heads up—to face the white men who try to hurt them and ridicule them—with patience and dignity. When I hear people talking about Communists being behind the colored students, I have to laugh. It's not Communists—it's Negro mothers who believe it's time for their children to fight for their rights and a good education.

Mahalia Jackson with E. M. Wylie, *Movin' On Up*
(New York: Hawthorne Books, 1966), pp. 100–101.

THE BLACK WOMAN IS
LIBERATED IN HER OWN MIND

DARA ABUBAKARI (VIRGINIA E. Y. COLLINS)
VICE-PRESIDENT, SOUTH; REPUBLIC OF NEW AFRICA

I feel that the role of black woman at this point in history is to give sustenance to the black man. At one time the black woman was the only one that could say something and not get her head chopped off. You could say certain things, you could raise the banner high. But the law was strictly against the black man. So he could not do anything. Now that he speaks, we speak together. We cannot separate, and this is what I say to the Women's Lib movement. You cannot separate men from women when you're black. The black woman is not undergoing the same kind of oppression that white women have gone through in the homes. The black woman is liberated in her own mind, because she has taken on responsibility for the family and she works. Black women had to get in the labor force, because black men didn't have jobs.

The black woman is independent. She's always been educated in the school of hard knocks. And she has had to make her way, even with the family, the children, everything. Not in my family. My father was a strong black man. My mother never worked. But it's true, that in the black family the woman often calls the tune. I'm against that, because that makes the whole family structure lopsided. I think the man should come forth. The man should be at the head of his household. Still, I don't mean we should take jobs away from black women.

The point is, that there are only two kinds of oppressed people in this country, and that is black people and women. Still, the struggle of black women and white women is not the same. Because the white woman is oppressed and is only now realizing her oppression. White women, middle-class women have to look at their problem and it is their husbands. He is the oppressor, because he is the system. It's a white male system. This is why she's got to look at him. The white woman can start there, but she can't solve her problem by saying, down with marriage. She has to start politicizing.

I also charge the white woman with complicity. When things went down with the black woman, if we had gotten together then, we would have been able to change things. But the white woman, up to now, chose to be a China doll. Even the woman's suffrage movement, after they got the vote, they did nothing else. They acquiesced. That was a disservice.

Now the black woman has been independent, but still she hasn't been able to make any decisions. She is liberated in her own mind, but the whole country still oppresses her as a woman. Women must be free to choose what they want. They should be free to decide if and when they want children. Maybe in this phase of the game we feel that we don't need any children because we have to fight the liberation struggle. So we won't have any children. We have the right to say so. Men shouldn't tell us. Nobody should tell us. Then I think women have a right to education. They have a right to knowledge.

Dara Abubakari (Virginia E. Y. Collins), taped interview with Gerda Lerner, New Orleans, Louisiana, October 11, 1970. Used by permission.

WOMEN'S LIBERATION HAS A DIFFERENT MEANING FOR BLACKS
RENEE FERGUSON

❦ *The author is on the editorial-page staff of The Washington Post.*

The women's liberation movement touches some sensitive nerves among black women—but they are not always the nerves the movement seems to touch among so many whites.

At a time when some radical white feminists are striving for a different family structure, many black women are trying to stabilize their families. They are making a special effort, in a great number of cases, to assume the wife and mother role more effectively. Whether a black woman feels that she can relate to the women's liberation movement and the extent to which she is or is not involved in it may well depend on her age and her experiences.

Dr. Anna Hedgeman, for instance, who takes pride in the fact that she lived in Harlem for most of the 30 years she has lived in New York, is a strong advocate of the women's liberation movement. She believes that there is no way in which black women in America are uninvolved in the movement. "We as Afro-American women have to face the problems of total discrimination in our society," Dr. Hedgeman says. "We have had the extra burden of being women. But if you just review the problems that women face you need only substitute the word Afro-American people for the word women and you have the same problems—job discrimination, want ads that discriminate and false stereotypes."

On the other hand, Howard University senior and Student Association Secretary Pamely Preston doesn't think that the women's liberation movement has any meaning for black women. "As far as I'm concerned the women's liberation movement is trite, trivial and simple. It's just another white political fad," Miss Preston says. "Black people have some of the same problems that they had when they were first brought to this country. That's what we've got to deal with." If the relatively modest turnout of black women for the recent Women's Liberation Day demonstrations is any indication of the black women's interest in the movement, then perhaps Miss Preston's attitude is indicative of the way most black women feel.

These vastly differing attitudes raise a real question about the extent to which the women's liberation movement means very much to black women. Do black women and white women have the same social, economic and political priorities and problems and how do they affect the status of the women's liberation movement in the minds of black women?

In a 1963 article which appeared in the *Washington Post*, the President of the National Council of Negro Women,

Dorothy Height, said, "A Negro woman has the same kind of problems as other women, but she can't take the same things for granted. For instance, she has to raise children who seldom have the same sense of security that white children have when they see their father accepted as a successful member of the community. A Negro child's father is ignored as though he didn't exist."

The instability of the black inner-city family has been the subject of concern and study by sociologists for years. . . .

Local singer Marjorie Barnes in citing the problems of the instability of black families as one of her main reasons for non-involvement in the women's liberation movement, says, "I don't think that black women can afford to be competitive with their men—especially now. Competing with them for jobs would just add to the problem that already exists. Black women have been able to find work when their husbands couldn't and have often been the head of the family not because they wanted to be but out of economic necessity. Some of those women's lib girls are asking for jobs that black men haven't been able to get."

Miss Barnes adds, "Black women have the additional problem of raising their children in crime ridden neighborhoods and they've got to see to it that their children receive a decent basic education. Most black women don't have time to take up a white middle class cause like women's lib unless they're trying to hide from the realities of the struggle for black liberation."

During a recent interview Miss Height, who served as a member of President Kennedy's commission on the status of women and who has been working actively for women's liberation for many years, explained the lack of black involvement in the movement this way:

"A few days ago we observed the fiftieth anniversary of women's suffrage, but in 1965 black women had to work for the passage of a voting rights act in order to make it possible for millions of black people to have their right to vote protected. I think that it is not that black women are not interested in the liberation of women, but many people have not recognized that everyone has to work for the liberation of black people—men and women."

Even those black women who vehemently oppose the women's liberation movement agree that some of the political and social reforms for which the movement is working and have helped achieve will help black women.

They agree that abortion reform and free child care centers would be of considerable value to black women. And they acknowledge the fact that a strong woman's lobby helped pass the New York State abortion reform law, which will have a positive effect on halting the heretofore growing rate of New York hospital emergency cases of black and other minority-group women who attempt to perform self-induced abortions.

They were also unable to deny the fact that black women are the victims of stereotypes which are not the same as white stereotypes but possibly more hurtful.

When asked to describe the black stereotypical woman Miss Preston replies, "Black women are pictured by some segments of white society and even by some black men as loud, obstinate, domineering, emasculating and generally immoral—that old Sapphire image. In contrast white women are stereotyped as blue-eyed, virtuous, to-be-put-on-a-pedestal types. But I don't think it's going to take any women's liberation movement to remove those stereotypes."

Miss Height believes that the main black stereotype of black women pictures them as the domineering matriarch.

"There is a complete denial by this society of the fact that since the slave ships brought the black woman to this country she has had to hold the family together," Miss Height says.

"She has been forced into a position of responsibility. These stereotypes have even caused the black male to think that he is dominated. The whole culture downgrades women. White women aren't treated as real human beings. They must be subservient to the male and are at his mercy for being called either beautiful and dumb or smart and aggressive.

"The black woman has had to struggle against being a person of great strength. She has had to demonstrate the skill to cope with what has happened to the whole black family. Black women have had to make for themselves services that white women have been able to take for granted. We had to take care of our own teen-age mothers when white women had the Florence Crittendon homes over the years. Our children had to carry the door key around their necks because there were no day care centers for black working mothers."

Another important issue of the women's liberation movement has been sexual exploitation. White women are rebelling against advertising that insults women and magazines that depict women as nonthinking, bosomy bundles of sexiness placed on earth for the benefit of the Playboy Magazine centerfold and the prurient interests of men.

To black women, the term sexual exploitation has a completely different meaning. Dr. Hedgeman describes the sexual exploitation of black women through the mass media. "We just weren't even there. We've had the greater sexual exploitation because we were ignored. We've not been seen. It's only been in the last couple of years that even the ads recognized the fact that we use toothpaste. And since then we've been used in the same stupid ways as women have always been used. In addition to that, Afro-American women have been sexually abused. During slavery we were chattel, breeders and often times at the mercy of slave owners. That was a form of sexual exploitation that affects us even today."

Perhaps the lack of involvement of black women in the women's liberation movement can best be explained in terms of priorities. The priorities of black women versus the priorities of white women.

Obviously the first priority of virtually all black people is the elimination of racial prejudice in America—in effect the liberation of black people. Second in importance is the black family problem of establishing a decent way of life in America as it exists today. When racism in America is eliminated, then perhaps the black family's stability problem will disappear and more black women will be able to give first priority to the elimination of oppression because of sex.

The Washington Post, October 3, 1970.

JIM CROW AND JANE CROW

PAULI MURRAY

❦ Dr. Pauli Murray is a graduate of Howard University, the University of California and of Yale Law School. She is a former Deputy Attorney General of the state of California, a poet, writer, teacher and practicing lawyer. A government consultant, a member of the NAACP, the National Organization for Women and the Women's Equity Action League, and for many years a leader in other feminist and civil rights organizations, Dr. Murray currently teaches American studies at Brandeis University. She is the author of an autobiography, Proud Shoes (New York: Harper & Brothers, 1956), of books and articles on the law and a volume of poetry.

Negro women, historically, have carried the dual burden of Jim Crow and Jane Crow. They have not always carried it graciously, but they have carried it effectively. They have shared with their men a partnership in a pioneer life on spiritual and psychological frontiers not inhabited by any other group in the United States. For Negroes have had to hack their way through the wilderness of racism produced by the accumulated growth of nearly four centuries of a barbarous international slave trade, two centuries of chattel slavery and a century of illusive citizenship in a desperate effort to make a place of dignity for themselves and their children.

In this bitter struggle, into which has been poured most of the resources and much of the genius of successive generations of American Negroes, these women have often carried disproportionate burdens in the Negro family as they strove to keep its integrity intact against the constant onslaught of indignities to which it was subjected. Not only have they stood shoulder to shoulder with Negro men in every phase of the battle, but they have also continued to stand when their men were destroyed by it. Who among us is not familiar with that heroic, if formidable, figure exhorting her children to overcome every disappointment, humiliation and obstacle. This woman's lullaby was very often "Be something!" "Be somebody!" . . .

Langston Hughes' poem, "Mother to Son" has great meaning for a generation which still recalls the washtub and the steaming wooden stove as the source of hard earned dollars which sent it to school. It reveals the great gift of the Negro woman for mothering, consoling, encouraging:

> Well, son, I'll tell you:
> Life for me ain't been no crystal stair.
> It's had tacks in it,
> And splinters,
> And boards torn up,
> And places with no carpets on the floor—
> Bare.
> But all the time
> I's been a-climbin' on,
> And reachin' landin's,
> And turnin' corners,
> And sometimes goin' in the dark
> Where there ain't been no light,
> So boy, don't you turn back,
> Don't you set down on the steps
> Cause you finds it kinder hard.
> Don't you fall now—
> For I'se still goin', honey,
> I's still climbin'
> And life for me ain't been no crystal stair.

In the course of their climb, Negro women have had to fight against the stereotypes of "female dominance" on the one hand and loose morals on the other hand, both growing out of the roles forced upon them during the slavery experience and its aftermath. But out of their struggle for human dignity, they also developed a tradition of independence and self-reliance. This characteristic, said the late Dr. E. Franklin Frazier, sociologist, "has provided generally a pattern of equalitarian relationship between men and women in America." Like the Western pioneer settlements, the embattled Negro society needed the strength of all of its members in order to survive. The economic necessity for the Negro woman to earn a living to help support her family— if indeed she was not the sole support—fostered her independence and equalitarian position. . . .

Not only have women whose names are well known given this great human effort [the human rights battle] its peculiar vitality but women in many communities whose names will never be known have revealed the courage and strength of the Negro woman. These are the mothers who have stood in school yards with their children, many times alone. These are the images which have touched America's heart. Painful as these experiences have been, one cannot help asking: would the Negro struggle have come this far without the indomitable determination of its women?

In the larger society, Negro and white women share a common burden because of traditional discriminations based upon sex. Dr. Gunnar Myrdal pointed out the similarities between the Negro problem and the women's problem in *An American Dilemma*. What he saw is common knowledge among Negro women, but it is interesting to see the United States through the eyes of a foreign observer. He said:

> "As in the Negro problem, most men have accepted as self-evident, until recently, the doctrine that women had inferior endowments in most of those respects which carry prestige, power and advantages in society.

. . . The arguments were used, have been about the same: smaller brains, scarcity of geniuses and so on. . . . As in the case of the Negro, women themselves have often been brought to believe in their inferiority of endowment. As the Negro was awarded his 'place' in society, so there was a 'woman's place.' . . . The myth of the 'contented women' who did not want to have suffrage or other civil rights and equal opportunities, had the same social function as the myth of the 'contented Negro.' . . ."

Despite the common interests of Negro and white women, however, the dichotomy of the segregated society has prevented them from cementing a natural alliance. Communication and cooperation between them have been hesitant, limited and formal. Negro women have tended to identify all discrimination against them as racial in origin and to accord high priority to the civil rights struggle. They have had little time or energy for consideration of women's rights. But as the civil rights struggle gathers momentum, they began to recognize the similarities between paternalism and racial arrogance. They also begin to sense that the struggle into which they have poured their energies may not afford them rights they assumed would be theirs when the civil rights cause has triumphed.

Recent disquieting events have made imperative an assessment of the role of the Negro woman in the quest for equality. The civil rights revolt, like many social upheavals, has released powerful pentup emotions, cross currents, rivalries, and hostilities. . . . There is much jockeying for position as ambitious men push and elbow their way to leadership roles. Part of this upsurge reflects the Negro male's normal desire to achieve a sense of personal worth and recognition of his manhood by a society which has so long denied it. One aspect is the wresting of the initiative of the civil rights movement from white liberals. Another is the backlash of a new male aggressiveness against Negro women.

What emerges most clearly from events of the past several months is the tendency to assign women to a secondary, ornamental or "honoree" role instead of the partnership role in the civil rights movement which they have earned by their courage, intelligence and dedication. It was bitterly humiliating for Negro women on August 28 to see themselves accorded little more than token recognition in the historic March on Washington. Not a single woman was invited to make one of the major speeches or to be part of the delegation of leaders who went to the White House. This omission was deliberate. Representations for recognition of women were made to the policy-making body sufficiently in advance of the August 28 arrangements to have permitted the necessary adjustments of the program. What the Negro women leaders were told is revealing: that no representation was given to them because they would not be able to agree on a delegate. How familiar was this excuse! It is a typical response from an entrenched power group. . . .

It is also pointedly significant that in the great mass of magazine and newsprint expended upon the civil rights crisis, national editors have selected Negro men almost exclusively to articulate the aspirations of the Negro community. There has been little or no public discussion of the problems, aspirations and role of Negro women. Moreover, the undertone of news stories of recent efforts to create career opportunities for Negroes in government and industry seems to be that what is being talked about is jobs for Negro men only. The fact that Negro women might be available and, as we shall see, are qualified and in need of employment, is ignored. While this is in keeping with the tenor of a male-dominated society, it has grave consequences for Negro women. . . .

At the very moment in history when there is an international movement to raise the status of women and a recognition that women generally are underemployed, are Negro women to be passed over in the social arrangements which are to create new job opportunities for Negroes? Moreover, when American women are seeking partnership in our society, are Negro women to take a backward step and sacrifice their equalitarian tradition? . . .

A fact of enormous importance to the whole discussion of Negro family life and one which has received little analysis up to now is the startling 1960 census figure showing an excess of 648,000 Negro females over Negro males. More than a half million of these were 14 years and over. In the past century, the ratio of Negro males to females has decreased steadily. In 1960 there were only 93.3 Negro males to every 100 females.

The statistical profile of a Negro woman which emerges from the latest census reports is that she has a harder time finding a mate, remains single more often, bears more children, is in the labor market longer, has less education, earns less, is widowed earlier and carries a heavier economic burden as a family head than her white sister.

Moreover, while it is now generally known that women are constitutionally stronger than men, that male babies are more fragile than female babies, that boys are harder to rear than girls, that the male death rate is slightly higher and life expectancy for males is shorter than that of females, the numerical imbalance between the sexes in the Negro group is more dramatic than in any group in the United States. Within the white population the excess of women shows up in the middle and later years. In the Negro population, the excess is present in every age group over 14 and is greatest in the 15–44 age group which covers the college years and the age when most marriages occur. Consider, for example, the fact that in the 15–24 age group, there are only 96.7 nonwhite males for every 100 females. This ratio drops to 88.4 in the 25–44 age group. Compare this with the white population in which the ratios for these two age groups are 102.2 and 98.1 respectively.

The explosive social implications of an excess of more than half a million Negro girls and women over 14 years of age are obvious. . . . The problem of an excess female population is a familiar one in European countries which have experienced heavy male casualties during wars, but an excess female ethnic minority as an enclave within a larger population raises important social issues. What is there in the American environment which is hostile to both the birth and survival of Negro males? How much of the tensions and conflicts traditionally associated with the matriarchal frame-work of Negro society are in reality due to this imbalance and the pressure it generates? Does this excess explain the active competition between Negro professional men and women seeking employment in markets which have limited or excluded Negroes? And does this competition intensify the stereotype of the matriarchal society and female dominance? . . .

I have stressed the foregoing figures, however, because it seems to me that the Negro woman's fate in the United States, while inextricably bound with that of the Negro male in one sense, transcends the issue of civil rights. Equality for the Negro woman must mean equal opportunity to compete for jobs and to find a mate in the total society. For as long as she is confined to an area in which she must compete fiercely for a mate, she will remain the object of sexual exploitation and the victim of all of the social evils which such exploitation involves.

In short, many of the 645,000 excess Negro women will never marry at all unless they marry outside of the Negro community. And many others will marry men whose educational and cultural standards may not be the same as their own. Add to the large reservoir of unmarried white women (22.3%), a higher proportion of widowed, separated and divorced nonwhite women than of white women, and you have factors which have combined to make the Negro woman the responsible family head in more than one fifth of all nonwhite families.

The point I am trying to make here is that the Negro woman cannot assume with any degree of confidence that she will be able to look to marriage for either economic or emotional support. She must prepare to be self-supporting and to support others, perhaps, for a considerable period

Why shd marriage be the preferred goal?

or for life. . . . Bearing in mind that everything possible must be done to encourage Negro males to develop their highest educational potential and to accept their family responsibilities and feel secure in their marital relationships, Negro women have no alternative but to insist upon equal opportunities without regard to sex in training, education and employment at every level. This may be a matter of sheer survival. And these special needs must be articulated by the civil rights movement so that they are not overlooked. . . .

One thing is crystal clear. The Negro woman can no longer postpone or subordinate the fight against discrimination because of sex to the civil rights struggle but must carry on both fights simultaneously. She must insist upon a partnership role in the integration movement. . . .

"The Negro Woman in the Quest for Equality," *The Acorn*, publication of Lambda Kappa Mu Sorority, Inc., June 1964.

POOR BLACK WOMEN

PATRICIA ROBINSON

It is time to speak to the whole question of the position of poor black women in this society and in this historical period of revolution and counterrevolution. We have the foregoing analysis of their own perspective and it offers all of us some very concrete points.

First, that the class hierarchy as seen from the poor black woman's position is one of white male in power, followed by white female, then the black male and lastly the black female.

Historically, the myth in the black world is that there are only two free people in the United States, the white man and the black woman. The myth was established by the black man in the long period of his frustration when he longed to be free to have the material and social advantages of his oppressor, the white man. On examination of the myth, this so-called freedom was based on the sexual prerogatives taken by the white man on the black female. It was fantasied by the black man that she enjoyed it.

The black woman was needed and valued by the white female as a domestic. The black female diluted much of the actual oppression of the white female by the white male. With the help of the black woman, the white woman had free time from mother and housewife responsibilities and could escape her domestic prison overseered by the white male.

The poor black woman still occupies the position of a domestic in this society, rising no higher than public welfare, when the frustrated male deserts her and the children. (Public welfare was instituted primarily for poor whites during the depression of the thirties to stave off their rising revolutionary violence. It was considered as a temporary stop-gap only.)

The poor black male deserted the poor black female and fled to the cities where he made his living by his wits— hustling. The black male did not question the kind of society he lived in other than on the basis of racism: "The white man won't let me up 'cause I'm black!" Other rationalizations included blaming the black woman, which has been a much described phenomenon. The black man wanted to take the master's place and all that went with it.

Simultaneously, the poor black woman did not question the social and economic system. She saw her main problem as . . . social, economic and psychological oppression by the black man. But awareness in this case has moved to a second phase and exposes on important fact in the whole process of oppression. It takes two to oppress, a proper dialectic perspective to examine at this point in our movement.

An examination of the process of oppression in any or all of its forms shows simply that at least two parties are involved. The need for the white man, particularly, to oppress others reveals his own anxiety and inadequacy about his own maleness and humanity. Many black male writers have eloquently analyzed this social and psychological fact. Generally a feeling of inadequacy can be traced to all those who desperately need power and authority over others throughout history. . . . But the oppressor must have the cooperation of the oppressed, of those he must feel better than. The oppressed and the damned are placed in an inferior position by force of arms, physical strength, and later, by threats of such force. But the long-time maintenance of power over others is secured by psychological manipulation and seduction. The oppressed must begin to believe in the divine right and position of kings, the inherent right of an elite to rule, the supremacy of a class or an ethnic group, the power of such condensed wealth as money and private property to give its owners high social status. So a gigantic and complex myth has been woven by those who have power in this society of the inevitability of classes and the superiority and inferiority of certain groups. The oppressed begin to believe in their own inferiority and are left in their lifetime with two general choices: to identify with the oppressor (imitate him) or to rebel against him. Rebellion does not take place as long as the oppressed are certain of their inferiority and the innate superiority of the powerful, in essence a neurotic illusion. The oppressed appear to be in love with their chains.

In a capitalist society, all power to rule is imagined in male symbols and, in fact, all power in a capitalist society is in male hands. Capitalism is a male supremacist society. Western religious gods are all male. The city, basis of 'civilization,' is male as opposed to the country which is female. The city is a revolt against earlier female principles of nature and man's dependence on them. All domestic and international political and economic decisions are made by men and enforced by males and their symbolic extension—guns. Women have become the largest oppressed group in a dominant, male, aggressive, capitalistic culture. The next largest oppressed group is the product of their wombs, the children, who are ever pressed into service and labor for the maintenance of a male-dominated class society.

If it is granted that it takes two to oppress, those who neurotically need to oppress and those who neurotically need to be oppressed, then what happens when the female in a capitalist society awakens to the reality? She can either identify with the male and opportunistically imitate him, appearing to share his power and giving him the surplus product of her body, the child, to use and exploit. Or she can rebel and remove the children from exploitative and oppressive male authority.

Rebellion by poor black women, the bottom of a class hierarchy heretofore not discussed, places the question of what kind of society will the poor black woman demand and struggle for. Already she demands the right to have birth control, like middle class black and white women. She is aware that it takes two to oppress and that she and other poor people no longer are submitting to oppression, in this case genocide. She allies herself with the have-nots in the wider world and their revolutionary struggles. She has been forced by historical conditions to withdraw the children from male dominance and to educate and support them herself. In this very process, male authority and exploitation are seriously weakened. Further, she realizes that the children will be used as all poor children have been used through history—as poorly paid mercenaries fighting to keep or put an elite group in power. Through these steps . . . she has begun to question aggressive male domination and the class society which enforces it, capitalism. This question, in time, will be posed to the entire black movement in this country.

Poor Black Women, pamphlet,
(Boston, Massachusetts: New England Free Press), 1970.

FACING THE ABORTION QUESTION

REPRESENTATIVE SHIRLEY CHISHOLM

In August of 1969 I started to get phone calls from NARAL, the National Association for the Repeal of Abortion Laws, a new organization based in New York City that was looking for a national president. In the New York State Assembly I had supported abortion reform bills introduced by Assemblyman Albert Blumenthal, and this had apparently led NARAL to believe I would sympathize with its goal: complete repeal of all laws restricting abortion. As a matter of fact, when I was in the Assembly I had not been in favor of repealing all abortion laws, a step that would leave the question of having or not having the operation entirely up to a woman and her doctor. The bills I had tried to help pass in Albany would only have made it somewhat easier for women to get therapeutic abortions in New York State, by providing additional legal grounds and simplifying the procedure for getting approval. But since that time I had been compelled to do some heavy thinking on the subject, mainly because of the experiences of several young women I knew. All had suffered permanent injuries at the hands of illegal abortionists. Some will never have children as a result. One will have to go to a hospital periodically for treatment for the rest of her life.

It had begun to seem to me that the question was not whether the law should allow abortions. Experience shows that pregnant women who feel they have compelling reasons for not having a baby, or another baby, will break the law and, even worse, risk injury and death if they must to get one. Abortions will not be stopped. . . . The question becomes simply that of what kind of abortions society wants women to have—clean, competent ones performed by licensed physicians or septic, dangerous ones done by incompetent practitioners.

So when NARAL asked me to lead its campaign, I gave it serious thought. For me to take the lead in abortion repeal would be an even more serious step than for a white politician to do so, because there is a deep and angry suspicion among many blacks that even birth control clinics are a plot by the white power structure to keep down the numbers of blacks, and this opinion is even more strongly held by some in regard to legalizing abortions. But I do not know any

black or Puerto Rican *women* who feel that way. To label
family planning and legal abortion programs "genocide" is
male rhetoric, for male ears. It falls flat to female listeners,
and to thoughtful male ones. Women know, and so do many
men, that two or three children who are wanted, prepared
for, reared amid love and stability, and educated to the limit
of their ability will mean more for the future of the black
and brown races from which they come than any number of
neglected, hungry, ill-housed and ill-clothed youngsters. Pride
in one's race, as well as simply humanity, supports this view.
Poor women of every race feel as I do, I believe. There is
objective evidence of it in a study by Dr. Charles F. West-
hoff of the Princeton Office of Population Research. He questioned 5600 married persons and found that 22 percent of
their children were unwanted. But among persons who earn
less than $4000 a year, 42 percent of the children were un-
wanted. The poor are more anxious about family planning
than any other group.

Why then do the poor keep on having large families? It is
not because they are stupid or immoral. One must understand how many resources their poverty has deprived them
of, and that chief among these is medical care and advice.
The poor do not go to doctors or clinics except when they
absolutely must; their medical ignorance is very great, even
when compared to the low level of medical knowledge most
persons have. This includes, naturally, information about
contraceptives and how to get them. In some of the largest
cities, clinics are now attacking this problem; they are nowhere near to solving it. In smaller cities and in most of the
countryside, hardly anything is being done.

Another point is this: not only do the poor have large
families, but also large families tend to be poor. More than
one fourth of all the families with four children live in
poverty, according to the federal government's excessively
narrow definition; by humane standards of poverty, the number would be much larger. The figures range from 9 percent
of one-child families that have incomes below the official

poverty line, up to 42 percent of the families with six children or more. Sinking into poverty, large families tend to stay there because of the educational and social handicaps that being poor imposes. It is the fear of such a future for their children that drives many women, of every color and social stratum, except perhaps the highest, to seek abortions when contraception has failed.

Botched abortions are the largest single cause of death of pregnant women in the United States, particularly among nonwhite women. In 1964, the president of the New York County Medical Society, Dr. Carl Goldmark, estimated that 80 percent of the deaths of gravid women in Manhattan were from this cause.

Another study by Edwin M. Gold, covering 1960 through 1962, gave lower percentages but supplied evidence that women from minority groups suffer most. Gold said abortion was the cause of death in 25 percent of the white cases, 49 percent of the black ones, and 65 percent of the Puerto Rican ones.

Even when a poor woman needs an abortion for the most impeccable medical reasons, acceptable under most states' laws, she is not likely to succeed in getting one. The public hospitals to which she must go are far more reluctant to approve abortions than are private, voluntary hospitals. It's in the records: private hospitals in New York City perform 3.9 abortions for every 1000 babies they deliver, public hospitals only 1 per 1000. Another relevant figure is that 90 percent of the therapeutic abortions in the city are performed on white women. Such statistics convinced me that my instinctive feeling was right: a black woman legislator, far from avoiding the abortion question, was compelled to face it and deal with it.

But my time did not permit me to be an active president of NARAL, so I asked to be made an honorary president. . . .

The question will remain "Is abortion *right*?" and it is a question that each of us must answer for himself. My beliefs and my experience have led me to conclude that the wisest public policy is to place the responsibility for that decision on the individual. The rightness or wrongness of an abortion depends on the individual case, and it seems to me clearly wrong to pass laws regulating all cases. But there is more to it than that. First, it is my view, and I think the majority's view, that abortion should always remain a last resort, never a primary method of limiting families. Contraceptive devices are the first choice: *devices*, because of their established safety compared to the controversial oral contraceptives. . . . Beyond that, still from the standpoint of public policy, there must be far more stress on providing a full range of family planning services to persons of all economic levels. At present, the full gamut of services, from expert medical advice to, as a last resort, safe "legal" abortions, is available for the rich. Any woman who has the money and the sophistication about how things are done in our society can get an abortion within the law. If she is from a social stratum where such advice is available, she will be sent to a sympathetic psychiatrist and he will be well paid to believe her when she says she is ready to kill herself if she doesn't get rid of her pregnancy. But unless a woman has the $700 to $1000 minimum it takes to travel this route, her only safe course in most states is to have the child. . . .

For all Americans, and especially for the poor, we must put an end to compulsory pregnancy. The well-off have only one problem when an unwanted pregnancy occurs; they must decide what they want to do and what they believe is right. For the poor, there is no such freedom. They started with too little knowledge about contraception, often with none except street lore and other misinformation. When trapped by pregnancy, they have only two choices, both bad—a cheap abortion or an unwanted child to plunge them deeper into poverty. . . .

Which is more like genocide, I have asked some of my black brothers—this, the way things are, or the conditions I am fighting for in which the full range of family planning services is freely available to women of all classes and colors, starting with effective contraception and extending to safe, legal termination of undesired pregnancies, at a price they can afford?

Shirley Chisholm, *Unbought and Unbossed* (Boston: Houghton Mifflin Company, 1970), pp. 113–122.

I WANT THE RIGHT TO BE BLACK AND ME

MARGARET WRIGHT

Margaret Wright is active in a number of Los Angeles community organizations, including Women Against Repression, a black women's liberation group. She is married and the mother of four children.

Black women have been doubly oppressed. On the job, we're low women on the totem pole. White women have their problems. They're interviewed for secretarial instead of the executive thing. But we're interviewed for mopping floors and stuff like that. Sometimes we have to take what's left over in Miss Ann's refrigerator. This is all exploitation. And when we get home from work, the old man is wondering why his greens aren't cooked on time.

We're also exploited in the Movement. We run errands, lick stamps, mail letters and do the door-to-door. But when it comes to the speaker's platform, it's all men up there blowing their souls, you dig?

Some white man wrote this book about the black matriarchy, saying that black women ran the community. Which is bull. We don't run no community. We went out and worked because they wouldn't give our men jobs. This is where some of us are different from the white women's liberation movement. We don't think work liberates you. We've been doing it so damned long.

The black man used to admire the black women for all

they'd endured to keep the race going. Now the black man is saying he wants a family structure like the white man's. He's got to be head of the family and women have to be submissive and all that nonsense. Hell, the white woman is already oppressed in that setup.

Black man have been brainwashed into believing they've been emasculated. I tell them they're nuts. They've never been emasculated. Emasculated men don't revolt. And if they were so emasculated, these blondes wouldn't be running after them. Black women aren't oppressing them. We're helping them get their liberation. It's the white man who's oppressing, not us. All we ever did was scrub floors so they could get their little selves together!

It used to be that only older women felt like this. But now the younger sisters, and the ones in college, are beginning to feel the same way. They see a brother walking around campus with a blonde on his arm just after he's left the BSU blowing black is beautiful. So it tees them off. Also, black women feel they have to move to the front now, because they're doing our men in. Whenever effective male leaders come up, they either get their brains blown out, or they're thrown in jail.

In black women's liberation we don't want to be equal with men, just like in black liberation we're not fighting to be equal with the white man. We're fighting for the right to be different and not be punished for it. Equal means sameness. I don't want to be equal with the white community because I don't think it's very groovy. And why do I want to be equal with something that ain't groovy?

Men are chauvinistic. I don't want to be chauvinistic. Some women run over people in the business world, doing the same thing as men. I don't want to compete on no damned exploitative level. I don't want to exploit nobody. I don't want to be on no firing line, killing people. I want the right to be black and me.

As cited in Mary Reinholz, "Storming the All Electric Dollhouse," *West Magazine, Los Angeles Times*, June 7, 1970.

IT'S IN YOUR HANDS

FANNIE LOU HAMER

✧ *Fannie Lou Hamer was born in Mississippi, one of twenty children of a sharecropper family. She began to pick cotton at the age of six and worked in the fields and as a plantation timekeeper until 1962, when she lost her job after registering to vote. Mrs. Hamer, who is the mother of two children and lives in Ruleville, Mississippi, was jailed in 1963 and severely beaten for attempting to integrate a restaurant. She has been under constant attack for her civil rights leadership and narrowly escaped being shot. Her home was bombed as recently as 1971.*

As a field secretary for SNCC, Mrs. Hamer worked to organize the Mississippi Freedom Democratic Party and was one of its spokesmen at the 1964 Democratic Party convention in Atlantic City, where MFDP challenged the lily-white state delegation. The same year, Mrs. Hamer was one of three black candidates running for Congress from her state and garnered 33,009 votes. Since then she has thrown most of her energies into the organization of economic cooperatives in Sunflower County and into political leadership in her state. She is a dynamic public speaker and an outstanding grass-roots leader.

The special plight and the role of black women is not something that just happened three years ago. We've had a special plight for 350 years. My grandmother had it. My grandmother was a slave. She died in 1960. She was 136 years old. She died in Mount Bayou, Mississippi.

It's been a special plight for the black woman. I remember my uncles and some of my aunts—and that's why it really tickled me when you talked about integration. Because I'm very black, but I remember some of my uncles and some of my aunts was as white as anybody in here, and blue-eyed, and some kind of green-eyed—and my grandfather didn't do it, you know. So what the folks is fighting at this point is what they started. They started unloading the slave ships of Africa, that's when they started. And right now, sometimes, you know I work for the liberation of all people, because when I liberate myself, I'm liberating other people. But you know, sometimes I really feel more sorrier for the white woman than I feel for ourselves because she been caught up in this thing, caught up feeling very special, and folks, I'm going to put it on the line, because my job is not to make people feel comfortable—(drowned out by applause). You've been caught up in this thing because, you know, you worked my grandmother, and after that you worked my mother, and then finally you got hold of me. And you really thought, people—you might try and cool it now, but I been watching you, baby. You thought that you was *more* because you was a woman, and especially a white woman, you had this kind of angel feeling that you were untouchable. You know that? There's nothing under the sun that made you believe that you was just like me, that under this white pigment of skin is red blood, just like under this black skin of mine. So we was used as black women over and over and over. You know, I remember a time when I was working around white people's house, and one thing that would make me mad as hell, after I would be done slaved all day long, this white woman would get on the phone, calling some of her friends, and said, "You know, I'm tired, because *we* have been working," and I said, "That's a damn lie." You're not used to that kind of language, honey, but I'm gone tell you where it's *at*. So all of these things was happening because you *had* more. You had been put on a pedestal, and then not only put on a pedestal, but you had been put in something like a ivory castle. So what happened to you, we have busted the castle open and whacking like hell for the pedestal. And when you hit the ground, you're gone have to fight like hell, like we've been fighting all this time.

In the past, I don't care how poor this white woman was, in the South she still felt like she was more than us. In the North, I don't care how poor or how rich this white woman has been, she still felt like she was more than us. But coming to the realization of the thing, her freedom is shackled in chains to mine, and she realizes for the first time that she is not free until I am free. The point about it, the male influence in this country—you know the white male, he didn't go and brainwash the black man and the black woman, he brainwashed his wife too. . . . He made her think that she was a angel. You know the reason I can say it, folks, I been watching. And there's a lot of people been watching. That's why it's such a shock wherever we go throughout this country, it's a great blow. White Americans today don't know what in the world to do because when they put us *behind* them, that's where they made their mistake. If they had put us in front, they wouldn't have *let* us look back. But they put us behind them, and we watched every move they made. . . .

And this is the reason I tell the world, as I travel to and fro, I'm not fighting for equal rights. What do I want to be equal to [Senator] Eastland for? Just tell me that. But we are not only going to liberate ourselves. I think it's a responsibility. I think we're special people, God's children is going to help in the survival of this country if it's not too late. We're a lot sicker than people realize we are. And what we are doing now in the South, in politics, in gaining seats for black people and concerned whites in the state of Mississippi, is going to have an effect on what happens throughout this country. You know, I used to think that if I could go North and tell people about the plight of the black folk in the state of Mississippi, everything would be all right. But traveling around, I found one thing for sure: it's up-South and down-South, and it's no different. The man shoot me in the face in Mississippi, and you turn around he'll shoot you in the back here [in New York]. We have a problem, folks, and we want to try to deal with the problem in the only way that we can deal with the problem as far as black women. And you know, I'm not hung up on this about liberating myself from the black man, I'm not going to try that thing. I got a black husband, six feet three, two hundred and forty pounds, with a 14 shoe, that I don't *want* to be liberated from. But we are here to work side by side with this black man in trying to bring liberation to all people.

Sunflower County is one of the poorest counties, one of the poorest counties on earth, while Senator James O. Eastland—you know, people tells you, don't talk politics, but the air you breathe is polluted air, it's political polluted air. The air you breathe is politics. So you have to be involved. You have to be involved in trying to elect people that's going to help do something about the liberation of all people.

Sunflower County, the county where I'm from, is Senator Eastland's county that owns 5,800 acres of some of the richest black fertile soil in Mississippi, and where kids, there in Sunflower County, suffer from malnutrition. But I want to tell you one of the things that we're doing, right now in Sunflower County. In 1969 I founded the Freedom Farm Coop. We started off with 40 acres of land. Nineteen-seventy in Sunflower County, we fed 1500 people from this 40 acres of land. Nineteen-seventy I've become involved with Y.W.D. —Young World Developers. On the 14th of January 1971, we put $85,400 on 640 acres of land, giving us the total of 680 acres of land. We also have 68 houses. We hope sometime in '71 we will build another hundred houses on a hundred of the 640 acres.

This coming Saturday . . . young people will be walking throughout the world against hunger and poverty. It will be forty countries walking, millions of people throughout the world. In the United States it will be over 377 walks. These walkers are young people that really care about what's going on. . . . And out of this walk—people will pay so much per mile for the kids that'll be walking—and out of this walk we hope to get a million dollars for Sunflower County. . . . If we get the kind of economic support that we need in Sunflower County, in two more years . . . We'll have the tools to produce food ourselves.

A couple of weeks ago, we moved the first poor white family into Freedom Farm in the history of the state of Mississippi. A white man came to me and said, "I got five children and I don't have nowhere to live. I don't have food. I don't have anything. And my children, some of them, is sick." And we gave this man a house. . . .

We have a job as black women, to support whatever is right, and to bring in justice where we've had so much injustice. Some people say, well, I work for $24 per week. That's not true in my case, I work sometimes for $15 per week. I remember my mother working for 25 and 30 cents per day. But we are organizing ourselves now, because we don't have any other choice. Sunflower County is one of the few counties in the state of Mississippi where in that particular area we didn't lose one black teacher. Because . . . I went in and told the judge, I said, "Judge, we're not going to stand by and see you take a man with a master's degree and bring him down to janitor help. So if we don't have the principal . . . there ain't gonna *be* no school, private or public." These are the kinds of roles.

A few years ago throughout the country the middle-class black woman—I used to say not really black women, but the middle-class colored women, c-u-l-l-u-d, didn't even respect the kind of work that I was doing. But you see now, baby, whether you have a Ph.D., D.D., or no D, we're in this bag together. And whether you're from Morehouse or Nohouse, we're still in this bag together. Not to fight to try to liberate ourselves from the men—this is another trick to get us fighting among ourselves—but to work together with the black man, then we will have a better chance to just act as human beings, and to be treated as human beings in our sick society.

I would like to tell you in closing a story of an old man. This old man was very wise, and he could answer questions that was almost impossible for people to answer. So some people went to him one day, two young people, and said,

"We're going to trick this guy today. We're going to catch a bird, and we're going to carry it to this old man. And we're going to ask him, 'This that we hold in our hands today, is it alive or is it dead?' If he says 'Dead,' we're going to turn it loose and let it fly. But if he says, 'Alive,' we're going to crush it." So they walked up to this old man, and they said, "This that we hold in our hands today, is it alive or is it dead?" He looked at the young people and he smiled. And he said, "It's in your hands."

"The Special Plight and the Role of Black Woman,"
Speech given at NAACP Legal Defense Fund Institute,
New York City, May 7, 1971.

BIBLIOGRAPHICAL NOTES

❦ Black women are mentioned, usually briefly and peripherally, in most Black history sources. A comprehensive bibliography of the subject would therefore cover substantially the same ground as a general Black history bibliography. There seems little point in attempting such a vast undertaking. Instead, information on sources consulted in the preparation of this documentary history has been arranged so as to serve the different needs of different groups of readers.

The sources cited directly in this book are in the footnotes following each item and should first be consulted by those wishing more information. For scholars interested in further research, the Notes on Sources (pp. xxix–xxxii) will provide the best guide. Readers who are seeking background and correlated readings may find the following bibliographical notes useful. The readings listed below constitute a partial list of sources used in addition to those footnoted in the text.

GENERAL BLACK HISTORY BACKGROUND

Excellent surveys of black American history are John Hope Franklin, *From Slavery to Freedom: A History of Negro Americans* (New York: Alfred A. Knopf, 1947); E. Franklin Frazier, *The Negro in the United States* (New York: Macmillan, 1949); August Meier and Elliot P. Rudwick, *From Plantation to Ghetto: An Interpretive History of American Negroes* (New York: Hill & Wang, 1966); Benjamin Quarles, *The Negro in the Making of America* (New York: Macmillan, 1964). However, none of these offer more than cursory information concerning black women. The *Negro Year Book* (Tuskegee, Ala.: Tuskegee Institute), started in 1912 under the editorship of Monroe Work, offers much valuable information. Biographies of many of the lesser-known women are contained in Clement Richardson (ed.), *National Cyclopedia of the Colored Race* (Montgomery, Ala.: National Publishing Co., 1919), which, despite its title, concentrates mainly on Southerners. John P. Davis (ed.), *The American Negro Reference Book* (Englewood Cliffs, N.J.: Prentice Hall, 1967) contains an excellent chapter entitled "American Negro Women" by Jeanne Noble, which synthesizes modern data on the subject. Margaret Just Butcher, *The Negro in American Culture* (New York: Alfred A. Knopf, 1956) is a valuable cultural history based on the research of Alain Locke.

Herbert Aptheker (ed.), *A Documentary History of the Negro People in the United States* (New York: Citadel, 1951) remains an indispensible collection of documentary sources. It is remarkably rich in materials pertaining to women. The same cannot be said for the many source books of Black history recently published, in most of which women are very poorly represented. A few notable exceptions are: Thomas R. Frazier (ed.), *Afro-American History: Primary Sources* (New York: Harcourt, Brace & Jovanovich, 1970) and Joanne Grant (ed.), *Black Protest* (New York: Fawcett, 1968). Martin E. Dann (ed.) *The Black Press: 1827–1890* (New York: G. P. Putnam's Sons, 1971) is a specialized source book which contains selections by black women journalists. A valuable collection of articles is August Meier and Elliot Rudwick, *The Making of Black America* (2 vols., New York: Atheneum, 1969). Although some of the interpretations are questionable, Gunnar Myrdal, *An American Dilemma: The Negro Problem and Modern Democracy* (New York: Harper & Row, 1962) provides a valuable compilation of sociological and statistical information, much of it concerning women. Appendix 5, "A Parallel to the Negro Problem," is a suggestive essay which points to the similar effects of lower-caste status on women and Blacks.

WOMEN'S HISTORY BACKGROUND

Eleanor Flexner, *Century of Struggle: The Woman's Rights Movement in the United States* (Cambridge: Harvard University Press, 1959) remains the best one-volume work on the subject. Gerda Lerner, *The Woman in American History* (Menlo Park, Calif.: Addison-Wesley Publishing Co., 1971) deals more extensively with black women's history as part of the general history of American women. The unique source on the Negro women's club movement is Elizabeth L. Davis, *Lifting As They Climb: The National Association of Colored Women* (n.p.: National Association of Colored Women, 1933), an uncritical and disorganized assemblage of records and documents pertaining to the National Association of Colored Women's Clubs. The six-volume *History of Woman Suffrage*, edited by Elizabeth Cady Stanton, Susan B. Anthony and Matilda J. Gage (New York: Fowler & Wells, 1881–1922), although badly organized, remains an invaluable source by virtue of its uniqueness. It contains scattered bits and pieces about individual black women, especially in Volumes I and II. J. W. Gibson and W. H. Crogman (eds.), *Progress of the Race* (Atlanta, Ga.: J. L. Nichols Co., 1903) has a chapter on the development of the Negro women's club movement written by one of its leaders, Fannie Barrier Williams.

ANTHOLOGIES

The various anthologies and biographical compilations concerning black women suffer from two defects: their facts are unreliable and they are frequently uncritical. The absence of critical standards on the part of editors of anthologies is a phenomenon which also occurs in the compilations of "famous women" made by the early feminists. The anthologists simply list any woman who achieved anything more than the standard housewife-mother role or who was mentioned in contemporary newspapers as a "woman of achievement." While this accurately reflects the degraded position of women during much of United States history, it obscures the significance of the real pathbreakers, trend-setters and influential leaders.

The reader may find secondary sources contradicting some of the biographical data in this volume. When such contradictions occurred, the information was carefully checked against primary sources before a correction was made.

Two of the earliest anthologies are L. C. Scruggs, M. D., *Women of Distinction* (Raleigh, N.C.: The Author, 1893) and N. F. Mossell, *The Work of the Afro-American Woman* (Philadelphia: George S. Ferguson Co., 1908). Sadie Iola Daniel, *Women Builders* (Washington, D. C.: The Associated Publishers, 1931) consists of brief biographical sketches of outstanding black women. Hallie Quinn Brown, *Homespun Heroines and Other Women of Distinction* (Xenia: The Aldine Publishing Co., 1926), although uncritical, contains a wealth of information about community, religious and educational leaders. Among the more recent compilations the most comprehensive and useful are: Sylvia G. L. Dannett, *Profiles of Negro Womanhood: Vol. I, 1619–1900* (Chicago: Educational Heritage, Inc., 1964) and Wilhelmina S. Robinson, *Historical Negro Biographies: International Library of Negro Life and History* (New York: Publishers Co., 1967). There are brief biographical sketches of important black women in Marcus H. Boulware, *The Oratory of Negro Leaders: 1900–1968* (Westport, Conn.: Negro Universities Press, 1969) and in Roy L. Hill, *Rhetoric of Racial Revolt* (Denver: Golden Bell Press, 1964). Mel Watkins and Jay David (eds.), *To Be a Black Woman* (New York: William Morrow & Co., 1970) anthologize autobiographical and fictional selections from printed sources. Josephine Carson, *Silent Voices: The Southern Negro Woman Today* (New York: Delacorte Press, 1969) offers an insightful group portrait of rural women engaged in self-help projects. Tony Cade (ed.), *The Black Woman: An Anthology* (New York: Signet Books, 1970) contains the writings of contemporary black women and defines their position towards women's liberation.

SLAVERY AND ABOLITION

The historiographic problems concerning the sources on slavery have been discussed more fully in *Notes on Sources* (see pp. xxix–xxxiii). The literature is vast and the recent proliferation of reprints has made most primary sources easily accessible to the reader. An exhaustive list of primary and secondary sources used in the preparation of this section would cover many pages. The following is a selective list.

Among the slave narratives by female slaves the most interesting are: Harriet Brent Jacobs, *Incidents in the Life of a Slave Girl, written by herself*, ed. by L. M. Child (Boston: The Author, 1861); *Narrative of Sojourner Truth, a Northern Slave* (Boston: The Author, 1850); Sarah Bradford, *Harriet Tubman: The Moses of Her People*, reprinted from the 1886 edition (New York: Corinth Books, 1961). Unusual and probably atypical slave experiences are related in Elizabeth Keckley, *Behind the Scenes, Thirty Years a Slave and Four Years in the White House* (New York: G. W. Carleton, 1868); *A Narrative of The Life and Travels of Mrs. Nancy Prince* (Boston: The Author, 1850); *An Autobiography of Mrs. Amanda Smith, the Colored Evangelist* (Chicago: Meyer & Bros., 1893).

Narratives by male slaves which offer a good deal of information on the condition of female slaves are: Charles Ball, *Slavery in the United States: A Narrative of the Life and Adventures of Charles Ball, a Black Man* (Lewistown, Pa.: J. W. Shugert, 1836); *The Narrative of William W. Brown, A Fugitive Slave*, reprinted from the 1848 edition (Reading, Mass.: Addison-Wesley Publishing Co., 1969); William Craft, "Running a Thousand Miles for Freedom, or The Escape of William and Ellen Craft from Slavery," reprinted from the 1860 edition in Arna Bontemps (ed.), *Great Slave Narratives* (Boston: Beacon Press, 1969); *A Narrative of the Life of Frederick Douglass, An American Slave, Written by Himself* (New York: Anti-Slavery Office, 1845); *An Autobiography of the Reverend Josiah Henson*, reprinted from the 1881 edition (Reading, Mass.: Addison-Wesley Publishing Co., 1969); *Narrative of the Life of Moses Grandy* (Boston: O. Johnson Publishing Co., 1844); *Narrative of Solomon Northup, Twelve Years a Slave* . . . (Auburn, N. Y.: Derby & Miller, 1853).

Travelers and foreign observers were, in general, quite unobservant regarding the condition of slave women. The most notable exceptions are Frances Ann Kemble and Harriet Martineau, whose strong feminist inclinations made them sensitive to the female experience of slavery and its differentiation from the general slave experience. See John A. Scott (ed.), Frances Ann Kemble, *Journal of a Residence on a Georgian Plantation in 1838–1839* (New York: Alfred A. Knopf, 1961); Harriet Martineau, *Society in America* (2 vols. New York: Saunders & Otley, 1837). Slave reminiscences collected in the 20th century are another informative source about women. B. A. Botkin, *Lay My Burden Down: A Folk History of Slavery* (Chicago: University Press, 1945) consists of a selection of such oral testimonies collected under the auspices of the Federal Writers' Project. See also *God Struck Me Dead: Religious Conversion Experiences and Autobiographies of Negro Ex-Slaves*, Social Science Source Document #2 (Nashville,

Tenn.: Fisk University Social Sciences Institute, 1945) and Social Science Document #1, *Unwritten History of Slavery: Autobiographical Accounts of Ex-Slaves* (Nashville, Tenn.: Fisk University Social Science Institute, 1945).

Charles Nichols, *Many Thousand Gone: The Ex-Slaves' Account of Their Bondage and Freedom* (Leiden: E. J. Brill, 1963) offers an excellent synthesis of the literature of slave narratives and evaluates their authenticity. The basic modern descriptive account of slavery is Kenneth Stampp, *The Peculiar Institution: Slavery in the Ante-Bellum South* (New York: Alfred A. Knopf, 1956). Allen Weinstein and Frank O. Gatell (eds.), *American Negro Slavery: A Modern Reader* (New York: Oxford University Press, 1968) provides a useful collection of recent essays on the subject.

ABOLITION

Abolitionist literature is an excellent source of information about slave conditions, insofar as abolitionists had direct contact with slavery and with ex-slaves or used contemporary Southern newspaper sources. A valuable compilation of contemporary sources is Theodore Dwight Weld, *American Slavery As It Is: Testimony of a Thousand Witnesses* (New York: American Anti-Slavery Society, 1839). William Still, *The Underground Rail Road* (Philadelphia: Porter & Coates, 1872) contains much fascinating material on slaves, slave escapes and the activities of black abolitionists, including a section devoted to Frances Ellen Watkins Harper. Another valuable contemporary source is Levi Coffin, *Reminiscences* (Cincinnati, Ohio: n.p. 1876). A modern interpretation stressing the role of Blacks in slave escapes can be found in Larry Gara, *The Liberty Line: The Legend of the Underground Railroad* (Lexington: University of Kentucky Press, 1961). Henrietta Buckmaster, *Let My People Go* (Boston: Harper & Bros., 1941) tells the story of the Underground Railroad in popular form. Benjamin Quarles, *Black Abolitionists* (New York: Oxford University Press, 1969) develops the story of black abolitionism with full awareness of the contributions of black women.

The autobiographies of female abolitionists contain reminiscences of their contacts with black women. See Laura S. Haviland, *A Woman's Life-Work, Labors and Experiences* (Chicago:

Publishing Association of Friends, 1889); John White Chadwick (ed.), *A Life for Liberty: Antislavery and other Letters of Sally Holley* (New York: G. P. Putnam's Sons, 1899). Several modern biographies of antislavery women contain scattered information on black abolitionist women. See: Otelia Cromwell, *Lucretia Mott* (Cambridge: Harvard University Press, 1958); Gerda Lerner, *The Grimké Sisters from South Carolina: Rebels Against Slavery* (Boston: Houghton Mifflin Co., 1969). Leon Litvack, *North of Slavery* (Chicago: University of Chicago Press, 1961), is an excellent and comprehensive treatment of northern racism which details many incidents involving black women.

The period of the Civil War and Reconstruction is described in Mary Elizabeth Massey, *Bonnet Brigades; American Women and the Civil War* (New York: Alfred A. Knopf, 1966), which has scattered information on black women. Bell Irving Wiley, *Southern Negroes, 1861–1865* (New Haven, Conn.: Yale University Press, 1938) and James McPherson, *The Negro's Civil War* (New York: Pantheon Books, 1965) are of great interest. Willie Lee Rose, *Rehearsal for Reconstruction: The Port Royal Experiment* (New York: The Bobbs-Merrill Co., 1964) is an excellent description of the conditions and experiences of freedmen in the Sea Islands of South Carolina. For the Reconstruction period there are a number of informative primary sources available, such as: E. H. Botume, *First Days Amongst the Contrabands* (Boston: Lee & Shepard, 1893); Mary A. Livermore, *My Story of the War: A Woman's Narrative . . .* (Hartford, Conn.: A. D. Worthington & Co., 1889); Henry L. Swint, *Dear Ones at Home: Letters from Contraband Camps* (Nashville, Tenn.: Vanderbilt University Press, 1966). Susie King Taylor, *Reminiscences of My Life in Camp with the 33rd United States Colored Troops* (Boston: The Author, 1902) is a fascinating autobiography by a black woman who lived and worked in a black regiment.

EDUCATION

Carter G. Woodson, *The Education of the Negro Prior to 1861* (New York: G. P. Putnam's Sons, 1915) is the earliest comprehensive history of Negro education. The subject is treated in great detail in the more recent Henry A. Bullock, *A History of Negro Education in the South, from 1619 to the Present* (Cambridge:

Harvard University Press, 1967). Both books contain some information about the vital contribution of black women to education. Jeanne L. Noble, *The Negro Woman's College Education* (New York: Teacher's College Press, 1956) and Marion V. Cuthbert, *Education and Marginality; A Study of the Negro Woman College Graduate* (New York: Columbia University Press, 1942) are useful sociological studies.

The few available autobiographical books by black female teachers are of great interest: Maria Stewart, *Meditations from the Pen of Mrs. Maria W. Stewart, Negro* (Washington, n.p., 1879); Fannie Jackson Coppin, *Reminiscences of School Life, and Hints on Teaching* (Philadelphia: African Methodist Episcopal Book Concern, 1913); Ray Allen Billington, *The Journal of Charlotte L. Forten: A Free Negro in the Slave Era* (New York: the Dryden Press 1953); Anna J. Cooper, *A Voice from the South by a Black Woman of the South* (Xenia, Ohio: Aldine Printing House, 1892). The story of the immense educational experiment undertaken during Reconstruction is partially told in Henry L. Swint, *The Northern Teacher in the South: 1862–1870* (Nashville, Tenn.: Vanderbilt University Press, 1941), which focuses on Northern, predominantly white teachers. A. D. Mayo, *Southern Women in the Recent Movement in the South* (Washington, D.C.: Government Printing Office, 1892) offers much useful information. The history of the black woman's contribution to education during and after Reconstruction remains to be written.

The development of a Negro educational system in the rural South and the contributions of individual women teachers can be traced in the following books: Phelps-Stokes Fund, *Twenty Year Report 1911–1931* (New York: n.p., 1932); Arthur D. Wright, *The Negro Rural School Fund, Inc. (Anna T. Jeanes Foundation) 1907–1933* (Washington, D. C.: n.p., 1933); G. E. Jones, *The Jeanes Teacher in the United States* (Chapel Hill, N.C.,: University of North Carolina Press, 1937); *Twenty-Two Years Work of the Hampton, Virginia Normal and Agricultural Institute* (Hampton, Va.: Hampton Institute, 1893). A wealth of information can be found in the publication of the Hampton Institute, *The Southern Workman*, 1872–1939, and in the pamphlets, publications and periodicals issued by *The Tuskegee Institute, Alabama, Departments of Records and Research*, Nos. 1–10, Tuskegee (1949–1961).

Reminiscences of contemporary women educators offer valuable insight into conditions in the rural South and provide excellent background reading for those wishing to understand the modern civil rights movement: Lura Beam, *He called them by Lightning: A Teacher's Odyssey in the Negro South, 1908–1919* (New York: Bobbs-Merrill Co., 1967); Rose Butler Browne, *Love My Children* (New York: Meredith Press, 1969); Septima Clark, *Echo in My Soul* (New York: E. P. Dutton & Co., 1962).

The story of school desegregation and of the Southern civil rights movement, with scattered references to black women, is told in Benjamin Muse, *Ten Years of Prelude: The Story of Integration Since the Supreme Court's 1954 Decision* (New York: Viking Press, 1964); Howard Zinn, *SNCC: The New Abolitionists* (Boston: Beacon Press, 1965); Len Holt, *The Summer That Didn't End* (New York: Wm. Morrow & Co. 1965); Elizabeth Sutherland (ed.), *Letters from Mississippi* (New York: McGraw-Hill, 1965); and Sally Belfrage, *Freedom Summer* (New York: Viking Press, 1968).

Anne Moody, *Coming of Age in Mississippi* (New York: Dial Press, 1968) and Daisy Bates, *The Long Shadow of Little Rock: A Memoir* (New York: David McKay Co., 1962) are autobiographical accounts by black women activists in the struggle. Robert Coles, *Children of Crisis: A Story of Courage and Fear* (Boston: Little Brown & Co., 1967), is a sympathetic psychological study of the ways in which school desegregation and participation in the civil rights movement have affected children. Polly Greenberg *The Devil Has Slippery Shoes: A Biased Biography of the Child Development Group of Mississippi* (London: The Macmillan Co., 1969), is the moving story of an embattled educational grass-roots effort as told by the participants.

BLACK WOMEN IN THE ECONOMY

There is no single book dealing with this topic. Readers interested in the economic role of women will have to extract the pertinent information from more generalized studies. Various publications by the Women's Bureau, Department of Labor are useful: the biennial *Handbook on Women Workers; Negro Women in Industry; Negro Women Workers* (1960). For an earlier period see *Negro Women in Industry*, Bulletin 20 (1922); also, U. S.

Department of Labor, *Negro Women* (1967) and *The Social and Economic Status of Negroes in the United States* (1969).

Informative general studies are: Lorenzo Green, *The Negro in Colonial New England* (New York: Columbia University Press, 1942); Lorenzo Green and Carter G. Woodson, *The Negro Wage Earner* (Washington, D. C.: Association for the Study of Negro Life and History, 1930); Sterling D. Spero and Abram L. Harris, *The Black Worker: The Negro and the Labor Movement*, reprinted from the 1931 edition (New York: Atheneum, 1968); Herbert R. Northrup, *Organized Labor and the Negro* (New York: Harper & Bros., 1944). Gunnar Myrdal, *An American Dilemma: The Negro Problem and Modern Democracy* (New York: Harper & Row, rev. ed. 1962) contains a vast amount of information on economic conditions. Some information on black industrial workers can be found in Grace Hutchins, *Women Who Work* (New York: International Publishers, 1934).

Specific studies of black domestic workers can be found in: W. E. B. DuBois, *The Phildelphia Negro: A Social Study Together with a Special Report on Domestic Service by Isabel Eaton*, reprinted from the 1899 edition (New York: Schocken Books, 1967); Elizabeth Ross Haynes, "Negroes in Domestic Service in the United States," *Journal of Negro History*, Vol. 8, No. 4 (October 1923), pp. 384–442; Lorenzo J. Greene and Myra Colson Callis, *The Employment of Negroes in the District of Columbia* (Washington, D.C.: Association for the Study of Negro Life and History, 1937); and Jean Collier Brown, *Household Workers* (Chicago: Chicago Science Research Associates 1940). A revealing fictional treatment of the subject by a black woman is Alice Childress, *Like One of the Family: Conversations from a Domestic's Life* (New York: Independence Publishers, 1956).

THE BLACK FAMILY

For over thirty years the views of E. Franklin Frazier as set down in his *The Negro Family in the United States* (Chicago: University of Chicago Press, 1939) have held sway over sociologists, historians and educators. Frazier's definition of the black family as matriarchal and disorganized, supposedly as the result of slavery and aggravated by mass migration to the cities, has remained undisputed until very recently. Subsequent studies of the subject have accepted Frazier's interpretation and his basically pessimistic thesis and have continued to measure black family life against white middle-class standards. Among these are: Kenneth Clark, *Dark Ghetto* (New York: Harper & Row, 1965); Allison Davis and John Dollar, *Children of Bondage* (Washington, D.C.; American Council of Education, 1940); Charles S. Johnson, *Growing Up in the Black Belt: Negro Youth in the Rural South* (Washington, D.C.; American Council on Education, 1941); and Hylan Lewis, *Blackways of Kent* (Chapel Hill, N.C.: University of North Carolina Press, 1961). Somewhat critical of Frazier's views are Jessie Bernard, *Marriage and Family Among Negroes* (Englewood Cliffs, N.J.: Prentice-Hall, 1966) and Andrew Billingsley, *Black Families in White America* (Englewood Cliffs, N.J.: Prentice-Hall, 1968).

The myth of black matriarchy was elevated to the level of governmental policy following the publication of Daniel Patrick Moynihan, *The Negro Family: The Case for National Action* (Washington, D.C.: Government Printing Office, 1967). The acceptance of the theory of black family "deviance"—which lay at the root of many, if not most, of the social, psychological and educational problems of Blacks in the United States—and its enshrinement in welfare and educational legislation focused the attention of critics on its basic assumptions. The theory and its critics are fairly represented in Lee Rainwater and William L. Yancey, *The Moynihan Report and the Politics of Controversy . . . including the full text of "The Negro Family: The Case for National Action" by Daniel Patrick Moynihan* (Cambridge, Mass.: The M.I.T. Press, 1967).

The Frazier thesis of black matriarchy with its historical origin in American slavery has recently been re-examined in the light of later research. Basing his critique and revisions on an exhaustive study of census data relating to the black family, Herbert Gutman challanged Frazier's methodology and conclusions, denied the existence of black matriarchy and refuted speculations about the direct connection between slavery and the twentieth century black experience. See: Herbert Gutman, *The Negro Family* (to be published by Pantheon Books, New York). Other challenges to the Frazier thesis are raised by behavioral scientists and anthropologists. See Joe R. Feagin, "The Kinship Ties of Negro Urbanites" and David A. Schulz, "Variations in the Father Role in Complete Families of the Negro Lower Class," both in Norval D. Glenn and Charles M. Bonjean (eds.), *Blacks in the United States* (San Francisco: Chandler Publishing Co., 1969); Nancy L. Gonzales, "Toward a Definition of Matrifocality" and Carol B. Stack, "The Kindred of Viola Jackson: Residence and Family Organization of an Urban Black American Family," both in Norman Whitten, Jr. and John F. Szwed (eds.), *Afro-American Anthropology: Contemporary Perspectives* (Glencoe, N.Y.: Free Press, 1970). Among more recent critics are Robert Staples, "The Myth of the Black Matriarchy," *Black Scholar*, Vol. 1, Nos. 3–4 (January–February 1970), pp. 9–16; and Joyce A. Ladner, *Tomorrow's Tomorrow: The Black Woman* (New York: Doubleday & Co., 1971). The latter, a sociological study, is unique in treating the subject from the point of view of the black woman.

WOMEN AND RACISM

The sexual dimension of American racism, a theme which had been a subtle undercurrent in abolitionist literature, was first openly explored by W. J. Cash, *The Mind of the South* (New York: Alfred A. Knopf, 1941). Another Southerner, Lillian Smith, in her *Killers of the Dream* (New York: W. W. Norton & Co., 1949), applied Freudian insights to the patterns of racist dominance and analyzed the effects of the racist caste system on the sexual adaptations of whites. A more recent study, Winthrop Jordan, *White Over Black: American Attitudes Toward the Negro, 1550–1812* (Durham, N.C.: University of North Carolina Press, 1968), explores the early history of racism, including a full discussion of its sexual aspects. Albert Memmi, *Dominated Man* (New York: Grossman Publishers, Orion Press, 1968), discusses sex-caste oppression and compares it to race-caste oppression.

Calvin C. Hernton, *Sex and Racism in America* (New York: Doubleday, 1965), approaches the subject from the black point of view. Eldridge Cleaver, in *Soul on Ice* (New York: McGraw-Hill, 1968) develops a provocative analysis of the connection between race oppression and sex. William H. Grier and Price M. Cobbs, two black psychiatrists, treat the subject impressionistically in *Black Rage* (New York: Basic Books, 1968). An entire issue of *Black Scholar*, Vol. 2 No. 10 (June 1971) is devoted to the subject, "The Black Male." The article by Robert Staples, "The Myth of the Impotent Black Male," pp. 2–8, is particularly interesting and insightful. There is, as yet, no comprehensive work dealing with race oppression from the point of view of black women.

AUTOBIOGRAPHIES AND BIOGRAPHIES

A glance at the list below will reveal the neglect of this subject on the part of historians and writers. There are very few black women who have been subjects of booklength biographies. This is due not only to cultural indifference, but also to the historiography of this subject. The amount of primary source material readily available usually determines the attention given a person in secondary sources. Yet this ready availability of sources bears little relationship to the actual importance of black women in history. The source list on some of the most important black women is woefully small, whereas others, who were frequently mentioned in the press and in literature were relatively minor figures in terms of historical significance. Cultural bias tends to give prominence to educated middle-class women at the expense of grass-roots leaders who were and are in many cases poor, less educated and not so likely to provide the historian with easily accessible written sources. Lastly the historical prominence given a particular black woman not infrequently represents the bias of white contemporaries who selected her as a "leader of her people."

Slave narratives are not listed here and may be found in the Slavery and Abolition section above. Where no booklength biography is available, articles have been cited. The list below is a selection of the best material and does not represent a definitive bibliography of the subject.

Marian Anderson
Anderson, Marian, *My Lord, What a Morning* (New York: Avon Books, 1957).

Maya Angelou
Angelou, Maya, *I Know Why the Caged Bird Sings* (New York: Random House, 1970).

Maria Baldwin
Porter, Dorothy B., "Maria Louise Baldwin," *Journal of Negro Education*, Winter 1952, pp. 94–96.

Ida B. Wells Barnett
Duster, Alfreda, ed., *Crusade for Justice; The Autobiagraphy of Ida B. Wells* (Chicago and London: University of Chicago Press ,1970).

Daisy Bates
Bates, Daisy, *The Long Shadow of Little Rock: A Memoir* (New York: David McKay Co., 1962).

Mary McLeod Bethune
Holt, Rackman, *Mary McLeod Bethune* (New York: Doubleday & Co., 1964).
Peare, C. O., *Mary McLeod Bethune* (New York: Vanguard Press, 1951).
Sterne, Emma Gelders, *Mary McLeod Bethune* (New York: Knopf, 1959).

Charlotte Hawkins Brown
Brown, Anna S. L., "Alice Freeman Palmer Memorial Institute," *Opportunity*, Vol. 1, No. 8 (Aug. 1923), pp. 246–68.

Rose Butler Browne
Browne, Rose Butler, *Love My Children* (New York: Meredith Press, 1969).

Shirley Chisholm
Chisholm, Shirley, *Unbought and Unbossed* (Boston: Houghton Mifflin Co., 1970).

Septima Poinsetta Clark
Clark, Septima with Le Gette Blyth, *Echo in My Soul* (New York: E. P. Dutton & Co., 1962).

Anna Julia Cooper
Cooper, Anna Julia, *A Voice from the South by a Black Woman of the South* (Xenia, Ohio: The Aldine Printing House, 1892).

Fannie Jackson Coppin
Coppin, Fannie Jackson, *Reminiscences of School Life, and Hints on Teaching* (Philadelphia: African Methodist Episcopal Book Concern, 1913).

Juliette Derricotte
Jenness, Mary, *Twelve Negro Americans* (New York: Friendship Press, 1936).

Katherine Dunham
Dunham, Katherine, *A Touch of Innocence* (New York: Harcourt, Brace & World, 1959).

Althea Gibson
Gibson, Althea, *I Always Wanted to Be Somebody* (New York: Harper & Row, 1958).

Charlotte Forten Grimké
Billington, Ray Allen, ed., *The Journal of Charlotte L. Forten: A Free Negro in the Slave Era.* (New York: The Dryden Press, 1953).

Anna Arnold Hedgeman
Hedgeman, Anna Arnold, *The Trumpet Sounds: A Memoir of Negro Leadership* (New York: Holt, Rinehart & Winston, 1964).

Billie Holiday
Holiday, Billie, with William Dufty, *Lady Sings the Blues* (New York: Doubleday & Co., 1956).

Jane Edna Hunter
Hunter, Jane Edna, *A Nickel and a Prayer* (Nashville: The Parthenon Press, 1940).

Addie W. Hunton
Hunton, Addie W. and Kathryn M. Johnson, *Two Colored Women with the American Expeditionary Forces* (Brooklyn, New York: Eagle Press, 1920).

Zora Neale Hurston
Hurston, Zora Neale, *Dust Tracks on a Road* (Philadelphia: Lippincott, 1942).

Mahalia Jackson
Jackson, Mahalia and Evan McLeod Whylie, *Movin' On Up.* (New York: Hawthorne Books, 1966).

Coretta King
King, Coretta, *My Life With Martin Luther King* (New York: Holt, Rinehart & Winston, 1969).

Louise Meriwether
Meriwether, Louise, *Daddy Was a Number Runner* (Englewood Cliffs, N.J.: Prentice-Hall, 1970).

Emma Frances Grayson Merritt
Woodson, Carter G. "Emma Frances Grayson Merritt," *Opportunity*, Vol. 8, No. 8 (August 1930), pp. 244–245.

Ann Moody
Moody, Ann, *Coming of Age in Mississippi* (New York: Dial Press, 1968).

Pauli Murray
Murray, Pauli, *Proud Shoes: The Story of an American Family* (New York: Harper & Row, 1956).

Sarah Parker Remond
Porter, Dorothy B. "Sarah Parker Remond, Abolitionist and Physician," *Journal of Negro History*, Vol. 20 (July 1935), pp. 287–293.

Amanda Smith

Smith, Amanda, *An Autobiography of Mrs. Amanda Smith, The Colored Evangelist* (Chicago: Meyer and Brothers Publishers, 1893).

Taylor, Rev. Marshall W., *Amanda Smith, or the Life and Mission of a Slave Girl* (Cincinnatti: Crouston and Stowe, 1886).

Maria W. Stewart

Stewart, Maria W., *Meditations from the Pen of Mrs. Maria W. Stewart, Negro* (Washington, D.C.: n.p., 1879). First published by Garrison & Knopp, 1932.

Ellen Tarry

Tarry, Ellen, *The Third Door: The Autobiography of an American Negro Woman* (New York: David Mckay Co., 1955.

Susie King Taylor

Taylor, Susie King, *Reminiscences of My Life in Camp with the 33rd United States Colored Troops* (Boston: The Author, 1902).

Mary Church Terrell

Terrell, Mary Church, *A Colored Woman in a White World* (Washington, D.C.: Ransdell Inc. Publishing Co., 1940).

Sojourner Truth

Fauset, Arthur Huff, *Sojourner Truth: God's Faithful Pilgrim* (Durham, N.C.: University of North Carolina Press, 1938).

Gilbert, Olive, *Narrative of Sojourner Truth, A Northern Slave* (Boston: The Author, 1850). Subsequent editions, 1853 and 1884.

Pauli, Hertha, *Her Name Was Sojourner Truth* (New York: Appleton-Century-Crofts, Inc., 1962).

Harriet Tubman

Bradford, Sarah, *Harriet Tubman; The Moses of Her People* (New York: Corinth Books, 1961). Reprinted from the 1886 edition.

Bradford, Sarah, *Scenes in the Life of Harriet Tubman* (New York: n.p., 1869).

Conrad, Earl, *Harriet Tubman: Negro Soldier and Abolitionist* (New York: International Publisher, 1942).

Maggie L. Walker

Dabney, Wendell P., *Maggie L. Walker and the I. O. of Saint Luke* (Cincinnati: The Dabney Publishing Co., 1927).

Ethel Waters

Waters, Ethel, with Charles Samuels, *His Eye is on the Sparrow; an Autobiography* (New York: Doubleday & Co., 1951).

Dr. Gerda Lerner was born in Vienna, Austria. She is currently teaching American and women's history at Sarah Lawrence College, in Bronxville, New York. Dr. Lerner is the author of *The Grimké Sisters from South Carolina: Rebels Against Slavery*, *The Woman in American History*, and the screenplay for the motion picture *Black Like Me*.